The Letters and Diaries

of

John Henry Newman

The Letters and Diaries
of
John Henry Newman

Edited at the Birmingham Oratory
with notes and an introduction

by

Charles Stephen Dessain

of the same Oratory

Volume XVI
Founding a University
January 1854 to September 1855

NELSON

THOMAS NELSON AND SONS LTD
36 Park Street London W1
Parkside Works Edinburgh 9
10 Warehouse Road Apapa Lagos
P.O. Box 25012 Nairobi

THOMAS NELSON (AUSTRALIA) LTD
117 Latrobe Street Melbourne C1

THOMAS NELSON AND SONS (AFRICA) (Pty) LTD
P.O. Box 9881 Johannesburg

THOMAS NELSON AND SONS (CANADA) LTD
81 Curlew Drive Don Mills Ontario

THOMAS NELSON AND SONS
Copewood and Davis Streets Camden 3, N.J.

SOCIÉTÉ FRANÇAISE D'ÉDITIONS NELSON
97 rue Monge Paris 5

First published 1965

Nihil obstat : die 29ª septembris 1964

JOANNES C. BARRY
Censor Deputatus

Imprimatur : die 1ª octobris 1964

✠ JACOBUS MONAGHAN
Vicarius Generalis
Sancti Andreae et Edimburgensis

PRINTED IN GREAT BRITAIN
BY R. & R. CLARK LTD., EDINBURGH

Preface

WITHOUT the gradual building up at the Birmingham Oratory of a very full collection of Cardinal Newman's correspondence (an account of which will be found in the Introduction to Volume XI), the present work could not have been undertaken. Its aim is to provide an exhaustive edition of Newman's letters; with explanatory notes, which are often summaries of or quotations from the other side of the correspondence. Some of these letters *to* Newman, when they appear to have particular importance, or to be necessary for following a controversy, are inserted in the text. Every one of the letters written *by* Newman is included there, in chronological sequence. Should there eventually be any of his letters, whose existence is known to the editor, but of which he has failed to obtain a copy, this will be noted in its place. On the other hand, no attempt has been made to include a list of letters written by Newman and now lost, nor the brief précis he occasionally made of his reply, on the back of a correspondent's letter, although these are utilised for the annotation.

In order that the text of each letter may be as accurate as possible, the original autograph, when it still exists, or at least a photographic copy of it, has been used by the editor as his source. (The very few cases in which he has been content with an authenticated copy will be noted as they occur.) Always the text of the autograph is reproduced, or, when the autograph has disappeared, that of the copy that appears most reliable. When only Newman's draft exists, that is printed. The source used in each case is to be found in the list of letters by correspondents.

Such alterations as are made in transcribing the letters aim, without sacrifice of accuracy, at enabling them to be read with ease. Newman writes simply and has none of those idiosyncrasies which sometimes need to be reproduced for the sake of the evidence of one kind or another which they provide.

The following are the only alterations made in transcription:

ADDRESS AND DATE are always printed on the same line, and at the head of the letter, even when Newman puts them at the end. When he omits or gives an incomplete date, the omission is supplied in square brackets, and justified in a note unless the reason for it is obvious. The addresses, to which letters were sent, are included in the list of letters by correspondents. The information derived from postmarks is matter for annotation.

THE CONCLUSION of the letter is made to run on, irrespective of Newman's separate lines, and all postscripts are placed at the end.

NEWMAN'S CORRECTIONS AND ADDITIONS are inserted in their intended place. His interlinear explanations are printed in the text in angle brackets ⟨ ⟩, after the word or phrase they explain. His erasures are given in footnotes when they appear to be of sufficient interest to warrant it. Square brackets being reserved for editorial additions; all Newman's brackets are printed as rounded ones (the kind most usual with him).

NEWMAN'S PARAGRAPHS AND PUNCTUATION are preserved, except that single quotation marks are printed throughout, and double ones for quotations within them. (Newman generally used the latter in both cases.) Further, a parenthesis or quotation that he began with the proper mark but failed to complete, or completed but did not begin, is supplied. All other punctuation marks supplied by the editor are enclosed in square brackets. Newman's dashes, which frequently do duty either for a full stop, a semicolon or a comma (especially when he is tired or writing hurriedly), are represented by a ' — ' with a space before and after. His spelling and use of capitals are left unchanged, but 'raised' letters are lowered in every case.

NEWMAN'S ABBREVIATIONS are retained in the case of proper names, and in the address and conclusion of each letter, since these are sometimes useful indications of his attitude at the time. In all other cases, abbreviations are printed out in full, where Newman employs them.

When he uses the initials of proper names, the full name is normally inserted in square brackets after the initials, at the first occurrence in each letter, and more often if it seems advisable in order to avoid confusion. No addition of the full name is made in the case of Newman's correspondent, whether his initials occur at the beginning of the letter or in the course of it.

When Newman uses only a Christian name, the surname is sometimes added in square brackets for the reader's convenience. The Christian names of members of the Oratory, since they are of frequent occurrence, are listed in the index of proper names and the reader is referred to surnames.

When transcription is made from a PRINTED SOURCE, typographical alterations clearly due to editor or printer are disregarded.

Sometimes Newman made HOLOGRAPH copies of his letters or of portions of them, when they were returned to him long after they had been written. In order that the reader may be able to see how much he copied and what changes he introduced, the copied passages are placed in quarter brackets ⌐ ¬, and all additions of any importance included in the text in double square brackets, or, where this is impracticable, in the annotation.

Newman's letters are printed in CHRONOLOGICAL ORDER, with the name of his correspondent at the head (except that those of each day are arranged alphabetically), and, when more than one is written to the same person on the same day, numbered I, II. In the headings the name of the correspondent is given in its most convenient form, sometimes with Christian names in full, sometimes only with initials.

THE LIST OF LETTERS BY CORRESPONDENT, at the end of each volume, shows whether the source used was an autograph, draft, printed source or copy, and in the last case, whether a holograph made by Newman later; and gives the present location of the source, as well as of any additional holograph copies or drafts. When a letter, or a considerable portion of it, has been printed in a standard work, references are given; but mistakes or omissions in these previous publications are noticed, if at all, in the annotation.

THE LETTERS WRITTEN TO NEWMAN, when inserted in the text, are printed in type smaller than that used for Newman's own letters, and headed by the name of the correspondent. These letters are not arranged in chronological order, but are placed either just before or just after the letter of Newman to which they are related. A list of them is given at the end of each volume in which they occur. These and the quotations from letters in the annotation are always, unless otherwise stated, printed from autographs at the Birmingham Oratory, and are transcribed in the same way as Newman's letters.

NEWMAN'S DIARIES cover the years 1824 to 1879 (with a gap from July 1826 to March 1828). They are written in a series of mottled copy books, $12 \times 18\frac{1}{2}$ centimetres, printed for a year each, and entitled *The Private Diary: arranged, printed, and ruled, for receiving an account of every day's employment* . . ., with the exception of the four periods July 1847–May 1850, January 1854–January 1861, January 1861–March 1871, March 1871–October 1879, each of which is contained in a somewhat thicker copy book.

These diaries are printed complete for each day in which Newman has made an entry, except that the lists of people to whom he has written or from whom he has received letters are omitted, as not being of sufficient general interest. The original diaries are, of course, available for consultation. At the end of each diary book are various notes, lists of addresses, of people to be prayed for, accounts, etc. These, also, are omitted, except for occasional dated notes of events, which are inserted in their proper place. Of the rest of the notes, some are theological and will be reserved for a volume of Newman's theological papers, and others will perhaps have room found for them in any fuller edition of *Autobiographical Writings*.

Newman compiled with his own hand, on quarto sheets sewn together, a book of *Chronological Notes*, drawn largely from the diaries. Any new matter in these *Notes* is printed in italics with the appropriate diary entry. (It should be noted that the diary entries themselves were sometimes written up considerably later than the events they record.)

Each volume is preceded by a brief summary of the period of Newman's life that it covers. Summary, diaries and annotation give a roughly biographical form to the whole, and will, it is hoped, enable the ordinary reader to treat it as a continuous narrative.

THE BIOGRAPHIES OF PERSONS are collected in the index of proper names at the end of each volume, in order to simplify the annotation of the letters. Occasionally, when a person is mentioned only once or twice, and a note is required in any case, biographical details have been given in the notes, and a reference in the index. Volume XI, being the first of a new period in Newman's life, contains an account of every person mentioned, with the exception of a few for whom a notice seemed unnecessary, and of still fewer who have not yet been identified. The indexes of Volume XII and of subsequent volumes contain notices of persons who appear in them for the first time, and references back, in the case of those who have been noticed in an earlier volume. (The editor will be grateful for information as to persons not identified.)

These notices have been compiled from such various sources—books of reference, letters at the Oratory, information supplied by the families or religious communities of the persons concerned, and by librarians and archivists—that the giving of authorities would be a very complicated and lengthy process. Like others faced with the same problem, the editor has decided usually to omit them. References are given, however, to *The Dictionary of National Biography*, or *The Dictionary of American Biography*, in all cases where there is an article there, and failing them, to Boase's *Modern English Biography* or Gillow's *Bibliographical Dictionary of the English Catholics*. When all the volumes of letters have been issued, a final index volume will be compiled for the whole work.

Contents

Abbreviations in Volume XVI

THE abbreviations used for Newman's works are those listed in Joseph Rickaby, S.J., *Index to the Works of John Henry Cardinal Newman*, London 1914, with a few additions.

References to works included by Newman in his uniform edition are always, unless otherwise stated, to that edition, which was begun in 1868 with *Parochial and Plain Sermons*, and concluded in 1881 with *Select Treatises of St Athanasius*. From 1886, until the stock was destroyed in the 1939–45 war, all the volumes were published by Longmans, Green and Co. They are distinguished from other, usually posthumous, publications by having their date of inclusion in the uniform edition in brackets after the title, in the list of abbreviations below. The unbracketed date is, in every case, the date of the edition (or impression) used for giving references. (Once volumes were included in the uniform edition the pagination usually remained unchanged, but there are exceptions and minor alterations.)

Add.	*Addresses to Cardinal Newman with His Replies etc. 1879–82*, ed. W. P. Neville, 1905.
Apo.	*Apologia pro Vita Sua*, (1873) 1905.
Ari.	*The Arians of the Fourth Century*, (1871) 1908.
Ath. I, II	*Select Treatises of St Athanasius*, two volumes, (1881) 1920.
A.W.	*John Henry Newman: Autobiographical Writings*, ed. Henry Tristram, 1956.
Call.	*Callista, a Tale of the Third Century*, (1876) 1923.
Campaign	*My Campaign in Ireland, Part I* (printed for private circulation only), 1896.
D.A.	*Discussions and Arguments on Various Subjects*, (1872) 1911.
Dev.	*An Essay on the Development of Christian Doctrine*, (1878) 1908.
Diff. I, II	*Certain Difficulties felt by Anglicans in Catholic Teaching*, two volumes, (1879, 1876) 1908.
Ess. I, II	*Essays Critical and Historical*, two volumes, (1871) 1919.
G.A.	*An Essay in aid of a Grammar of Assent*, (1870) 1913.
H.S. I, II, III	*Historical Sketches*, three volumes, (1872) 1908, 1912, 1909.
Idea	*The Idea of a University defined and illustrated*, (1873) 1902.
Jfc.	*Lectures on the Doctrine of Justification*, (1874) 1908.
K.C.	*Correspondence of John Henry Newman with John Keble and Others, 1839–45*, ed. at the Birmingham Oratory, 1917.
L.G.	*Loss and Gain: the Story of a Convert*, (1874) 1911.
M.D.	*Meditations and Devotions of the late Cardinal Newman*, 1893.
Mir.	*Two Essays on Biblical and on Ecclesiastical Miracles*, (1870) 1907.

Mix.	*Discourses addressed to Mixed Congregations*, (1871) 1909.
Moz. I, II	*Letters and Correspondence of John Henry Newman*, ed. Anne Mozley, two volumes, 1891.
O.S.	*Sermons preached on Various Occasions*, (1870) 1927.
P.S. I-VIII	*Parochial and Plain Sermons*, (1868) 1907-10.
Prepos.	*Present Position of Catholics*, (n.d. 1872) 1913.
S.D.	*Sermons bearing on Subjects of the Day*, (1869) 1902.
S.E.	*Stray Essays on Controversial Points*, (private) 1890.
S.N.	*Sermon Notes of John Henry Cardinal Newman, 1849-1879*, ed. Fathers of the Birmingham Oratory, 1913.
T.T.	*Tracts Theological and Ecclesiastical*, (1874) 1908.
U.S.	*Fifteen Sermons preached before the University of Oxford*, (1872) 1909.
V.M. I, II	*The Via Media*, (1877) 1908, 1911.
V.V.	*Verses on Various Occasions*, (1874) 1910.

* * *

Boase	Frederick Boase, *Modern English Biography*, six volumes, Truro 1892-1921.
Culler	A. Dwight Culler, *The Imperial Intellect*, *a Study of Newman's Educational Ideal*, New Haven 1955.
D A B	*Dictionary of American Biography*, London 1928-36.
D N B	*Dictionary of National Biography*, to 1900, London, reprinted in 1937-8 in twenty-two volumes, the last being a Supplement, *D N B*, Suppl.
D N B, 1901-11	*Dictionary of National Biography*, 1901-11, three volumes in one.
D R	*Dublin Review*.
D T C	*Dictionnaire de Théologie Catholique*, Paris 1903-50.
Gillow	Joseph Gillow, *Bibliographical Dictionary of the English Catholics*, five volumes, London 1885 and later.
Harper	Gordon Huntington Harper, *Cardinal Newman and William Froude, F.R.S. A Correspondence*, Baltimore 1933.
Liddon's *Pusey* I-IV	H. P. Liddon, *Life of Edward Bouverie Pusey*, four volumes, London 1893-7.
de Lisle	E. S. Purcell, *Life and Letters of Ambrose Phillipps de Lisle*, two volumes, London 1900.
McGrath	Fergal McGrath, S.J., *Newman's University Idea and Reality*, London 1951.
Trevor I	Meriol Trevor, *Newman the Pillar of the Cloud*, London 1962.
Trevor II	Meriol Trevor, *Newman Light in Winter*, London 1962.
Ward I, II	Wilfrid Ward, *The Life of John Henry Cardinal Newman*, two volumes, London 1912.

Introductory Note

IN the autumn of 1851 Newman had been chosen by the Irish bishops to be the first Rector of the Catholic University, but not until October 1853 was he actually called to Dublin to begin his task. His summons came from a meeting of the University Committee at which only two bishops were present, and he was asked to do nothing public, lest he should antagonise those bishops who were opposed to the scheme, or who thought it too much under Archbishop Cullen's control. The end of 1853 saw Newman insisting that if he were to set up the University, it could only be after some form of public recognition. The very hesitation over granting him this implied a failure to grasp that a University was a public institution, not a mere college or seminary. Also, if professors were to be secured, and arrangements made for an autumn opening, he must be seen to have a mandate.

Archbishop Cullen bowed to Newman's representations early in January 1854, but meanwhile Cardinal Wiseman was acting more effectively in Rome. He suggested to Pius IX that a new brief should be drawn up approving the University, confirming Newman as Rector, and authorising him to make appointments. At a later audience with Pius IX, Wiseman, who had already secured Cullen's agreement, proposed that Newman should be made a bishop, in order to give him a position among the disunited Irish bishops, and enable him to overcome opposition and inertia.

Newman learned on 31 January 1854 of his proposed elevation, and welcomed it for its practical advantages. Others had heard the news too, and it soon became public. Congratulations came in and friends sent presents of the insignia that would be needed. In February Newman crossed over to Ireland and began a tour of the Irish bishops, to interest them in the University and secure their support. Letters home give a vivid and entertaining account of his journeys and impressions.

In March 1854 the papal brief was issued and on 18 May the Irish bishops met in synod to erect the University. Not a word was said about Newman's bishopric. Cullen had written urgently to Rome that it should be postponed. But neither he nor Wiseman nor any of those who had though it so expedient ever said to Newman a word on the matter, or explained that what had been so publicly announced was not to be.

Newman's friends were first puzzled and then annoyed. Newman himself asked no questions, and later reflected how much more difficult it would have been to extricate himself from the University and return to his Oratory, if he had received the honour proposed for him.

On Whit Sunday 1854 Newman was installed as Rector of the University, in the Pro-Cathedral at Dublin, in the presence of Archbishop Cullen. Before and after this he was busy gathering advice, engaging professors, buying and adapting buildings. He realised the importance of advertisement and of bringing the idea of the University before men's minds. In June he began the weekly *Catholic University Gazette*, acting as editor until the end of the year. It contained information about the University and articles of his own, including those on University Subjects and the Rise and Progress of Universities, now to be found in the second part of *The Idea of a University* and in *Historical Sketches III*. Later in the summer Newman purchased the medical school in Cecilia Street, for the use of the Faculty of Medicine. This was inaugurated in 1855, and was a lasting success, its courses being recognised by the chartered medical bodies. He also made preparations for the Faculty of Science and tried to start an Observatory. In the summer of 1855 he began the building of a University Church, finding the money for it himself, in part from the surplus of the Achilli trial fund.

Newman was above all anxious to obtain the support of the laity, whom the University was intended to serve, many of whom, as the correspondence reveals, were distrustful of clerical domination or inclined to support the Government and its colleges. This led him to collect the names of prominent laymen besides those of bishops and clergy, as associates of the University. He hoped in this way eventually to be able to give laymen certain powers of control, but it was not to be. They were excluded from the administration and allowed no direct voice in matters of policy, with results fatal to the University which was thus deprived of strong lay support, and fatal also to Newman's plans for the formation by means of the University of a body of educated and responsible laymen.

The first term began on 3 November 1854, the feast of the Irish St Malachy, when the Faculty of Philosophy and Letters was opened. Newman had collected a brilliant team of professors who gave inaugural lectures in successive weeks, Newman leading off on 9 November with the lecture on 'Christianity and Letters.' An account of the first term will be found in Appendix 2. Towards the end of the term the number of undergraduates rose to twenty-seven, and when the Spring Term began they numbered sixty.

During all this time Archbishop Cullen was in Rome whither he had gone to be present at the definition of the doctrine of the Immaculate Conception, and where he remained to defend himself against his Irish nationalist opponents Frederick Lucas and Archbishop MacHale. He wrote to Newman on 12 January 1855 warning him against the Young Irelanders, who included some of the most talented Irishmen. Newman was unwilling to give up men who were his friends, or to keep them out of the professorships for which they were the best available candidates, when they agreed to eschew politics within the University. Cullen took grave offence at this, and, although he did not return to Dublin until the middle of July, never wrote again to Newman, leaving unanswered his letters on urgent University matters. Thus during the very first year while other bishops held aloof because they considered Cullen had assumed sole control, the latter too withdrew his support. Even after his return, Cullen still did not reply to letters, and Newman's request for a financial committee of laymen, who would guarantee that the funds of the University were competently administered, was a further cause of offence. In fact Cullen wrote again to Rome urging that Newman's bishopric should be held over. He seemed not to appreciate either the intellectual or the physical freedom necessary for a University, since he at the same time complained of Newman's lax discipline. The letters show Newman at grips with these difficulties, ordinary and extra-ordinary, of a nascent Catholic University, and his efforts to open new Faculties in preparation for the second year.

Yet the University represented only part of Newman's responsibilities. He remained Superior of the Oratory at Birmingham where strain was caused by his being absent for more than half the year. He kept in touch by letters which tell of the internal difficulties with which he had to grapple. In 1854 he bought land at Rednal for the cemetery where he now lies buried. He corresponded with Bishop Ullathorne about the possible use of the vernacular in services at the Oratory. During the summer vacation of 1855 which he spent at Birmingham, he wrote the greater part of his second novel *Callista*.

Early in the period covered by this Volume the Crimean War began. Newman's letters show how he detested it and the spirit in which it was waged. In the spring of 1855 he wrote for Henry Wilberforce's *Catholic Standard* a series of articles on the lessons of the War, 'Who's to blame?,' now included in *Discussions and Arguments*. He sent long letters on the subject to Mrs William Froude, and to her too he wrote, for her husband's sake, on the possibility of attaining certitude in religious matters.

Summary of Events covered by this volume

*   *   *

1854

7–27 Feb.	Newman visits the Irish Bishops, at Dublin, Kilkenny, Carlow, Waterford, Cork, Thurles, Limerick, returning thence to Dublin.
20 March	Papal Brief issued, instructing the Irish Bishops to meet within three months, under the presidency of Archbishop Cullen, in order to set up the Catholic University.
22 March	Opening of the London Oratory at Brompton. Newman goes there from Dublin, and blesses the church.
22 April	Newman back in Dublin, and attends Bishop Moriarty's consecration.
3 May	Newman preaches at the opening of the church attached to Mother Margaret Mary Hallahan's convent at Stone, Staffordshire, returning at once to Dublin.
18 May	Synodal Meeting of the Irish Bishops. The Statutes of the University are approved. Newman is formally recognised as Rector and Patrick Leahy is appointed Vice Rector.
23 May–2 June	Newman goes to Birmingham for the Feast of St Philip and then visits St Edmund's College, Ware, and Ushaw College, Durham.
4 June	Newman is installed as Rector of the Catholic University, in the Pro-Cathedral at Dublin. He begins the *Catholic University Gazette*, writing many of the articles himself, and remains editor until the end of the year.
3 July	Newman returns to Birmingham. Land is bought for a house and cemetery for the Birmingham Oratory at Rednal.
5 Sept.	Newman goes to Dalkey near Dublin, where the Oratorians come in turns for holidays.
29 Oct.	Newman moves into 6 Harcourt Street, Dublin, St Mary's House.
3 Nov.	The University is opened, and the first term begins.
9 Nov.	Newman delivers the Inaugural Lecture for the School of Philosophy and Letters.
23 Dec.	Newman back at Birmingham.

1855

12 Jan.	Newman leaves for Dublin to begin the second term of the University.
6 Feb.	Newman in Birmingham to lecture on 'The Three Patriarchs.'
11 Feb.–3 April	Newman back in Dublin. He goes to Birmingham for Holy Week and is in Dublin again on 16 April.

3 Mar.–21 April	Newman's articles 'Who's to blame?' appear each week in the *Catholic Standard*.
1–9 June	Newman at Birmingham for the Feast of St Philip. Robert Wilberforce comes to stay for a few days. Newman returns to Dublin.
13 July	Newman calls on Archbishop Cullen, just returned from Rome, where he has been since the autumn of 1854.
16–19 July	The Terminal Examinations at the University.
20 July	Newman arrives in Birmingham for the Vacation. Several Oratorians from London come to visit Birmingham.
22 July–31 Aug.	Newman takes up again and completes *Callista*.

The Letters and Diaries
of
John Henry Newman

SUNDAY 1 JANUARY 1854 we got in to the Refectory at last, after the decorations etc — having been two months out of it. *the decorators having been 2 months in it.*

TO JAMES HOPE-SCOTT

Edgbaston. Jany 1. 1854

My dear Hope Scott

A happy new year to you, to Mrs H S. to Mary Monica, and to all of yours — to Badeley, and to ⌈the Bishop of Southwark on condition (not else) he gives us his blessing⌉[1] up to December 31 inclusive. I was with you this time year, when you took such care of me — and made me so happy when I had various troubles within — (premit alto corde dolorem)[2] Dear Father Gordon was sinking, and old Campbell was sharpening his weapon for his pound of flesh.

Your suggestion is a very happy one, and those who have heard it, have caught at it — but it is impossible. I wont take up your time in saying why. However, I will bear it in mind.[3]

I inclose a copy of a letter which I wrote to the Archbishop a day or

---

[1] Newman altered this, when copying in 1872, [[Ask the Bishop of Southwark for his blessing for me . . .]]

[2] *Aeneid*, I, 209. For Newman's troubles over the summary dismissal of Brother Bernard see the letters of Jan. 1853. On 31 Jan. 1853 the Judges presided over by Lord Campbell sentenced Newman at the end of the Achilli trial. Joseph Gordon died on 13 Feb. 1853.

[3] Archbishop Cullen kept postponing the official installation of Newman as Rector of the Catholic University, which meant that he could not begin work nor make appointments and other necessary arrangements. Writing on 28 Dec. 1853 to Hope-Scott Newman asked whether the time had not come for him to say that unless he were installed as Rector he would be forced to resign. In his reply of 30 Dec., part of which is in *A.W.* p. 308, Hope-Scott urged Newman not to resign, since this would probably bring the whole University scheme to an end. He then went on to say that he learned from Bishop Grant about Newman's idea of founding an Oratory in Dublin. The Bishop suggested, wisely in Hope-Scott's opinion, that Newman should set about this plan independently of the University project. He would thus have a locus standi in Dublin, be able to make a beginning of lectures at the Oratory, and prepare the way for the University.

The reasons which made this suggestion impossible Newman has given in *A.W.* pp. 308–09. 'When a University was actually set up, then an Oratory would be its natural attendant, as being what may be called the School of Devotion for its members.' It would follow the University, rather than be a preparation for it. 'Moreover, to have commenced proceedings at Dublin with an Oratory, would have been to impress upon the Dublin public that I had a private and personal end in coming there, not the good of Ireland. . . .' Further, Cullen would not have borne with an Oratory in practice, a group of secular priests more or less independent of the Bishop. Lastly Hope-Scott and Bishop Grant appeared to think of Oratorians as being in the normal course 'academical Lecturers.'

3

two ago, and have kept by me till I had your answer, It goes tonight.[1]

Also I inclose a memorandum of my own — which contains a skeleton of the sum total of my thoughts.

⌜I must get my way [[with the Archbishop]] [with] him — and if I don't, though I believe you are right in bidding me not resign *on* the correspondence, yet I shall bide my time, and resign quietly.

Yet I believe it will not come to this. I believe I shall get my way — and plunge myself, apertis, if not siccis, oculis into the deep with its monstra natantia.⌝[2]

Ever Yrs affly in Xt J H N

P.S.   Some time or other let me have my two inclosures back.

MONDAY 2 JANUARY 1854   hard frost with snow lying for about a week past.

TO CARDINAL WISEMAN

Edgbaston. Birmingham. Jany 2/54

My dear Lord Cardinal,

Your Eminence has enough to trouble you without my inflicting any additional matter, but a letter of yours to Mr Northcote which this post has brought me and in which my name is mentioned, has put it into my head that I ought to make you acquainted with the actual state of my own Irish affairs, and that, though a most delicate matter it is for you even to know any thing about, you would not be unwilling to know without seeming to know, and might befriend me without seeming to befriend.

I have been called over by the Committee to commence the University, as last October. In the beginning of November I went — made some preparatory arrangements — and, finding every thing was committed to me, actually made some appointments with salaries to commence next Autumn. In consequence, since then, one person at least has given up his house with a view to his prospective engagement — and another has given formal notice to his Bishop of his intended removal.[3] These are but specimens of the real and serious consequence

---

[1] Letter of 30 Dec. 1853 to Cullen. The Memorandum Newman also enclosed is printed in *A.W.* pp. 305–07, and in *McGrath*, pp. 221–3.

[2] Horace, *Odes*, I, 3.

[3] These were E. H. Thompson at Clifton and W. G. Penny at St Chad's, Birmingham.

of what I have done, and of the inconveniences I shall cause, if I do not as soon as possible tell these friends what they are to expect after all.

This brings me to the point of my letter. Dr Cullen wished me to be made the Vicar General of the Bishops for University purposes — as Dr Ram was at Louvain. He has not been able to effect it. I do not ask for it — Still, I do ask for *some* sanction or other to my prospective proceedings in Ireland.

For instance, Dr Mullen etc go as collectors of subscriptions to America — would they dream of going without Episcopal letters? — I am to come to Ireland, nay perhaps to visit, certainly to correspond with America — can I rest my claims on common report that I am Rector, or an invitation to go to Ireland from a committee partly lay, which has not been directly recognised by Episcopal authority for these three years?

What then I have asked for, is simply this, and nothing more; viz *to be allowed to take the usual oaths* in acceptance of the 'Creed of Pope Pius iv' (so called) etc. The very fact of having taken them before the Archbishop of Dublin would be quite enought for my purpose; it would imply a recognition on the part of the Irish Church.

However, *I have not succeeded*, and on grounds which are still less satisfactory to me than the refusal itself. (1.) because I must avoid *all* public acts, and (2) that, because the majority of the Bishops of Ireland are not with me.

Now see what a position I am in.

1.   By avoiding public acts, I believe is meant, for example, that I must not advertise the time of the Schools opening, advertise the subjects of the examination for entrance etc etc — but if I comply with this advice, I shall have my staff of lecturers etc in the Autumn at Dublin and *they will have no one to teach*. How then can they be paid?

2.   Since the Bishops are not with me, if I exert myself to get students, professors, etc throughout Ireland, I actually shall be engaged in an underhand proceeding something like Dr Pusey's in going to hear confessions in the Dioceses of Canterbury or Worcester without leave of his Bishops. I have no authority either from Ireland or from Rome.

I am still urging my point strongly, and hope to gain it — but, if the Bishops are any how against me in heart, how can I possibly succeed in my plans, even if I gain this particular point? I shall not think of resigning, till I have exhausted every expedient, but will it not come to this, that at length I *must* resign? I ask nothing else but a fair stage, nothing but a locus standi, if it be but an inch of Irish ground, or the point of a needle — but, unless they let me come in, I can do nothing.

I ask nothing of authorities at Rome — they will judge and decide what is best. I only wish it understood that, if I do not act, it is not my fault. For two years I have been entreating to be allowed to act. This year just gone is nearly lost to me — for I have kept myself free from all engagements, to come over to Ireland at a moment's notice. I have not been called till October — and now when I have commenced acting, I suddenly find myself stopped — for to tell me to do nothing public, is to stop me.

Dr Cullen from first to last has given me the *most generous support*, but he cannot do every thing he wishes at his mere will

Begging your Eminence's blessing & kissing the sacred purple I am, My dear Lord Cardinal, Your affecte friend & servant in Xt

John H Newman of the Oratory[1]

P.S.   I have doubled my letter thus oddly, that the transparency of the paper may not publish it to the world.[2]

TUESDAY 3 JANUARY 1854   went up to Oscott in fly with Shortlands (leaving him there)[3] to call on Dr Weedall   at night a most violent wild wind

TO GEORGE RYDER

Edgbaston Jan 3/54

My dear Ryder

I have nothing to say, but, as boys are bad message-carriers, I send you by hand-writing my most affectionate congratulations to you and all yours on the Sacred Season and best wishes for the new year.

I did not answer your last, thinking you would have more to tell me, and I have been anxiously expecting a letter since from you.[4]

I was going to Ireland yesterday, but *fresh delays*! and, though I suppose I shall beat them at last, yet it is not at all off the cards I may have quietly to resign.

Will you ask Harry what he did with the paper on Latin Composi-

[1] Wiseman's reply of 20 Jan. will be found before Newman's letter of 1 Feb. to him. Wiseman translated Newman's letter of 2 Jan. for Pius IX, and made comments on it, which are now in the Archives of Propaganda. *S.R.C. Irlanda*, Vol. 32, f. 1 seq.

[2] As always when writing to correspondents out of England, Newman used thin paper, folded and sealed, without an envelope.

[3] John Rutherford Shortland (1814–81), at Oriel, became a Catholic in 1851 and was studying to be a priest. In 1856 he was made a Canon of the Plymouth Diocese.

[4] This refers to Ryder's plans for himself. See letters of 25 Sept. 1853 and 8 Jan. 1854.

tion which I lent him. If he has got it with him, only let him carefully bring it back. But if it is in his room, perhaps he will tell me where.[1]

Ever Yrs affly in Xt John H Newman of the Oratory.

WEDNESDAY 4 JANUARY 1854 [a most violent wild wind] into and through this day with snow drifting and in the day half melting

TO J. M. CAPES

Edgn Jan 4/54

My dear Capes

Thank you for the sight of the Cardinal's letter. It contains a beautiful plan — but what time and strength shall *I* have for writing, while life lasts, if I have this University on my hands?[2]

A fresh hitch! When I am on the point of starting. Suddenly I find my hands tied. It is a crisis which will decide my going or not; but I *fear* I shall get my way.

Every thing really good and happy to you also for the New Year.

Do you know poor Mr Rhodes?[3] His wife is now dying. She is a Protestant — He has long been wearying Heaven for her conversion. And now he has had Masses on Masses and Novenas on Novenas; and wishes every one to help him. If she could but make a good act of contrition at last, his prayers and exertions will not be in vain

Ever Yrs affly John H Newman

THURSDAY 5 JANUARY 1854 the snow drifts all through the country the worst since 1814

[1] This paper must be *Hints on Latin Composition*, eight pages drawn up by Newman at Oriel in 1824. It was published by V. F. Blehl, S.J., in *Classical Folia*, xv (1961), pp. 1–10, 'John Henry Newman on Latin Prose Style.'

[2] Capes was the editor, with Northcote and Thompson, of Burns and Lambert's 'Popular Catholic Library,' in which Wiseman's *Fabiola or the Church of the Catacombs* appeared towards the end of 1854. Wiseman suggested to Capes that Newman should write a tale to illustrate the next period in the history of the Church. See the preface to *Fabiola*, and also the advertisment to *Callista*.

[3] Matthew John Rhodes (1817–91), son of a Leeds banker, went up to Trinity College, Cambridge, in 1835. He was married in 1839, and lived at Eardstone House, Worcs. Manning received him into the Church in 1852.

TO JOHN EDWARD BOWDEN

Edgbaston Jan 5/54

My dearest John

What a bad man of business you must think me when actually I have got Dr Dingli's answer from Malta before I have paid for the present which has elicited it. So he has roused my conscience, and behold the money, which you have nothing to do, but to send to your Banker, I am faithfully assured.[1]

I expect if all is well, to see some of you at Westbury; Thursday the 12th I believe is the day.[2]

As to poor Dr Bonavia, I have done nothing from not knowing what to do. I shall send him £10. I suppose it will reach him if directed to 'Protestant Mission College, Malta.'[3]

It is a shame I have not written to dear Father Richard. Tell him of my deep compunction, which I fear is not contrition, till I *do* write.

The best wishes of the Tide to your very Revd Father,[4] to him, and to all of you.

The Irish people are jibbing again, when I am going over — and I am going to tell them that they must take me or give me up.

Ever Yours most affectionately in Mary & Philip

John H Newman of the Oratory

P.S.   If I possibly have a copy over, I shall send your Congregation my Opus Magnum on the Turks — but I can't tell yet, how many copies I have. Liverpool takes up a good many.[5]

Another Confession. I have for half a year been asking Mr Finlayson to accept a book from me. Tell me his direction that I may write to him.[6]

[1] Dr Adrian Dingli was the Maltese lawyer who had been of such help in the Achilli trial.

[2] Bowden's sister, Marianne, was to make her profession as a Visitation nun, on that day.

[3] Vincent Bonavia, a Maltese lawyer who had become a Protestant and a teacher at the Malta Protestant College, was one of Newman's witnesses at the Achilli trial. He returned to Catholicism, and was trying to find employment in England. See also letter of 15 Aug. 1854 to John Bowden.   [4] i.e. F. W. Faber.

[5] *Lectures on the History of the Turks in its relation to Christianity,* by the Author of Loss and Gain, Dublin 1854. The book was dedicated 'To the Members of the Catholic Institute of Liverpool, in the confidence that they will kindly welcome what was written for their information, and comes to them in St. Philip's name.' These *Lectures* were later included in *H.S.* i, pp. 1–238.

[6] William Francis Finlason (1818–95), a barrister at the Middle Temple, received into the Church by Faber in 1849, published *Report of the Trial and Preliminary Pro-*

TO J. M. CAPES

Edgbaston. Jany 5. 1854

My dear Capes,

Certainly the article on St Alfo should have an answer and a good one.[1]

The subject is one which must before now have employed all our minds and made us anxious.

It is not only difficult in itself and logically, but unless it was answered in a way rhetorically good, and suitable to persuade the British Lion or at least to silence him, it would be of no use.

It requires to go back to first principles, if the answer is to be logical and philosophical; and how can you possibly introduce new first principles rhetorically? Such an introduction cannot convince — though it might dazzle, perplex, and silence. Yet even this is something, I grant; — and it is all that can be done.

What strikes me is, first

1. St. Alfonso's views are not binding on us, we may dissent from them.
2. It must be carefully examined whether the approbation pronounced on his theology at Rome applies to his abstract principles or their concrete applications. E.g. as no act is indifferent in the individual, though indifferent in itself, and as all *may* keep from venial sin, and no one *does*, so it may be abstractedly allowable to equivocate in this way or that, but never in the case of any individual.

Or at least the cases may be only *extreme* ones. (And the treatise is not a *popular* one, but scientific — though Protestants put it into English.)

Or at least the cases may only exist in particular states of society; and be inadmissible among Catholics in England at this day.

3. Again, it is to be considered that where rules are laid down what is lying and what is not, there is a provision against *deceit*. E.g. A.B.

ceedings in the case of . . . G. Achilli v. Dr. Newman, London 1852, with an Introduction and notes calling attention to the issues involved and the frequent prejudice and unfairness shown.

[1] *The Christian Remembrancer*, XXVII (Jan. 1854), Article II, pp. 38–87, 'St Alfonso de Liguori's Theory of Truthfulness.' Capes's answer, making use of the advice Newman now proceeds to give, appeared in the *Rambler* (April 1854), pp. 307–36, 'Equivocation as taught by St Alphonsus Ligouri.' See also letters of 15 Jan. and 15 June to Capes, and 11 May to Badeley; and cf. *Apo.*, note G, pp. 348–63.

The article in the *Christian Remembrancer* was by Frederick Meyrick, and was republished in his *Moral Theology of the Church of Rome*, Baltimore 1856, pp. 5–78, followed by a few pages in reply to the *Rambler,* and to an article in *D R* (Dec. 1854), pp. 326–403, 'St. Alphonsus and the Christian Remembrancer.'

tells me in strictest confidence that he wrote a certain book. C.D. says to me 'Did A.B. write it?' I answer — 'No, he did not — but I am surprised at your question, and I tell you fairly that, had I known it was his, I should have considered it quite fair to have answered in the negative.' Is this taking C.D. in? is it more than blunting, in the only way that is possible, his unfair question? When then a theologian lays down generally beforehand that I may thus speak in the case of an unfair question, what is he doing more but protecting A.B.'s secret, and defending me in my faithfulness to it?

4. Protestants *do*, what we *teach* — the difference only is, that we make a theory, and say what may be done, and what may not. So of persecution — the Church defines and draws lines — Putting aside the question of the real exactness of its distinctions etc, at least it keeps persecution within bounds — and so in like manner, it tells us what we may say without lying, whereas Protestants become reckless. Moreover, Protestants are hypocrites, for they denounce[,] when stated[,] what they do. Thus I believe Copleston always maintained he might say 'I don't know,' when a person asked him whether a certain person wrote a certain book, when he did know. I think this was the case as regards Tremaine.[1]

You shall hear from me again.

Ever Yrs affly J H N

P.S. Another thought strikes me — though I say it *quite under correction*, and only as affording matter for consideration. It is ten times more honest to say boldly 'It is allowable to say the thing that is not in particular cases,' or 'to say the thing that is not is not necessarily lying,' than to have recourse to such subterfuges as St Alfonso and some[2] Jesuits use, of *double* words etc etc. So that I should admit their *conclusions*, and *prove* them in some other way. I am told that some one has been writing in a French work to say that under circumstances we may say the thing that is not, without attempt at getting off by an equivocation — I like this far better than St Alfonso's way. An equivocation is cowardly. But I throw this out. J H N.

One word more. I believe that the judgment pronounced at Rome on St A's works, is not so much as an approbation, but that *they are not worthy of censure*.

Another thing. It would be well to bring out clearly and boldly *what* the Church did *not* allow, so that Protestants might see that what

---

[1] *Tremaine, or the Man of Refinement*, the first novel of Robert Plumer Ward (1765–1846), the politician, published anonymously in three volumes, London 1825.
[2] Newman first wrote 'the,' and corrected it.

they stumble at, are exceptions. E.g. a man must not swear falsely in a Court of law etc etc.

FRIDAY 6 JANUARY 1854 My volume on the Turks came out just now

TO VISCOUNT FEILDING

Edgbaston. Jany 6/54

My dear Lord Feilding,

I fear there has been some mistake about your letter, since you have not come today, as you proposed.

It came to me *this* morning, but it speaks as if it ought to have come yesterday, in time for me to answer it.

I expect to be here continuously until Wednesday next[1]

Very sincerely Yours in Xt John H Newman of the Oratory

The Viscount Feilding

TO JAMES HOPE-SCOTT

Edgbaston Jan 6/54

My dear Hope Scott

⌐You will be pleased to read the inclosed[2] — but don't suppose I think myself out of the wood yet, even as regards commencing⌐

Ever Yrs affly J H N

SATURDAY 7 JANUARY 1854 a thaw

TO GEORGE RYDER

Edgbaston. Jany. 8. 1854

My dear Ryder

Thank you for the information. Don't suppose you have taken any steps which had better not be taken. You thought Providence was

[1] Lord Feilding dined at the Oratory on 20 Jan.

[2] The enclosure was Cullen's reply dated 4 Jan. to Newman's letter of 30 Dec. 1853. See note there. Cullen suggested that some official recognition on the part of the Bishops, of Newman as Rector of the University, should be made by means of a written document. Cf. *A.W.* p. 312.

making an opening for a certain change of life in your behalf. You thought the opening would not last. You asked yourself what was God's will, and, against your own wishes, you put yourself to do God's will. Abraham, I suspect, was not sorry for offering to surrender Isaac, on the ground that Almighty God let him off. Leave yourself ever to Him, and He will do what is best for you.

For me, you may be quite sure that I never shall act otherwise than I have done — never, that is, mention such subjects to you, till you see the signs of a Providence so striking that you think it right to mention the subject to me.

Ever Yours most affectly in Xt John H Newman

P.S. Northcote is sending his children ⟨girls⟩ to some one at Stone — I think they are older than yours — but he must be very anxious about them. Is it worth while your inquiring?[1]
P.S. Thank dear Harry for this letter just received. F Nicholas wishes notice of their return in good time.

MONDAY 9 JANUARY 1854 Anderdon went (after 14 weeks *in the House*) about this time

TUESDAY 10 JANUARY a wild wind again at night

WEDNESDAY 11 JANUARY went down to Clifton, putting up at the Bishop's house dined at Northcote's at night

THURSDAY 12 JANUARY went to Westbury for M B's *Maryanne Bowden's* profession preached the Sermon[2] dined with Northcote and came back to Bm [Birmingham]

TO F. W. FABER

Edgbaston Jan 13/54.

My dear Fr Wilfrid,

The Countess de la Pasture recommends herself to your prayers and to those of the Confraternity of the Precious Blood. Include also her daughter, a dear child, who with her mother, has given up wealth to become Catholic.

The mother is confined to one position by a sort of rheumatism in the knees, and is sinking under it — and has great internal troubles, her daughter says.

[1] Ryder was in need of a school for his daughter. See letter of 16 Nov. 1853.
[2] The striking sermon Newman preached on love and virginity is as yet unpublished. It is described in Meriol Trevor, *Newman The Pillar of the Cloud*, p. 90.

I have never spoken to you about your book.[1] I think. 1. it is extremely necessary for these times. 2. most engagingly or rather fascinatingly written. 3 (the conclusion) likely with God's blessing to do a great deal of good

Ever Yrs affly J H N.

Please tell F Antony I want a line from him in answer to mine.[2]

TO ROBERT ISAAC WILBERFORCE

Edgbaston Jany 13/54

My dear Wilberforce

Owing to Irish dilatoriness, I shall doubtless be here to the end of this month

Ever Yrs affly John H Newman

TO J. M. CAPES

Edgbaston. Jany 15/54

My dear Capes,

The Review shall go back to you tomorrow.[3] I talked to Northcote the other day on its subject. I fully think, as I said to him, that the Tu quoque must be taken. I recollect Lord Brougham saying, in the Reform Bill debates, that there *must* be a dispensing power somewhere — and of course Parliament was it. Think of the Oxford oaths to Statutes; of the Epinomis[4] in the Statute Book etc etc. Again, the quotations from St Alfonso, etc should be closely sifted, for there are mistakes, doubtless.

---

[1] *All for Jesus*, first published in 1853 and already in its third edition.

[2] Hutchison had replied affirmatively to an enquiry of Newman's as to whether he and others would assist the Catholic weekly the *Lamp*, but had sent his letter to Dublin.

[3] i.e. The *Christian Remembrancer* for Jan. 1854. See letter of 5 Jan. to Capes.

[4] ἐπινομίς, appendix to a law. Capes adopted Newman's argument: 'At Oxford (and we believe at Cambridge also) the Fellows swear to observe the college statutes, without the remotest intention of so doing. There is not a word of limitation to the promise, so as to confine it to things enforced. They swear as the original founders bade them, i.e. to do the very things which the founders intended to be actually and always done . . . There is no recognised authority for dispensing with the observance; yet the swearing goes on. . . . Public opinion sanctions the lie as a lawful one . . .' The *Rambler* (April 1854), pp. 326–7.

My only fear is, that you will have so much matter, that you will not be able to do justice to the subject in an article in the Rambler.

I don't think you can get Dr Cullen to look over it — he has barely time to write a letter now and then. If you know Dr Moriarty of All-hallows, he would be a very good man — or one of the Maynooth Professors.

I am getting my way in Dublin. Perhaps I shall go to Rome

Ever Yrs affly in Xt John H Newman of the Oratory

TO JAMES HOPE-SCOTT

Jan 15/54

Private

My dear Hope

Rome is speaking in the matter — Perhaps I shall have to go there

Ever Yrs affly J H N

TO J. I. TAYLOR

Edgbaston. Jan. 15/54

My dear Dr Taylor

I thank you very much for your welcome letter and its inclosure.[1]

It has struck me whether it would not be well for me to go to Rome

---

[1] For Taylor's letter and his enclosure, which was a copy of a letter of 27 Dec. 1853 from Wiseman to Cullen, see *A.W.* pp. 312–13 and *McGrath*, pp. 238–9. This letter from Rome explained that Pius IX had several times spoken with great interest about the University, and had offered to issue whatever Brief would set it going. Wiseman suggested to Cullen that the Brief should confirm Newman as Rector and give the power of choosing professors to such persons as Cullen might name. Wiseman ended his letter, '"Vedo," the Pope said to me a few days ago, "che bisogna che il primo colpo venga dal Papa". If your Grace thinks so too, the thing is done.'

When sending his enclosure on 13 Jan., the day Wiseman's letter reached Dublin, Taylor wrote that, 'It has afforded to his Grace the greatest consolation and joy: He sees the dark cloud so long hanging over our project beginning to clear off: the Holy Father will again put his hand to the wheel and will set all again in motion.

Dr. Cullen has already written to Rome for authority to convoke the Bishops *synodically* on the subject and he expects to have that power very soon . . .

Meanwhile he hopes that you will come over, as soon as business beyond will permit. . . . The Archbishop will write to him [Wiseman] at once requesting him to act upon the views he submits. . . . Would it not be well that *you too* would write to the Cardinal and suggest whatever plans occur to your mind? This from myself—But I am sure his Grace would like it also.'

14

myself, rather than to write to the Cardinal. It is so difficult to say exactly or all one wishes in a letter. Perhaps the Archbishop will kindly give me his opinion.

What I should recommend would be a mere *initiatory* step — If a Brief could be drawn up to this effect — to appoint me Rector, or Vicem Rectoris gerens, for this object, viz the setting up of the University — and to give me power to take measures towards that end, under the approbation and sanction of the 4 Archbishops. At the end of a year or two we might come again for a more definite Act on the part of the Holy See, and more formal provisions for the constitution of the University.

I am rather frightened lest Cardinal Wiseman should do too much. He is always full of kindness and very sanguine — and if I did not explain matters fully to him, we might find ourselves as perfectly formed as Louvain, with no means of working the system, and no students.[1]

If I went to Rome, of course the Archbishop would give me his full advice and instructions.

Very sincerely Yours in Xt John H Newman of the Oratory

TUESDAY 17 JANUARY 1854   a great deal of wind in these weeks

TO MRS J. W. BOWDEN

Jany 18. 1854 Edgbaston

My dear Mrs Bowden,

Your letter and Emily's took me quite by surprise, and startled and distressed me.[2] I cannot doubt that we shall feel quite reconciled to it soon. All along I have felt for you far more than another can know —

---

[1] In 'Memorandum about my connection with the Catholic University,' Newman quoted a note made at the time about why he wrote to Taylor proposing to go at once to Rome: '"My reasons are, 1. I fear the Cardinal will do too much, and that we shall have a University set up before we know where we are; at all events that something would be done *different* from what is wanted. 2. I shall be able to leave the matter in Manning's hands then" (who at that time was in Rome,) "but I cannot put it into them without talks with him. 3. I cannot really do any thing in Ireland, till the Brief comes; and now Dr. Cullen presses me to go to Ireland at once, *while* it is coming." (which I did not relish.) "If I don't go to Rome, it won't be done so quickly, meanwhile, I shall have a long kicking my heels and time-wasting in Ireland, when I am so wanted here." (i.e. in Birmingham.) "4. I shall come back from Rome with a prestige, as if I had a blunderbuss in my pocket."' *A.W.* pp. 313–14.

[2] Emily Bowden wanted to follow her sister's example and become a Visitation nun at Westbury.

J.H.N.—C   15

though far more removed from any one's understanding, except your Lord and Saviour's, is the extent of the trial which is apparently coming on you. He will sustain you, as you know well — and I suppose it is right and safe for you at present to make up your mind that it *is* to be — but I have not yet quite sufficient grounds to content me.

I do not think that Emily's feelings are to be judged of by her present state — Certainly at this moment she is opening her heart to the idea, which is before her, and would be sadly disappointed at finding that her hope was a fancy — but to go to Westbury, to see her sister, and her profession etc etc was enough to excite her.

It really seems to me, then, that *she must not go for a retreat there* after Easter or any time. It is no fair trial. I feel quite decidedly on this point. Could you fancy any other place or person she could go to? Several have occurred to me — which I throw out, thinking they may suggest something to you.

I hear a good deal of Abbé Vesque the Confessor of the Norwood Nuns. And the Revd Mother is, I believe, a most excellent sensible person, and a lady by birth and education.[1] And Norwood is so near London, that Emily might go there without an effort.

Again, people who know Fr Ravignan speak most strongly of his great discernment of character and state of mind. But I am not certain that you have any drawing to Paris.[2]

The Visitation vocation is so very peculiar, that, if Emily *has* a vocation, it is as unfair to *it* to let her attempt a noviciate *there*, ⟨and that might be the result of a retreat⟩ as the special feelings the place creates make it unsuitable to her, if she has *not*.

You will not suppose any thing I have said is in disparagement of the judgment of Sister Frances Angela[3] — I only say that a retreat at Westbury would not be a real and fair confirmation of it.

Ever Yours affly in Xt   John H Newman of the Oratory

P.S.   Of course I shall not forget you, nor do I, in mass etc.
Give my truest love to dear Emily and thank her for her letter.

[1] Désiré Michel Vesque, the chaplain of the Norwood nuns, became Bishop of Roseau, the capital of Dominica, in 1856 and died on 10 Aug. 1859 in his 41st year. In 1848 Henriette le Forestier d'Osseville (1803–58), in religion Mère Sainte Marie, brought the Daughters of the Faithful Virgin from the Mother House at La Délivrande, Bayeux, to Norwood, and died there.
[2] Gustave Xavier de Ravignan (1795–1858), Jesuit, succeeded Lacordaire in the pulpit at Notre Dame in Paris, 1837–46, and especially in his later years exercised great influence as a director.
[3] See next letter.

TO SISTER FRANCES ANGELA VAUGHAN

Edgbaston. January 19. 1854

My dear Sister M. Frances Angela,[1]

It was a great kindness and favour in you to write to me. I feel myself happy in being known to you and your holy community, for I cannot help being sure that my name will sometimes occur in the good prayers of you all, as it has already, and that I who live in the world and am so far from God, shall participate in your merits who are all of you so inexpressibly, intimately dear to Him who has redeemed us all.

It must be a great rejoicing to dear Emily Bowden to find you give her hopes of a vocation — and, severe as will be the bereavement to her Mother, I am sure she will go through the trial in the heroic spirit which I have always admired in her. It will be wonderful indeed if it shall turn out to be God's will that you should have both her daughters.

I feel the justice of what you say, and trust most fully the experience and judgment of a person who has opportunities such as yours — nor have I anything to add or to remark.[2]

One point there is on which I do not see my way, but it has relation to something future. I think Emily's friends would have clearer proof what God's will is concerning her, if she made up her mind, not at Westbury but at a distance from her sister. I know how clear-sighted you would be in detecting human motives and human feeling, which she might not be conscious of herself, but it must be recollected that she has various friends, some of them Protestants, who, though kind-hearted and kind to her, and ready to yield to what is the clear dictate of her reason, might think that her reason had not fair play, in a case where her feelings would be so much excited. Even if she never spoke a word to her sister, still it might be said that the consciousness she was near, and the imagination of her presence, would first bias her will and her judgment, produce an excitement in her heart, and lead her to fancy she had resolutions which otherwise would not be clear to her — and secondly would lead her and others to fancy that the vocation, which she had, was towards the Nuns of the Visitation. They would say, that, going to you, she was going to dear and honored friends, and that it was not religion which she sought, but you. Do not suppose I meant

[1] Frances Angela Vaughan (1805–61), one of the Vaughans of Courtfield and an aunt of Cardinal Vaughan, entered the Convent at Westbury in 1823, and was three times Superior there.

[2] Sister Frances Vaughan had put forward the Reverend Mother's proposal that Emily Bowden should make a retreat within the enclosure, in order to decide whether she had a vocation.

17

that you could be so deceived; but it seems to me to be well to avoid even the appearance, of what is not likely to happen really.

You will see I have written to you quite unreservedly, and I know you would wish me to do so.

With my best respects to your Revd Mother and all the Community, and repeating my hope of your holy prayers for me and mine.

I am, My dear Sister M. Frances Angela, Sincerely Yours in Jesus & Mary

John H Newman of the Oratory.

TO HENRY WILBERFORCE

Edgbaston Jany. 19. 1854

My dear H W

Day by day have I been waiting to write to you, expecting a letter from Dublin — but it has not *yet* come — but now I shall write any how.

⌐I trust I have got my way. Unless a letter comes absolutely negativing it,[1] I am going to Rome, to return as soon as I can, meanwhile I shall for a day or two come over to Dublin.

You may tell Ornsby this, who must wonder at my silence.⌐ But I shall wait one or two posts more before I take steps — so don't speak of it either of you till you hear it from others. ⌐My first act will be to write to Mr O Ferrall for money for my trip.[2]

My object in coming over would be to put out an advertisement, saying that the Schools would open in the Autumn — that names of candidates for admission are requested in order to provide lodgings for them — that the entrance examination will consist of such and such subjects, and any other points which appear necessary.⌐

I would have you and Ornsby turn in your minds these points. e.g. whether there *should* be an entrance examination, and if so in what. ⌐My first idea is in something which will admit of great *latitude* of proficiency in the examinee — e.g. the first book of Homer's Iliad — the first book of Virgil's Aeneid — the first book of Euclid, or Algebra up to Quadratic Equations.⌐

You shall hear again as soon as I have any thing to say.

I am hoping (entre nous) that Robert [Wilberforce] will call here.

---

[1] [[my resolution]].
[2] James O'Ferrall was a member of the University Sub-committee.

I do trust you and Ornsby are getting out of your great family anxieties

Ever Yrs affly J H N

P.S. You may tell Ornsby whatever I have told you.

⌐P.S. I have just heard from Ireland — I do *not* go to Rome — but I have got my way.[1]

I shall be coming to Ireland *at once* —¬ I shall call on you in my way to Dublin.

FRIDAY 20 JANUARY 1854 Lord Feilding called and had dinner

TO FRANCIS RIVINGTON

Edgbaston. Bm Jany 20. 1854

sent in substance

Dear Sir,

In reply to your letter which came to me last evening, I assure you that I will attend to its subject directly I return from Ireland, whither I am on the point of going, which will be about a fortnight hence.[2]

It perplexes me to think how any copies of Dr Pusey's notes on Number 70 can possibly remain. I doubt whether more than a second edition was ever printed and he published it in 1834 or 1835. Besides this, you have (I believe) 300 copies of all the remaining Tracts still in your hands, which with the 180 you say have come down to us leaves 480 on hand, which in the case of the second edition of a Tract of which the former parts are long out of print is at first sight incredible.[3]

Perhaps before I pull to pieces the packet you would be so good as to set me right on these points.

I have referred to Messrs Gilbert and Rivington's Account from February to December 1839, and find that *I* paid (and not Dr Pusey) for the re-editions of Numbers 18 and 66 in that year — and therefore I conceive there is no doubt that Dr Pusey paid only for the original

[1] See letter of 20 Jan. to Taylor.

[2] Francis Rivington wrote on 18 Jan., 'Among the Tracts for the Times which we recently returned to you we sent 180 copies of Number 70 being the Notes to the First Edition of Dr Pusey's Tract on Baptism. I find from a letter lately received from Dr Pusey that these copies belong to him as he paid for the printing. . . . I find myself obliged to ask the favour of you to return them to us, if possible, as Dr Pusey wishes to have them for his own use. . . . .'

[3] This point is developed in a further paragraph, which has alternative versions intertwined.

edition in 1834.[1] The account stands thus — Messrs G and R's bills
are two, first £801. 4. and then £160. 11 for No 81, which they seem
to have sent in some months later, from this I have, in a memorandum
at the foot of the page deducted the expence of 2 Editions (of 1000 and
2000 copies) of the *enlarged* Tract Number 67 (on Baptism) of Dr
Pusey's which Dr Pusey paid for, which came to £155. 15. 6 and
186. 15 respectively, and then state the date of my payment of the
remainder — thus

	801.	4.	
155. 15. 6.			
186. 15. 0	342.	10.	6
	458.	13.	6
Number 81 omitted —	160.	11.	0
	619.	4.	6

1840
paid — Messrs Rivingtons

	March	–	300.	0.	0
ditto	April 30	–	319.	4.	6
			619.	4.	6

It will be observed that I also paid for printing of Dr Pusey's Tract 81
— which I doubt not (though I have not time to refer) you have ever
paid to me.

Also it is clear that Number 67 (the first part of Baptism was out of
print in beginning of 1839 — therefore the 'Notes' or original Number 70
for which Dr Pusey sends could not have continued in print much later.

TO J. I. TAYLOR

Jany 20 [1854]

My dear Dr Taylor

I write a hurried line to say that I am trying to get off to Dublin
every day — and hope to do so very soon, as the Archbishop wishes.

[1] Pusey was also enquiring about Tracts 18 and 66, copies of which had been returned to Newman. Rivington wrote that the conclusion from his own accounts was
that Newman had paid for these. See also letter of 28 Jan. to Rivington.

I shall have to come back here for a few days at the Purification and shall then return to Dublin[1]

Very sincerely Yours John H Newman

SATURDAY 21 JANUARY 1854 Mr Lynch came — *going* [?] *in two days.*

TO J. M. CAPES

Jany 21/54

My dear Capes

A great deal might be said about the Catholic *definition* of virtues.

E.g. Viva says (as I *suppose* St Alfonso would) 'Qui dicit, "voveo castitatem, sed nolo illam servare," *certe non mentitur*, est tamen Deo infidelis.'[2]

The Protestant stops at 'non mentitur,' and cries out, 'so a man may take an oath, and yet not lie, if he never meant it.'

True, he does not sin in what we call lying, but in unfaithfulness — and *mortally*

That occurs constantly in moral theology, and it requires a treatise to bring it out.

Thus a person does not sin against *faith* in this or that, *but* — he is guilty of contempt of God.

Animals have not *rights, but* — cruelty is in itself a sin.

I cannot recollect instances, but it is a most fruitful subject, and would much disabuse the public mind.

[1] Taylor wrote on 17 Jan., 'The Archbishop [Cullen] seems to think it would be better of you not to go to Rome just now.

In his last letter to Propaganda to which he is daily expecting an answer he consulted them as to the fitness of calling together the Irish Bishops. . . . He would like you to be on the spot when the answer arrives.

Again he thinks it most probable that the issuing of the Brief whenever it does take place will be accompanied by some mark of distinction to yourself as its Rector . . ., it would appear more appropriate that you should not be on the spot at the time . . .'

This was the first hint Newman received of the plan to make him a titular bishop, in order to give him freedom of action in the University. Wiseman had obtained the 'hearty concurrence' of Cullen in this plan in Oct. 1853, when they met at Amiens, and had just written to inform the latter of Pius IX's agreement to it, authorising him to tell Newman 'as much as he thought proper.' See Wiseman's letter of 20 Jan. to Newman, placed before Newman's of 1 Feb., and Newman's letter of 23 Jan. to Taylor. Cf. also *A.W.* p. 314, and *McGrath*, p. 240.

[2] Dominic Viva, S.J., *Cursus Theologicus*, IV, *De Fide, Spe, et Charitate*, Padua 1755, I, iv, p. 11.

E.g. Such and such an act is no sin against the divine law, *but* it is forbidden by the human, and in things indifferent it is a sin not to obey the human.

This or that is not irreverence, *but* it is a scandal etc etc.

Ever Yrs affly J H N

P S. I trust I have weathered my difficulties in Dublin, and am going there tomorrow night.

'Veracitas conformat *verba menti*, Fidelitas conformat *verba rebus.*'[1]

TO JOSEPH ALEMANY, ARCHBISHOP OF SAN FRANCISCO

Jany 22/54

My dear Lord Archbishop

You may fancy with what extreme satisfaction and gratitude I have received the very munificent mark of their charity which the clergy and laity of California have sent me, conveyed to me by your good priest, Father Accolti, which is still more welcome as coming to me with the sanction and co-operation of your Grace, whom I have never ceased to remember with sentiments of deep veneration from the day that you so kindly allowed me and mine to make your acquaintance and ask your blessing.[2] The only alloy in my feelings or qualification is my deep consciousness how unworthy I am both of the consideration you have shown me and the words you use of me. But to dwell on such thoughts, however well founded, would be a very ungracious way of meeting the warm hearted sympathy of such friends, and therefore I put them aside and do but thank God that He has deigned to make me, such as I am, an object of it.

You draw my attention to the various nations which severally in the persons of priests under your jurisdiction have joined in it. This is a most striking addition to its value to me; and, many and dear to me as have been the proofs given me during my late anxieties that one heart and but one beats all through the Catholic Church, there needed but this, to make a present from California the most striking instance of all

[1] Dominic Viva, *loc. cit.*

[2] Father Accolti brought from Archbishop Alemany a letter conveying the congratulations and sympathy of himself and his flock over the Achilli trial, together with a nugget set in a gold ring of great thickness, weighing in all over seventeen ounces. On the ring was inscribed, 'Reverendo Admodum Doctori J. H. Newman, Vero Fidei Defensori Catholici California.'

Archbishop Alemany visited the Oratory at Birmingham, on his way to California, on 2 Sept. 1850.

The present has besides a singular interest in itself. All people here feel the utmost curiosity to see so beautiful a specimen of the far famed gold fields of California. I should not be surprised if soon it was the wonder of all Birmingham and, if St Philip blesses us, it will go down in this house to posterity and will be gazed upon when we are gone, by antiquarians as the precious relic of an era which then will have become historical[1]

TO MISS M. R. GIBERNE

Edgbaston. Jany 22/54

My dear Miss Giberne

I did not answer your letter sooner, because there was a chance of my coming to Rome on this University matter — indeed (tho' I do not wish it mentioned) there is still some prospect of my coming. In that case I should have brought with me the books you speak of.[2] If any were to be translated into Italian, it ought to be my Oscott Sermon called 'The Second Spring.' I go to Dublin tomorrow, and shall come back for the Purification, hoping to stop till dear Fr Joseph's anniversary, which is on the 13th February. If I don't come to Rome, I think of sending you a parcel. I hope you got my letter inclosing one to Cardinal Brunelli.[3] The report here is that the Queen is going mad, and that the people won't bear Prince Albert as Regent.[4] Poor thing, a war will try her certainly, for she has had nothing but peace and plenty hitherto. I want very much to get, if I could, the name and address of the lawyer at Naples who was so kind to Fr Joseph in the Achilli matter — as I wish to make him a present. I have not a dream how your politics are at Rome in this quarrel between the North and England and France. Perhaps no one there thinks much about it. Every body is wearing moustache or beard now — all the snobs in Birmingham — people you must know, though I don't like to mention their names. Today I heard that my dear brother Frank wears a moustache! I hope you have got

[1] Newman later presented the nugget to the Oratory at London, where it is still preserved.

[2] In her letter of 8 Dec. Miss Giberne spoke of wanting the tenth of the *Discourses on University Education*, and *Hymns for the use of the Birmingham Oratory*, Dublin 1854.

[3] See letter of 14 Dec. 1853 to Miss Giberne.

[4] Faber wrote to Newman on 14 Jan., 'There was a report in town yesterday that ministers feared the queen's reason going. She is excited about the Prince Albert question, and it is said the country won't bear him for Regent. Rumour is that the success of the Exhibition turned his head.' To the Queen's annoyance Prince Albert had not yet been given the title of Prince Consort, and was personally unpopular. The Crimean War was about to begin, and he was thought to be pro-Russian.

out of your low spirits now. It is very trying to be a stranger in a place —
but the feeling brings us nearly [sic] to our unseen strength, our Lord
and His Mother. What are Protestants, when so situated, without the
Blessed Sacrament! Marian Bowden was professed at Westbury the
other day — I went down to preach the Sermon.

You know I suppose that the London House have given us Fr
Dalgairns to make up the loss of F Joseph. The London Oratory is not
yet finished. You see I have nothing to tell you — but I don't like to
delay writing

Ever Yours affectly in Xt J H N

MONDAY 23 JANUARY 1854   was starting for Ireland, when a letter gave me a
reprieve   Mr Lynch went   Lord Dunraven called for several hours

TO JOHN EDWARD BOWDEN

Edgbaston Jany 23. 1854

My dear John

I shall be much obliged by your contriving to send, as you offer me,
£10 to M. Bonavia. And you must tell me how I can write to him, to
tell him I have done so[1]

Ever Yrs most affly J H N

TO JAMES HOPE-SCOTT

[[The Oratory]] Edgbaston ⌈Jany 23. 1854⌉

My dear Hope Scott

⌈We shall gladly receive, as far as we are concerned, Lord Ralph
Kerr, if things turn out as you expect. We were rejoiced to hear of his
and his brother's reception.[2]

[1] See letter of 5 Jan.

[2] Hope-Scott wrote on 21 Jan., 'The other day two of Lady Lothian's sons—aged
respectively about 17 and 13—were received into the Church—against the wish of some
of the guardians, and under circumstances which are likely to cause some disturbance.'
Lady Lothian and her two daughters were already Catholics, and the two boys went
with their mother secretly to Edinburgh, in order to be received. Hope-Scott asked
if Newman would undertake to finish the education of the elder boy, Lord Ralph
Kerr, 'very nice—clever gentlemanlike and good—' at Edgbaston, provided the guardians allowed it. Lord Ralph Kerr arrived at Edgbaston on 17 Feb. His own narrative
of these events is in Cecil Kerr, *Cecil Marchioness of Lothian*, London n.d. [about 1920],
pp. 121–34.

24

I was starting for Dublin last night: but there is virtue in dawdling, at least in going to Ireland. This morning comes a letter putting me off till after the Purification. It is no real delay. Dr Cullen had expected daily a letter from Rome, which he wished me to see at once — but it has not come — so he has no immediate call for me. I am satisfied now that things are progressing — but you recollect the German story of the Broomsticks — I only fear too much will be done — and this is why I wished at once to go to Rome.[1]

Ever Yours affly in Xt John H Newman of the Oratory

J R Hope Scott Esqr

TO RICHARD STANTON

Edgbaston. Jany 23. 1854

My dear Richard

What a shame I have not written to you — but *necessary* letters make one so languid and inert, but [that] one does not write where silence is not taken as an insult.

I hear a good account of your health, which consoles me — but I wish your F. Superior gave a better account of himself.

Thanks for your valuable Form of Elections.[2] I like much the idea of your drawing up a Formularium.

As to reception, I thought at Rome they followed the novice (or Triennial?) with lighted candles? I prefer the Roman to the Neapolitan way as to the *vestments* — blessing them seems monastic.

Should not the Novice (and lay brother) on admission make a profession of obedience etc, to Superiors, Rule etc, and especially that he means to remain in the Congregation till death?

We are making up our accounts and are sadly minus — Our *board* is £1100, for 24 or 25 mouths — our rates etc £130 — our whole expences little short of £1400. This has made me look with great anxiety at the prospect of yours in a dearer place — and this war will make every thing so dear and put on taxes

Ever Yrs affly in M & Ph [Mary and Philip] John H Newman

[1] The sorcerer's apprentice used a spell to make the broom do his work and then could not stop it.

[2] i.e. for an Oratorian community. Stanton was also drawing up a Form for the Reception of Novices.

TO J. I. TAYLOR

Edgbaston Jan 23/54

My dear Dr Taylor

Your letter just caught me before starting. Thank his Grace for his consideration.[1] However, I am packed up, and if it turn out he wants to see me before the Purification and sends me a line, I will come by the first Train[2]

Very sincerely Yours in Xt John H Newman

TO HENRY WILBERFORCE

Edgbaston ⌐Jany 23/54⌐

My dear Henry

⌐I was packing up and starting, when I had a letter to say I need not come till after the Purification.

This is *no delay* — entre nous, if I did not tell you before, Rome is moving, and will act — and we can do nothing till the act is done.⌐ I may be tempted to wish to stop here till after dear Fr Gordon's anniversary — but there is no real delay now. You may tell this to Ornsby, under strict secrecy

Ever Yrs affly J H N

[1] Taylor wrote on 21 Jan., 'The Archbishop bids me beg of you not to put yourself to the inconvenience of coming over before the Purification. It will be time enough after that.

It is no season of the year for exposing yourself to unnecessary journeys.

He has written to the Cardinal this day—He waited the entire week before doing so to see if there should be a letter from the Propaganda. None came.'

Cullen wrote on 21 Jan. to Wiseman in Rome about the plan to make Newman a bishop 'that perhaps it would be better to wait a little,' [*D R* (Spring 1960), p. 33] but Wiseman had already on 20 Jan. written to tell Newman that the Pope had given his assent.

Taylor did not tell Newman the contents of Cullen's letter of 21 Jan. to Wiseman, nor did he explain that Cullen had also written on 21 Jan. to Tobias Kirby his agent in Rome, who passed his views on to Propaganda, '. . . Mgr Cullen adds that, having heard that people have been pushing to have Father Newman made bishop *in partibus*, he would be delighted at such an appointment, but he is of opinion that it would be better to wait till the affairs of the university are put a little more in order.' Propaganda Archives, *S.R.C. Irlanda*, 1854–6, ff. 116 and 104, quoted by J. H. Whyte, *D R* (Spring 1960), p. 32, 'Newman in Dublin,' the use of whose excellent translation is gratefully acknowledged, and by V.F. Blehl, *Thought* (Spring 1960), pp. 117–18. See also letter of 7 April to Hope-Scott.

[2] Taylor replied on 25 Jan., 'I have not seen the Archbishop since ere yesterday—but I *know* he does not expect you until *after* the *Purification*.'

TO CARDINAL WISEMAN

Edgbaston. Jany 23. 1854

My dear Lord Cardinal

I do not like to plague your Eminence with letters, but having seen with great gratification a letter of yours to the Archbishop of Dublin, I write at his suggestion.[1]

My first wish was to run off to you at Rome instead of writing, for I feel I cannot say all I would in a letter, because there is *so much* to say, but his Grace, who is in a position to judge of the expediency of the step, advises me not.

It takes many words to put you in a condition to enter into what I wish about the University. I am perfectly sure we must be at first in a *provisional* state — any Brief then which set up Professors etc *at once* would be doing too much. The Louvain case was quite different — it was the restoration of an old University in a country, when Bishops and clergy and laity *understood the value and the drift* of the Institution. I think too the eventual Rector and officers had been already going on quietly for some years, before they were formally erected into a University.

What we must do at Dublin is to have an external *manifestation* and the beginning of an inward and real *formation*. These two objects will be at first distinct. 1. For the latter, we must have a few persons who thoroughly understand each other and whom I entirely know, who can quietly and without show be bringing into shape the students who come to us. 2. For the former, we want some popular Lecturers, Preachers, etc who *might or might* not ultimately belong to the body.

I think then the preliminary Brief which is contemplated at Rome should be very vague — it should appoint me Rector, or *Rectoris vicem gerens*, to take the steps necessary for erecting the University — it should give me the power, subject to the approbation of the (Bishops or) Archbishops, of appointing Lecturers and Tutors, for a space not exceeding three ⟨3⟩ years — and of taking such other steps as I thought necessary for the purpose. But it must not enter upon the question of the *normal constitution* of the University. It might give me the power of *admitting members* to the University, without touching the question of *Degrees*, which for various reasons is inexpedient at the moment.

You will smile at my laying down the law thus, in writing to *Rome* — but I am convinced that as much harm would come of attempting too much just now, as of doing too little. We must *feel our* way — and

[1] See letter of 15 Jan. to Taylor.

get over a mass of prejudice and opposition. *No rules* can do this —
but the zeal, energy, and prudence of the individuals employed in the
work.

Begging your Eminence's blessing & kissing the sacred purple I am,
My dear Lord Cardinal Yr affectionate friend & servt in Xt

John H Newman of the Oratory

TO HENRY WILBERFORCE

Edgbaston Jany 26/54

My dear Henry

I have just had your letter. A letter is lying for you from me at
Kingstown, unless it has been forwarded to you. If so, send it back to
Ornsby. I think I said he was to see it. We can give you a bed here.[1]
I don't go till after the 2nd of February

Ever Yrs affly J H N

All kind remembrances to Serjt and Mrs Bellasis

TO FRANCIS RIVINGTON

Edgbaston. Jany 28. 1854

My dear Sir

As I have been detained here a few days, I have opened the parcel[2]
— and I find, as you led me to expect, a number of copies of the Notes
on the Tract on Baptism. I also find a portion of Tract 69.

These I will send you as they have come. At the same time I propose also to send you nearly all of Numbers 18, 66, and 81, which I
shall put at Dr Pusey's disposal. I do not suppose he will find any
difficulty in accepting them from me; but I will gladly accept in return,
you may say, should he be willing, one or two copies of my three
volumes of St Athanasius in the Library of the Fathers.[3]

I shall also send you in separate parcels Mr Keble's Tracts, and Mr
Williams's — at the same time writing to them to ask them to tell you

[1] Wilberforce had left Ireland and was staying in London.
[2] See letter of 20 Jan. to Rivington.
[3] *Select Treatises of S. Athanasius in controversy with the Arians,* Oxford 1, 1842.
II, 1844, and *Historical Tracts of S. Athanasius,* Oxford 1843.

where they would like them sent. I wish you to put to my account any expences which the carriage involves.

I have ever considered the *copyright* of the Tracts as the property of their respective authors

I am, My dear Sir, Very faithfully Yours John H Newman

F Rivington Esqr
Sunday Jany 29.   I wrote the above yesterday, but there was no post last night — Your letter dated the 27th has not come till this morning[1] You will observe I had *no intention* at all of breaking up the Series, but had been negociating for the sale of the *whole*, (except 67-70), but your letter of the 18th stating Dr Pusey's wish to have his own Tracts (18 etc) had determined me to do so, in spite of overtures which had been made to me[2]

TO BISHOP ULLATHORNE

Edgbaston. Jany 28/54

My dear Lord,

I do not like to leave for Ireland, without expressing to your Lordship the interest I take in the Birmingham Catholic Association. It is an institution very much needed in the place, and, I feel sure, will be productive of very great good. It seems to me likely to make Catholics better acquainted with each other, and in consequence to increase their mutual esteem and kind feeling, to facilitate their cooperation for objects and on emergencies, which concern the Catholic body generally,

---

[1] Rivington wrote that 180 copies of *Notes to Dr Pusey's Tract on Baptism* had been sent to Newman under a misapprehension. 'Dr. Pusey requests us to ask you to return them to us for him and also the surplus copies of his other three Tracts, viz: 573— No 18 / 331—No 66 / 392—No 81 / He begs me to add that he will be glad to refund any loss which may have been occasioned by printing the Editions.' Newman cancelled the first draft of his present postscript, which began, 'I am sorry that Dr Pusey should have requested you to *ask me to return* the surplus copies of his Tracts. . . .'

[2] Rivington replied on 23 Feb. that he had sent Pusey the *Tracts* for which he asked. Pusey then wrote to Newman asking him to correspond with Rivington about his three volumes of St Athanasius. Newman's reply is lost, but Pusey wrote again about 7 March,

'My dearest N.

I am so glad that I wrote. I did not like to write about a few copies of a Tract when I could not write about all which was nearest my heart, my daily dying, or my daily life, the achings of the heart, or God's mercies. So I thought that he would settle it, as a matter of business, in which I supposed him to have made a mistake. But amid all these heartaches, I could not write about a few tracts.

Pray print whatever you like of your S. Athanasius. It is yours of course, without asking me. Rivington has nothing to do with it. . . .' Newman replied on 11 March.

and to enable them to act as protectors and champions of their poorer or oppressed brethren.

I am sure that you, and all the members of the association, will believe the regret I feel, before I express it, at my absence from their public dinner in the course of this week. I thought over the matter a good deal, but I could not persuade myself, that it was not a less evil to abstain from their annual meeting, than to run the risk of displeasing St Philip, by transgressing his rule and tradition,[1] which puts upon us so few restraints and exacts of us such little sacrifices, while it makes us such great returns

Begging your Lordship's blessing, I am, My dear Lord, Your affte friend and servt in Xt

                                   John H Newman of the Oratory
The Lord Bishop of Birmingham

                        TO ISAAC WILLIAMS

                              Edgbaston Birmingham Jany 28. 1854
My dear Williams,

As the Volumes of Tracts for the Times are now so fragmentary as scarcely to admit of sale, I think you and dear Keble will let me send you the remaining stock of your own Tracts respectively. The *copyright* I have always considered as simply yours.

For this purpose I have had yours and his done up in parcels, and by the time you get this, they will be at Rivingtons' for your orders where to send them. They have, I believe, a difficulty in giving room for them at their warehouses.

                              Affectionately Yours John H Newman

SUNDAY 29 JANUARY 1854 Mr Gibson of Liverpool called from Mr Nugent

MONDAY 30 JANUARY fine bright mornings for some time with high wind.

TUESDAY 31 JANUARY Northcote came for some months

WEDNESDAY 1 FEBRUARY Captain Patterson dined in passing thro' Lord Campden called.

[1] i.e. as to not dining out. Ullathorne read this letter publicly at the dinner on 31 Jan. See letter of 5 Feb. 1854.

Rome Jan 20. 1854[1]

Private

My dear Dr Newman

It is a delicate thing perhaps for me to learn any thing from *you*, about the University; but it is not so for me to speak about it to the H.F. [Holy Father] for two reasons.

First he has several times spoken to me; and 2ndly my position here is naturally different from what it would be in England. While I am *in curia*, no one can consider me as merely an English Bishop, in whom it might be impertinence to meddle in the affairs of another country or Church. As Cardinal, however unworthy, I am bound to assist the H.S. [Holy See] by my advice on any matters proposed to me by it, without reference to country. In fact I am of the Pope's Council.

From the first audience I had of the H.F. I did not hesitate to say that the University would never, could never be started except by a Pontifical Brief, and that so great a work deserved, and required this flowing from the Fountain of jurisdiction. His Holiness said that if materials were furnished him, he would gladly issue such a high document. He spoke to me again, and agreed to the same conclusion.

At a third audience I begged to make a suggestion long on my mind, and about which I consulted Archbishop Cullen at Amiens,[2] and obtained his hearty concurrence — indeed I had mentioned it in England I think to H. Wilberforce. It was that H.H [His Holiness] would graciously please to create you Bishop *in partibus*, which would at once give you a right to sit with the Bishops in all consultations, would raise you above all other officers, professors, etc of the University, and would give dignity to this itself, and to its head. The holy Father at once assented. I wrote to Dr C. and authorised His Grace to tell you as much as he thought proper.[3]

Your letter[4] to me came after this; and you must pardon me, if I communicated it to the H.F. of course in all confidence; for it showed better than any studied narrative could possibly do, the real difficulties of the case. I made my own observations on it.

This day I had another audience, in which H.H. graciously told me, that he had commissioned Mgr Pacifici (who has been ill since October) yesterday to draw up a Brief, establishing the University and naming Archbishop Cullen Chancellor; and smilingly drawing his hands down from each side of his neck to his breast, he added: '*e manderemo a Newman la crocetta, lo faremo Vescovo di Porfirio, o qualche luogo.*' This was spoken in his kindest manner. Of course, Porphyrium was only an *exempli gratia*, as it is filled up. But I thought it would be pleasing to you to have the Pope's own words.

I trust that the impulse thus coming from above downwards will be efficacious. I trust you will keep good heart, and not be discouraged by that

---

[1] Newman noted beneath this date, 'received Jany 31.'

[2] On 12 Oct. 1853, at a great meeting for the translation of the relics of St Theodosia.

[3] See note to letter of 20 Jan. to Taylor. Cullen allowed Newman to be told that he would receive 'some mark of distinction.'   [4] i.e. that of 2 Jan. 1854.

opposition, which San Filippo would have considered a good augury in a great and holy work.

To return to yourself, I will not hurt your feelings by what would be painful to them; but I must add, that I have long wished to do what I have done, even independently of the circumstances which appear to me to *require* it: for it appears to me to end many difficulties, and place things on their right basis. But ever since the Achilli judgment, I have felt that a mark of honour and favour, and an expression of sympathy *from the Church* was requisite; and this seemed to me the proper mode of bestowing it.

I have only one thing to add, that I request the consolation and honour, of conferring on you the proposed dignity, when the proper time shall come.

Today also I obtained the degree of D.D. for Mr now Dr Manning, which the Pope granted with great and manifest pleasure.

I find myself in very much better health than I have long enjoyed. Business however will keep me something longer, I fear quite into spring.

I will offer no congratulations as yet. You will use quite your own discretion about this letter.[1]

Yours ever affectly in Xt   N. Card. Wiseman[2]

TO CARDINAL WISEMAN

Edgbaston. February 1. 1854.

My dear Lord Cardinal,

Your Eminence's letter arrived yesterday evening, the very *anniversary* of the day of my having to appear in Court, and of the sentence from Coleridge. And tomorrow, the Purification, is the sixth anniversary of the establishment of our Congregation, and completes the fifth year of our settlement in Birmingham. As to the Holy Father's most gracious and condescending purpose about me, I should say much of my sense of the extreme tenderness towards me shown in it, did not a higher thought occupy me, for it is the act of the Vicar of Christ, and I accept it most humbly as the will and determination of Him whose I am, and who may do with me what He will. Perhaps I ought to remind your

[1] Newman thought it best to keep the matter secret, but Ullathorne heard of it independently, and made it known. See second note to next letter. It was also reported in the *Tablet* on 11 Feb. See letter of 9 Feb. to Flanagan.

[2] Newman commented, when he copied this letter in 'Memorandum about my connection with the Catholic University': 'This letter was a great satisfaction to me. I really did think that the Cardinal had hit the right nail on the head, and had effected what would be a real remedy against the difficulties which lay in my way. I wrote to Dr. Grant of Southwark, who congratulated me on the Pope's intention, that I never could have fancied the circumstances would exist such as to lead me to be glad to be made a Bishop; but that so it was, I did feel glad, for I did not see, without some accession of weight to my official position, I could overcome the *inertia* or opposition which existed in Ireland on the project of a University.' *A.W.* p. 316.

Eminence that, to do it, the Holy Father must be pleased to supersede one of St Philip's provisions in our Rule, which runs thus:—'Dignitates ullas nemo possit accipere, nisi Pontifex jubeat.'[1]

As to yourself, I hope without my saying it, you will understand the deep sense I have of the consideration and attentive kindness you have now, as ever, shown me. I shall only be too highly honored by receiving consecration from your Eminence[2]

Febr. 6. I do not know that I have any thing to add to the 2nd letter I sent your Eminence about a fortnight ago.[3] I go to Ireland to-night or tomorrow morning. My purpose is to call on different Bishops about the country, and to try to talk them into feeling interest in the University. Now that I am to be recognised as having a position in it, I have no hesitation in doing so at once. I wrote to Dr Dollinger about 6 weeks ago,[4] asking him to assist, if only for a time, but I have not had his answer yet.

The reports in England are that your health is much better for your change of scene and work — it was very pleasant to have your own confirmation of them.

Pray convey my hearty congratulations to dear Dr Manning — I hope he is not ailing as he was last winter

Kissing his Holiness's feet and your Eminence's purple I am, My dear Lord, Your affectionate friend and servant in Xt

John H Newman of the Oratory

The Cardinal Wiseman &c &c.

SATURDAY 4 FEBRUARY 1854   Mr [Terence] Flanagan came
SUNDAY 5 FEBRUARY   Mr Flanagan went[5]

[1] *Instituta Congregationis Anglicae Oratorii S. Philippi Nerii*, Rome 1847, Decretum LXXII, p. 31.

[2] Cullen succeeded in postponing and preventing Newman's becoming a bishop. See notes to letters of 23 Jan. to Taylor and 7 April to Hope-Scott. Meanwhile Ullathorne had learned of Newman's proposed elevation, and already on 31 Jan. mentioned it publicly in Birmingham, see letter of 5 Feb. to Ullathorne, and it soon became known generally. Wiseman's letter of 20 Jan., to which Newman is now replying was 'the beginning and the end of his appearance in this transaction. His concluding words were that he hoped to have the consolation of consecrating me.' 'The Cardinal never wrote to me a single word, or sent any sort of message to me, in explanation of the change of intention about me, till the day of his death.' *A.W.* pp. 318–19.

[3] i.e. that of 23 Jan. 1854.

[4] i.e. letter of 15 Dec. 1853.

[5] This entry is repeated on 6 Feb.

TO BISHOP HENDREN

Febr 5/54

(Sent nearly verbatim)

My dear Lord

I do not like to start for Ireland, which I expect to do tomorrow, without expressing my regret that I do not obtain your Lordship's blessing viva voce, before I go — but I doubt not I may reckon on it still.

I trust that this sharp winter has not been the occasion of any of those painful attacks, from which I know you sometimes suffer — I believe winter is not so bad for the gout as autumn and spring

We have been very careful of your room and books; a fire has been frequently kept up there, and frequent dustings administered.[1]

I must not end without touching on to a very unpleasant and prosaic subject. We have been making up our accounts for the year, and we find what with the expences of the house and its situation, and what with the rise of prices and the prospect of war taxes, we cannot support our establishment on the rate of charges which I mentioned to our Bishop when your Lordship came in May last. I told Dr Ullathorne that we charged our Fathers a guinea a week — we find that their board, lodging etc individually amounts at least to a *guinea and a half* per week. This is a most serious matter to us: but it obliges our Treasurer much against his will, to impose *the same increase* of pension for the time to come on your Lordship.

With all our kindest respects and united request for your Lordship's blessing

I am &c J H N

TO RICHARD STANTON

Edgbaston. Febr 5/54

My dear F Richard

I should have written to you before this in answer to your and your Father's letters,[2] had we not been so busy. I suppose I certainly go to Ireland tomorrow.

[1] Bishop Hendren, after resigning the See of Nottingham owing to ill-health, came to live at the Birmingham Oratory. He was at this time on a visit to Taunton. Cf. letter of 6 March to Flanagan.

[2] Stanton and Faber, the 'Father' i.e. Superior, wrote on 2 Feb. The latter described 'the shocking occurrence which took place today while I was ill in bed. Mr

How shocked and troubled you must all have been! and an inquest of course! it is seldom that any thing so dreadful occurs to any one. We wish of course to send our special sympathy to poor Plater. A most terrible event — I hope the shock has not been too much for any of you.

I trust St Philip has enabled us to arrange our officers in the very best way which our body admitted, and, since I am going away, it is a comfort. I write this for your Father, but, as I am writing to you, I do not begin a fresh letter. He will have a formal announcement soon.[1]

I am confirmed as F Superior the four F Deputies are Ambrose, Nicholas, Stanislas, and Edward, all exterior or managing men. F Bernard is Confessor, and (against our wish, but we could not help the pluralism) Novice Master — F Ambrose is Minister, F Frederic Musician, F. Austin Ceremoniere and Prefect of buildings, F Nicholas Sacristan, F. Stanislas Treasurer, F Henry Infirmarian and F Edward Prefect of the Oratory, and Procurator. I am Corrector of faults and Librarian.

Entre nous, our accounts are in a sad way — we are £530 minus — and *we cannot reduce*. The deficiency is owing to the additional cost of our House, which has obliged us to borrow the Fathers' private money, and thus burdened us with interest. If we do not get Lady O A's [Olivia Acheson] money,[2] I cannot *conceive* what is to be done — (but St Philip, I trust, will land that freight safe) but even it will not set us straight. Our living etc is about £1100 counting in boys and all, and we cannot bring it under — our whole expences about £1400 —

Now *we* began, intending to build a £11000 house. *You* have begun intending a £18.000 *We* began with £10.000 for the purpose distinct from private property — What have *you* begun with? I assure you I am made *very anxious* indeed about you. I do not say this to tease you, but to get you to look at it *practically*. If you are all doing this, I have not a word more to say — and would not, for it is disspiriting you

Ever Yrs affly J H N

Plater came to see F. Louis, and after 10 minutes very kind conversation in the recreation room, dropped down dead. . . . The body lies in our only room, waiting for the inquest; and we have sent for the relations. . . .' Mr Plater disapproved strongly of his son F. Louis, becoming a Catholic. See first note to first letter of 8 Feb. to St John.

[1] The election of the officials of the Birmingham House was held on 2 Feb. Not until 1856 did Newman realise that the Brief setting up the English Oratory had constituted him Superior at Birmingham for life. See letter of 17 Jan. 1856 to Caswall. The four deputies with the Superior formed the governing council.

[2] Lady Olivia Acheson left between five and six thousand pounds to Alexander Fullerton, her residuary legatee, intending it to be given to the Oratory. See letters of 15 Oct. 1854 to St John, and 12 Jan. 1855 to Wiseman.

P.S. Will you thank Fr Alban for his announcement and letter.
Tell him I and F Ambrose, perhaps more, said Mass at once for dear
Fr Delle Valle. I send back his letter with thanks.[1]

Thank your Father *for his intention of saying Mass for me*. I grieve
to hear his account of himself.

TO BISHOP ULLATHORNE

Edgbaston. Febry 5. 1854

My dear Lord,

I am now leaving for Ireland tomorrow — and before I go let me
write one word of acknowledgment for your mention of me at the
dinner. I have not heard any particulars of what you said, but I am
perfectly sure from the general account of it which has reached me, it
was something which was far more than I deserve, and what it would be
well indeed with me, if I did.[2]

I wish also to mention another thing to your Lordship, which I
have not told to any one yet, except my immediate brothers here. It is
that I have had a private notice from Rome, that it is the Holy Father's
most gracious intention to make me a Bishop in partibus. I have not
allowed myself to think of it except as an act coming from the Vicar of
Christ, and as such most exceedingly gratifying to me, and demanding
my most humble and grateful acceptance. It is also a touching evidence
of the tender regard of the Holy Father for one of the least of his children.
I suppose I shall know more about it in due time.[3]

[1] Wells had written about the recent death of Fr Delle Valle, the Superior of the
Naples Oratory.
[2] This refers to the first annual dinner of the Birmingham Catholic Association.
Ullathorne, who had already heard of Newman's proposed Bishopric, called him Right
Reverend, to the surprise of everyone present, and in a speech which filled almost two
columns of the *Tablet*, spoke of him in the highest terms, as 'one of those men, who,
from time to time, are raised up to form an epoch. One of those men around whom
great events group themselves as on their centre.' He had lead a great movement in
the Church of England, and had then had much to do in establishing 'a firmer and
more elevated tone' among Catholics in England. The *Tablet*, xv (18 Feb. 1854), p. 99.
See also letter of 24 Feb. to Estcourt.
[3] Ullathorne replied on 8 Feb., 'The announcement in your kind note does not
take me by surprise, I had a hint of his Holiness's intention a fortnight since, and it
appeared to me that the Episcopacy was the suitable mode of expressing the estimation
which both his Holiness and the Catholic episcopacy entertains of you. And whilst this
dignity, so conferred, as to make the distinction peculiar, will be universally applauded,
so it will be useful to the cause of the University and to your own position in reference
to that arduous but important undertaking. . . . The report of your elevation has been
rumoured through England for some time. . . .

36

Meanwhile, help me to thank God for his mercies towards me, and, begging your Lordship's blessing, believe me to be, My dear Lord, Your affectte friend & Servt in Xt

John H Newman of the Oratory

P.S.   I open my letter to express my additional thanks for your having read my letter at the dinner.

TO MOTHER FRANCES DE SALES WELD[1]

Edgbaston, Birmingham February 6. 1854

Dear Revd Mother

I send you by post the Univers giving an Account of the *Association for Prayers*. Will you send it back when you have done with it?

Begging your good prayers for us, I am Dear Revd Mother, Very sincerely yours in Xt

John H Newman of the Oratory

TUESDAY 7 FEBRUARY 1854   started at noon for Dublin, where got between 11 and 12 P M

WEDNESDAY 8 FEBRUARY   called on Dr Cullen (away) Dr Curtis, Ornsby (out)

TO AMBROSE ST JOHN (I)

⌐16 Harcourt Street Febr 8/54⌐

My dear Ambrose

F Faber's letter will painfully interest you — but you know his way of writing.[2]

I hope that when you receive your Briefs some of the brethren will tell me, and as I suppose this is the last time I shall ever give you my blessing I do it very heartily. . . .
Your devoted brother in Xt   W. B. Ullathorne.'

[1] Frances de Sales Weld (1792–1881), born at Lulworth Castle, joined the Visitation Convent in 1812, and was Superior 1852–8. She was a sister of Cardinal Weld.

[2] Faber wrote on 6 Feb. an account of the inquest on Mr Plater, 'They did all they could to annoy us. Poor Louis's examination was most harrowing, his conversion, his quarrel with his father, altercation, etc etc. . . . They say in the place we kidnapped the son and killed the father. . . .' then after details as to blood and stench, 'the body is now removed, by coroner's warrant, partly dressed in my clothes and partly in F. Albans. . . .'

I had a very stiff passage — and, though not sick, might have been sick any moment, had I chosen, but I was afraid, if I once began, I should not stop — It was a temptation for the pain of *not* being sick was considerable — I think I have heard described that latent or implicit sickness, which is not nausea but a convulsive compression of the stomach, a sense of burning there, a bad taste in the mouth, and a difficulty in breathing. I have not go[t] over it yet.

⌐I have seen no one but F Curtis — who however true [[in his prophetic utterances]], certainly is not a bird of good omen as regards the University.[1] The Archbishop is away — Dr Taylor [[when I called,]] was out — Ornsby and I have missed — H W [[Henry Wilberforce]] is away — Dr Quin is away — Duffy is away, not being yet convalescent. Dr Dixon called yesterday, but is gone, is away, The Revd Mother of the House of Mercy is away.[2]

My goods [[at Dr Quinn's]] are dispersed to the four winds — my room is devoted to a billiard table and⌐ its consequences — also it has ⌐pianos and gives concerts. I am to be quartered in the room over it,⌐ which I like better — when it is put to right, ⌐but the wind comes in bodily at top, bottom, and side of the door, and the closet won't shut. However, I feel happy, and am putting my things in order⌐ Love to all

Ever Yrs affly J H N

P.S.   Perhaps Fr Faber would not like his *accounts* read out.[3]

[[H. Wilberforce had lent me an Escrutoire [sic], when I left in 1852 — but on my return in February 1854 I found it had been broken open and the contents, which I had arranged and locked up so carefully, were scattered abroad. My pocket handkerchiefs, perhaps a new set, had disappeared and I never got them back — my nice Roman breviary was in actual present use in the House — my new razors a gift, with my name engraven on them, which I had never once used, were smeared and dulled, having been taken out and put back unwiped and unstropped. etc etc]]

[1] Fr J. Curtis, the Provincial of the Irish Jesuits, said that 'the class of youths *did not exist* in Ireland, who would come to the University,' and that there were really no youths, to fill evening classes in Dublin. He concluded by saying 'My advice to you is this, to go to the Archbishop and say, Don't attempt the University—give up the idea.' *A.W.* p. 323, *McGrath*, p. 252, *Ward* I, p. 333, *Trevor* II, p. 34.

[2] This was Robert Whitty's sister, Ellen Whitty, the Superior at Baggot Street Convent.

[3] Faber's letter included a statement of the London Oratory accounts, which he said were 'as bad as they can be.'

TO AMBROSE ST JOHN (II)

⌐Febr. 8 1854 or 1855?[1]

Thank you for your long letter As to the preachers in Lent, the Congregatio Deputata must decide.

I have put the whole German glass matter into Stanislas's hands.

I have no prospect of coming back I will help you to keep Charlie.⌐

THURSDAY 9 FEBRUARY 1854   went down to Kings town, to see Mrs Wilberforce, and dined at the Hotel there.   saw Scratton   called on Dr Meyler.

TO JOHN STANISLAS FLANAGAN

16 Harcourt Street Febr 9. 1854

My dear Stanislas

I have nearly established myself in my rooms, though I have not yet got by [my?] bed, bedding, washhandstand, candlesticks, coal skuttle, inkstand, kettle, horse, table, or footpail. Dr Taylor called last night — I suppose, from what he says, the Synodal meeting *must* be held within a month of the arrival of the Brief, which is expected without delay.[2] Then I should go to Rome before Easter, *after* the Synodal meeting, at which, I suppose, I should assist as Bishop elect. This makes it necessary I should do as much in Ireland now, as possible — and I shall set about sounding people at once, whether I could not pay my visits now to the Bishops. The report of my elevation is in London, and will be in the Tablet next week.[3]

All this of course is private to the Fathers. One thing I wish you to do still more privately — so don't go on reading out, till you have read it yourself. Learn from Robert, without his knowing it comes from me, *when* the great heats *begin* in the United States, and when they *cease* — and whether a pestiferous season follows as in Italy. Also, *how*

---

[1] Newman added the year with a question mark. Charlie was the Rednal pony.

[2] The Brief arranging for the Irish Bishops to meet was issued in Rome on 20 March. The Bishops met in Dublin on 18 May 1854.

[3] The report appeared within two days in the *Tablet*, xv (11 Feb. 1854), p. 84: 'THE VERY REV. DR. NEWMAN.—We understand from a well-informed correspondent that it is rumoured the illustrious President of the Catholic University of Ireland will shortly be raised to the dignity of Bishop *in partibus*. This report will doubtless be welcomed with great satisfaction by Catholics both here and abroad.'

long, with moderate exertion, it would take to visit the *principal* Catholic cities from New York to New Orleans.[1]

It is very blowy and blustery here — and I have not got over my implicit sea sickness.

Tell Philip I find myself wrong about Eccles Street

Ever Yrs affly J H N

FRIDAY 10 FEBRUARY 1854   Mr Buckle called with Scratton.   went down to All Hallows College and dined there.   long talk with Dr M. [Moriarty][2]   called on Marshall (away)

TO F. W. FABER

16 Harcourt Street Febr 10. 1854

My dear Fr Wilfrid

Thank you for your two letters.[3] What a horrible business you have had fall on you — I hope poor Louis [Plater] is getting better; but time alone can restore him.

As to your question, of course I know nothing at all of Canon Law, and cannot contemplate that side of it.[4] We have made an entry in our books that the last elevation to the decennium was to be the last. It is difficult to say what is meant by *necessary*, and who is to be the judge of it. E.g. suppose, if you do not elevate, only one Father can be confessor and he is one who is utterly unfit for the office — and who, if elected, is likely to tend to break up the body — is this a necessity? I should have thought at the beginning of societies there must be a latitude. Who was that Vincenzo, or whatever his name, who was a great benefactor to the infant Chiesa Nuova, and I think was raised to the triennium or decennium at once?[5]

[1] Flanagan replied fully on 11 Feb., allowing two months to visit the chief Catholic cities. Newman's letter of 28 Feb. to Stanton shows him still hoping to visit America in the interests of the University.

[2] 'He mentioned as possible lecturers several persons whose names I took down He spoke most highly of Mr McCarthy the poet. He also gave me a list of preachers.. (Newman's contemporary University Journal, as to which see *A.W.* p. 279.)

[3] Of 6 and 8 Feb.

[4] It was proposed in London to give to some of the triennial fathers, benefactors of their House, the rights of decennials, i.e. of those who had been for ten years members of the Community. Stanton maintained that this was only permissible in cases of 'sheer necessity,' since the Oratorian Rule was 'part of canon law.'

[5] When the first Oratorians came to occupy their present site at Rome in 1577, Alfonso Visconti gave them the use of his house, which was next to theirs, and he was

40

I am so cold I can hardly write. So they are going to submit to my pastoral superintendence, in addition to the Birmingham Oratory, or the Irish University, the diocese of Ptolemais, Megalopolis, or Rhinocorura — I then shall have a field of action on which pretty nearly the sun will never set

Ever Yrs affly J H N

SATURDAY 11 FEBRUARY 1854 went down to Kingstown with Scratton, and called on Mr Errington, Mr James O Ferrall, Mrs Ornsby (all three out or engaged) and Mrs Buckle, where lunched. called at Presbytery in Marlborough Street

TO F. S. BOWLES

[11 February? 1854]

My dear Frederic

Read the inclosed out in Recreation, and *keep it for me*.

Tell Robert to be so good as to send me the Evening Mail on Tuesdays, Thursdays, and Saturdays, directed here (16 Harcourt Street) I cannot tell yet *when* I return.

Ever Yrs affly J H N

TO AMBROSE ST JOHN

16 Harcourt Street Febr 11/54

My dear A

What a shame you should not get one of the Novices to send me the Evening Mail — Here am I in ignorance how my friends the Turks and Russians progress.

All right about the Handsworth question — you had the letter, to which it alludes, in your hands — It went to Mr Ivers's ultimately.[1]

I have talked and dined with Dr Moriarty yesterday — he is on the point of going to Kerry.[2] I hope he will be of considerable use to me. The Archbishop is not yet returned.

almost at once made a member of the Community and a deputy. Giovanni Marciano, *Memorie historiche della Congregatione dell' Oratorio*, Naples 1693, 1, Book 1, ch. xiv, p. 51.

[1] This presumably refers to the Oratorians' serving the Convent at Handsworth. Bernard Ivers was the priest at St Peter's, Broad Street, Birmingham.

[2] David Moriarty had just been appointed Coadjutor Bishop of Kerry.

On Thursday I went to see Mrs Wilberforce, who was in a most low way — A dead silence what Henry is doing in London. I fear it must be some disagreeable matter — at first I thought he was getting some appointment — Scratton says she is not commonly low; else, I took it as the shadow of the hooping cough etc.[1]

She *just* asked me 'if I would have any thing,' I was prepared for her having dined early, but also prepared for her getting me some cold meat. She mentioned it, as Charles[2] flourishes beer and bread before me, to make a Tantalus of me, to offer, and to mock — so I declined.

I left the house pensively, as I had lost my dinner in Harcourt Street, from the late hour. What was I to do? My bad genius suggested that I could get some cold meat at the 'Royal Hotel' — so thither I went, by the back streets. I said indeed there was no one that would know me — but I thought it would look absurd to any friend, and that Mrs W. would hear of it; so I kept to the back streets, and darted down upon the 'Royal Hotel.' I was congratulating myself, when, *just* as I was mounting the steps, up rushed old Scratton full of congratulations — it is always the way. Well, I hoped he was going to give me some dinner — but no — he was sorry to say he was a batchelor, he had hoped indeed he had a bed for me, but had found it was too short — but not a mouthful of dinner hot or cold — so I had to enter the coffee room — Then, there was no cold meat — and for a small steak so small that I ate it to the bone, with a bare glass of porter they charged me 4 shillings! almost as bad as the 5/ mutton as we were starting for Rome. Nor was this all — I had cautioned Scratton not to blab — but to my annoyance the waiter called me Doctor, and Mr Buckle, who called next morning, said he heard I had been *wandering about* Kingstown, and begged I would never scruple to take my dinner with him. So, you see, it will be hard if Mrs W. does not hear of it

Ever Yours affly J H N

P.S.   I fear Lord R. Kerr will slip thro' our hands.[3]
Please, post up the inclosed notices.
I suppose my grate is fixed all right.
I have forgotten the penance you gave me.

[1] Mrs Wilberforce, who was the friend of St John as well as of Newman, had recently had whooping cough in her family, and lost her youngest child. On 12 Feb. Wilberforce wrote to apologise for his absence, in London, where he was exploring the possibility of becoming editor of the *Catholic Standard*. See letter of 14 Feb. to him.

[2] The lay brother at Birmingham.

[3] He arrived at the Oratory on 17 Feb. to complete his education there.

TO CATHERINE ANNE BATHURST

16 Harcourt Street Dublin Febr 12/54

My dear Child,

You went with a very good heart to Loughborough, and I was thankful to witness it, you felt you could almost volunteer to do so, and I would not for the world damp so promising a purpose.[1] Do not be discouraged and give up, merely because trials come upon you which were sure to come.

There are only two courses before you, either to be a nun, or not to be; either to live religiously with your friends and to prosecute your own (religious) objects — or to give yourself up entirely to others. I thought you went to Greenwich for the first of these — I was surprised to find you had the grace to contemplate the second, and wished to go into the noviciate at Loughborough. But since you have been led there, do not shrink — go on, and go through it. Should you *not* have a vocation, God will make this known to you — but let it be determined by the event; do not by any act of yours anticipate His decision.

You have hitherto found so much comfort by having your course determined for you from without, from acting from obedience, and by rule, that, if you *are* able to give yourself up, there is reason for thinking it would be a great relief to you. While you have the management of yourself, you will, I fear, always be fretting. However, God will decide — ask Him to do so. I do not forget you

Ever Yours most affly JHN

MONDAY 13 FEBRUARY 1854 dined with Ornsby Dr Cullen returned — called on him, and went over the house.[2]

TUESDAY 14 FEBRUARY had a *bad* cold and stopped indoors

[1] After joining the group of convert ladies under Miss Lockhart, the Sisters of Charity at Greenwich, Catherine Bathurst in the autumn of 1853 became a novice with the Rosminian nuns at Loughborough, only to leave the following March. Later in 1854 she returned to the Greenwich community, but left again in 1861 and retired to Bruges, where she became a Dominican tertiary. In 1878 she returned to England and founded the Dominican Convent at Harrow.

[2] i.e. the University House, 86 Stephen's Green. Newman went over it, 'marking out the alterations in order to turn it into rooms. It will make 17 (single) rooms in two upper stories—' (University Journal).

TO JAMES BURKE[1]

[14? February 1854]

Dear Sir,

As far as I have a voice in the appointment of University officials, I trust I shall be guided, as you do me the justice to think, by the fitness of the persons who are selected, to discharge the duties respectively imposed upon them — and in judging of their qualifications, I mean to be guided by the opinion of the public and of those in whose judgment I place confidence.

I thank you for your offer to assist me in a literary way — but I am not likely to have any call on your services you so kindly tender to me.

J H N

TO RICHARD STANTON

[14? February 1854]

My dear Richard,

I am ashamed to find that your Father has taken my clumsy jest in earnest[2]. I am *not* to be Bishop of Ptolemais, nor Megalopolis, or Rhinocorura (if there be such a place) nor of Agropotamos or Taganrog; I cannot go beyond a negative. I shall not know till it is decided by brief.

What are you anxious about, my dear Fr R.? the *colour* of my stockings?[3]

Ever Yrs affly J H N

[1] James Burke (1819–86), B.A. Trinity College, Dublin, and Barrister at Kings Inns, Dublin, 1842, was the author of *Life of Thomas Moore*, Dublin 1852, *The Speeches of the Right Hon. Edmund Burke*, with memoir and historical introductions, Dublin 1854, as well as of legal treatises. In his letter of 13 Feb. asking for a Professorship at the Catholic University he said that he did not think Newman capable of partiality or of favouring Englishmen, and explained that he felt 'competent to lecture in history, belles lettres or legal science.' He also offered to help with the 'periodical in sustainment of the views of the Catholic University,' which he had learned Newman intended to start.

Burke was either editor or joint editor of the Catholic weekly the *Lamp*, 1855–62. In 1859 he published *Gems from the Catholic Poets*.

[2] See the end of the letter of 10 Feb. to Faber.

[3] Newman guessed right, since he was evidently writing *before* the arrival of Stanton's letter of 12 Feb., which must be the one referred to in the second postscript. In it Stanton wrote: 'We have just heard the certain confirmation of the reports about the bishopric.

'We feel the great propriety of the thing on a thousand grounds, and therefore

P.S.   I am soon going to make the tour of Ireland, calling on the Bishops.

P.S.   Your letter is just come — it is very kind of you. I will abide by it.

TO HENRY WILBERFORCE

16 Harcourt Street ⌈Febr 14. 1854⌉[1]

My dear Henry

⌈A paper is a most desirable thing, and you would edit it well — but Richardson won't give any decent terms. He picks the brains of authors, and there is the whole of it.

I would have you as a *sine quâ non* be guaranteed your salary for *five years*. It is the only way in which you can be independent — If he thinks you are to make any thing of a newspaper in a shorter period, he ignores all his experience as a publisher. *If* this is not done, he may throw you up, having begun by throwing you out.

It is for you to consider what terms you will require, yourself — but, besides your own salary, you should bargain for a hundred a year, to be put absolutely at your disposal, in order that you may buy good articles with it. An Editor cannot know all things under the sun, nor can he get good writers without pay. You must be able to say to a friend, 'Here is the Trust Question — or the War question — or the Anglican Convocation Question,⌉ making a row — ⌈This is, I know, your subject — give me a dozen articles on it during the Session of Parliament and I will give you £2 for each.⌉ Of course *Richardson* must look at it as a portion of the (abstract) Editor's salary — and so it is — but,

rejoice heartily at it. I have no doubt it will be greatly for the good of the University. . . . We are all for Ptolemais. I am anxious to give you my views of what your dress ought to be—

In private I think you ought to wear the black Cassock with red edges and buttons, but made *with our collar* . . . You must have violet stockings, I should say of fine wool, and I should recommend shoes like ours, but of shining leather. . . . Your berretta and zucchetto must be black, those of violet which some of our bishops wear are a French abomination. . . .' and so on. Stanton concluded, 'You will be amused with this; but I am persuaded you agree with me, that externals if minor are not little matters.'

[1] [[H W W. was now in London]] Wilberforce wrote on 12 Feb. '. . . I wanted to consult you about a private matter. Mr Bagshaw[,] Bellasis and others want me to come and edite [sic] the Catholic Standard. My own opinion is that if Richardson will offer fair terms I could not be more usefully employed. What do you think. Of course it would imply my giving up the hope of working with you at Dublin but really this seems in any event so uncertain. . . . I should like to know what you feel.'

⌐depend on it, *unless he does the thing really well*, it will be a simple failure — and an *additional* discouragement to Catholics.

Further, if you ask my opinion, R. not only *won't* but *can't* pay — I mean, that I don't think a Catholic Newspaper *can* succeed in England. It must be supported at a dead loss. It must be supported, as the Morning Chronicle by Beresford Hope, by the zeal of the rich.

You seem to speak despondingly about the University. Think it over seriously, and, if you are confirmed in the view, give it up. I own, that all along, as I have expressed to you once especially, it is only *your zeal* which makes me come to the conclusion that teaching is[1] your line. *I have faith in that*, while I see it lasts. When it goes, and in proportion as it goes, I fall back to what would be my natural opinion⌐[2]

Ever Yours affly J H N.

WEDNESDAY 15 FEBRUARY 1854   dined with Dr Cullen

THURSDAY 16 FEBRUARY   Dr Taylor gave me 3 £50 notes (Bank of Ireland) sent to Nicholas for Stanislas in registered letter one of them — viz 139 No 198298 Sept 13. 1853

FRIDAY 17 FEBRUARY   dined with Dr Cullen to meet Dr Denvir

TO THE EARL OF DUNRAVEN

16 Harcourt Street Febr. 17 1854

My dear Lord Dunraven,

I shall rejoice to come over to Adare to lunch there as you propose. As far as I can calculate my movements, I shall arrive at Limerick on Friday (the 24th) evening, this day week, and shall start for Galway on the following Monday. I am to be the Bishop's guest, and shall aim at coming over on Saturday the 25th

Ever Your Lordship's sincere and attached friend

John H Newman of the Oratory

The Earl of Dunraven

P.S.   I very much wish to see Mr Aubrey de Vere, if I could manage it.

[1] [[can be]] Cf. letter of 23 Nov. 1853.
[2] [[I think H W did not give up his house at Kingstown during this Spring—which will account for no letters till June, for I was in Dublin all that while.]]

TO AMBROSE ST JOHN

16 Harcourt Street Febr 17. 1854

My dear Ambrose

I am pleased to hear the result of your visit to Stone, and am sorry I shall disappoint Mother Margaret again.[1]

I do not set off till tomorrow (Saturday) I am to meet Dr Denvir of Belfast at the Archbishop's at dinner today, and this will save me going to the North at all.

I hope to be present at the Chapter on March 8. *Then* I can receive the return I asked for — without distressing F Frederic lest the sigillum communitatis be broken by the post, or obliging you to lay your perplexities before Fr Bernard.[2]

I suppose in like manner you have some scruple of my making you read addresses from me in Chapter.

I *will not believe* that other Fathers share your and F Frederic's sentiments — but if so it is, that I am neither to ask questions nor address you, what is this but inflicting on me the fact, that I cannot be a

[1] St John had visited Mother Margaret Mary Hallahan at Stone on 14 Feb., and obtained from her a promise of some of her nuns to settle and work in the district round the Oratory at Birmingham. St John added, 'She is very wrath against you, says you have more to do with her convent than any others, that they have all prayed their knees off for you, and you have not kept your promise, and she wont pray for you any more till you come. You are to be sure to be at the opening of their new Church at Stone.' Newman preached on that occasion. See diary for 3 May. Mother Margaret was hoping to see Newman as she passed through Birmingham on 20 Feb. Hence the disappointment in store for her.

[2] Newman had asked that during his absence in Ireland, reports or returns should be sent to him, by the various fathers responsible, as to how some of the rules and regulations of the Oratory were being observed. This was an expedient, as he wrote in a paper of 8 April, 'to keep myself continually before the Congregation, as if present; e.g. by incessant letters, questions, messages, addresses, and the like, as well as by frequently coming over from Ireland.' Newman, the Superior, wished to overcome the difficulty inherent in his Irish appointment, and keep in touch with his Community. His request was resented, 'as if,' he complained in the same paper, 'we were a boy's school, and the Fr Superior head-master of it.' Thus St John wrote on 15 Feb., 'Your paper of returns which I have duly posted has caused a slight effervescence. F. Fredk said (*not* grumpily) it was against the sigillum communitatis and F.F. Nicholas and Stanislaus thought it a very strong measure, and discussed it in the Congregatio Deputata. I have sounded F. Bernard, he thinks you have a perfect right to ask all you have asked of us, but doubts whether it will work for a continuance. As you are coming home soon, D.G. [Deo Gratias] you will talk more to us all about it. . . .' St John's letter ended: 'Give us your blessing, dearest Father I am never going to call you any thing else, and don't half fancy this Bishopric.'

Newman's reflections of 8 April on the difficulties of an absent superior, which he delivered as a Chapter address to his community, will be included in the volume that contains his Oratorian papers.

J.H.N.—E

non-resident Superior? See what you are doing? Incola ego sum in terrâ.[1]

I sent Nicholas a registered letter yesterday — which he ought to receive this morning.

It blows a tempest, and rains furiously. I cannot think such weather will last. Next Sunday I am at Carlow — On Wednesday 22nd at Cork — Sunday 26th at Limerick — Ash Wednesday at Belfast. Sunday March 5, I trust in Birmingham.

The first week I was here was simply lost, the Archbishop being away. Since then, I have engaged one Lecturer, and almost another — both distinguished persons here —[2] I have laid the foundations of a quasi Oratory, with priests to confess the youths, and set up a debating society etc[3] — and have thrown lawyers, architects, painters, paperers, and upholsterers into the University house, with a view of preparing for our Autumn opening.

Love to all Ever Yrs affly J H N

SATURDAY 18 FEBRUARY 1854   started for Kilkenny *in snow*, where dined with Dr Walshe — thence to Carlow to Mr Hughes[4]
SUNDAY 19 FEBRUARY   saw Dr Hely[5]   at Carlow   raining
MONDAY 20 FEBRUARY   went to Waterford — to the Bishop, Dr Foran[6] — where dined and slept

TO PETER LE PAGE RENOUF

Waterford. Febr 20. 1854
my address is '16 Harcourt Street, Dublin'
or 'Oratory, Edgbaston, Birmingham.'

My dear Renouf,

I am making a circuit of good part of Ireland to pay my respects to the Bishops. I am shortly in England again, and then back to Dublin.

[1] Psalm 118:19. For St John's reply, see first note to letter of 26 Feb. to St John.
[2] Newman's University Journal shows that these were D. F. MacCarthy, who was to be the Lecturer in Poetry, and T. O'Hagan, Lecturer in Political Economy.
[3] This met for the first time on 9 March 1855 or 1856. See *Centenary History of the Literary and Historical Society of University College Dublin 1855–1955*, edited by James Meenan, Tralee n.d. [1957], p. 1, *Culler*, p. 166.
[4] James Hughes (1810–76), was Dean of Carlow College, 1841–55, and parish priest of Naas 1858 until his death.
[5] Francis Haly (1785–1855), Bishop of Kildare and Leighlin from 1838, resided at Carlow. Newman noted in his University Journal that he 'told me to go to Mr James O Ferrall for information about gentry in Co. Kildare,' in order to get names of supporters for the University.
[6] Nicholas Foran, educated at Maynooth, was Bishop of Waterford and Lismore from 1837 until his death in his seventy-fourth year, in 1855.

I wish very much to hear from you. At this moment, I have not the fullest powers to engage persons, but, if I do not anticipate the future, I shall be losing valuable weeks.

If I offered you the Lectureship of French Literature for 3 years (we shall have no Professor at all at present) at £150 a year *at least*, would it be worth your acceptance?

We must begin all of us *con amore*, with zeal to do a great work as the first motive, with other motives in the back ground.

I suppose our session would be 8 or 9 months, with some little cessation at Christmas and Easter — Dublin is a very cheap place to live in. But what your work would be and what your remuneration, it is impossible to calculate at first. We are making a great *experiment*. When you came, French perhaps might fail of a Professorship (though I don't know why it should, and I have given it above a trial of three years) — but, if so, is there any other subject which would tempt you? It is difficult to write — easy to talk[1]

Most sincerely Yours in Xt   John H Newman of the Oratory

TUESDAY 21 FEBRUARY 1854   after seeing Ursuline Convent etc started for Cork for the Vincentians where arrived late in evening

TO AMBROSE ST JOHN

Cork. Febr 21. 1854
½ past 10 P M

My dear Ambrose

I have got here after a fatiguing day, just now, and find ⌐F Nicholas's letter, which is satisfactory, except that you are unwell. What do you

[1] The friends of Renouf, who was still tutor to Louis, the son of the learned Count de Vaulchier near Besançon, had thoughts of getting him into the French diplomatic service, when his pupil no longer needed him. 'But Newman's invitation had all the precious Oxford associations to lend it weight. . . . The French Lectureship did not tempt Renouf, but the idea of helping Newman appealed strongly to him.' *The Life Work of Sir Peter Le Page Renouf*, IV, Paris 1907, p. xlvii. He wrote his acceptance on 1 March, adding, 'My favourite and persevering study is Christian Antiquity, and my delight would be to lecture on Eusebius, or the Pseudo-Clementine literature or the Arian controversy or the "Introduction" to the New Testament. . . .' After a year as Lecturer in French Literature, Renouf became Professor of Ancient History and Geography. Count de Vaulchier could not bear to part entirely with Renouf, and said that he must continue to be his son's tutor, and take him also to Dublin. In April 1854, Renouf wrote to his parents, '. . . I look upon my new vocation not merely as a means of bettering my position, and coming out before the public on a theatre to display my powers, but as a call from God to do upon a large scale what everyone is bound to do in his degree, to advance the spiritual Kingdom of his Son. . . .' (*loc. cit.* p. xlviii).

say to going to Dr Duke for a week? I will frank you —⌉ I suppose a return ticket would give you a week, but perhaps the rail companies do not act together — Any how, go for a week.

My own letter to Fr O Sullivan here miscarried — it is a wonder that Nicholas's came right — I suppose it was for the happy word 'Michael —' I did not know his proper direction. To complete it, not only did not the letter get here, but *he* was away — and he returned *with* me (without my knowing it) nearly all the way from Waterford, and had got home a few minutes before I made my appearance.[1]

Of course I shall see fewer Bishops than I had hoped — and I can't tell whether I shall not be knocked up by the time I get to Limerick. ⌈I started with a cold and cough, the weather has been trying,⌉ and I am now out of order besides, and have a difficulty in travelling, as you coming from Naples,[2] which is unlike myself, and therefore difficult to manage.

I was received most hospitably at Carlow, and Stanislas has heard of me from Dr Hughes. The Bishop of Ossory too at *Kilkenny* (which place I always hit by an act of memory before speaking, of which the formal object is the Kilkenny cats; else I should infallibly say Killarney — indeed I was on the point of taking a ticket for Limerick instead of Waterford till Dr Hughes set me and the ticket man right, and I always say England instead of Ireland) but to return, — was most hospitable — for he took me in the right way, giving me dinner and not urging me to stay. However, he made me ascend up to the top of his unfinished cathedral (a noble building) along planks and up corkscrews, in doing which my only support was that it was impossible that I could be fated to die the death of a hodman, whatever be its logic. I trembled when I saw the mutton, and how it blushed on the first cut, but his Lordship was merciful, and let me dine in the brown.[3]

At the Ursuline Convent at Waterford this morning I saw a lady, a nun, who inquired after 'Philip Molloy,' as knowing his family intimately, though not him — she did not know Stanislas. I travelled here with a most fervent Waterford Catholic, who seemed to hate the English, but not less the young Irelanders, 'the triumvirate,' and, nefas dictu (not to hate, but to shrink from) the lion.[4] I liked the young

---

[1] Newman was staying at the Vincentian House in Cork. The Superior there was Michael O'Sullivan, and Newman's letter to him went astray for want of the Christian name. O'Sullivan, the Vicar General of the Diocese, had founded a school for boys in the old Mansion House, Cork, which in 1848 he handed over to the Vincentians, and having joined their Congregation himself, was made the Superior at Cork. He died in 1855. [2] In Sept. 1847.

[3] Edward Walsh, who was Bishop of Ossory 1846–72, completed the exterior of his cathedral at Kilkenny in 1857.

[4] i.e. 'the Lion of the West,' John MacHale, Archbishop of Tuam. As to 'the

clergy about the Bishop of Waterford exceedingly — Every where the greatest praises of Fr Faber's book — but in Dublin I was told that Fr Bernard's had done even more good than it.[1] People seem to say that pious people are not unfrequently deficient in doctrinal knowledge, and dont understand what was the matter with the Jansenists.

I said Mass this morning for all those who think of me religiously this day, according to their several needs. Love to all — ⌜kindest thoughts of the unknown Lord Ralph⌝[2]

Ever Yrs affly J H N

P.S.   I should say £150 for Lord R. I will write to Hope Scott.

WEDNESDAY 22 FEBRUARY 1854   at Cork with Fr O Sullivan   visited Convents etc.[3]   Fr Leahy at dinner[4]   The Bishop, Dr Delany called on me.

TO AUSTIN MILLS

Cork. February 22. 1854

(I shall not put this into the post for a day or two)

My dear Austin,

Though you are not Secretary, yet as Fr Edward is a new hand, perhaps you will inform him how best to bring the following before the Congregatio Deputata. I submit part of a sketch of a *new work*, which must be submitted to *two Fathers*; I propose to call it 'The triumvirate,' 'This title is not found elsewhere in contemporary writings. It may apply to Sadleir, Keogh and a third member of their party, possibly John Reynolds, who was their colleague in the Catholic Defence Association. Or it may designate the three prominent newspaper editors, Gavan Duffy, Lucey and Gray.' *McGrath*, p. 256, note.

[1] Faber's book was *All for Jesus*, and Dalgairns's *The Devotion to the Sacred Heart of Jesus; with an Introduction on the History of Jansenism*, both London 1853.

[2] 21 Feb. was Newman's birthday. Darnell's letter of 17 Feb., referred to above, called Lord Ralph Kerr, who had just arrived as a boarder at the Birmingham Oratory, 'a fine young Scotchman.' The Oratorians did not know what pension to suggest to his mother, Lady Lothian, £200 or £150. See letter of 24 Feb. to Hope-Scott.

[3] Among the convents Newman visited was that of the Sisters of Charity. In March the foundress of the Order, Mary Aikenhead, wrote to one of her nuns at Cork, 'I am glad you and yours have seen Doctor Newman, who, I believe, is a really holy man. I have not seen his Reverence, nor do I expect to do so. He has, however, been several times to St. Vincent's Hospital [in Dublin], and sent a portion of money at his disposal (five pounds) as a donation for its support, lately.' Quoted in *The Life and Work of Mary Aikenhead*, by a Member of the Congregation of the Irish Sisters of Charity, London 1924, p. 411.

[4] This was John Piers or Pius Leahy (1802–90), the Irish Dominican Provincial and Prior of the house at Cork. In the autumn of 1854 he was consecrated as Coadjutor to the Bishop of Dromore.

doleful disasters and curious catastrophes of a traveller in the wilds of the west.' I have sketched five chapters as below.

1. The first will contain a series of varied and brilliant illustrations of the old proverb, 'more know Tom Fool than Tom Fool knows.'

2. The second will relate how at Carlow a large party of priests was asked to meet the author at dinner, after which the said author, being fatigued with the day, went to sleep — and was awakened from a refreshing repose by his next neighbour on the right shouting in his ear, 'Gentleman, Dr N is about to explain to you the plan he proposes for establishing the new University,' an announcement, which the said Dr N. does aver most solemnly took him utterly by surprise, and he cannot think what he could have said in his sleep which could have been understood to mean something so altogether foreign to his intentions and his habits. However, upon this announcement, how the author was obliged to speak and answer questions, in which process he made mistakes and contradicted himself, to the clear consciousness and extreme disgust of the said author.

3 Chapter third will detail the merry conceit of the Paddy who drove him from the Kilkenny station, and who, instead of taking him to the Catholic Bishop's, took him to the Protestant Superintendent's palace, a certain O Brien, who now for 15 years past has been writing against the author and calling him hard names[1] — and how the said carman deposited him at the door of the Protestant palace, and drove away, and how he kept ringing and no one came — and how at last he ventured to attempt and open the hall door without leave, and found himself inside the house, and made a noise in vain — and how, when his patience was exhausted, he advanced further in, and went up some steps and looked about him, and still found no one at all — all along thinking it the house of the true Bishop, and a very fine one too. And how at last he ventured to knock at a room door, and how at length out came a scullery maid, and assured him that the Bishop was in London — whereupon gradually the true state of the case unfolded itself to his mind, and he began to think that, had that Protestant Superintendant been at home, a servant would have answered the bell, and he should have sent in his card or cartel with his own name upon it, for the inspection of the said Superintendant.

[1] James Thomas O'Brien (1792–1874), appointed Protestant Bishop of Ossory by Sir Robert Peel in 1842, was a strong evangelical. In the advertisement to *Jfcn*, p. vii, Newman in 1838 mentioned O'Brien's *An Attempt to explain the Doctrine of Justification by Faith only, in Ten Sermons*, London 1833, 'though no reason has occurred for alluding to it elsewhere, as it does but advocate, in opposition to Bishop Bull and the great number of English Divines, the pure Lutheran theory . . .' O'Brien's two Charges of 1842 and 1845, were directed against Newman and Tractarianism.

4. And the fourth chapter of the work will go on to relate how the Bishop of Ossory pleasantly suggested when he heard of the above, that the carman's mistake was caused by a certain shepherd's plaid which the author had upon his shoulders, by reason of which he, the author might be mistaken for a Protestant parson. And this remark will introduce the history of the said plaid, and how the author went to F Stanislas Flanagan's friend, Mr Geoghegan, in Sackville Street, and asked for a clerical wrapper, on which the said plaid was shown him. And he objecting to it as not clerical, the shop man on the contrary assured him it was. Whereupon in his simplicity he bought the said plaid, and took it with him on his travels, and left behind him his good Propaganda cloke; and how now he does not know what to do, for he is wandering over the wide world, in a fantastic dress, like a merry andrew, yet with a Roman collar on.

5. And the fifth chapter will narrate his misadventure at Waterford — how he went to the Ursuline Convent there, and the acting Superior determined he should see all the young ladies of the school to the number of 70, all dressed in blue, with medals on, some blue, some green, some red; and how he found he had to make them a speech, and how he puzzled and fussed himself what on earth he should say impromptu to a parcel of school girls — and how in his distress he *did* make what he considered his best speech — and how, when it was ended, the Mother Schoolmistress did not know he had made it, or even begun it, and still asked for his speech. And how he would not, because he could not make a second speech; and how, to make it up, he asked for a holiday for the girls, and how the Mother Schoolmistress flatly refused him, by reason (as he verily believes) because she would not recognise and accept his speech, and wanted another, and thought she had dressed up her girls for nothing — and how he nevertheless drank her rasberry's vinegar, which much resembles a nun's anger, being a sweet acid, and how he thought to himself, it being his birthday, that he was full old to be forgiven if he would not at a moment act the spiritual jack pudding to a girl's school.

This is as much as I have to send you — Would you kindly add your own criticisms on those of the two Fathers? Love to all

Ever Yrs affly J H N

THURSDAY 23 FEBRUARY 1854 went to Thurles — the Archbishop's guest — dined with Dr Leahy and a party of priests.[1]

[1] i.e. Michael Slattery, Archbishop of Cashel, and Patrick Leahy, who became Vice-Rector of the University under Newman.

TO THE ORATORIANS AT BIRMINGHAM

Thurles. Febr. 23/54

I am in a great difficulty whom to write to. For Austin I have a letter already written. Henry has been answered through Edward; and I am literally fixed. So I shall write to the *supper* recreation.

Well then, the Bishop of Cork was cold and courteous — stiff and donnish — and I should never get on with him, I am sure. He is the only Irish Bishop I have met unlike an Irishman; I think I had rather be pawed by the lion.[1] Observe, by the bye, the Recreation must *never* let out any thing I say, especially against the lion. The bird of the air to a certainty will carry the matter. Already I think I smell that reports of my not liking him, or rather of my thinking myself rudely pawed by him are in circulation — and, *if he thinks I think* he does not like me, he at once will set himself against me.

The dissentions [sic] in Ireland are awful — as many and sub divided and cross divided as dissenters in England. I have nothing to rely on but God, the Pope, and myself, and as yet I have not any sort of misgiving — but I do not know what encouragement I see.

I have so bad a cough and cold that I should like *much* to beg off going further than Limerick, and to get back to Birmingham by Ash Wednesday — but I fear it would be a great mistake not to seek the lion's habitat. Alas, it is 18 Irish miles (11 to 13) off Galway,[2] and how I am to get there and back in a day I see not — (with one horse!) and I dread a night in so awful an abode.

The Archbishop of Cashel, with whom I am lodging here, is a most pleasing, taking man — mild, gentle, tender and broken. My dear Fathers,

Ever Yours affly, J H N.

FRIDAY 24 FEBRUARY 1854 went to Limerick — where arrived about 3 P M went to the Bishop's to dine and put up.[3]

[1] In his University Journal Newman wrote, 'The Bishop, Dr Delany, called on me—he cautiously came with his Vicar General—he wished to show his respect, he said, to my *character*. Directly I got so far as to say that I wished the advice of the Bishops, he rose and went away.'
[2] The distance from Galway to Tuam is 21 statute miles. The Irish mile is 1¼ statute miles.
[3] On this visit to John Ryan, Bishop of Limerick, see letter of 28 Feb. to Flanagan.

Thurles. Febry 24/54

My dear Estcourt,

I do not like to tease the Bishop with letters — but I should be much obliged to you, if you would take an opportunity of presenting to him my acknowledgments for the speech I see in the last Tablet.

Of course it is not for me to do more than to thank him for the extreme kindness and charitable affection which he shows towards me — hoping and praying that I may labour more successfully in time to come to fulfil the idea of me which he has too indulgently formed — but I may with propriety observe, and I cannot help doing so, that he has hit off one truth, as I really think it to be, which I have no where else seen noticed, and has been as happy and graceful in the expression of it, as kind in the thought itself. I do believe it was in no slight measure from a sense of admiration and a confusion and joy at the objects which were opening upon us, that we were hindered from realizing sooner our own position with relation to them — and this I say without at all wishing to disguise the truth, that, had we had more faith, simplicity and earnestness, we should have become Catholics much sooner.[1]

I am in the middle of a course of visits to the Bishops; but am so knocked up with a cold, I suppose I shall be obliged to give over.

Most sincerely Yours in Xt John H Newman of the Oratory

The Revd E. E. Estcourt.

Thurles. Febr 24/54

My dear Hope

I am very glad to find that Lord Ralph is at Edgbaston. They write to me to know what he is to pay. Well I say this — I should be glad to

[1] Ullathorne in his speech at the dinner of the Birmingham Catholic Association on 31 Jan., spoke of how Newman had revived the Catholic doctrines in the Church of England, and the surprise of Catholics that he did not, in consequence, leave it sooner. 'To us it was a marvel how they [Newman and his followers] could so think, and so speak, and so act, and so remain. But we took not into account that they were inebriated with the new wine of doctrine; that they were occupied with the operation of self-enlargement; that they were engaged with the new sensations that moved within them through the advent of new truths; that employed so fully within they were not disposed as yet, to look beyond themselves, and to survey and appreciate the real nature of their position.' The Tablet, xv (18 Feb. 1854), p. 99. See also letter of 5 Feb. to Ullathorne.

ask £150 a year: but if this seems too much, do not name it, but £100. Now you know what I think.[1]

⌐So, the Pope has most graciously determined to make me a Bishop in partibus — by way of strengthening my hands here.

I am making a tour of episcopal visits, and am received by Bishops and clergy with open arms. Whatever manifold dissentions there are here, on this one point they are unanimous — and it is certainly a most wonderful outfit for beginning. It will be hard indeed, as time goes on, to keep from entangling myself in this party or that — and I mourn over my great deficiencies in circumspection and presence of mind. Please, say a prayer for me that I may have my eyes about me⌐[2]

Direct to Edgbaston

Ever Yrs most affly in Xt John H Newman of the Oratory

J R Hope Scott Esqr

TO J. I. TAYLOR

Thurles Friday Febr 24/54

My dear Dr Taylor,

I thank you very much for your letter. It is with regret I say that my cough and hoarseness are so troublesome, that I am afraid to extend my travels just now beyond Limerick, whither I go today. In a week or two I may renew them. As I have business in England, I propose to cross the water on Monday evening next. How many hours I shall be in Dublin, I don't know — but I shall be found on call in Harcourt Street. If you would kindly drop me a line there, with Mr Butler's address, I would go and call on him.[3] I should *like* to arrive in Dublin early in the day — but the chance is I do not get there will 4.15 P M — which will give me very little time, as I shall dine in Kingstown. I wonder whether *he* would call on me at 5 P M in Harcourt Street.

Very sincerely Yours in Xt John H Newman of the Oratory

The Revd Dr Taylor

P.S.   My travels have been very successful. I have been received with *great* kindness and have been much pleased with the Bishops and others I have seen.

[1] For Hope-Scott's reply see letter of 6 March to Flanagan.
[2] Hope-Scott replied on 3 March, 'I rejoice at your prospects in Ireland. They have warm hearts yonder—would they had cool heads.'
[3] Edward Butler was a Chief Inspector of the National Board of Education. He became Professor of Mathematics in the Catholic University.

SATURDAY 25 FEBRUARY 1854   went over, with Mr Barry,[1] to Adare   lunched with Lord Dunraven   a beautiful day

TO EDWARD CASWALL

Convent of Mercy Limerick Saturday Morng Febr 25/54
My dearest F Edward

Your letter has just been brought me here, where I was breakfasting, and tho' I dare say I shall not say all I wish to say, still I think it right to answer it immediately, since what you begin with shows I have not made myself understood, and therefore may have misled others as well as you.[2]

This then is for others besides yourself. My dear Edward, how could you *fancy* I meant you to *count who* were at discipline! how was it possible! I am not saying the fault was yours, the fault might be mine — but a mistake it is.

You see, I have felt deeply that the Father Superior is bound to see the rules of the Congregation executed — I have felt too I have not done this as much as I ought. In the very matter, of which you write, I felt that, having half dispensed with the Oratory Exercise, we run the great risk of dispensing with the Discipline.

The rules of the Congregation are those which are contained in the *Rule*, or the *Decree Book*.

If I personally have imposed any, it has only been *pro tempore*, by way of *trial*, before they were formally enacted. I cannot at the moment tell whether any, which were the subject of the Paper, which occasions your Return, were imposed simply by me; but, if so, this is the explanation of them.

I have felt then very much, that as I am to be so much away from you, it was still more necessary than before, that I should rouse myself to do what I have been so tempted to forget.

My memory is not good — even when I am with you, things go out of my head as soon as they come in; — I often say, I will put them down. The list of points I set down in the paper are such as have long

---

[1] Presumably Michael Joseph Barry (1817–89), poet and barrister, a Young Irelander, who wrote vigorous poems for the *Nation* but recanted after 1848, and became editor of the Cork *Southern Reporter*.

[2] The first paragraph of Caswall's letter of 23 Feb. ran 'During the last fortnight the attendance at the Oratory [community prayer] on Discipline evenings has been good but not of the best. On one occasion I counted twelve present, but I have not liked to look too curiously with my short sight lest it should be noticed. I think on the whole it has been slightly under the mark.'

been floating in my head, and which at last I thought I *would* set down once for all.

I set them down, thinking, as I do still, that to *name* them was to correct the deficiencies (at least gradually) which they implied.

But never did it enter into my mind to put on you the kind of office which you have understood, when you say in words,[1] — I am not at all denying I did not explain myself — What I wanted was that any omissions in discipline should come through the *Chapter of faults*. You would only be reporting the confession at the Chapter. *I should only be as if I were present* — Therefore I said 'once a fortnight —' nay, I think I said 'after the Chapter of Faults.'[2]

Any thing inquisitorial never entered into my mind. I wanted simply to be put into the position, in which *I should be if present*. I wanted to ask questions, which I *should* ask if present, did I recollect to do so.

Any how what am I to say? may not I fairly desire to think of you all, and to be sollicitous, and to pray for the congregation, and to desire to be refreshed (as a refreshment it truly is) by letters from you, and about you, when I am absent? Will you really cut me off from this?

And then again, I now begin to have some fears lest you do not like the addresses which I send you from me at the Chapter — I *cannot* send them, if I suspect so — I shall not have the heart to do so — But my dear Fr Edward (though I am not speaking to you, but to all the Decennial Fathers,) will you cut me off from speaking to you, as well as from hearing of you? Will you thus, I may say, in my old age, throw me on the world without a home? No one knows but myself the desolateness I sustain in leaving Birmingham, and being thrown among strangers — I trust it will be taken as my penance, and be of eternal good to me — but it has been my lot through life, to make friends and to be sent away from them.

If I neither speak to you nor you to me, how am I one of you? I am conscious to myself, that my heart is with you all, and no where else. Husbands and wives write to each other daily, when separated —

---

[1] Newman here inserted a line and a half from the first paragraph of Caswall's letter. This was erased in accordance with the instruction at the end of Newman's present letter.

[2] At the fortnightly Chapter, faults against the Rule were publicly acknowledged.

Caswall wrote on 27 Feb., 'how much it pains me to think that my letter should have occasioned you any uneasiness.

The words on the paper were "The Father Prefect to state whether there are any omissions on the part *of any subject* of the congregation as to attendance at the time of the discipline." I at once thought this to mean that I was to make a report drawn from my own immediate observation . . . It seemed to me a most *reasonable and natural* thing to make such a report to you . . .' Caswall added that others had shared his mistake. See letter of 22 March to Caswall, and letter of 17 Feb. to St John.

When I come to a place, like Limerick, I say, 'I wonder whether any letters from Edgbaston, will be lying for me.' I write you to you [sic] when ever I have half an hour, and wish to find sympathy in you — Well, I know I commit a thousand faults when I am with you; — let it be my penance, when I find myself disappointed.

I wish this read by all the Fathers, though I have written it in a great hurry. Excuse faults from your love for me, and *scratch out, before you lend the letter*, the words at the very beginning of page 4,[1]

Ever Yrs most affly J H N

SUNDAY 26 FEBRUARY 1854   rain in afternoon

TO AMBROSE ST JOHN

⌐Limerick. Sunday Febr 26/54

My dearest Ambrose

Your second letter is quite unexceptionable, and cancels the first.[2]

I have said Mass, since I have been away, several times for the Congregation, several times for the Fathers, and several times for the Brothers. I have said Mass this morning for the Congregation,⌐ to return good for evil.[3]

[1] At this point also, on page 7, a few words in brackets have been erased.

[2] St John, in his first letter, that of 18 Feb., replied to Newman's of 17 Feb., '. . . When I read your letter [asking for reports from the Fathers in Birmingham] nothing entered my head, when I heard F. Fredk [Bowles] words I thought it an absurdity—and think so now, but when in Deputy Congregation I heard another Father [Nicholas Darnell] whom you do not believe has said anything[,] take the paper[,] read it formally and say he should make his protest against it and call on the other Fathers to protest against it, I thought it my duty to you to tell you what passed. My words to him were "take care lest what you say makes the Father talk about resigning." . . . It has now come back on me and you believe me the only offender. It is very hard. Your letter is ice. . . .'

Next day, 19 Feb. St John wrote his second letter, 'Dearest Father I am so sore that I will not trust myself to say more . . . It is very selfish to feel so much for myself, and so little for you, but I can't help it in this matter.

'My best love to you.   Yr affect child

Ambrose of the sore head.'

[3] St John replied on 1 March, 'I am more and more displeased with myself for my second letter not withstanding what you so very kindly say—The affair was an absurd burst which ended in a splutter, and I ought not to have made any thing of it—All the Congregation to the time I left were heart and soul carrying out every thing you wished, most heartily—I have just come from Sydenham [,] Father, and have seen a good deal there, and had F. Wilfrid's account of the extraordinary perfection and obedience of the house and I must say I blessed God for our own imperfection and

⌐I return through you Edward's paper — thank him for it. I wish you to get the Congregatio Deputata to appoint a Praefectus studiorum or the like — whose duty it will be to superintend the whole matter of the School boys.

Also, bring the matter of sitting in Refectory before the Congregatio Deputata, and let it settle it.⌐

I wish my poor paper ⟨⟨of Returns⟩⟩ posted up in the Congregation Room, if it is not done so, already, and to remain there, *till* I call for the returns.

⌐My cold is so bad that I shall stop in Dublin, and there nurse myself, and not come on to Birmingham.

God bless you, My faithful Ambrose, Ever Yours affectionately

J H N

Thank you for what you have done about the Library stove —⌐ I must ask you to act for me there, or to depute Philip

MONDAY 27 FEBRUARY 1854   left Limerick, not for Galway, but for Dublin, my cold being very bad

TUESDAY 28 FEBRUARY   my cold and cough still very troublesome   it has been on me a fortnight today

TO F. S. BOWLES

Dublin Febry 28/54

My dear Frederic

Please to order for me at Maher's a Vesperal bound for Brother Frederic — and give it to him from me with my love, telling him it is in fulfilment of a promise which I made him last Christmas four years in Alcester Street, when he sang by himself one evening, at the time I (!) played the organ. I have never forgotten it, tell him, but have not had time to think of what I should give him.

And tell Austin, that I fear much there is no chance of his going to Rome.[1] Of course some fine day the Brief will come — but perhaps

disobedience. I am most thankful for the hearty loving spirit of our house, and I love our own Fathers more than ever—Father, they love you, and you may do what you like with them, spite of a little blustering; and I would not exchange our blustering for the Londoners obedience—There is very hard riding there I am sure. . . .'

[1] i.e. with Newman, who planned to go to Rome, after the Bishops had met to inaugurate the University in accordance with the expected Brief from the Pope. Cf. letter of 9 Feb. to Flanagan.

not for weeks — after that a good month will elapse before the Bishops are called together — indeed, I consider it *certain* they will not meet before Easter.

My last exploits have been to make an eloquent speech to perhaps 80 or 100 persons at Thurles, on my health being drunk — and to escort a school girl with bandboxes up to London [sic] from Limerick. What strange uses we are put to! My cold won't go — and has something to say in its defence, till I manage to get coals in my room, and to get my door and window made tight against the draughts, which are killing; but I have been here three weeks and cannot yet get it done. As to my new coalscuttle, etc etc they are gone irrevocably — and I have this morning bought over again nearly every thing I bought 2 years ago. A school house can't be otherwise — I did not like to lock up things, on Lord Clarendon's principle, that 'a policy of suspicion' was bad[1] — but now I have at once had locks and keys fitted to my desk and drawers and closets.

I see the papers little — but am interested to hear that the Greek insurrection is spreading and that the Abyssinians have risen! — of course we and the French will put the rising down, but that will not be the end of it.[2] I see also that there is a 'quadruple alliance' (!) between Russia, the Khan of Khiva, the Khan of Bukharian, and the Afghans.[3]

And now I have told you more politics than the Civiltà will tell you for six months to come

Ever Yrs affly J H N

TO R. A. COFFIN

Febr 28/54

answered that, not I, but people, made these objections—[4]
1. the work unbound will be nearly 7 guineas — and bound £10.

[1] It was a favourite phrase of the Foreign Secretary Lord Clarendon in his instructions to Lord Stratford de Redcliffe, the British Ambassador, during the summer of 1853 that 'a policy of suspicion towards the Czar was neither wise nor safe.' Lord Clarendon's despatches had just been published in the Government Blue Book, *Eastern Papers*.

[2] *The Times* of 28 Feb. gave news of the rebellion of the Greeks and *Albanians* in Turkish provinces in Europe, and of French and English support for the Turks.

[3] *The Times* also reported that 'The intelligence of the establishment of a Russian army on the Oxus is confirmed; also that an alliance offensive and defensive has been concluded between the Russians and Dost Mahomed, the Khan of Khiva, and the Khan of Bockhara.'

[4] This is Newman's summary of his answer to R. A. Coffin, now a Redemptorist at Clapham, who sent Newman on 18 Feb. the prospectus of a complete edition of the works of St Alfonso translated into English, asking for his support.

2 that St Alfonso is not of the *calibre* of Suarez and Bellarmine — that £10 would buy a good deal of theology (not of course in those *words*)

3 that St Alf., as a practical writer, repeats himself — so that the very fact that a reader has one of his works is the reason why he does not want another.

4. that the best are translated already — and that F. Coffin in his Prospectus only meets this by saying, that, without knowing *all* St A's works, a reader has no idea of the number of subjects he has treated — as if he read, not for his own edification, but to estimate Alfonso's mind!

5 that so large a series is beset with this inconvenience, — if the issues are slow, the subscriber may be dead before the series is completed, or it may never be completed — if quick, they are a tax upon his purse.

Of course I said all this in gentle and subdued language.

TO J. D. DALGAIRNS

16 Harcourt Street Febr 28/54

My dear Fr Bernard,

Since I have been gone, I have several times said Mass for the Congregation, several times for the Fathers, and several times for the Brothers — and I have especially remembered you and your charge.[1]

You come in with great advantage — as being comparatively a stranger. All parties will bear from you, what they would not bear from another. As to the labour, of course it is greater with the *giovani* at first — as to the anxiety, time has no tendency to lessen it, and the worst is, that, in the most delicate and responsible matters, from the nature of the case, you can take no other person's judgment.

As to dear Robert [Tillotson], I should certainly advise his going to Dr Duke for a month, as far as I can judge at a distance. He should not go for a *little* time, or he will come back worse.

I don't think your report arises from any thing I set down on my *Paper* — but in case it does, I wish to say that I wrote to Fr Ambrose (unless I am greatly mistaken) on Friday February 17, to say that I did not wish reports *sent* me, but would wait to receive them in person. I have long had on my conscience that I was not doing my duty to St Philip in not forcing the subjects of the Congregation to keep the Rule or Decrees which they lie under — and I have wished very much to

[1] Dalgairns had the charge of the novices, Robert Tillotson being one of them.

remind them of this duty in many points. It is another thing whether I can succeed. They cannot bear, or at least some of them, the slightest exertion of authority, and it is a question whether another could not govern them better than I, being, as I am, at a distance.

Ever Yours most affectly J H N

Father Bernard Dalgairns

TO JOHN STANISLAS FLANAGAN

16 Harcourt Street Febry 28. 1854

My dear Stanislas

Thank you for your report — but on Friday the 17th I wrote to Fr Ambrose to say *that I would receive these reports in person in Chapter on my return, and not by letter.* Please let the Fathers know this. As I destroyed the first letter I wrote to F. Ambrose on that day, it is just possible that in the second which went, I omitted by accident to express this wish — yet I shall be surprised if I have.[1]

I wonder whether the list of Benefactors has been read, but I am afraid to inquire, lest I should be offending some one. How can I be Superior, yet not have the power to enforce the Rule and the byelaws of the Congregation?

I have sent dear Br Frederic a message through Fr Frederic.

Does Patterson's £20 note require my endorsing?[2] I don't like keeping notes in one's desk — but perhaps his Bank is as secure as ours.

⟨(Don't repeat any part of this)⟩ I got what I would from the Bishop of Limerick. He is a man I like very much — a down-right, honest, bluff person — very hearty and very positive — arguing and laying down the law, and abusing his young priests, who take his kicks and stick out against him. He is the cleverest bishop I have met, and certainly to me the kindest. He has twice over given me faculties in his Diocese — and this time he has made me formally one of his priests, and given me power to confess Nuns (as far as he has it to give) and (as I understood him) to give absolution in reserved cases![3]

---

[1] Newman had not omitted this wish. See letter of 17 Feb. to St John.

[2] See letter of 9 March to Patterson.

[3] George Butler, a Limerick priest, later to succeed the Bishop John Ryan, wrote to Newman on 12 Feb., about the latter, '. . . you must be prepared to find him full of prejudices against the University and indeed labouring under the most absolute conviction of its utter impracticability. . . . We (the Clergy) are all most anxious that our Bishop and our Diocese should have an honourable place in connexion with a project recommended by the Holy See, and commended by its own excellence and its manifest

I went over to Adare, a most splendid place, for which I was quite unprepared.

Ever Yrs affectly J H N

I wish you would be so good as to send me one copy (*smallest size*) of the Proprium of the Oratory, and also a Proprium S. Philippi (two copies?) to bind up in a 4 volumed Breviary. I suspect I have not asked for the right number of copies — but you see what I want — I am going to bind a Breviary of 4 parts — and I want, both the Proprium Sanctorum of the Oratory, and the Office of St Philip, for each of the Quarters.

TO RICHARD STANTON

16 Harcourt Street D. Febry 28/54

My dear Richard

Your letter has followed me about — I returned here yesterday.[1]

There is little chance indeed of my quitting Ireland till Holy Week — I was cut short in my travels by an obstinate cough and hoarseness — when I had got as far as Limerick — and as soon as I and the weather are better, I mean to set out again on the Galway line — and then on the Belfast line. Besides these journeys, there is a great deal of work to be done here — so that, much as I should like it, there is not a chance of my being able to preach at Brompton. If I went abroad, or my teeth obliged me, I might come to London — but not else, and I can't tell when.

There is little chance indeed of my going to Rome — what I desire more is to go to New York on University matters — but I am so weak, that I do not know how to venture it.[2] I am very well, when I keep quiet — but travelling knocks me up — ⟨⟨*don't tell all that follows* to any one⟩⟩ and the little annoyances of strange houses, of being in the

necessity.' Butler hoped Newman would win over the Bishop, who thought a University independent of the State could not succeed. When inviting Newman on 18 Feb. to be his guest, the Bishop wrote, 'There is one point however of which I have the strongest conviction that if success be not attainable it cannot nor will not be imputable to any defect on your part.'

Newman noted in his University Journal for February 24–27, 'Bishop of Limerick very strong against the *possibility* of the University answering. However he has consented to have his name put down on the Books, on condition (which *I* proposed) that he should not be bound to give money, and also (which he proposed) that he should not be supposed to prophesy anything but failure.' Cf. *A.W.* p. 324.

[1] Stanton wrote on 20 Feb. to ask Newman to preach at the opening of the Oratory at Brompton on 22 March. See the diary for that day.

[2] Cf. letter of 9 Feb. to Flanagan.

hands of others who do not know what hurts one and what not, who protest one does not take care of oneself, at the time they are keeping the said one standing in draughts, and press one to eat and are distressed at one's abstinence, while they offer raw mutton which would turn a Tartar's stomach, I say such annoyances, and moreover the having to make speeches after dinner, to refuse sermons, and to explore unknown regions a mile from the dwelling house, tease mind as well as body in a wonderful way.

I, as you, had the fear of a Roman examination in Canon Law before my eyes — and mean to get an understanding on the point, before I venture into such predicament.[1] The Cardinal has very kindly asked to consecrate me.

Tell this all to F Wilfrid — I have heard nothing about his health an age.

Ever Yrs affly J H N.

WEDNESDAY 1 MARCH 1854 gave ashes to and said Mass for the boys in Harcourt Street. Mr Errington called.[2]

TO MRS WILLIAM FROUDE

16 Harcourt Street, Dublin March 2. 1854
My dear Mrs Froude,

Your kind congratulations have just come to hand, having followed me over Ireland, through which I have been ranging. I *thought* you were thinking of me on the 21st and I did not forget you and William on the 28th, when my intention at Mass was the repose of the souls of Hurrell, Mr S. Wood, and my dear friend John Bowden, who, all three (humanly speaking) would have been Catholics, had they lived till now.[3]

[1] Stanton reminded Newman that if he went to Rome for his consecration as bishop, he would have to undergo an examination there.

[2] Newman copied out from his Journal Errington's remarks '. . . "he said that Mr. James O'Ferrall had a more desponding view than ever of the University, from things which came out in the Maynooth commissions." I suppose clerical jobs. "He thought there was simply no demand for it. He told me last November," I continue, "that the Catholic party had been obliged to move in order to oppose the Queen's Colleges. Perhaps many will content themselves with their [the Queen's Colleges'] failure, looking on the project of a University merely as something negative." If this use of me was what called me to Ireland . . . this might be a great object, but a very different one from that which filled my own mind.' *A.W.* p. 325.

James O'Ferrall was a member of the Royal Commission to enquire into the management of Maynooth, which was in receipt of a Government grant.

[3] Cf. letter of 28 Jan. 1846 to Miss Giberne. Newman's birthday was on 21 Feb. 1801, and Richard Hurrell Froude died on 28 Feb. 1836.

I grieve to hear you confirm what I have long felt, the mysterious antipathy of our population to Catholicism. The surplice controversy first clearly brought it out — unless you say that Devonshire is more Protestant than the rest of England —[1] I don't suppose that Hurrell or I had ever any *real* idea of the English *population* being influenced by Church principles — though sometimes doctrines may, in order to their elucidations, have been now and then thrown into the shape of anticipations — but certainly every event since 1833 has gone to show those, who would be Catholics, that they must come out of their own people as Abraham or St Paul. I forget minutely all that has passed between us, and may be saying what is inconsistent with, or a repetition, of what has been said before, but, My dear Mrs Froude, *do* you pray for 'effectual grace' —? Suppose I come to a high wall — I cannot jump it — such are the moral obstacles which keep us from the Church. We see the Heavenly City before us, we go on and on along the road, till a wall simply crosses it. Human effort cannot clear it — there is no scaling, no vaulting over. Grace enables us to cross it — and that grace is called effectual grace. Our first grace is sufficient to enable us to pray for that second effectual grace — and God gives grace for grace.

Excuse this Sermon, and with love to William and the dear child you brought to see me Ever yours affectly

John H Newman, of the Oratory.

P.S.   I have nothing to tell you about Ireland. The Pope is taking my part, i.e. he is making me a Bishop; but the great difficulty(!) *between ourselves* is, that, what with emigration, campaigning, ruin of families, and the μικροψυχια (pusillanimity) induced by centuries of oppression, there seems *no class* to afford members for a University — and next, there is a deep *general impression* that this is the case, which is nearly as hopeless a circumstance as the case itself, supposing that case to be a fact. Don't repeat this.

TO MRS JOHN MOZLEY

16 Harcourt Street Dublin March 2/54
My dear Jemima
    Your kind letter has just come to hand, having followed me about over Ireland. I have returned here to nurse a bad cough, which has

[1] There were Protestant riots in the church of St Sidwell at Exeter, in 1844 and in 1848, when the preacher wore a surplice.

been on me for a fortnight. I caught my other by going about — I am very well, when I keep quiet.

War has been all but certain for a year past — but it is difficult to realize — and difficult to acquiesce in.[1] We are starting with every advantage, and are pretty certain of success, if we are quick about it, as we seem likely to be — but it is morally impossible that English, French, Austrians, and Prussians can pull together for any time — and Russia can be as slow and obstinate, as we are energetic — She is looking out for the chapter of accidents, for the jealousy of the Powers, the weakness and fanaticism of the Turks, and the insurrection of the Greeks. So that, it is impossible to say what the end will be. It is a year since the Emperor was said to have propounded two things:—1. that the solution of the Eastern question would not be without war, for an amicable partition of Turkey was impossible — 2 that he was prepared for the annihilation of his navy, since, his military power being his real strength, he was content to pay that price for success. When I press people on the subject, the only termination at which they seem to look, is the assassination of the Emperor by his nobles. The heir apparent is for peace, I believe.

Ever Yours affectionately John H Newman

TO AMBROSE ST JOHN

16 Harcourt Street March 2. 1854

Charissime,

My birthday letters have just come from Cork — and another — making two envelopes from Cork. I received two letters, whether in one cover or two I don't know, from Carlow. Was this all? Were any sent to Waterford or elsewhere?

How is your cold? pretty well, I thank you — how is yours?

What do you mean by a hankerchief for me from Derby? I cannot

[1] Early in 1853 the Czar Nicholas I made known his claims against the Turkish Empire, and England gradually 'drifted' into war. On 4 Oct. the Sultan declared war against Russia, and at the beginning of 1854 the British and French fleets entered the Black Sea. Early in Feb. the Czar withdrew his ambassadors from London and Paris, and the ultimatum of England and France followed. On 12 March these two countries became the allies of Turkey, and before the end of the month the Crimean War had begun.

Newman disapproved of the war as unnecessary, and thought Russia had more claim to be considered Christian, than Turkey, the protection of whose Christian minorities was an ostensible cause of the war.

conceive what it can be — when you return to Edgbaston, you can open it, and forward it or not, as you judge best.[1] I am well employed here, and could not leave just now for England, and do not know when I shall.

By all means have the kitchen coloured or painted, as you say. ⌐I am not aware what you mean by the 'bath room' —⌐ did we settle on it? if so [[if you mean the one close to mine]], ⌐I should like very much, *supposing it is only lath and plaster*, a door broken into my [[short, cross]] passage out of it, close to my door, and opposed [[opposite]] the glass door of the guest room (Number 2) if the Congregation would not object.⌐ I would pay for it — but I did not know we had settled to make it is [sic] a bath room.

⌐The Saturday's Mass is for the Sanctification of both Houses — put any thing else in you will. For 20 years I have said my work was that of raising the dead! I have said so in my fourth University Sermon,[2] quoting Aeschylus, before the movement of 1833 began. Well, if that was a raising the dead, emphatically more so is this Irish University — for every one almost seems to agree that no where in Ireland are the youths to be found to fill it.

Ever Yours, My dearest Ambrose, Most affectionately⌐ in Mary & Philip

John H Newman of the Oratory

TO J. D. DALGAIRNS

16 Harcourt Street March 4/54

(Private)

My dear F Bernard

It has some time struck me that the Giovani should know more of Scripture than I suspect they do — and really their spiritual reading might most suitably include some part of the Old and New Testament.

I have thought before now whether I should make it one of the conditions of Ordination — but perhaps it had better come through

---

[1] See postscript to letter of 9 March to Mrs John Mozley.

[2] [[now fifth]], 'Personal Influence, the Means of Propagating the Truth,' *U.S.* pp. 87–8, '. . . What was the task of an Apostle but to raise the dead? and what trifling would it appear . . . when such a one persisted to chafe and stimulate the limbs of the inanimate corpse, as if his own life could be communicated to it . . . in the poet's words, θράσος ἀκούσιον | ἀνδράσι θνήσκουσι κομίζων. [Agamemnon, 803–04.]

. . . .Yet (blessed be God!) the power of Truth actually did, by some means or other, overcome these vast obstacles to its propagation . . .'

you in the way I have suggested. But let me have your opinion upon it.

Thank you for your affectionate note, which is solitary.

Ever Yrs affly J H N

TO F. W. FABER

16 Harcourt Str March 4/54

My dear Fr Wilfrid

Thank you for your good news.[1] I congratulate you. I fear there is no prospect of my being in London soon.

I shall say mass for your 'Introitus' on St Thomas's Day and St Gregory's.

Ever Yrs affly J H N

TO JOHN STANISLAS FLANAGAN

16 Harcourt Street March 4/54

My dearest Stanislas

Nothing can be kinder and truer than your letter.[2] I had no doubt at all of you. Till Edward's letter[3] came I had no suspicions of any one, but of Fr Ambrose and F Frederic, and of them not suspicions, but more — for Fr Ambrose told me that he stumbled at my Paper, and that Fr Frederic did too. Also he said, (as I understood it, to defend himself,) that it created surprise in the Congregatio Deputata. I dare say he does not recollect himself what he said and what he did not — *and if taxed with gossipping about others, may* [have] *admitted against himself, out of wish to be candid, what is not true.*

But F. Edward used words, which at once struck to my heart, and the more so, because so gentle and mild a person never would have used such words, unless he spoke them from others. And his apology

---

[1] Faber took possession of the new house of the Oratory at Brompton on 28 Feb.

[2] Flanagan wrote on 3 March what he understood by Newman's paper which asked for reports: 'I took it that we were each in our several offices . . . after each Chapter, to let you know how matters were going on. This seemed to me a very natural proceeding and a wise one. . . . I thought it a kind and affectionate way of getting us all to write to you, and of making us live together, although separated.'

[3] Edward Caswall's letter is that quoted in the first note to the letter of 25 Feb. to him.

simply was in answer to mine, when I wrote, that others felt as he.

He and he alone pained me, and on the day following I could hardly get thro' the Mass, which I said for all of you, for crying. Edward's letter was quite a surprise to me. Father Ambrose had not been the cause of it, or prepared me

Ever Yrs affly J H N

P.S.   Thank Henry for his affectionate letter, and tell him to condole for me with dear William and Robert respectively.[1]

I find the Guards *used* to be in Dublin.[2] My cold and cough are gone

TO AMBROSE ST JOHN

⌐16 Harcourt Street March 4/54

Charissime

Thank you for your affectionate letter just received —[3] F. Bernard sent me an affectionate one also.

My cold and cough are gone. I believe I got them by the state of this room — into which the wind poured with a liberality and continuance,⌐ which no other room could possibly show. ⌐I began my travels with hardly any voice, except that of coughing.⌐ (*Do not* read this out.) ⌐Then,⌐ on my journey, as here, ⌐I fell in with raw coarse beef and mutton —⌐ and for three weeks kept fast.

⌐However, these things are at an end — I have *just* managed to get my door listed, and a curtain put outside. I have at length got a coal skuttle, and I have this very morning had my first joint in from a pastry cook's, being a loin of cold mutton —⌐ so I hope now to do quite well.

⌐I have a good deal of *business* here though not much *work* — i.e. I have *appointments*, with a good deal of *leisure*. Had I a good subject, I could write a new book⌐

Ever Yrs most affectly J H N

SUNDAY 5 MARCH 1854   went to Vespers and dined at All Hallows

---

[1] The former had sprained his ankle and the latter had been unwell.
[2] Flanagan had served in the Guards for a short while.
[3] That quoted in second note to letter of 26 Feb. to St John.

MONDAY 6 MARCH   Mr Errington and Mr O Reilly[1] with Mr Butler, the architect, all day with me about the plans for the alteration of the University House,
and other matters

TO JOHN STANISLAS FLANAGAN

16 Harcourt Street March 6/54

My dearest Stanislas,

I forgot to tell you before I came off, that Northcote readily assented
to the guinea and a half per week.[2] Dr Hendren, you see, is leaving. I
wrote to Hope to say for Lord R.H [Ralph Kerr] £150 — but *not to ask
more than* £100, if he thought £100 better — we must not be Jews. I
trust the Lady O.A [Olivia Acheson] money is moving.

I want to hear something about the Vault for which your cousin
Terence said he should sketch a plan.[3]

I am very sorry to give you more trouble — but I had miscalculated
the size of the Breviary — it is just a thought larger than the smallest size
of our Proprium. So you must send me, if you please, a copy of the
next large size, which I must cut down. Please put the expence of both
postages, either to me, or to Laurence whom I will repay.

Afternoon. I have just received from Birmingham a letter from
Hope Scott, in which he says '£150 is not thought by me, or by Lord
Ralph's mother and Lord Henry too much, so you may consider that
settled.' This being so you may tell Fr Minister (not, however, letting
out to the world that this is the reason of it) that I think Lord R. should
go into the Bishop's rooms, if he does not object. The want of a
book-case is the only difficulty. A blind must be added to one of the
windows.

I am afraid I must have taken you in with my account of my after
dinner speech to 80 people. It was only a priest's dinner, after which all
the boys of the (Thurles) College and the servants came in, to hear the
wonderful eloquence which was going on.[4]

Monday morning. I am answering the inclosed giving your name,
and saying that you will give a receipt for me, if the money is sent to
you —

Ever Yrs affly J H N

[1] Newman noted in his University Journal, 'Offered Mr [Myles] O Reilly a Lectureship—he thought of Political Economy—I wished him to talk with Mr Thomas
O Hagan and he consented.'
[2] Northcote was boarding at the Oratory and studying there for the priesthood.
[3] There was a plan for a burial vault beneath the church at the Oratory.
[4] Cf. letter of 28 Feb. to Bowles.

WEDNESDAY 8 MARCH 1854   the Archbishop called and took me out to various schools.   dined with Fr Curtis

TO WILLIAM MONSELL

16 Harcourt Street Dublin March 8 1854

My dear Monsell,

Thank you for your very valuable letter, which will be of great service to me, though I hope you have got over the disagreeable affection to which I am indebted for the leisure necessary for your writing to me.

As yet nothing is done here, and I am not in loco. I should not be here at all, unless I had a moral certainty that it is a matter of days, or at least of a few weeks, for the time to come when a start is really to be made — but I can do very little.

It would indeed be good, if I could spirit up people to your £5000 a year plan — I do not think it is out of the question — but it requires a good deal of zeal — and I think we must first show what we can do, or at least that we are beginning. I should rather propose to take the £5000 for the first year from the sums already collected, (though, alas, the fall of the stocks has been a very serious thing to them) and then see how much comes in that first year, from the fact of beginning; and then after this, when we had some claim, viz during the second year, to commence your applotment subscription, the idea of which is capital.[1]

Were I strong enough, I should like to go to New York on the matter — but a little thing knocks me up, and it would not do to be ill all the time I was there — so I am frightened about it.

I was at the Bishop of Limerick's a day or two, and gained all I ventured to ask, which was indeed enough for the present — viz leave to put down his name on the books of the University. This will enable me to go about to the laity, M Ps, country gentlemen (as many as there are) in his diocese, and get their names too. It is intended as at once a compliment to them, and a sanction from them. It involves no payment. I shall come to you in this way in due time — but I can do nothing publicly, till I am publicly recognised.

I was extremely pleased to see Lord Dunraven in his own place — and what a fine place it is![2]

Ever Yrs affly in Xt   John H Newman of the Oratory

[1] Monsell wrote suggesting how the amount required for the University might be shared among the parishes.   [2] See diary for 25 Feb.

TO THE EARL OF SHREWSBURY

16 Harcourt Street Dublin March 8. 1854

My dear Lord Shrewsbury,

I have been moving about in various parts of Ireland; this and the difficulty of commanding time under such circumstances must plead my excuse for seeming delay in acknowledging your Lordship's most friendly letter.[1]

It is true that a communication has been made to me to the effect, that it is the Holy Father's condescending intention to raise me to the Episcopate. I have, however, no reason to suppose that this involves any removal of me from the duties which have been already put upon me here, or any imposition of more onerous duties elsewhere. Indeed it is my comfort to think that my present undertaking, which is more suited to me, will be an effectual guarantee that I shall have no part in responsibilities of a higher and more sacred kind, for which I have had no preparation and am altogether unfit. I have been here some weeks, waiting for some formal announcement from Rome of the honor intended me, which in fact will be the commencement of active operations here in behalf of the establishment of the University.

Till the University is actually set up, we cannot tell what its success will be. This has always been the case with the schools of learning. Paris and Oxford would not have succeeded, let the desire of education have been ever so great, till they actually had shown they had men to produce who were able to educate. No one could have predicted the growth of Universities there, rather than in any other spots of the world, till they had great Professors to show, an Albertus Magnus or a Duns Scotus.

But I must not occupy your Lordship with such truisms — and begging my best respects to the revered and kind relatives you have with you, whose health, I trust, nothing avails to affect injuriously, I am, My dear Lord Shrewsbury, Most sincerely Yours in Xt

John H Newman of the Oratory

The Rt Honble The Earl of Shrewsbury.

[1] Lord Shrewsbury wrote to Newman on 19 Feb.,
'My dear Lord Bishop (Elect.)
    . . . Long have I wished that you might receive the mitre, and now my desire is accomplished. Deo Gratias—but my dear Lord Bishop, although delighted to name you by that title I wish that I could call you Archbishop, and that I might address you as the Metropolitan of England. . . .' Lord Shrewsbury, thinking that Wiseman was about to become a Cardinal in Curia, went on to say he hoped Newman would be translated to Westminster.

THURSDAY 9 MARCH 1854   went down to Kings town to see H W[Wilberforce] who was returned, and dined with Mr Buckle, where he was to dine.

TO MISS M. R. GIBERNE

16 Harcourt Street. Dublin. March 9. 1854

My dear Miss Giberne

Your letter of February 27 came to me here yesterday. I have this morning said a Mass for the repose of the soul of Mary Woodmason. Tell Jemima W. [Woodmason], when you see her, that the housewife ⟨(is this the right spelling?)⟩ she gave me, when I left Littlemore for Oscott, is in the drawer of the table on which I am writing, that it is as blue as ever, though it has travelled to Rome and back, and that its inexhaustible black silk still threads its ever brilliant and ever sharp needles.[1] I was using both only yesterday in a wonderful attempt to mend my clothes. For the poor Naples lawyer,[2] for whom a present lies packed up in London, which, consisting of razors, would not suit his wife and children, I shall say three black privileged Masses, if all is well, on the

14th, 15th, and 16th of this month.

We are waiting for the brief of my appointment, before which I cannot do much here in the way of overt preparations. I think it will be of great use to me with reference to the University, and so alone I look at it, except of course as a most consolatory proof besides, as it is, of the Holy Father's condescending consideration and thought for me. There seems little chance *now* of my going to Rome, because the time is passing. I know full well that I shall be beset with engagements when I once begin — my own leisure was before Easter, but there were very good reasons which made it inexpedient for me to go to Rome before the brief came.

I have not the book here and cannot tell you fully St Philip's immediate companions — I should say, e.g. Baronio, Tarugi, Manni, Gallonio, Consolini, Ancina, Bozzio, etc. But don't do too many. I like the crying B. Valfre. But I fear you are taking a deal too much trouble.[3]

Northcote is with us for a few months — but there is no notion of

[1] For the Woodmason family, see the Index to Volume XI.

[2] On this lawyer, who was found to have died, see letter of 22 Jan. to Miss Giberne.

[3] Miss Giberne was making copies of the portraits of St Philip's companions at the Roman Oratory, for the refectory of that at Birmingham, where they are still to be found. B. Valfre is Blessed Sebastian Valfré of Turin.

his becoming an Oratorian. Manning *does* preach indefinitely better than I, say what you will. I send you some books by Captn Patterson, which I hope will save a box.

Denison, Bishop of Salisbury, is dead — so is little Jenkyns, the head of Balliol — and Richards, head of Exeter, and the old soldiers of the poor Duke are dying, before the new war begins — e.g. Lord Londonderry.[1] The cholera has begun again — The Baltic fleet is just setting off. France is successfully keeping off the hands of England from revolutionizing Italy in this war.[2]

TO MRS JOHN MOZLEY

16 Harcourt Street March 9/54

My dear Jemima

I have just got a letter from Harriet Fourdrinier to the effect that she wants to borrow £10 of me.[3]

This is impossible — not only because I have not the money to give, with[out] simply impoverishing myself — but that to lend is to give.

I have said I would give her £3, and that, as I don't know her post office, I would send it to you.

Excuse this liberty — I will send it in a day or two — as soon as I have the money

Ever Yours affly J H N

P.S.   I hear of a beautiful mat or the like having come from you at Birmingham — thank you for it.

[1] Edward Denison (1801–54), Bishop of Salisbury from 1837, Richard Jenkyns (1782–1854), Master of Balliol College from 1819, and Charles William Stewart third Marquess of Londonderry (1778–1854), who served under Wellington in the Peninsular War, all died on 6 March. Joseph Loscombe Richards (1798–1854), Rector of Exeter College from 1838, died on 27 Feb.

[2] Newman sent this letter unfinished.

[3] Harriett was Newman's first cousin, daughter of his uncle, Henry Fourdrinier. He and his brother Sealy Fourdrinier lost money over their inventions of paper-making machinery, owing to the defective law of patents, and were cheated by the Czar of Russia. In 1840 Parliament voted £7000 to Henry Fourdrinier, but this was thought inadequate, and firms in the paper trade raised a subscription to purchase annuities for him and his two daughters. According to *D N B*, VII, p. 519, this ensured them a comfortable income.

TO JAMES LAIRD PATTERSON

16 Harcourt Street. Dublin March 9. 1854

My dear Patterson,

I fear you have expected an answer from me before now — Your letter was opened at Birmingham, and the cheque taken out and put in safety,[1] and then the letter wandered after me into the South and West of Ireland, where I was roaming in quest of episcopal sanction to the Decree of the Synod of Thurles touching the Catholic University. But this fact, that such sanction is any where still to be sought, seeing it is one too profoundly hidden from the public to get out from any other quarter, must not, if you please, get out in Rome *from me* — else, it is plain, I shall seem to be hitting a defect some where or other in the Irish Hierarchy. I am received every where, by both Bishops and Priests, with the greatest cordiality and affection — and I may say most truly and thankfully, that, many as are the varieties of opinion in Ireland, on one point it seems quite agreed, to be kind to me.

But I have forgotten you and your most kind gift. I really was ashamed to take it — and had hoped you would not think it necessary to send it — now, however, it has come, I will take care it is applied to some very good purpose, such as I trust you would approve as well as that for which you originally intended it.

We were much gratified by a visit from your brother[2] — who by this time I suppose is with you. Pray say every thing kind and respectful from me to him. Today's paper gives notice of the sudden death of the Bishop of Salisbury — and yesterday's of the Master of Balliol. Richards of Exeter, long expected, went shortly before him and Harrington, I think, before you left.[3] What a clearance! and in the army too, as if the war were to begin without the old soldiers — Lord Londonderry is just dead — Sir C. Napier followed the Duke, Lord Anglesea, I suppose, is dying — and I think another has gone.[4]

The cholera has begun its own campaign — it has fallen on Leeds

---

[1] Patterson, on 5 Feb., sent a cheque for £20 towards the Achilli trial fund, wishing it to be simply at Newman's disposal. Patterson, who wrote from Rome, congratulated Newman on his 'approaching elevation to the High Priesthood, which is the subject of universal rejoicing here.'

[2] Captain Patterson. See diary for 1 Feb.

[3] Richard Harington (1800–53), Principal of Brasenose College from 1842, died on 13 Dec.

[4] Sir Charles James Napier (1782–1853) died on 29 Aug. The Marquis of Anglesea, Henry William Paget (1768–1854), who commanded the cavalry at Waterloo, died on 29 April.

with great fury. I had a kind letter from Pusey yesterday, whose daughter is going to be married.[1]

And now I have told you all the news I can think of

Ever Yours most sincerely in Xt

John H Newman of the Oratory

FRIDAY 10 MARCH 1854 H W[Wilberforce] with me the whole morning

TO CATHERINE ANNE BATHURST

16 Harcourt Street Dublin March 10. 1854

My dear Child

Of course I was very sorry to find what disappointment and anxiety you were in, and grieved for the perplexities which still beset your course, but I could not feel any surprise at what you told me, and I have a consolation in thinking that, though you may not see it yourself, the good Hand of Providence is bringing you forward, and by means of your trials bringing you nearer to Him.[2]

Recollect I never intended you for the serious ordeal you have passed — it took me by surprise when you proposed to go to Loughborough, and I only gave in upon your eager wish, under the notion that I could not of course be sure that the Hand of God was not in it. It took me by surprise to find that you aspired to be a real nun — it cannot be any surprise to me, that, whatever may one day be the Divine Will, such it is not just now.

Do not be cast down because your Loving Father is bringing you to Heaven in His own way. He sees that way is quite as necessary, as in this world a physician's regimen is for the sick — though the sick child wonders that he must do this and he must not do that. You will see it all clearly enough, please God — hereafter. *Now* the only question is, what should you do at the moment. I can give you no hopes of my being in Birmingham, or in Dublin, or in London, or any where else — and, when you are tried by the uncertainty of your own future, think, please, that it must be some trial to me at my age thus to be without a home, and say a Hail Mary for me. I do not know whether I am going to Rome, whether I am going to America; so that I cannot promise to see you. The best chance would be for Birmingham in Holy

[1] See third note to letter of 11 March to Pusey.

[2] Catherine Bathurst had left the Rosminian noviciate at Loughborough. Cf. letter of 12 Feb. to her.

Week — but I only know all my anticipations and appointments have failed hitherto — so that I place confidence in nothing. What is becoming of your brother? is he a priest, or soon to be? could you keep house for him on his Mission? this would give you time to think over things. Cannot you be with Miss Lockhart for a time, though not of the body?[1]

I sometimes ask myself whether some very anxious and energetic employment, as that of the Good Shepherd, would not keep you from thinking of yourself — have you ever thought of Miss Ryder?

Ever Yours affly in Xt John H Newman of the Oratory

TO J. D. DALGAIRNS

16 Harcourt Street March 10/54

My dear Bernard

My conscience has been uneasy some time, because, I have not renewed license to eat as usual this Lent. You said something in a PS. which I took as sufficient, but in the letter it is not.[2]

I want leave neither to fast nor to abstain — though abstain I can and will, please God — but sometimes my dinner fails me after the first mouthful, and then I can't touch meat again at a later hour, unless I have full leave.

Mr Babington told me I must not weaken myself, and I believe it necessary I should have the discretion

Ever Yrs affly J H N

Revd Fr B.

TO JOHN STANISLAS FLANAGAN

16 Harcourt Street. March 10/54

My dear Stanislas,

I have no objection to Mr Canning, but I thought you considered Mr N. a sharper man. I have the reverse of an attachment to Mr N. personally.[3]

---

[1] Stuart Eyre Bathurst was ordained priest at Oscott on 24 Aug. 1854, and became the priest at Stone. Catherine Bathurst returned to Elizabeth Lockhart's community at Greenwich, later in the year.

[2] Dalgairns, the official confessor at the Oratory, could give lenten dispensations.

[3] Flanagan was dealing with a claim for payment, where the advice of a solicitor such as Walter Canning might be required. The next sentence refers to a debt owed by a man in London which was paid within a day or so.

What do you mean by 'the money from the London Gent'?

I like your plan of borrowing Edward's money, and think you had better act on it.[1]

I had not heard the Morning Herald's absurd rumour.[2]

A young priest ran yesterday morning to do his daily Dublin work — at confirmation, Dr Cullen says 'What would you say if I sent you as chaplain to the Catholic soldiers embarking for the East?' he put himself at the Archbishop's disposal, and off he is. I want to raise a fund for Catholic chaplains, if government would accept it.[3]

Would it be possible, and respectable, in me to get my name on the list of some Club House here? and of which? This is the best way I can think of for securing my dinner.[4]

I doubt now whether we shall open our University till Christmas — but I am getting clearer in my plans, and shall surprise people by the splash I make, if I can manage it.

Thank FF Frederic and Edward for their letters, but please to repeat to them that I said I should not receive their Reports.

Between ourselves. F Frederic complains of T. McKenna being sent away to Ireland, seeing he is a boss singer.

Thank you for the Proprium.

Ever Yours affectly John H Newman

[1] It was proposed to borrow £1000 from Edward Caswall, to meet the current debt of the Oratory.

[2] i.e. that the Russians had captured Constantinople.

[3] It was estimated that one-third of the soldiers in the British Army were Catholics, and the provision for chaplains was most inadequate. The Government agreed to authorise and meet the expense of Catholic chaplains, and the first of these left for the Crimea in Sept. 1854.

[4] Flanagan replied on 12 March, 'There is only one club in Dublin into which you would gain admittance . . . the Stephen's Green Club, which is the opposite side of the Green to the University. . . . Into this, altho' I think any other priest would be blackballed, *you*, I feel sure, would be admitted. It is not the crack Club of Dublin, but it is, of course, a most respectable one. Myles O'Reilly, and the O'Ferralls (I believe) are members. *I* know shoals of its habitués—I wish much you *were* a member, because I am of opinion it would be the most efficacious way of gaining over to your views those who are now opponents. It would serve all the purpose of dinners, without the bore and loss of time—But would it *do* for you to put your name up? This is a point upon which you would have to feel your way among Ecclesiastics. It would astonish them no doubt, and perhaps the Archbishop might not like it. I believe I am right in saying that there is no priest in Ireland a member of the club.'

TO AMBROSE ST JOHN

16 Harcourt Street — March 10/54

Charissime,

I have for some days wished to write to you about Lord R. Kerr — and your report of his having the measles gives me an additional reason for doing so.

First, his mother ought to know his illness — this, I suppose, has been attended to.

I hope he is quite comfortable in his room. Would not the Bishop's ⟨[[Hendren]]⟩ bed rc n be more so? I shall write to Henry by this post about him. Recollect *we are here put on our trial* — for the doubt in the world is, whether men can nurse a sick youth.

As he gives us so handsome a sum, I think he must be well taken care of. His shoes etc etc, all those little things which are necessary for a young man, and a trouble to him when they go wrong, should be carefully attended to. He should want for nothing. I have a great difficulty so to throw my mind upon the subject as to go into detail, but I must ask you, as Fr Minister, to do so. He should have some one to attend on him — does Charles do so enough? he may want hot water of a night, or plenty of towels, or a hundred little things, which would make him more comfortable. He should have pegs put up for his clothes — and, if he is put into the Bishop's rooms,[1]

⌐I am pleased at your plans for Laurence. If any one could come from Brompton uncorrupted, it would be he. But you must think of this difficulty.¬[2]

TO E. B. PUSEY

16, Harcourt Street Dublin March 11. 1854

My dear Pusey

I hope you will receive very shortly a copy of my Discourses on University Education, to which you allude, if you will kindly accept it.

[1] St John wrote on 7 March of Lord Ralph Kerr '. . . he is very unlicked, but not unhopeful. His devotion to St P. [Philip] and possible vocation to the ecclesiastical state is all fudge . . . he is only half converted yet.' Lord Ralph Kerr wrote long afterwards of his coming to the Oratory, '. . . the Fathers were all delightful—Father Ambrose St John, Father Bernard Dalgairns, and Father Edward Caswall were of the number—and it was there that I learned to be a true Roman Catholic, for Rome and St Philip were the joy of their lives.' *Cecil Marchioness of Lothian*, edited by Cecil Kerr, p. 134.

[2] Newman cut out most of the second page of this letter, but recopied and stuck back this paragraph. It was proposed that Brother Laurence should stay at the Oratory at Brompton, while he took lessons in cooking at Pagliano's Restaurant, Leicester Square.

I should value much your answer to Vaughan.[1] I have read the Report of the Heads of Houses, and smiled to find that, after all the rubs they had given you, they were at last obliged to have recourse to you as their best champion.[2]

Thank you for your leave about the volumes of St Athanasius.[3] It is just possible I might wish to turn them into Latin, or in some way or other to use them.

Give my best love to Philip and to Mary,[4] and believe me to be,

Ever affecly Yours John H Newman

SUNDAY 12 MARCH 1854 went down to Kingstown and dined with H W [Wilberforce]

TO AMBROSE ST JOHN

16 Harcourt Street March 12/54

My dear Ambrose

I should not like my Stations [of the Cross] to be used till they are put up for good, and the walls are not dry enough yet for that. Let them remain quietly *in Number 2*. the room next to mine, where I put them.

I think you do not care for the Telegraph at Edgbaston. If not, pray stop it. You alone can do it, because it comes to you; you must explain to them that Mr Ambrose, is St John's Oratory. You may tell them to send the bill to me at 16 Harcourt Street.

[1] Pusey wrote, about 7 March, 'I am just now answering Vaughan and defending the state of the Colleges of the 12th–14th centuries . . . I have seen the outside of a book of yours upon them; and heard much of it from Isaac [Williams]. It would be strange to buy each others books. I know not whether you would like my last volume of Parochial sermons, (it is practical) for my sake or use of the library'

H. H. Vaughan, Regius Professor of Modern History, championed the professorial system. His *Oxford Reform and Oxford Professors*, London 1854, Pusey answered in *Collegiate and Professorial Teaching and Discipline: in answer to Professor Vaughan's Strictures*, Oxford 1854. Pusey argued that the recommendations of the Oxford University Commission would destroy the collegiate system.

[2] The Heads of the Oxford Colleges welcomed Pusey as an ally, and praised his defence of their position. Liddon's *Pusey*, III, pp. 381–94; C. E. Mallett, *A History of the University of Oxford*, London 1927, III, pp. 318–23.

[3] i.e. leave to print whatever he wished. See Pusey's letter, quoted in fourth note to that of 28 Jan. to Rivington.

[4] Pusey wrote about his children, 'Ph. [Philip] is working on here at the higher mathematics; Mary is going to be married to a kind religious man; I longed that she should have chosen to belong to our Lord, Alone.' Mary Pusey married the Rev. J. G. Brine on 13 July 1854.

March 15. ⌐I return Stanislas's letter from Mr Flanagan — which has just come. I have nothing to add to what I said yesterday in returning the Plan — except that I think 7 feet should be allowed for the length of the coffins.⌐ It would not do to have a difficulty in getting their handles in. And I think ⌐since it is his recommendation that we should enlarge the vault in time to come, in the way he shows, we should carefully keep his letters, or copies of them, with the Plan, for our Successors.[1]

We have had most delightful weather here, ever since I returned from Limerick —⌐ and I am prophesying that every day as it comes, is to [be] the last of the fine ones. ⌐The leaves are half out,⌐ but I suppose frosts are in store.

If Jewsbury is in the House, (which I have not heard yet,) I wish Frederic to have nothing to do with the Sacristy — and to be concerned with the Church *only* in the sweeping and cleaning, as far as it is necessary. If any inconvenience arises from this, I cannot help it; as I am cut off from asking questions before I determine on things.

Will you give the inclosed Essay back to Edward? It wants unity, and that, because it has a term, not a proposition, for the thesis.[2]

⌐It seems to me shocking that, instead of any religious act whatever, Lord Palmerston (who has lately put his mockery of Providence on record) Sir James Graham, and Sir Wm Molesworth (a known sceptic, I believe) should send Sir C. Napier off with after dinner speeches,⌐ (to say nothing of the indecorum in Cabinet Ministers,) ⌐when Sir C. Napier, who is the only one to introduce the subject of God, does so to call the Russians blasphemous for appealing to Him.⌐[3]

Ever Yours affectionately John H Newman

[1] Nothing came of the plan to construct a burial vault beneath the church at the Oratory.

[2] It was an essay by Lord Ralph Kerr, sent for Newman's inspection.

[3] All this was during a great banquet at the Reform Club, on 7 March, in honour of Admiral Sir Charles Napier who had been appointed to command the Baltic fleet. Sir William Molesworth, unbeliever and radical, who was in the Cabinet, said, 'On false and flimsy pretexts two provinces of the Turkish Empire had been invaded . . . blasphemous appeals had been made to the Almighty; a crusade had been preached . . .'

Newman was not the only one shocked. In the House of Commons on 13 March John Bright said, 'I have read the proceedings of that banquet with pain and humiliation. The reckless levity displayed is, in my opinion, discreditable to the grave and responsible statesmen of a civilised and Christian nation.' Macaulay, an admirer of Palmerston, commented, 'I heard Bright say everything I thought.' G. O. Trevelyan, *The Life and Letters of Lord Macaulay*, popular ed. London 1889, p. 607. Newman preserved in a scrap book the parliamentary report in *The Times* of this speech by John Bright.

Palmerston's mockery of Providence was occasioned by a request to him as Home Secretary from the Moderator of the Edinburgh Presbytery, for the appointment of a

TO RICHARD STANTON

16 Harcourt Street Dublin March 12. 1854.

My dear Richard,

Private. I say Private, for your Congregation is a very ear of Dionysius, and whatever is even whispered there, is known to all the world

It is my hope to commence with a University Church, which will bring the University, as a University, once a week before the public. Now for this we must have costume. Should it come from Belgium or Rome? It must not be expensive, if possible. Nor cumbrous, like the rigmarole nondescript at St Edmund's.

Turn your thoughts this way, please. First we must have a Chancellor's gown. Then a D D's, (for D D's of other Catholic Universities etc will be ad eundems) which *perhaps* need not be more than the tippet or cappa, or whatever you call it. However, must the buttons etc be of any particular colour? any sash? any thing in short easily added and take-off-able from the common cassock? — Then Doctor in Philosophy — and I suppose something for undergraduates — this last, however, though necessary for lecture, need not figure in the University Church. Then should there be Bedells etc? there must be one or two Vergers and the like — and how are they to be dressed? *If* we might choose a colour, as at Oxford the D D is red, I suppose green would be the most popular. And what kind of cap? a beretta? without tassel for the undergraduates?

Then again consider how, in me, the two characters of Bishop and Rector, not to say D D, are to combine?

Also turn your thoughts to what the ceremonial should be. The time, *I suppose*, will be the after noon — it might always close with benediction — which would give opportunity to have a choir.

I want the whole *imposing*. There is some chance of our actually getting a Church of our own. If so, I should in due time try to tempt you to Dublin in order to lay it out for me — with thrones, pulpits etc all very grand. It would be the place too, where degrees were conferred. The Blessed Sacrament would never be there, unless (I suppose) in the Sacristy on Sunday, and thence brought for Benediction.

Please tell me whether in *England* (as it is here) it is allowable to

national fast day during the cholera epidemic the previous year. The reply sent at Palmerston's direction maintained that sanitary measures must come before prayers, and concluded 'When man has done his utmost for his own safety, then is the time to invoke the blessing of heaven to give effect to his exertions.' Evelyn Ashley, *The Life of Henry John Temple, Viscount Palmerston, 1846–65*, London 1876, II, pp. 13–15.

have vestments of Irish poplin — which is a mixture of silk and something else.

If John (Bowden) is with you, tell him that the poor Naples lawyer is dead — and I am just saying some black Masses for his soul.[1] So I must give John more trouble unless indeed I come to town myself — but I will wait to see

Ever Yrs affly J H N

P.S. *Ultimately*, I shall try to get the Rector always a Bishop with jurisdiction over the University Church and Premises, as Propaganda is the seat of a Bishoprick. Then he could lord it in his own diocese; or he might be (a Priest) Vicar Apostolic for it of the Archbishop of Dublin.

MONDAY 13 MARCH 1854   went with Mr Errington to the Archbishop's for the meeting of St Laurence's Association.[2] Saw Mr O Reilly and H W[Wilberforce]
TUESDAY 14 MARCH   dined with Mr Flanagan P P[3] to meet the Archbishop

TO F. W. FABER

16 Harcourt Street — Dublin March 14. 1854
My dear Fr Wilfrid,

It is an ungracious thing to you to say I am coming up to London *because* I have broken two teeth — but it is a very gracious thing to you, not to me, for my teeth so opportunely to break. It is ungracious again in me, so coming up, to ask not to preach still — but, if it gets into the Paper that I have been preaching, it will be over with me here. I am ever keeping the waters out, which ever threaten to inundate me with preaching engagements, by the most violent assertions, which would be floored once and for all by the fact of my appearing in a pulpit.

I dare say you will not be able to give me a bed — nor need I ask for one. As to the day I come, it is quite uncertain. I don't know how long my Dentist will keep me.

I had thoughts of even leaving for London next Sunday night — but it depends on the weather etc etc. I shall take a return ticket — if that is consistent with my going to Birmingham, I shall do so on my return

Ever Yrs affly J H N

[1] See letter of 9 March to Miss Giberne.
[2] A newly founded charitable society.
[3] Parish priest of St Nicholas Without, Dublin.

TO JOHN STANISLAS FLANAGAN

16 Harcourt Street. March 14/54

My dear Stanislas

Thank you for so speedily sending Terence's plan. I think I am right in saying you have not sent his *letter*, tho' you say you have.

I have nothing to remark except that it seems as if the expence would be something. Your cousin has taken a good deal of trouble about it, and it would be very complete, if done — ⟨I don't see how it could *be less.*⟩ Also, I have still a misgiving, lest, when constructed Lord Palmerston should interfere — but I suppose we must run that risk.[1] I know of no let why Nowell could not give in his estimate. It had better come before the Congregation at once.

I am much pleased at Fr Bernard's report that the Sunday Services are more frequented. I have great expectations of the Month of Mary.

As to Thomas McKenna, try to make out what his voice is *worth*. Fr Frederic seemed to disparage him some time ago — I am uneasy about the Choir. I have promised money, and shall be much disgusted if nothing comes of it. To this moment I don't know if Jewsbury is in the House or not. However, you have nothing to do with all this. If you think it is a mere grumble of Fr Fred's, which I think it is likely to be, take Thomas away without scruple

Ever Yrs affly J H N

TO DENIS FLORENCE MACCARTHY

16 Harcourt Street. March 14/54

My dear Mr Mc Carthy,

I am very glad to understand you now. I had feared you declined the subject of Poetry, as such; now I understand you wish to be Professor or Lecturer on '*Poetry*,' as a science, an art, an historical fact etc etc. just as another might be Professor of Ethics, or of Politics, or of Political Economy.[2]

Of course the Poetry of all countries will fall under such a province — I only heartily wish I were my own master, so as to enable me to

[1] The Home Office might object to a burial vault underneath a church. Palmerston was Home Secretary.

[2] MacCarthy, who became Lecturer in Poetry at the University, at first wanted to include in his subject the rise of European literature, beginning with that of Spain.

make use of you to the full. But I suppose suspence and difficulty are the necessary trials of the undertaking put on me. It is now two years and a half that I have been kept in uncertainty myself, unable to form an engagement or plan or undertake any work a month in advance, thinking I might be called to Ireland. So that I can sympathise in the trial, so far as it comes on others. But I do trust a very few weeks will put an end to it now.

Very truly Yours John H Newman

D. F McCarthy Esqr

TO J. D. DALGAIRNS

March 16/54

My dear F Bernard,

I think I should come into your notion of a three day's retreat yearly — but I don't like *going any where*, if it were only for the precedent[1]

In great haste Ever Yrs affly J H N

Revd Fr Bernard

TO JOHN STANISLAS FLANAGAN

16 Harcourt Street March 16/54

My dear St

It is not as if any thing followed for you *to do*, but you may like to hear my thoughts, as they are at present, about my publications. Well then, I really doubt whether I, and all Catholics who publish, shall not be acting wisely in giving up the Protestant world. I suspect nothing whatever has come of the advertisements in the Times — first from the resolute determination of the Protestants to ignore me and all of us — next from the stupidity of our own people.

I talked to Duffy about the depot in Pater noster Row — this, you know, was my idea as well as his — but now what can come of it? for Protestant Publishers it is all very well to be near each other — but what is the good of a Catholic publisher being in the thick of Protestants, especially if he is an Irishman? they and their correspondents simply ignore his books. I don't deny that a bold energetic person with £50.000

[1] i.e. going away from the Oratory for the retreat.

86

capital could not force his way upon the English public and bring his books into Protestant circulation, but it is the only way in which it could be done.

But see what is the state of the case — If what I have said is true, then we have nothing left us but to retire upon the consumption of *Catholic* readers and the *retail* trade at the West End. Observe then — Duffy lately, when in London, wished to get my University Discourses — he went to Jones's (?) and to Burns's in vain — then he went to Dolman's in Bond Street — the shop man denied he knew the existence of the book — Duffy looked round and picked it off the shelves.

Here then we seem, by the ineffable stupidity of shopmen, cut off even from Catholic circulation — but so much we must aim at correcting. We must, I think, in future make it a sine quâ non with Duffy that Dolman should have a real shopman. And this being secured, I really think we must consider our simple mission to be to write for Catholics.

But I am interrupted

Ever Yrs affly J H N

P S   I have not time to read this over.

TO WILLIAM MONSELL

16 Harcourt Street Dublin March 16/54

My dear Monsell,

Can you say, 'Yes,' or 'no' or 'I don't know' to the question in the inclosed note, in which your name comes in? I don't ask more in these times of the Clerk to the Ordnance.

Direct 'The Oratory, Brompton Road, London,' as I [am] expected to be there for their opening

Ever Yours affly J H Newman

W Monsell Esqr M P

TO MRS JOHN MOZLEY

16 Harcourt Street March 16/54

My dear Jemima

I write that you may not be in suspence. I am sorry to say that you must not pay the £3 for me yet — as I cannot send it; and probably shall not be able till next pay day. Meanwhile it may happen that I shall send it *direct* without troubling you — so don't pay it, please, unless you hear from me — else, we shall be paying it twice over — and there will be no refunding.[1]

How sad, and almost shocking, that, in so awful a matter as the commencement of a war, instead of any religious manifestation, three cabinet ministers should joke about it with the admiral in chief over the bottle — and how undignified and vulgar! was such a thing ever heard of before!

Ever Yrs affly J H N

TO E. B. PUSEY

16 Harcourt Street Dublin March 16/54

My dear Pusey,

I have observed that the Briefs for Universities are, as regards the preamble, constantly taken one from the other; I suppose from the wish to go by precedent — at least I can give no other reason. I don't know whether they are properly Bulls or Briefs — I suspect Briefs, though called Bulls.

I will try to get you information on the other point you ask; but I know nothing of M. Montalembert. I have fancied him somewhat a touchy man, but I may be wrong.

Affectionately Yours John H Newman

TO MRS WILLIAM FROUDE

16 Harcourt Street Dublin March 17/54

My dear Mrs Froude

Indeed your last letter was a very kind one, and had nothing confused or reserved in it. Now, as to your present question, I forget so many things I once got up, and have outlived so many questions and doubtings, that I shall not answer you easily, but I will say what I can.

First I will say that in many points the Church leaves questions open, and hence, as one individual takes a different view from another, so does one country from another country. Certainly some foreign nations, particularly in the South, do identify the Object with the material image in a way in which an Englishman hardly could, if he

---

[1] See letter of 9 March.

tried. The word 'Il Crocifisso' shows it. It means to an Italian 'the crucified One' primarily, directly, and naturally — but 'Crucifix' to an Englishman means primarily the wooden image. Hence, you have the greatest difficulty in translating Italian devotions, for the Crocifisso is 'He,' and you find 'He' loves you, and can do you all mercies and bestow on you all blessings.

Still, were an Italian asked 'Do you think that wooden image hears you or can think about you?' he would answer 'How can you think me such a fool?' However ardent then his devotion to it, he *really* only holds it to be a symbol or sacramental of his Lord and Saviour and he prays not *to* it, but *before* it, which is the *sober, formal* language of *theology*.

But here you seem to have an antagonism among Catholics — viz *Italian devotion*, against *English teaching*. Italian devotion is Catholic, English teaching is Catholic — yet each nation is startled, I may say, at the other, when unused to it — the Italian devotee would think the language of Suarez or Bellarmine cold, and the English (Catholic) student or catechumen is confounded when the Protestant brings against him the practice of Italian Saints.

If all this is true, which I believe it to be, it is unfair to say that English Catholics try, in their representation of Catholic doctrine, 'to please the English taste' — (tho' I don't think William means quite this) they please their *own* taste. This, I say, of the mass of them, though some may make statements which, while agreeable to their own tastes, they feel to be agreeable also to those whom they are addressing — and a few, with whom I do not at all sympathise, if they do it consciously, may conceal or deny the foreign ways of Catholics, and try to blind or puzzle an inquirer by objecting the *doctrine* of the *Church*, which, authoritative as it is, and again apparently distinct or divergent from those foreign ways, is not really inconsistent with them.

The only question which I think may be asked, is as to the truth, or (as a Protestant would say) the *Scripturalness* of the doctrine *as interpreted by the practice* — there is no harm in praying *before* an image — but if this, practically considered and understood, is to all appearance a praying *to* it, then how is it defensible?

Now I am *approaching* your immediate question about the Commandments — and here I say first, before closing with it, that nothing has yet occurred to make me doubt the correctness of my position in my Essay on Development of doctrine, that a *ceremonial* prohibition of image worship was imposed on the Jews in the Decalogue, which, like the ceremonial enforcement of the Sabbath, was abolished when Christ came to introduce the New Law.

Now, if this be true, you see I might take the bull by the horns, and boldly answer any Protestant who accused us of leaving out the greater part of a commandment (assuming the 1 and 2 Protestant commandments are one) by saying 'Certainly, I *do* leave it out, because the Decalogue does not bind us as coming from Moses, but as being a declaration of the Eternal Law re-sanctioned, republished, by the Gospel.'

As to my reasons for saying this, I cannot recollect them all. But I do not see how else to answer an object [sic] which Coplestone used always to make to Davison's lecture on the fulfilment of the divine threatenings on the Jews —[1] He said that D. had left out *the* very difficulty of the case — for the threatenings were to come upon the people for their neglect of their Law vid Levit. xxvi. 1 and 30. Whereas in the event they were inflicted on account of its over rigid fulfilment. Nothing in fact is more remarkable [than] that, after the captivity, the Jews had simply unlearned the temptation to idolatry, and sabbath breaking, and, when they were not infidels like the Sadducees, were over formal observers of Moses and the Prophets.

It is usual to answer this by saying, that they observed the *letter*, not the *spirit*. Well, this is true — but carry it out — do not make your 4th commandment spiritual, and not your 2nd — do not recur to the Jewish Law in order to oppose the Catholic image-worship, while you shrink from the Jewish Law in the matter of Sabbath-breaking. The ceremonial law is abolished; query *is* in matter of fact the abhorrence of images, like the abhorrence of pork, part of the ceremonial, or not?

The present Archbishop of Canterbury has written a book, in which, borrowing (I think) from Spencer, he says that the Jews were pre-eminently the witnesses of *the one God*, of Creation, etc and that the Jewish rites are framed with this great object.[2] Thus the law of the Sabbath was a commemoration of the rest after *creation*; that the infancy of the world required this, etc etc. Now I want to know why the precept against imageworship may not be directed against the gross carnal views of the Godhead which St Paul speaks of to the Athenians, and necessary at that Day, though not afterwards?

And the New Testament does more, I think, to support this view, than for the spiritual interpretation of your 4th commandment. St Paul pointedly speaks twice of *covetousness* as idolatry, which is that

---

[1] John Davison, *Discourses on Prophecy*, 2nd ed. London 1825, Discourse IX, pp. 435–55.

[2] John Bird Sumner, *A Treatise on the Records of Creation and the Moral Attributes of the Creator*, London 1816, 6th ed. 1850, Chap. III, ii, p. 31, and vi, p. 85. The work of the Hebraist, John Spencer (1630–93), was only superseded in the nineteenth century.

very spiritualizing of the sin for which we might look out, if my view of the Decalogue is correct.

Now to come to the *division* of the commandments. We divide them into 3 and 7 — Protestants into 4 and 6.

I cannot go through the subject, for want of memory, but the whole matter of their arrangement and division is very confused. I recollect very well nearly 30 years ago, falling in with three passages of St Augustine in which the division is into 3 and 7, as we divide them now — and I believe *he* knows no other division. I believe it was the *common* division of the Church in his day, as far as there was any rule. As to the order, St Chrysostom, I recollect (I think on the Colossians) inverts them. In Matt. xix, our Lord put the (Protestant) 5th after the 9th, leaves out the 10th and adds another as a summing up from Levit xix, 18. In Mark x He puts the 7th before the 6th, the 5th after the 9th, and inserts another between them — leaving out the 10th. St Paul in Rom xiii puts the 7th before the 6th, inserts the 10th and leaves out the 5th and adds as Our Lord in Matt. xix the Summa Legis. *This* shows how little there was a *formal text*.

Well then — when the Catholic division and order was put forth (as I believe from the first) for the people and for children, it was natural that, *when there was no reason to the contrary*, each commandment should be put as *shortly* and *tersely* as possible. Thus, if my memory fails me not, the Decalogue is put into *rhyme* in some Protestant prayer books, each commandment being expressed in a few words. Thus 'I believe in God the Father etc' in the Anglican Catechism is the short summary of the *Creed*. And *in this* way the *first words* of the longer commandments have often been put down in Catholic catechisms — that is, of the (Catholic) first and third — and *that the more, because the greater part of them was ceremonial, Jewish, and in the letter unappropriate*. Thus St Paul in Romans xiii, as above referred to, says 'Thou shalt not covet,' and our Lord '*Honour thy father and mother,*' without going through the whole text of the commandment.

This is what would be *natural* to do, if we were left to ourselves. It is equally natural, when we are *not* left to ourselves, but taunted with suppressing what we think inapplicable, that we should print the whole text.

I have but one remark to add to the above — viz that we consider idols *still* forbidden by the commandment, and even representations of God which are unauthorized. Thus we allow a representation of the Eternal Father, because Scripture supplies us with it in Dan. vii. 9. 10. Ez. i. 26. 27 viii, 2 but we do *not* allow the pictures, sometimes found in Catholic countries of the Holy Ghost under the figure of a man.

And now I don't know what more I have to say, but to send my love to William and to tell you the old tale that I am

Yours very affectly John H Newman of the Oratory

TO F. S. BOWLES

16 Harcourt Street. March 18/54

My dear Fr Frederic,

I am very anxious about the choir. I forget exactly what was settled, but it seems *natural* that Mr Wood should look out for Boss singers. As a matter of strict duty, I shall not be able to go on giving the money, if nothing comes of it. I wish, without bringing in my name *as writing to you*, you would contrive to frighten him with what will probably be my disappointment etc He ought to know it. I want very much to see *the terms* which I drew up for Mr Wood — I fear I gave him the *whole year*, but I certainly shall not renew them at the year's end, unless he has done a good deal in it.[1]

People here say they never knew so long a spell of fine weather — it has lasted three weeks. I only fear we may suffer for it afterwards — unless indeed we have suffered for it beforehand, which is the better thought.

I shall pass through Birmingham at the end of next week, (about the 25th or a little before) in my way from London to Dublin; so I suppose. Will you ask Fr Minister, with my love, either to let my mattress etc be put to the fire, or (what may be better) to put me into a stranger's room, if it has been lately slept in? I want to consult several books in the Library, which I suppose I cannot get in London.

Tell Philip [Molloy], whom I should have written to about it, unless I were writing to you — that I do not expect, what with his examination and ordination, he can have had much time to give to the Library for me, but that I shall be able to talk with him on the subject, when I come — if he has any thing to say.

The Irish seem to be startled that the war has not made the Government kinder to them or more afraid of them. Here are two nunnery bills — a committee in favor of Archbishop Whately — besides the income tax, and nearly all the soldiers withdrawing.[2] Of course I only see the

[1] See letter of 12 Dec. 1853 to Mr Wood.

[2] Soldiers were leaving Ireland for the War, and the Income Tax of sevenpence in the pound was to be doubled. Archbishop Whately of Dublin hoped to use against Catholics the Committee appointed to enquire into the national system of education in Ireland.

On 28 Feb. a motion was passed in the House of Commons for a Committee to

clergy — they seem to eschew both parties in politics. I very much doubt whether any but the Archbishop of Tuam and the Bishops of Meath and Clonfert are for Lucas. Dr Cullen always speaks highly and gratefully of his services in the House — but excepting him, all the Bishops, I have heard speak of him, are most energetically against him, as an agitator.[1]

Ever Yours affly John H Newman of the Oratory

TO F. W. FABER

16 Harcourt Street March 18/54

My dear Fr Wilfrid,

I hope to leave this place tomorrow evening — and to be with you between 12 and 1 on Monday.

Ever Yrs affly J H N

SUNDAY 19 MARCH 1854[2] went down to Kingstown to go to England — but the wind violent — dined and slept at H W's [Wilberforce]

MONDAY 20 MARCH went to London arriving at the Brompton Oratory at 12 midnight

TUESDAY 21 MARCH went to Dentist (Lintott) Badeley etc FF Edward, Henry, Stanislas, Frederic came up

WEDNESDAY 22 MARCH opened [sic] of the Brompton Oratory I blest the Church and gave benediction in evening F Wilfrid preached twice[3]

inquire into the number and rate of increase of monastic and conventual institutions in the United Kingdom, and on 14 March a Bill was introduced to secure to persons under religious vows the free exercise of their rights in the disposal of their property.

[1] The war between the two parties in the Irish Tenant League was at its height, the one supporting the Government and approved by Cullen, the other with Lucas and Duffy faithful to the policy of independent opposition, and approved by MacHale, Archbishop of Tuam.

[2] There is no entry in the diary for 18 March, but Newman wrote in his University Journal: 'Had a very interesting conversation with *Mr* [*O'*] *Curry*, who is willing, or wishes, to be Professor or Lecturer of Irish Antiquities in the University. He showed me a mass of interesting *ecclesiastical* documents ⟨MSS⟩, which the Protestants will not print for him. I said the University *would*. He said it would be the most popular thing I could do in Ireland, if I connected the University with such a work. He says he wants me to get the Irish MSS from St Isidore's at Rome. He has got a Mass, a Litany, etc etc. He is not a Theologian. Would it be possible to put *Dr Croke* with him to comment historically and theologically upon the documents, while under publication. Mr Curry seemed to enter into the matter con amore, and though he is engaged six hours a day for Government in Trinity College, I think he would prefer to be with us altogether.' For the St Isidore's manuscripts see letter of 5 June 1854 to Talbot, and *Campaign*, pp. 299–300. [3] For Faber's account see *Trevor* II, p. 43.

TO EDWARD CASWALL

London. March 22. 1854

My dear Edward,

You may think how much I was touched by your affectionateness last night — but it was impossible I could at a moment, and at that moment, say what you wished me.

I will say it now. I have not for an instance thought, that by your letter you meant to hurt me; nor to be inconsiderate to me in any way.[1] I think you meant to exercise the virtue of obedience, and to do just what I wished. Indeed, I know perfectly well that you love me, as I love you.

But I think that you thought my order a strange one —and, while you obeyed it, you were not unwilling to show me the inconvenience of it; whereas, were it in appearance a strange one, the question which might suitably have suggested itself to your mind, was, 'Have I really mastered it?'

I think you meant to show me the inconvenience of it, when you spoke of your shortness of sight, and your not liking to look narrowly.

And then, if you say that these impressions of mine are incorrect, I have to consider whether you are the competent and decisive witness to more than your *main* motive — which I allow to have been a wish to obey — and whether I may not fairly set the obvious force of your words against your negative assertion, which I know well you make most sincerely, that you were not at all influenced by the feeling which they seem to me so obviously to suggest.

Having said all this, I have said all I have to say on the subject — I feel most grateful to you for your affection, as shown to me last night, and I am much distressed that I should have been obliged so much to pain you.

But I have more to say — I wish to pass it all over and to think no more about it, for the following reason, which weighs very much with me. My dearest Edward, I have long had it on my conscience, that from time to time I have behaved very rudely to you in conversation — and it certainly is not for me to complain of any real or supposed inconsiderateness of you to me. So begging you to forgive me for what I have so often done amiss, and begging God to give me grace to forgive you as a first step to my being forgiven, I am, My dearest Fr Edward Ever Yrs affly in Mary & Philip

John H Newman

[1] See letter of 25 Feb. to Caswall.

THURSDAY 23 MARCH 1854   went to Badeley's to breakfast
FRIDAY 24 MARCH   dined with Hope — and Badeley   Stanislas went to Belgium
SATURDAY 25 MARCH   breakfasted with Monsell   came down to Birmingham
MONDAY 27 MARCH   engaged these weeks in collecting matter for projected University Gazette.

TO THOMAS MOZLEY

The Oratory, Hagley Road Birmingham. March 28/54
My dear Mozley

Your welcome letter has just come. I know what labour it is looking over, sorting, reserving and destroying letters, and thank you for sending me mine.[1]

I can't tell at the moment what I shall do with them. If I have time to think about them, I shall[2] come at once to some conclusion — My present feeling is to add to them all others of the same sort I have by me, and to send them all to some one or other who would care to have them. Henry Wilberforce is the only one who strikes me. As to Jemima, it is only giving her the trouble of keeping them, and the responsibility of disposing of them. As to destroying any, I feel deeply the truth of what you say, that I can be no judge in the matter — and, though it might be a sore trial to me to keep my hands off some, yet it would only [be?] a very extreme case (e.g. where others came in) which would satisfy me in getting rid of one of them, directly that I have made up my mind to keep any.

As to the school and college books, I really shall be obliged by receiving them — for, though the Editions are old and the notes young, yet I am very short in classics, and just now am likely to want them.[3]

[1] Many of Newman's letters to his brother-in-law Tom Mozley are preserved at the Birmingham Oratory. From those to his sister Harriett, who died in July 1852, Newman copied long extracts before destroying the autographs.
[2] 'not' has been written above the line in pencil at this point, perhaps by Newman at a later date.
[3] Newman wrote reminiscences on the first pages of two at least of these books, when they reached him. In R. Turner, *An Easy Introduction to the Arts and Sciences*, eleventh edition, London 1806, he wrote:
'This book I had at Ham, i.e. before September 1807. I have just received it from T. Mozley, and on opening it at pp. 186–190, I recollect perfectly rhodomontading out of it to my nurserymaid in the shrubbery there, near the pond, at the end of the diagonal of the paddock or field from the house, and telling her that, when I was at Brighton I had seen four different fish, describing from pp. 186–190, the whale, the shark, etc. and when she could not make out what the fish were, and guessed wrong, I said "it was a whale," "it was a tortoise" etc which I saw.
Edgbaston April 17. 1854 Easter Monday'
In Lucy Peacock, *Visits for a Week; or Hints on the Improvement of Time.* . . .

I had come here for two days from London, and was returning to Dublin — but am detained by the indisposition of one of our party here, who has the measles somewhat seriously.

Ever Yours affectionately John H Newman

The Revd T. Mozley

P.S.   The letters have come. Do not pay carriage for the books, when you send them.

TO MRS J. W. BOWDEN

The Oratory Edgbaston March 30. 1854

My dear Mrs Bowden,

I should have called on you on Saturday, as I was passing the end of Grosvenor Place — but I changed my mind thinking you were either started or on the point of starting, for the Isle of Wight. I had nothing to say — but thought something might occur to speak of.

You seemed to think of taking an early opportunity, should Emily decide as appears likely, of mentioning the matter to your own family — and I cannot help thinking it better to do so; though *you* will see what is best.[1]

Tell Emily, the days I say Mass for her are Tuesday Thursday, and Saturday.

Don't doubt, nor do you, that you will be supported through every thing. Recollect when God gives faith, and strength, He tries them. He does not give them for nothing, or, as it were, for ornaments, but for use. It is the solemn privilege of those who have more gifts, that they have more suffering.

I am going to begin a weekly Mass for you, as soon as I have done with Emily — not that I forget you in her Mass.

Pray for me, as you do, and believe me, Ever Yours most affectionately in Jesus & Mary

John H Newman of the Oratory

Original Tales . . . for the Instruction and Amusement of Youth, sixth edition, London 1806, Newman wrote:

'I must have had this in 1808 or 1809 I was in the little school at the time, and I was out of it by June 1809; I can't tell how much before. J H N' 'I was in the little school in Ealing, when this book was given round to us to read in class. I believe the date to be as I have put it in the beginning of the book. Instead of keeping it for school time as a lesson, I put myself in the large open window my legs hanging out or along it and read it right through, or at least as far as time would allow, one half holy day.' 'I have thought of this book—and thought it was lost for ever. I was thinking of it only a week or two ago. It has just come to me from T. Mozley. April 17. 1854'

[1] This refers to Emily Bowden's wish to become a nun.

P.S.   The inclosed was new to me lately. I think it may be well said for poor soldiers and sailors on both sides of the contest.

TO JAMES HOPE-SCOTT

Oratory. Hagley Road. Birmingham April 4. 1854
My dear Hope Scott

I found your Pix and its casts had been lying for you ever so long at Hardman's, and have now got them in my room. I doubt whether you will think them well done — and indeed wondered at your going to H. For glass and brass he has no equal — but in bijouterie and small matters, nay in chalices, I think he does not succeed — I don't think it is his line.

⌐It was with great concern I heard the other day from Rome that Mr Monteith and his family had been prostrated by some dreadful fever at Rome, and that one child is dead.¬ You spoke of them the other day, and never said any thing about it. It must surely be they — I was told 'Mr Monteith, a Scotch man.'[1]

⌐I am amused to see that, not only the Czar, but your friends the Peelites (according to the 'Secret Correspondence' as brought out in Parliament) seem certainly to have intended Turkey to fall to pieces into their mouths, and each great power to have a share; — which is the very view which you seemed to think so greedy and disgusting in me, on that fast day when I dined with you in Albemarle Street.[2]

Stewart writes me word that he cannot hope to get me Bulaeus[3] — Is it asking too much to look for the loan of your copy *here*? I shall stay here several weeks, and it would be useful to me. I tried to use yours when in the Temple the other day; indeed, it was one reason of my going to London; but the right people were not in the way to get it me.

[1] Robert Monteith's daughter, Caroline Agnes, died in Rome at the age of 4, and her father devoted the fortune of £35,000 intended for her to building the Catholic church at Lanark.

[2] This was on 24 March. Newman refers to the secret papers laid before Parliament and debated in the House of Commons on 31 March, concerning the negotiations with Russia which had led up to the Crimean War. They showed that in June 1844 Lord Aberdeen, when Foreign Secretary under Peel, had accepted a Memorandum from the Russian Minister, Count Nesselrode, which discussed arrangements to be made on the dissolution of the Turkish Empire. Then in 1853 Aberdeen, now Prime Minister in a Coalition Government of Peelites and Whigs, had allowed his Foreign Secretary, Lord Clarendon, to discuss similar proposals with Russia.

[3] Caesar Bulaeus, *Historia Universitatis Parisiensis*, six vols, Paris 1665–73.

I have kept your other books most creditably, in the box in which they came close by the fire place.

Badeley will tell you what he thinks of the article in the Rambler on 'lying,' this month. I have only just now received the Number,⌐ and cut open the pages[1]

> Ever Yrs affectly John H Newman

TO SISTER MARY IMELDA POOLE

The Oratory Hagley Road. Bm April 4. 1854

My dear Sister Imelda

If all is well I will gladly preach for you on May 3 tell with my respects Mother Prioress, though I have to come from Connemara or the Giant's Causeway on purpose: — that is except under two conditions.

The first is, unless the Cardinal has put me in retreat before he makes me a Bishop just at that time.

The next is, unless the Chairman of the Nunnery Committee of the House of Commons has by that time put Mother Prioress and all of you in Charge of the Sergeant at Arms for Contempt of the said House.

Meanwhile, whether she and the rest of you are in prison or not, don't cease to pray for me and us, and to believe me Yrs affectionately in Xt

> John H Newman of the Oratory

FRIDAY 7 APRIL 1854 about this time the Brief came for the Synodal meeting of the Irish Bishops about the University which was fixed for May 18 ⟨Dr Taylor's letter on the subject is dated April 6⟩

TO JAMES HOPE-SCOTT

Birmingham. April 7/54

My dear Hope Scott

⌐I see you are the modern Aboulcasem.[2] The books have come this morning, and beautiful ones they are. If it would not make you angry,

---

[1] See letter of 11 May to Badeley, and those of 5 and 15 Jan. to Capes.

[2] Newman appears to refer to a Prince of the Seljuk Turks in the eleventh century, whose treasures became a byword. *Biographie Universelle*, Paris 1811, p. 89.

I should make a stand against taking them, and would consider that they remained here, till you asked for them. I don't half like your saying you never shall have any use for them — Are you to go on with the laterum labor[1] to your old age? is the time never to come when your books are to be of use to you? I hope some day you will claim again these, and I am tempted to leave a memorandum, that, if I die, they are to come back to you.⌐2

But I dont write this to bother you for any new letter, when you have so much on your hands.

⌐Mean while, I shall show best my gratitude for your gift, by beginning to use it at once⌐

Ever Yours affly in Xt John H Newman of the Oratory

J R Hope Scott Esqr

⌐P.S. I have *just* heard that the expected Brief for convoking the Bishops is come — the Pope *confirms* my appointment to the Rectorship in the most flattering terms. So now, I suppose, we *shall* begin. I expect to go over early in Easter week.⌐3

[1] The baking of bricks.

[2] The volumes of Bulaeus appear to have gone back to Hope-Scott, for the set now in the Oratory Library was presented some fifteen years later by the Dowager Duchess of Argyll.

[3] This was the Brief for which Cullen had asked. See notes to letter of 15 Jan. to Taylor. Taylor wrote from Dublin on 6 April, 'At length the Brief has arrived for the convocation of the Bishops. . . .

You are specially mentioned by His Holiness in the highest terms and your appointment as Rector *confirmed by him.*

Is not *that* formal and decisive enough? can any thing more be requisite for *you?*'

This Brief, dated 20 March, is printed in *Campaign*, pp. lxxix–lxxxii. Taylor copied out for Newman the lines at the end which mentioned him: 'Cum autem noverimus a Vobis jam electum fuisse Dilectum Filium Presbyterum Joannem Henricum Newman ut eamdem Universitatem regat et moderetur, tum ejusmodi Vestram electionem approbantes volumus, ut idem Presbyter egregiis animi ingeniique dotibus ornatus, ac pietatis doctrinaeque laude, et Catholicae religionis studio praestans ejusdem Universitatis curam et regimen suscipiat, eique veluti Rector praesit.'

The Archives of Propaganda make it clear why there was no mention of Newman's bishopric in this Brief of 20 March. Cullen, besides his January letters delaying it (mentioned in the first note to letter of 23 Jan. to Taylor), wrote on 18 Feb. to Kirby, his Roman agent, who quoted to Propaganda, the following extract from his letter: 'I am of opinion that it would not be prudent to make Dr Newman a bishop for the present. It is better not to begin with too much fuss; otherwise we shall make ourselves ridiculous. In Belgium the Rector Magnificus is not a bishop. Moreover the episcopal character will bring with it yet greater expenses; and the people will complain about it.'

Cullen evidently thought this was not sufficient for he wrote again on 21 Feb., directly to Barnabò, the Secretary of Propaganda, urging his view 'that I should have the greatest pleasure in seeing a man so learned and saintly as Dr Newman raised to the highest dignities, but, that perhaps it would be better to wait a while until things

TO J. I. TAYLOR

Hagley Road Birmingham April 7. 1854

My dear Dr Taylor,

I thank you very much for your letter just received. I have been detained here, first by the illness of one of our novices, and then by the unexpected and unluckly absence of our Fr Treasurer, whom I must see. But now I should come over directly, were we not close upon Holy Week.

Will you tell his Grace I will come early in Easter Week. The Cardinal is expected back in Easter Week — and perhaps will have something to say to me, but nothing, I suppose, which he could not write.

Since I have been here, I have written about the University House — and I did all *I* had to do, before I went away. I should have written to *you*, but I thought you might feel some delicacy about interfering.[1]

Very sincerely Yours in Xt John H Newman of the Oratory

The Revd Dr Taylor.

SUNDAY 9 APRIL 1854 Palm Sunday celebrated High Mass and sang Xtus in Passion

TO J. SPENCER NORTHCOTE

Edgbaston April 9/54

My dear Northcote,

I confess it is very disgraceful not to engage to write a life of St Philip — but what would you have? You cannot eat your cake and have it. Fr Dalgairns, I dare say, would do it, if you let him off his Church

are in better shape,' and giving the additional reason that jealousy would be aroused if the English Cardinal Wiseman were known to have intervened in the matter.

These two letters were endorsed at Propaganda as having been taken into account in the Brief of 20 March. Propaganda Archives, *S.R.C. Irlanda*, 1854–6, f. 114 and ff. 116–17, quoted by J. H. Whyte, *D R* (Spring 1960), *art. cit.* pp. 32–4, and by V. F. Blehl, S.J., *Thought* (Spring 1960), *art. cit.* pp. 117–19. In July and Oct. 1855 Cullen was again to write to Rome urging that Newman should not be raised to the episcopate.

Newman was never told that he was not to be made a bishop. See note to diary, 29 April.

[1] Taylor wrote on 6 April that he believed nothing had been done to prepare the University House, 86 Stephen's Green. For the rest of Taylor's letter, see the previous note.

History. I should like nothing better than to do it myself, for I want to see a life of him written which is *not* devotional, but historical — which, I suppose, would be the thing your Library would want — for which I think there are a certain quantum of materials, but how can I with a safe conscience promise, what I might not be able to do for 10 years to come, or even till the last volume comes out of Fr Coffin's edition of St Alfonso?[1]

At length the expected Briefs are come to Dublin, though you had better not say so, till you see about them in the Papers. The Pope has confirmed me as Rector, and the Irish Bishops are to meet synodically on the matter in no long time. I am at Dr Cullen's disposal, but you may tell Dr Newsham, with my affectionate regards that if Dr C. gives me time, I shall be coming to Ushaw soon to interest him and my friends there, and the whole College in my work — and to stimulate them to come in mass, St Cuthbert and all, and place themselves, without deserting Ushaw, in Dublin bodily.

Entre nous, do you think Paley would do this for me. Draw out carefully lists of the best grammars, lexicons, critical books, editions of the classics etc. that is, a kind of report as to the best tools for working youths in latin and greek — with remarks what classics should be preferred to others, what parts read etc etc — in fact such a report as a Praefectus Studiorum would draw. If it were really a good thing, such as I know he could do, if he threw his mind into it, I suppose £50 is an acknowledgement, which he would think enough, and which I could get for him. But, if you sound him, don't mention any sum to *him*, which I mention to you, in order to have your opinion on the idea. Without *having* him, I might perhaps thus be able to use him, and he might consent to be used.[2]

Ever Yours affectly in Xt John H Newman

FROM WILLIAM FROUDE

Dartington 3rd April 1854

My dear Newman

I enclose you a Bankpost bill for 30£ which I have received from Lumley on account, for the copyright of the Arians. I do not know exactly how soon

---

[1] Cf. letter of 28 Feb. to Coffin. Northcote was one of the editors of the 'Popular Library of History, Biography, Fiction, and Miscellaneous Literature,' and wished Newman to write for it a life of St Philip. Newman had begun the first draft of such a life of his patron as he here describes in Lent 1853, and it is hoped to include it in the projected volume of his Oratorian papers.

[2] See Newman's letter to Paley of 10 May.

the edition will be out: but probably in the course of this month or early in the next, it will be ready — the printing has been rather a slow process owing to the scarcity of copies of the work which made it impossible for Mr Forbes to put on many hands at once. The remainder of the money will be paid as soon as the work is ready to be issued or is issued — or at all events very shortly afterwards. That which I now send I have had in my possession for several weeks. But I have deferred from day to day to send it to you wishing and hoping that the inspiration would come which would enable me to say to you many things which it is often on my mind that I ought to say, and the thought of saying which was lately 'borne in upon my mind' all the more, by the arrival of the enclosed 'dead letter' which found its way to me the other day after a long pilgrimage, during which it has perhaps lain in a state of suspended animation or lost in the wilderness of foreign post offices — not indeed quite 'Seven twelve months and a day' as the ballad says — but yet not very far short of that term, for it is dated April /47.

You may remember I told you I had written to you at Rome,[1] and that you had never received the letter — and this is it. If you have time to read it you will I think see that its arrival will have quickened any wish of mine to explain myself to you, not in the way of testifying or as if what I had to say could be of any importance to you or weigh with you but because I always feel that your continued and unwearied warm and kind affection, makes some explanation — some openness on my part, of the nature of a debt which I owe you, and which as this letter reminds me if I needed to be reminded of it I have often acknowledged — and which I never can deny.

It seems safe enough — if not mean and cowardly to go on acknowledging debts when in the same breath, one admits the inability to pay. Yet such is my position — and it is one which I do not quite expect you to sympathise with — for you not long since told me it 'was a paradox to say we' (i.e. people in general) 'could not express our thoughts to each other in words.' But the difficulty to me is a most real and serious one and seems the essence of almost all other difficulties, and at all events a key to the position which on Religious questions my mind occupies. I find it not less remarkably however on *all* questions — and its existence is most tangibly verified in cases when it ought to exist least — e.g. in questions of practical science — in which all men are agreed in the desirableness of making language the instrument of exact thought — and in which they have the greatest and most complete means which can exist anywhere of verifying and comparing the meanings of words, and of expressions which are intended to convey modes of thought. I do not say in questions of this kind words do not *help* — do not convey a *good deal*, and set people on investigations etc etc but dogmatic statements in these matters *do* fail absolutely to convey definite meanings or ideas — and to carry out (conclusively to others) the reasonings which they perhaps logically enclose. And on the other hand you will find that people agree precisely in their dogmatic statements on such questions, and yet in conversations and discussions it will come out perpetually that real differences lie hid beneath these words which no amount of talking will serve to clear up or dissipate.

I do not wish to tempt you on to write a treatise on this difficulty — by my

---

[1] Newman inserted in pencil at this point 'It is dated April 1847.' Cf. letter of 8 April 1848 to William Froude.

own showing I should not understand it if you did so. I only wish to let you know why I do not attempt explanations which I admit to be of the nature of a debt, both in the way of duty and of affection.

But I must say something in reply to your kind letter about Kate.[1]

I had no scruple in shewing it to her, and I am glad I did so — for though I had before known pretty well the nature of the conflicting thoughts and feelings which govern her position, the conversation to which your letter gave rise, led me to see that I had not accurately struck the balance between them.

I fully believe that as far as reasonable or reasoning conviction goes, her judgment is against Catholicism — as far as feeling goes it is in its favour — the feeling being partly what might be called fascination occasioned by the magnitude and endurance of the system, and what appears to her the adaptations of its ceremonial to her own peculiar turn of mind — and partly her entire love and admiration for the few Catholics she has known — a love and admiration which goes entirely beyond that which she feels for any other persons whatever.

My conversations with her, have led me to see that I had if anything underrated the force of this fascination, and it would not surprise me if it were some day or other wholly to outweigh all opposing influences of whatever kind.

I cannot say that such a result would not be painful to me — and perhaps the knowledge which she would naturally have that the result would be painful to me, being of the same description to a certain extent as those which load the opposite scale, would to a certain extent, steady the beam: With this exception no obstacle to her progress would occur on my part — for indeed I should have none else to offer, at least of a nature commensurable with the force of those springs which push her forward.

You will readily understand I am sure that it is with no very cheerful feelings that I contemplate as almost a probable result a change which though it could not impair affection, would in its very nature make an end of that full community of thought and judgment in which affection has had such scope. I cannot trust myself to think or speak of it.

Believe me ever   Yours affectionately   W Froude

TO WILLIAM FROUDE

Oratory Edgbaston. April 10, 1854.

My dear William,

Your letter with the Bank Post Bill for £30 has just come to hand. I have known my own movements so little, that I could not, till the end of last week, give directions to those in Harcourt Street to forward my letters here.

Thank you very much for your long letter, and the inclosure.[2]

[1] This letter about Mrs William Froude is not to be found.

[2] i.e. the letter of 3 April above, and that of April 1847, returned from Rome. The latter is not to be found, but Newman's eventual reply to it is printed after this present letter.

I have not forgotten the one you wrote me about a year ago — and have it safe in the desk I am writing on.[1] If I did not answer it, it was not that I did not feel interest in it — and I shall read most anxiously what you now send.

God ever bless you, my dearest William, I know I don't pray for you and your wife near so much as I ought.

Ever yours most affectly John H. Newman.

P.S.   Let me add, that Catholics hold it would be wrong in any one becoming a Catholic without his *judgment* being convinced. This you know. At the same time you know my writings well enough (e.g. my University Sermon)[2] to understand, that, at least in my opinion, persons may have very good reasons, which they cannot bring out into words. Your dear wife has said she would not write to me again — and I assure you, my dearest William, I shall not write to her — but you can't hinder me (nor wish to hinder me) praying, whatever the prayers are worth.

2nd P.S.   Your second letter has just come.[3] I am very sorry you should have had the trouble and anxiety. I had better tell you, my Bankers are 'Birmingham Banking Co Bennett's Hill, Birmingham', and their London correspondents 'Messrs Jones, Lloyd and Co.'

[1] This appears to be the letter of 21 March 1853, in which, among other things, Froude wrote: 'Perhaps much irritation is felt towards you by the bulk of the Anglican body; yet of this, a very large portion is due I am sure to that peculiar sensitiveness which is induced by a difficult or uncomfortable position. They are on slippery ground —on skaits, perhaps for the first time . . . and you have shouted to them: and pushed them in the direction of least equilibrium; perhaps made them sensible that there was something awkward, ungainly and absurd in their position . . . and for the most part I do not think the irritation of the better sort of Anglicans is of a different description— But those who used to be so near to you,—feel I am persuaded very differently: by them (At least as far as my experience goes) I never heard you spoken of except and [in] words and in a manner that belonged (if one may use the words) to tender affection —but they feel your power, and feel keenly that it is (in a way) used against them. Perhaps it has never fully forced itself upon you, what a blank was left among them by your going—or how differently the change of relative position must affect you, and them; putting a restraint upon them which it does not tend to put upon you; when they are so certainly the losers, by whatever test the "loss and gain" is tried, and when you feel that you are so certainly the gainer by the change—'

[2] 'Implicit and Explicit Reason,' *U.S.*, pp. 251–77.

[3] Froude wrote again on 9 April, because his Bankpost bill had not been acknowledged.

TO MRS WILLIAM FROUDE[?][1]

[1854 or 1855?][2]

N B.   As to dear W.F.'s letter of April/47 it contains two arguments against inquiry in religious matters, and [for] acquiescence in doubt.

He speaks of a state of mind 'certainly different from a long and anxious condition of change' — one in which one is 'taking *no steps* for oneself or apparently getting nearer to a change.' And he thinks there is 'an intelligible reason for following it.'

One of his two grounds is, that, whereas I once said 'that, if I am right in my doubts, what had happened to me might *happen to others* also,' '*till then* the least unsatisfactory course seems to be to stand still.' He refers particularly to Keble and Pusey. He says too that perhaps 'some happy re-union may be yet in store.'

Now as to Keble and Pusey, perhaps it is more wonderful that a person of my age (when I left them) should have embraced a new religion, than that they should not have done the same. But valeant quantum; I will not touch the argument, as derived from them, here. Yet my anticipation, as W.F. has recorded it, has been remarkably fulfilled. One after another, moving not as a party, but one by one, unwillingly, because they could not help it, men of mature age, from 40 to past 50, in all professions and states, numbers have done what I have done since the date of W.F.'s letter; — such as Manning, R. Wilberforce, H. Wilberforce, Allies, Dodsworth, Hope Scott, Badeley, Bellasis, Bowyer, Monsell, Sir John Simeon, Dr Duke, Biddulph Phillips, Dean Madavori,[3] Bishop Ives, the de Veres, H. Bowden, Mrs Bowden, Lady Lothian, Lady G. Fullerton, Lord H. Kerr, etc. I

[1] This important letter or memorandum is in the collection of copies of letters to William Froude and his family. It is placed between those of 14 July 1849 and 11 August 1851. It is headed '*Note of unknown date, unaddressed, presumably written to Mrs W. Froude* (By the handwriting it should come at about this point in the Correspondence) R E F.' i.e. Robert Edmund Froude, son of William.

[2] This letter is placed here because it replies to and illustrates William Froude's of April 1847, which only now reached Newman, and which is no longer to be found. It also answers Froude's letter of 3 April 1854. Its date cannot be fixed with certainty. Internal evidence shows that it was written after Robert Wilberforce became a Catholic in Nov. 1854. It was perhaps written in the latter part of 1855, when Mrs Froude was reaching conviction on the subject of Catholicism. On the other hand, Newman seems to refer to William Froude's letter of April 1847 as still unanswered, when writing to him on 2 Jan. 1860, so that, although written earlier, it was possibly not sent until much later. The dates, 1850 given in *Ward* I, p. 622, and 1851 in *Harper*, p. 84, are obviously incorrect.

[3] The copyist has put a question mark above this word. It is safe to say that what Newman must have written was 'Wm Maskell.'

cannot help thinking it was dangerous for W.F. to have recourse to this argument. It is surely much easier to account for Keble and Pusey not moving, Catholicism being true, than for all these persons moving, Catholicism being not true. And, whereas it was the fashion at first to use this argument, as W.F. does in 1847 *against* us — I think it ought to have its weight *now for* us. It was the fashion then to say 'O, Newman is by himself. We don't deny his weight — but no one else of any name has gone — and are we to go by one man?' Times are altered now.

Alas! this was not W F's real reason, this, which solvitur ambulando. I did not get his letter at Rome — I had not the opportunity of answering it; but, so far, Time has answered it for me —

which solves all doubt
By bringing Truth, his glorious daughter, out.[1]

The second ground is his real reason, which Time will solve too — tho' not so soon — alas! that he will not anticipate its unsoundness, as he has not anticipated the unsoundness of the former.

The second argument which W.F. uses with himself is that he has got less and less to see his way in any such questions; and that there is least private judgement in making no judgement at all.

This means, when brought out, this:—that, without denying there is a truth, which would be absurd, (for either Catholicism, as we hold it, is from God or it is not,) we have not been vouchsafed means sufficient for getting at the truth; and therefore if we attempt it, it is like attempting to fly, or to sail on the atlantic in a pleasure boat without compass — we shall be lost — or we shall go wrong — or we shall be ever at sea — or, if we attain any thing better than what we start from, it will be by accident.

I do not undervalue at all the speciousness of this argument. But I would remark at once, that almost all truth 'lies in a well.'

Does not this saying imply two things 1 that it is hard to find, yet 2. that it may be found?

If it is so in other subject matters, may it not be so in religion too?

Is it not likely to be so, inasmuch as the difficulty of arriving at truth seems to vary with the preciousness and refinement of its kind? I have observations on this at length in one of my University Sermons.[2]

---

[1] George Crabbe, *Tales of the Hall*, IX, 'The Preceptor Husband,'

Leaving the truth to Time, who solves our doubt,
By bringing his all-glorious daughter out—
Truth! for whose beauty all their love profess,
And yet how many think it ugliness!

This quotation comes near the middle of the poem; in the Oxford edition, p. 393.
[2] 'The Nature of Faith in relation to Reason,' *U.S.*, pp. 215-21.

Is it not a coincidence (not to speak of the authority of Scripture declarations,) that so much is said of 'crying after wisdom,' 'asking and knocking' etc etc in Scripture?

When then a certain portion of our race are certain they have found religious truth, should we not feel as we might do, if, while ignorant of mathematics, we found a number of educated persons simply confident of Newton's conclusions? I mean, admit that truth was attainable in religion, though *we* had not attained it.

Nor do I think it matters that many men are 'certain' of what is opposite to Catholic truth — or 'certain' that Catholicism is false — for men have been 'certain' that Newton was false — yet that would not move me against Newton, because, though we are no judge of Newton's reasonings, we may be judges of the persons who use and embrace them, and all the Dominicans in the world might not move us in favor of any theory *but* Newton's — though we understood the arguments on neither side. In like manner there are men *rationally* certain in religion — and irrationally certain — and we may be judges of this, though not as yet judges of their reasons.

And here, recurring to what I said before, I do really think the character and variety of the converts to Catholicism of late in England form a most powerful argument, that there is such a thing as ascertainable truth in religion — and I am willing that a man should set against them, Luther, Cranmer, and Company, if he wishes.

Next it must be considered that, though there is a profession of certainty among Protestants, and pious earnest persons among them, yet their certainty commonly relates to, and their religious life is seated in, doctrines which are included *in* Catholicism. So that their certainty cannot be considered to contradict and invalidate the certainty of Catholics.

I do not think then, that any primâ facie incompleteness or unsatisfactoriness of the arguments for Catholicity are sufficient to lead me to acquiesce in the notion that truth cannot be attained about it. ⟨My argument is that against the probability adverse to Catholicism, arising from the *primâ facie* incompleteness of its proof, must be put the primâ facie probability in its behalf arising from the 'certainty' of Catholics.⟩ For whatever probability there is, from the persons professing certainty about Catholicity, that they are rationally certain, such degree of probability is there that those arguments are *only* primâ facie and not substantial[ly], of this incomplete and unsatisfactory character.

On the other hand, taking the two instances, to which W.F. refers, Keble is not certain of *any* thing — and if I put him on one side, and

107

men like R Wilberforce, Hope Scott, or Allies on the other, he does not pretend to collide with them; he only has not what they have.

Again, as to Pusey, he indeed is most 'certain' — but the greater part of things far, of which he is certain, are those of which Catholics are certain — and as to other points, in which he differs from Catholics, how he can be said to be certain of them I cannot tell, for, if his words are fairly quoted, he contradicts himself continually, or affirms to one person, what he denies to another.

Then, when, quitting this view of the subject, we fall back to the consideration of the arguments themselves, it must be recollected that in all departments *cuique in arte suâ credendum.* By which I mean that, as I have said above, a man cannot suddenly get up a subject, and see the drift and bearing of it, the relative importance of its parts, and the value of its arguments.

Men who have lived in the dark, see things with a clearness un-intelligible to those who enter it from the broad day. That religious truth is an obscure subject is granted; but that does not prove that we cannot find out its roads and their termination.

We are told by Bishop Butler, that this difficulty of finding is the very trial of our earnestness, and the medium of our reward.

Every science requires a preparation, that we may feel and appreciate its principles and views. Is it unnatural that the subject of religion needs a preparation too?

Is it wonderful, if, considering religion is a special subject, this process should be peculiar? Is it wonderful, considering that its scope and its subject are supernatural, its preparation should be supernatural also?

Perhaps then what divines call grace, the supernatural assistance of the Father of Lights, may be the necessary preparation for our understanding the force of the arguments in the subject matter of religion; and perhaps prayer may be the human means, in the way of cause and effect, of gaining that supernatural assistance.

I do not see then that I am bound to believe W.F's statement of the unsatisfactoriness of religious inquiry, and the necessity of an everlasting suspense, until I am sure that he contemplates the probability of that being true, which is not improbable in itself, and which all those who have attained certainty say *is* true — that a preparation of mind of a particular kind is indispensable for successful inquiry — and till he makes it clear to me that he duly appreciates that probability.

I should like an inquirer to say continually 'O my God, I confess that *Thou canst* enlighten my darkness — I confess that Thou *only* canst. I *wish* my darkness to be enlightened. I do not know whether Thou wilt; but that Thou canst, and that I wish, are sufficient reasons for me to *ask*, what Thou at least has [sic] not forbidden my asking. I hereby promise Thee that, by Thy grace which I am seeking, I *will embrace* whatever I at length feel certain is the truth, if ever I come to be certain. And by Thy grace I will guard against all self deceit which may lead me to take what nature would have, rather than what reason approves.'

If a man tells me he has thus heroically cast himself upon God, and persisted in such a prayer, and yet is in the dark, of course my argument with him is at an end. I retire from the discussion, and leave the matter to God.

In W.F's other letters there is a great deal which seems to me philosophical and deep, but it does not seem to bear, nor to be meant to bear, on religion.

As to what he says of the difficulty of understanding one another's words, I don't suppose it applies to the above, which, according to my view of the subject, is engaged upon the root of the whole matter.

TO ARCHBISHOP CULLEN

Oratory Birmingham April 12. 1854

My dear Lord,

I shall be anxious at your leisure to hear from Dr Taylor your movements and arrangements. He has told me, as you know, that the Briefs are come — which was a great satisfaction.

I will come over, whenever you tell me. At present I am very well employed here. I am in the midst of my books, hunting out and making extracts, (which I could not find the means of doing in Ireland,) which will be of service for the University in various ways. Also, now I am actually appointed Rector, I wish to go round the English Colleges to stir them up in our favor. I will do this at such time you can best spare me — but of course the sooner I do it, the better.

Begging of your Grace the blessings of this Holy Season, I am, My dear Lord Archbishop Yours affectionately & faithfully in Xt

John H Newman of the Oratory

The Lord Archbishop of Dublin

TO MISS HOLMES

April 12. 1854 Oratory, Birmingham

My dear Miss Holmes

This is the 32nd Anniversary of my election to a Fellowship at Oriel, which was a turning point in my life.[1] are turning points, but this was the greatest, I think, of any — un[less my going][1] to Oxford instead of to Cambridge be greater.

I have got all your letters safe —[1] [mu]ch pleased to find how you go on — I have been saying Mass for you[1] It will be a great comfort for me to believe that the family you are in suits you *permanently*. I know how difficult it is for any one to get permanently attached to strangers; but they seem to be very amiable people, and I shall be anxious how you continue to get on with them.[2] You need not fear Ireland — the Irish Priesthood is a nobly devoted body of men. You must not judge of them by the newspapers. I admire them exceedingly. Many of them are persons of cultivated minds generally. Those I have met about the country are zealous, hardworking men. You, who are getting so philosophically liberal about Italian architecture and Italian ways, will soon understand that, being intended for the *people*, they are taken *from* the people. There are but few in the upper classes Catholic in Ireland, and if the Bishops looked out for parish priests among the upper classes, even if they could get them, they would not suit the classes for whom they have to work. They are commonly taken out of the families of small farmers, they have strong constitutions, they know the habits of the people, and are fully trusted by them. As to the few who come forward in public and spout, they are generally as unpopular with their brethren as they would be unattractive to you.

The Pope has confirmed my appointment to the Rectorship of the new University, and the Irish Bishops are to meet synodically about it — so now I suppose we are really setting off. It is with the view of strengthening my position and giving me weight, that he has most considerately determined to make me a Bishop. This will give me no duties, for my see will be Ptolemais[1] or Sinope, or Sebastopol, or some other unknown place, and I shall be able to *rank* as Bishop.

I was very glad to make acquaintance with your niece at Kingstown

[1] A piece more than one inch in breadth and two in length has been torn out of the fragile paper.
[2] Miss Holmes was at Florence, with the son of Lord Gormanston, Thomas Preston and his family. Preston lived near Dublin and was a Commissioner of National Education in Ireland.

lately — and trust she will see her way plain before her, now she is entering life.

Pray present my respects to Mr Preston, who, I think I am right in saying, was very obliging to me when I began my Dublin Lectures.

Ever Yours affectionately in Xt

John H Newman of the Oratory

TO FORTUNAT DE MONTÉZON, S.J.

Birmingham, April 12, 1854

My dear Revd Father

When I was in London lately, I received your valuable present, consisting of the volumes of the P. Daniel and of M. L'abbé Maynard.[1]

I thank you very much for them — they are very useful to me just now, when I am very busy with University and literary questions. I have begun both and feel great interest in reading them. Pray convey to these good authors the instruction I get from them.

Thank you too, my dear Father, for the kind way in which you speak of your visit, which you so condescendingly made to us.[2] I hope you will come again. You will find us in a better house, better able to entertain you, with three Fathers who will talk French to you all the day long, though I cannot.

Begging your good prayers & those of your holy Community I am, My dear Revd Father, Your Reverence's faithful servant in Christ,

John H. Newman of the Oratory

The Revd Father F. de Montezon S.J.

THURSDAY 13 APRIL 1854 celebrated in the function Stanislas returned from Belgium.

FRIDAY 14 APRIL celebrated in the function

SATURDAY 15 APRIL celebrated in the function

[1] Charles Daniel, S.J., *Des études classiques dans la société chrétienne*, Paris 1853. Abbé Maynard, *Des études et de l'enseignement des Jésuites à l'époque de leur suppression (1750–1773) . . . suivi de l'examen général de l'histoire du pontificat de Clément XIV*, Paris 1853.

[2] On 23 Aug. 1850.

TO MRS J. W. BOWDEN

Holy Saturday. [15 April] 1854

My dear Mrs Bowden,

The time when Emily was to decide is so near, that I prefer to send you an answer which will avail for the moment, instead of waiting to think over the whole matter as carefully as I can.

It seems to me then that there is no reason at all why we should not advise her to put aside her ultimate decision for 3 or 6 months. And, since it *may* be done, your scruple is quite a reason for doing it.

Therefore I think you had better tell her so — and you will be able to explain why

Ever Yours affectly in Xt John H Newman of the Oratory

P.S.   All good Easter greetings to you. The Irish Bishops are to meet in Synod on May 18 to set the University going. I expect to go over in the course of Easter week — probably at the end of it — my direction will be 16 Harcourt Street, Dublin.

TO ARCHBISHOP CULLEN

Oratory Birmingham April 15/54

My dear Lord

I return your Grace's inclosure,[1] which came to me this morning, with many thanks. Dr Taylor had been kind enough to transcribe the portion which related to myself, but I was very much encouraged to see the Holy Father's strong desire to expedite matters.

I will come to Dublin at the very beginning of Low Week, that is, by the day of Dr Moriarty's consecration.[2] In the meantime, as I mentioned to your Grace, I am not idle here. I am very much rejoiced to think that we are moving at last.

Begging the blessing of the Season I am, My dear Lord, Your affectte friend & Servt

John H Newman of the Oratory

The Most Revd The Archbp of Dublin

---

[1] This was the Brief of 20 March about the University. Cullen announced that the Bishops would meet on 18 May, and asked Newman to come to Dublin as soon as convenient after Easter.   [2] 25 April.

P.S. I propose to commence on June 1st a small periodical, giving information about Universities, our University etc. When I see you, I will ask you two questions — 1. Whether any thing strikes you on the plan itself — 2. Whether you see any reason against putting it forward before the Synodal meeting[1]

EASTER SUNDAY 16 APRIL 1854 took Vespers

TO MRS J. W. BOWDEN

Oratory Edgbaston Birmingham April 20. 1854
My dear Mrs Bowden,

I hope you got my letter, which I wrote on Saturday.

Since then, I have thought over Emily's case, and said Mass about it — and, as far as I am concerned, you may say this to her from me:—

'that her long continuance in one and the same state without advancing, and her own indecision and doubt whether she has a vocation or not, are as unlike as possible what she ought to feel, if she really had a vocation. Accordingly I advise and wish her *absolutely and entirely* to put the thought from her once and for all, and to make up her mind that she is *not* called to a religious life.'

1. You will observe this is not telling her to put off the thought for a month or two, but for good and all.

2. You must take care, this does not seem an abrupt change in *me* — else, it may perplex her, and frighten her — so that she may be *unable* to give up the thought of religion.

3. I don't know what her *present* state is — or what effect this three weeks of [un]certainty for the future has had upon her, or how she received my letter of Saturday, putting off the decision again. If she received it with *great distress*, we must think whether it is not a proof, as far as it goes, of a vocation.

4. You must see the *effect* of this absolute dismissal of the idea of a vocation, (if she consents to it,) on her, in the course of the next *three months*, say. You will not tell her you are watching her — but if, as weeks go on, she is quite reconciled to a secular life, it will certainly look as if she had no vocation. If on the other hand, at the end a certain number of weeks, the wish recurs, and she says 'really, I *cannot* get it out of my mind, —' I suppose we must reckon that she has a vocation.

5 During this time that you are trying her, of course you must keep

---

[1] Taylor wrote on 17 April Cullen's warm approval of the plan for a periodical.

her from all external influences, which would win her to a secular life. Nothing can be more quiet than your mode of living — nothing less likely than that you should be going out into society — but I think you must make a *point* of keeping her sheltered — for this, I suppose, is what is meant by directors who say that you must act without taking too much time to decide: — they mean that a lady, who is living in the *world*, is every day exposed to the chance of committing herself to another kind of vocation

Ever Yours affectly in Xt John H Newman

P.S. I go to Ireland (16 Harcourt Street, Dublin) tomorrow.

FRIDAY 21 APRIL 1854 set off at midnight for Ireland

TO E. B. PUSEY

Edgbaston Bm April 21. 1854.

My dear Pusey

I ought to have thanked you before now for the copies of St Athanasius.[1]

By this post I send you a copy of a pamphlet I published at Rome, which perhaps you have not seen. I go to Dublin tonight.

Affectionately Yrs ever, John H Newman

TO J. B. ROBERTSON

Oratory. Birmingham April 21. 1854

My dear Sir

I am very sorry to find from your letter just received that my letter from this place has occasioned you some pain — which of course I need hardly say was very far indeed from my intention.[2]

---

[1] See letter of 11 March. Newman sent in return *Dissertiunculae Quaedam Critico-theologicae*, Rome 1847, *T.T.* pp. 1–91.

[2] Newman had offered Robertson a Lectureship in German Literature, at £150 a year, secured for three years. This Robertson declined, or rather asked for a Lectureship in History to be combined with it. He was told on 12 April that there was nothing else available to offer him, and that for a Lectureship with so little responsibility £150 was thought enough. Newman noted in his University Journal for 21 April, 'letter from Mr Robertson to the effect that [he] had not, as I thought, declined and that he would now accept my offer—He wanted an early answer.'

Undoubtedly every one has a right to his due remuneration, and I was ashamed of offering you the poor sum I did. You were perfectly justified in being influenced by the question of remuneration and in asking whether two lectureships could not be joined together so as to increase it.

It seems to me however that you hardly realize how very unformed our plans are at present, when you speak as if we were not each of us *equally* dependent on circumstances and emergencies. In any new plan fresh combinations are continually rising, and I, as little as you, can promise that, what is not at once settled today, will admit of being settled just in the same way tomorrow. My offer, such as it was, was made two months ago February 21. If it was not accepted then, of course it is not in my power, much as I might wish it, to *continue it on* an indefinite time. Else, it would come to this surely, that *I* should be bound, and any one to whom I offer any office, *not* bound. Day by day questions are asked me, and plans proposed — new views are opened — the equilibrium, so to call it, of chairs is changed — influences superior to my own are brought to bear. It is impossible for me to do more than wait for the answer expected, and to act upon it.

You say indeed, 'I neither definitely accepted nor definitely rejected your offer of the Lectureship in German Literature.' But, my dear Sir, you could not be indefinite; you could not but answer when you wrote — you proposed something else instead. I am sure you would see, if you were in my situation, that I could make no progress at all, if every offer I made was to be a promise, to be held and used by the person addressed, when he would.

You will understand from what I have now said, that, much as I wish for the sake of the University to have the benefit of your services, that which is past is over, and that any negociation between us must begin again, when I am in a position to recommence, if you will allow me to do so.

The Bishops are soon to meet, I do not know how far they will take things into their hands — they may ask me what is settled and what is not settled; they may choose to accept what is done or over — but cut short negociations. I do not say it will be so — but I say this to illustrate the impossibility of my doing more than offer

After the trouble I have given you already, you will see that it is simple prudence in me not to repeat just now any anticipation of the future with relation to the lectureship in History.[1]

Let me in conclusion repeat my sorrow if I have said any thing

[1] In Oct. 1854 Newman appointed Robertson Lecturer in Modern History and Geography.

calculated to hurt your feelings and to beg you to pardon it, and to subscribe myself

J H N

SATURDAY 22 APRIL 1854   passed the day at Kingstown with H W[Wilberforce][1] to Harcourt Street at night

SUNDAY 23 APRIL   went down and dined with H W

TUESDAY 25 APRIL   Dr Moriarty's consecration — present at it

WEDNESDAY 26 APRIL   called on Bishops of Limerick, Killaloe, and Cloyne dined at Dr Cullen's with large party for Dr Moriarty.

TO F. W. FABER

16 Harcourt Street. Dublin April 26/54

My dear Fr Wilfrid,

I am only too happy to have any such memorial as you offer me from your Fathers and youths of the London House.[2] At the same time I hope the very fact of their offer is a proof that I shall be securing as *cheap* mitres as possible. I mean, not only, as they will know well, that as much love goes with the gift of a cheap mitre as a grand one, but really for my own comfort let me not have about me more precious things than I absolutely *need*. 'The abundance of the rich, says Ecclesiastes (at least in the Protestant version) does not suffer him to sleep.'[3] At present I sleep in a rail-carriage or a steam boat tolerably well — but, if I know that in the van behind I have a lot of precious things to lug about with me, which I must be seeing after, with no 'Newman' (such as the Cardinal's) to be my cad,[4] why all I can say is, it is next door to travelling with nursery maids, and their paraphernalia, and a worse penance than St Philip's cat, or 'cruel scourge of human minds.'[5]

Your letter has come to me from Birmingham, or I would have replied sooner — but I am sorry to say, that, even as it is, I have delayed a post

Ever Yrs most affectly J H N

[1] See letter of 13 June to Wilberforce.
[2] Faber wrote on 21 April asking if the London Oratorians might present Newman with the three mitres he would require as a bishop.
[3] Ecclesiastes, 5: 12.
[4] Newman was the name of Wiseman's (and later Manning's) manservant.
[5] St Philip used to mortify his disciples by making them look after his cat. J. Bacci, *Life of St Philip Neri*, Book II, ch. xix.

TO AMBROSE ST JOHN

16 Harcourt Street April 26/54

My dear Ambrose

Perhaps Stewart will be sending me to Birmingham a parcel of books, which I shall trouble you to bring over to me to Stone on this day week — (Wednesday) and I can take them back with me to Dublin.

Also ask, please, Fr Bernard, whether his article on Dante and Ozanam in the British Critic, does not go into the details of the row which the heretical intellect was making in St Thomas's time. I want to see it, as throwing light upon the intellectual movement in Oxford etc now.

If he says it does, then you must be so good as to bring me the volume from the Library to Stone — (getting leave of the Congregatio Deputata on Monday) and I will make some extracts from it there, and you shall take it back to Birmingham.

If *you* happen to have the number, I will borrow it and take it back with me here, and you need not bring the Library copy.

Perhaps Bernard can suggest some other book of the same kind.[1]

I consider the congregational music comes under neither the Prefect of music, nor the Ceremoniere — nor again the Sacristan — and that it falls to me. I say this, lest any complaint or protest follows what I am going to say, that you may be prepared what to answer.

I wish *you* then to oversee for me the May Service at our Lady's Image in Church. By which I mean that you will signify for me to Br Frederic what I want done, and to the singing girls generally, and to Jewsbury. And I wish you would tell Fr William to order for me at Parker's some candles sufficient for lighting up (not sump —[2]

THURSDAY 27 APRIL 1854 dined at Kingstown with Mr J. B. O Ferrall meeting J. O Hagan and H W[Wilberforce]

[1] Dalgairns's article 'Dante and the Catholic Philosophy of the Thirteenth Century,' *British Critic*, XXXIII (Jan. 1843), pp. 110–43, was a review of A. F. Ozanam's *Dante et la philosophie catholique au treizième siècle*. The two stories which Dalgairns recounted, p. 128, against pride of intellect, Newman quoted in the *Catholic University Gazette* (3 Aug. 1854), *H.S.* III, p. 187.

[2] The second sheet of this letter is missing.

TO F. W. FABER

Thursday April 27/54

My dear Fr Wilfrid,

I am deeply concerned and alarmed at what you say.[1] Do write again, when you have any thing to say. I will say Mass for your intention in the matter tomorrow

Ever Yrs affly J H N

TO AMBROSE ST JOHN

16 Harcourt Street April 27/54

Charissime

⌐Since Stanislas is gone, some one must write to M. Denouelle to find out the *process* for fixing Miss Giberne's 7 pictures on the apse⌐ which had better be done as soon as possible.

As to the Sunday notices, I think I had better undertake them, and you in my absence. There is, however some difficulty in the circumstance, that I ordered Fr Nicholas to get the notice book; so you must explain to him, that, on second thoughts, I thought it fell under me rather, as representing the mission.

⌐As to the Sermons [[list]], they were made upon a cycle, or something like it — the 4 o'clock Sermon was Frs Bernard and Stanislas alternately and the short post gospel sermon was taken by three or four fathers successively. Had I the names here, I would draw it out at once — but from what I have said, you can draw it out for me and affix it to the board, adding after your name, 'according to the directions of the Father.'

I am very much concerned about your house window. Were other windows blown in, or is yours badly built?⌐

Mrs Bowden has always said poor [Manuel] Johnson has become liberal — I thought you knew it. I suppose Lord Ralph did not go.[2]

You may ask the Bishop in my name for the same leave of Benedictions we had in Alcester Street. You may say I took it for granted —

---

[1] See final paragraph of next letter.

[2] St John wrote on 26 April, that Dalgairns, with Flanagan, had taken the novices to Oxford the previous day, and that they seemed 'to have had a very jolly day with Johnson. He was extremely kind, so was his wife. F. Bernard thought he was more *liberal* I fear in a bad sense. He seemed absorbed in astronomy and a magnificent telescope which had cost some £1000s.' The party also met Bloxam.

but feel I had better ask for it. ⌈I sent the May services yesterday.⌉

The Post which brought your letter brought one from F Wilfrid to the following effect:—

'We must now have a strong prayer: there is a certain Act of Parliament which prohibits any dissenting place of worship being opened within three hundred yards of a protestant church. Irons[1] has held a large meeting; and we are told the Parish is going to shut our Church up.

Even the Oratory is not 300 yards off.'

Ever Yrs affly J H N

FRIDAY 28 APRIL 1854   dined at All hallows, where introduced to Dr Corrigan

TO J. D. DALGAIRNS

16 Harcourt Street April 28/54

My dear F Bernard

Your letter has just come. You yourself hinted to me before the difference of which you speak, and you must not be annoyed at it. It is no new matter. F. Ambrose once got them to swear an eternal friendship, and things went on well for a while. The one is somewhat sawney, and the other in the opposite extreme — I suspect it is the third who (unconsciously) does the mischief.[2] What would you have to *do*, my dear Bernard, if your charges were already perfect? It would be the case of the English soldier without the grand Monarque.

I have just seen F. Stanislas, who is full of Oxford — but I wish the leaves were out. As to Keuffel,[3] thank you for your thoughtfulness — but I have already read it and taken extracts from it — and so do not want it. I should not wonder if I had to come round by Birmingham in my way back — as I find I have left my collars, card case etc etc. there — and I want to poke about Huber[4] and some other books a little. It is so provoking, *I have not been wanted here.* I could have remained

---

[1] W. J. Irons, incumbent of Holy Trinity, Brompton.

[2] Dalgairns wrote that the noviciate was 'split up into two parties, Robert [Tillotson] and Philip [Molloy] versus William [Neville].' Tillotson was the sawney (i.e. sentimental) one, and Molloy was the one who made the mischief.

[3] Georg. Gothofr. Keuffel, *Historia Originis ac Progressus Scholarum inter Christianos*, Helmstadt 1743.

[4] *The English Universities from the German of V. A. Huber*, an abridged translation edited by Francis W. Newman, three vols., London 1843.

quietly at Birmingham till the 18th, and have saved the journey to Stone from this place. I am from my books, which I *want*. I have seen Dr Cullen for about 5 minutes this week. Next week *I* go to England Tuesday, *he* on Friday. I will be bound, I shall not see him between his return and the 18th except for another 5 minutes. At the same time DOUBTLESS it is a good thing being on the spot; and I should have had a great difficulty in escaping Dr Moriarty's consecration — and am not unwilling under my circumstances to have seen it.

I have no objection to your setting up the Sacred Heart, if you are sure it is not set up at St Chad's.[1] You had better of course take the Bishop's judgment. I don't suppose he can object.

Alas, I have ordered Meiners' book on Universities from Stewart, and find it is in German! Tell F Ambrose to be so good as to undo the parcel, and, if my suspicion is confirmed by his inspection, not to bring it me.[2]

Ever Yrs affly J H N

Thank F Frederic for his letter.

P.S. The wind blows so, that I shall come over to *Birmingham* on the first lull. Tell Frederic, please, to light my fire, and place my sheets *open* to them, [sic] *at once*.

TO F. W. FABER

16 Harcourt Street Dublin April 28 [1854]

My dear F Wilfrid

Mr Cotter was the Priest of St George's who mentioned to me what I told you about the books. It has seemed to me a pity you did not at once pursue his information which I gave you two years ago — and I am very glad you are going to do so now.[3]

I hear with pleasure the Cardinal seems in excellent health

Ever Yrs affly J H N

[1] Dalgairns wished to set up the confraternity of the Sacred Heart in the Birmingham Oratory church.

[2] Christoph Meiners, *Geschichte der Entstehung und Entwickelung der hohen Schulen unsers Erdtheils*, four vols., Göttingen 1802–05.

[3] See letter of 2 July 1851 which told Faber that the bound set of Newman's works intended by the London Oratorians for presentation to Wiseman, had been sent in error to Rome. Faber wrote on 26 April 1854 to say that the set had been discovered in Rome, at the English College.

SATURDAY 29 APRIL 1854   called on Archbishop[1]
SUNDAY 30 APRIL   O Reilly and Mr Th. O Hagan called   went down and dined with H W[Wilberforce].   intending to cross to England
MONDAY 1 MAY   F Stanislas called in his way to Roscommon,   crossed to England

TO ARCHBISHOP CULLEN

Monday May 1 [1854]

My dear Lord
    I hastily finished, just in time for Post, my Sketch yesterday, expecting to go off by the 7 o'clock boat.[2]
    I now write this to say that I am not at all sure I have hit your wishes in what I have sent you — and that if you will make pencil marks and alter it, I will write another Paper
                          Yrs faithfully & affectly John H Newman

[1] As has been explained in the last note to the letter of 7 April to Hope-Scott, Newman was never told that he was not to be made a bishop. Friends continued to send him presents and congratulations. Ullathorne treated him as a bishop, and as late as June was asking why the consecration had not been arranged. Newman later realised that 'long before this Dr. Cullen knew that I was not to receive the honour proposed. I judge so from the way in which he commented on the University Brief of March 20. He had sent me word January 19 [see letter of 20 Jan. to Taylor] that the Pope most probably would *accompany* the issuing of the Brief by some "mark of distinction" in my favour, and Cardinal Wiseman told him distinctly that that distinction was elevation to the Episcopal dignity. To this I was to offer no *opposition*—But now, showing me the University Brief he pointed out to me the words "Newman, egregiis animi dotibus ornatus" etc [quoted in last note to letter of 7 April to Hope-Scott.] and said in an awkward and hurried manner, "You see how the Pope speaks of you.—*here* is the distinction."'
    This episode must have occurred at the interview of 29 April, since Newman's letter of 28 April to Dalgairns shows that he had as yet had no real audience with Cullen, and was still expecting Consecration. Newman never asked a single question about the postponement and abandonment of the plan to make him a bishop, the prospect faded out of his mind, and no explanation was given him. Neither did Cardinal Wiseman nor 'Dr. Cullen, nor Dr. Grant nor Dr. Ullathorne, nor any one else, ever again say one single word on the subject; nor did they make any chance remark by which I might be able to form any idea why that elevation which was thought by Pope, Cardinal and Archbishop so expedient for the University, or at least so settled a point, which was so publicly announced, was suddenly and silently reversed.' 'Memorandum about my connection with the Catholic University,' *A.W.* pp. 317–20. See also letter of 1 Feb. to Wiseman, and last note to letter of 11 May to Cullen.
    [2] This was Newman's Memorandum of 29 April on the objects of the University and how they were to be realised. See letter of 11 May to Cullen, and Appendix I, p. 557.

TUESDAY 2 MAY 1854   got to Birmingham early

WEDNESDAY 3 MAY   went over with Fr Ambrose to Stone, — preached at opening of Church of Sisters of Penance[1] — called at Aston[2] — back in evening

THURSDAY 4 MAY   went back to Dublin

FRIDAY 5 MAY   arriving there at 6 A M.   dined with Mr James O Ferrall

TO MRS WILLIAM FROUDE

16 Harcourt Street Dublin May 5/54

My dear Mrs Froude

I have been to England for a day and found your letter, and brought it with me here where I have just arrived — and now sit down to thank you for it and the former one.

Be sure I shan't forget you and Wm [William] please God. I shall for some time give my Friday's mass (excepting the 26th inst) to that intention.

Do not fancy you can put me in a painful position to dear Wm. I don't mind differing with him. I don't mind giving you advice in which he would not concur. But I wish to be sure I tell him so when I do it. He is so true and tender, that I leave you safely to him. But I never can disguise from him what I think and feel about you.

As to your reference to my letters, of course I may forget about myself — but just consider, since you have them with you, whether I am not right in saying, that I never was in doubt what *my duty was* — I doubted what was true, but I used to say 'To join the Church of Rome would be against my conscience. I *could not* do it'. I don't say this was not a false conscience, but a conscience it *was*, and it is ever right to go according to one's conscience, though a false one.

Moreover, it is a Catholic principle, that no one can be in doubt what he ought to *do* (i.e. without fault). We are often left 'speculatively' doubtful, to use the theological word, never 'practically'. Shortly before my reception, when my book was partly printed, I saw I *ought* to be a Catholic — and I did not then wait till I had finished the printing, but left the book unfinished, as it stands.[3]

When my dear friend Bowden lay dead, I wept bitterly over his body, saying he had gone, and left me without light;[4] this was the same

[1] 'Dr. Ullathorne treated me as a Bishop, refusing to give me the benediction before the Sermon.' *A.W.* p. 317.
[2] i.e. the Passionist monastery which Newman had visited at the end of 1845.
[3] Newman became a Catholic on 9 Oct. and *An Essay on the Development of Christian Doctrine* was published at the end of Nov. 1845.
[4] *Apo.* p. 227. J. W. Bowden died on 15 Sept. 1844.

feeling as far as I recollect — I don't think I was remaining a Protestant, thinking I ought *not* to remain, but with a sense of duty that I *ought* to remain *till* I got clear light.

I am not defending myself, but I am writing with reference to you, my dear Mrs Froude. See then whether your doubt be merely speculative. Can you say 'I am certain I ought now and here, at this time and place, to remain a Protestant'? — Are you sure that, whatever remaining *speculative* doubts or difficulties you may have, you have not a secret feeling at times[1] that you ought to be a Catholic? I am not attempting to answer this question *for* you, but I really cannot help having an opinion on the subject.

I hope I make this clear, but am somewhat anxious lest I should not

Ever Yrs affly J. H. N.

TO MANUEL JOHNSON

16 Harcourt Street Dublin May 5. 1854

My dear Johnson

I was very glad to have pleasant tidings of you and your wife thro' our Birmingham party.[2] I have long been wishing you would run over to us, some time when I am at home. Perhaps in the summer Birmingham will be your and Mrs Johnson's way to Ireland, which is a great place for tourists just now, and there is no sea sickness to fear except in winter. H Wilberforce and Ornsby are here, and perhaps others whom you know.

I should like very much to have your advice on a subject on which you can give it better than any one else. I want to set up an Observatory here. You know, *you* are, of all men in the terraqueous globe, '*the* Observer,' as St Paul is 'the Apostle' and Aristotle 'the philosopher,' and Peter Lombard 'the Master.' The best of all would be, if you would fling off that shabby Protestantism of yours, and come here yourself — Since that, alas, cannot be, give me your advice on the whole matter — first on the existing state of the Dublin Observatory under Hamilton — then on the project itself — what it will cost, with how few instruments it can get on — what really good instruments

---

[1] The copyist noted that these two words were added in pencil.

[2] Johnson replied on 29 May, 'That visit from your people was a very pleasant event indeed both to my wife and to myself. To see that "Boy" [Dalgairns] was of course a pleasure but it was hardly less agreeable to make acquaintance with those who are your constant associates.'

would come to, and whether you know a Catholic (not a 'Christian') Observer —[1]

Is there any chance of your running up to us for the 26th our great day? I shall then be in Birmingham.

Give your wife and her sister my affectionate remembrances. I recollect them before they recollect themselves[2]

Ever Yours affectly John H Newman of the Oratory

SUNDAY 7 MAY 1854   dined with Serjeant Howley[3]

TO F. W. FABER

16 Harcourt Street May 7/54

My dear F Wilfrid,

The Very Revd Austen Killeen, the bearer of this, wants to get cheap lodgings for two months. I suspect Brompton will be out of the way for him — but some of you may have penitents in London whom it would be a service to mention to him — and thus — mutual advantage will follow. So I think it worth while sending you this.

Thank you for your note of the other day Certainly Irons' statute did not *sound* new to me but it may be a popular error.[4]

I am glad to believe things are going on at high quarters in London

Ever Yrs affly J H N

TO EDWARD BADELEY

16 Harcourt Street Dublin May 11. 1854

My dear Badeley,

I have wished to write to you some time, to ask what you thought of the article against the Christian Remembrancer in the Rambler for

---

[1] See letter of 11 June to Johnson. Sir William Rowan Hamilton (1805–65), the mathematician, was appointed superintendent of the Observatory at Dublin in 1827, and soon after was made Astronomer Royal for Ireland. Johnson's view was that nothing was done at this Observatory.

[2] They were the daughters of J. A. Ogle, Newman's private tutor and close friend.

[3] John Howley (1789–1866), at Old Oscott and Trinity College, Dublin, was called to the Irish Bar in 1815. He was Chairman of Quarter Sessions for County Tipperary 1835–65, and Queen's First Serjeant in Ireland from 1851 to death.

[4] See letter of 27 April to St John.

April — would it do to publish separately? with expansions?[1]

I have another thing to trouble you with now. It is not your affair, and you are a busy man — but Hope is a busier, and I have more chance of an answer from you. Next week, May 18th is the meeting of the Bishops here, and I suppose that then I shall be formally placed into my Rectorial chair. My first act will be to invite a number of lay men in both countries to place their names on the University books. (This will involve no trouble or expence.)[2] Now of course my best way will be to begin with several names which will carry others — so before going to Lord Arundel etc etc I must have Hope's, that is Hope-Scott's — you know the individual, as you are a lawyer, what ever be his aliases.

I don't think it likely he will have any scruple — the only condition he might like to make, which I can anticipate, would be, that his name should not be printed unless a definite number, which he might fix, of other names could be got.[3]

Ever Yours affectly John H Newman of the Oratory[4]

E. Badeley Esqr

[1] See letter of 5 Jan. 1854 to Capes. Badeley replied on 16 May, 'I have read the Article in the Rambler and so has Hope, and so has Bellasis. We were all disappointed with it, thinking that it was not sufficiently pointed . . . if it was largely expanded and the subject well followed out, the case would be very different . . . a vast deal of most important matter might be extracted from Jery Taylor, and other Protestant writers, which would effectually silence such hypocrites as the Christian Remembrancer.'

[2] Newman was anxious to compile a 'list of honorary members of the University, principally laymen from Ireland and elsewhere.' He hoped they would compensate for the absence of a body of graduates, and he wished eventually to confer certain rights on them, and thus use them as a means for giving the laity a place in the administration of the University. It was all the more necessary to secure lay support in view of the suspicion and disapproval of the University that existed among influential groups of laymen, e.g. among those who favoured the Queen's Colleges. Newman's plan for getting names of associates of the University, although sanctioned by the Synod of Bishops on 18 May 1854 (*Campaign*, p. 90), 'was not viewed without jealousy by Dr. Cullen, and at Rome they gave it no countenance.' *A.W.* pp. 324–6, and cf. letter of 12 May to James O'Ferrall.

Newman's correspondence also shows him aware of the importance of advertising: the University needed to be 'brought before the world,' since the whole weight of the Government was on the side of a rival system. Cf. *Campaign*, pp. 94–5. There is a note in Newman's University Journal, at 8 Feb. 1854: 'The young priests here [Dublin] said that the vanity of the Irish character would lead them to take up any thing that had a name.'

[3] Badeley replied on 16 May that Hope-Scott agreed at once to give his name. That of Lord Arundel was also forthcoming. The names began to be published in the *Catholic University Gazette* from Oct. 1854 onwards, and they were listed in the first University Calendar. The most famous name among ecclesiastics other than bishops was that of Döllinger, and among laymen, those of Acton and Montalembert.

[4] Badeley's letter continued, 'What about your consecration? When and where is it to be? . . . we hear nothing.'

TO ARCHBISHOP CULLEN

⌜May 11/54⌝

My dear Lord

I send the corrected statement, and am pleased that the substance of it has met your approval.[1]

⌜It occurs to me that I ought as a matter of duty to represent to your Grace the absolute necessity of your bringing one point before the [[Synodal]] Meeting[2] which I know has long been on your own mind.

I cannot, I ought not at this very critical time to forget the way in which I have been received by two of the Irish Prelates. The one was most courteous to me *personally*, when I went into his Diocese, but pointedly directed his courtesy to my person not my office[3] — the other[4] was condescending enough to second my appointment in Committee two years ago — but he has since expressed much distrust of me personally.

With facts such as these before me, I find it imperative to ask that their Lordships should do me the kindness of taking the distinct step of constituting me, after the precedent (I believe) of Louvain, their Vicar General (say for 3 years) for the establishment of the University — if they do not, it is very plain I shall not know where I stand. When the meeting separates, I may find to my perplexity that majority of votes does not bind the minority; and that the decision of the Episcopal body is considered no rule for the acts of its members, taken individually.

Such things have occurred before now, but would be precluded by an arrangement such as I now propose which alone can give me courage to engage in a work, most arduous, undertaken by me from a simple sense of duty, and already hanging over me and keeping me from other employments without result for two years past.

Should your Grace see your way to suggest any other expedient

---

[1] This was the Memorandum of 29 April on the objects of the University and the means for attaining them, which Newman sent to Cullen on 1 May, and which was to be read at the Synod on 20 May. The corrected version is printed in *Campaign*, pp. 93–100, cf. *McGrath*, pp. 297–8. The original uncorrected version found among Taylor's papers after his death, was returned to Newman in 1879. It is printed in Appendix I, p. 557. See note there.

[2] [[This was the formal meeting, convoked by Brief of the Holy See and held in May 1854, at which the Fundamental Constitution of the University was settled]]

[3] This was the Bishop of Cork, William Delany. See letter of 23 Feb. to the Oratorians at Birmingham.

[4] [[Dr McHale]]

to the Vicar Generalship in gaining me the sanction of the Bishops severally and personally, of course I shall be content[11]

I am &c J H N

TO F. W. FABER

16 Harcourt Street May 11/54

My dear Fr Wilfrid

The inclosed will explain itself. There was a talk of a Russian privateer in St George's Channel the day I came over — but I got over without a chase

Ever Yrs affly J H N

TO AMBROSE ST JOHN

16 Harcourt Street May 11/54

My dear Ambrose,

As to Denouelle's job, *I* don't know who can do it — can Philip tell? could one of Hardman's men do it? —

Thank you for the trouble you have been at about Mr Robertson's letter.[2] I find I can manage.

As to the Antiphons, *I* do not give you power to do any thing — and it is for you to consider what power you have of your own.[3] Do not get into scrapes, by exerting a power which will not be allowed you. Certainly it would seem to me, that, if people loved me, they would show their love by attending a little more to my wishes, considering

---

[1] [[Of course nothing came of this appeal!]] As late as 28 April, Newman took for granted that he was to be made a bishop, since in his letter that day to Dalgairns he spoke of the advantage of seeing Dr Moriarty's consecration. On 29 April Newman saw Cullen, who showed him the laudatory reference in the University Brief, and said hurriedly that here was the promised mark of distinction from Rome. See note to diary of 29 April. This much was clear as to the bishopric: 'The Brief had been silent on the point, Dr. Cullen had been pointedly evasive, and there was no sign from Wiseman. With the prospect of his work as Rector commencing in the near future, he thought it incumbent on him to demand the lesser dignity which Dr. Cullen himself had suggested as a means of securing the support, not merely of the hierarchy as a whole, but of the individual bishops.' *McGrath*, p. 293.

[2] It had been mislaid.

[3] St John wanted to insist on the rule that the Fathers should attend a singing practice.

the paper still is fastened to the board. Till I find the practical consideration for me, I cannot have confidence in them. Somehow I fancy I am not in the habit of asking much.

⌜You say 'the Deputata agreed to £30 being applied from the boys to their Tutor whoever he is.' But till Mr Wilson goes, he is their Tutor,⌝ unless Fr Edward has expressly waived the £30. If he waives it, he is literally giving it — which he cannot be expected to do. However, if he has waived it, then ⌜the Deputata may or may not, as it pleases, choose Mr Hamilton for Tutor, and pay him at the rate of £30 —⌝ and then *he* will be able to pay the House at the rate of £30. And then the Deputata must consider whether it thinks £30 per annum enough for his board and lodging. I am not quite sure I understand you — but I have tried to draw out my answer so full, as to meet whatever you exactly mean.[1]

Ever Yrs most affly J H N

FRIDAY 12 MAY 1854   dined with Mr James O Ferrall

TO JAMES MORE O'FERRALL

16 Harcourt Street May 12. 1854

Private
not sent[2]
My dear Mr More O'Ferrall,

I was very much obliged to you for letting me see Mr More O'Ferrall's letter.[3] To one like myself who knows so little of Ireland, it is a great point to have the opportunity of seeing the view which he would take of our prospects and duties at this moment.

---

[1] Charles Hamilton was a clergyman, just converted, whom St John wanted to live at the Oratory.

[2] These words appear to have been added at a later date.

[3] Richard More O'Ferrall wrote on 5 May to his younger brother James: 'I concur with Dr Newman that it is desirable to connect a large portion of the Catholic body with the new University, but there is some difficulty in deciding on the course most likely to effect that object. . . . [O'Ferrall thought that those, chiefly laymen, who supported the University, should elect a Council which the Rector could assemble in emergencies.] The Protestant party will endeavour to raise a cry in which many Catholics are disposed to join that the new University is got up for the purpose of placing Catholic education entirely in the hands of the Clergy and for the exclusion of the Laity from all interference; the plan proposed by Dr Newman if fully carried out by the Bishops will meet that objection and give satisfaction to the Catholic Laity myself among the number.

I would have no objection to have my name among the members, provided it was

I most entirely concur in what he says upon the necessity of laymen having a direct part in the management of the University. The University is mainly for the sake of the laity; and it is a proof of my own feeling on the subject, that I hope, as far as ever I can, to fill the Professorial Chairs with laymen, except those which are more or less theological; though it would create misapprehension to give this out to the world. Now the Professors with the Rector will be the governing body; here then will be a distinct provision for even more than Mr More O'Ferrall requires, and that, independently of the presence of laymen in the constituent body, which was the object of the letter I sent you.

I do not think he will ask more than this, and I will tell you why. It flattered me very much to find the confidence he places in me. Now, if he insisted on more now, he would destroy my power of doing any thing. I have ever contended that the University must start in a provisional state, without any constitution; that the whole power must be vested in one person, that is, the Rector, whose appointment indeed is revocable, but who, while he holds it, is unshakled [sic]. I revere and admire such Irish Bishops as I have had the opportunity of knowing; but I am resolute in requiring to be free in this work. ⟨⟨(i.e. except an Episcopal *Veto*.)⟩⟩ Now, if the laity determine to have any *immediate* recognition of their right in the administration, will it be possible to separate this abstract right contended for from a de facto interference with me on the other hand on the part of the *hierarchy*? One claim will provoke another. As soon as the question of Academical constitution is mooted, I am put under restraint; — whereas, if the laity are but forbearing now, is it not certain that, when the provisional state ends, say in 3 or 7 years, the laity, holding a good number of professorships and being members of the University, must necessarily secure their due weight in the ordinary government? If they join the University now, they secure their due weight in it, when it really deserves the name.

Will you kindly bring these considerations before your Brother's

taken as a recognition of the right of the Laity to a voice in the management of the University. It does not follow that because the right is recognised, that it should be exercised. Practically I would desire to see the management of the University entirely in the hands of Dr Newman, and such I believe would be the general feeling, but in founding an establishment we must look beyond the present time, and have some security that if it ever fell into bad hands there should be a means of redress.

In my opinion the Constitution of the University should be framed, and an abstract sent to all those persons whose names you desire to have. I do not think it likely that the Bishops would agree to any such proposal unless strongly urged by Dr Newman, but if he can carry his point into practical effect I have no doubt it would obtain for the University very general support.' Cf. Note to diary, 1 March, letter of 11 May to Badeley, and *A.W.* p. 326. See also end of letter of 26 July 1855 to Cullen.

notice, and believe me, My dear Mr More O'Ferrall, Sincerely Yours in Xt

John H Newman of the Oratory

James O'Ferrall Esqr

SATURDAY 13 MAY 1854 dined with Ornsby to meet Mr Dalgairns[1]

TO JOHN STANISLAS FLANAGAN

May 13/54

My dear Stanislas

It has struck me I seemed to discourage you getting me to know your cousin, Mr Wolf Flanagan.[2] If so, I misrepresented myself. I should like to know him very much.

Thank Fr Bernard for his letter just received

Ever Yrs affly J H N

SUNDAY 14 MAY 1854 dined with H W [Wilberforce]
MONDAY 15 MAY dined with Dr Cullen, as did Dr Moriarty

TO J. D. DALGAIRNS

16 Harcourt Street May 15/54

(Private)
My dearest Fr B

You need not in any way be distressed or cast down.[3] When one hears a thing of this kind, one looks back at one's own time with respect to it, and my first feeling has been about myself. I dare say I have had a good deal to do with it. If he had taken to me he would *perhaps* have taken to St Philip; — but I never took to him. I respect him exceedingly — I think he makes a great effort to overcome those points in which I do not take to him. He started, as far as I was concerned, with bad auspices. I was much surprised that the Redemptorists should send him here, and he came here, κατὰ τον δεύτερον πλοῦν —[4] and when

---

[1] Ornsby's father-in-law and the father of J. D. Dalgairns.

[2] Stephen Woulfe Flanagan, Master of the Incumbered Estates Court.

[3] Philip Molloy, one of Dalgairns's novices, was making up his mind to leave. See letter of 7 June to Dalgairns.

[4] Second scheme when the first fails. Aristotle, *Eth. Nic.* II, 9, 4. Before coming to the Oratory Molloy had wished to be a Redemptorist.

he came, he thought his immediate admission certain — at least so it seemed. Well, this I resisted, and it is a satisfaction to me that I did, though I was importuned to do otherwise. There is one other thing I was strongly against, but, being still more strongly importuned again and again, have to my sorrow weakly given way — and that is his ordination. I never wished him to enter sacred orders till he was a Father. I have been weak enough to let him be ordained first Subdeacon then Deacon. It is very hard, I find, to act firmly when I have so little confidence, as I have, in my own opinion. If I prayed more, and lived more in the next world, I should not give way half as much, for I should have more trust in myself, which every Superior should have. It is an awkward thing to part with a Deacon — we must have some security what he means to do. I am anxious what the Bishop will think. I must suffer for my weakness.

Well, but to come to the point. I cannot be sorry he is not to be a Father. He is an honest minded man, and he sees that he cannot be a Phillipine, with the love of St Alfonso in his heart — for this we ought to be very grateful to him. Next, nothing could be more propitious than the fact of his Sister's needing him — it will give so good an excuse, and *Stanislas has suggested it*, as you know, 'Tell him from me, with my love that I thank him much for the honesty I have been speaking of, viz of his seeing that he could not be St Philip's child with a devotion to St Alfonso — tell him that I feel this the more, from the deep certainty I have of his love and consideration for us personally — that I do not wish the matter finally settled now, *unless* he presses for it — but, since he feels it a duty to go to his sister, I should like him to go to her — and then, in the course of a month or two to write to you on the subject again. One thing more you must tell him — that it makes me anxious that he leaves us in sacred orders, lest the Bishop should be disturbed — and that I should — if he leaves us, like to know distinctly what I should tell the Bishop about him.' read him the part under ' '

And now I have nothing more to say except to bid you *burn* this, as soon as you have given Philip the message. Tell him not to tell any one but you *why* he is going (whether he finally decides before he starts, or not). '*He is going to his sister*' — that is enough. This will hinder the house being unsettled. Above all, he must not tell the Novices. As I presume Stanislas has been long back, he had better go *directly*. Tell no one but Stanislas about it. He may leave his things, i.e. in such a state that they can easily be packed up. I suppose I shall see him here, as he passes through.

Ever Yrs affly J H N

P.S.   I have seen your Father. He seems to be as you say, — a drawing towards the Church, without an understanding of the sacrifice. I suppose he was pleased at the largeness of our House at Birmingham, and at the pleasant Catholics whom Ornsby has introduced to him here — but every thing must have a beginning, and you must be very thankful for so much as this.

TO MISS M. R. GIBERNE

16 Harcourt Street Dublin May 15/54

My dear Miss Giberne,

It is a great shame and very ungentlemanlike, and worse ungrateful, in the Fathers not writing to you. I can only hope that you have got a letter before this. I account for it, first in their being so busy, and next in each thinking the other has written. However, this does not excuse. Another reason may be this, you do not send things *to us*, but to the London House. If you directed them to Birmingham (the expence to us would be only a few shillings more) our Fathers would be inexcusable. We have got the two Portraits, and vestments, and your other pictures which you meant for us — but I should tell you, tho' I don't wish you to repeat it, (for I should be hurting some one) they remained in London till it could be proved for certain to the satisfaction of the Fathers there that they could not possibly have any claim to them. I believe all you sent, has come — the vestments were all put out for a show, and much admired. As to the pictures of Oratorians, please send them to us *straight* — and I should be much obliged if you would get me a small white marble copy of the St Cecilia, as she lies before her altar, as they are commonly sold.

The Bishops all meet here in Synodal Meeting on Thursday next the 18th — when they are formally to instal me, and I am to set off at last. The brief has not yet come for my consecration. We shall not be able to have our grand opening till after Christmas, but perhaps we may open schools in October. Mrs Anstice and Josephine are here for a while — I have not seen them yet — I saw Miss Poole lately at Stone, and had not seen her since she was at Rome — I did not know her.[1] Henry Wilberforce talks of being called to the bar, but *you must not mention this*, as, though it cannot be a secret ultimately, it may be kept

[1] Mary Imelda Poole came to Rome in 1846. She was now one of Mother Margaret Hallahan's nuns at Stone. Mrs Anstice was Imelda Poole's widowed sister, who was in Dublin with her only child, Josephine.

as such for a long time — and he might change his mind again, before
he had to publish it. I am beginning a short weekly periodical of a few
pages each number, on University subjects — I suppose at the beginning of June. Fr Dalgairns's Lectures on the Sacred Heart are doing
a good deal of good.

There is literally no news to tell you — I have been ransacking my
memory and thoughts in vain. We have a wonderful run of fine weather
— for Ireland marvellous — since the beginning or middle of February.
Your seven pictures were put on the wall — and then we got afraid of
the damp and took them off — now they are going to be put on for
good.

Ever Yrs affly in Jesus & Mary J H N

Thank you for the relics

You will judge what you are to do when your charge marries. I
think you should be slow in accepting any invitation to *go* with her.
To a certainty you would have some unpleasantness with her husband.[1]

TO AMBROSE ST JOHN

16 Harcourt Street May 16/54

My dear Ambrose

Your letter has just come. First, ⌐see that the Bishop is asked at
once to the banquet on the 26 — we thought *supper* the more convenient
meal last year, didn't we?¬ Whether he should be asked to pontificate or
not, is as you all please. ⌐He pontificated on St Cecilia's day, so I don't
suppose it is *necessary* [[now]] —¬ All the clergy too should be invited,
throwing the declining upon *them*. Then the great Mr Barth. (is it not?)
Bretherton, your friend should be asked — and whom ever else you
think right. Two or three Oscott luminaries. On second thoughts ⌐it
strikes me best to ask the Bishop to sup and to *give Benediction*¬ and
not to sing Mass. This too will save him the double journey.

⌐As to advertisements about Fr Bernard's preaching, it is the sort
of thing I proposed *last October*, and he (with Fr Edward) extinguished
it — If it is done, he should determine on a course —¬ and take a good
subject. ⌐⟨⟨I do not think the Sacred Heart will do⟩⟩ I am still in favor
of it. At the same time I think you, as well as he, are fidgetting about the
4 o'clock Service, in a way I do not approve. You, I believe, are one of

---

[1] Miss Giberne's charge was Princess Agnes Borghese (1836–1920), granddaughter
of the sixteenth Earl of Shrewsbury. On 31 May 1854 she married Rudolph Prince of
Piombino, Duke of Sora.

the authors of that service —⌐ and from the time I gave my consent you have been making objections. Do you know I have come to the resolution, in consequence of something which has occurred, not to be swayed by your objections in future? which, I have almost to confess as a sin, I have yielded to, when I should not.[1]

⌐You will be of great use, if you keep Fr Bernard from fidgetting. I must have some talks with him. He really must guard against an anxious disposition. It will kill him.⌐

The question of the pattern for the Font must come before the Congregation with an estimate of its expence — and must be voted. This might be done when I am at Birmingham. ⌐I cannot tell what day I shall come — if all is well, between the 23rd and 25th.⌐ Let my room, please, be ready. ⌐It is not likely that I shall stay. They talk of inaugurating the University on St Peter and St Paul's day.⌐ I have not got a rochet.

⌐Ever Yours most affectly⌐ John H Newman

WEDNESDAY 17 MAY 1854   F Stanislas passed thro' to Birmingham about now.

TO EDWARD BADELEY

16 Harcourt Street May 17. 1854

My dear Badeley

I write, not only to thank you for your welcome letter, which I do heartily, but to give expression to my wonder and curiosity what in the world can be my anxiety, and what its cause. How did Dr Grant get up or pick up any such vision? I am ignorant simply and entirely what he can mean. Pray tell Hope so — and that I am not anxious or ill, and that I thank him very much for his message.[2]

I put an 'etc' after Lord Arundel's name, and I trust to come to London (if they let me here) soon after St Philip's day to get names — i.e. to inflict degrees of D.C.L.

Ever Yrs affly J H N

P.S.   Turn in your mind whether it would frighten people, as if implicating them with the Government, e.g. Lord Arundel, in giving

[1] See the first paragraph of Newman's letter of 15 May to Dalgairns.
[2] Dr Grant thought Newman was ill with anxiety at the threatened legal obstacle to the building of the London Oratory church. See letter of 27 April to St John. Badeley described the obstacle as a mare's nest.

them a *D.C.L.* It is not in *Arts* — nor in any thing which the Law of England recognises — for it can hardly be said to recognise *Civil* Law. Would D.Ph. . . . . Philosophy be less objectionable?[1]

TO ARCHBISHOP CULLEN

May 17 [1854]

My dear Lord

I send you the two draughts of letters, such as they are.

As to the title Rector, as is well known, it comes from ruling, regere, in the Schools. *Master* has the same meaning, and is sometimes used — There are three Heads of College called 'Masters' in Oxford. Praepositus too might be used — but as to President, I much suspect, it came in with the (so called) Reformation — and is not, I do think, an *ecclesiastical* title. If you mean the Head of the University, to be *a layman*, by all means call him *President*, as the President of the Royal or the Geological Society

I will be at home tomorrow, in case you want me.

Ever Yr affte friend & servt

John H Newman of the Oratory

The Most Revd Dr Cullen

THURSDAY 18 MAY 1854   dined with Dr Cullen to meet the Bishops   the beginning of the Synodal Meeting[2]

[1] Badeley replied on 23 May, 'I don't think the Government would trouble themselves about the matter—' Honorary Degrees were not conferred during Newman's Rectorship of the University.

[2] Newman's 'University Journal' adds some details for this day: 'Mr O'Hagan has today accepted the Professorship of Political Economy (I offered him the choice of that and Philosophical Law)—*Ward* I offered that of Philosophy of Religion, which he is taking a fortnight to think about. [W. G. Ward declined.]

The meeting of the Bishops is today. When I hear it is all settled right, I shall despatch letters I am writing or have written *to Allies* . . . to Mr Paley . . . to *H W* [Wilberforce] offering him Political Science, on *my* understanding of the subject, which I will explain (i.e. a *practical* view, e.g. such questions as should the State centralize and how far—should it take *religion* into its hands—*education*. What the legal constitution—working rules, by laws, customs etc etc. of the two houses of Parliament—on diplomatic relations, and international law—so that his subjects would go into details, statistics etc etc very much.)'

16 Harcourt Street Dublin May 18./54

My dear Allies,

I am this day put into possession of my office. The Bishops are now in Synodal Meeting, and I suppose in the course of the day, I shall hear they have made over their administrative powers over the University to me.

My first act is to inquire if there is any way in which you can be connected with us. Considering how much of an experiment we are engaged in, I much fear I can offer you nothing at once, which will be an inducement to you to give up any thing you have, but still it might be possible so far to take part in it as to have an opportunity of seeing whether it gave scope to duties sufficient to justify you in coming here.

What would you think of the 'Philosophy of History' for your Province? If you thought of it, would it be possible for you to come over (not to reside, but) to give two courses of lectures a year? In this way, you might feel your ground. I fear the emolument would be very little at first. Say the course was one of 10 Lectures, and we paid your expenses of journey, and gave you £50 a course, this would be no more than the rate of paying an (Oxford) University Sermon. Perhaps you will tell me it is impossible for you to prepare lectures at all with your present occupation. I shall be very sorry, if you say so. If you wanted a year to get together preliminary matter, which afterwards you might work up, I suppose we could easily let you have it.

As you know the resident Professors are, as matters stand, placed at no more than £300 year pay, but when the system was commenced and able men in possession as non-resident Lecturers, and the time came for changing into the normal state of things, say three years hence, it would be difficult to resist their representation that £300 was insufficient.

I propose to be in Town shortly, and, in the meantime you can think over what I have said.[1] I go to Birmingham some day next week.

Ever yours most sincerely in Xt
John H Newman of the Oratory

P.S.   I wrote this in anticipation. I am only *just* in possession, 3 o'clock Sunday.

[1] Newman noted in his University Journal for 6 June that Allies accepted the Lectureship in the Philosophy of History.

FRIDAY 19 MAY 1854 dined in Harcourt Street
SATURDAY 20 MAY dined with Mr J O Ferrall to meet Mr O Reilly and Mr Errington

TO J. D. DALGAIRNS

Saturday [20 May 1854]

My dear Bernard

Your letter has just come. I think it would be civil to go for Sunday the 28th to Liverpool, and I have written to Mr Nugent to say you shall.[1]

Bye the bye, I shall ask you to preach at Waterford Rosary Sunday, 1st Sunday in October, for the sisters of mercy.

This is the *third* day the Bishops are sitting — and I hear not a word what they are doing. I fear there are sad disputes, but cannot tell of course.

I have made up my mind I will serve under *no committee* — but what I shall *do*, if they so determine, is not so clear; whether to retire, or to ignore the committee. Most probably the former. But perhaps all my anticipations are groundless[2]

Ever Yrs affly J H N

TO F. A. PALEY

16 Harcourt Street May 20/54

My dear Sir

I trust you will let me take the liberty of writing to you without any other introduction than the momentary sight it was my good fortune of having of you some years ago at Alton Towers.

Perhaps you have heard we are soon to lay the foundations of a Catholic University of the English tongue in this country. Our plan I suppose will be to give the first two years but not more of an under-graduate's course to classical studies, and the age of his coming may be taken to be 16.

I could not hope to get better advice than yours on the books and

---

[1] James Nugent wanted Dalgairns to preach in his church at special services 'for the purpose of asking St Philip to establish the Oratory in Liverpool.'

[2] The Synodal Decrees gave Newman power for the time being to designate professors, their final appointment being reserved to the Bishops, and also the right to appoint other officials. He was subject only to the Bishops. *Campaign*, pp. 88–92.

the subjects of examinations of which this course should consist; and it has struck me you might be willing in a great Catholic work to draw up for us a sort of formal Report, as it might be called, on the subject. I beg you will pardon me if I am abrupt or inconsiderate in making this proposal.

The sort of questions I want answered are, 1. what should be the subjects of entrance examination (in Arts) for a boy of 16? — 2. what the subjects of examination (in Arts) of a boy of 18, for a pass and for honors. 3. what the course of classical studies from 16 to 18. 4 what are the Greek and Latin Grammars and dictionaries to be recommended — the critical help to the classical student, what the editions of those classics which come into the course. What the Latin, and best Greek histories, or historical helps — histories of literature — etc etc — the geographical and chronological works — 5 any other suggestions which you would be kind enough to make —

I dont know whether I need add it will be one object to oppose ourselves to the slovenly mode of reading the classics so common in many quarters, and to require of the student a few books done well rather than many done imperfectly; the object being that of cultivating his taste, and imagination, and judgment, rather than giving him a smattering of a great many authors.

Hoping to have a favorable answer to this request

I am etc.[1]

SUNDAY 21 MAY 1854 dined in Harcourt Street for the music Mr J E Pigot called

MONDAY 22 MAY dined with Mr Wolf Flanagan said Mass at the Jesuits' church and breakfasted with them

TUESDAY 23 MAY crossed to England early — went from Rhyl to St Beuno's to see Fr O Reilly and back, getting to Birmingham at 2 A M of Wednesday

TO F. W. FABER

The Oratory Edgbaston Birmingham May 24 [1854]

My dear Fr Wilfrid

I propose leaving this place for London on *Saturday* afternoon — can you give me a bed?

[1] Newman has preserved three long letters in which Paley replied to his request.

I wish to catch the Cardinal — can you tell one of your youths to answer me here *when* he goes out of town. He will tell you himself on Friday. I should get the letter on Saturday morning.

Ever Yrs affly J H N

TO JAMES STEWART

Birmingham May 24/54

My dear Mr Stewart

At last I am set off, but we shall not really open till after Christmas; when I shall want you.

I write in a great hurry. I don't know what I have to tell you, except that I am to be installed on Whit Sunday.[1]

Very truly Yours John H Newman

THURSDAY 25 MAY 1854 Ascension I gave Vespers

FRIDAY 26 MAY I sang High Mass. Mr Jeffreys preached.

SATURDAY 27 MAY went to Brompton to Oratory F Bernard went to Liverpool to Mr Nugent's and thence to Kingstown.

TO ARCHBISHOP CULLEN

Birmingham. May 27/54

My dear Lord,

It would be a great favor, if you let me have the *resolutions* of the Synodal Meeting, that I may compare them with what I am inserting about it in my Gazette. But perhaps this is impossible till they return confirmed from Rome.[2]

At all events will you kindly cast your eye over *what I am printing* on the subject. It shall be sent to you in type — and Mr Scratton (of Constantine Lodge, top of Northumberland Avenue, Kingstown) will call on your Grace on Friday morning next to receive your remarks upon it. It must be ready for press *next day* — so that I am sorry to

---

[1] Stewart had heard of the Bishops' meeting and wrote to ask when he would be wanted.

[2] Cullen replied on 30 May that the resolutions adopted by the Bishops, too long to copy, were, with only verbal changes, those corrected by Newman and Dr Moriarty. They were not to be published until approved by the Holy See. See *Campaign*, pp. 88–92.

have the chance of incommoding you with a request which may be unseasonable — but I hope not.[1] I am going to London today, and shall see the Cardinal and some of my legal friends tomorrow

    Begging your Grace's blessing, I am, Yr affte Friend & Servt in Xt
                    John H Newman of the Oratory

The Most Revd Dr Cullen

SUNDAY 28 MAY 1854 called on the Cardinal — on Scott just converted.[2] rain Monsell called dined with Hope Scott to meet Badeley and Manning

MONDAY 29 MAY called on Manning Allies hard rain F Robert went to St Leonards?

TUESDAY 30 MAY breakfasted with Mrs Bowden

WEDNESDAY 31 MAY went off to St Edmund's where lunched thence to the Great Northern sleeping at York

THURSDAY 1 JUNE thence to Ushaw where Dr Newsham took me out to their country place for dinner

FRIDAY 2 JUNE went off mid day from Ushaw to Holyhead by Manchester and Chester F Bernard crossed back from Kingstown to Birmingham

SATURDAY 3 JUNE arrived in Dublin 7 A M in time to say Mass

TO JOSEPH DIXON, ARCHBISHOP OF ARMAGH

                      June 3. 1854 16 Harcourt Street
My dear Lord

    I do not quite understand why your Grace's letter was not forwarded to me in England. I am just returned, and find it on my table, and write at once to acknowledge it.

    Of course it pleases me to be let off — And I feel quite sure that

---

[1] Cullen suggested some changes in the proof and on 30 May, wrote to emphasize the need to 'be cautious not to publish any thing that might be interpreted in a wrong sense.' The first number of the *Catholic University Gazette* was dated 1 June 1854. It described the Synodal meeting of the Bishops, who 'after recording their past nomination, made by means of the University Committee, and already confirmed by his Holiness, of the Very Rev. Dr. Newman, Priest of the Oratory of St. Philip Neri, to the office of Rector, proceeded to commit to him the execution of the great work which it will be, in years to come, the glory of their Lordship's time to have designed . . .

They then proceeded to the selection of the Vice-Rector, which they made in favour of the Very Rev. Dr. Leahy, President of the College of Thurles . . .'

This number contained the essay now to be found in *H.S.* III, pp. 1–5.

[2] W. H. Scott of Trinity College, Oxford, having heard Newman was to be in London, wrote to ask to see him.

Miss Richardson knows the state of things better than her good Priest.[1]

Begging your Grace's blessing, I am, Your faithful & affte Servt in Xt

John H Newman of the Oratory

The Most Revd the Archbp of Armagh

P.S.   I have been to St. Beuno's, to Birmingham, to London, to St Edmund's College, Ware, and to Ushaw — and have found satisfaction and encouragement every where, on the commencement we are making with the University.

TO AMBROSE ST JOHN

⌐16 Harcourt Street June 3. 1854⌐

My dear Ambrose

⌐This is the Anniversary of our first Mass. I returned this morning — having been travelling, walking or talking since 8 o'clock A.M. on Wednesday. I hope I shall not go to sleep tomorrow in the High Mass or at the Archbishop's Sermon. Monday and Tuesday in London were frightful days for rain — else, I have had beautiful weather — especially in my journey, part of it, in an open carriage, from St Edmund to St Cuthbert.[2] Lord John (?) Kerr at Ushaw is one of the nicest little boys I ever saw — he came into my bedroom laughing with all his might with William Manning, and did not cease to wriggle about, and distort his face all the time he was in it.⌐ Dont tell his brother so.[3] ⌐The said William was so impatient to see me, ⟨he was a child at St Leonard's in 1844–5 when last I saw him⟩ that, after two attempts in the evening, he came into my room in the morning when I was half dressed, and I had to turn him away — and then he served my mass. After breakfast he showed me his relics.[4] In St Joseph's chapel they have St Philip and

[1] Cf. letter of 4 March 1852 to Cullen, asking him to provide a confessor for this recently converted Protestant lady, who lived near Armagh.

[2] i.e. from the College of St Edmund, Ware, to that of St Cuthbert, Ushaw.

[3] Lord John Kerr, born 24 April 1841, became a Catholic at the same time as his brother Lord Ralph, in Jan. 1854, and, when the latter went to the Oratory at Birmingham, John was sent to Ushaw. Everyone found him a most attractive child. See Newman's letter of 26 Jan. 1855 to Lady Lothian condoling at his death two days earlier, and *Cecil Marchioness of Lothian*, edited by Cecil Kerr, pp. 144–7.

[4] William Henry Manning (1837?–79), a nephew of H. E. Manning, was the second son of Charles Manning who became a Catholic with his family in 1852. William later joined his uncle's Oblates of St Charles, and was the first Rector of St Charles's College at Bayswater.

St Aloysius side by side in stained glass⌐ by Hardman. He came to see our picture to do it *well*. ⌐The face of St Aloysius is very nice — St Philip is the sourest looking ghost I ever cast eyes on. It would frighten any boy to look on it.⌐ The structures are magnificent. ⌐I was struck with the Exhibition Hall, and thought, as I could fairly praise it con amore, I would do so for Pugin's sake — alas! it was the only work, which was not Pugin's, but Joseph Hansom's.⌐ So, alas at Liverpool, in the Jesuit's church, the only glass I did not like turned out to be Hardman's. I have had a successful expedition, I trust.

The difficulty about a Cottage at Dublin is, that the summer is *just the time* I expect to be able to come to Edgebaston — the only time.[1]

⌐As to Frederic, if he had spoken but a word to me, he might have set things right.[2] It is as you say, elsewhere I am received as a prince — They received me with Canticles at St Edmund's — they threw bouquets into the carriage, and followed me shouting like Bacchanals, as I left Ushaw. At Brompton the Fr Minister and a Brother watch my motions.⌐ I do not want this at home — but really I may ask at least not to be *molested*. I come back here — I had given the same charge about my sheets — there they are as they were — Had I knocked in at 11 last night, I could have gone to bed as usual. ⌐I will bear the soot, dust, and neglect — if⌐ I am let alone

Ever Yrs affly J H N

P.S.   I shall send the copies of my Gazette to the *Oratory*, not to any publishers at Birmingham, and Maher etc may receive any number they want *on payment beforehand*. I do *not* send them to *give away*. I can't afford it.

I am glad about Robert.[3]

WHIT SUNDAY 4 JUNE 1854   installation as Rector of the University *in Cathedral by Dr Cullen*   took the oath to Pope Pius's Creed[4]

[1] Newman had offered to pay half the expense of a furnished cottage at which the Oratorians would take holidays in turns. St John wrote 'We are all agreed that nothing would be so jolly,' and suggested Dalkey or Killiney near Dublin.

[2] The laybrother, Frederic (Thomas Godwin), was downcast because of his neglect of Newman during the latter's stay at Edgbaston. St John in his letter of 2 June contrasted the attentive brother who looked after Newman when he visited the London Oratory, 'with the soot, dust and forgetfulness you meet with from us. . . .' See letter of 11 June to Godwin.

[3] Tillotson's health had improved during a stay at St Leonards.

[4] i.e. The *Professio fidei Tridentinae*, imposed by Pius IV on holders of ecclesiastical offices.

TO AMBROSE ST JOHN

⌐In fest Pentecost. [[4 June]] 1854⌐

My dear Ambrose

⌐I have just got home after the ceremony; H.W. [Wilberforce] is sitting by me reading Gazette Numbers 1 and 2. The church was more crowded than ever known. The Archbishop ended with a very touching address to me.[1] How I am to continue in Birmingham (entre nous) turns my head.⌐

Ever Yrs J H N

MONDAY 5 JUNE 1854   dined with H W [Wilberforce]

TO SIR JOHN ACTON

Monday in Pentecost. June 5/54 16 Harcourt Street, Dublin

My dear Sir John,

I hope you will allow me to write to you without more introduction than that of having seen you at Oscott, and of your having shown interest in our University in a letter you wrote to Mr Badeley.[2]

It is a great disappointment to us that Dr Döllinger cannot give us at least his name — but it cannot be helped.[3] I now write first to ask you to let me put down your name on the University Books — This involves nothing at all except your goodwill to an Institution which the Church has sanctioned and which is now commenced, since I took the oaths yesterday, the feast of Pentecost.

[1] This sermon was summarised in the *Catholic University Gazette* for 15 June; reprinted in Peadar Mac Suibne, *Paul Cullen and his Contemporaries*, Naas 1962, II, pp. 163–5. Cf. *McGrath*, p. 314.

[2] Newman first met Acton when the latter was a boy at Oscott in 1845. He was now studying under Döllinger at Munich, and had just written at great length to Badeley, urging that Brownson should be invited to lecture at Dublin, not on Geography, but 'on philosophy or the philosophy of history.' Acton had seen much of Brownson the previous year in America, and now learned through the latter's son, who was at Munich, that the chief obstacle to his lecturing in Dublin was the subject that had been proposed to him. See letter of 6 June to Brownson. Cf. diary 25 May 1851.

[3] Döllinger not having replied to the letter of 15 Dec. 1853 inviting him to lecture at Dublin, Newman asked Badeley to try to obtain an answer through Acton. For Döllinger's own reply on 15 July, giving his name only, see the letter of 18 Aug. to him.

I also wish to be allowed to enter on the books in like manner the names of Dr *Döllinger*, Dr *Windishman* (I know I do not spell his name rightly) and Dr *Phillipps*; and should be much obliged to you to obtain them for me.[1] Mr Hope Scott and Mr Badeley in London are going soon to send me a number of London names, such as Lord Arundel and Surrey etc etc. Excuse this abrupt letter, which is rendered, more so than it might have been by the various letters to friends, which I have to write at this time

Pray give my best respects to Dr Dollinger and believe me My dear Sir John Very truly Yours in Xt

John H Newman of the Oratory[2]

Sir John Acton Bart &c &c.

TO GEORGE TALBOT

Monday in Pentecost June 5/54

My dear Mgr Talbot

I write at once thinking the Holy Father will be gratified to know that the University is now begun. Yesterday after High Mass, at which Dr Moriarty, the new Co-adjutor Bishop of Kerry, celebrated, I took the oaths, and then the Archbishop of Dublin preached a very impressive sermon. The Church (at Marlborough Street) was more crowded than it was ever recollected to be.

I have this to tell and no more — but this is a good deal, if dimidium qui coepit habet. We have begun on the most suitable of days, and I trust we shall put ourselves under the patronage of the Sedes Sapentiae — and that St Thomas and St Catherine and other saints who are

---

[1] Acton replied on 15 July, sending the name of Friedrich Heinrich Windischmann (1811–61), orientalist and exegete, who was Vicar General of Munich. George Phillips (1804–72), a learned professor of Canon Law at Vienna, gave his name through Döllinger.

[2] Acton concluded his reply of 15 July, 'I am deeply sensible of the honour of being thought worthy to bear a part in so good a work [as the University]. I hope you have forgiven my presumptuous interference in the matter of Dr Brownson. I was impelled by my great friendship for him and by the certainty I felt that a visit to Dublin would be of great service to him and would also greatly increase his usefulness in Europe.

The opening you have given me towards making your acquaintance, which has long been my most earnest wish, I shall not readily lose sight of, and I trust you will allow me to make use of it hereafter in order frequently to consult you and speak to you, always with the greatest confidence and respect on my own plans and proceedings.'

patrons of learning, will help us — and that St Philip will not refuse to bless us.

Zealous friends in England and Ireland are putting their names on our books. I want *yours*, and the sooner the better. It involves nothing beyond giving your name. I want also those of FF. *Perrone* and *Passaglia* — F *Bresciani* — F. *Modena* — F. *Salua* — F *Theiner* — F *Benigno* (of S Francesco a Ripa, if he is alive) — You see I have selected those whom I knew *personally* and can seem to be paying a *personal* attention to — for, if I took any other rule, I should not know where to stop. Is it giving you too much trouble, to ask you to get these names? I dare say some other friend of mine at Rome would relieve you, of good part of it — and would explain that the fear of giving the expence of postage hinders me writing separate letters. I would ask for the names of Mgr *Hohenlohe* and Mgr *Barnabò*, if they would not think the request a liberty.[1]

Dr Cullen has been writing to stop the reported sale of some MSS at St Isidore's to Trinity College, Dublin — which we wish to make use of ourselves — just in time![2]

The Cardinal is going to write to his Holiness to get a formal leave of absence from the Oratory for so many months every year — lest my absence should be a *precedent*

I am beginning a *weekly University Gazette*. I wish there was some way of getting it to you — if I could, it would keep his Holiness in continual information how we were going on. I shall inquire whether it is possible to do so

Ever Yrs most sincerely in Xt   John H Newman

To the Very Revd Mgr Talbot &c &c.

[1] For all these except Modena and Sallua see Volumes XI and XII. Vincent Modena and Vincent Leo Sallua were two Roman Dominicans, members of the Holy Office. Talbot promised to secure all these names and they appear in the published list, with the exception of those of Fra Benigno, who had perhaps left Rome, and of Alessandro Barnabò.

[2] Eugene O'Curry had already spoken to Newman about these manuscripts at the Irish Franciscan church in Rome. See note to diary for 19 March. On 28 May, John Edward Pigot wrote to Newman the report that negotiations had actually been opened in Rome for the purchase of the manuscripts by Trinity College, Dublin. Newman must at once have asked Cullen to intervene at Rome. See also letters of 8 Oct. 1854 to Cullen, and 30 June 1856 to Talbot, and the letter to Pius IX printed after it. Newman tried to obtain the manuscripts, when he was in Rome in Jan. 1856. *Campaign*, p. 300. They were transferred from St Isidore's to the convent of the Friars Minor, Merchant's Quay, Dublin, in 1872, and are now at the Franciscan House of Celtic Studies and Historical Research, Killiney.

TO BISHOP ULLATHORNE

16 Harcourt Street Dublin June 5. 1854

My dear Lord,

Yesterday, the day of Pentecost, I was admitted to my office. I took the oaths after High Mass, and the Archbishop preached. I lose no time in conveying to you this information.

I wish very much that you would let me set down your name in our University books. This involves neither trouble nor expence. We hope to get the name of all Irish, English, Scotch, and American Bishops.[1]

Excuse this short note, & give me your blessing, and believe me to be, my dear Lord, Your Lordship's affte & faithful friend & servt

John H Newman of the Oratory

The Rt Revd The Bishop of Birmingham

TO CARDINAL WISEMAN

16 Harcourt Street June 5. 1854

My dear Lord Cardinal

We are at length set off. I took the oaths yesterday after High Mass, and Dr Cullen preached. I have written to Rome that his Holiness may have the intelligence.

What I wish your Eminence to be kind enough to get me from the Pope, is a permission such as is implied in the following:—

'The Very Revd J H N. Father Superior of the Birmingham Oratory, provolutus etc. begs that, in order that he may undertake the charge of the new University of Ireland, he may receive such a *license for absenting himself*, from his Congregation for the next (3?) years, as will at once save him from *undutifulness to St Philip*, and prevent his case from *becoming a precedent for others*. And he further begs that the permission asked may extend to *seven months* in each year.' I do not

---

[1] Ullathorne replied on 8 June giving his name for the University, and, after fervent accounts of his visits to La Salette and the Curé d'Ars, added, 'One of the first questions I asked on reaching England was about your consecration. But I have not yet heard of the when and the where.'

know how it should be drawn up, but I hope you will excuse its informality, and put it in the right shape.[1]

Excuse this trouble, My dear Lord Cardinal, and give me your blessing, and believe me to be, Your Eminence's faithful & affectionate friend in Xt

John H Newman of the Oratory

His Eminence The Cardinal Wiseman

TO ORESTES BROWNSON

16 Harcourt Street Dublin June 6. 1854

My dear Sir

I thank you very much for your kind letter, which I received a few days ago.[2] As to what you say about myself, I deeply feel, that this is a day above all others in which the children of Holy Church need to be united, and bear upon her enemies with their entire and concurrent

[1] On 20 Dec. 1854 Wiseman presented a petition drawn up in his own hand to Pius IX, who wrote at the bottom of it the date and that he granted the desired permission:

'Alla Santità di N.S. Pio P.P. IX

Beatissimo Padre

Il P. Giovanni Enrico Newman prostrato ai Sagri Piedi, umilmente supplica la Santità Vostra nel sequente caso—

Come è ben noto alla Santità Vostra, egli sostiene un doppio incarico, cioè di Superiore dell'Oratorio dei Padri Filippini a Birmingham in Inghilterra, e di Rettore della novella Università di Dublino. Siccome questa seconda incombenza richiede la sua assistenza personale, ed è incompatibile con una residenza non interrotta nella sua Casa a Birmingham, quindi per quiete della sua coscienza prega la Santità Vostra di dispensarlo da tale residenza, per alcuni mesi nell'anno, per il termine di tre anni, Che,

Roma 20. Decembre 1854

Concediamo all' Oratore che possa con piena tranquillità di coscenza risiedere in Irlanda per quel tempo che esige il bisogno dell Universita

Pius PP IX.'

[2] To Newman's letter of 15 Dec. 1853, inviting him to lecture in Dublin, Brownson did not reply until 8 May 1854, when he regretfully declined, and said his long delay was caused by inability to decide what answer to return.

Brownson added 'Permit me, Very Rev. Sir, to avail myself of this occasion to express the hope that nothing unpleasant may ever hereafter occur to affection [sic] our personal relations. To yourself personally I have never had any feelings but such as you would approve, and whatever I may have written in connection with your name or that of your friends, it was solely in relation to a theory [i.e. the development of doctrine], which rightly or wrongly I deemed it my duty to oppose. Circumstances have changed since 1844, and I am most anxious that the bonds between English Catholics and American should be drawn as close as possible.'

force. Much more should those be one, who have been so wonderfully brought out, each in his own way, according to the will of Sovereign Love and Power, from darkness to light. If there is one misery greater than another, it is division among Catholics, when their walls are beleaguered by the united powers of darkness. If we have traitors among us, of course let them be duly dealt with — but, in cases where treason is not suspected, let us interpret each other's words in meliorem partem, and aim at cultivating that charity, which 'thinketh no evil.' As for me, these are the sentiments which I have ever felt towards you, and it is a great satisfaction to me, and I feel grateful to you, to find that you reciprocate those sentiments towards me.

Of course it disappointed me that you did not see your way to assist us in the University in the way I pointed out.[1] Theology and Metaphysics will, I suppose, be given by the Bishops to Ecclesiastics. The Philosophy of History is already in the hands of a man of ability and name. It has struck me you would not be disinclined to take the chair of 'the Philosophy of *Religion*;' i.e. of the Evidences of Christianity, or of the Notes of the Church, especially as viewed in reference to the needs of this age. This would open upon you the fields of *logic* and of *history*, in both of which you are so well practised —would not the subject you mention of *civilization* come into it, without going into the subjects of theology or metaphysics, which, as I have said, the Bishops will reserve for ecclesiastics? Again, the mythical theory and its attendant errors are now making their way in these islands — nor are Catholics secure from the infection — any logical or historical attack upon them would be of the greatest service to us. As to politics of the *day*, I suppose it will be our prudence to abstain from so exciting a subject.[2]

[1] Brownson wrote in his letter: 'I feel my own utter disqualification for the duty you would assign me. I have neither the manners nor the learning you have a right to demand in a University lecturer. . . .

On a few topics I could possibly give a passable course of lectures. But I am by no means well versed in Geography . . . The subject I am most familiar with after theology and politics, which you do not want is philosophy, and the only course of lectures I should dare undertake to give in connection with any university would be on philosophy, or the philosophy of history, contrasting the questions of Gentile and Christian civilizations. But I could not give them under the head of Geography.' Cf. letter of 5 June to Acton, and Theodore Maynard, *Orestes Brownson*, New York 1943, pp. 205–208. Maynard says of Newman's invitation that 'It was perhaps the highest and the handsomest tribute that Brownson ever received.'

[2] Brownson replied on 11 July accepting this proposal, on the conditions that the Bishop of Boston approved, and that satisfactory arrangements for the editing of *Brownson's Quarterly Review* could be made. Meanwhile Brownson aroused the anger of the Irish in America, and in the end did not come to Dublin. See letter of 23 Aug. to him.

Excuse this short and unceremonious letter and believe me My dear Sir, with true esteem Very sincerely Yours in Xt

John H Newman of the Oratory

Dr Brownson &c &c.

WEDNESDAY 7 JUNE 1854   dined with H W [Wilberforce]   Lockhart there

TO J. D. DALGAIRNS

16 Harcourt Street June 7/54

My dear Bernard

Your letter came last night, and I have been dreaming about Fr Lans.[1] As Ambrose will tell you, on no point am I more touchy. He is always interfering in our matters. You have burned your fingers, and I don't pity you. I think you broke the confidence of the Congregation, when you spoke to him, and then you were rewarded by his breaking yours. (As I understand that Philip spoke to him *without our leave*, by that act *he* implied that he had ceased to be our subject. Ambrose will tell you about Br Bernard.)[2] Fr Lans would be very glad, if Philip proved a decoy duck. You must write to him, as soon as he writes to you, (which he is sure to do to the effect that he is leaving) that *he must not write to any of the novices* — he is too good a fellow to do so, when you tell him not. If they write to him, you must tell him he can *return a message through you.*

You must at the next Chapter confess, that 'You have without leave spoken of internal matters of the Congregation to a member of a Religious congregation.' And I will send a notice to Fr Ambrose to be promulgated, (in which of course you will not be mentioned.)[3]

If *you* speak of things to strangers, who can be trusted not to do so?

[1] Dalgairns, who had just returned to Birmingham after a visit to Ireland, wrote on 5 June that the Redemptorist Fr Lans at Liverpool insisted on talking to him confidentially about the Oratorian novice Philip Molloy, with whom (unknown to Dalgairns), he had been corresponding about his vocation. 'I made no difficulty of saying to him [Lans] that I thought Philip had no vocation and that I considered the matter virtually, though not formally settled. To my astonishment when I returned here [to Birmingham], Stanislas read me a letter from Philip [who was away] in which he said that Father Lans had written to him (Philip) an account of our conversation. I had all along purposely avoided telling Philip my opinion, as I wanted the decision to come from him; and I cannot help thinking this a breach of confidence on Father Lans's part.'   [2] See letters of 10 and 11 Jan. 1853 to St John.
[3] Letter of 8 June to St John.

However, I have nothing at all on my mind — you have done all you could afterwards, by at once telling me. And it is over — but think with yourself, should I have known any thing about it (I don't mean you would have *concealed* it, but would not have thought of mentioning it, especially as I am out of the way) unless Fr Lans most happily had blabbed to Philip?

It is this *free and easy* way of going on — this want of recognizing the Congregation as a sacred thing, which makes me more than any thing else anxious about the future. There seems an enormous tendency in our subjects to act each for himself, as if [he] were in a lodging house, and to be impatient of control. On the other hand there have been those, and Fr Lans has been the most ancient of them, who have had the indelicacy to try to insinuate themselves between the Congregation and its subjects. What would he say if a Redemptorist novice wrote to me? what would any one of us do under such circumstances? simply refuse to correspond with him without his superior's leave.[1]

I was very much pleased to hear that they thought you looking well here, and pleased, yet sorry, you wished to remain longer. I should have insisted on it, but you *asked* to return by Saturday. I was pleased because it showed the change did you good.

As to Mr Nugent's place,[2] you know last October one of my schemes was to make Liverpool in a certain sense the seat of our Oratorium Parvum — and I urged its easy distance from Birmingham — This was with you and Fr Edward, in the room next mine, while mine was colouring. We cannot now. But I feel deeply the importance of Liverpool. Could you get any persons from Liverpool to come *to us* for our noviciate? if so, we might feel a claim to do something for them at once, in spite of our engagements. Humanly speaking, Birmingham is not our place, but Liverpool and Dublin — I say 'humanly' — for I cannot really believe that a choice made from simple obedience, as ours was, will not in the end, turn out to be best.

Ever Yours most affly J H N

THURSDAY 8 JUNE 1854 dined with Scratton The University Gazette began — 2 numbers published, dating, *however*, from the 1st

[1] See letter of 19 June to Dalgairns for his reply.
[2] i.e. the Catholic Institute, founded by James Nugent, which he hoped would develop into an Oratory. Dalgairns wrote of Liverpool that he 'was immensely struck with the go of the place, and especially with the generosity of the merchants. Many persons are crying out for an Oratory. Mr Nugent is evidently perfectly ready and asked me what was the best way of setting to work.'

TO HENRY BITTLESTON

Harcourt Street June 8. 1854

My dear Henry,

I think the Sacraments will be a very good subject for you — The Catechism of the Council, I think, the best text to go to — but you must avoid any thing which is too much 'ad parochos.'[1]

I fear the subject of Heresiarchs — you will be getting some apocryphal story from St Alfonso's popular works.

I have a great desire that something should be done about a *Scripture* lecture — However, at present Fr Ambrose reads, I think, a chapter of the gospel before his Lecture. If it is dropped, you may do so instead — merely reading it distinctly, and making no remark.

I will not forget little Elinor Bretherton on Corpus Christi in Mass. It surprises and sorrows me to hear you say her life is precarious.[2]

In consequence of your wish, I have sent a Freeman's, giving an account of my Installation — but long as it is, it contains very little. As you suspected, F. Bernard's tale was a mares nest.[3] You will observe the Tablet has as yet taken no notice of our start. I can't tell why not. Perhaps next week will show it was an accident. I believe it *was* — but people here are speculating on the *effects* in Ireland of its keeping silence[4]

Ever Yrs affly John H Newman

P.S.   Let me hear how F Ambrose's sprain goes on. F. Frederic's useful letter has just come. Thank him for it.

TO JOHN STANISLAS FLANAGAN

16 Harcourt Street June 8. 1854

My dear Stanislas

The three sums, amounting to £28. 10. 10 must be paid to Bishop by me, and I should be obliged by your paying him for me. I think the carpeting (£2. 0. 4) high.

[1] Bittleston had written for advice as to the subject of his weekly lectures in church. The Catechism of the Council of Trent is addressed 'ad parochos,' to parish priests.

[2] Elinor Bretherton used to go to confession to Newman. He had dedicated her to our Lady, when her health had been restored after he gave her a relic of St Philip. She was about to make her first communion.

[3] Newman sent a copy of the *Freeman's Journal*. Dalgairns had brought back a story that Cullen was insisting on certain insertions and omissions in the *Catholic University Gazette*.

[4] The *Tablet*, xv (10 June 1854), devoted a leading article and all its p. 366 to Newman's installation.

I think we can accept Mr Jeffries's terms for the Vault — the transaction must be entered in the Register under authority of a *Congregatio Generalis*.[1]

I think it will be a good thing if you take the Sunday Instruction at Smethwick alternate weeks, if you see no difficulty.

Fr Lockhart gives a bad account of the Pope's health — It comes from Talbot. He *did not* hear at Rome that he had the dropsy — but if he *has* the dropsy, his life is not worth many years.

It was told in the North that the poor Middy who lost his legs and life in the Tiger was Wilkinson's brother — but the Papers make him a relation and namesake of the Captain.[2]

Did you see a few weeks ago by the Examinations before Committee in the Papers that Priests *may* say Mass in Workhouses — i.e. that leave will never be refused? I think I am right — Fr Antony would tell you all about it, for he was examined[3]

Ever Yrs affly J H N

TO AMBROSE ST JOHN

[8 June? 1854]

My dear Fr Ambrose,

Will you read out at the next chapter to all our subjects, Fathers and Brothers the two following notices?

Ever Yrs affly J H N

1. The Father wishes that every subject of the Congregation who asks leave of absence from home, should name *the number of days* during which he wishes it to extend, and put up a *notice* to that effect in the Congregation Room.

2. The Father thinks it right to remind every subject of the Congregation that it is never lawful, without distinct leave from Superiors,

[1] The Oratorians were to pay rent for a burial vault in the crypt of St Chad's Cathedral, Birmingham.

[2] John Gifford, a Midshipman on H.M. steam frigate *Tiger*, and a relative of the Captain, lost both his legs when the ship was sunk in the bay of Odessa on 12 May, and died soon after being brought ashore. Thomas William Wilkinson (1825–1909) was a convert at Ushaw, later Bishop of Hexham and Newcastle.

[3] Hutchison's examination was presumably in connection with the Return ordered by the House of Commons on 19 Aug. 1853 of the religious provision made in the workhouses of England and Wales for the poor of each denomination, ordered to be printed 18 July 1854. *Accounts and Papers, 17, Poor: England and Wales. 381.*

Flanagan was chaplain to the Birmingham Workhouse.

to mention any matter which takes place within the Congregation, to any one outside of it.

———————————

You need not post these up, but read them distinctly.

FRIDAY 9 JUNE 1854   went over to Maynooth for the day, where was the Archbishop   Dr Ellis carried me back to Dublin
SATURDAY 10 JUNE   dined with Mr James O Ferrall?
TRINITY SUNDAY 11 JUNE   dined with H W? [Wilberforce]

TO THOMAS GODWIN

16 Harcourt Street June 11/54

My dearest Frederic,

I am very glad to have your letter, and wish, my dear Child, you had spoken to me before I left Birmingham. It is always best to get these things over and off, as soon as possible — and I love you too well not to be pained when they remain unremoved. The only advantage now is, that I can write more distinctly than I could speak.[1]

My dear Frederic, you have a very easy life at the Oratory, and you must not let it do you harm. You have one yoke upon you, and far from me be it to say that it is not in its nature to all of us a severe one. God's grace does all things for us, as He has promised; and those whom He calls to a single life, He enables (blessed be His Name) to lead it in all purity and honesty. This necessity is your yoke, as it is the yoke of all of those around you; and what makes you dear to them, as they to you, is that you and they are all partakers in one and the same calling, and sympathise one with another; that you and they are all sons of St Philip, the most angelic of saints, and are imitators of him, as he of our Lord and Saviour.

This certainly is your yoke, as it is ours by vow — severe in itself, by God's grace light — but, with this exception, (which you see, I am not forgetting,) have you not my dear child, every thing your own way? and is there not the greatest danger that you should *take out* (if I may so speak) the indulgence, which you cannot have in one direction, in *another*? Is there not great danger that you may in other ways get into a careless mode of going on? I look on, in my thoughts, 20 or 30 years, when I am gone, and you all alive — and I try to fancy what you will be then. I think of you in imagination, my dear Frederic, as a

---

[1] See letter of 3 June to St John, and fifth note there.

middle aged man of 40 or 45, and I ask what you will be then, in mind and habits. Depend upon it, it is your wisdom, to ask St Philip to make you more and more his child now — to refashion you — to break up the natural man, to eradicate your natural infirmities and propensities, and to bring you through God's grace into that happy state of mind, that your sole and only thought is to please God and get to heaven.

Now, my dear Frederic, I judge of you by what I see — and that is, for the most part, by what concerns myself — and I certainly do think that there is a great deal whether of indolence or selfindulgence, or something or other in you, which, did I know you better, I could give a truer name to, which needs correcting. And I feel it the more, (naturally,) because it touches me more personally. I think I take pains to give as little trouble in the House, as I can — but I assure you, my dear child, that often I say nothing about things I wish done, and either do them myself, or let them pass undone, because I know I shall not get them done without asking half a dozen times. Did I give ten times the trouble, I should be much better attended to. If you think about it, you would understand, that it is a very great trial to me to leave home — and when, after sending distinct notice I shall return, I come twice and thrice and find nothing ready, what is this, but as if saying to me, that my portion is not here, and that I am a stranger and sojourner upon earth? Well — it is good I should so be reminded, and, please God, it will *turn* to my good — but it is hard, that the lesson should come from those at home. It is hard, that, when I desire as some momentary refuge, to come home, I should be treated as if I were unwelcome. It is hard, that, when I express a wish, and give an order, I may not discharge it from my mind, but must remember to give it three or four times over, with a certainty that, unless I do so, it will not be done. That Cotta of mine hung for 24 hours on my chair, after I had told you to let it go to the wash; and I said to myself 'When will it be taken?' and was on the point of putting it up again, when it vanished. Whether you took it or Charles I know not; but, had you taken it when first I told you, there could have been no mistake. Then either you or Charles, not asking what my *wishes* are, (though I had given them) come and pull my blankets, or my sheets, off my bed, and away with them — letting fresh ones come by chance, when a fair wind blows them in at the windows — with no thought at all, that I am not a school boy, whose room may be pulled about as a house maid pleases, but have a certain right to have a room of my own, and think it quite as strange that you should pull my room about, as you would, did I do the same to yours. And all this, I must say, from a want of real *practical* reverence towards me. And then I think that the time will come, when you will

154

not have me; and will be sorry, that you did not treat me with more consideration.

However, I will say no more — and though I have but imperfectly brought out what I mean, yet you will perhaps make it out fully, when you think over it.[1]

Ever, My dear Frederic, Yours affectionately in Mary & Philip
John H Newman of the Oratory

P.S. I don't like to interfere with Fr Ambrose, in the question about your going away.

TO MANUEL JOHNSON

16 Harcourt Street Dublin June 11. 1854
My dear Observer,

Thank you for your valuable letter.[2] I will explain myself more fully, and you will see whether it modifies what you have said.

Nothing is done well, which is not done slowly, and with feeling your way, unless you have success in your power. Hence, as regards the University *itself*, I am going as slowly as possible; but, if any particular department was really practicable *beyond doubt*, I would put it into shape at once.

I will tell you why. For reasons, which it would take long to explain, it is desirable to make a *show* — though it is *impossible* that the *real growth* of the University can be but *slow*. It has struck me then to set up certain institutions or schools which will have their worth in themselves, and will command respect, while the real University, (i.e. the bodies and minds of its constituents,) is growing in number and in intellect under their shadow. Such institutions are, a medical school, a school of the useful or industrial sciences, an archaeological department with a Press; and, in like manner, an *Observatory*.

If then I was sure of a really good Observer, who would set to work from a real love of the science, I would *call* him an Observer from the first. For the look of the thing, and to prove *what* he could do with *little* means, I should not set him up with £20,000 worth of instruments all at once — but I would give him a telescope, and let him *print* his

[1] St John wrote on 14 June, 'Frederic has picked up since your letter, though he wants a great deal to set him up. He has been down a long time. . . . His own account of himself is rather sad. . . . He has no energy or heart for any thing. . . . I find him of little or no use for work.'

[2] Johnson wrote on 29 May suggesting that Newman should begin his Observatory in a small way, with a telescope costing £100.

observations. If he nourished his beard, smoked, and talked broken English, so much the better, if he was a clever fellow and a good (respectable) Catholic. If then you thought by turning your glass towards Paris, Spain, Italy, or Germany, you thought you could find such a star, who would come to us with the kind of testimonials which a friend of mine once showed to Sir Robert Peel,[1] I think I could appoint him sine periculo (and given him enough to maintain his family). But he must not be one of your French Red republicans or Socialists. He must be a man who would do us credit at home and abroad.

Now you have my *idea* — and you are free to tell me that it won't do — if you think it won't — but this is why I *wish* it, if possible.

Of course all this is in confidence. I was so sorry to miss your wife and her sister. Say every thing kind from me to them Ever Yrs very affectly

John H Newman

M. Johnson Esqr

TO ARCHBISHOP CULLEN

Monday June 12/54

Private

My dear Lord

Though this is not Saturday, I come to your Grace, for time presses.

I got leave to mention the matter of the Medical School to Dr Leahy, Surgeon O'Reilly, Mr Myles O Reilly, and Mr James O'Ferrall, besides yourself — and have seen and talked with them every one. I think we are all of opinion, that (subject to the Title deeds being made good, the place pronounced in good repair, etc etc.) it will be good to buy the medical school — going as far as £1500 for it, if we can give no less. From circumstances I need not go into, we must buy at once or not at all.[2]

When I say we *can* buy; I mean, if all the proprietors can be induced to sell — which can only be done, by keeping the matter very quiet.

---

[1] i.e. Johnson himself.

[2] Newman learned from Dr Ellis on 11 June that the house in Cecilia Street, which had been opened as a Medical School in 1837, by a group of members of the Dublin Apothecaries' Hall, was about to be sold, two of its ablest professors having left. It was necessary to keep the identity of the purchasers secret until the sale was effected later in the summer. The School became one of the permanent successes of the University. It was the first Catholic Medical School in Dublin, where, in 1854, as Newman calculated, 'out of one hundred and eleven Medical Practitioners in situations of trust and authority, twelve are Catholic, and ninety-nine Protestant.' *Campaign*, p. 65.

The house in Cecilia Street also put the 'Medical Faculty in a bodily, visible shape before the Dublin public.' *Op. cit.* pp. 64–7 and 295–7; *McGrath*, pp. 327–9.

Unless then I hear any thing from your Grace to the contrary, I shall proceed to make an offer.

I would add that the Funds being up just now, it would be a good time to *sell out* Stock to the amount of £1500 whether we wanted it or not. Even if we bought in again, we are sure to gain by the transaction, for they will fall again. They were touching 94 — now at 91. They have been at 87

        Ever Yours affectly and obediently John H Newman
The Archbp of Dublin

P.S.   If you decide on selling out, will you tell me how to proceed? — whom should I write to?

TUESDAY 13 JUNE 1854   H W went to England?

TO JOHN MACHALE, ARCHBISHOP OF TUAM

                 16 Harcourt Street, Dublin, June 13, 1854.
My Dear Lord
    I want to ask your Grace's permission to enter your name on the University Books. This permission will neither involve trouble nor expense to you. And, if you do not see any objection, while to us it will be a great gain, to you it will be no loss.

Also, I am about to make a request, which I should not have ventured upon, unless Dr Leahy had encouraged me to hope I might succeed. I am making a list of University preachers, — and I hope your Grace will condescend to be one of them. It will not involve more than one sermon in the year, which, I trust, would be possible. If so, here again we shall be the gainers, while you are not the sufferer.

There is a still further request which I now lay before you. I want to have your countenance and aid in obtaining *students*. Bishops, indeed, have their own work, and it is pretty commonly sufficient to occupy them; but it might so happen that, without effort, opportunities might fall in your way which might turn to our advantage.

Begging your Grace's blessing, I am, my dear Lord Archbishop, Your faithful servant in Christ,
               John H. Newman, of the Oratory.[1]

The Most Reverend The Archbishop of Tuam.

[1] MacHale replied on 16 June, '. . . you have my cordial permission to enter my name in the University books.

As to preachers, you cannot fail in securing a sufficient number of persons qualified

TO H. E. MANNING

16 Harcourt Street Dublin June 13. 1854

My dear Manning

I wish to write a great many letters, but am so cold, neither my brain nor my fingers will work. But here I am left as I thought I should be — Hope and Badeley undertook what I knew they had not time for — but they undertook it, and I am left in the lurch.

Now it will be the greatest service to me, if (without saying a word to them *from me*, which I should not like) you could get me some of the following names by Sunday morning (i.e. Sunday's i.e. Monday morning's post *here*).[1] I suppose the letter must leave town by 5 P M on Friday. viz

Honbl T. Stonor,	Bowyer
Lord Cambden [sic],	Lord Lovat
Lord Arundel and Surrey	Lord Stafford
Lord Arundell	Lord Vaux of Harroden [sic]
Lord E Howard	Lord Dormer
Lord Kenmare	Sir John Simeon
Lord Castlerosse	Mr Maxwell of Everingham
Bellasis	Lord Fingall

I do not know *who* is in London — *any* Catholic nobleman or gentleman, of good name, will do — the more the better.

If I once am able to print a dozen good names, I will collect the rest myself.

Every thing is going on as well as it can do — but we want names.

Any names you can get me of *students*, even if they *cannot come for a year or two, so that* at present their friends bonâ fide intend to send them, would be a great gain.

As to the above names of noblemen etc., they will be simply names

for the task in your own vicinity: our feeble efforts we ought to reserve for our own poor people.

Although I cannot promise many students from this quarter for some time at least; I shall not be wanting in taking an interest in the Catholic University, and I trust that its management will earn the confidence and support of the Catholics of Ireland.'

[1] Manning had written on 12 June offering to get names for the University. Of the list in this letter, the following did not give their names: Lord Arundell of Wardour (although his son did so), Lord Edward Howard (later Lord Howard of Glossop), the Earl of Kenmare, Viscount Castlerosse (son of the Earl of Kenmare), Lord Lovat, Lord Vaux of Harrowden, Lord Dormer, and the Earl of Fingall. See also letter of 19 June to Bishop Grant.

on our books. I mean the owners of them will have no trouble or expence

Ever Yours affly in Xt   J H N

P.S.   I consider I have *got your* name.

TO A. LISLE PHILLIPPS

16 Harcourt Street, Dublin June 13. 1854.

My dear Mr Phillipps,

I wish you to do us the favor of allowing us to place your name on the books (or as Cambridge men call them, the boards) of our University. It will involve neither trouble nor expense — for us it would be an honor.

And if among your Catholic friends, you know any parents who intend to send their sons to us, I should be much obliged to hear of them. Their sending them, of course would not *bind* them to send them. All that is wanted, is a real intention *now*. We should not *print* the names, but they would be added into the total of expected students.

With my best regards to Mrs Phillipps believe me, My dear Mr Phillipps Very sincerely Yours in Xt

John H Newman of the Oratory

A. Phillipps Esqr

TO HENRY WILBERFORCE

⌐June 13/54

Charissime,

I have certainly thought you were trifling with the University for some time, and I have said to people 'O he will never take part in it.' And now I don't think you would wish it, except you see it begun — did the Bishops not meet till next month, and were things now in the unsettled state they were in April, you would still be shilly shallying. I have under date of April 22 this entry — 'It seems to me that H W is simply putting aside the notion of being one of the four Tutors — and I told him so, as once before — and he seemed to assent — nay [[the notion]] of assisting me at all.'[1]

[1] Newman quotes here from his University Journal. Cf. letter of 11 Feb. to St John, third note.

And now you still are going on on your shilly shally way. I have offered you a *Professorship* and you won't say whether you will take it or not. It is true that at present it is £50 under a Tutorship ⟨[[£200]]⟩ — but, if the University prospers, it will increase — and if it does not prosper, the Tutorships will go too.

From the first you have taken up the whole matter in quite a different way from Thompson or Stewart. *They* have thrown themselves into it with enthusiasm. But I have long said to Ambrose, 'H W never comes into any of my plans, much as he loves me.' Never since the famous Hampden pamphlet, I think, have you done so.[1] Perhaps you [[had]] enough of it then (and perhaps you might fairly think so — as I have often reproached myself) — You would not read Number 90 before it came out; and, did my memory serve, I could mention half a hundred similar things. But I only say this, to justify myself, in despairing you would help me now. And I repeat it, as I have written to you within the half year, I *don't wish* you to do so, merely *because* I ask you; — unless you do it con amore, I don't want you to do it at all.⌐[2]

I wish, please, you would write to young Mr Langdale, and ask him for me to allow me to put his name on our books. It involves no responsibility or expence[3]

Ever Yours affectly, very, J H N.

THURSDAY 15 JUNE 1854 Corpus Christi went down to All hallows for the Procession, and dined there

TO F. S. BOWLES

Allhallows. June 15/54

My dear F Frederic

I have come here for the Procession, and am employing myself in writing letters.

[1] In the controversy with R. D. Hampden over the admission of Dissenters to Oxford, H. Wilberforce wrote a famous anonymous pamphlet *The Foundations of the Faith assailed in Oxford*, London 1835. See Meriol Trevor, *Newman the Pillar of the Cloud*, London 1962, pp. 173–5.
[2] Letter of 23 Nov. 1853.
[3] *Old* Mr Charles Langdale gave his name, but not his son Charles, who was important because he had married an Irish wife, Henrietta, eldest daughter of Henry Grattan of Celbridge Abbey, Co. Kildare.

Thank you for yours, and for the information it contains — I hardly know how to get an opinion of the *worth* of the convert professor, but must try.[1]

I was lately told, it came indirectly from the Cardinal, that they were waiting at Rome till the University actually began, before they sent me my brief. Whether they will consider the inauguration enough, I do not know —[2]

What I am most anxious to get is the *names* of candidates for entrance — It does not matter, though they cannot come for a year or two, if they *are* to come — If their friends have a bonâ fide intention of sending them, it is enough, though they should change their minds before the time of residence.

I am extremely busy, and do not know how long it will last. As to the Gazette, of course I could write it as well or better at Edgbaston, but I have so many things to *do*, and people to *see*. If I manage to get the medical, engineering, astronomical and physical departments into shape, I may leave with a tolerable conscience.

The Jesuits have refused me Fr Christie[3]

Ever Yrs affly J H N

TO J. M. CAPES

16 Harcourt Street Dublin June 15/54

My dear Capes

Your welcome letter has just arrived. I have long been writing to you, ever since your article on St Alfonso came out. I was very anxious to know what people thought of it — and asked in every direction. Had they agreed with me, I should have asked you to publish it — but the general feeling was that, though *very good as* far as it went, it was not long enough and developed and methodical enough for the purpose.[4]

---

[1] i.e. Morgan William Crofton. See the letter of this day to Johnson.

[2] This refers to the brief for Newma'ns consecration. Manning, who had written on 1 May of his great joy that Newman was to be made a bishop, 'It is the due and fitting end of your long life of work,' wrote again on 12 June, 'On the point affecting yourself I gathered from the C[Cardinal Wiseman] that it was thought right to wait till the University had a formal existence. This I suppose will be accomplished already by this inauguration.' Cf. *A.W.* p. 318 and letter of 7 April 1854 to Hope-Scott.

[3] Wiseman suggested to Newman that the English Jesuit Albany Christie who was at St Beuno's, North Wales, should be appointed Professor of Theology at the University.

[4] See letter of 11 May to Badeley.

I am persuaded something should be published with the author's name to it. Think whether you could make a longish pamphlet of it. If so, I will ask for criticisms in detail.

I agree with you entirely about not frightening the Queen — and shall be very glad to see your article. A third person would write it better than I, even had I time.[1]

If you can circulate my University Gazette do — it only costs a penny. Duffy will send it you for another penny, if you pay a quarter in advantage [sic] (2d × 13) 2/- in stamps.

And if you can get me any *names* to set down for students, you will do me a *great* favor. Their parents are not *pledged* to send them — and they may be coming 2 years hence — but it will be a great thing to say 'We have 25 names, etc etc.'

I wish you could give me a better account of Mrs Capes. Yet God is not forgetful of you, though He tries you so much — you are better, when she is afflicted.

Ever Yrs affectly in Xt   John H Newman of the Oratory

TO MANUEL JOHNSON

16 Harcourt Street June 15. 1854

My dear Johnson

Thank you for your valuable letter.[2]

As to what terms I can offer, you must recollect that Dublin is a much cheaper place, I won't say than London merely, or Oxford, but than any part of England. I know a friend of a friend of mine who lives comfortably with a wife and young family, not a large one, and keeps a gig, for £300 a year. This is truly 'respectable,' as good authorities tell us — but, to be sure, it was before the war taxes. Now this I could offer to a good article, but, in the commencement of the University, I fear not more. Printing of course would be an extra.

I know two persons, who, if they felt willing, and you thought them promising, might be turned into astronomers. One is Penny of Ch Ch [Christ Church], who 20 years back got the mathematical prize

---

[1] This refers to an article in the *Rambler*, (Sept. 1854) pp. 189–209, 'The Queen's Government and the University,' showing that the Catholic University would not encroach upon the State's privileges.

[2] It contained advice as to the choice of an astronomer.

— his age is 39. He is going to help me, as it is — but, being a priest, he might scruple at being turned into a star-gazer.

The other is a convert who was a professor at the Galway Godless. He is a T.C.D. [Trinity College, Dublin] man of perhaps 25 — he took high honours, I believe — he is a mathematician — and still more a physicist.[1]

Would it be possible to send either of these, if they were willing, to learn their trade at some Observatory? What more is necessary to a mathematical head, than the *taste*? and how long would it take them?

Ever Yours affectly John H Newman of the Oratory

M. Johnson Esqr

P.S.   I don't mind the subject being told to persons you can trust. But I should not like it to get round here.

TO AMBROSE ST JOHN

⌈16 Harcourt Street June 15/54

My dearest Ambrose

On my return from the Procession at Allhallows I find your affectionate letter. I quarrel with its length on account of your wrist, and I really do put you under obedience to spare it.

What you say about Frederic makes me melancholy.[2] As to what you say of yourself and me, unsay it — God's ways are unscrutable, but I will not anticipate so great a trial as being separated from you. I generally like to anticipate evil — this I cannot anticipate.[3]

As to Austin, he had better go to Mr Butt's, if he will kindly take him, when Robert returns.[4] Here I think he would be a fish out of water

---

[1] i.e. Morgan William Crofton. Johnson replied on 25 June that the proposed remuneration was 'very handsome,' but that a mathematician would not necessarily make a good astronomer. See also letter of 1 Aug. to Johnson.

[2] See note to letter of 11 June to Godwin.

[3] St John wrote on 14 June, 'I have been with you on every occasion of importance since we were Catholics until this inauguration. . . . *Now*, the separation is realized, our courses will run no more together, who can tell when they will meet again if ever?'

[4] Tillotson was staying for his health with John Butt, the priest at St Leonards, who was a friend of the Oratory.

—⌐ wishing to see me, and I not able to see him — but it is of course his own look out.

⌐I think your plan of a meat safe will do very well — (except I don't like the *small* court — it should be out of the kitchen door.)⌐ I have nothing to send to Miss Giberne but my love. ⌐I think of going over to Howth soon to see it — they say it is as pretty as Killiney and lodgings much cheaper. I know a person who was lodging at a *hotel* there.⌐ It struck me whether some of us might not be there for September and October, except that perhaps they are expensive months. Without *saying all* this, you might quietly pump Stanislas. ⌐If an hotel were even as much as three guineas a week; and we were three there together, we could be 8 weeks there for 70 or 80 £;⌐ which I think would be cheaper than housekeeping and you *would know your* expences. ⌐In this case Frederic might have a turn. I should aim at being at Birmingham from the beginning of July till Assumption, and then at Howth. If I did this, it must not be so done as to seem to *oblige* any one to take his holy day there — which it might easily be made to do, and so defeat its purpose altogether. I can't conceive any thing so miserable as Nicholas or Edward thinking they *must* go there.⌐ Stanislas must *not*, for he has had his holyday. Bernard will have his passage paid by his Waterford trip, and will be a proper person. So will Henry, if his ladies will pay his journey.[1] ⌐If Austin goes [[to Butt's]] now, *he* will be superseded.⌐ Frederic might come. ⌐I asked William once to come to Ireland, and he would *not*. Thus I have made out you, Bernard, Frederic, Henry, Br Frederic — add Laurence, and he might learn cookery even at the Hotel!⌐ (by the bye has Stanislas done any thing in Dublin about it?) Well, 2 beds a week for 8 weeks is 16 among 6 persons or $\frac{16}{6}$ or $2\frac{2}{3}$ a week for each — or giving each brother just a fortnight, then it will be 16 ⟨weeks⟩ – 4 = ⟨weeks⟩12, or $\frac{12}{4}$ i.e. just 3 weeks for each Father. ⌐Mind, I am not excluding Nicholas or Edward or Austin,⌐ but (between ourselves) I think they should pay for themselves. ⌐I am willing to pay (except journeys) for you, Bernard, Henry and the 2 brothers, and for Frederic so far as he cannot pay himself.

I want you to get a wooden rack for my Gazette — let it have 12 openings to put 12 numbers in — and let there be a money box with a slit — let it be put up as quickly as possible in the recreation room — and then any one who came to the door (Maher or other) for any numbers might give his pence to the brother etc who would deposit them in the box,⌐ and take the numbers asked for — and so any of

---

[1] Dalgairns was engaged to preach at Waterford at the beginning of Oct. The Misses Farrant would pay for Bittleston.

you also. If a closet was under it, — this closet would contain all but the last 12 numbers, and form a stand for it.

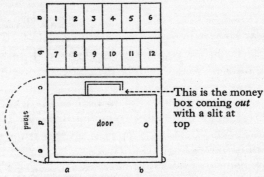

The height of the stand (which has a closet in it) is that of *3* lengths of the Gazette — so that the whole height of the machine is 5 Gazettes — which I have marked on the side a b c d e The breadth is 2 Gazettes, which I have marked a, b. ⟨*I have not allowed for the thickness of the shelves.*⟩ I want it done in a rough way, by a common carpenter — and not *dawdled over*.[1]

Tell Brother Frederick with my love that I think my list of the hymns must be running out, and to let me know.

Ever Yrs affly J H N

TO THOMAS JOSEPH BROWN, BISHOP OF NEWPORT

16. Harcourt St Dublin June 17/54

My dear Lord,

I beg to ask your Lordship's permission to put your name on our University books. It will involve neither trouble nor expense — And we should be very much obliged, if, in like manner, you could obtain for us the names of any noblemen, country gentlemen, or literary men, such names, that is, as would do us service.

Also, if you could send us any students, without putting yourself to inconvenience, we should be very much obliged. Even if a youth did not propose to present himself for a year we should be very glad to have his name.

You may think how arduous and troublesome the commencement is of an undertaking such as we are engaged in — give us your blessing, My dear Lord, and believe me Your faithful Servt in Christ

John H. Newman of the Oratory

The Rt Revd The Bishop of Newport

[1] One sentence of a letter to St John, dated 14 June 1852, which must belong to 1854, has been preserved in a copy: 'It [The *University Gazette*] is selling very well; but how long shall I be able to keep it up? J. H. N.'

TO HENRY WILBERFORCE

16 Harcourt Street June 17/54

My dear Henry

Thank you for your letter just arrived. I never thought of printing the candidates' *names* — only their *number*. I will gladly use Arthur's[1] in this way.

⌐I shall have a good deal to bear in the way of discouragement — and I fear some difficulties from the Bishops. A very little thing casts me down, but of course, I foresaw all this from the first. My Gazette hitherto is succeeding,⌐ Deo Gratias.

Any names, especially of Peers etc. you can get me, will be thankfully received

Ever Yrs affly J H N

SUNDAY 18 JUNE 1854 went down to Kingstown and dined with Ornsby

TO ARCHBISHOP CULLEN

16 Harcourt Street June 18. 1854

My dear Lord,

As you asked me yesterday about one or two points connected with the appointment of officers of the University, I think you will like me to put down on paper what I meant to say in conversation.[2]

I should think it well to limit the period of Professorships at present to *three years*; and to have very few Professors, the greater part of the teachers being Lecturers for the year. Indeed I have ever questioned whether it were well to have at first any Professors *at all*: whether it

---

[1] Henry Wilberforce's eldest surviving son.

[2] Newman noted in his University Journal for 17 June: 'I have just had a long talk with the Archbishop. He wishes me to consult Mgr Vecchiotti on the safety of appointing Sulpician or Louvain Professors; and Mgr Reisach at Munich about any German. He tells me I cannot make any appointments to professorships, without the four Archbishops—on my asking explanations, *he says I may appoint ad interim lecturers for a year*. He seemed nervous about English appointments. I said as to emoluments and influence and power, as to Professorships, they might be [held by] Irishmen—but my own people *about* me, must be those I knew and trusted. Also as to Classics, I must take the *best*—classics were more the English line—besides, the Irish *sent* their children to England as it was, i.e. that class out of whom our students were to come; it would be impolitic to have Irish *Tutors*.' When recopying this entry Newman explained the last word 'i.e. what in Oxford we should call "*Private* Tutors."'

would not be better to call all Lecturers; but on this point I readily yield to your Grace's judgment.

⌐If I were *able* to get Irishmen for the purpose I should always prefer an Irishman to a native of any other country; and I hope the *great majority* of Professors *will* be Irishmen; but I never will recommend an Irishman, or any one else, who in my judgment is not the man for the situation.

In the classical department I feel it more likely that I shall be able to find Englishmen than Irishmen. And in preferring Englishmen I shall carry with me the very class from which we are to get our students, for they so much prefer Englishmen, that they send their children to England.⌐ I am persuaded that to exclude Englishmen from places they *ought* to hold, is not the way to make the University succeed.

⌐For Deans of Residence (or more properly as they should be called, Deans of twenties) I should always take young Irish Priests — except in some extraordinary case as Mr Marshall's.⌐ It is not the case that I ever made him or promised to make him, a Dean — I said, '*If* you collect your 20 youths, you shall be *their* Dean.' But, however, it is scarcely possible that another English Priest *knowing Ireland and the Irish*, (which is his qualification) will occur — So I should say they would be all *Irish*.[1]

June 20. ⌐Lastly, for my own private assistants, to be immediately about me, and to fill places not of great emolument or power or honor, but of work and familiarity, I should take personal friends of my own, Irish or English, as it might happen to be.⌐[2]

I began this letter two days ago — but have been so very busy, that it has remained unfinished

I am, My dear Lord Your Grace's affte friend & Servt in Xt

John H Newman of the Oratory

The Most Revd The Archbp of Dublin

[1] The University Journal for 21 June explains: 'The conversation I had last Saturday ⟨17th⟩ with Dr Cullen makes me somewhat cautious of my appointments, so far as he thought me (I consider) making *English radical* ⟨extreme⟩ appointments. I had said to Marshall "If you get your youths I will get you a house and make you head of it." He has led Dr Kirby to write back from Rome "Dr N. has made Mr Marshall *the* Dean of the University!" Dr Cullen on the 17th said that Marshall must be put aside altogether, which I consented to do—and took Mr Flannery at his suggestion,' i.e. as a dean of residence such as Marshall would have been. On 16 June Newman had said to Flannery exactly what he said to Marshall. Henry Johnson Marshall, one of the Oxford converts, renowned for his girth and wit, was at this time working as a priest in Dublin. See also next letter.

[2] Newman's holograph copy of this letter, as of many others in the Irish University correspondence, was made not from the autograph but from a draft.

P.S.   I have heard from Mr Ellis. He says that the formal decision is to be on Friday.[1] He hopes to succeed 'if (he adds) strict secrecy (with a line under the words) shall be continued.' He evidently thinks I cannot keep a secret. One person (not he) said 'No priest must know, or it will get out.' They say the same in England. It is not the *Roman* way.

TO J. D. DALGAIRNS

16 Harcourt Street Dublin. June 19. 1854

My dear Fr Bernard

I saw Dr Cullen the day before yesterday — and he said that certainly he thought the devotion could be set up without a picture — that was his impression; but I do not think he would say without an Altar.[2]

Your letter was quite satisfactory — I have not answered it, waiting for the above information. I never fancied that *you* did not regard the Congregation as something sacred.[3] But I think one thing has to be said which we none of us perhaps (naturally) recollect — that we ought not to gossip with our London Brothers. Things come round to me sometimes in an odd way. I must take an opportunity of speaking upon this matter.

You must not notice to Molloy what you have found out. It would only lead to irritation, and I dont see would do any good.

Next Thursday I go over to Maynooth to meet the Bishops. I shall have great difficulty in doing things my own way — and every individual Englishman, who helps me, will be grudged — but please God, I *will* do things as I think best — making every allowance consistent with this. But it is a most forlorn thing in a strange country thus to be set up as a mark — for the time will come when I shall have to go through evil report as well as good. Fancy its coming back from Rome, as if on Marshall's authority, that I have made the said Marshall *the* Dean of the University! All that I did was to say that, *if* he brought his 15 or 20 men, I would give them a house for them and him. In consequence, an English job is apparent — and the said Marshall has to turn into the

---

[1] As to the purchase of the Medical School.
[2] Dalgairns wished to erect a confraternity of the Sacred Heart.
[3] Dalgairns on 12 June acknowledged his fault in talking of private Oratorian matters to Fr Lans, and denied any disloyalty. 'I entreat you to have no anxiety on that score. I feel certain that I only live for St Philip. . . . I have felt bitterly the defect of which you speak in the Birmingham Oratory . . .'

outer darkness till things change. People are much annoyed at him certainly, all through Ireland

Ever Yours affly J H N

TO THOMAS GRANT, BISHOP OF SOUTHWARK

16 Harcourt Street Dublin June 19. 1854

My dear Lord

Thank you for all the trouble you have been at — The names you have sent are, with others, printed — and in course of circulation to obtain Irish names. Any others which come in your way would be most acceptable, but a Bishop has something else to do than to go *out* of his way.

Lord Fingall, Lord Kenmare, and Lord Castlerosse, are, I believe, in London. If you see Henry Wilberforce, Manning, or Mr Woodward, perhaps they would be able to get them for me.[1]

Begging your Lordship's blessing, which I need very much, and all the blessings I can get. I am, My dear Lord, Your affectionate friend & servt in Xt

John H Newman of the Oratory

The Rt Revd The Bp of Southwark

TO SIR JOHN SIMEON

16 Harcourt Street Dublin June 19. 1854

My dear Sir John Simeon,

I am very much obliged indeed by your letter and name. The latter will be very useful to me. It is already in print with others — and we shall first circulate the list, with such additional names as come in, among Irish gentlemen — and then publish them in the Irish University Gazette.

It is very difficult to get people to commit themselves here — but I

---

[1] A note by Grant on the autograph shows that he passed it on to H. Wilberforce. On 13 July, Monsell wrote to Newman, 'I applied to Lords Kenmare, Castlerosse and Fingall to give their names to the University and was surprised to find that they objected to do so—

I think their names of great importance and therefore think it would be well for Dr Cullen to write to them.' The names were never given.

trust the English names will decide the matter — as they will not like to be left behind, when the Pope has distinctly settled the matter.

Pray give me some of your prayers and believe me to be, My dear Sir John, Most sincerely Yours in Xt

John H Newman of the Oratory

Sir John Simeon Bart.

TO J. H. WOODWARD

16 Harcourt St Dublin June 19 1854

My dear Mr Woodward,

I thank you very much for the trouble you have been at for us, and also the gentlemen who have given you their names. Already they are in print — I am first circulating them by letters, and then publishing them.

If you, or Serjeant B [Bellasis], or H Wilberforce or anyone else, saw the way to getting me Lord Fingall's name, or Lord Kenmare, or Lord Castlerosse, all of whom are in London, or anyone else especially Irish, I should be very grateful. I don't know whether Lord Gormanstown would give his. — Mr Preston is abroad.[1]

Our great difficulty is making a show at first. There seems no doubt of ultimate success — but we must expect very uphill work. I want as many good prayers as I can possibly get — and I hope you will give me yours.

Very sincerely yours in Xt   John H Newman of the Oratory

J. H. Woodward Esq.

TO JAMES STEWART

16 Harcourt Street, Dublin June 21. 1854

My dear Stewart

Your letter followed me about — and I wrote to you before I received it   I have not been in a position to tell you any thing till now — nor indeed am I now — but I will not delay to write.

In confidence I must say, that we have as yet hardly any names of students given into us — and that is our pressing difficulty. As I said

---

[1] Neither of these gave his name.

in my last letter, there is no chance of our doing anything before Christmas. I have put down in my circular November 3, but this is because, whatever time I mentioned the *real* opening would be later.

I wish I could say any thing to Mr Gainsford's purpose about his boys. Do you mean whether *you* can take them for a *longer time*, or whether he can elsewhere dispose of them? Or does he think of sending them to the University? If so, it would be a great favor, if he would tell us so. Of course we should not print their names, but we should number them in our scanty list.

You may think how it fidgets me to be standing with you in this precarious way. All I can say is, that, directly we have promises enough to enable us to set off, I will let you and Thompson know at once.

We may open our schools in November as we advertised, but then it will be simply externs, and others who have *no* connexion with the University, whom we expect to fill them

Yours very sincerely in Xt   John H Newman of the Oratory

James Stewart Esqr

THURSDAY 22 JUNE 1854   went over to Maynooth, where the Bishops for the annual meeting, and dined there

TO J. D. DALGAIRNS

16 Harcourt Street Thursday June 22 [1854]
My dear F Bernard

As you have *passed the place* where you could modify or explain what you are thought to have implied in re Jesuitarum versus Missionarios Saeculares, I don't think it matters.[1]

You may tell Philip that, on his month being now at end, I consent to his going, and wish him godspeed. Perhaps I shall see him here. Tell Stanislas first, that he is going — and then every one else.

Tell Robert he is a goose for changing with the hour[2]

Ever Yrs affly J H N

[1] A priest from Ushaw had complained of Dalgairns's account of the history of the English devotion to the Sacred Heart at the end of the first chapter of his *The Devotion to the Heart of Jesus*, London 1853, the second edition of which was all but printed.
[2] Tillotson had suddenly decided to return from his health cure at St Leonards.

TO HENRY BITTLESTON

16 Harcourt Street June 23. 1854

My dear Henry

We shall have all sorts of miscarriages in the transmission of the Gazette at first — but its not coming to Edgbaston is unpardonable — already I find stoppages at Limerick and Manchester. As to the Advertisements, the Angel has them — or the Leader — or the Literary *Gazette* — all Gazettes have advertisements. I am glad you like Number 3. I assure you I put out *every* Number as it comes with much anxiety — and in spite of all my care, I expect some day to make some egregious floor. I rather shiver about the Mr Brown and Mr Thomas of Number 4. in which there are two false prints — stopping for stepping — and first class for really good.[1]

Your plan of a Middle School is a very good one,[2] but I am surprised you should not know the whole matter is in Fr Edward's hands — and that he spoke to some one, I think the Bishop, on the subject — Since that, I have heard nothing on the subject, as far as I recollect.

Thank you for your hospital return[3] — I am glad to find, that, bad as it is, it is not quite equal to that [of] my friends the Russians in the Dobruscha, who are catching it where no one thought they would catch it.

I was at Maynooth yesterday to meet the Bishops. The Archbishop of Tuam shook his hand with so violent a cordiality, when I kissed his ring, as to punish my nose. I am in the midst of two grand Operations, as military men say, and of one I expect tidings of success or failure every hour. The other is to come off tomorrow at half past 9.[4]

Ever Yours affly in Xt J H N

TO ARCHBISHOP CULLEN (I)

16 Harcourt Street June 23. [1854]

My dear Lord

I forgot to give you the list of names for the Archbishops. They are as follows:—

[1] Cf. *Idea*, pp. 336–47.

[2] Bittleston writing on 21 June, hoped that this school might 'grow into a good Grammar School, and rival the great King Edward's, and be able to send boys to the University.'

[3] i.e. a humorous account of the ailments of members of the household at the Oratory. The Russians had just been defeated by the Turks at the mouth of the Danube.

[4] The operation of 23 June was the purchase of the Medical School, due to be concluded that day, the other was the list of Professors to be approved.

Ad interim till the meeting of the coetus Episcoporum, (for this I understand is the arrangement) Professors (i.e. really Lecturers)

In dogmatic theology Fr *Edmund O'Reilly* S.J.
In Exegetics   Dr *Leahy*
In Archaeology and Irish language Eugene *Curry* Esqr
In Political Economy John *O Hagan* Esqr
In Philosophy of History T. W. *Allies* Esqr
In Poetry   D. F. *McCarthy* Esqr
In civil engineering   Terence *Flanagan* Esqr
In logic   The Revd Mr *Forest*

The last two I have not spoken to you about, and leave to your discretion to propose — About Mr Forrest I have inquired and thought a good deal — but your Grace knows him so well that no one can decide the question better than yourself.[1]

Mr Flanagan is a very good Catholic, and extremely well known in England as an engineer. He has lately been employed in Belgium, and is now engaged in Portugal. I know him quite well enough to know that he would throw himself into our service with great devotion, if he found himself once in it. I consider, from the inquiries I have made that it will be difficult to get a man like him if we lose him. He is of County Roscommon

Ever Yours affly & obtly in Xt

John H Newman of the Oratory

The Most Revd The Archbp of Dublin

TO ARCHBISHOP CULLEN (II)

16 Harcourt Street June 23/54

(Second)
My dear Lord
Since writing to you just now it strikes me to mention Dr Ford's name with Mr Forest for the Logic *Lectureship*
Will you determine which you think best of the two.

Ever Yours affte and faithful John H Newman

[1] John Forest, a priest of the Dublin diocese who had made his studies in Rome, was a professor at Dr Quinn's school in Harcourt Street. He never became a professor at the Catholic University, and in 1857 he was chosen as the first President of the Catholic College at the University of Sydney, where he remained until his death.

TO CARDINAL WISEMAN

16 Harcourt Street June 25/54

My dear Lord Cardinal

Your Eminence's present is most acceptable, as well as most hand-some — and we shall rejoice to have it.[1] I beg to acknowledge it in the name of the University — It will be a sort of appropriation and recogni-tion, on the part of the Holy Father, of the University House, when the picture is put up there. I wish we heard more of students — here of course will be the pinch for some time — till we get a character.

I took your suggestion, and tried to get Fr Christie — He would have been most useful — but the Fr Provincial would not hear of it. As to Mr Bingley,[2] the difficulty is that there are one or two Chemists of *name* here — who must be thought of, but I have got his testimonials, and shall use him, if I can.

Thank you for your hint about the Pope's exertions in the Univer-sity way.[3] I am about to write to Mgr Talbot in a few days, and will take advantage of it to ask him for the particulars.

Every thing promises for us, as well as it possibly *can* — but things cannot promise *much* at first. It is a great thing that indisposition to the *idea* of a University is slowly giving way, and that men, who have not yet given in their adhesion, wish an excuse for doing so — which is the case

Give us your blessing, My dear Lord Cardinal and believe me to be Your Eminence's faithful & affte friend in Xt and dutiful Servt

John H Newman of the Oratory

His Eminence The Cardinal Wiseman

MONDAY 26 JUNE 1854   dined at Dr Cullen's   went down in morning for the disputatio at All-hallows

[1] This was a portrait of Pius IX, for the *aula maxima* of the University.
[2] A friend of Wiseman.
[3] Wiseman suggested on 23 June that the *Catholic University Gazette* might de-scribe these exertions, 'the establishment of the Seminario Pio at a cost of 500,000 dollars, of the Collegio Pio for British subjects, and his great College, a quasi university at Senigaglia, to which he sent eighteen Jesuit professors at once from Rome.'

TO JAMES STEWART

16 Harcourt Street Dublin Jun 26. 1854.

My dear Mr Stewart

I am starting for Birmingham the first week in July — and cannot tell *where* I shall be on the 5th.[1]

I will let you know when I know myself. Will you drop me a line to Birmingham on the 4th or 5th? I will answer it at once if there. This will be a less journey to you than Dublin.

It is not that we have less prospect or greater prospect of students than before — only that in fact names have not come in. At first sight I am not at all against your going to Dublin; but I will talk with you.

Yours most sincerely in Xt   John H Newman of the Oratory

James Stewart Esq.

TO HENRY BITTLESTON

16 Harcourt Street June 27/54

My dear Henry

Thanks for your very affectionate letter, which came this morning. As to the Middle School, Edward seems a fitter Father than you to take it up, as he has given himself to that line. At the same time he may have done it for the sake of Mr Wilson only, and that failing, does not care to continue the project.[2] By the bye, I wish you would tell him that the Diocese of Kerry wants to set up a middle boarding school at Tralee, a town of many thousand people, I believe. It is just possible that Mr Wilson may think of the Mastership. They would be glad to get him, I suspect.

As to your reference to my Chapter Papers, you must know, that, though when younger I could write off things, now I suppose from declining vigour, I feel it very hard to get up the steam.[3] I am like an

[1] Stewart wished to consult Newman before deciding to take a house in Dublin.

[2] At the beginning of the year Caswall had suggested that Wilson should undertake the Middle School, but Ullathorne 'wished for someone more used to old Catholic ways, etc etc.' (Bittleston to Newman on 25 June).

[3] Bittleston wrote on 25 June of his great regret that Newman no longer sent papers to be read in Chapter, 'they were a real delight, and refreshment, and consolation to us in your absence. . . . It was indeed our own fault that we lost them.' Bittleston added, 'The reading of your dear letters at recreation is a great comfort, and the weekly

old horse, who, when warm, goes well, but stumbles at starting. It has cost me, for instance, a deal of labour to begin the Gazette — now I am in the work — and at present write very fast, am well in advance, and have a great many subjects in petto. Did I leave off for a few weeks, I could do nothing. Now I *had* got up the steam for the Chapter Papers, and I think they would have gone off swimmingly — a number of subjects seemed to open — I hoped it would have been, on the part both of yourselves and me, a constant intercourse of affection — and I thought to myself, that, when I was gone, it would have been a memento after me in the Oratory to have left such a series of papers behind me, interesting both historically, as showing our state, and for their own worth — such as they were. As far as I see, this is quite at an end. How can I get up the steam with my present engagements? and where are the coals and the fire to get it up withal? It was in a simple confidence in the *sympathy* of the *whole* community for me, that I wrote to them. I did not expect, that, hardly would my back be turned, when a *spontaneous* exhibition of a different feeling would take place.[1] You may *tell* me that every one now wishes for the papers — but how am I to realize it? how is a feeling, which hitherto I freely indulged, the grounds for which I took for granted, to be restored? I may speak with the utmost confidence to a or b — but how am I to speak confidently to all together, which is the very thing you ask, when you want a paper for the Chapter?

Ever Yrs affly J H N

P.S.   I think you had better delay the further question of the Middle School, till you see me.

TO THOMAS SCRATTON

Tuesday [27 June? 1854][2]

My dear Scratton

Soon after you went today, I found I wanted to ask you the following question:

excitement of the Gazette is an enjoyment, but the latter is external to the Congregation, and the other too much for individuals to supply at all the place of those addresses in Chapter. There was a certain sacredness about them, and sweet solemnity—and so appropriate . . . as an expression of your common paternal love and care, and a ready vehicle or instrument of paternal admonition and advice. . . .'

[1] See the letters of 17 Feb. and 25 Feb. 1854 to St John and Caswall.

[2] Newman noted in his University Journal for 26 June that Ornsby did not want to be Secretary to the University. The previous autumn Newman had offered Scratton a place as tutor.

What would you say to be appointed Secretary of the University, with the understanding that it would be a *permanence*, and would be a *gradually increasing* salary (with the increase of University business) *though beginning with* a *small* salary? And on this understanding giving up the Tuition?

Ever Yrs J H N

P.S.   If you could answer me at once, I should be obliged.

TO EDWARD BADELEY

16 Harcourt Street Dublin June 28/54

My dear Badeley

It was very kind of you to write, and I did not expect you would do more than you have done.[1] I know it was unreasonable to think of it. We are getting on very fair. I want and hope to bring over the quondam favorers of the Queen's Colleges,   mostly lawyers, and important persons — so I printed and circulated the English names — and they are doing good service.

I had written to Sir John Acton, directing to Döllinger.

I go to England next week, if all is well, for a month.

Ever Yours affectly in Xt   John H Newman of the Oratory

Ed Badeley Esqr

TO F. W. FABER

16 Harcourt Street Dublin June 28. 1854

My dear F Wilfrid

I *lost* the paper of your considerate Fr Felix giving me the name of the St Sulpice author of M Olier's life and disquisition on St Mary Magdalen.[2] I am obliged to ask him for it again. And will you get some one to ask the name of another Sulpician which the *Cardinal* gave me,

---

[1] i.e. getting names of supporters of the University.

[2] Félix Philpin de Rivière, a French priest and novice at the London Oratory, had sent Newman the name of Étienne Michel Faillon (1800–70), who joined the Sulpicians in 1821 and was the author of *Vie de M. Olier*, Two volumes, Paris 1841, 2nd edition 1853. In 1848 he published *Monuments inédits sur l'apostolat de S. Marie Madeleine en Provence*. Wiseman was a great admirer of *Vie de M. Olier*, but Faillon was accused of being anti-Jesuit in some of his writings. See the letter to Mgr Vecchiotti placed at the end of June.

and I wrote down but cannot read. It was La Hue or La Haye or La Hire —[1] Will you get one of your subjects to do me this job, and to direct to me at Birmingham, whither I hope to go on Monday next the 3rd.

We are going on well, but slowly — This is my best time for getting away, but it is a nuisance to go with my beginnings of work half done.

Ever Yours affectly J H N

TO JOHN STANISLAS FLANAGAN

16 Harcourt Street June 28/54

My dear Stanislas

Your letter has just come. As to Denuelle what I said I would pay was £160 If *I* paid the £75, — I owe £85. How much of the rest I owe, especially as regards the Refectory, — I do not know. I will pay all I can. £30 is unnecessarily gone in that glass. *You* must pay it — and we will arrange when I come.

Will you tell Fr Dean to let my room be ready for me by Monday evening next. I can't tell exactly when I shall come. It is *very* difficult to *get away* here.

Unless Robert is already come back, or set off, tell Fr Bernard to write to him to the effect that he may go to the London House for a night, but he is to talk nothing at all about us or our doings — that every thing connected with the house is secret

I am glad you like the Gazette — you should look at the Postmark — Duffy protests he sends it on Thursday evening.

Ever Yours affly J H N

TO JOHN LEAHY

Catholic University House, Stephen's Green, Dublin.
June 28th, 1854.

My dear Fr. Leahy,

Will you kindly allow me to put down your name as one of our University Preachers? We shall not ask more of you than one sermon a year; and our gain will very far exceed your trouble.

---

[1] Arthur Le Hir (1811–68), biblical scholar and orientalist. He joined the Sulpicians in 1833 and was the teacher of Renan.

Not forgetting the pleasant glimpse I had of you at Cork last February,

I am, my dear Fr. Leahy, Very truly yours in Xt.,

John H. Newman, of the Oratory.

The Very Rev. Dr. Leahy.

TO WILLIAM MONSELL

16 Harcourt Street Dublin June 28/54

Confidential

My dear Monsell,

Lord Brougham was in conversation with Serjt Shee the other day and asked whether the new University here wished a Charter from the Government, or what its views were — and whether he in the House should ask Lord Aberdeen a question as to the Government's views on the subject. I suppose it would be apropos of the Oxford Bill; but this may be a misconception.[1]

Our first question is this — would Lord Aberdeen's answer *do us harm* by showing the government was opposed to us — else, even if nothing else came of it, the recognition of us in Parliament as existing, would be valuable.[2]

As to a Charter, I cannot fancy the Government giving one in the present stage of proceedings. If it did, it would, I suppose, impose *an oath of allegiance* — as to which there would be no difficulty, if it were drawn up in the terms of the Oxford oath 'I. A. B do sincerely promise and swear, That I will be faithful, and bear true allegiance to his

[1] Gladstone's Oxford University Bill, introduced in March, received the royal assent in August. Its chief reform was to abolish religious tests for degrees. Lord Aberdeen was Prime Minister 1852–5.

[2] Monsell replied on 30 June, 'I think it would be unwise now to moot in any way the question of a charter.

Until the University exists it will not be recognized.

To recognize it at any time will be unpopular and therefore its recognition will be avoided even by our friends as long as it can be with decency. When it becomes a power, and shows signs of being a permanent one, it will be indecent to ignore it, but not till then.

It would be unwise to commit the Government to hostility towards it. . . .

I do not see the advantage of creating a grievance at this moment.

The Government are in advance of the Country. They wish to do more for us than the Country will allow them to do. It seems to me a great point to make Catholics feel this—to make them realize their actual position in relation to that public opinion which is after all the governor of the country.

It always seems to me that Lord Aberdeen's government goes as near to the wind as it can . . .'

179

Majesty King George' (I quote from my own copy, for I don't know what late changes there may be)

But nothing on earth should make me, for one, take the Maynooth oath, 'that the Pope has neither directly nor indirectly temporal power,' not that I have any view on the subject, but because I haven't; because I won't have my private judgment as a Catholic interfered with; and because I have had quite enough of Number 90s ⟨nineties⟩ without bringing on myself by my own act the necessity of writing a new one[1]

Ever Yrs affly in Xt   John H Newman of the Oratory

Wm Monsell Esqr M P

THURSDAY 29 JUNE 1854   went to Allhallows to dine

TO AUSTIN MILLS

16 Harcourt Street June 29/54

My dearest Austin

I am glad to hear so good an account of you. It was my intention to get off for Edgbaston on Monday — and I may still — but thank God, I am prospering so much in various little plans preliminary to our set off, that I may be kept a day or two longer — but Fr Minister must *expect* me on Monday.

This post brings me a letter from Mr Phillipps as well as you[2]

Ever Yrs affly J H N

P.S.   I was very sorry to hear from Dodsworth of Cardinal Fornari's death.

I said mass for Fr Ambrose on St Peter and St Paul[3]

[1] The Oath of Allegiance laid down in the Catholic Emancipation Act of 1829 included the sentence, 'I do declare that I do not believe that the Pope of Rome, or any other foreign Prince, Prelate, person, state or potentate, hath or ought to have any temporal or civil jurisdiction, power, superiority or pre-eminence, directly or indirectly, within this realm.' This was taken almost verbatim from the form of oath proposed by Bishop Milner and approved by the four Irish Archbishops and six Irish Bishops at a meeting in Maynooth on 26 June 1821. Many Catholics held that the Pope had 'indirect power' in temporal matters, when the good of religion was at stake.

A Bill for the revision of the Catholic oath was before Parliament, but no effective action was taken until the oath was removed in 1866. See also letter of 1 May 1855 to Monsell.

[2] Mills had been staying with Ryder near Phillipps's house in Leicestershire.

[3] This was St John's birthday. Cardinal Fornari, who died on 15 June, was reputed the best theologian among the Cardinals.

TO WILLIAM MONSELL

16 Harcourt Street June 29/54

My dear Monsell

Your letter[1] has just come, or rather I have just come in and find it on my table.

Your consent to give your name rejoices me, and is very apropos. Tomorrow morning I go to Serjeant O Brien with whom and other lawyers I am negociating this fortnight past for their names. His first question, when I first went to him, was 'Have you got Monsell's?'

I don't suppose you will mind my showing your letter to him. He and his friends have already pretty well made up their minds to give me their names, but it would be a comfort to him to know that you give yours. Perhaps he has written to you.

I am, thank God, prospering so much, in various ways, that perhaps I may be kept here a day or two longer. However, as to the Cross, for which many thanks, please send it to Birmingham.[2]

Thank you for your munificent donation. I think you had better give it at the October collection at Limerick. It will be a support to your Bishop — and, in getting your name now, and your money then, we shall get you twice over

Your letter has crossed one of mine to you. Our *great* want of course is *students*, which we anticipated. But we *must set up* before we are able to do any thing in the way of attracting them

Ever Yours affectly in Xt   John H Newman of the Oratory

W Monsell Esqr M P

TO LE COMTE DE MONTALEMBERT

University House. Stephen's Green. Dublin.
June 29. 1854

M. le Comte,

I am emboldened by some friends of mine to address to you this letter. We are at present engaged in this country, in setting up a Catholic University of the English tongue, which it is to be hoped, will be of

---

[1] That of 28 June, giving his name to the University.

[2] Monsell wrote, 'I hope to send your pectoral cross in a few days,' i.e. for Newman, when he became a bishop. Monsell also offered £25 to the University, and promised an annual subscription of £5.

service, not only to Irishmen of the upper and middle class, but to Catholics in England and the United States also. It is a great point to us to have the adhesion of eminent men, and those not only of our own countries, but those on the continent, who are known for their zeal for Religion. Among them what name is so illustrious as that of M. de Montalembert? and whom could we more anxiously wish to show us some countenance?

Might I then ask the honor of entering your name of [sic] the University Books? We have already the names of Lord Arundel and Surrey, Mr Hope Scott, and other leading Catholics of England.[1]

I am M. le Comte, With profound respect, Your humble obedient Servt in Xt

John H. Newman Rector of the University

M le Comte de Montalembert &c &c.

TO THE EARL OF SHREWSBURY

University House, Stephen's Green. Dublin
In fest. Apostol. 1854

My dear Lord Shrewsbury

I feel the kindness of your Lordship's letter, and have had the greatest satisfaction in entering your name, in accordance with your wish, on our Books. It will be interesting, and honorable to the University, in time to come, for a name, so historical in Ireland as well as England, to have had a place in its commencement.[2]

Thank you also for your expressions of sympathy in our work, and the offer of your good offices, in promoting it.[3] It seems to be not impossible that the Government may give us a Charter — but we do not exactly know their intentions. I shall be fortunate, if I am able to secure any person so able as Mr Scott, for our classical department.

Should it be in your power to get us any names of candidates for admission, it will be a very great service.

I beg my respects to Lady Shrewsbury and Miss Talbot — and

[1] Montalembert gave his name.
[2] Lord Shrewsbury was Earl of Waterford in the peerage of Ireland.
[3] Lord Shrewsbury wrote on 18 June from Paris:
'My dear Lord Bishop (elect)
'. . . . I suppose your Lordship intends getting a Charter to confer degrees, and if any influence I possess with the present Government might be of use I put myself entirely at your disposition.
I am very glad that you have so kindly given a Professorship to Mr Scott . . .'

their good prayers, and yours too, My dear Lord, and am Your Lordship's faithful Servant in Xt

John H Newman of the Oratory

The Rt Honble The Earl of Shrewsbury

TO GEORGE TALBOT

University House. Stephen's Green Dublin
In festo Apostolorum 1854

My dear Mgr Talbot,

Dr Cullen wishes me to ask you the name of the Louvain Professor. The Chair is not filled up, but we are anxious to get as good an occupant as we can. We have heard of a Mr or Dr des Coux of Louvain, do you know any thing about him? I dont suppose it is he?[1]

The Cardinal tells me you can give me information about the Pope's *foundations* — e.g. the Collegio Pio etc. I should very much like to be able to publish some account of them here.[2]

I feel your kindness in sending me the Apostolical Benediction — in my present very arduous and anxious undertaking it is the one stay I have — and this is the Feast especially to remember it. Mgr Gerbet is consecrated at Amiens to day.[3]

We are getting on as well as we can. We have some little difficulty, naturally, in getting the adhesion of gentlemen who have supported the Queen's Colleges, but I think we shall get it

Ever Yours very sincerely in Xt
John H Newman of the Oratory

TO SEPTIMIUS VECCHIOTTI

[End of June? 1854][4]

Il est nécessaire que je commence tout d'abord par demander pardon de votre Grandeur. Inconnu que je suis, je n'oserais jamais

[1] Talbot had written on 13 June, offering Newman a Belgian professor of Canon Law. In the event Laurence Forde, an Irishman, was appointed.

[2] See letter of 25 June to Wiseman.

[3] Olympe Philippe Gerbet (1798–1864), a former disciple of Lamennais, became a friend of Newman in Rome in 1846. He had been appointed Bishop of Perpignan.

[4] Newman has written at the top of this draft, which is in Dalgairns's handwriting, 'was this to Mgr Vechiotti in consequence of Dr Cullen's suggestion of June 17. 1854?' See letter of 18 June to Cullen, first note.

vous donner la peine de lire cette lettre, si ce n'était que Monseigneur Cullen Archevêque de Dublin ne m'eût donné l'assurance que je pouvais écrire sans indiscrétion. Muni de son autorisation, j'ose donc m'adresser à votre *Grandeur*?[1] Il a cru que par votre connaissance intime et profonde de l'état actuel de la France religieuse, vous pourriez nous donner quelques renseignements qui nous seraient d'une extrême utilité dans l'oeuvre si pleine de solicitudes de la fondation de l'Université Catholique. Il m'a prié de vous demander si vous connaissiez en France des hommes d'érudition qui pouvant parler la langue Anglaise seraient utiles en qualité de professeurs ou autrement à notre Université naissante. On m'a cité le nom de M. Rio. Il se peut faire que l'état de sa santé serait un obstacle: cependant, si d'après le jugement de votre Grandeur cela serait possible, nous attacherions un grand prix à son concours, quelque court fut le temps qu'il pût nous donner.[2]

Monseigneur de Dublin m'a chargé de vous demander en confidence si vous pouviez nous rassurer sur les opinions théologiques de M. Faillon et M. Lahir de St Sulpice. Il désirerait savoir si ces Messieurs sont imbus des préjugés Gallicans qu'on impute à cette Congrégation d'ailleurs si respectable.[3] Il voudrait aussi vous prier d'avoir la bonté de nous donner de pareils renseignements sur le Docteur Kempences, du diocèse de Liège en Belgique et vice-préfet de la Bibliothèque de Louvain.[4] Il nous serait bien important de savoir si les opinions de ce monsieur en fait de droit Canon sont conformes à l'enseignement approuvé par Rome. On dit qu'il n'est pas très bien avec l'Evêque de Liège.[5]

Je vous prie, Monseigneur, de croire que c'est à grand regret que je viens empiéter sur votre temps, déjà si rempli et si précieux à l'Eglise. Je compte sur votre extrême bonté pour me pardonner, et je suis persuadé que votre zèle et votre charité vous porteront à nous aider par la communication de vos lumières et de vos avis.

---

[1] Dalgairns evidently hesitated as to the title to give Mgr Vecchiotti, who was not a bishop, but a Roman canonist, employed on various papal missions in Europe. In Nov. 1855 he became internuncio at The Hague.

[2] Vecchiotti, who was not in Paris as Newman thought but at Osimo, replied to Wiseman on 6 Oct., that Alexis François Rio (1797–1874), author of *L'art chrétien*, would not be able to leave Paris.

[3] See letter of 28 June to Faber. Vecchiotti replied: 'Mr Lahire de St Sulpice est ultramontain; c'est un homme solidement instruit . . .', while as to Mr Faillon, 'Il n'est peut-être pas aussi décidement [sic] ultramontain, que Mr Lahire; mais ses doctrines sont sûres . . .'

[4] This was the canonist Augustin Kempenaers, author of *De Romani Pontificis Primatu*, Louvain 1841.

[5] Vecchiotti approved thoroughly of Kempenaers, 'd'une doctrine à tout égard sûre, dans les meilleures idées par rapport aux droits et prérogatives du Saint Siége.'

C'est avec le plus profond respect que je vous prie d'agréer l'hommage de ma vénération et de croire que je suis bien sincèrement, etc.

Votre serviteur tres humble et tres obéissant

SATURDAY 1 JULY 1854 dined with H W ?[Wilberforce]

TO ARCHBISHOP CULLEN

July 1/54

My dear Lord,

I have not a great deal to say before I go — but I wished to call. Dr Taylor has been kind enough to answer my questions.

1. The Hibernian Bank people want your Grace to go there, to sign your name in their book. The cheques drawn in *either* of our names can be cashed — but they seem to wish you to go even though you do not draw. I lodged £1500 in our joint names.

2. Of this £1500 I drew out yesterday £*100* for Mr Kelly the sollicitor [sic] (Kelly and Maxwell) as an earnest money for the Medical School. I am glad to say we have got as far as this. The lawyers are to look over the title deeds this week and to get every thing finished — and then I suppose the rest of the money (in all £1500) will be paid. As things have gone as far as this, should you not sell out stock to the amount of £1500? the funds are very high just now. If you decide not to do so, I shall write to your Grace in about ten days to beg you to ask a Bishop's signature in addition to your own, for that sum from the floating balance.

3. I will bring back the Hib-Dominicana and Monck Mason tomorrow.[1] I have brought back your Louvain book and l'Abbé Cruice's now[2] — and taken away my own Louvain pamphlet.

4. I dare say you know that Mr Monsell has given us his name

Ever Yours affly & obedtly in Xt

John H Newman of the Oratory

The Most Revd Dr Cullen

[1] i.e. Thomas de Burgo's *Hibernia Dominicana*, Kilkenny 1762. Monk Mason is probably the work of William Monck Mason (1775–1859), *The History and Antiquities of the Collegiate and Cathedral Church of St. Patrick near Dublin . . .*, Dublin 1819; or else some work on Ireland by his brother Henry Joseph Monck Mason (1778–1858).

[2] This was probably *Études sur de nouveaux documents historiques empruntés à l'ouvrage récemment découvert des Philosophumena et relatifs au commencement du christianisme et en particulier de l'Église de Rome*, Paris 1852, by Patrice Cruice (1815–66), founder and director of the École des Hautes Études set up by the French bishops. Cruice was Bishop of Marseilles, 1861–5. He had been born in Ireland, which he visited in the summer of 1854, but, to his regret, missed Newman.

SUNDAY 2 JULY 1854   went to lunch with the Buckles   dined with Marshall to meet F Curtis Dr Moriarty etc.

TO JOSEPH DIXON, ARCHBISHOP OF ARMAGH

16 Harcourt Street July 2. 1854

My dear Lord,

I do not know whether I am not taking a liberty in applying to your Grace, but I do not know what better to do.

Will you kindly place to the fund for building the Cathedral at Armagh the inclosed post office order for £5?[1]

His Grace The Archbp of Armagh

TO JOHN STANISLAS FLANAGAN

16 Harcourt Street Sunday July 2/54

My dear Stanislas

I thought I had said, I meant to have done so, that I was so soon coming, I thought the vault question might wait till then.

As to Mr Lynch, I have some delicacy of introducing him to Hope, since it is to be followed up with the objects you mention.[2] There are very few persons I am on such terms as to make it possible for me to be instrumental that way, even though I was only accidentally so — and of course it is kind, as well as delicate in Mr Lynch, telling me.

I hope you will see me soon, but I never can promise I am going, till I am gone

Ever Yours affectly J H N

MONDAY 3 JULY 1854   dined with Ornsby   set off in evening
TUESDAY 4 JULY   arrived in Birmingham

[1] Work on the Cathedral, interrupted by the Famine, was resumed in 1854. The conclusion of this letter has been cut out.

[2] Flanagan's cousin, Henry Lynch, learned that Hope-Scott had recently appointed an agent for Lord Shrewsbury's estates. Lynch wanted an introduction, in order to apply for a similar appointment.

TO MRS J. W. BOWDEN

The Oratory Hagley Road Birmingham July 5. 1854

My dear Mrs Bowden

I have been thinking a great deal of Emily the last fortnight — As she has not written to me, I suppose she has nothing to say. It seems to me that I am very likely to make up my mind without more delay. But she may perhaps wish to write to me.

Ever Yours affectly in Xt   John H Newman of the Oratory

TO JAMES STEWART

The Oratory, Hagley Rd Birm July 5/54

My dear Mr Stewart,

Any day will suit me, on which you choose to come. Of course you will take a bed.

Very truly Yours in Xt   John H Newman of the Oratory

James Stewart Esq.

TO HENRY WILBERFORCE

The Oratory. Hagley Road July 5. 1854

My dear Henry

Since I saw you the following scheme for myself has come up in my mind. I wish you to keep it to yourself, but to make the inquiries you will see it involves.

I have £400 a year as Rector — put aside a £100 for contingencies, and leave £300 — Now I want to do as follows:—

I want to rent a large house (yearly rent would suit me best) — as large a house, say in Eli [Ely] Place, Hume Street, Leeson Street, or Harcourt Street, as I could get for £60 to £80 a year with £20 rates and taxes. Then I shall furnish a bedroom, receiving room, and Chapel — all on one floor; the ground floor, if possible. The rest I should leave at first unfurnished, except one or two bedrooms.

Then I should try to get a man and his wife without children to live in the house as servants on board wages — what would they cost? say, £60.

Then I should try to get my dinners sent in — and call my board altogether (£1. 10. 0 a week for (allowing for absences from Dublin) 40 weeks) £60.

There would be coals, candles, washing, say £30. You will smile at some of my calculations.

All this comes to (House rent, taxes etc £100 — servants £60 — board £60 — coals etc £30) £250. I don't know of any other great expence. The remaining £50 would do for clothes and books.

Well then, the rest of the rooms I should use, as I had youths who wanted them — Harry Ryder would want a room — I should charge him his board etc. and so with others — but I should not be sollicitous, if I had none. I might want a private ⟨or public⟩ Secretary, and offer him board and lodging with me etc. At all events I should have elbow room — and should be solving one of our actual difficulties — viz the necessity of beginning with *several* houses for different classes of students.

Now you see my plan, which I shall be willing to commence on the 1st of August, if I could manage it.

Tell me what you think of this. If you think it possible, just look out for a house as you walk through the streets.[1]

Ever Yours affly J H N

TO ROBERT ORNSBY

The Oratory Hagley Road July 7/54

My dear Ornsby,

I directed to you at the Tablet office yesterday, and do now, because I have not got your direction at Kingstown quite exactly — I think it is Millicent ⟨font⟩ Avenue, number unknown.[2]

Please, tell Fowler the Printer (Number 3, Crow Street) to put these two Errata at the end of Number 7 July 13, and to correct the text in *future* impressions —

p 45 column 1 line 14 from end after Dryden, add and Gray.

p 46 col 2 line 5 from end delete such

Am I not right in saying that 'fallen, fallen' is Dryden, and 'without a friend to grace his obsequies' Gray?[3]

Before the 'Specimens' etc to the notices, which I sent yesterday, must be put as a date at the right hand

'Catholic University House
July 8. 1854

---

[1] Wilberforce noted down on Newman's letter the addresses and rents of several houses.   [2] 16 Claremont Terrace.

[3] See *Idea*, pp. 355 and 357. Newman did not add 'and Gray' in the middle of the latter page, since the whole passage is taken (with an alteration) from Dryden, *Alexander's Feast*, lines 78 and 83.

Specimens of examination in
Grammar for the classical exhibition'

You will have some work to correct Fowler's *Greek*.

Paley mentions the following — you are not obliged to give all or just his — but I send them you.

Liddell and Scott's Lexicon

Riddle or Andrew's Dictionary (he has not seen the latter, but believes he is right in the name, and that it is a good work)[1]

Smith's Greek and Roman *Antiquities*.

Bekker's Gallus and Charicles

'I prefer' he says 'Donaldson's Complete Greek Grammar.' and Ditto Latin. 'as short and very accurate.'

'But they cannot be called easy and are opposed to received notions.'

Key's Crude form Latin Grammar and Zumpt's abridgment by Schmitz are very good. As a Greek Grammar, I think Buttman's larger or intermediate one about the best.

Jelf's and Matthiae's are of little practical use except for advanced scholars.

In *History* (of language)

    Carr's Greek and Roman

    Schmitz's Roman

    Dr Smith's Greek   These are compilations, and embody the results of greater *philological* works.

The Editions of G Bell's 'Grammar School Classics' and 'Bibliotheca Classica' are well adapted for College use.

Buttman's Lexilogus and Irregular Verbs, Donaldson's Theater of the Greeks and Verronianus, Dr Smith's Classical Dictionary small edition in one volume Merivale's *short* history of the decline of the Roman Republic — Wordsworth's Athens and Attica

'I have not found T. K. Arnold's books particularly serviceable' (Others praise them. J H N)

Geography — Butler — but Mr Long's, which is about publishing, is worth waiting for.

You should *see* any books you mention. Get them in my name at Smith and Hodge's[2]

                                        Ever Yrs J H N

P.S.   Your welcome letter is just come. I have not time to read it yet. But the paper will not be for *next* week (July 13) but for July 20, so there is time.

---

[1] Ainsworth's Latin Dictionary is meant.
[2] Hodges and Smith, medical and general publishers, 104 Grafton Street, Dublin.

The Oratory, Hagley Road Birmingham — July 9/54

My dear Mrs Bowden,

I feel I am writing you a very anxious letter. I suppose I had better say at once, I have come to the conclusion that Emily has a vocation. I thought I would let yesterday's Mass go over before I wrote — I got F Dalgairns to say Mass for your intention about her in addition to my own Mass.

During the last three weeks she has been a great deal on my mind, and I have thought about her as she has described herself in her letters and as she is now. It seems to me my only reason for trying her was because I did not see my way to say she had a vocation — but, if I have come to the conviction that she has, I have no right to go on trying.

I shall not write to her till I have heard from you — or rather till after this day week. Thus I shall be able to say Mass for her next Saturday and Sunday (B.M.V. de Monte Carmel.)

If she considers it then settled, that does not involve the necessity of any sudden movement on her part.

You will be much happier when it is all over, than you can be now — and I shall begin saying Masses for your consolation and strengthening, as soon as I cease hers.

I wish I could say any thing at the moment to comfort you, which will not suggest itself to your own mind

Ever Yours very affectly in Xt

John H Newman of the Oratory.

TO THOMAS SCRATTON

The Oratory Hagley Road July 9/54

My dear Scratton

Thank you for your trouble.

1. You need not trouble yourself with the letters directed to me at 'Harcourt Street,' which will be private — except so far as to inclose them and send them in an envelope — and then I must pay you for the stamps and covers. The 'University House' letters are your subject matter.

2.   I *had* spoken to the Porter to tell the Postman to put letters in the box you have set up — but it will come with more force from you direct to the latter.

3.   Merivale I suppose is Martindale

4.   Bishop of Derry, I suppose is Dr Derry, Bishop of Clonfert

5.   I am surprised that Dr Kilduff does not mention about his being a *preacher*, only about his name being on the books.[1]

I have not more to say this moment, except that Stewart, who is going to settle in Dublin is tomorrow going to cross over, and it would be kind of you to show him any attention. He takes a letter to Mr Buckle. Ask Wilberforce and Ornsby to be civil to him also. I don't know where he will be findable — but the Buckles will know — I have warned him against the Kingstown Hotels

Ever Yrs affly J H N

P.S.   My parcel of Gazettes may remain in my room at Harcourt Street, as they come.

I am sorry to tell you that what Fr Harold asks is not possible —[2] None of us are preachers in any sense but Fr Dalgairns — and our rule, as you know, is so much against our preaching out of our own houses, that we have only done so on particular occasions when Bishops have asked us, and not always then. Fr Dalgairns will not be, and cannot be in Ireland in August. Say all this as civilly as you can.

MONDAY 10 JULY 1854   Henry Bowden and his wife called this week?

TO EDWARD BUTLER

[10 July 1854][3]

P.S.   I hope you will excuse the ignorance I may show in the following — it is about 25 years since I turned my mind to any thing of the kind. I only put them down by way of suggesting to you thoughts for a really apposite paper.

---

[1] John Kilduff was the Bishop of Ardagh.

[2] John Harold was one of the curates at Kingstown.

[3] Edward Butler destroyed the letters he received from Newman as being 'too private.' See Cuthbert Butler, *The Life and Times of Bishop Ullathorne*, II, London 1926, p. 213. This postscript must have been returned to Newman, who kept it with Butler's letters from which its date can be fixed.

Specimens of *oral* examinations in Mathematics.

1.   The Candidate is told to turn to Eucl. i. 47 in the Schemata. He is asked the *medium* of proof, then the previous theorems generally on which the proof depends. Then in turn he is made to analyze them all, viz 41. 14. and 4 to their first principles.

2.   He is made to prove Eucl. i. 32. Corr. 1 and 2.

3   Eucl. v. 16 is put before him; and the examination turns on these points — (1) Why in the enunciation of the Theorem is it said, 'of the same kind.' (2) What is the force of the words 'any equimultiples *whatever*'? Will it do, e.g. to take four times or ten times or even thousand times — and if not, why not. (3) *How can* we take and represent any multiple *whatever*? (4) the previous theorems on which the proof depends.

4.   (1) When is the motion of a body said to be uniform, when accelerated, when retarded? (2) When is a force said to be uniform? (3) If two bodies have gone over the same space $T \, \alpha \frac{1}{V}$; if a body is impelled in a right line by a uniform force V and T: reconcile these two formulae by explaining the terms and conditions of each.

5.   The Candidate is asked to *construe* the following formula, in treating of the descent of a body down an inclined plane, $V = \frac{H}{L} . 2 \, m \, T$.

6.   He is asked the respective velocities, after direct impact, of two bodies, A and B, if perfectly elastic, compared to their respective velocities after that impact on the supposition of their being perfectly hard — the proof — and the definition of hard and elastic.

7.   What is the *meaning* of the *words* 'ellipse' and and '*h*yperbola,' (according to their *derivations*.)

8.   'If two straight lines touching a conic section (or opposite hyperbolas) meet one another, the diameter bisecting the line joining the points of contact will pass through the point of concourse.' Let him draw on paper before the examiner the four cases of this theorem.

9   Define the asymptote of the hyperbola geometrically, and prove that, if it and its curve ⟨the curve and its asymptote⟩ be continually extended, they will approach nearer and nearer to each other, yet can never meet.

Now you may see reasons to question the utility or advisability of putting out any such papers. But, if you do not, I should be very much obliged to you for some specimens 1 of oral 2 of written examinations. The above is all *oral*.[1]

---

[1] The questions as eventually drawn up by Butler will be found in the *Catholic University Gazette* (28 Sept. 1854), pp. 138–9, and (26 Oct. 1854), pp. 170–1.

TO ROBERT ORNSBY

Hagley Road. July 10/54

My dear Ornsby,

I like your Remarks very much — you will see I have made some observations, as I went.

I think that the *Questions* should come under the dating 'Catholic University House' in the *official* part of the Gazette.

But that the *Remarks* should be unofficial and be inserted under the 'Sedes Sapientiae —' as the Remarks on the Entrance Examination in Number 1. This being the case, I retract my wish that they should be under 1. 2. 3. etc. And you should put some signature, perhaps your initials at the end. They would come *after* my Essay. After you have corrected them, I should like them to appear in Number 8 (July 20) or Number 10 August 3, whichever has room for them — (Number 9 July 27 will *not* have room.) There is no great harm that they (the Remarks) are postponed — for it is well to bring out the Questions first, and see if there are any criticisms which make explanations necessary, and then explanations will come into the Remarks.[1]

I think you should define Philology.

You have given examinations in Grammar, and History (you may add the other parts of Philology if you will —) (by the bye they are not *pure* grammar, which fusses me, for the οὐ μὴ is something more, and there is no time now to correct the Press).

As to your Questions on History, I should make this criticism on them, that some of them are rather subjects for *distinct Papers* than for simple *answers*. The fault of many examinations (say the Ireland)[2] was that the Questions were so vast that it was absolutely *necessary* for Candidates to *cram* for them. All the time I had any thing to do with the Oriel Examination I set my face against this and (as I think) prevented it, by always writing on the top of the Paper of Questions '*One or two* of these are to be taken, instead of answers to *all.*' This we need not do here — but, what I think will be better, to make the historical questions enter more into the *Grammar* of History, so to speak. E.g., 1 Who was Camillus, what is his date, what is his position etc in Roman History. 2. What were the Roman Generals concerned in the Mithridatic war, and what countries were involved in it. 3 What Greek authors were contemporary with Pericles. etc.

For this reason I send you back your Questions on Ancient History,

[1] The Remarks appeared on 17 Aug., in Number 12.
[2] Dean Ireland's Scholarship at Oxford, founded in 1825.

for Revision, with my notes upon them. I should like the Questions on Ancient History to appear in Number 8 (as those on Grammar appear in Number 7) and please send them (without sending them to me) to the Printer, *as soon as you can*. And tell him to let me have a proof of the whole Number (8) set up in columns.

I have sent you a Message by Scratton about Stewart, who crosses tonight. Be civil to him — I think you will like him

Ever Yrs affly J H N

P.S.   I will attempt a paper on Composition, as a specimen, and send it to you.

TO ARCHBISHOP CULLEN

July 12/54

My dear Lord

I have this minute opened a letter from the Archbishop of New York — about which I shall have to write to you. It is *most encouraging* as to our prospect of students from the United States.[1]

But I write without any delay on account of the following sentence — tho' I don't know what your Grace can do.

'Though I know not how far his Grace may have authority to act in the matter, I beg of him for God's sake to arrest the advent of the Revd Dr Cahill, whose presence here at this moment can have no other effect than that of betraying us into a worse position than what we now occupy.'[2]

Monsell thought it premature to talk about a charter, and would only do harm.[3]

The Archbishop of Munich writes most kindly with warm remembrances of your Grace — but he does not know any thing definite of M. Gfroer[4] I will write to some one else.

[1] Archbishop Hughes of New York, on 24 June, besides giving his name for the University, and being very optimistic as to the money and students that would flow to it from the United States, invited Newman to cross the Atlantic for a lecture tour, before the term opened in Dublin in Nov.

[2] The Nativist agitation especially against Irish Catholics was at its height, and Daniel William Cahill was a fiery Irish Nationalist and lecturer. His visit to the United States was postponed until 1859.

[3] See letter of 28 June to Monsell, second note.

[4] August Friedrich Gfroerer (1803–61), a Protestant and a church historian, became a Catholic in 1853. He was never a professor in Dublin.

194

Begging your Grace's blessing I am, My dear Lord, Yrs affectionately & faithfully in Xt

John H Newman of the Oratory

The Most Revd The Archbp of Dublin

TO JOHN HUGHES, ARCHBISHOP OF NEW YORK

The Oratory, Birmingham, July 12th, 1854.

My dear Lord,

I am quite overpowered at receiving from Dublin the letter with its
munificent enclosure, which has come to me from your Grace.[1] I beg
you to receive, as the best offering I have to make, poor as it is, my
warmest acknowledgments to the kind and sympathetic hearts from
whom it has proceeded, and my grateful prayers for their welfare
present and future, and to assure them how great an encouragement I
find it to be in the fulfilment of the duties which are at present upon me
to have received such an expression of their favour.

It is a pledge to me, that what I have done or am doing, full of
imperfections as it is, will have a worth and a success, not its own, as
being accompanied by the good wishes and availing intercessions of
distant friends who have taken so charitable an interest in me.

As to my past anxieties, to which your Grace alludes, I adore the
mercy of a good Providence, who has never forsaken me in trial, and
who, on this occasion has, by the instrumentality of Catholic liberality,
carried me so triumphantly through them.

Will you let me add I have long wished to be able to provide a
cemetery for the members of the Birmingham Oratory? It has struck
me I could put the present I have now received to no better purpose.
It will be the place whither if God fulfils my wish, I shall one day be
carried myself, and it will remain after me a memorial to those who
succeed me in this house of the kindness of American Catholics towards
one who had nothing to recommend him to them but a small portion
of their own zeal for the honour of religion.

Begging your Grace's blessing, I am, my dear Lord, your affectionate
friend and servant in Christ,

John H. Newman, of the Oratory.

The Most Rev. the Archbishop of New York.

[1] Archbishop Hughes wrote on 26 June, that, at a meeting of clergy and laity at
New York in March 1853, it had been agreed to send Newman a testimonial of the
respect and admiration felt for him on account of the Achilli trial—'a private purse
for your own specific and personal use—' amounting to £223.

TO HENRY WILBERFORCE

Hagley Road July 12/54

My dear Henry,

I don't care whether I have youths or not, *if* I can do it for the sum I calculated; £280 was not it? of course, *should* they come, it will diminish my expences — but I can afford £280. I shall not mind taking the house from the first of August. I should at once furnish one or two rooms, and get into it by the Assumption or there abouts. This would save me the expense of going to Howth, and allow us to go out to the 7 Churches[1] etc as expeditions.

I have offered Duffy the place of University Bookseller — but am not sure he will accept it. It will require some outlay in stock.

Poor Mrs Whitty! — as to Dr Corrigan — She told me what she told you. He has given *me* no encouragement. *I* cannot move more than I have done. If any one can make overtures *from him,* I shall be glad.[2]

⌈The Archbishop of New York has just sent me from his people £223 as a present in memory of the Achilli matter. Ornsby might know this for the Tablet. He promises me in a year or two from 60 to 120 students.⌉

Ever Yrs affly J H N

TO ROBERT ORNSBY

⌈July 15. 1854

I do not like you to have any thing to do with the leading Articles of the Tablet. It will be my object to make it worth your while to give up the Tablet altogether, if you will . . . Any change which involves (your) taking leading Articles I don't like.

J H N⌉

[1] At Glendalough, south of Dublin.
[2] Dominic Corrigan was the most eminent Catholic physician in Dublin at this time, but a supporter of the Queen's Colleges, and indeed an active member of the Senate that governed them. He was also connected with the Jervis Street Hospital run by the Sisters of Mercy of Baggot Street, where Ellen Whitty, Mother Mary Vincent, was the Superior. Cf. Newman's letters to Corrigan in June 1855.

TO EMILY BOWDEN

The Oratory Bm July 16/54

My dear Emily,

You are expecting a letter from me. Dear Mama thought it best to speak to you a week ago, and, I believe, has told you I should give your matter a last Mass today.

I had intended not to decide till the Assumption — but my mind is quite clear a month before it. And I have no reason to delay to tell you what I deliberately think.

It is, that you have a vocation to a religious life. You cannot help thinking I have gone to and fro — but I have not. I have wanted to see whether your own thoughts on the subject would undergo a change — and I wanted calmly to reflect on what I already knew about you. Now you seem to me precisely where you were — in your last letter you express in a simple natural way just what you expressed months ago. When left to yourself, you seem to me to look one way and one way only.

It comes home to me forcibly, that I know various persons who desire to have a vocation and have not, and would be content indeed to find in themselves those marks of a vocation, which show themselves in you.

My opinion is, that, if you find the right convent, you will never wish to leave it.

At the same time, you will see, my dear Emily, that the trial is the proof. If I am wrong, the trial will show it. If you determine in the way I suppose, you are taking no step which you cannot recall. Of course no one would make the trial without good grounds for doing so — still to try is not to anticipate the event of it.

I do not like to lose the Post, and write in a great hurry

Ever most affectly Yours in Xt
John H Newman of the Oratory

Miss Bowden

TO MRS J. W. BOWDEN

The Oratory July 16/54

My dear Mrs Bowden,

The inclosed letter to Emily is a very painful one for me to write — and I have had great difficulty in writing it. It will read to her, I fear, quite cold.

I can say nothing but what occurs to yourself — God's will be done, if it is His will. My comfort is, that, if I am wrong, a noviciate will show it. But I do not think I am wrong.

197

Of course there is no *hurry* about her taking any step, if she determines on one.

> Ever Yours very affectly in Xt
> John H Newman of the Oratory

MONDAY 17 JULY 1854   Mr Knott called
TUESDAY 18 JULY   walked with Mr Knott[1]
WEDNESDAY 19 JULY   Harry Bowden and Mr Trevilyan passed through this week?

TO ROBERT ORNSBY

Hagley Road. July 19/54

My dear Ornsby

At last I find a quarter of an hour to begin to write. Your criticisms on my Composition Paper are very valuable — and please always give me your remarks, whether I always take them or not — for they are always a guide to me, even when I do not literally act upon them.

What you say about the 'taste of blood,' at first I did not understand, owing to ellipses which you have made (naturally) in stating the drift of your remarks. On reading you several times, I think all you say about 'physical taste,' 'tasting,' 'sensation' etc in fact all you say on it is only to bring out the fact that I have in one place put 'taste of' in another 'taste for.' You shall see it again, and then tell me if I have met your objections.[2]

⌐Paley's having recommended books exceptionable on the ground of faith and morals, has again thrown me back in thinking of asking him to help us —⌐ What do you think yourself?[3]

I have had some time an idea that if to certain books we printed *Prefaces*, which we took care to bind up with the copies we allowed, they would be made safe. e.g. Donaldson's Theatre of the Greeks. When *attention is drawn* to such errors, their effect is almost neutralized, even though they are not refuted. It is the *surprise* which does most

---

[1] This was probably John William Knott whose family came from the neighbourhood of Birmingham. He went up to Wadham College in 1840, at the age of 18 and was a Fellow of Brasenose College 1844–67. At Pusey's request he became Vicar of St Saviour's, Leeds, in 1851, and remained there until 1859. He died in 1870.

[2] Cf. the *Catholic University Gazette*, (10 Aug. 1854), pp. 81–2, and *Idea*, pp. 363–4.

[3] Ornsby replied on 26 July against inviting Paley, 'not so much on account of recommending those books, which he might only maintain are the current school literature, as because he seemed to take a desponding and depressing view of what is possible to be done.' Thus Paley was not invited to Dublin. In 1874 he was appointed Professor of Classical Literature in Manning's Kensington university.

mischief.[1] What youth, who read the Cantica Canticorum, but would have the thought rise up in his mind 'This is very human?' We cannot prevent this — we can *suggest indeed* to him, which is enough for a religious youth, the Catholic idea and theory of it — but we cannot expect to prove it to him — he must be thrown on the authority of the Church. There the matter will stand — and then when he sees the idea in a book like Donaldson's it does him no harm. But, if suddenly in the midst of the illustration of a philosophical *law*, the Cant. C. is brought in as one instance of it, of course he is startled and perhaps damaged.

I cannot stomach the Jesuit mode of pasting leaves together. Nothing but the distinct authority and bidding of the Church would make me consent to it. Lemprieres Classical Dictionary unless altered from what I used as a boy, is utterly inadmissible.[2] I must talk with you about a Classical Dictionary if you don't see your way. I don't see great harm of an attack on St Jerome. It overdoes itself.

Ever Yrs affly J H N

⌐I wish you could learn from John O'Hagan something about the *turn of mind* of Mr McCarthy, if you cannot speak about it yourself . . . If he were a person to take up the cause of literature generally, I should like to make a good deal of use of him, if he would be used.[3]

J H N.⌐

TO HENRY WILBERFORCE

Hagley Road. July 19/54

My dear Henry

Thank you for your valuable information. Number 7 Ely Place seems out and out the best. It is provoking the terms had not reached

---

[1] *The Theatre of the Greeks*, first edition Cambridge 1827, was revised for the fourth edition in 1836 by J. W. Donaldson, and thenceforth appeared under his name alone. In the first chapter Donaldson suggested that the Song of Songs was derived from the idolatrous neighbours of Israel, and had no religious reference.

[2] *Bibliotheca Classica; or, a Classical Dictionary containing a full Account of all the Proper Names mentioned in Antient Authors*, Reading 1788, with many later editions, by John Lemprière (1765?–1824), of Jersey, educated at Winchester and Pembroke College, Oxford. Lemprière, whose life was spent as a schoolmaster, took orders, and in 1788 was assistant master at Reading grammar school.

[3] This postscript exists only in the holograph copy. Ornsby replied that MacCarthy was 'mainly a literary man, and his literary tastes are rather of the magazine description;' but he had 'a remarkably painstaking and industrious mind, and . . . a good deal of real genius.' MacCarthy was appointed Lecturer in Poetry at the University.

you. Stanislas thinks they will not be very high, as far as the locale goes. I would take a lease of a house for 3 years; but I don't see I could do more.

Scratton wrote me word that the owner of the house next to the University House, on the other side to Judge Ball's, proposed to sell it to us — but I suppose that would be far too large a concern for me.

I suppose Mr Arthur O'Hagan is partner to Mr Kavanagh. It is quite necessary I should go to a lawyer, and if he will let me pay him I cannot go to any one better than to him. As the University sollicitors are likely to be Kelly and Maxwell, I should be delicate of doing any thing which might compromise me with Mr A. O'Hagan — which taking his assistance and not paying him would do.

Of course I should be glad of Ornsby knowing it too — and you may tell him — but I am afraid of its getting out, because there will be so much talking — and 'why doesn't he go to the University House etc etc?' so I want at present as little said about it as possible.

⌜Any news about the Catholic Standard? You are prepared I suppose for its having got out.⌝

From your experience of the badness of drains, this is a point to be looked to in Number 7. And is there any water closet?

Some money is owing to me from the Achilli Fund — and I want the account made up. Mr Kelly of Sackville Street refers me to Star, and Star refers me to you — I wish you would all three agree about it

Ever Yrs affly J H N

P.S.   You do not say any thing about the Harcourt Street Houses. I suppose they are out of repair.

THURSDAY 20 JULY 1854   went over with F Ambrose to Bromsgrove to see some bits of ground for a burial ground

TO J. M. CAPES

Hagley Road. July 20/54

My dear Capes

Thank you for the sight of your article, which has interested me very much.[1] In returning it, I have set down a few remarks, which struck me, as I read — valeant quantum. Thank you especially [sic] of what

---

[1] 'The Queen's Government and the University,' the *Rambler*, (4 Sept. 1854), pp. 189–209, an article which justified the setting up of the Catholic University.

you say of me.[1] There have been numerous attacks on my past conduct, especially in detail — but from the nature of the case, no opportunity of any friendly consideration of it. With (I dare say) many inconsistencies in detail, it has not been inconsistent, I think, (I am not talking of opinions, but of conduct) on the whole.

I could not insert more than one additional heading of the Essays — 1st because I am not sure of the order in which they will come — 2. because the more probably following one, (before August) is nothing more definite than 'Objections answered.' If you want, however, the August Essays, I suppose they will be such as 'Professorial and Collegiate systems contrasted.' 'Athenian and Imperial Schools —' but it is almost unsafe to put them, as I may change them.[2]

Thank you for trying to circulate the Gazette

Ever Yrs affly in Xt   John H Newman of the Oratory

J M Capes Esqr

TO ROBERT ORNSBY

Thursday Evening July 20/54

My dear Ornsby

I write in a great hurry Many thanks for your valuable criticism. In case I do not see the revise, which I *trust* Fowler will let me, I must ask to commit to you the following and beg you to see it is done.[3]

1.   'this Irish' for 'an Irish' — will do

2.   'undertaking' may do — but I fear will be flat

3.   'one scrape or other' must stand as it is.

4.   'England as well as Ireland,' will do.

5   the word 'noble' will not do. You are making Richard or me *speak* from the stage to the boxes. You may put 'fine,' 'grand' 'great,' 'Catholic' or 'large.'

6.   I shall keep myths.

[1] *Loc. cit.*, pp. 199–201. Capes wrote concerning Newman '. . . we believe it would be impossible to name any person, of whatever station, who has in practice, and in the most difficult of circumstances, more consistently acted upon his professions, and personally made every submission which authority could possibly require of him, without grudging, without ostentation, and without reserve. Obedience to authority, spiritual or secular, elevated or humble, has been a doctrine which he has uniformly taught, and which he has uniformly practised. That such a man should be ready to convert a University into a focus of disloyalty and discontent, is simply impossible. . . .'

[2] Capes had ended his article by praising Newman's papers in the *Catholic University Gazette*, and expressing a wish to announce forthcoming titles.

[3] Newman is referring to his article 'Objections answered' in the *Catholic University Gazette*, (27 July 1854), now 'Discipline and Influence' in *Rise and Progress of Universities*, H.S. III, pp. 60–76. See pp. 65–6, 60 and 67.

I would *not* alter this objection — at the moment I forget what the Eastern story is.

Don't hurry yourself about the Remarks.

Ever Yrs affly J H N

P.S.   I trust earnestly I may not offend the Irish — is there any one who could give an opinion? I suppose not; and it is *not* worth while to ask. What consoles me is that you do not find fault with the line of argument only with the *expressions*

TO CARDINAL WISEMAN

The Oratory Bm. July 20/54

My dear Lord Cardinal,

I shall be sure to attend to your Eminence's recommendation and will bear it in mind. Whether I shall be able in the event to act upon it, at the moment I cannot tell. So much depends upon the number of students we have. At present I have rather over done my engagements, and am only afraid that I may not get work equal to them. And besides, there is considerable jealousy of English appointments, and I am kept in constant anxiety lest I should go too far. The papers Mr Sankey sends evidently merit great attention.[1]

I will take care the Gazette is sent to your Eminence and kissing the Sacred Purple

I am, My dear Lord, Yr affectionate friend & Servt in Xt

John H Newman of the Oratory

His Eminence The Cardl Wiseman

FRIDAY 21 JULY 1854   Bishop of Boston called: or yesterday or tomorrow.

TO ANDREW ELLIS

The Oratory, Hagley Road, Birmingham, July 21/54

My dear Sir,

I felt the kindness of your letter, and rejoiced to hear your good news.[2] As you have mentioned about it to several of our friends, I

[1] William H. Villiers Sankey, at Trinity College, Dublin, who became a Catholic with his wife and four children in 1846, had been practising as a civil engineer since 1840. He wanted to be appointed to the Professorship of Engineering.

[2] Ellis reported on 17 July that the purchase of the Medical School in Cecilia Street was almost completed, the University solicitors having confirmed that the title was perfect.

conclude it is no longer a secret, and may be made public.

As to the question of the University appointing Protestant Professors, you were kind enough to ask my opinion one of the times I had the pleasure of seeing you; and I answered, as I should answer now, according to my present state of information, that it was *impossible*. A Catholic University cannot by any possibility appoint Protestant Professors.[1]

I can fancy two ways of proceeding.

1. not to open the Schools this autumn — but to let out our buildings (for I suppose I may call them ours) for a year — and then of course the University would not be responsible *who* lectured there.

2. to place there *only such Catholic Professors* as we could find of eminence — and to suffer our students to go *elsewhere*, to Protestant Lecturers, for those subjects of professional learning which we did not yet supply.

I cannot at present fancy any other course.

But it is so large and so anxious a subject, that it is impossible it can be decided without consulting various persons, and consuming much time.

I should have written to you, sooner, except that I had thought it possible that I might have soon heard from Mr Maxwell

I am, My dear Sir Very truly Yours in Xt

John H Newman

A Ellis Esqr

TO ROBERT ORNSBY

Birmingham   July 21/54

My dear Ornsby

Scratton wishes me to take the Roman kings into the period of history for the Examination. But surely very little *is* known about them, unless we enter upon deep disquisitions. We shall oscillate be-between Goldsmith and Niebuhr.[2] The era of Pisistratus being fixed will take in something, I think, like 50 years of the Roman kings — and

[1] Ellis had consulted Myles O'Reilly, Charles Bianconi and Michael Flannery, who were anxious to open the Medical School in the autumn. Sufficient qualified Catholic lecturers would not be available in time, and Ellis wrote that his three advisers were unanimously in favour of obtaining some who were Protestants. When the School was opened in the autumn of 1855, all the Professors were Catholics.

[2] i.e. Oliver Goldsmith's unreliable compilation, *The Roman History from the Foundation of the City of Rome to the Destruction of the Roman Empire*, 1769, and B. G. Niebuhr's scientific *Roman History*, English translation 1847–51.

it is a definite and convenient date. However, if you are strong about it, let me know your reasons.

July 26. Thank you for your trouble about the Houses. I still prefer 7 Ely Place; and any how, think the other two decidedly will not do. I must not have a small house. I want nine persons in it — besides a servant, who might be down stairs; myself, a dean, two tutors etc, and 5 youths. (All this is in confidence, except to Wilberforce) I propose to live on the ground floor myself, and want a (back) bed and working room, with a door into the front room, which would be reception and dining room — and I want a chapel. All this would be provided in Ely Place. Then I want a sort of common room for the youths, this would be the front drawing room. The back drawing room, on the other side of the pillars, I could board off, and perhaps, with a partition turn it into two bedrooms. According to Wilberforce's account there are 6 bed rooms on the two upper floors — (you say 5) this would just make 9. A number of persons living together of different ages and pursuits require a large house. ⟨You have not said whether there are *Stables* — which would be room for servants.⟩

Whether 7 Ely Place will do or not, or whether it be dear or not, I fear I must have as large a house. Has it stables?

6 P M Your letter just come. I think I shall try to do without a *leading article* on August 3, since my Composition Paper does not come in for tomorrow (July 27). There will be 1. Mr Butler's papers,[1] which, I wonder, Fowler has not sent me in type yet — *if* you have time, ask about them — (it is not worth while going on purpose) 2 your Philology[2] 3 my composition. 4 I am going to begin a digested table of Catholic works[3]

I understand your 'Remarks' will be for August 10 — Accordingly, please see that Fowler puts Essay B which *was* to have been in August 3, to August 10 also.[4]

Since there is time now to make any alteration in my paper on Composition, send me a proof with the passage marked against, which you think obscure. I shall keep your Philology a post, as I was pressed for time.

Ever Yrs affly J H N

[1] 'Heads for questions to be answered vivâ voce by Candidates for the Mathematical Exhibition.' The *Catholic University Gazette*, (3 Aug. 1854).

[2] 'Specimens of Examination in Philology for the Classical Exhibition.' *loc. cit.*

[3] These last two items were postponed a week, until 10 Aug. For the Latin Composition paper see *Idea*, pp. 362–5.

[4] Ornsby's 'Remarks on the Examination for the Classical Exhibition' were postponed to 17 Aug., and with them appeared Newman's 'Macedonian and Roman Schools,' *H.S.* III, pp. 90–104.

TO MRS J. W. BOWDEN

The Oratory Bm July 23/54

My dear Mrs Bowden

Thank Emily for her letter of this morning.

It strikes me to say one thing. It is possible of course, if Emily determines in the way I have suggested to her, for her to remain for a time, at present indefinite, with you; though of course she must not do so except under direction.

I mean, she could take a vow of devoting herself to religion (if a religious house would take her), yet with the intention of remaining a year, two years, three years with you.

The chief difficulty of this would be whether it would be a temptation to her to wish to recall her vow — or whether a half and half state would be painful to her; — which a Confessor alone could determine.

It would involve, I suppose, a sort of religious life with a rule at home — it would keep her out of society. Whether it would expose her to remarks from friends who came very near her, as at Capheaton, I do not know.

I think it worth while to mention this. Of course there must be times as in the early centuries, whether [sic] persons, dedicated to Christ, lived by themselves or in their own families. It is a mere question of expediency

Ever Yours most affectly in Xt
John H Newman of the Oratory

P.S. She might try it for half a year, or a year, and see how it answered. In a case where you were poor, and she was gaining a livelihood for you, of course it would be right So that there may be cases even now.

TO D. B. DUNNE

The Oratory Birmingham July 25. 1854

My dear Dr Dunne,

I assure you I should like nothing better than to have you connected with us in the University. It would be really a gain to us; — but, as you will easily understand, there are difficulties in the way.

As to a Professorship, I do not think that would be possible. We must have men who have in some way or other fought their way on, and have some tangible claims, by age, publications, or the like, since there is no concursus — or at least, who happen to be before the world. It does not follow that these must be always the best men, but we must begin the University on the basis of *faith in individuals*. The Professors must, if possible, create trust in them by their *names*. This is one of those tyrannical circumstances, which arise out of the nature of the case, and which hamper *me*, as much as they may be an obstacle in the way of *others*.

Should we be able to form a number of houses, I shall wish to put Tutors in each — They will form with the Dean the governing body of the House, and will have a certain salary and their board. I do not know whether this is a kind of thing, which you would like, if we prosper. It is in this way a man of talent will make himself known, and in course of time make his way to the Professorships.[1]

With every kind feeling, I am Very truly Yours in Xt

John H Newman of the Oratory

TO JAMES NUGENT

The Oratory, Birmingham July 25. 1854

My dear Mr Nugent

I brought the subject of your letter before the Fathers yesterday. You may easily believe that they were much pleased at what you say and wish, and will not forget it in Mass and prayer. For myself, I will make a point of saying a number of Masses for your intention, as there expressed.

The first question in setting up a religious body is, 'Have you the men?' The second in setting up an Oratory is, 'Can they live together?' Since we have no vows, *this* till a Congregation actually is set off, and gains a momentum, and is able to carry away, and carry on with it, the subjects who then from time to time join it, is the great thing. First get a number of Priests who can live together for a fair space of time — say three years. You and Mr Gibson can do it, but you are not enough.[2]

This seems to me the point at present. Our noviceship is three years. Should you get four priests to live together for that space of time, we

---

[1] Dunne had studied for the priesthood in Rome, but gave up after obtaining a distinguished Ph.D. and D.D. in 1852. He was now teaching at Dr Quinn's school, 16 Harcourt Street.

[2] Nugent's aim was to establish an Oratory in Liverpool. His companion at the 'Catholic Institute, Oratory of St Philip Neri,' was a young priest, Henry Gibson.

will make your actual novitiate after that, very easy. But you must come to us, and say, 'Here, we have been living together for three years, and we verily believe we know and understand and can bear with each other, and get on together, very well.' Without this agreement nothing can be done.

Give my kindest remembrances to Mr Gibson.[1]

P.S.   Nothing you have suggested as an objection is really such.

WEDNESDAY 26 JULY 1854   Dr and Mrs Ives came[2]   F Bernard went to give mission at Clifton convent   Mr Burgess, F Robert's American friend, with us about this time

TO MRS JOHN MOZLEY

Birmingham July 27/54

My dear Jemima

I have forgotten Harriet Fourdrinier's *Post Office* — and perhaps it will not do now. So I am obliged to trouble you with the £3 — which at your convenience perhaps you will convey to her[3]

Yrs affly John H Newman

FRIDAY 28 JULY 1854   F Stanislas drove me over to see the bits of ground at the Lickeys —   chose one for certain and made a bargain with Mr Davis[4]   Lord Ralph Kerr went home?

TO D. B. DUNNE

Oratory   Hagley Road 28 July, 1854

My dear Dr Dunne,

As to Tutors, my great difficulty is that I have not a dream how many youths will come to us, whether externs or interns.

What I want is to place young unmarried men *in* the houses or Halls. They would have nothing whatever to do with discipline directly. They would give Lectures for (say) three hours a day. The rest of their time would be their own. I should wish these to be intermediate between

---

[1] The signature had been cut off at the time this letter was copied.
[2] i.e. the American convert Episcopalian bishop and his wife.
[3] See letter of 16 March to Mrs John Mozley.
[4] i.e. for the purchase of ground for a cemetery and country cottage at Rednal.

the Dean who would be a Priest and the young men — to gain the confidence and intimacy of the young men — and, in this way, to smooth the Dean's work. This implies they have *nothing* to do with Discipline — for else, good bye to the confidence I speak of.

I have already engaged two or three of my own personal friends to begin the classical system, who are married men. It seemed to me necessary to get persons who had been members of the English Universities, where the classics are especially attended to — and, from what I have heard, I think Irish people wish it. I think they have an idea that the English Universities have given more attention to the classics than they have — and there seems to me truth in this.

Your line would on the contrary be the scientific. We must, I think, soon have an opening for it — but, from what I have said, you will see I cannot speak more confidently about our prospects than you could yourself.

I suppose we shall not *really* commence till after Christmas — I mean, that, in November we shall merely be sounding our bell for a rendezvous, as the first dinner bell or train bell on a rail road. Probably I then could tell you for certain whether I could avail myself of your services after Christmas[1]

Very truly Yours in Xt   John H Newman

SATURDAY 29 JULY 1854   went to Alton Towers, where the Earl, Miss Talbot, Hope Scott, Mr Butler[2]

SUNDAY 30 JULY   preached in morning

MONDAY 31 JULY   returned to Birmingham   F Edward went from home   The Ryders went home

TO W. H. SCOTT

The Oratory Hagley Road Birmingham July 31/54

My dear Scott

Thank you for your letter and its inclosure — I should have written to you before this, had I had any thing to say about the University. Things are as yet just as they were.

But I wish to ask you *in confidence* one question — Do you think that *literary work* would be tanti? — I have no right to say it, but I know that Lady Shrewsbury is contemplating a life of Lord Shrewsbury —

[1] In Oct. Dunne was appointed Lecturer in Logic.

[2] This was Robert Jackson Butler, at Brasenose College, Oxford, and a clergyman, who became a Catholic in 1850. He had just been appointed Lord Shrewsbury's agent.

though perhaps she may not put her idea into execution or may already be provided with a biographer.

It just struck me that, considering your intimacy with the family, you might be willing to undertake the work. There would be very little labour, as all the documents are ready collected and arranged — but it would require some tact, and some knowledge of the state of Catholic affairs. I should think it would be a very interesting, though a delicate, task. I have a sincere admiration of Lord Shrewsbury, and though I knew little of him and never had more than civilities from him, yet I have those feelings in regard to his simplicity, zeal, kindness of heart, and munificence, that I would gladly honor his memory in the way now talked of, if I could — and I should consider I had done a good work, in getting him a good biographer. There would be a handsome remuneration.

If I have a favorable answer from you, I would proceed to find out how matters stand at present with Lady Shr. It would be a great thing for her, I conceive, to get a writer of your calibre, and would be mortifying on the other hand if I found the task going to some second rate person.[1]

Ever Yours most sincerely in Xt   John H Newman of the Oratory

TO MANUEL JOHNSON

Oratory Bm. August 1. 1854

My dear Johnson,

I have not been ungrateful for your valuable letter, though I have not written to you.[2] I wrote off at once to my Irish friend, who is wandering in France. He had given me his direction, and I wrote according to it but he does not reply — which is very provoking. Before taking your offer to get your Bonn friend [to] look out for a man there, I wish to take the chance of the youth in question[3]

Ever Yours affectly John H Newman

M Johnson Esqr

[1] See letter of 3 Aug. to the Earl of Shrewsbury. The Scotts were an ancient Staffordshire family.

[2] See letter of 15 June to Johnson, who wrote on 7 July that he had been in touch with his friend the Astronomer at Bonn, who offered to find a Catholic astronomer for Newman.

[3] i.e. M. W. Crofton, who wrote from Brittany on 4 Aug., to decline the appointment as Observer. Crofton added, 'It was only since I have been here that I heard of the Pope's intention to raise you to the episcopal bench—I trust and am sure it will be to your own and the Church's advantage.'

TO WILLIAM MONSELL

Oratory, Birmingham. August 1. 1854

My dear Monsell

Sir John Simeon has mentioned to me the name of Mr Aylward of Waterford, whom he had met at your house, as a person who could help us in the University.[1] Could you tell me any thing about his qualifications and his likelihood to look our way — or refer me to any one who can. Don't refer me to the Baron Schröter, who is an excellent religious man, but too much in the clouds.[2]

I have just returned from two days at Alton Towers — where I found Hope Scott as well as the Earl. After hearing so much of Hope's overwork, I was pleased to find him so flourishing. Lord S. [Shrewsbury] looks very well, though delicate.

I have got Mr Meagher's name, of Waterford for our list.[3] Before I put the list into our Gazette, I shall send you the Irish names for you to judge whether they are enough for yours to appear. The Maynooth people are holding back somewhat. These difficulties do not annoy me, because they do not tend to retard us ever so little — what *is* of course the serious anxiety at the moment, is the poor prospect of students, which must continue for some time.

Ever Yours affly in Xt   John H Newman of the Oratory

Wm Monsell Esqr M P.

TO SIR JOHN SIMEON

Oratory Hagley Road Bm August 1/54

My dear Sir John Simeon

I am very much obliged to you for your suggestion, and for the interest it shows you take in our proceedings. I will write to Monsell at once.[4]

[1] Simeon wrote thus on 29 July, adding 'Baron Schröter too, whom you doubtless know, is of the same opinion.' Monsell reported on 5 Aug. that John Aylward was learned in many subjects, but wrote more cautiously next day, that he really knew nothing of Aylward's capability.

[2] Von Schroeter was staying with Sir John Simeon, at Swainston, in the Isle of Wight, at this time. Wilfrid Ward, *Aubrey de Vere*, London 1904, p. 227. For von Schroeter's relations with Newman see Volumes XIII and XIV.

[3] Thomas Meagher (1796–1874), M.P. for Waterford 1847–57, was the father of the Irish Nationalist, 'Meagher of the Sword,' who was at this period in New York, having escaped from Van Diemen's Land, to which he had been transported.

[4] See the preceding letter.

Our difficulty at present is with the Irish laity. They are in one way or other pledged to the Whigs or bound to the Government in a way in which Catholic gentlemen are not bound in England. The consequence will be, if they do not look sharp, for it is their business more than any one's else, we shall be thrown only upon a section of Ireland instead of representing the whole. This would matter little to them, if it were a mere Defence Association or Political Union — but since it is an institution set up by the Holy See, and must go on, they at least should feel the difficulty they are in and some do. Begging your good prayers for us, I am, My dear Sir John, Very sincerely Yours in Xt

John H Newman of the Oratory

Sir John Simeon Bart.

TO CARDINAL WISEMAN

The Oratory Birmingham August 1. 1854

My dear Lord Cardinal

I was truly surprised and vexed to hear the day before yesterday that the action with which your Eminence had been threatened was actually in progress and to be tried this month. We had heard it was all at an end.[1]

One good thing is that it will be over so soon — and another that, come what will, it can but be an exposure of the animus and conduct of the parties who have set it on foot. But it seems hard that any additional trouble should come upon you, who have so many cares upon you already — and so I have been saying Mass for your Eminence this morning, with the full confidence that all these trials are only heaping up for you a greater amount of merit.

Of course this letter requires no answer — but I should be sorry you should not know the anxiety I am ever feeling in the anxieties of which you are the subject — and understand that, not in word, but really, I am, My dear Lord, Your affte friend & servt in Xt

John H Newman of the Oratory

His Eminence The Cardinal Wiseman

[1] Richard Boyle a Westminster priest with a grievance against Wiseman was sueing him for libel. The trial to which Newman refers, held on 18 Aug. at Guildford, went in Wiseman's favour, but was followed by an appeal and a second trial, when £1000 damages were awarded against Wiseman. A threatened third trial in the summer of 1855 was averted by a compromise. See Wilfrid Ward, *The Life and Times of Cardinal Wiseman*, 2nd edition, London 1897, II, pp. 93–5, and *DR*, (Sept. 1855), pp. 146–64.

WEDNESDAY 2 AUGUST 1854   Dr and Mrs Ives went   F Bernard returned

TO THE EARL OF SHREWSBURY

Oratory, Hagley Road, Birmingham. Aug. 3/54

My dear Lord Shrewsbury,

Father Dalgairns returned last night, and, on talking over the matter this morning, we came to the conclusion, on the subject of which your Lordship spoke to me, which I anticipated on your opening it. He could not, I feel persuaded, with his present engagements, undertake so sacred a task consistently with the feelings with which he regards the memory of its deeply regretted subject, and with the responsibility which a Biographer will contract towards the Catholics of England.

I take the liberty of inclosing letters from him and me to Lady Shrewsbury, explaining the necessity he is under of declining what he is sensible is a great honor offered to him. I have ventured to suggest Mr Scott to her Ladyship.[1]

The day before yesterday some venison came to us from your Lordship, for which kind present we beg our respectful thanks.

I am, My dear Lord Shrewsbury, Your Lordship's faithful Servant in Xt

John H Newman of the Oratory

The Rt Honble The Earl of Shrewsbury

TO RICHARD STANTON

Oratory Bm Aug 3/54

My dearest Fr Richard,

I have been at the Towers, that is one reason of my silence. My load of letters is another. A third is the unpleasantness of the subject you write about.

I wish you could come down here, while I am still here, and let us have a talk. Now do. I remain here over the 15th.

Your letter is (necessarily) too vague, to answer. I suppose he is a

---

[1] Lord Shrewsbury replied on 18 Aug. that the widow of the Sixteenth Earl of Shrewsbury would at once ask W. H. Scott to be her husband's biographer, but nothing came of this.

child — but you do not mention any thing which is specifically un-philippine.[1]

The Earl of S. [Shrewsbury] is very kind — has sent us half a buck — and given me £100 for the University.

We think we have bought a burying ground, if the title is made good. If you came, you should see it.

Ever Yrs most affly J H N

P.S. I am rather over worked. We shall be hard up for Students at first. We have plenty of money

TO ARCHBISHOP CULLEN

Birmingham August 5. 1854

My dear Lord

I have just heard from Mr Kelly that the purchase money for the Medical School must be forthcoming next Wednesday. May I then beg your Grace to have it ready? It is £1450. Mr Kelly will call on you.

He also wants the names of the *Trustees* for the property. Will you think who they shall be — e.g. Your Grace, Surgeon Ellis, and Mr James O'Ferrall?

I have this evening heard from Dr Brownson, and inclose his letter.[2]

I have got M. Montalembert's name, but cannot get Lord Fingall's or Lord Kenmare's. If any thing leads you to write to me, I will ask you to say *whom* I shall write to at Paris, for a list of Paris people, for our books.

The following comes from Fr Rosmini, but I have no right to quote *it as his*.

'Ho ricevuto communicazione autentica che il risultato dell' esame delle mie opere in Roma si fu che nihil inventum est censurà dignum. Se poi si publichera, quando, e come, non si sa ancora.'[3]

Begging your Grace's blessing, I am, My dear Lord, Your affte friend & Servt in Xt

John H Newman of the Oratory

The Archbp of Dublin.

[1] It is not clear to whom this refers.

[2] Dated 11 July, replying to Newman's letter of 6 June. See last note there, and letter of 23 Aug.

[3] After lengthy examination of Rosmini's works, a meeting of the Holy Office, presided over by Pius IX, decided that there was in them nothing deserving of censure. However the decree giving effect to this, although it was communicated to Rosmini, was to be kept a secret, and attacks on him were still able to circulate. See Claude Leetham, *Rosmini*, London 1957, pp. 433–6.

SUNDAY 6 AUGUST 1854   F Nicholas went away at night to Captain Phillipps's at Paris

TO VISCOUNT FEILDING

The Oratory, Birmingham Aug. 9, 1854

My dear Lord Feilding

I am very much obliged by your consent to my request. No subscription or trouble of any kind is implied in your giving your name. I want it for its own sake.

I wish you all success in the conversion now on your hands and will not fail to remember it,[1] and am, begging your good prayers Your Lordship's faithful & affte Servt in Xt,

John H. Newman of the Oratory

The Viscount Feilding

SATURDAY 12 AUGUST 1854   [W. G.] Ward and his wife and child came   Mr Flanagan came

TO F. W. FABER

Sunday August 13. [1854]

My dear Dr Faber

Accept my best congratulations on the well deserved honor, which I have heard of this morning. We all rejoice.[2]

Tell Fr Richard, if he comes down here after the Assumption, I will show him our new burying place

Ever Yrs affly J H N

TO CARDINAL WISEMAN

Oratory Bm August 13. 1854

My dear Lord

It was very kind in you to write so soon. We had been waiting for news with great anxiety, and been saying Mass for your Eminence's intention. It was a great relief to have your letter. I suppose it means

[1] Perhaps the conversion hoped for was that of Lord Feilding's father, the Earl of Denbigh, to whom he had been reconciled in the previous year.

[2] Faber wrote on 12 Aug., 'You will smile when I tell you that the Pope has made me a D.D. because of my book.' i.e. *All for Jesus*.

that the opposite party could not bring the letter home to you — any how, he is non suited.[1]

The news of Fr Faber's doctorate was very gratifying to us

Ever Yr affte friend & Servt in Xt   John H Newman

The Cardl Wiseman

MONDAY 14 AUGUST 1854 news that F Nicholas had had a touch of the Cholera or tomorrow Mr Flanagan went for good to Lisbon F Edward returned
TUESDAY 15 AUGUST [W. G.] Ward and his wife and child went

TO JOHN EDWARD BOWDEN

Oratory Bm In fest. Assumpt [15 August] 1854

My dearest John,

A happy feast to all of you in St Philip's House — and congratulations from all of us on your Father's honours. They are an amusing answer to the criticisms or rumour of criticisms which have been going about concerning passages in his book.

However, I do not write merely to say what you must know we feel without our saying it, especially as I wrote a line to the Revmo P. Superiore himself, but to say that poor Bonavia has written to me for money — I really am very hard up — and don't know what I shall do. However, if you recommend, I will give him £4 (four) more; that is, if you will give it him for me. Then I shall owe you £14, I think, which I will try to persuade Fr Stanislas to send to you. I think your bankers are Coutts.[2]

I shall be going back soon, and am melancholy at the thought. It is a sad thing having two homes, or, if it makes it better, being more than half one's time away from home

Ever Yrs affectionately in Mary & Philip

John H Newman of the Oratory

P.S.   Your Father's second letter has just come — when I have some precise information *from whom* the chain of the Cross comes, I must write thanks. I am very much pleased and grateful. If Fr Richard brings it down, he can also bring your dear Mother's chain and rochet.[3]

[1] See note to letter of 1 Aug. to Wiseman.
[2] See letter of 5 Jan. 1854 to John Bowden.
[3] Bowden replied on 18 Aug. from Capheaton, 'I have not heard anything about the second chain which you mention. I hope that now your things are collecting fast,

TO THOMAS SCRATTON

The Oratory. Bm August 15. 1854

My dear Scratton

Your letter has just come. I find I shall not be able to return for several weeks yet. The reason is, that I cannot dispense with my books while certain prospective Numbers of the Gazette are still unfinished. This is a difficulty I cannot get over. It is not for want of working that I don't get on faster.

I inclose a letter to R. W. [Wilberforce][1] I wrote to you last night. Do you think if I looked towards Grafton Street or any of the streets between Stephen's Green, and the Trinity College Gardens and the Kingstown Station, I should have better luck? I should have been very glad, if, when I returned, I could have stepped into my house — but that I suppose is impossible.

I thought of asking you how it would suit you to be one of my inmates — but there is no hurry of settling the point

Will you tell Henry W. [Wilberforce] with my love that it would be a real kindness, if he would settle the Achilli account with Mr Kelly and Mr Star, and send me the balance to my account at the 'Birmingham Banking Co, Bennett's Hill, Birmingham.'[2]

P.S.   Do you know whether Myles O'Reilly is yet at the House, and furnishing it, or preparing to furnish? etc etc. I want to know, but I don't want to be known to be asking.

As to the Lawyer, I had already employed Messrs Kelly and Maxwell — which was the reason I mentioned them.

TO ROBERT ISAAC WILBERFORCE

The Oratory, Hagley Road, Birmingham August 15/54

My dear Robert Wilberforce,

I am truly sorry I do not see you in Dublin — it will be impossible for me to move for some weeks from this place.

there is some hope of your being consecrated soon. I am afraid that Father Richard will not be able to bring down my mother's chain and rochet, as I have left them locked up at home.'   [1] See next letter.
     [2] The conclusion and signature have been cut out.

216

It would give me so much pleasure to see you. I dare say you may think it out of place to visit me here — but no one possibly could know, so it would be no scandal. Except Frs St John and perhaps Dalgairns, no one knows you here by sight. And no one would even see you. It is a large house. People are ever coming in and out — there are plenty of rooms — and no one sees any one else. It is not as if it were a congregation which knew your *name* — but except a few, they are Brummagem snobs and factory girls, who know nothing of the theological world whatever. Since I wear a quasi archidiaconal dress, you would be taken for Fr Faber or some London Oratorian, if anyone saw you. So do come

Ever Yrs affly J H Newman

The Venble Archdn Wilberforce

TO MRS J. W. BOWDEN

The Oratory Bm August 16. 1854

My dear Mrs Bowden

Fr Brownbill's letter is quite satisfactory. You had better *not* send mine to him, but destroy it.[1]

I return the letter. I am very well, and have no very great trouble at the moment, thank you — but am overworked. My Gazette keeps me from having a holiday, which I should most covet — I expect to go back to Dublin soon

Love to Emily Ever Yrs affly in Xt

John H Newman

THURSDAY 17 AUGUST 1854   F Frederic's brother came   Monsell called in passing through to Ireland?

TO ARCHBISHOP CULLEN

The Oratory Hagley Road Bm Aug 17/54

My dear Lord,

Mr Monsell happened to be here, when your Grace's letter came — and he agreed with me that we might safely put the matter into Mr Kelly's hands, as a matter of business, the like of which must often occur — Accordingly I propose to send him today £1400, which is the

[1] Cf. Newman's letters of 16 and 23 July.

balance in the joint name of yourself and me at the Hibernian Bank.[1] I suppose it is very near enough, if not over the mark — for I gave £100 as earnest money before I left. I will write to the Archbishops as you suggest. As to money I am now nearly swept clean — except £270 of the whole £2000, which I transferred to my private account, for accidental needs. But I almost doubt whether *I* ought to ask for more, as soon as we get a Procurator.

I am much pleased at your account of the judgment passed on our purchase — I trust from every thing I hear it is a good hit. I have already (from the first) told Dr Leahy, I considered him to represent Dr Slattery in the matter, which he quite agreed to.[2]

It is a trouble to me, not to have returned to Dublin before now — but I cannot go on with the Gazette, without being a little longer time with my *books* here. You will not suppose I am not writing for the University — on the contrary it is my one business from morning to night, and I want a holy day sadly — for brain work is to me the most fatiguing of work. It is like manual labour, tho' I do not mean to say I should be able to bear up against a tread mill or hemp picking better.

Will you be so kind as to return me Dr Brownson's letter — he wants an early answer — and as I knew the Bishop of Boston wished some confidential conversation with your Grace I did not like to write till I heard from you.[3]

Begging your blessing I am, My dear Lord, affectionately yours

John H Newman

P.S.   Since writing this, I hear from Mr Kelly that you have paid the money. I am almost sorry *I* did not. Mind the *full* responsibility is *mine*.

TO JOHN MACHALE, ARCHBISHOP OF TUAM

The Oratory, Birmingham, August 17, 1854.

My Dear Lord

You will be pleased to hear that I have been able to accomplish the purchase of a Medical School in Dublin for something like £1500. I

---

[1] This was for the purchase of the Medical School, but see Postscript.

[2] Patrick Leahy now Vice-Rector of the University, was the Vicar General of Michael Slattery, Archbishop of Cashel.

[3] See letter of 23 Aug. to Brownson. The Bishop of Boston, John Fitzpatrick, passed through Birmingham on 21 July. He not only knew the situation in America but was a personal friend of Brownson.

trust it will be a very serviceable building, although we shall not be able to open our classes in it in the ensuing autumn.

I have not liked to conclude the transaction without having the satisfaction of feeling that I have your Grace's congratulations and blessing, though I do not expect, nor does the occasion need, that you should put yourself to the trouble of answering this.

I am, my dear Lord Archbishop, with profound respect, Your obedient, faithful servant in Christ,

John H. Newman, of the Oratory.[1]

The Most Reverend the Archbishop of Tuam.

TO JOHN MACLACHLAN

The Oratory Hagley Road Birmingham Augst 17/54

Revd Sir,

Will you allow me the favor of placing your name on the books of our new Irish University? It will involve neither expence nor trouble to you, and will be a satisfaction to us.[2]

I am, Revd Sir, Very faithfully Yours in Xt

John H Newman of the Oratory

The Revd J. Maclachlan

TO H. E. MANNING

The Oratory Bm Aug 17. 1854

My dear Manning

Monsell, who was here yesterday, urges me to set you upon Aubrey de Vere and to get you to oblige him, as a matter of duty, to become our Professor of Political Science.[3]

It seems a very hard thing, that he will not take his part in a work,

---

[1] MacHale wrote on the back of this letter, 'Dr. Newman's letter about a purchase for the new University. *No answer*, he says, *is required*.' See also MacHale's letter of 6 Oct., placed before Newman's to him of 8 Oct.

[2] John Maclachlan (1826–93), one of the priests at Glasgow, gave his name. In 1878 he became the first Bishop of Galloway in the restored Scottish Hierarchy.

[3] De Vere wrote to Newman on 12 Aug. that he was too ignorant to accept a professorship. See also Newman's letter to him of 21 Aug.

which he confesses to be very important, and which every one but himself thinks he could materially serve. What right has he to set up his own opinion against every one's else?

However, you will know, better than I, how to move yourself successfully — but you really must succeed.

I have heard nothing about you for some time. So poor Mr Gubbins had to knock under. I have heard no particulars

　　　　Ever Yours affectly in Xt　John H Newman of the Oratory
The Revd Dr Manning

TO J. B. MORRIS

　　　　　　　　　　The Oratory Hagley Road Birmingham Aug 17/54
My dear Morris,

Some months ago I wrote to Bastard asking him to give us his name to put on our University Books. As I have never heard from him, I suppose he is out of the country.

At the same time, if my memory serves me right, and this is what leads me to inflict this letter upon you, I asked him to get me your Reverence's for a like purpose. Let me now repeat my request to you in propriâ personâ.[1]

I trust you are well and flourishing — and making converts, which some one told me you were.[2] Fr Darnell, I am sorry to say, has had a touch of the Cholera at Paris — as we do not hear again, I trust he is progressing towards recovery
　　　　　　　　Ever Yours affectly in Xt　John H Newman
The Revd J B Morris

TO GEORGE RYDER

　　　　　　　The Oratory Hagley Road Birm August 17/54
My dear Ryder,

I am on the point of taking my house in Dublin — where I should recommend Harry [Ryder] to be placed. I should recommend it, be-

---

[1] Bastard apologised on 21 Aug. for not answering Newman's letter, and gladly gave his own and Morris's names for the University.

[2] Morris was Bastard's chaplain at Yealmpton in Devon, where he opened a new chapel in July 1852. 'There he received several distinguished converts into the Church.' *Gillow*, v, p. 130. Bastard, however, wrote, 'it is very uphill work. His converts hitherto amount to 7.'

cause he would be with English people he knew, and not with strangers: and because, as we consider him to have an ecclesiastical vocation, as I suppose you do yourself, he will be able to take care of himself better when he is with me, than elsewhere.

There is, however, this difficulty, that I cannot take any one into my house under £100 — first, because my house will be expensive in point of rent and taxes — and servants — and next, because I shall have no means of avoiding taking any one, unless I name a high sum — and, I suspect, I shall have some difficulty even then of making both ends meet.

At the University House, I hope we shall *do* for youths at from £40 to £50 — but it will be in every sense a rough place — it must be so.

I hope this sum will not be a difficulty in your way. You should consider that Harry will be there only for *two* years of necessity, since he is now 17, I believe — though of course you might keep him there longer. Also he will be there continuously from the beginning of the Session to the end — the only vacation, being from the end of June (I suppose) or July, to October — so that the £100 goes for more time than in an English University.

If there is any other question you wish to ask, let me know. I told him to mention to you, we thought it would be well for him to receive minor orders before he went.

Ever Yours affectionately in Xt

John H Newman of the Oratory

G. D. Ryder Esqr

P.S.   Since writing the above we have had a long meeting on the subject of our Treasurer's halfyearly statement — and I regret to say the upshot is very unfavorable. We find we are exceeding our income frightfully, the main expence being our Chapel. However, we find that one difficulty arises from the boys — and at Christmas we have settled to close that portion of our establishment. This of course affects the little boys especially — it will be a great trouble to part with Charles and Cyril — but we cannot help it — As to Lisle, his time is naturally so nearly run out, that it is no great matter. This will vex you as it does us — but we cannot help it, as you would see clearly, if you were to go through our accounts J H N[1]

[1] Ryder replied on 19 Aug., 'I shall very much like Harry to be in your house. He is very anxious for it, though, dear boy, when I read your account to him, he took for granted that all that was possible for him was the University House, and he was for choosing that with all its roughness in preference to an Indian cadetship . . . But, as you say, I do believe he has a vocation for the Priesthood . . . I shall feel it to be an

TO THOMAS SCRATTON

Oy. Bm. Aug 17/54

My dear Scratton

I wrote to Mr Bianconi some weeks ago that I thought it important to get the lease for 150 years, and he answered he thought Mr J. O Ferrall could best sound the people — which was one of the subjects of my answer-less letter — It is a pity there should be delay.[1]

I believe I alone am answerable about the fittings up [sic] of the University House. If any of the subcommittee is on the spot, he might answer for me — but, if Mr Butler[2] put them on paper, 1. 2. 3 etc. I would answer them by return of post. It is not as if *I* did not wish you to save me the trouble, which would do me a great service, but I am bothered more than you know perhaps, with the sensitiveness of some Irish people — tho' this must not be mentioned.

O'Reilly has taken all the furniture upon himself. He is a person you can safely say to, all you think about it.

Ever Yours affly J H N

P.S.   Aug 20. I am very sorry to hear of your boils. As to Number 21 and 22 Ely Place, as you describe them, I don't know what the rates and taxes are — but I will assume that *together* they are not more than £30 or very little over. If so, if *both* the houses are, or are put, into repair (e.g. the *drains*,) I would gladly have them for £100 a year — and would take them for 3 years or, if very much pressed, for 5 years. Would I go above £100? I don't like to do so — They ask £63 for the one and £55.7.8 (for 5 years) for the other. Supposing I got each for £55, that is £110 the two . . . And they are the *same* Landlord . . . Well, I would go as far as £110 for the two for 3 years — but grudgingly. However, I am very sorry to see that, in my previous calculation, I find I cannot allow /6d more than £*120* for *rent, rates and taxes together* — and *this* (110 + 30) will make £140. Unless I do it for not more than £120, I shall for the £20 extra depend on my lodgers, which will be a bore.

Please, if you are well, go and look over our University Medical

honour and a pleasure as well as a religious duty to assist. The 100£ a year I can certainly only meet by selling out. But so it must be. . . .'

After referring also to his second son Lisle, who wanted to go to Newman's University, and the two young ones, Ryder concluded, 'Many many thanks, my dear N. for all your persevering kindness to them.'

[1] This refers to the University House, 86 Stephen's Green.
[2] i.e. the architect.

School at the end of Crow Street. Use Mr Ellis's name or Mr Peirs Kelly's the lawyer's. I have two plans for it for the coming year. 1. To make it a medical *lodging* ⟨boarding⟩ house — only indirectly connected with the University. or 2. a second Stephen's Green formal University Hall, to give us elbow room.

J H N

TO MICHAEL SLATTERY, ARCHBISHOP OF CASHEL

The Oratory. Birmingham August 17. 1854

My dear Lord,

I think Dr Leahy has mentioned to your Grace the interesting negociation in which we have been engaged with respect to the purchase of a Medical School in Dublin. It is excellently situated, and has both a very good character — and is considered a very good investment of the money, which is between £1400 and £1500.

I am glad now to tell you that the transaction is concluded and the place ours.

Begging your Grace's blessing, I am, My dear Lord, Your faithful and affte Servt in Xt

John H Newman of the Oratory

The Most Revd The Archbp of Cashel

TO WILLIAM CLIFFORD

The Oratory Hagley Road Birmingham. 18 August 1854

My dear Dr Clifford,

Would you kindly consent to be one of our University Preachers? It will only take you one day in the year, and you shall have plenty of notice.

Some one said you were rather delicate just now, and would be unwilling to preach. I hope it is not so — but any how, I want your name, if you would kindly give it — and then, if when the time came, you felt unequal to the exertion, which I trust would not be the case, we could postpone your turn.

I do not know where you are, but beg your Bishop's blessing, if you are with him.[1]

Ever Yours very sincerely in Xt

John H Newman of the Oratory

The Honble W. Clifford D.D.

TO WILLIAM DODSWORTH

The Oratory, Birmm. Aug 18/54

My dear Dodsworth,

I have wished to write to you ever since I got your letter, which was most welcome.[2] How strange that I should have missed you whether in London or *elsewhere*, since you have been a Catholic. My time is so cruelly taken up, not least with letter writing, that I have been hindered from answering you. Yesterday, e.g. I wrote 20 letters — today I shall have to write a host — and when I have got through business correspondence my hand gets so tired that I cannot hold my pen without pain which is the case even now, so that letters to friends go to the wall.

I got your letter in Dublin, but have been here for some weeks, nominally on holiday — but, alas, I have been harder worked than I should have been in Dublin. All things are going on, as well as they can — a beginning is not an ending, and we have the many difficulties of a beginning, of which we must not complain. Do you mean *soon* to send your boys? We shall have, I suppose, 'the Nations' in distinct houses, We expect soon, not at once, from 60 to 120 Yankees — and I am beginning at once an English house of *my own friends*. That is the sort of excuse, I make, for the sake of drawing a line. I suppose I shall have a fair *number*, and the difficulty is about getting bed-rooms enough in one house. If you keep the intention of sending your boys to us, I should rejoice at taking them in, if I have room — but I so little know what my room will be. At present I seem to have about seven youths, or eight, coming to me, but I don't suppose they will come all at once — and some may not come at all. G. R's [Ryder] sons, e.g. H. W's [Wilberforce] son, Hy. B's [Henry Bowden] son etc etc — but at present every thing is uncertain in these matters of detail. We shall not begin *in form* till after

[1] Clifford, who gave his name, was living with his Bishop, George Errington, at Plymouth.

[2] Dodsworth wrote on 20 June from Como, having spent nearly two years in Italy. He became a Catholic in 1851, but of his family, only his two boys had followed his example. He congratulated Newman on the University and hoped to send his boys there, a hope which was not realised.

Christmas. There will be a great many small local jealousies, which I must not mind — and I must get my friends to pray that I may have, not only the gift of wisdom, but of tranquillity. The *ordinary* expenses of the University residence, taking in every thing, we hope to be from £40 to £50 a year. But I can hardly recommend a friend to accept it. It stands to reason that to be as cheap as that, things must be very rough. I mean to charge myself £100. The course consists of two years, or four years, or seven years — and the session, including three terms, will be about thirty-eight weeks.

We are expecting more persecution here — but wise men read the signs of the times differently. The Peelites are much frightened — some of them talking even to the repeal of the Emancipation Act. Others go no further than to anticipate the loss of the Maynooth grant, and some inconvenience in the holding of our property. Others, as Hope Scott, think that John Bull is only fighting in gloves, which he never will take off, [f]or he cannot *bear the sight* of real cruelty or injustice, big as he may talk beforehand. The war will not create a diversion, unless it were some great disaster, which does not seem likely.

Ever Yours affly John H. Newman of the Oratory

P.S.   I have forgotten to thank you for your name, which on *many* accounts is most welcome to me.

TO J. J. IGNAZ VON DÖLLINGER

Oratory — Hagley Road — Birmingham. August 18/54

My dear Dr Dollinger

I thank you for your very kind letter, and for all the encouragement you give me — while I am much disappointed that you cannot give us your most valuable assistance in any shape, though we had no right to expect it.[1]

Yet this has struck me — We shall not begin the Theological Classes

---

[1] Döllinger replied as follows to Newman's invitation of 15 Dec. 1853:

'Munich 15 July 54

My dear Sir,

I have tarried so long in answering your kind letter respecting the part you wish me to take in the lectures to be delivered in your University, because I really felt and am feeling still a great desire to accept such a honourable and flattering invitation and to contribute my mite towards an undertaking, which if the old antipathy between the Anglosaxon and the Celtic race doth not frustrate it, will be an invaluable benefit to the Catholic Cause. But I have not yet been able to discover a way, by which, without neglecting duties nearer home, I might make myself serviceable at Dublin. You will agree with me, when I tell you, that I am regularly delivering two lectures every day;

for a year to come — and even then, they may be delayed, or at least we could put off one particular set of Lectures or course of subjects, or get a substitute to lecture for the occasion — Now you cannot be *certain* that a little time hence, say this time two years, you might not be able to help us — At least then let me enter your name *now* as Professor of Ecclesiastical History — when the time actually comes, you can but withdraw it — Sufficit diei malitia sua.

If you let me do this, I would set down your name in the beginning of September, when I go to Dublin

You know how conclusive a blow you are considered to have struck at Bunsen and the Hippolytus-mongers.[1]

Ever Yours most sincerely in Xt

John H Newman of the Oratory

The Very Revd Dr Dollinger etc etc.

TO MISS M. R. GIBERNE

Oratory Birmingham August 18/54

My dear Miss Giberne,

I think you have had a message from me about St Cecilia — You were to do any thing you liked, so that St Cecilia was not black — ditto about the carriage As to your own prospect of things, I really don't know what to recommend you. I am rather glad there has been no offer to you to continue with the young Princess — it might have been awk-

it is true, that there are two vacations in the year; but one, at easter-time, requires my service in the church or chapel, and the other would nearly coincide with your vacations, as you will and must keep them too. Besides, to say the truth, at the beginning of August I generally find myself so tired, not to say exhausted, that I am sighing for a season of relaxation and a change of occupation, whereas lecturing in English would be rather hard work for me, and require careful preparation.

Of course Dr Phillips and myself we feel honoured in having our names put down in the University-list, and give you carte blanche in this respect.—May God bless your efforts, I cannot express the joy it gave me when I read that you had accepted the task, for which an equally competent man could not be found in all England and Ireland!

I have read with the greatest interest and pleasure your lectures on the Turks, in constant admiration of the versatility of your genius, and the correctness of your historical views, pray let us soon have an other fruit from the rich stores of your mind.

Begging to be included in your memento's I remain, Dear Newman Yours most devotedly J. Doellinger'

[1] Döllinger published at Ratisbon in 1853 *Hippolytus und Kallistus*, which was considered to have proved Hippolytus's authorship of the *Philosophoumena* and to have vindicated Pope Callistus, against Chevalier Bunsen's *Hippolytus and his Age*, four volumes, London and Leipzig 1852.

ward.[1] Perhaps the best course will be, not to decide at once, but to wait and see the turn things take. I hope you continue well, and your knee. I should have thought a warm climate good for it. We are expecting more persecution here, but not in a way which would come home to us. What does come home, is the expence of the war — what with the rise of prices and the increase of taxes, it is very hard for an honest m[an to c]ontrive to make both ends meet — and I suppose this is only the beginning. I am amused at *your* being interested in the war — I thought you were so intensely unpolitical.

H. Wilberforce has become editor of the Catholic Standard, and leaves Ireland.

We are gradually, though slowly, increasing our chapel congregation — though about this you hear doubtless from better correspondants than I. I am sorry to say that Mrs Poncia is far from well — with the erisipelas in her head, which is a very serious thing — Fr Nicholas has just had a touch of the Cholera at Paris — Mrs Gordon has been in serious danger, but is convalescent.[2] We have bought (I trust) a burying place — under the Lickey hills, just about 8 miles off — it is a most beautiful spot. The deed of sale is not yet signed, so it is not quite ours yet. We are going to build a cottage there, and ultimately a mortuary chapel. Fr Ambrose has bought some ground next to it, so we shall have an estate of 3 or 4 acres. The good Catholics of New York sent me a present of £200 — and I had put aside £300 from the Achilli fund —[3] we have done it with these two sums together.

Ever Yrs affly J H N

I have sent you the University Gazettes by Northcote

TO MISS HOLMES

The Oratory Birmingham August 18. 1854

My dear Miss Holmes,

I know that people abroad always look for letters from home, as if they were to bring some great news to them. They fancy that many

[1] See letter of 15 May 1854.
[2] An undated letter to Philip Gordon perhaps refers to this:
'My dear Philip
It is with the deepest concern I have just got your letter.
I write a hasty line, with the post boy in the room, to say that we shall all say Mass tomorrow morning (Saturday) for your dear Mother. Tell her so.
I was saying mass for dear Joseph this morning Ever Yrs affly J H N'
[3] i.e. surplus which the donors put at Newman's disposal.

things are happening, of which they hear nothing, and think themselves cut off from their own world; while in truth things are going on so quietly that there is nothing to be told. You seem to ask a letter under this feeling, though I have nothing to write about. I was pleased to find from your letters that, with some drawbacks, you were on the whole well pleased with your Italian sojourn. However, wherever you go, I think it is a good rule to observe, to expect nothing. So I say, if you are going to Rome. There indeed you cannot expect too much in a super-natural line — but, according to my impression of it you gain that privilege by a great many human and earthly discomforts, which make it, as it should be, a place of pilgrimage. The climate shifting from heat to cold, the heavy and insidious atmosphere, the alternative of whisking dust in clouds and ankle deep mud, and the ever lively ever hungry insects, make it pre-eminently, to me at least, a place of penance — and the want of pavements, the water pipes emptying the clouds upon your head, if you walk in rain, the forlorn untidy ruined palaces, and the faded churches, would be insupportable, were not the ground you tread on the dust of martyrs, and the wonderful dome, which you see from all parts of the city, the roof over the body of St Peter. I do not know whether you are still likely to go to Rome or not — but if you do, prepare for all this, and for a degenerate people.

I have been here for some weeks, not exactly for a holyday, for I have been more busy than I like — but I could be spared from Dublin, whither I return soon. I have been saying Masses for you lately. I only wish you had some settled prospect before you, but it is God's will. We are expecting the Catholics to be more and more oppressed in England — the only vulnerable point is the property — but that is a very serious one. The war as yet has made no diversion — nor will it, unless there are some great reverses, which does not seem likely

Ever Yours affectly in Xt   John H Newman of the Oratory

TO F. R. WARD

The Oratory. Hagley Road. Birmingham. Aug 18/54.
My dear Mr Ward

Mr Monsell, who called here the day before yesterday, on his way to Ireland, informed me that he intended to take my advice as to the disposition of a sum of money left to him and Mr Fullerton in trust by Lady Olivia Acheson.

He told me that the sum of money, which he and (I understood) Mr Fullerton, wished to put at my disposal (he was not sure whether principle or yearly interest) was £1900, and that it must be given, in some shape or other, as charity to the poor.

He also wished me to write to him a formal letter on the subject, proposing some object or objects, and advised me first to write to you, in order to ascertain whether I was naming purposes which would fulfil the intention of the Trust.

I have no hesitation in naming one at once, should it approve itself to a legal judgment. It is this; — A person intimately connected with our community has built us a chapel, which has cost him as near as possible the exact sum of £1900. He has not given up the money, but has lent it to us for a term of years, till we are rich enough to build our own church — The chapel was built for the *poor*, and is used by the poor, and by very few others. We have no means at all of paying the interest, and as yet have *not* paid a farthing of it, and the lender, though he would not urge us for it, is not a rich man, and simply wants the money. Thus we have incurred a debt, which we cannot pay, principle or interest, for the sake of the poor.

Now I suppose it would not be possible to give us the principle of the trust money, to pay off our debt, because it *is* a debt — , and the law might not like a charitable bequest to go on payment of a debt: — though if this could be done, it is the simplest arrangement, (and when the chapel was pulled down, we might engage to produce the sum, and give it to the church to be built; and not pull it down till then).

If it cannot, at least the interest of the sum left, might go, I suppose, in securing free seats for the poor. Say there are 60 days of obligation in the year, and that a poor person paid 1d per attendance — then a free sitting for him would cost 5/ a year or £1 would buy four free sittings, and £50 (supposing such was the interest) 200 sittings, or £70 (supposing that the interest) 280 sittings.

We would put up a board with an inscription, to the effect that 'In this chapel 200, or 280 etc etc. sittings are reserved without payment for the poor in consequence of a yearly sum given us for that purpose by the Trustees of Lady O.A.'

When we built our Church, we would burden it with a similar obligation.

Excuse the trouble of this application & Believe me Very truly yours in Xt

John H Newman of the Oratory

F. Ward Esqr.

SATURDAY 19 AUGUST 1854   F Frederic's brother went

TO F. R. WARD

The Oratory Hagley Road, Birmingham Aug. 20. 1854.
My dear Mr Ward

I am much obliged by your speedy answer to mine, and, as you wish, I write by return of post.

We have read your case over — and I have one or two things to remark.

1. You imply the lender of the £1900 has engaged to take no interest. This is not so — only — he has not pressed for it; and we have not paid him, *simply because we* cannot. We intended to give him interest *from the seat-letting* — but it has been a failure. We have taken nothing from the poor for sittings. We have thought and talked of it, but we have not liked to do so — I do not know that we can honestly say that the lender of the money would not give it us, if he could afford it.

2. I am not clear on the legal definition of 'poor.' Is it a married man with a number of children, who has from 10 to 15 shillings a week? is it a young woman in a factory who supports herself?

3. We should not like to make the *ground* trust property.

4. There is another suggestion for the disposition of the money. We are giving away in shillings and halfcrowns at the very least £60 a year — *which we cannot give of our own* — and are in consequence in considerable distress. Sometimes we have tried to screw the money out of the Offertory, but the offertory *never* has paid the expences of the Chapel Service. The consequence has been it, (the charity money) has been a debt on the Chapel Account carried on and accumulating year after year. It would then be a direct charity to the poor, if 'the principal or interest of £1900 were given to the Head Clergyman for the time being of the Oratorian House in Hagley Road to be dispensed in alms for the *temporal* necessities of the poor.'

5. I understood Mr Monsell to say that the money was left for the Catholic *poor*. Your letter suggests it is left for *religion*. If so, the simplest plan would be to leave it 'to the Head Clergyman of the Oratorian House for religious duties rendered by the House to the Catholics of Birmingham.'

You may think it strange we do not name some such objects as schools. But, the truth is, we are too poor to undertake schools — We cannot sustain our *present* religious liabilities. Did we take it as school money, *at present* it would simply be an additional expence to us.[1]

Very sincerely yours in Xt   John H. Newman

P.S.   Your letter came open.

TO WILLIAM MONSELL

The Oratory. Hagley Road Birmingham Aug 21. 1854

My dear Monsell,

Thank you for your attempt to see Dr Cullen and Sergt O'Brien. It is rather good, Dr C. writes reproachfully to me about my absence from Dublin, and he absent too! And for your letters to Sergt O'B and Mr Fitzgerald.[2] I am afraid you said you were leaving Ireland by September 10. If so, I must look forward to your second visit there.

I fancy you did a good service to me by putting it into Lord Shrewsbury's head to send to the Dublin Post Office for his letters; which had not struck him.[3]

As to the titles, perhaps you did not observe how I had evaded the point in my first number of the Gazette —[4] would it do? viz

'The Archbishops and Bishops of Ireland, as present at the Synodal Meeting etc.

> The Most Revd Dr Cullen of Dublin, Apostolic etc[5]
>
> The Most Revd Dr Dixon of Armagh, Primate etc.
>
> The Most Revd Dr Slattery of Cashel
>
> > etc etc.'

Is it against the Law to call them Bishops of Ireland? or to call Dr Slattery 'of Cashel' subaudi Bishop?[6]

Ever Yours affly in Xt   John H Newman

W Monsell Esqr M P

[1] As Ward explained on 22 Aug. the money was left for 'the advancement and maintenance of the R.C. religion,' and it appears to have been used for sittings for the poor in the chapel.

[2] Monsell's letter of 19 Aug. shows that this was J. D. Fitzgerald, a barrister and M.P. for Ennis. Monsell was trying to get names for the University.

[3] Newman's letter of 3 Aug. had been at the Poste Restante there.

[4] Monsell wrote that to use the rightful (although now illegal) titles of the Irish bishops, except where this was essential, gave great offence.

[5] Apostolic Delegate and Primate of Ireland.

[6] Monsell replied on 31 Aug., 'Your way of getting over the difficulties of the titles bill seems to me unexceptionable.'

TO THOMAS SCRATTON

The Oratory Bm Aug 21/54

My dear Scratton

Every thing promises well about the two houses. I shall be obliged by your signing the proposal. I sent you yesterday my ultimatum and ultimatissimum. It seems now really as if I might come at once to them on returning. I don't want furniture. At least I shall get it quite piece-meal as wanted; — as you send tea and sugar into a house.

Will you be so good as to tell Duffy to send Number 1 and Number 2 of the Gazette to 'W. Carberry Esqr, Green Park, Youghal.'

I am *very* anxious to get some *good* information of the points of Mr Butler the Mathematician — and as soon as possible. I have delayed saying so. It is not what I think or you say — but I must have something to appeal to — Does John O'Hagan know him? Who can definitely speak of him? *What were his honors*? Surely this can be executed *at once*. I should be very much obliged to you, if you would get me at least this point, and as much more as you can.[1] I suppose I shall come to Dublin next week — and it would be great thing if I could enter into negociation with him *before* I go.

Ever Yrs affly J H N

TO AUBREY DE VERE

The Oratory Hagley Road Bm August 21/54

My dear Mr de Vere,

I thank you very much for your valuable letter about Mr A [Aylward]. I think I now have all the information I can have about him — and the question only is, what is the next step. Does he ever come to Ireland? Where I expect to be next week.

But I cannot really let matters stay with yourself as they are. Because you cannot promise to do any thing *now*, is no reason why you should not do something in a year to come — and no reason you should not *promise* you will do something then — There is Mr John O'Hagan — he has undertaken the province of Political Economy. He says 'I cannot promise to begin at once — but you may set down my name on the

---

[1] Scratton obtained a strong testimonial, the only one now to be found, from Edward Butler's former tutor at Trinity College, Dublin, William Digby Sadleir. Butler was chosen as Professor of Mathematics in Sept.

understanding I have a year for preparation.' There is Dr O'Reilly S.J. who is to be our dogmatic Professor, whose Superiors will not agree to his coming till next year. There is Mr Flanagan, our civil engineer, who cannot begin till November 1855. There are the medical schools which cannot commence till the same date. What indeed shall we commence with now, but some grammar schools? Really if I may take the liberty of saying it, it is to me incomprehensible, how you can profess so great an interest in our goings on, and yet will not give us the benefit of your *name*, will not go so far as to *promise* us *any* thing, and only hold out some mysterious hope, that the day will come when you in your own judgment will think yourself quite equal to a Professorship.

Now, why will you not let me offer you the Professorship of Medieval History on the terms that you do not begin to lecture till November 1855? Then you may take *one* period. Depend upon it, very few persons have an accurate or comprehensive knowledge of a subject, till they are called on to have it. Every year you will add to your own circle of historical attainments by the stimulus of lecturing. Where are we to look, if every one refuses on grounds like yours?[1]

Very sincerely Yours in Xt   John H Newman of the Oratory

A de Vere Esqr

TO ROBERT ISAAC WILBERFORCE

The Oratory Hagley Road Bm August 21. 1854

My dear R W

Your letter of course interested me very much.[2] I have been saying Mass for you often for a long while — and, both as a Community, and (without your name) in Church, we have been praying for you from time to time — So, I know, have a great many others. I doubt not at all that the grace of God will prevail, for it is a matter of grace.

I quite understand your feeling. Your logical ground against such men as Mr Brock is perfectly good — but they will not understand that 'non me tua terrent dicta ferox, dii me terrint etc[3] You must let them

[1] De Vere replied on 5 Sept. that he had offered to take the Professorship of Poetry, 'the only one for which I am even tolerably qualified.' He knew nothing of mediaeval history, but might be able to deal with 'philosophical and social subjects.' In 1855 he was appointed Professor of Political and Social Science.

[2] This letter is not to be found, but see that of 1 Sept. to Robert Wilberforce.

[3] *Aeneid*, XII, 894–5. William Brock, from 1833 onwards for many years Rector of Bishop's Waltham in Hampshire, was attacking Robert Wilberforce's book *The Holy Eucharist*, for teaching the full Catholic doctrine. The latter would have welcomed a prosecution to decide whether his views were permissible in an Anglican, and when this test was not forthcoming, resigned his preferments.

have their most inglorious victory. You will not be so cruel as not to write to me, if you have any thing to say. How life is wearing away! how long it is since I have seen you! I am getting an old man now — and have too much to do, and it is telling on me — yet it is so difficult to hinder it.

Ever Yours affectly John H Newman of the Oratory.

The Venble Archdn Wilberforce

TUESDAY 22 AUGUST 1854   M. l'Abbé Segonde came for a month?[1]
WEDNESDAY 23 AUGUST   Mr Lucas came

TO ORESTES BROWNSON

Oratory Birmingham August 23. 1854

Dear Sir

My delay in answering your letter of July 11 is not owing to me. I sent it to Ireland at once, and had it back only yesterday evening.[2] By the same post, I received letters from different places which have perplexed me very much, as well as surprised me — so that, now that I write to you, I write, to my great disappointment and concern, with considerable difficulty. But I will neither delay my answer, nor be otherwise than open and straightforward in what I have to say.[3]

[1] F. Segondy was a young French priest of the Diocese of Montpellier, whom his Bishop (de Cabrières, later a Cardinal) made Vicar General in 1874. Segondy died in 1885 at the age of 64. He published *Essai sur l'Église anglicane*, Paris 1878, six hundred pages, and had evidently kept up his interest in England. He paid a tribute to Newman's work as a Catholic, and defended his attitude during the Vatican Council, pp. 381–2.

[2] Newman sent Brownson's letter to Cullen on 5 Aug.

[3] Cullen, when returning Brownson's letter, wrote on 21 Aug., 'I enclose a letter from Dr Donnelly now collecting in America [for the University]. He is of opinion that Dr. Brownson should not be appointed professor. I believe Dr Kenrick and Dr OConnor are of the same opinion. It would be well to weigh the matter well before you make any appointment.'

An authoritative correspondent also wrote from America on 4 Aug. to Dr Taylor in Dublin, 'It will be a bad business to bring Brownson to the University. He is a man, long regarded with distrust by some and dislike by many; but the last number of his review has evoked a perfect tempest of odium and indignation against him;' *McGrath*, p. 218 note. *Brownson's Quarterly Review*, II, 3rd Series (July 1854), pp. 329–54 contained an article 'Of Native Americanism' on the Know-Nothings. It has been summarised as follows: 'The gist of what he wrote in 1854 may be stated in a sentence. While Brownson condemned the excesses of the Native Americans in their new guise as "Know-Nothings," he stood firmly on his own Americanism and told the immigrants that, if they were regarded with hostility, it was because they often acted in such a way as to give Americans offence. It was an opinion that had at least a great deal of truth in it, but as usual Brownson put it tactlessly. What many readers got out of

I am urged then, now for the first time, in quarters to which I cannot but listen, to ask you whether it would be convenient to you to postpone your visit here, on the ground of some offence which happens to have been taken *just now*, in America, and, I believe, in Ireland, at something you have lately written.

It will be a serious loss to us, if you cannot take part in our undertaking; and I know I have no right to suppose you will consent to come at all, if I take a liberty so great as to ask you to postpone your coming. But still I must take things as I find them; and, since it rests with me to do what is at once unpalatable to me in itself and apparently uncourteous to you, I think it best to state the case as it really stands, trusting that I may not, besides my own disappointment and inconvenience, have the additional misfortune of disobliging you.

I might offer some mere excuse for proposing a postponement, but I think you will be better pleased that I should speak the plain and entire truth. I earnestly trust that this change of purpose on our part may not put you to inconvenience. I am very sorry to see, on looking again at your letter, that you have recalled your Son from Munich apropos of your coming to Europe.[1]

I am, Dear Sir, with much respect, Your faithful Servant in Xt
            John H Newman of the Oratory
O A Brownson Esqr LL D etc etc.

THURSDAY 24 AUGUST 1854   Wenham came

TO THOMAS SCRATTON

Thursday [24 August 1854]
My dear Scratton
    I have just got your letter
    I will take Number 21 for five years for £45 with the first ½ year allowed me for repairs, as your propose
                    Ever Yrs J H N

i.e. ON CONDITION I get the Number 22 for £50 or £55[2]

his articles was that he was defending or palliating Know-Nothingism. And they took this as an attack on the Irish.' Theodore Maynard, *Orestes Brownson, Yankee, Radical Catholic*, New York 1943, pp. 193-4.
    [1] Brownson's son, who was with Acton at Munich, was being recalled to edit *Brownson's Quarterly Review*, during his father's absence in Dublin.
    [2] Newman's negotiation for 21 and 22 Ely Place came to nothing. See letter of 2 Sept. to St John.

FRIDAY 25 AUGUST 1854   I, Ambrose, Stanislas, Edward, Robert, Victor [Duke] went with Mr Nowell to Rednal to measure out the ground for our house and burial ground   W H Scott called
SATURDAY 26 AUGUST   Wenham called   Scott went

TO ARCHBISHOP CULLEN

The Oratory Birmingham August 27. 1854
My dear Lord
    I return your Grace the letter about Dr Brownson, for the sight of which I am much obliged. I wrote to him by the first post, *postponing* our engagement, on the ground of the excitement in which the American Catholics at present seemed to be. It was awkward matters having gone so far.
    I hope in a few days now to be able to ask your blessing in person and to assure you that I am,
        My dear Lord, Yr faithful & Affte Servt in Xt
                    John H Newman of the Oratory

The Most Revd The Archbp of Dublin

TO F. W. FABER

The Oratory Bm Augst 27/54
My dear Fr Wilfrid,
    I did not write to the Pope, as far as I recollect — but wrote to Mgr Barnabò who was the agent, as I understood in getting the Degree. I thanked him for his trouble and zeal, and begged him to kiss the Pope's foot for me.[1]
    Thank you for your anxiety about the Gazette. Of course I cannot go on with it for ever — but the weekly form was the only one which would tell, or which I could undertake. You see it requires no *editing*. It is only an effusion. If I had it monthly, one Essay four times as long would be heavy and absurd without any thing else — and if more must go in, I should have to look about for writers, must select, arrange, and correct them, and must charge a price which would limit the sale.
    On the other hand, I never know but I may have some piece of

---

[1] Newman was explaining who should be thanked for the degree of Doctor of Divinity. Newman's letter was that of 12 Aug. 1850.

news to put in which I can't defer — and a publication which comes out once a month would not answer this purpose. Moreover I wanted to keep clattering in people's ears till the University opens — and a monthly publication would not do this. Enjoy your holy day

Ever Yours affly J H N

P.S.   I want you to be one of our University Preachers — you will only be called on for one Sermon a year. If you don't say 'no', I shall clap down your name.

TO A. J. HANMER

The Oratory Hagley Road Bm. August 27. 1854

My dear Hanmer,

Your letter dated the 18th and directed to Dublin, did not reach me here till the 24th or 25th — which must explain my silence.

Of course every thing which you have to tell me of yourself is always a subject of interest to me, though it would please me more if your difficulties and trials were less than they seem to be.

At first sight I should have been against your plan. You are a traveller, more, I believe, than I — and again I, as being older, must be more particular and squeamish than you — but still, to give my opinion, I think going to California will be a far greater trial than you can anticipate. The Bishop was in Birmingham several years ago — and a most pleasing man he is — and we offered to lend him two fathers to teach some Spanish Oratorians English, for a while.[1] So that my thoughts were drawn that way. On the whole I am glad that we had not to put our plan into execution. No one but hardy men, or monks, can go through what would await a person who had to go there. But you are going to unknown people, as well as a rude state of society.

It distresses me a good deal to hear you say that you are dissuaded from becoming a secular priest. Your line seemed to lie that way. But if not, why should your minor orders be a difficulty or separation between you and a secular life?[2] Surely there are many things which would open upon you, if you began to look about — though it would be some time before you decided on any thing to suit you.

Ever Yours very sincerely in Xt

John H Newman of the Oratory

The Revd J A Hanmer

---

[1] See diary for 6 Sept. 1850.
[2] Hanmer had been a novice at the London Oratory until Sept. 1850.

TO JAMES HOPE-SCOTT

The Oratory Hagley Road Bm. August 27. 1854

My dear Hope Scott

A letter has come from Hardman here, saying that you are inquiring for your cast, and that I have it.[1]

I very much regret to say that I *might* have brought it to you at Alton,[2] and did not. It came to me, I think, a few days before my visit — and much provoked I have been with myself. I had sent to Hardman for it shortly before, thinking him very long about it. What shall I do with it now?

You know that Lord Henry [Kerr] thinks of sending his boy to Dublin, and to the Oratory here up to Christmas. We shall be very glad to have him.[3] What do you think about Lord Ralph? how is his mother pleased? It has fidgetted me that we should have so few companions for him — and now, I suppose, after Christmas he will be alone. We have taken all the care of him we can, but I feel the great difficulty of keeping a boy to rules, when he is almost alone. He is as well off in that respect as a Protestant youth is in a parson's family — but perhaps that is not much.

⌐I trust you and Mrs Hope Scott are enjoying your holy day, and that the weather is as good with you as it is here. Lord Shrewsbury writes word, the weather in Ireland is wretched — but, you know, that is Ireland — it is otherwise in Scotland⌐

Ever Yours affly in Xt   John H Newman of the Oratory

J R Hope Scott Esqr

P.S.   (Private) ⌐After all old Brownson's coming is suspended. He has been treading on the toes of the great Irish nation — and advocating something like mixed Education.

P.S.   Father Darnell has the cholera or cholerine at Paris. We have been much alarmed.⌐

P.S.   When you write tell me whether Mr Stothert is a *preacher* (i.e. for University Pulpit)[4]

---

[1] This was the cast of a communion pyx. Cf. letter of 4 April.
[2] i.e. Alton Towers, on 29 July.   [3] See next letter.
[4] James Stothert (1817–57?), at Trinity College, Cambridge, and an Edinburgh lawyer, became a Catholic in 1844, and a priest a few years later. He was attached to St Patrick's, Edinburgh. Hope-Scott did not mention him in his reply, and although Stothert gave his name for the University, he was not among its preachers.

TO LORD HENRY KERR

The Oratory Hagley Road Bm August 27. 1854.
My dear Lord Henry,

I am ashamed at my delay in answering your kind letter, and hope you will excuse it — It has arisen from a great pressure of work this last day or two —

I do not see any difficulty in the plan on which you have resolved. It will give me great pleasure to make your son's more intimate acquaintance and we shall be pleased and ready to see him here whenever you send him.[1]

I am, My dear Lord Henry, Yours most truly in Xt
John H. Newman of the Oratory.
The Lord Henry Kerr.

TO EDWARD WALFORD

The Oratory Hagley Road Bm August 27. 1854
My dear Walford,

Had I not been so busy the last day or two, I should at once have answered your letter, which interested me very much.

I assure you that we shall have every disposition to use your books — or rather, shall be obliged to you for publishing them. And I will not fail to bear them in mind from this day forward.[2]

What you say to me about yourself, of course is very painful — I will not permit myself to believe that you have suffered more than a temptation. We will all bear you, and your intention in the matter, in mind, though I shall not of course say any thing of what you have told me. I am truly glad that Dr Manning has been of use to you.[3]

Yours, My dear Walford, Very truly in Xt
John H Newman of the Oratory

P.S.   I suppose some day or other the University will get into motion — but we do not see a furlong in advance.

[1] Lord Henry Kerr proposed to send his third son, Francis, aged 14, to be educated at the Oratory until Christmas, and then at Newman's University. He arrived at Birmingham on 6 Sept.

[2] Walford had recently published text books for Latin prose and Latin verse.

[3] In 1860 Walford returned to the Church of England, and then, after becoming a Catholic a second time, died an Anglican.

27 AUGUST 1854

TO J. WALKER, OF SCARBOROUGH

The Oratory Hagley Road Birmingham. August 27/54

My dear Mr Walker,

Will you be so kind as to let me put down your name on the books of our University. It will involve neither trouble, nor expence. But we shall have the satisfaction of counting you one of our members.[1]

Very truly Yours in Xt   John H Newman of the Oratory

The Very Revd Canon Walker

WEDNESDAY 30 AUGUST 1854   The Cottage at Rednall begun about now.

TO JAMES HOPE-SCOTT

Oratory Bm Augst 30/54

My dear Hope Scott

Your letter has just come and I send at once the Pyx in a registered cover. As Hardman says he is on the point of sending you a parcel, I shall let him send the casts himself, since you do not seem to want more than the very Pyx. However, if I am mistaken, and you will take the trouble to say a single word by post, I will send the casts too. I was very sorry to hear of Mr Wallace's illness — yet it is a very unmeaning sorrow, and I am glad to have seen him. It will be a sad event for Lord Traquhair and his sister.[2]

By the bye, this is not a moment to ask him, but why have I not got his name on the University List, or others of the Scotch peers who are Catholics?

We have not heard of Fr Darnell for some days, which is good. The difficulty was keeping him quiet. He had fever about him which they said was good as far as Cholera was concerned. He had gone for his holyday for the great Paris doings on the 15th, and was taken ill the day before.[3] He is with friends of ours, a lady and her daughters converts, Captain

[1] Walker gave his name.
[2] Mr Wallace lived with the seventh Earl of Traquair and his sister, Lady Louisa Stuart, at Traquair House, Peebles-shire.
[3] There were elaborate decorations and illuminations in Paris for the Fête Napoléon, 15 Aug., Napoleon I's birthday.

240

and Mrs Phillipps — and is most carefully tended. That is, as far as he will be tended, for we were obliged to send him instanter a telegraphic despatch — to keep him from starting to be here last Sunday. This shows he is up, but he is very weak

Ever Yours affly in Xt   John H Newman of the Oratory

J R Hope Scott Esqr

P.S.   Thank you for getting Lady Lothian to write to me.[1]

TO AMBROSE ST JOHN

Bm ⌐Sept 1/54

My dearest Ambrose,

I am sorry you should have so much trouble about houses. Mrs or Miss Kelly's will not do — ⌐ I know her lodging houses and her boarding house. The former are cabins planted on the earth. ⌐The Jesuits' house at Dalkey is too far from the rail, and too expensive.[2] You must not take it. I don't know what I shall do if I come on Monday, as at present I propose.⌐

You should have gone with *Scratton* to Ely Place, as I said. 1 not to do so, is to slight him, and you must explain this to him, lest he be put out. 2. He alone can show you the *right* house. You do not mention the number — and I have not a notion whether you have got to the right house or not. I am taking *two* not one. Thus you see, not knowing how the houses stand, I shall wait patiently for Scratton's letter to report proceedings, if it comes before I leave.

⌐The brothers went over to Rednall the other day, and were much pleased. I am glad you have such fine weather.

I have not yet got my own conveyance from the lawyer. The ground is turned up, but no bricks are yet upon it.

The Times in a leading article has a strong denunciation of excursion trains, as most dangerous.[3]

Mr Jewsbury asked me whether he might take the boy O Hare to his room to teach him Tenor. I gave him no leave, after I had spoken (I think) to you about it. I found out yesterday the boy went regularly upstairs. On my taxing Mr J. with it, I could not get him to say he did

[1] This concerned the sending of Lord Ralph Kerr to Dublin.
[2] This house, Mount Salus, was the one Newman eventually took.
[3] St John, who had gone to stay with Henry Wilberforce at Kingstown, complained of the excursion train he took as far as Holyhead.

241

get leave or not.⌐ At length I said 'It seems to me that you did *not* get leave, yet will not confess it.' ⌐He was still silent, and I could not get him frankly to own it. He began to evade — and then to make excuses — but he would not say 'I had no leave.' I shall leave the matter till you come, when Edward will decide about it. If he is guilty of such an act again, he must leave the house. He is far too free and easy.⌐

Ever Yrs affly J H N

P.S.   Have you given up the thought of Booter's town.

TO ROBERT ISAAC WILBERFORCE

The Oratory Hagley Road, Birmingham. Sept 1/54

My dear Robert Wilberforce,

I have been saying Mass for you this morning, and have just received your letter, which you may be sure I read with great interest.[1] Of course I can enter into your special pain, better than anyone else except Manning. In my own case, the separation from friends was the one thing which weighed on me for two years before I became a Catholic — and it affected my health most seriously. It is the price we pay for a great good. Every one has to give his best — there are few things, besides, which either you or I had to give; for I don't suppose that either of us cared much for any thing else.

---

[1] Wilberforce wrote:

'Burton Agnes Hull Aug 30. 1854

Private

My dear Newman,

You will like to know that I have tendered my resignation of my Preferments to the Archbishop of York this day. Say nothing about it, till it becomes public.

I thank you for the affectionate tone of your last letter: and hope that we may meet before long.

Should you like to have a set of the Transactions of the French Ecclesiastical Assemblies in 29 Folio volumes for your University Library.

Also should you care to have a set of Luther's works in 8 folios, in German, printed soon after his death, for the same.

I would that titles and effects were all I had to divest myself of. But the friendships of a life are not broken off without rending the heart.

Believe me ever affecy yours R I Wilberforce.'

On 30 Aug. Wilberforce wrote to the Archbishop of York that he could no longer accept the Royal Supremacy, and that in consequence he resigned his preferments, and put himself in the condition of a lay member of the Church. His resignation was accepted by return of post. Wilberforce became a Catholic at Paris on 1 Nov.

242

As to the books, we shall prize them very much, and be very grateful. Your name, I dare say is in them, but please, add in your handwriting that you give them to the Irish Catholic University. I expect to leave this place for Dublin on Monday.

Bear your agony, which is but a little while. The last death bed I attended some time ago, the poor sufferer kept saying 'will it soon be over?' It is a terrible stream to pass — but you will be soon through it. We have been praying for you here some time — So has Miss Ryder at the good Shepherd — and my dear child, Mary-Anne Bowden at the Visitation — and Fr Burder and his Trappists at St Bernard's.

Ever Yours affly John H Newman of the Oratory

P.S.   We shall be very grateful for the books.

TO AMBROSE ST JOHN

The Oratory Sept 2/54

My dear Ambrose

Your letter has just come. Thank you for all your zeal — I don't like delaying to come since your time is shortening, and I am wanted in Dublin — but I have not realized your account quite.

First you seem quite to have given up what was most on my mind — something very common at Booters town (e.g.) and then excursions e.g. to the 7 Churches.

Again Howth has not been in your mind.

Further, at least, if we were to have a place, a *down* and the *sea close* at hand, were two requisites — which *were* at Howth and at Killiney — are they at Bray?

Again, as to the houses you mention, you say of number 3 'one sitting room, *2* good bed rooms — a servants room and kitchen —' how is that enough? we talked of *three* fathers.

I really think the safest thing will be for you to take at hazard some lodging near Dublin and near Kingstown *for a week* for you and me — and then I can decide on the spot. You will have this on Monday morning — I will come on Tuesday, arriving at Kingstown at 11 PM. I will sleep at the Inn there, if you shall have not succeeded in getting a lodging. On Wednesday morning I will go to Dublin, and see some people I wish to see.

Our negociation about Numbers 21 and 22 [Ely Place] is all off. Scratton thinks a priest (you) going there had something to do with it.

This shows I was right in being sorry you did not go to *him*. Every thing is just as unsettled as 2 months ago!

Ever Yours affly J H N

P.S.   In the lodging we can adopt the plan you proposed — have a piece of cold meat in — and some tea, sugar, and rolls.

TO T. W. ALLIES

The Oratory Bm Sept. 3 1854

My dear Allies,

I am surprised and disappointed at what you tell me, and am concerned you should have any anxiety rising out of your connexion with us, but I trust that October will set all things straight.[1] I go to Dublin tomorrow.

My notion of the Philosophy of History is the science of which historical facts are the basis, or the laws on which it pleases Almighty Providence to conduct the political and social world. The fault of Schlegel's work, as far as I recollect it, is that it has no *view* — only a number of detached remarks. Gibbon's is a philosophical history, i.e. a history written not as Fleury writes, viz as a collection of facts, but with reference and subservience to a certain philosophy, and a bad one![2]

One subject, and a very useful one for us, while we are employed chiefly with the junior schools would be the *preparation of the pagan world for the coming of Xt*, i.e. to show how the four empires, the literature of Greece, and the organization of Rome ministered to Christianity vid. Clement of Alex.'s view of heathen philosophy as an οἰκονομία. Another would be the uses of ancient history in education. Another would be the history of Diplomacy. But of course it is like calling spirits from the deep, the putting down subjects.[3]

Ever affecly Yours in Xt   John H Newman of the Oratory

[1] Some members of the Catholic Poor School Committee, of which Allies was the Secretary, were objecting to his accepting a lectureship in Dublin, but leave was in the end forthcoming. See letter of 22 Oct. to Allies.

[2] Allies wrote on 1 Sept., 'Do you know that your hints of subjects give me a far better idea of what you want than I had before. Schlegel is grievously disappointing to me, vague and unsubstantial, and but half a Catholic. I should like to try the first subject you give, "the effect of the revival of learning on the European Kingdoms."' Friedrich Schlegel (1772–1829), convert and Catholic apologist, was the author of *Philosophie der Geschichte*, 2 volumes, Vienna 1829, English trans. by J. B. Robertson, London 1835. Newman published an English trans. of part of the twenty-volume *Histoire ecclésiastique* of Claude Fleury (1640–1723), 3 volumes, Oxford 1842–4.

[3] Cf. *Henry IV, Part I*, III, i, 53.

TO J. WALKER OF SCARBOROUGH

The Oratory Bm Sept 3/54

My dear Mr Walker

Thank you for your kind and suggestive letter. My first act, after my appointment, was to go round to the different English Colleges. I should like a month's holy day at Scarborough very much — but when shall I have one? I have been busy all the time I have been here, and tomorrow am going to Dublin

Very sincerely Yours in Xt   John H Newman of the Oratory

MONDAY 4–TUESDAY 5 SEPTEMBER 1854   crossed to Ireland to the Wilberforces where Fr Ambrose

TO H. MACLEAN

Dublin Sept 6/54/

Sir,

I am looking out for a house for myself in the neighbourhood of Stephen's Green and have been today to see Number 6 Ely Place, for the letting of which, I believe, you are Agent.

The roof and the drains and the offices seem to be in a bad state and the repairs would be considerable. I wish to make an offer for it, but I could not do so on the condition of putting it into repair. But as it is a large house it need not all be used. I make you the following offer.

I will give £100 a year for it for five years and engage to leave it in no worse state of repair than that in which I find it. However I should wish to make this exception. I do not wish to be bound to do anything to the offices, their state is so bad. I would engage not to let them off to any one else.

I am, Sir, Yr. obed Servt. J. H. Newman

Address to me at

H W. Wilberforce Esq. 2 Crosthwaite Terrace Kingstown.[1]

[1] H. Maclean was a house agent at 6 Westmoreland Street. He wrote this same day that Newman's offer was not accepted.

TO J. D. DALGAIRNS

Thursday [7 September 1854]

My dear Bernard

I had a letter from Bm [Birmingham] from Lord Henry Kerr last night to the effect that at the very hour the letter came here, his son was to arrive at Bm. Fr Edward will take care of him, he may go into Ralph's room till his own is prepared etc. or wherever Edwd has put him.

Whoever comes here, should bring *work*, in case of rain — the weather is changing today.

A Catholic has written to me to protest against my not acknowledging the Turks to be a 'power that bes' — and, quoting besides St Paul, Kenelm Digby and Judas Maccabaeus against me. Please tell me, if I may say this in answer — 'I believe Catholic divines do not oblige me to consider that Christian governments have any duties towards the Turks, except as arising out of distinct engagements.'[1]

Ever Yrs affly JHN

TO EDWARD CASWALL

Mount Salus. Dalkey. Sept 8/54

My dear Edward,

I have not a clear idea of the room you speak of, as you do not mention its *number*; but I see no objection, since you think it best to use it for the boys.[2] But are we doing any thing towards *getting* them a master? I don't think Jewsbury would do. Some one spoke of a 'Private Tuition' man with a brass plate near us — *something* ought to be done. I wish you would call on him, or make *some* application — putting down on paper *what* subjects we want. How many hours a day, and how many days a week. Is Scratton's brother doing anything at Oscott? Dr Weedall seemed to say he was *not* — could any arrangement be made in *that* quarter?

Does not the new Congregation Room want its *colouring*? has it *ever* been coloured? If not, it had better be.

Fr Ambrose sees no objection to Sutton instead of Smallwood —[3] if you can warrant him — I am not in a position yet to engage him here.

---

[1] Cf. *Lectures on the History of the Turks*, pp. 131–8. *H.S.* I, pp. 108–14. No reply of Dalgairns's is to be found.   [2] i.e. as a schoolroom.
[3] As a servant at the Oratory.

Mr Nugent is here.

I wish Stanislas was able to say that he had got my deeds from Mr Davies.[1]

P.S. It looks as if some letter from F Nicholas must have miscarried. Has not Mrs Poncia heard from Mrs Phillipps? I hope the case is not, that, though not worse, he has not rallied; and they don't write, waiting for something definite to say. Dolman wants a list of our Oratory (from Fr Austin or you, the Ceremoniere or Secretary) for his Calendar.

TO F. W. FABER

The Oratory Kingstown Sept 8. 1854

My dear F Faber,

I have given our Villegiatura a fine name; mortals call it 'Mount Salus, Dalkey —' Some of our Fathers are coming over here; and, if any of you are invalided in the cholera, we have two bedrooms for you — and an altar in the house. We cannot afford you board, but it is a most *beautiful site* looking over the sea, and its healthiness is conveyed in its name. We shall have it till November 1. I fear this is no great temptation on the whole, but we should rejoice, if you would come.

I shall say Mass for you, while you are upon the Cholera mission, once a week — You know Nicholas has had a touch of it at Paris — he is with most kind people, the Phillipps — but it perplexes us that it is a fortnight, since we have heard any tidings of him.

Ever Yrs affectly J H N

TO WILLIAM MONSELL

H Wilberforce's Kingstown. Ireland Sept 8. 1854

My dear Monsell

Thank you for the trouble you are taking. We must not be discouraged — I wish exceedingly to get such persons as Mr [J. D.] Fitzgerald's — but they will come in time — I have seen Sergeant O Brien this morning, and am to meet him and Mr T. O Hagan with Dr Cullen on Sunday. Somehow I don't expect to get any of them just yet — meanwhile Mr F. speaks of the 'convincing reasoning' of your letter — and

[1] i.e. for the land at Rednal. The conclusion and signature have been cut out.

247

only contemplates 'keeping back at present —' so I hope he really wishes to join us, and there is no doubt your letter has done good.[1]

Thank you for your hint for a subject for the Gazette — I will think over it.[2]

I am for some weeks at 'Mount Salus, Dalkey;' where several of our Birmm Fathers are to pay me a visit. Our London Fathers are to be in the thick of the cholera, having offered themselves to the Vicar general of the diocese.

I am going over with James O'Ferrall to his brother at Ballina shortly.[3]

Ever Yours affectly in Xt   John H Newman of the Oratory

Wm Monsell Esqr M P

SATURDAY 9 SEPTEMBER 1854   left the Wilberforces, and went with F Ambrose up to Mount Salus, which I have taken till November 1   F Ambrose's asthma came on at night   —*a long attack*

TO ARCHBISHOP CULLEN

Saturday [9 September 1854]

My dear Lord,

I hoped you would have returned to Dublin before this — but I shall meet your Grace at Sergeant O Brien's tomorrow.

I wish you would persuade him to give his name to the University. Mr Monsell has been pressing me to get you to do this some time.

It is my intention to send round to the four Archbishops very soon a number of names of ad interim Professors. We must not delay longer, for I am told that the delay is keeping back names of students. People wish to see *who* the Professors are, before they send in their sons'

[1] Monsell wrote on 5 Sept. from Tervoe, 'I send you Fitzgeralds letter—it is very disheartening—

I wish much that Dr Cullen would get hold of O Hagan and O Brien—If we can only get one of them the rest will follow—In my answer to Fitzgerald I have shown him that he and I, both, do what he objects to, when we support both the National Board and the Christian brothers. . . .'

O'Brien gave his name to the University but not Fitzgerald nor O'Hagan.

[2] Monsell wanted Newman to point out the exceptional advantages of the first students of the University, who would be few, with a large staff of eminent men, dedicated to teaching them and to making a success of the University. Newman seems not to have acted on this suggestion.   [3] i.e. Richard More O'Ferrall of Balyna.

names. I shall try to give you the list tomorrow privately — but you will receive a formal letter from me soon.

Is it too much to ask leave to erect an Altar in the House on Mount Salus which some of our Fathers at Birmingham have taken for some weeks? It is the house the Jesuits lately have had. And will attendance on our Masses be a fulfilment of the obligation (on days of obligation) for the *members of the Oratory* in the House?

Also, unless it is something unreasonable, I would ask *faculties for confession* for myself, Father St John, and Father Dalgairns *as far as subjects of the Oratory are concerned*, while we are in the House at Mount Salus Begging your Grace's blessing, I am, My dear Lord, Your affecte friend & Servt in Xt

John H Newman of the Oratory

SUNDAY 10 SEPTEMBER 1854   dined at Sergeant O'Brien's
MONDAY 11 SEPTEMBER   Austin and Lawrence came

TO EDWARD CASWALL

Mount Salus. Dalkey. Kingstown Ireland Sept 11/54

My dear Edward

The voyagers are just come, Lawrence after much sickness. Ambrose is in bed with the worst attack of asthma he ever had—and I am anxious lest this most beautiful place, from its purity of air, may have some thing to do with it. Two nights he has had no sleep. He has got a monster mustard plaister on him. I shall go in to Dublin, or send Austin, today to get the vestments. We *suppose* they were directed to Harcourt Street. Thank William. I ought to have told him where to direct.

Tastes so differ, that I do not like to talk, but I think this is one of the most beautiful places I ever saw.

The inclosed is for the Bishop, if you will kindly send it to him in an envelope. I have in it made apologies for the absence of the Fathers etc. Make him understand that Ambrose is ill abed here — Nicholas in Paris (when *will* he be heard of?) and Bernard *on the Bishop's business* at Mother Margaret's.[1]

As to Henry's letter which is just come, *of course* we cannot answer

---

[1] Dalgairns was giving a retreat to Mother Margaret Hallahan's nuns at Stone. Bishop Ullathorne proposed to hold a Visitation at the Oratory on 14 Sept. and had sent a list of questions to be answered, to several of which Newman now refers.

about the mission etc. more than we *know* — We must do as well as we can. As to the question about Masses of obligation left us — *we have none.*

Ever Yours affly J H N

P.S.   You may tell Henry that I shall expect him, *unless he has some better reason* than Fr Ambrose's penitents, as soon as the Visitation is over. F Ambrose's conversions are 8.

TO MRS JOHN MOZLEY

Mount Salus Dalkey Kingstown Ireland Sept 11/54

My dear Jemima

Will you kindly forward the inclosed. I cannot read H's [Harriett Fourdrinier] direction. No one can be surprised at what has happened.[1]

I am at the above queer-named place till November — its name, though queer, is true — and the place is as beautiful as it is healthy. It is, I really think, the first time since Horsepath that I have been in such an occasional dwelling.[2] I have invited some of our Birmingham party to see me.

The house is on the rocks which rise above Dublin Bay — and commands a view of the whole coast and headlands. The Wicklow mountains are seen out of one window, and Howth and Kingstown out of the other. I never saw a place out of Italy and Sicily like it for beauty of rock and sea, and that is why Dublin Bay is compared to the Bay of Naples, I suppose — for in nothing else does it resemble it, except that both are Bays. The Isle of Wight is very beautiful, but there are no real rocks, only chalk cliffs there. Here it is granite. There are houses innumerable scattered about — but, being all of stone, and nothing red about them, and the ground being very irregular, they do but furnish and set out what otherwise would be bare and rugged. They group into small towns, and run off upon outlines, and then terminate on heights with the effect of castles, and spread over the plain, with a variety ever fresh, and in spite of a brilliant sky and plenty of wind, the soil is too bare to generate dust. Hills, of rock and heather mixed, run behind up for some miles, affording endless rambles. Ever since I knew Horsepath, I preferred

[1] Henry Fourdrinier, Harriett's father, died on 3 Sept. 1854, in his eighty-ninth year. Newman was evidently sending a letter of condolence at his uncle's death.

[2] Newman took a cottage at Horsepath for his mother and sisters in the summer of 1829, and used to come out to them from Oxford.

this sort of scenery to meadow, wood, and stream, — i.e. for a *continuance* — the other palls upon one — nay oppresses one. When I went down to Devonshire in 1831 with H Froude, the rich depth of the vegetation stifled me — I could not enjoy a leafy feather bed.[1] In all this I curiously agree with Arnold and Whately[2]

Ever Yrs affly J H N

THURSDAY 14 SEPTEMBER 1854   Accident — broke a fibre of a tendon in my left calf   laid up.

TO EDWARD CASWALL

Mount Salus. Dalkey Sept 14. 1854

My dear Edward

Thank Fr Nicholas for his letter; I hope he will get back well.

I don't like the Bishop's *leave* asked about Scratton's coming to teach the boys. He either is the Bishop's subject, or he is *not*. I think he is *not*. But *he* (Scratton) must decide all that. If we cannot treat with Scratton himself, we must treat with no one else.[3]

Tell Wm [William Neville] he did quite right about the vestments, and that they came quite right. It was Austin's mistake who said that Wm had directed them to Dublin, and who in consequence was all Monday running about Dublin for them.

I think the Crucifix should be put up *flat* against the wall, in a socket.

Tell Henry it is nothing to *me* when he comes — (if he comes) but the thing to be settled is *Birmingham*

Ever Yours affly J H N

P.S.   I inclose the receipt for Stanislas.

[1] Cf. *Moz.* 1, pp. 241–4.
[2] Cf. the extracts from Arnold's Travelling Journals in Appendix D at the end of A. P. Stanley's *Life of Thomas Arnold*, London 1844. Newman presumably learned Whately's opinion direct, but cf. Whately's letter of 24 June 1839 in E. Jane Whately's *Life and Correspondence of Richard Whately, D.D.*, new edition, London 1868, p. 151.
[3] James Scratton, a student at Oscott, ceased being a subject of Bishop Ullathorne on 15 Aug. See also letter of 22 Sept. to Caswall.

TO J. M. CAPES

Mount Salus. Dalkey Sept 15/54

My dear Capes,

Your letter has come to me here, and I have read your Remarks with great interest.[1] Of course the *end* is important, more than any other almost which can be named just now, and I am rejoiced to find that it is meeting with attention in so many quarters.

As to the *means*, it requires more experience than I can have, to say what is feasible. At first sight I cannot understand persons who have been working at their worldly employments for 6 days, entering *with spirit* into an exhausting spiritual occupation, even for an hour, on the day of rest. I should be overcome by *facts* immediately; but, not having the means of obtaining them, I hesitate.

I should like some statistics relative to Sunday School teaching. There is, I suppose, very little exercise of *mind* in Protestant Sunday Schools. The teaching consists mainly of hearing the Bible read, or the collect or gospel said by heart. If we are to *amuse* youths from 15 to 21, we must *exert* ourselves. It strikes me that you should write a paper stating in detail the kind of thing you propose, before you can expect it taken up, at least with the prospect of success. But forgive me, if I have misunderstood you — and let me hear from you again, if you wish me to say more.

Brownson was as civil as could be expected — but nothing out of the way. However, for the present, at the last moment his coming to us is stopped. He can't keep out of scrapes — and his late articles on Nativism and Education are exciting such strong feeling in America, not to say in Ireland, that the highest authorities in both countries are against our having any thing to do with him. But I do not wish all this mentioned.[2]

Ever Yours affectly in Xt   John H Newman of the Oratory

P.S.   As to Hardman, he has more young Catholic men than any one in Birmingham — and you know how zealous he is — but (quite in confidence) his young men are not spoken of in the most flattering terms.

[1] Cape's remarks, approved by the English Hierarchy, were about to appear in a signed article in the *Rambler*, ii, New Series (Oct. 1854), pp. 277–90, 'An Appeal to the Catholic Laity on the Present Condition of the Poor.' Capes urged that lay people should establish Sunday Schools for poor Catholics, especially those above school age.

[2] See second note to letter of 23 Aug. to Brownson.

TO S. M. MACSWINEY

Mount Salus. Dalkey Sept 15. 1854

My dear Sir,

I have to acknowledge the receipt of your letter, announcing your intention of becoming a Candidate for a Professorship in the University Medical School, and will not forget your application, when the proper time comes to make a selection.

As we have not been able to commence this year, of course the appointments are not likely soon to occupy our attention. None have been made as yet.[1]

I am, My dear Sir, Yours very truly John H Newman

C. M. Mac Swiney Esq

TO EDWARD CASWALL

Sunday Sept 17. [1854]

My dear F Edward

As William is not coming at once, and *must* be at Birmingham on the 29th I think one of the other novices had better come at once, if any one is coming, which depends on them. We shall not have our additional beds in till *Wednesday* — so he might come on Wednesday night or Thursday Wm might come *after* the 29. The weather is splendid — love to all

Ever Yrs affly J H N

TO J. D. DALGAIRNS

[18 September 1854][2]

My dear Bernard

The post is just going out as your letter has come in. I write in a great hurry, and will answer your letter at length soon.

I gave Mother Margaret a *week* at Clifton, and, when you exceeded it, I thought it was not for *her*, but for *yourself* — and that you *ought*

---

[1] MacSwiney was appointed Professor of Medical Jurisprudence in 1855.
[2] Dated from postmark.

to have a day of rest after your labours — So I was quite content you should be away a day longer.[1]

You will recollect I objected to a *full* retreat for *you* at Clifton, and in consequence the nuns *began* it themselves.

I thought I was granting now for as much as I granted at Clifton, i.e. *not* for a full retreat.

Of course I know the length of a retreat. I grudge very much, your being so much away from Birmingham, *since* you are coming here.

I have sent word to Birmingham I should like you to come here from Waterford.[2]

Well, then, as you left the Oratory on Thursday, I think you should come back on Thursday

I know to what you allude — and am deeply sorry at the pain it must cost you[3]

Ever Yrs affly J H N

I hope you will have here the fine weather we have now.

WEDNESDAY 20 SEPTEMBER 1854 Fr Frederic came went to Dr O'Farren [O'Ferrall] about my leg for first time.

TO ROBERT ISAAC WILBERFORCE

Mount Salus Dalkey Sept 21/54

My very dear R W

I wish there was a chance of my being at Birmingham at the time you mention. It is not probable I should quit this till Christmas.

Thank you for your books, which have arrived.[4]

The packing is a terrible trial — it is another form of the grief of friends

I do not forget you

Ever Yrs affectly John H Newman

[1] Dalgairns, who at the end of July gave a retreat to Mother Margaret Hallahan's nuns at Clifton, had begun one on 15 Sept. for her nuns at Stone. He explained that if he gave a 'full' eight day retreat, he would have to be absent for ten days.

[2] See diary for 29 Sept. and 4 Oct.

[3] Dalgairns wrote on 16 Sept., 'May I ask you to pray for me. I have anxieties which I *must* not tell you. I am looking forward to seeing you with great joy.' This seems to refer to Dalgairns's dissatisfaction with his Oratorian vocation.

[4] See letter of 1 Sept.

St Matthew 'at once he rose' etc.[1] does not Keble run so? It makes me think of you.

FRIDAY 22 SEPTEMBER 1854   Victor [Duke] came (with his brother)

TO EDWARD CASWALL

Mount Salus. Dalkey Sept 22/54

My dear Edward

We have enchanting weather but it is too keen for poor Fr Ambrose — so, having been laid up 10 days and getting at best not better, he goes off tonight to Dr Duke. ⟨Perhaps he will go straight to Birmingham — so please let two sheets be put to the fire.⟩ Victor has not yet made his appearance.

I write in a great hurry. I dare say, it is my fault, and I ought to have spoken more at length, but it took me by surprise, and was a new idea to me, that Scratton was to *be in the house*.[2] It is done now, but this is the difficulty, that, since he has no place to go to, we shall find it very hard to get rid of him. If we give him board and lodging, is he to have any thing besides? I certainly think no room need be *papered* for him — *we* have slept in unpapered, uncoloured rooms and why should not he? it is only a matter of *look*.

I suppose the Bishop will be satisfied if the red curtains are taken away from the confessionals — that is all you mentioned, I believe. If so, take them away directly. Begin the prayer for the Queen by all means — but I have said how I think it had better be done.

We have two posts coming in — one about 9 AM the other about 2. Two go out — one at 10¼ AM the other at 4¾ or there abouts.

It was the rheumatism in my knee before — now it is a bursting or rupture of one of the fibres of my calf. I bandaged it, but not bandaging from the toes, the consequence was the blood was forced down to my ancles [sic], which swelled (they always are apt to swell) greatly. I went to a surgeon in Dublin the other day — and he makes me lay my leg

---

[1]   'At once he rose, and left his gold;
               His treasure and his heart
           Transferr'd, where he shall safe behold
               Earth and her idols part;'
                                   'St Matthew' in *The Christian Year*.
The feast of St Matthew was on 21 Sept.
     [2] Caswall had arranged that James Scratton, who had left Oscott, should come as the boys' tutor until Christmas.

on a table, tell Robert, but I generally put it on a chair, in spite of him — I am now going on for my second week with all this lovely weather about me! Austin and Frederic went up the sugar loaf yesterday —[1] and Austin hurt his heel, and *he* is limping about this morning

Ever Yrs affly J H N

P.S. Ambrose *certainly* comes to-morrow to you, if he leaves this place.

TO MYLES O'REILLY

Mount Salus, Dalkey Sep 23. 1854

My dear Mr O'Reilley

I propose to advertise as follows directly — Will you give me your opinion whether *guineas* is too high; Also, what do you think of my scheme founded on yours, drawn out on the opposite leaf?[2]

Yours most sincerely John H. Newman

[1] Hills south of Dalkey.
[2] '*Copy*

Expences of a Student in the University House.

N.B. The University takes upon itself the Rent, Taxes, and House Porter of the University House.

The Students take on themselves Laundress, and the Grocer and Chandler.

The Dean and Tutors take on themselves firing in addition (I think we shall be able to give them this in.)

1. Dinner, (as by Mr M. O R's calculation) per week .. .. 11.8.
2. Breakfast (minus tea and sugar.) .. .. 1.6.
3. Supper (2/3 of Breakfast.) 1.0.

14.2 say 15.0

	£. s
Board 38 weeks at 15/-	28. 10.
Firing 30 weeks at 3/-	4. 10
Attendance for 38	
at 15/ a month for 9 months	7. 0
£6.15—say £7	
Tuition from two Tutors	4. 0
Share in Dean and Two Tutor's board	
viz £28. 10s × 3 ÷ 15	
(3 being the Dean and Two Tutors	6. 0
and 15 the number of students)	
	50. 0

N.B. As to attendance, the perquisites of the two under servants will be so considerable that I think £50 (£25 apiece) which is Mr O'R's calculation is too high. Again

The whole expences of a Student residing in the University House for the 38 weeks of the ensuing session, (including board, lodging, firing, servants, public lectures, and private tuition, to the exclusion of laundress, and of grocer and chandler,) will amount to 50 guineas; of which one half will be paid on his coming into residence, and the other half by the feast of St Mathias, Feb 24 1855.[1]

TO ORESTES BROWNSON

Mount Salus — Dalkey Sep 27. 1854

My dear Sir

Your welcome and generous letter came yesterday, and I lose no time in answering it.[2]

I cannot prevail on myself to give the coup de grace to an arrangement, which I still hope will come into effect, by putting the notice into the Newspapers which you propose.[3] There are so many changes in men's minds, and public affairs are at present in that uncertain state, that it is not at all improbable that our present difficulty may blow over — and, when it had done so, I should be vexed to have committed myself. I shall not fill up the Professorship which I offered to you, and we will see the turn things take. At the same time I do not mean to say a word to inconvenience you, or to oblige you to consider it a suspended

since cook and kitchen maid will get their board from what is over, I think £30 and £20 too high. Considering, moreover, the Hall Porter is paid by the University, I think that £7 × 15 or £105 is enough for servants.'

[1] O'Reilly thought Newman's calculation too high, and the sum of fifty guineas, which appeared in the notice on the first page of the *Catholic University Gazette* for 28 Sept., was reduced a fortnight later to forty.

[2] To Newman's letter of 23 Aug., Brownson replied from Boston on 12 Sept. that he was 'neither surprised nor disappointed' at being asked to postpone his visit, since this suited him for private reasons. He was ready to come later 'if desirable,' but gave his opinion 'that it will be best all round that I should not be in any way or manner connected with the University. Your position is one of great delicacy and difficulty, and to succeed in carrying your University through you have got to make concessions to national prejudice. Here, and unless I am misinformed, also in Ireland there is a large party by no means pleased to see an Englishman the Rector of an *Irish* University. This party were able for a time to use me against you and your friends, and now that they find I will no longer be their tool, they would break me in pieces. Never will the *Irish* party as such consent to support a university in which I could be a lecturer. I ought to have known this . . .' See also *McGrath*, p. 218, and Theodore Maynard, *Orestes Brownson, Yankee, Radical, Catholic*, pp. 207–08.

[3] Brownson asked Newman to 'let the Tablet or Telegraph say that I finally decline the Lectureship, I think it the best way, and I really do so, if you will permit me, though not because of your request.'

engagement, or to hinder you entertaining a renewal of my proposition as a really de novo matter.

What you say about Loss and Gain has given me heartfelt satisfaction, and I know such friends of mine as you are kind enough to contemplate will be as much pleased as I am at your message[1]
(My direction is Dublin — this is a watering place)

TO ARCHBISHOP CULLEN

Wednesday [27 September 1854][2]

My dear Lord

On thinking over it, I cannot be sure I did not speak of the chance of Dr Forde's appointment to Mr O Reilly, though I don't recollect I did. Assuredly I did not say you hindered the appointment, because it never came into my head to think so. I was very wrong in speaking at all.

I am now writing to Dr Forde to correct this misapprehension

Ever Yrs affly in Xt   John H Newman

TO T. F. KNOX

Mount Salus Dalkey Sept 27/54

My dear Fr Francis

Thank you for your hint about Hurter — I have already availed myself of your former one about Prescott.[3]

I have just heard from Brownson. He says 'I have just read for the first time Loss and Gain. If I had seen that work at an earlier day, many things which I have written concerning you and your friends, the Oxford converts, would never have been written.[4] Forgive me, Revd Father, whatever injustice etc' This is all very pleasant ⟨This must not go beyond your House.⟩

Very affly Yours J H N

¹ See letter of this day to Knox. The conclusion here has been cut out.
² The autograph has '1854' in another hand, and Forde's reply of 29 Sept. thanking Newman for his letter referred to below, enables the date to be fixed. Laurence Forde, who was Cullen's chaplain, hoped for the Professorship in Canon Law, which fell to him in the autumn of 1855. He had heard a report that Cullen was opposed to his appointment, and had asked him if this was the case.
³ These appear to refer to the *Catholic University Gazette*.
⁴ Brownson's letter continued, 'I have taken occasion in my Review for October to say as much, and to do what I could to repair the injustice I had unwittingly done

THURSDAY 28 SEPTEMBER 1854   Fr Ambrose went, having been somewhat better since Sunday

FRIDAY 29 SEPTEMBER   Robert came, with Bernard who went on to Waterford to preach.   went in to Dublin to see the Archbishop and Dr O'Farrell

SATURDAY 30 SEPTEMBER   F Austin went.

TO ARCHBISHOP CULLEN

Mount Salus. Sept 30/54

My dear Lord

I am happy to say that Dr O Ferrall pronounced me much better yesterday — and I do trust I am rapidly advancing.

I saw Dr O'Reilly and had a long talk — and am to have others with him. He quite gives up the idea of medical lectures this year. He says, 'Where will you get your *audience*?' Again 'Unless you are first rate, you will damage the University.' I can't help agreeing with him.

Could you without trouble let me have the *words* of the Synodal Meeting, of which your Grace spoke to me yesterday, giving me a power of acting under circumstances?[1] I have nothing at all to say against your plan of the 4 Archbishops — So that there were *definite times*, say once a quarter when things came before them — leaving me to act in the interval provisionally.

Mr Butler has accepted the appointment of Professor of Mathematics. So that I now can formally propose to you my list — and to the other Archbishops

Ever Your affte Servt in Xt   John H Newman of the Oratory

The Most Revd Dr Cullen

to men whom I love and reverence, and with whom I wish in my humble sincerity to cooperate in the defence of our holy religion. Forgive me, Reverend Father, whatever injustice I may have done you, and ask them in my name to forgive me also. Believe me I was moved by no personal consideration, and thought I was doing only my duty.' See also *Campaign*, p. xxxiii. Newman sent Brownson's letter to Birmingham, for the Oratorians there to read.

When he reviewed *Loss and Gain* Brownson still held to his strictures against the theory of development, but expressed his 'entire confidence in the whole class of converts' he had formerly opposed. *Brownson's Quarterly Review* (Oct. 1854), p. 525.

[1] Cullen does not appear to have sent the words of the Synod, as to which see note to letter of 20 May 1854 to Dalgairns. For Cullen's reply see letter of 1 Oct. to him.

TO JOSEPH DIXON, ARCHBISHOP OF ARMAGH

Mount Salus Dalkey Sept 30. 1854

My dear Lord,

I am very sorry it has been out of my power to send you the list of gentlemen, whom I propose for Professors and Lecturers, till now, when your Grace is on the point of starting for Rome. But the delay has been no fault of mine — it was not till this morning that I received a letter I had been waiting for, and without which I could not proceed. The list is as follows —

1 Professor of Classics — *Robert Ornsby Esqr*, late fellow of Trinity College Oxford, and highly distinguished in his University.

2. Professor of Mathematics. *Edward Butler Esqr* of Trinity College, Dublin, at present an Inspector for the National Board — he has the highest testimonials from the College.

3 Professor of Civil Engineering — *Terence Flanagan Esqr.* Late Engineer on the Blackburn Railway line — He has lately been employed in Belgium, and now is on professional business in Portugal.

4. Lecturer in Geography — *J. B. Robertson Esqr* the translator of Moehler, Schlegel, etc — he is a friend of Dr Russell's of Maynooth, and a frequent contributor to the Dublin Review.

5 Lecturer in Ancient History — *James Stewart Esqr* of the Universities of Aberdeen and Cambridge — in both of which he got many honors.

6. Lecturer in Logic — *D. B. Dunne Esqr* of the Irish College, Rome.

7. Lecturer in French language and literature — M. P. le Page Renouf, of Pembroke College, Oxford; his conversion deprived him of the opportunity of distinguishing himself. He is a most accomplished man, a native of Guernsey. He has given great attention to French literature, and speaks French better than English. He is a good English writer. He has been for the last 7 years tutor in some Frenchman's family.

When the names are published, I propose to accompany them with some account of the persons.

I showed this list to the Archbishop of Dublin yesterday — but should be much obliged, if your Grace let him read this letter — and would kindly give him the inclosed[1]

[1] This was a paper in Newman's hand:
'Scheme
A Rector—
3 Professors at £300 a year 900. 0. 0
Lecturers and Tutors at £100,
which the Rector may increase up to 10, and} 1000. 0. 0
take out of the Professors if he will.

Begging your Grace's blessing, I am My dear Lord, Yr faithful & affte Servt in Xt

John H Newman of the Oratory

The Most Revd Dr Dixon

SUNDAY I OCTOBER 1854   Robert came

TO ARCHBISHOP CULLEN

Mount Salus. ⌈Oct 1. 1854⌉

My dear Lord,

I do not know whether your Grace is acquainted with Baron de Schroeter, the writer of the letter I return.[1] If so, I think you will corroborate me, when I say that he is a very pious, but a somewhat censorious and busy person. As to Dr D. [Döllinger] I have always heard, and his books show, that he has not quite the circle of opinions, which would be called Ultramontane — and the Bishop of Boston the other day spoke doubtingly of him; and I thought was going to speak of him to you. But I have always considered that he was an *historian*, not a theologian, and only professed to depose to historical testimony; not to doctrines[.] I should be very much concerned if I had to think any thing beyond this.

I very much fear that it will not be prudent in me to come into Dublin tomorrow — If I do not make my appearance, will you convey my apologies to the Primate, as well as accept them yourself. I wrote to him yesterday, inclosing a letter to your Grace.

Thank you for your remarks on the appointments. ⌈I quite recognise the wisdom of Mr Hope Scott's advice, that we should consider ourselves

A Vice Rector, who may be taken from Deans or Professors, Lecturers and Tutors, so that he be an intern. }	at	50. 0. 0
A secretary	at	50. 0. 0
2 Deans of discipline at £150 a year		300. 0. 0
		£2300. 0. 0
Exhibitioners (on merit) at £30, £20, and £10 a year Prizes of £5 a year. } up to		1000. 0. 0'

[1] Cullen had evidently sent Newman a letter from von Schroeter, suggesting that Döllinger should be appointed Professor of Theology. For von Schroeter's dealings with Newman see Volumes XIII and XIV.

in a preparatory [[or provisional]] state, and begin quietly.[1]

I hardly think, however, that appointments can be made only for the *year*. [[i.e. all.]]⌐ I know perfectly well that every thing must be referred to the Bishops; but, ⌐unless there was a reasonable expectation of the appointments continuing, no man of talent would accept them. No one will change his place and home, much less give up his situation for a mere chance; and, unless we can persuade men to do all this, we must put up with the absence of superior men from our staff of University teachers.

Again — I consider it quite necessary to publish the names of the persons engaged, as a sort of advertisement of what is going to be done.⌐ I have been told from Limerick some time back, that we should not get students, till I published the names of Professors and Lecturers. ⌐And I know five or six persons, who are coming, and will not come without a guarantee that the arrangements stood pretty much as I have proposed

Thank you also for your suggestion about Dr Leahy.⌐ He has already most kindly offered to be of use in philosophy. It has struck me ⌐he would do us an important service,⌐ and in accordance with his own Professorship, ⌐if he gave to all the Students catechetical lectures in exegetics; e.g. in the Greek Testament.⌐[2]

As to Mr Stewart, perhaps your Grace would think it enough, if I did not *publish* his name, and, if I dropped his connexion with Aberdeen, leaving him 'Trinity College, Cambridge.' He is perhaps the best *worker* of my whole lot. I have chosen him and the rest, from no personal feeling, (not one of them is my intimate friend, some of them I never saw,) — but simply because I thought they would support me and enable me to get through my undertaking, better than any one else;

[1] Cullen wrote on 30 Sept. marking his letter *Private*, 'I recollect that about two or more years ago Mr Scott Hope [sic] in a conversation I had with him insisted very much on the necessity of making every one understand that everything done about the University in the beginning was only a preparation for a university, and that the real university was still at a distance. . . . I think it would be prudent for us to act in the same way, and if you could supply professors in a temporary way for the first year, or get the one professor to act for another perhaps it would be better Dr Leahy for example might start something connected with classics this year. He is an excellent classical scholar. I fear that it will not be prudent to bring in a *Scotch* man for the present—the Scotch are looked on by the people at large as their worst enemies—and it is the policy of the gentry to introduce as many Scotch as possible in the Country. Treating of a catholic they should not apply these reasons—but you must make allowances for prejudices—Besides I think the Scotch have not contributed as yet one shilling to the University—[when copying this letter Newman noted here, [[Not Mr Hope Scott?]]]

I write these lines in a great hurry just as I am starting for Cork—They are intended only for yourself—' Newman noted in his University Journal, 'The object of the letter is apparently to get rid of Ornsby and Stewart.'

[2] In the draft Newman added here '(and this in fact would be helping in Classics.)'

that in short they, of all men, would do what your Grace suggests, help one another, putting their shoulder to the wheel, and undertaking any work which was wanted with ability and cheerfulness.

If I withdraw Mr Stewart's name from the published list, perhaps you will let me substitute Mr E. H. Thompson's — of Trinity College, Cambridge for the Lectureship in English Composition.

It does indeed require a very delicate and nice judgment to steer between doing too much and doing too little. People expect a great deal; if we do nothing public, we shall disappoint them. A provisional state is one, in which we are engaged in feeling our way — but to do nothing public, is to take a definite line — instead of temporising, adjusting, beating about, and making attempts.

Further, will you let me say, that, ⌐for the very reason that we are in a provisional state, I ought to have,⌐ during that state, an influence in ⌐the appointments⌐ which otherwise I could not expect. I have not to preside over some existing institution, but to set one going. The Bishops must put confidence in me. ⌐An extra-ordinary work demands extra-ordinary powers. I have to begin; every one has his own way of beginning;⌐ unless I begin in my own way, I cannot promise I shall succeed in making any beginning at all. It is in the power of the Bishops to end the provisional state of things when they will, and, together with it, to put an end to my office; but, while that state continues, that office surely must continue too.

It seemed to me at the time, as if some of the resolutions at the Synodal Meeting assumed that a provisional state is the normal one. I should have said so then; except that of course I am most unwilling to throw difficulties in the way of so great a work as a University; and I felt that words often will not work and become dead letters, and that events of themselves manage to clear a way for us out of difficulties, if we are but patient. But it is well I should say it now to you; for ⌐I wish none of my views or intentions unknown to one whom I love and venerate so much as I do your Grace.⌐ To you then I wish to say, that, ⌐if I am to get through the initial difficulties of my undertaking at all, I must have my arms free;⌐ that I must be able to use my own judgment, and my own instruments.

⌐When I say 'my own instruments,' I am speaking of the persons who actually are to co-operate with me in the *launch* of the vessel; I do not mean the body of the Professors [[who belong to its normal state]]⌐. Those whom I have already recommended, those whom I may in time to come recommend, as Fr O'Reilly, or Mr Currie, or Mr O'Hagan, have their own sufficient sphere, in which I should not think of interfering. ⌐I am speaking of those, who, in the very commencement, at the first stroke, are immediately around me. I ask for this privilege on the principle,⌐ on which I am sure I shall have your Grace's sanction, ⌐that he who has the *responsibility* should have the *power*.⌐¹

As I am writing, will you let me add that I think I should like placed in the joint account of your Grace and myself at the Hibernian Bank before you go, the remaining £500, of the £2500 which was voted me in May — and an additional £1500 — out of which I should repay you the £1350 which you have advanced for the Medical School. Excuse this trouble.

Begging your Grace's blessing, I am, My dear Lord Your faithful & affte friend & Servt in Xt

John H Newman of the Oratory

The Most Revd the Archbp of Dublin

TO ARCHBISHOP CULLEN²

Mount Salus. Dalkey. Octr 3. 1854

My dear Lord,

It has vexed me much, that I have been able neither to send to your Grace sooner, nor on the other hand to postpone for the present the list of Gentlemen, whom I submit to your Grace hereby for ad interim employment in the lecture-rooms of the University.

That I have not written sooner to you on the subject has not been owing to any want of diligence on my part, but to the unavoidable slowness with which the correspondence has proceeded which was preliminary to any satisfactory arrangement.

On the other hand, I have reason to fear that the publication of a list cannot be postponed with a due regard to the probable wants of the

¹ [[(These last sentences refer to what Dr Cullen said Sept 28 about Dr Leahy and Mr Flannery)]] Cullen wrote on that day: 'I have heard that some complaints are made of Mr Scratton as a manager. I do not know what grounds for them—but I think you would do well to call Dr Leahy and Revd Mr Flannery to you once or twice a week, and as they are well versed in the management of temporal affairs, they would be of great assistance to you.'

² Newman's identical letter to MacHale is printed in Bernard O'Reilly, *John MacHale Archbishop of Tuam*, New York 1890, II, pp. 504–06, and that to Slattery is in the archives of the Archdiocese of Cashel.

Newman noted in his University Journal on 10 Oct., 'In answer the Archbishops of Armagh and Dublin assented simply—of Cashel, if the others did—all three resting it on confidence in me. Archbishop of Tuam neither approved nor disapproved—referred the matter to the meeting of the Bishops, and implied that I had in this matter, and as regards the Medical School, assumed a power which I had not.' See also below 6–8 Oct.

University, or with out impairing the confidence of the public in the reality of our commencement.

As to the schools of Theology, Law, and Medicine, they certainly may wait. What presses is the School of Arts; and here the ad interim appointments, which I would submit to your Grace, together with those already made, run as follows:—

1. Professor Dogmatic Theology — Fr O'Reilly D D. S J.
2. Professor Exegetics — Very Revd P. Leahy D D. V G. etc
3. Professor Archaeology and Irish History. Eugene Curry Esqr
4. Professor of Classical Literature — Robert Ornsby Esqr
5. Professor of Mathematics — Edward Butler Esqr
6. Professor of Civil Engineering — Terence Flanagan Esqr
7. Lecturer in Political Economy — John O'Hagan Esqr
8. Lecturer in Poetry — D. F. McCarthy Esqr
9. Lecturer in the Philosophy of History — T. W. Allies Esqr
10. Lecturer in Geography — J. B. Robertson Esqr
11. Lecturer in Logic — D. B. Dunne Esqr D D.
12. Lecturer in Ancient History — James Stewart Esqr
13. Lecturer in English Literature — E. H. Thompson Esqr
14. Lecturer in French Literature — M. P. le Page Renouf.
15. Lecturer in Italian and Spanish — Signr Marani

Most of these gentlemen must be known to your Grace by reputation — and do not need any commendation of mine. Mr Butler is of Trinity College, Dublin — and bears a high name for mathematical attainments. Dr Dunne is of the Irish College at Rome, and is most highly thought of by all who know him. Mr Flanagan has much experience of English Railroads, has been employed in the Railroads of Belgium, and is now similarly occupied in Portugal. Mr Robertson, who has been living in Germany, is the translator of some of the works of Moehler and Schlegel, and is a contributor to the Dublin Review. Mr Ornsby and Mr Renouf are from Oxford, Mr Thompson and Mr Stewart from Cambridge. They are all men of well known ability, and I am convinced would do justice to their appointment. M. Renouf is a native of Guernsey, and speaks English and French with equal facility. He has been living for the last 7 years in a family of distinction in France. He is a classical scholar, well versed in theology and history, and generally well informed. Mr Ornsby gained the highest honors at Oxford, was Fellow and Rhetorical Lecturer in his College, and held the University office of Master of the Schools. He, as well as M. Renouf, is a successful writer. The two gentlemen from Cambridge are equally well qualified. Signor Marani has high testimonials from persons in Dublin, in whose family he has taught, or who know him — and I have heard what is to the credit of his religious character.

I trust your Grace will believe the anxious care with which I have prepared this list for your Grace's approval. I am sanguine that, when tried, it will deserve it. Of course none of the Gentlemen who are upon it, will be employed till actually wanted; nor paid till employed.

I have addressed a copy of this letter to the other Archbishops — and am, My dear Lord, begging your Grace's blessing, Your faithful Servt in Xt

John H Newman of the Oratory, Rector

His Grace The Most Revd The Archbp of Dublin

TO RICHARD STANTON

Mount Salus, Dalkey Octr 3/54

My dear Fr Richard

I ought before this to have answered your letter, and conveyed to you the grateful and affectionate thoughts I have of you all in return for your kind present.[1] I am very much gratified, and shall like much to see it. The Mitres etc. had better stay at Brompton till an opportunity, and then must go to Birmingham, not here.

We have still splendid weather — I shall have every one in turn here, I suppose, but Nicholas and Edward.

I am now just coming to the rub — and may have a few shocks, from certain indications about me, but I don't expect to be thrown off the line. I want some good prayers.

I am saying a weekly anti-cholera Mass for you all — and gave you, of course, Michaelmas Day besides

Ever Yrs affly J H N

WEDNESDAY 4 OCTOBER 1854   Bernard came having been at Waterford to preach

TO EDWARD CASWALL

Mount Salus Dalkey Oct 4. 1854

My dearest Edward

I have to tell you *in strict confidence* that Frederic is going to leave the Oratory.

[1] Stanton wrote on 25 Sept., 'The mitres which you consented to accept from us, have just arrived—The case also includes the vimpas or little veils to hold them with, and pontifical gloves of the different colours . . .'

The reason he gives is, that you have treated him like a servant.

You said to him something like this; that the Brothers were like Servants waiting on Gentlemen.

I do not write to you, however, about him but merely to say, that I think you will find it your wisdom, as I have found it mine, *not to interfere with the brothers*. Leave them to the Father Minister.[1] *I* do not interfere with the Brothers' work at all — If I did, they would have *two* masters, the Minister and me.

Therefore I should recommend you to have nothing whatever to do with the Brothers, as such, except as *a private Father* — nothing as Rector.

I have already heard you had some words with John who is gone — who, though not a brother, was in loco fratris. I have serious anxiety lest you should hurt *Laurence's* vocation on his return.

All this makes me say, Leave the brothers to the Fr Minister.

I am somewhat pained, my dear Edward, to hear you speak of us as 'Gentlemen —' We are not Gentlemen in contradistinction to the Brothers — they are Gentlemen too, by which I mean, not only a Catholic, but a polished refined Catholic. The Brothers are our equals in the same sense in which a Priest is a Bishop's equal. The Bishop is above the Priest ecclesiastically — but they are both sacred ministers. The Father is above the Brother sacerdotically — but in the Oratory they are equal.[2]

Excuse this hint, my dearest Edward, and forgive me, and believe me Ever Yours affly in St Philip

                                                              J H N

TO ARCHBISHOP CULLEN

                                                  Mt S. D. Oct 4/54

My dear Lord

I have addressed a formal letter to the four Archbishops on the subject of the appointments. There is nothing in it which I have not already said to your Grace and Dr Dixon — except that I have added

---

[1] The lay brothers were under the care of the Minister, St John. Frederic (Thomas Godwin) complained to St John about the way he was treated by Caswall, who was Rector or Superior in Newman's absence.

[2] Caswall's defence was that he had on one occasion described a dirty lamp as 'not fit for gentlemen,' meaning it as a proverbial phrase.

Signr Marani, concerning whom I have had a very good account this four or five months.

I inclose your Grace's and the Primate's copies of it

Ever Yours affly and obtly in Xt

John H Newman of the Oratory

The Most Revd Dr Cullen

TO AMBROSE ST JOHN

⌐Mount Salus Dalkey Oct 4. 1854

My dearest Ambrose

I wish you were well. For me, I get better daily, thank God — but it will be a while before I am right.

I am passing through a crisis about University appointments — but hitherto all goes well.⌐

As to F. [Frederic] tell him I wish you to see the inclosed letter to him after he has read it. And advise with him.

⌐I have written to Fr Edward, to have nothing to do with the Brothers.⌐ You will find he will *tacitly* leave them alone. Do not speak to him about it — leave him to himself, but write to me

⌐Bernard came today — Robert on Friday⌐

Ever Yrs affly J H N

Thursday Oct. 5. ⌐I think it will be best for [[Brother]] Frederic to come here till Christmas⌐ as my helper — for I want a help very much. When I first get into Number 6,[1] he can be of great use to me — and therefore there could not be a better reason for his leaving Bm. [Birmingham] ⌐Rednall might follow in time, if it suited him;⌐ but his coming here would be no mere excuse, but a real service to me.

⌐Had John Smallwood a voice? I think not. T. Ford has. The greatest loss of F. will be in the singing,⌐ and I wish you would turn your thoughts to this at once.

Thank God, ⌐I am every day better — but it will be some considerable time before I can take a walk. It happened three weeks today. The weather still *beautiful*. The Fathers seem enjoying themselves as much as I could wish.⌐ Can Frederic cook? If so, Laurence might go back with Fr Frederic in the middle of next week, and Frederic come with Stanislas. But ⌐I should like very much to hear that old Simcox had

---

[1] Newman had just taken a lease of 6 Harcourt Street, which became St Mary's House. See *McGrath*, p. 342.

finished the deed.⌐ ⟨*If* Frederic can cook for you or you can get on without Laurence, Laurence had better stay here for several weeks longer⟩

Monsell was here last night. He says or implies that the probable opinion is that Sebastopol after all *could* be taken by a coup de main on the land side. If so, since every one said *not*, I suppose the generals etc had kept it to themselves and encouraged the opposite idea in order to conceal their plans. Thanks for the Newspaper. Monsell seems to think that Sir C Napier has shown the white feather! The captains of the fleet are almost in mutiny. What a reverse![1] J H N.

TO THOMAS SCRATTON

Mount Salus Oct 5/54

My dear Scratton

Thank you for your zeal about the coals.

As to the board being given, I think I may say I never said a word to you on the subject.[2] I took at once, and have, a note of what I said last November, and think I have been cautious about it, because I did not know if I *could*

You may be *quite sure* I wish to do much more than I do — and *directly* the University fills, you may be sure I shall be looking about me for the purpose; but at first I must do what I can.

What I may have said to O'Reilly, of course was another matter.

Further, supposing I had ever thought of it, I should have felt anxious on hearing your question about giving dinners. I do sincerely fear, residence in the University House will not suit you — whether your board was provided or not, and I cannot help advising you not to do so.[3]

---

[1] The heights on the opposite side of Sebastopol Harbour to the City were captured on 20 Sept. at the Battle of the Alma, and people thought the fortress had fallen. The heights were then abandoned in favour of an attack on the land side, from which the fortress was not taken until a year later.

The fleet in the Baltic under the command of Sir Charles Napier, after sailing about ineffectually, began to return home at the end of Sept., but the order was counter-manded. Napier was severely criticised and was accused of losing his nerve.

[2] Scratton wrote on 2 Oct., 'Shall I say what I have it in my mind to say? It appears to me that the University is rather sharp upon us not to allow us our board? . . . I thought Myles O Reilly had informed me differently and that it was intended to give us a free table . . .'

[3] Scratton replied next day, 'Your excessive kindness confuses and overwhelms me and I am determined to do nothing rashly. As I never found that I was the worse for taking your advice so in this case . . .'

I don't know that I have any thing more to say at the moment — but I shall be quite ready to talk it over with you

Ever Yrs John H Newman

TO ARCHBISHOP CULLEN

Mount Salus — Dalkey Oct 6. 1854

Private

My dear Lord

I sent my list of 15 Professors etc. to Dr Slattery through Dr Leahy — and I am glad to say that Dr L. writes back thus :—

'I have read over your letter to Dr Slattery and am sure he must be pleased with your list of appointments. Though not acquainted with the merits of each one, he may and will take them upon trust from you.'

Dr Dixon has written a most kind letter of the same kind.[1] I shall go to Fr McNamara to see what *he* thinks about the whole list frightening any one. If he does not think it will, I shall consider you will not object to my publishing all 15

Ever Your affte friend & servt in Xt

John H Newman of the Oratory

The Most Revd Dr Cullen

TO JOHN STANISLAS FLANAGAN

Mount Salus. Dalkey October 6. 1854

My dear Stanislas

⟨Fr Fred goes to Bm [Birmingham] at one. The sooner some one comes, if any one comes, the better⟩

I cannot endorse the Abbé Chaillot's bill or whatever it is. I inclose his letter to me; from which it appears that the copies to the end of 1852 were my due. I think I kept the *second* number of the Analecta, taken in my absence.[2] Perhaps the third too. However, it is easy to see how many, because Dulan has only sent me one. If on looking over the numbers I

---

[1] Dixon of Armagh wrote on 4 Oct., 'The list is most acceptable to me; as indeed any list should be, which meets with your approval.' Slattery of Cashel wrote personally on 7 Oct., '. . . I have every confidence in your experience and judgment,' and '. . . if the other Archbishops are satisfied, so am I.'

[2] This refers to a bill for copies of *Analecta Juris Pontificii*, which Newman had not ordered.

have (between my windows) you can not make out *when* Dulan began,
I must trouble you to write to Messrs Dulan, Soho Square, and ask.
All *before* Dulan I have had from Rome. They will be those, which you
actually *find* between the windows + the Number which Robert brought
here, viz Number ⟨Livraison⟩ 3 Then, from those numbers must be
subtracted those which belong to 1852 — and the remainder are those,
or is that, (if those *be* one or more) for which I owe the Abbé Chaillot.
I am sorry to give you so long a sum. This, however, does not interfere
with the *bill* — which I cannot accept. Could not Dulan settle it for me
with M. Francois Terwagne?[1]

As to Simcox, if you are morally satisfied that the title is good and
the deed sure to be executed, do not wait at Birmingham. The fine
weather is still lasting — how long I do not know — knowing people
say, *not* long. Father Fred. was *suddenly* going this morning — he is
either gone or in bed. Before I close the letter, I will make him fix a
day. At present we have only room for his substitute, who would have a
back room. Give my love to Wm [William] — thank him for his letter —
say I shall be most glad to see him — but that there is no room at the
moment, and I so fear that he has let the fine weather slip, that, glad as
I shall be to see him, he must look the chance of bad weather, and a bad
voyage to and fro, in the face.

Pray break up the ground for potatoes.[2]

I suppose you think it hopeless to get Simcox to speak to Lord
Calthorpe's agent.

Ever Yrs affly J H N

P.S.   F. Bernard came on Wednesday

SUNDAY 8 OCTOBER 1854   William came

TO EDWARD CASWALL

Octr 8/54

My dear Edward

Thank you for your letter. I think, under the circumstances, you
had better let matters remain as they are. Frederic will come to me here
for a time

Ever Yrs affly J H N

---

[1] A Belgian banker in Rome.

[2] i.e. the field beside the cottage that was being built at Rednal, to the title deeds
of which reference is made above.

TO ARCHBISHOP CULLEN

Mount Salus. October 8. 1854

My dear Lord,

I am afraid this will not catch you in England — I send it to Liverpool with hopes it may.[1] Thank you very much for your kind letter.[2] I have great responsibilities on me which make me very anxious — I can only trust I may have a wisdom superior to my own as I rely on the prayers and good offices of my friends, and of those especially who have been concerned in placing me under these anxieties, to get me through them happily and to the greater glory of God.

I hope to get as far as Phibsborough to Mr McNamara tomorrow — and as soon as I am able, to Castleknock.[3]

Mr Curry called here today — and wished me to remind your Grace of the Irish Manuscripts at St Isidore. If he cannot get the possession of them for the University, he much covets the *loan* of them.[4]

I see by the Papers that Cardinal Mai's Library is coming to public auction. I suppose it could not be bought for the University.[5]

Overleaf you will find the cause of my writing. I have transcribing [sic] Dr McHale's answer to my letter, addressed to the four Archbishops, with the reply I have made to him

Begging your Grace's blessing, I am, My dear Lord, Yr affte friend & Servt in Xt

John H Newman of the Oratory

The Most Revd the Archbp of Dublin

[1] Newman changed his mind and sent it to Rome.

[2] Cullen wrote from Liverpool on 7 Oct., 'I place so much confidence in your judgment and prudence that I cannot hesitate once more to give my sanction to their [the professors and lecturers] appointment. You may now proceed with confidence in the matter as you are certain of a majority of the Archbishops.'

[3] Cullen's letter continued, 'I think it will be most useful for you to consult Revd Mr McNamara and Mr Dooley on all practical matters as they are intimately acquainted with the state of public feeling in Ireland.

I need scarcely add that I shall be always ready to give you every possible assistance in my power.'

Thomas MacNamara, Superior at Phibsborough, and Philip Dowley, Superior of Castleknock College, were the founders of the Vincentian Congregation in Ireland. Newman consulted MacNamara in a long letter on 9 July 1856, but the latter found its questions much too grave and difficult for him to answer.

[4] See letter of 5 June to Talbot.

[5] Angelo Mai (1782–1854), the palaeographer who was Prefect of the Vatican Library, died on 9 Sept. In his will he said he would gladly have left his library for the use of the Roman clergy, but that since he could not provide premises for it, it

FROM JOHN MACHALE, ARCHBISHOP OF TUAM

Tuam October 6 1854

My dear Dr Newman

I am in receipt of your letter of the 3rd Inst. as I have been of that of the 17th of August, to which I would have replied, were it not for the concluding words that no answer was needed. From this it appears that to consult the Archbishops on the purchase of Schools or the fitness of Professors is a matter of mere courtesy

On the subject of the list forwarded, I am unable with few exceptions to express approval or disapprobation, even if I considered this the appropriate occasion. I purpose freely to express my opinions, when the opportunity shall offer of meeting assembled and acting together the Prelates to whom the provisional and permanent appointment of the Professors is entrusted.

I remain, My dear Dr Newman Your very faithful Servt

+John Mac Hale.

Very Revd Dr Newman

TO JOHN MACHALE, ARCHBISHOP OF TUAM

Mount Salus, Dalkey, ⌐Oct. 8, 1854.⌐

My Dear Lord,

⌐I hope this letter will find you still in this country, for I should be very sorry not to have the opportunity of submitting to you a few words in explanation of my letters of August 17 and October 3, which I am concerned to find have not met with your approbation.

It would be a serious trouble to me to have it brought home to me that I had misconceived the powers which your Grace and the other Irish prelates have, in so flattering a way, bestowed upon me as rector of the new University; and, if I have really overstepped them in consequence, I beg to offer you my sincere and humble apology.

It is very plain that, whatever powers I have, come from the Irish episcopate; and that, as it gave them, so it may at any moment withdraw them. But it seems to be equally plain, that the confidence their Lordships have placed in me is very full, and the powers in consequence instrusted to me are very ample; and you will have, I am sure, no difficulty in entering into my feeling when I say that, unless I have that full confidence and those ample powers, it would have been the height of presumption and folly in me to aspire to such very anxious responsibilities as I have accepted.

was to be sold. However, he gave the Papal Government the option on it at half the valuation. Pius IX bought it, and it is preserved in a room in the Vatican Library. Cardinal Wiseman, *Recollections of the Last Four Popes*, new and revised ed., London n.d., p. 311.

273

The purchase of the Medical School was one of those measures which I certainly did think came upon me by virtue of my situation. I never should have ventured to trouble the bishops with a matter of business which was nothing else than a part of the work which they had imposed upon me; nor should I have been able to form any clear idea of my duties, had I been told that this was not included in them. Accordingly I acted on my own responsibility. When, however, the negotiation was brought to a satisfactory issue, the feeling, never absent from me, that I am acting for the bishops, prompted me, on the other hand, at once to acquaint you with my success, by way of offering you an evidence that I was not idling at my post. Writing under these circumstances, I wrote without form, and did not keep a copy of my letter; I cannot, however, but be surprised and deeply pained to find that I so expressed myself as to admit of the interpretation, foreign from my real meaning, which you have been led to put upon my words.

As to the *ad interim* appointments of professors and lecturers, still more distinctly do I bear in mind that they rest with a power more authoritative than my own. At the same time, I thought I was required to suggest them to your Grace and the other archbishops; and, if we are to open our schools without delay, it is surely undeniable that, had I not moved in the matter, the schools would be opened without lecturers to lecture in them. The meeting of the bishops to which your Grace postpones the *ad interim* decision will take place, by the very force of the terms, at a time when the *ad interim* season has expired. [[for my appointments are 'ad interim *donec* coeant Episcopi.']]

I do not like to keep anything back from your Grace; and, since you have opened the subject, you will, I know, suffer me to speak, with the generous condescension which is so much your characteristic. From the bishops, then, I hold whatever power I possess in the University; they have the appointment of professors, and they can exert their Veto at their pleasure upon the names which I present to them. But I am deliberately of opinion, that, if they exercise it except on definite grounds, sufficient in the judgment of each other, they will be making the commencement of the University an impossible problem to any one who is not better fitted for the work than I am. Having so many instances of their consideration for me, I do not fear any such misfortune.[1]

I am, my dear Lord, with profound respect, your Grace's obedient servant in Christ,

John H. Newman, of the Oratory.[1]

The Most Rev'd The Archb'p of Tuam.

[1] MacHale's biographer, after printing the above, adds: 'As the Archbishop of Tuam was then setting out for Rome, he may not have received this letter in Ireland,

TO AMBROSE ST JOHN

Oct 8 [1854]

My dear Ambrose,

My difficulty, looking narrowly at the matter, to his being my porter, is considerable.[1] I meant him rather for another post in my house — but this perhaps would be a needless expence to me.

Have him I must (i.e. as long as he likes) but how? would he buckle to being cook? I suppose not. But he could not do me a greater service. I would send him between November and Christmas to the Club to be taught. You could sound him. If he were not, he would be in the position of an attendance on me and my household. The only difficulty about this is, that the youths might bully him. Is this likely?

I trust you are getting on. I am, but slowly. William came today.

The Lion, solus, has roared at me — and I have roared again — and the two roarings are done up in a letter and sent to Dr Cullen at Rome

The Archbishop of Sidney is here, and inquired after you.[2]

Ever Yrs affly J H N

Oct 8

If you *can* get rid of Kushnig, I should be very glad.[3]

TUESDAY 10 OCTOBER 1854   Frederic went?
WEDNESDAY 11 OCTOBER   Monsell called

or been able to return an immediate answer to it. His quarrel was not with Dr Newman —but with the men who deliberately, systematically, and unjustifiably set aside the authority of the Irish episcopate in the government of the University, [understand *Cullen*] and only made use of the shadow of authority left to that body as an instrument for their own purpose, and a cloak for proceedings which ended in discrediting and ruining the University itself.' Bernard O'Reilly, D.D., *John MacHale Archbishop of Tuam*, II, p. 509.

[1] St John suggested this post for Br Frederic.

[2] The Archbishop of Sydney was John Bede Polding, O.S.B., whom Newman and St John had met at Alton Towers in 1846 and at Rome in 1847.

[3] This refers to the Croatian cook at the Birmingham Oratory, who was about to leave.

TO J. M. CAPES

Mount Salus. Dalkey Octr 11. 1854

My dear Capes,

I don't think I had any particular criticisms to make myself on your Article.[1] I am *very glad* you are going to reprint it. The criticisms I heard were that the article was too sketchy, and ought to be worked out in *detail* more.

Thank you for your remarks on my Book List, which I have used.[2] Tell me any books of weight in their own line which I may add, if any strike you.

Thank you very much for your name, which I gladly add to our List. I am in great anxiety about [W.G.] Ward's health.

Ever Yrs affly in Xt   John H Newman of the Oratory

J. M. Capes Esqr

TO W. J. O'NEILL DAUNT

Mount Salus. Dalkey. Octr 11. 1854

My dear Sir

I thank you for your contribution of £1 to the University, which I will take care to send to the University Treasurers.

Lady Lothian has two of her sons received — the two eldest are Protestants — and I think there is a third who is in the navy[3]

Very truly Yours John H Newman of the Oratory

W. J. Daunt Esqr

THURSDAY 12 OCTOBER 1854   Shepherd of Oriel College called[4]

[1] 'Equivocation, as taught by St Alphonsus Liguori,' in the *Rambler* (April 1854), pp. 307–36. See letter of 15 June 1854 to Capes.

[2] Capes sent corrections to the list in the *Catholic University Gazette*.

[3] Lady Lothian's son the eighth Marquis of Lothian, and his brother who succeeded him, did not become Catholics. Lord Ralph and Lord John had already been received, and Lord Walter, serving with the Baltic Fleet, became a Catholic in 1855.

[4] William Sheppard (1813–60), Scholar of Trinity 1831–6, Fellow of Oriel 1836–40, and a clergyman, wrote to Newman on 4 Oct. to say that he was 'in Dublin in very great pecuniary distress, owing to a three months illness.' He begged for help, explaining that he had no friend in Dublin.

TO EDWARD CASWALL

Oct 12/54

My dear Edward

I must put a little trouble on you. Fr Frederic has paid the choir up to June 21. I wish you to be so good as to pay it up to Michaelmas. He will give you the tables I drew out, and other papers.

The way of doing it is this:—1. You get a certain sum from Stanislas (which comes from the Offertory) and £10 from me. 2. You then ask Fr Frederic for the quarterly sum due to each performer — 3. From this you deduct his *absences* — which are calculated as so much a time in Fr Frederic's papers — 4. and you pay each performer the remainder.

Ever Yrs affly J H N

TO JOHN STANISLAS FLANAGAN

Mount Salus Dalkey Octr 12. 1854

My dear Stanislas

Of course when Fathers are away for holyday their duties, as far as not imperative, should be dropped. I said so to Fr Ambrose, about his own Lecture, when Fr Henry made an excuse of his taking it for not coming here — and I say so now, and, please, tell Fr Edward, I wish this carried out as far as possible. I do not at all forget the forlorness you must at present experience, confessor, novices, cook, and others being away — but depend upon it the *annoyance is worth* while. Austin and Frederic were both much better for their sojourn here. Dear Ambrose was a sad misfortune, which we could not reckon on — The Fathers now here are enjoying themselves very much, and I think no one will grudge it eventually. For that reason I wish you here — the weather is still splendid. Tell Fr Minister to order Victor's and Laurence's room to be got ready. I shall send them back as soon as possible — and as soon after they come as convenient, I should like you and Frederic to start. Read all this to Ambrose.

No 1 of the Analecta, I suspect, I sent back. *Certainly* I sent back one number — i.e. I did not take it in, and Dulan must get it etc.

I settled with Noel [Nowell] the direction of the sewerage when I was on the field[1] — Fr Ambrose perhaps may recollect. I wish you to exercise a supreme discretion and to settle 1. 2. 3. 4 — i.e. about the sewerage and

[1] This paragraph refers to Rednal.

277

every thing else, which you have mentioned and which you have not. I fear there is not a chance of my being with you till Christmas — at all events I must not count on it. As to the gravel, I should like a terrace — but if it will wait, let it wait.

I am sorry to give you additional trouble — can you send £5 to Fr Antony for me?

As to your want of funds, for coming here, why I wont press you, if you really feel it — but, if you will, you may borrow £5 from me to be repaid when you will.

I am very anxious about Lady O A's [Olivia Acheson] £6000 — i.e. because nothing is done. I think it might be a good thing to have a Novena to St Philip. Ask the other Fathers about it.

Ever Yrs affly J H N

P.S.   I will write to Edward about the choir.
I WANT INSTANTER SOME PARTICULARS OF YOUR COUSIN TERENCE'S CAREER. A few words will do.
Robert is laid up today with *a bad leg*. Laurence has a bad toe. You know Austin had a bad ankle. I am getting on.

TO AMBROSE ST JOHN

Mount Salus. Dalkey Octr 12. 1854
Private
My dear Ambrose

I am exceedingly displeased to find that Frederic has actually made a proposal to a young woman, *being in our house and having our habit on.*[1] This seems to be so great an offence that I do not know what to say about it. I hereby through you distinctly forbid him to hold any communication, or to send or receive any letters while he is in our house — and I trust to his good feeling, that he will not be in a hurry to leave our house till we give him leave. It will be a poor return indeed to our kindness, if he does not obey these distinct commands, and will bring a great scandal on St Philip's house, to which he may find St Philip not insensible. All this you may tell him from me. You may read this letter to him, and tell him, that, if he wants a blessing on his new line of life, he does not go the way to get it.

[1] Oratorian laybrothers are not bound by vows and Frederic (Thomas Godwin) was soon to cease to be a laybrother.

278

What I have said only goes a very little way to express my sense of the extraordinary act which he has allowed himself to commit.

Ever Yrs affly J H N

P.S.   This letter is *only* for yourself and Frederic — and if you did not know any of the facts before, you must not repeat them from me.

TO AMBROSE ST JOHN

Mount Salus Dalkey Octr 15/54

My dear Ambrose

⌐Will you tell Fr Edward to communicate in confidence the following to the Congregatio Deputata:—Yesterday Monsell, who called here, opened the subject of Lady O A's [[Olivia Acheson's]] money.⌐ He was in his way to London, and went to see Mr F. [Fullerton]. ⌐He said that we could have the *interest* of the trust money, the lawyers said, in the way we proposed but not the principal — since we could give no legal guarantee for our continuance as a body. He would take care that it was placed in Rail road security, and would bring us in 4½ per cent (which for £1900 is £85. 10)

I then went on to speak of the £6000 — and said that we were much inconvenienced by the suspence. He said he must touch up Mr F's [[Fullerton's]] memory, for, from what Mr [F.R.] Ward had said, he did not think Mr F. quite realized just now our close connexion with the money, over other charitable dispositions of it. I said 'We should be much surprised, if he did not — but, any how, the suspence was a great trouble to us.' He replied 'O, it was nothing — there was no doubt we should have it — he would set it right.' I suggested that we had fancied that Mr F. was scrupulous about a secret trust. He said he thought it was not so — [[but]] Dr Whitty had said something as if Dr Jones had said that the family would contest the money.[1] I answered that it seemed most unlikely that they should *pay over* the money [[as they had done?]], if they meant to contest it. He said, yes, but it might make Mr F. nervous lest it should be claimed of him when he had given it up to us. What should we think of a first mortgage on our house? In that case the money would actually be made *over to* us, as a loan to us without interest, on the security of our building — I said I saw no objections — but should we give us [[up]] the title deeds? However, I

---

[1] [[bequest]] This was left to Fullerton as residuary legatee, and Lady Olivia intended it to go to the Oratory. Dr Jones was her physician.

thought he might propose it to Mr F. and we should hear about it within a fortnight.

The plan would be that at the end of 20 years, (or whatever the term is) he would simply *destroy* our deed of mortgage; but we must look sharp that an heir does not enforce it.⌐

————————

As to Frederic, I have heard from him this morning and the *tone* of his letter, as I can make it out, is *against* his coming here. 1. As far as I ⟨(i.e. Harcourt Street)⟩ am concerned it would be no object his coming here — but if he does not come, I think William must be spared to come here and *wait* on us. We *have* a (man) cook. 2. ⌐It is absurd to suppose that the laurels etc and making the cemetery at Rednal can occupy F. [[Frederic]] *long* —⌐ and what is to become of him then? for ⌐*Hansom must go there*, as you propose.⌐ And are we to *pay* F. while there? 3. I wished him *here*, to avoid the *scandal*, which will be *very great*. It is a most cruel thing for the other brothers — and for the Congregation — Here he would be out of the way, and things would settle down — I should propose to keep him till Christmas, and then let him follow his own devices. 4. I object to his going even for *a day* to Rednall, if he is courting during it. While he is in our house and under our shadow, he must observe most perfect chastity — which in a certain sense courting is not.[1]

Tell Stanislas, I think the windows of the house must have shutters. As to the Privy, he must do what is best

Every Yrs affly J H N

TO BISHOP ULLATHORNE

Mount Salus Dalkey Octr 19. 1854

My dear Lord

I thank you very much for your kind letter and for the assurance you give me of your sympathy, in the most effectual manner, in the very anxious work in which I am engaged. A little time may make our prospects clearly [sic], but we are now just on the brink of an experiment, which, though not so bad as landing on the Crimea, is in a little way parallel to it.

I am rejoiced to find you contemplate a work on the Immaculate Conception — it will, I am sure, do extensive good. Not only Catholics

————————

[1] The part of this letter that concerned him was read to Br Frederic, who without hesitation expressed his desire to go to Dublin for as long as Newman pleased.

but a number of inquiring Protestants need and ask information on the subject — and any thing which came from your Lordship would be received with great respect and read with interest. I hope you will write it so far popularly, that all classes may read it. Your sketch of chapters seems exceedingly good.[1]

Does Father Perrone in his recent work dwell on the distinction you mention as throwing light upon the meaning and drift of the early Fathers when they speak of the Immaculate Conception or approach the subject?[2]

I am sorry to hear your Lordship say that conversions have diminished since 1846. Have the lists been kept accurately before and after that date?

Those of our party who are here desire your Lordship's blessing, in which I join, and beg you to believe me to be, My dear Lord, Your faithful & affte friend & Servt in Xt

John H Newman of the Oratory

The Rt Revd the Bp of Birmingham

TO CATHERINE ANNE BATHURST

Octr 21/54 Dalkey

My dear Child

I have just got your letter of Tuesday. If I did not speak more strongly, it was because I had not seen you lately.

I certainly think that it is God's will you should try the religious life with the convent at Greenwich, as you propose.

Ever Yrs affly J H N

P.S. Do not mention it about, but we are anxious for Fr Ambrose, who I fear will have to go abroad for the winter. Give him and us your prayers

[1] This was Ullathorne's *The Immaculate Conception*, London and Baltimore 1855. Cf. *Diff.* II, p. 127.
[2] Cf. *The Immaculate Conception*, pp. 129–31, where it is maintained that no Father denied the doctrine in formal terms.

TO T. W. ALLIES

Mount Salus Dublin Oct. 22./54.

My dear Allies,

I am exceedingly pleased and relieved by your letter.[1]

Do you think you can give us a set of Lectures between Christmas and Easter? If I could put into the Gazette 'The Lecturer on the Philosophy of History will deliver a course of Lectures on the Balance of Power in the course of the Term between Christmas and Easter,' it would have a good effect now, and would prepare for a full audience then. If you saw fit to change or modify your subject in the interim, n'importe. The great thing is to impress general ideas of a University and what we are doing, upon people.

There will be no ceremonies of opening now. I shall try to get up a series of inaugural Lectures (of Professors etc) between this and Christmas. Would you give one, explaining what is meant by the Philosophy of History? but I do not press it, though I *wish extremely* you should *come* and make a good hit.

Private. Some one writes to me dating 'Reform Club,' and signing 'Wm B. Sills' and wishing his name put down on our books. Who is he? he says he has been on the continent the last 2 months.[2]

Ever Yrs affly J. H. Newman

TO AMBROSE ST JOHN

⌜Dalkey. Octr 27/54

My dearest A

We move to 6 Harcourt Street, i.e. Stan. [Stanislas] Wm [William] I and Fred.[3] on Monday next. On the same day Bernard and Robert return to Edgbaston. Let their beds be got ready. Thank Henry for his letter.

Of course it would be a great relief to find you had the gout formally instead of those troublesome precursors. When you go to Dr Watson[4]

---

[1] Allies wrote on 20 Oct., that he had received permission from the Catholic Poor Schools Committee to accept the Dublin Lectureship. Cf. letter of 3 Sept.

[2] Allies replied, 'Mr Wm B. Sills *is* a member of the Reform Club; has been so long; appears from his acquaintance to be a Catholic; and is not known to be in any profession. That is all I can extract from the Porter. I never heard of him before.'
William Bernard Sills gave his name to the University.

[3] [[(Godwin)]] i.e. the former laybrother.

[4] The London doctor whom St John was about to consult.

take Fr Richard with you and let him know first hand what Dr W. says as well as yourself. For, though I know you will be honest, yet it will be a comfort to you not to convey to me your own impressions.

As to Tonks, I do not feel great zeal about his return, but I acquiesce. One thing I should like to stipulate, that he *does not go into the kitchen*. You talk of his honest face, but he has a sharp eye, and a grasping hand.

Charlie must not be ridden. We must get a parson's pony chair for Rednall. Stanislas is looking out for one here.⌐

I shall keep Frederic to Christmas, and no longer. I *must* make up my mind now. What astonishes, perhaps hurts us, is his utter absence of distress at breaking so old a tie. He is simply relieved and happy — and sings in the kitchen with astonishing compass and volume.

Thanks, for Mr Beeky's list[1]

Ever Yrs affly J H N

Weather beautiful up to today, which is gusty. ⌐This day three years the Achilli proceedings began.⌐

TO CARDINAL WISEMAN

[November 1854?][2]

To the Cardinal Archbishop
&c.

The Archbishops and Bishops of Ireland, being on the point of inaugurating the University, to which a few years since they sollicited the attention of their brothers in England, have committed to me the pleasing duty of informing your Eminence of the fact; and of expressing through you to the Fathers of the Synod of Oscott, their warmest acknowledgments of the interest and sympathy, with which the Synod, responded to their call, and of the sums collected in consequence through England in their behalf.[3]

They have also to convey their special thanks to your Eminence and other Bishops, who, in spite of the many domestic objects which press upon them, have found ⟨felt⟩ themselves at liberty to advocate the cause of their University in the pulpit.

Next to the consciousness of the divine blessing on a work, to which they have been called by duty to the Catholic faith, and to the souls of

[1] Of furniture hired for Dalkey.

[2] Newman's draft of this letter is preserved in the Dublin Diocesan Archives.

[3] The Synod of Oscott, the first Provincial Synod of Westminster, was held in July 1852.

their people, no encouragement can be greater than that thus afforded by a sister Church, which is sharing with them a continuance of those trials and sufferings for religion, to which in greater or less severity it has been the good and holy will of God to subject them for the last 300 years.

They offer their humble prayer, (in which they have the cheering certainty that they are joined by your Eminence and the other English Bishops, and the confident hope that it will not be offered in vain,) that the great Institution, which now occupies their thoughts, when carried into effect, may, while it affords the necessary protection to the faith and morals of the youths submitted to its teaching, also promote the mutual edification of the Catholics of both countries, and join together more and more the hearts of populations, who are partakers, as of the trials, so of the grace and truth and consolations of this same holy religion.

TO FRANCIS KENRICK, ARCHBISHOP OF BALTIMORE

[November 1854?][1]

I have great satisfaction of fulfilling the commission of the Archbishops and Bishops of Ireland, to express to your Grace and the other Fathers of the Synod of Baltimore our united thanks for the cordial and fraternal interest, which they have shown in the great undertaking, in which we are at present engaged, of establishing a University in Ireland where science and literature may be cultivated in the widest aspect without prejudice to the faith and morals of those who avail themselves of it.[2]

That interest, as we gratefully acknowledge, has been effectual as well as warm. The Fathers of the Synod recommended our cause to the liberality of their flocks, and the munificent contributions which followed fills us, in the midst of our special trials with a double consolation, as furnishing, not only seasonable aid to our immediate object, but also a fresh and encouraging evidence, if any were needed, of the zeal of transatlantic Catholics for the cause of religion, and their affection for the people and land, to which by birth or relationship so many of them belong.

We have considered, that we could not select a more auspicious moment for conveying to your Grace, and through you to the Hierarchy of the United States, the expression of these feelings, than the present,

---

[1] Newman's draft of this letter is preserved in the Dublin Diocesan Archives.
[2] The first National Council of Baltimore was held in May 1852.

when it is also my gratifying duty to inform you that we have actually begun our work by a formal inauguration of the University.

You will, I am sure, join with us in a sentiment of religious hope and confidence, that this our first step, important as it is, will be by the Divine blessing, only the humblest in a long series (of successive movements) which are to follow; that, many as may be our difficulties, we shall, by the generous prayers and the persevering alms of the faithful, be carried over them; and, that an undertaking, founded in the union of Catholics so widely dispersed and so various by circumstances, will issue in more than corresponding benefits, external and temporal, to many countries and many generations.

(N B.   A Sentence perhaps on the Archbishop of Baltimore's expressions of respect personally for the Primate, Dr Cullen.)

TO A. J. HANMER

6 Harcourt Street Dublin Novr 1. 1854

My dear Hanmer,

Though I am surprised and concerned at Dr U's [Ullathorne] decision, I cannot be sorry you have gone to him; for it makes matters clear.

I shall be at Edgbaston at Christmas — till then I am here.

You should look out for some lay occupation which would occupy your mind, or semi-lay, I think — but not amateur occupation, but really obligatory upon you.

I am very busy, as you may think. Say every thing kind from me to your Sister

Ever Yrs affly John H Newman of the Oratory

A J Hanmer Esqr

TO HENRY WILBERFORCE

6 Harcourt Street, Novr 3/54

My dearest H

I write a line to congratulate you. Dear R. wrote to me too[1] — and, as soon as I get a minute, I will write to him.

[1] Robert Wilberforce's letter ran: '4 Rue du vieux Colombier Paris Eve of All Saints 1854

My dear Newman,

to you first, after my own family, I must announce what has befallen me—that by God's mercy I have been received into the Catholic Church May my few remaining years be more worthy of so high a privilege.

I owe this, of course, under God to you, more than to any man. "Primus Graius

By *the same post* as he wrote to me, a letter was received at the Tablet Office stating the fact — and I am told it is in the Tablet.[1]

Will you hand on the subscriptions you spoke of as a debt to the new Treasurer? they are not paid.

We number more than 60 — but not in residence or lecture; which is good for a beginning. Those actually in lecture at once, are of course much fewer — E.g. *my* house is not yet come.[2]

Ever Yrs J H N

TO J. D. DALGAIRNS

[4? November 1854]

My Dear Fr Bernard

Pray thank the Miss Farrants for their kindness to us and to our people at Smethwick.[3] I should accept their munificent offer without a word, except that they ask me a question relative to it. They say 'the thing to be known is whether Fr Newman means to go on with the school at Smethwick, and would like the plan for a room.'

Will you let them know that, tho' at present Smethwick is included in our mission, an opinion is entertained, at least by some of our body, that it never can really depend upon Edgbaston as its centre, and must, to be efficicably [sic] worked, become a centre itself of missionary exertion. Accordingly, the time will come, sooner or later, when the Oratory must decide on undertaking what really will be a second mission, or of separating it off altogether from its own spheres of exertion. It may decide this point very soon, or not decide it for years, but, while it is undecided, I feel I cannot answer what I understand to be their question, that is, to pledge the Oratory to continue the preaching and schools at Smethwick.

homo" etc. [Lucretius, *De Rerum Natura*, I, 66] I have never met you since you were a Catholic yourself, but your words have been in me as a fire.

Please not to mention the fact for a few days. Family reasons suggest this; and no one knows it but my confessor Pere de Ravignan. I stay here probably a fortnight, and then go South for the Winter. Perhaps I may settle on the Continent, or else in Ireland.
Your affect disciple in Christ   Rob I Wilberforce'

[1] The *Tablet* (4 Nov. 1854), p. 694, announced, 'We rejoice to be able to inform our readers that the Rev. Robert Isaac Wilberforce, formerly Archdeacon of the East Riding, was, a few days ago, received into the Catholic Church by the Bishop of Southwark at Paris.'

[2] On 3 Nov. the University was opened. For an account of this and of other University events see Appendix 2, p. 562, 'The Autumn Term, 1854.'

[3] The two Miss Farrants wanted the Oratorians to accept £200 to be spent on the missionary centre at Smethwick. Caswall on 2 Nov. had reported to Newman the views of the Oratorians on the matter.

This of course does not interfere with our glad and thankful acceptance of their charity, but only concerns the question whether the Oratory will or will not remain trustees of a bounty by which the poor of Christ's flock will any how be the gainers.

One point, besides, has to be considered, on which the other Fathers are more qualified than myself to decide — viz whether the spot selected is well adapted to be the centre of the independent mission of Smethwick.

Ever Yrs J H N

TO MISS M. R. GIBERNE

6 Harcourt Street Dublin Nov 6/54

My dear Miss Giberne

We have begun, and prosperously. We have about 60 names given in for Lectures, tho' all do not come at *once* — We have 20 in Lecture at present — and might increase them if we pleased. E.g. I have six to come in this house, perhaps 10, whom I have *postponed* till Christmas, that we may get things more in order. The youths are a very nice looking set of fellows.[1]

I broke the fibre of my calf — which has required rest — that is all. It is tedious. I have been steadily getting well from the first — but, though it is nearly 8 weeks since it happened, I am not well yet.

There is no news but R Wilberforce's reception — which is of course great news, but you will have heard it before you receive this.

Fr Ambrose is still uncomfortably unwell. They now call it a kind of gout — gouty asthma.

Thank you for your Masses — I doubt not they have done a great deal for us. We are carried over the difficulties with great ease — tho' there are of course breakers ahead. It is very kind of Mr Lyons.[2]

Thank you [for] what you tell me of yourself and your letter to the Princess. I shall be glad when you are settled in lodgings — let me know about it.[3]

[1] For an account of Newman's address to the students on 5 Nov., see Appendix 2, 'The Autumn Term,' p. 563.

[2] In her unpublished autobiography Miss Giberne speaks of the kindness to her at this time of Richard Bickerton Pemell Lyons, later Lord Lyons, who was attaché at Florence, but resided in Rome as unofficial British representative. His father was playing a vital part at Sebastopol as second in command of the British Mediterranean Fleet.

[3] This refers to Princess Borghese, recently married, who was Miss Giberne's pupil and friend. Cf. letter of 15 May 1854.

We have a French Viscount in this house — a youth of about 17 — Mr Renouf's pupil — he will attend the University.[1]

       Ever Yrs affly in Xt   John H Newman of the Oratory

TO AMBROSE ST JOHN

6 Harcourt Street Nov 6/54

My dear Ambrose

    I write in a great hurry. ⌈Go to St Leonard's by all means — Stanislas's⌉ business will keep him till next week here — and he is ⌈going down one day to see our Chapel.

    As to the poney carriage,⌉ Stanislas says if you like to think of it, you must *first go to Bretherton* and make him examine and give a good account of wheels, etc etc and the whole concern. ⌈If he *warrants* give £15 for it.

    Thank you, Edward, Bernard, and Henry for your letters about Smethwick — AS soon as ever I can *effect a meeting* between Stanislas, William and myself we will consider them all.⌉

    All is going on well. The Viscount with Renouf is already come to this house — and Sir Reginald Barnewall, aged 17, comes next week

       Ever Yrs J H N

P.S. ⌈I will write about the Music, I will put down £10 (tell Fr Frederic) to head the subscription.⌉

TO J. D. DALGAIRNS

6 Harcourt Street Nov 7/54

My dear D

    I wish Victor to be tonsured. Thank you very much for getting Mother Margaret etc a praying for us here. As to your Mass for me, give me a stray one now and then, and I shall be too thankful, but don't burden yourself with a promise or a rule. I send back Miss F's [Farrant] letter. I have written to Ambrose about it. I have written to Ambrose about Henry — let him have *enough* work to keep him from wasting his time in those conversational etc excursions

       Ever Yrs J H N

[1] This was Louis de Vaulchier.

TO AMBROSE ST JOHN

⌐6 Harcourt Street November 7. 1854⌐

My dear Ambrose,

⌐As to Henry⌐ — I am quite surprised at the question! — Of course ⌐I asked him to take William, and Robert's preparation for Oscott — and Victor's for Dublin. ⟨N.B. You and Bernard take care that Henry has not *too much*, but I wish to keep him from his women.⟩⌐ ⟨as to V's attending F. Nicholas, I thought he would not have *time* — but that he *would* attend Scratton.⟩

I meant to write on another matter — the *popular* music. ⌐As to the Mass and Vesper music, we must find what the subscription does for us, before we determine any thing. But we must think of the popular music at once. The only idea I have is to confine ourselves at present to those tunes we know best,⌐ such as the Evening Hymn, (supposing the congregation does not join.) I talked to Henry about it, and I wish you would consult with him.

⌐I have had a talk with Stanislas and Wm [William] — on the subject of the £200.⌐ They will write to you what they think, I say for myself as follows:—

1. ⌐Miss Farrant's letter⌐ (which I inclose and wish you to return to Fr Bernard with thanks for his letters)[1] ⌐puts us quite at ease — She wishes to do good to the Oratory's work, leaving *to us* absolutely to determine absolutely *what* work we shall choose.

2. This being the case, I am distinctly of opinion that there are objects *more* necessary than doing good to Smethwick.⌐

3. Next, if (as seems decided) Smethwick must be a centre of operations or nothing, Smethwick will drain from us men we want for Edgbaston — and therefore to spend the £200 on Smethwick is to give men as well as money to it.

4. And since I think we *never* shall be able to get Smethwick off our hands, if we once take it as a missionary centre, it will be a *perpetual* drain while the Oratory is.

5. If one mission is an extra-oratory work, much more are two missions.

6. Either say that Edgbaston does not do for the seat of an Oratory Church, or consolidate *there*, instead of undertaking two inchoations. Recollect the words of the Gazette, which apply to a mission, 'an imperial power comes to nought, if its acquisitions outrun its organization.'[2]

1 The sentence in brackets has been erased, apparently by another hand than Newman's.

2 An article in the *Catholic University Gazette*, (2 Nov. 1854), p. 180, 'On the opening of the School in Arts,' explained that beginnings would be small, 'for a University

7. As to *what* has to be done at Edgbaston, I am not enumerating our desiderata, ⌜but will mention one, viz a boys school.

8. In this object we could employ the interest of Miss F's money, if we rented a cottage or small house.

9. Or, if it were free to *spend* the money in what might not last above 20 years, I should recur to my old idea of putting an anti-chapel across the entrance of our temporary church —[1] which would 1. be a boy's school, 2. be a place of confession — 3. have an altar of the Sacred Heart. 4. keep the church warm.⌝ Fr Ambrose (i.e. you) had £100 from some one at one time — which added to Miss F's £200, would do the thing well.

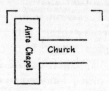

Ever Yrs affly J H N

P.S.   ⌜As to the chalice,[2] it is too kind of you all — but don't get it now —⌝ wait a while — don't do any thing without letting me hear again from you.

Thanks for your papers.

⌜Get the laurels by all means and plant them on each side of the *drive*.⌝

TO T. W. ALLIES

6 Harcourt Street Dublin Nov. 8/54.

My dear Allies,

What do you mean to do about the Inaugural Lecture?

They will take place every Thursday evening. I start tomorrow, Dr Leahy next Thursday, Ornsby the next.

I wish you could. The 21st of December will be the last.

Ever yrs John H Newman

---

is like an imperial power, which will surely come to pieces, if its acquisitions outrun its organization.'

   [1] [[Or if our temporary church is to last twenty years, I should recur to my old idea of putting anti-chapel across the entrance,]]

   [2] This was to be a present from Newman's Community for use in his chapel at Dublin.

TO JAMES HOPE-SCOTT

6 Harcourt Street Dublin November 8. 1854

My dear Hope Scott

I have advised Lord Henry [Kerr] to send Frank to *the University* at *once*. He is quite fit for the classes, and he will get the advantage of good tutors.

The only difficulty is the matter of *Terms*. I ask in my house £100 a year. Considering the various expenses of an establishment, I could not ask less (on calculation). But as I have asked it of *poor* George Ryder, who can ill afford it, I dont know how to ask less of any one else. Yet persons, who give up livings to join the Church, may not have the treasures of Croesus. I wish very much to have Frank, I hear such a pleasant account of him from Edgbaston, and if you tell me that £100 is too much, I will contrive some expedient to meet the difficulty. Harry Ryder is — I suppose, four years older than Frank[1]

Ever Yrs affectly in Xt   John H Newman of the Oratory

J R Hope Scott Esqr

TO LORD HENRY KERR

6 Harcourt Street Dublin Nov. 8 1854.

My dear Lord Henry,

I am now in my house and I have set apart a room for Frank who is very popular at Edgbaston.

From what I see here, and hear from Edgbaston, I should advise his entering at the University *at once*. The lectures would not be above him.

Excuse a short letter, but I am very busy

Yours, My dear Lord Henry Very sincerely in Xt

John H. Newman of the Oratory.

The Lord Henry Kerr.

[1] Hope-Scott wrote on 13 Nov. advising Newman to abide by £100, 'Henry Kerr can afford it as well as most of the Clerical converts—and better than many.' But see Newman's letters of 11 Nov. to Hope-Scott and 15 Nov. to Lord Henry Kerr. Hope-Scott added, 'I think I have forgotten to tell you that your Morse and Ring were sent some time ago . . . to the London Oratory.' See note to letter of 25 April 1855 to Hope-Scott.

TO T. W. ALLIES

6, Harcourt Street Dublin Nov. 11./54

My dear Allies,

Thank you for your letter. I know how vexatious it is to be pressed, and yet I wish to be importunate.[1]

I must fix some one else, if you do not lecture on the 21st and this I cannot at a moment's notice. Rather than lose you, I would leave the turn vacant, but I wish you *could* accept it. You will have plenty to say on the subject of what is meant by the Philosophy of History and your views will clear as you write.

I don't know what exactly I said to you, but I should define it pretty much as you have expressed it.

Of *course* I want to be able to advertise your name.

Ever yrs J H N.

P.S.   I should laugh at Ward's accident, except for his state of health. You say nothing of that.[2]

P.S.   I think your instances in illustration apposite. Davison's book on Prophecy[3] seems to me of this same nature, though of course it is too

---

[1] Allies, who did not want to bind himself to give an Inaugural Lecture, wrote on 10 Nov., 'Have you not set me a science almost new, about the meaning of which even people are not agreed?

On the continent the Philosophy of History seems to be mixed up with Psychology.

I am disposed rather to take your definition, as "the science of which historical facts are the basis, or the laws on which it pleases Almighty Providence to conduct the political and social world." [See letter of 3 Sept. 1854] That is, I suppose, the results of history viewed by the light of final causes.

I suppose instances of the philosophy of history are

The De civitate Dei, in some degree

Bossuet sur l'histoire universelle

Guizot, civilization in Europe and in France.

What others would you name?

Neither Faber nor Ward seem to me to have any fixed idea on the subject.'

[2] Allies added in a postscript 'On Monday [W. G.] Ward had the most extraordinary adventure at Brighton, he went out a couple of miles in a boat, and found himself suddenly in the midst of three whales. For half an hour he was prepared for certain death; but they rowed into shore, and the whales did not touch them.' On 13 Nov. Allies added, 'Ward is in a very queer state. The Doctors can make nothing of him. I confess that I fear the result. He lives but for the theological lectures, and they say these will kill him.'

[3] John Davison, *Discourses on Prophecy, in which are considered its Structure, Use and Inspiration*, London 1825. Cf. 'John Davison, Fellow of Oriel,' in *Ess.* II, pp. 375–420.

theological, as perhaps your first instances are (Augustine etc. *not* Guizot).

Gibbon takes a philosophical view of Christianity. Fleury does not. When Schlegel contrasts the characters of Persians, Egyptians, etc I think he too exemplifies the same definition.

'Providence' comes into the definition accidentally. In physical nature, an atheist talks of efficient causes, and the theist of final, but the *laws* are the same.

I consider the Lecture which will appear in the Gazette of next week November 16 has something of the Philosophy of History in it.[1]

TO JAMES HOPE-SCOTT

6 Harcourt Street Dublin Novr 11. 1854

My dear Hope Scott

Had I waited, I could have sent you a letter more to the purpose.

I have just now agreed with a builder to run up a chapel at the back of my house. This puts a small room (without a fireplace) at liberty. Frank [Kerr] is welcome to it. (Of course he shall not have to read in the cold.)

By this arrangement I shall consider him an *extern* of the University, accidentally lodging with me — and propose to charge him for lodging, board, tuition, and all extras £60

Forgive me, if, in the number of letters I have to write and persons to see, I have said any thing inconsistent, or abrupt, or other wise absurd.

I am sure it is the best thing for him to enter at once — or I would not propose it

Ever Yrs affly J H N

J R Hope Scott Esqr

[1] i.e. Newman's Inaugural Lecture 'On the place held by the Faculty of Arts in the University Course,' delivered on 9 Nov. It was published in the *Catholic University Gazette*, (16 Nov.), pp. 193–200, and became 'Christianity and Letters,' in *Idea*, pp. 249–67. Cf. *McGrath*, p. 334.

Saturday [11 Nov 1854]
My dear Scratton

I have looked at the proof as well as I can — but what can they mean by having cut it up so?[1]

Thank you for the docket — I thought the sum was £50. nor does the docket say the money came from *me*, or from *you*.

There is a draft I wish you to be so good as to take from me — and give to Mr Mooney

Ever Yrs J H N

TO CATHERINE ANNE BATHURST

6 Harcourt Street Dublin Nov 14/54
My dear Child

Your books have come quite safely — and we are very glad indeed to have them, and shall profit by your kind thoughtfulness

Ever Yrs affly J H N

TO MRS J. W. BOWDEN

6 Harcourt Street Dublin Nov 14/54
My dear Mrs Bowden,

I was glad to get your letter this morning, and hear of your movements. I have little to tell you of mine. As to my accident I can walk, but not naturally, with ease or fast. However, it has annoyed me far less than I could have fancied.

I have got a friend's house on very favorable terms, and am engaged

---

[1] This refers to a document or form for use in the University. The following note, also only dated 'Saturday,' seems to belong here:
'My dear Scratton

It has struck me there should be a *last* column to the Register Page, to enter when a member of the University took off his name   Ever Yrs J H N'

Another undated note runs:
'My dear Scratton

I want handsome labels to paste into the University books—and a catalogue books [sic]. We must talk together when first we meet.   Ever Yrs J H N'

in putting it to rights. With my utmost efforts, I can only make seven bedrooms for young men. Six are taken, and Harry,[1] if he comes, will be the seventh. One is a French boy, a Viscount de Vaulchier, whose Tutor, Mr Renouf, our French Professor, is luckily required, since the boy is delicate, to sleep in the same room with him. Thus I get a locum-tenens in my absence.

We are getting on very well, I am thankful to say, though with anxieties. Two of my Oratorians are still with me. I shall be loth to part with them; but I shall be home at Christmas for three weeks, and shall bring back with me Victor Duke and Harry Ryder as University Students. My other inmates are two Kerrs — the French youth, and a young Irishman, Sir Reginald Barnwall

Ever Yrs affly in Xt   John H Newman of the Oratory

With love to Emily

TO EDWARD CASWALL

6 Harcourt Street Dublin Nov 15/54

My dear Edwd

Your letter has just come. Stanislas is down looking at our property.[2]

Miss Farrant's letter made it *quite plain* that the *disposition* of the money was a secondary matter — so Fr Bernard must write to her thanking her warmly and accepting at once.

This solves the immediate difficulty — When he ⟨S.⟩ [Stanislas] returns, he shall write to you — and I will talk to him about your letter just received — and say what I think about it.

I have heard from Mr [F. R.] Ward about Lady O A's [Olivia Acheson] TRUST money, and should have written to you, except that I am waiting for Stanislas — He went away last Friday.

W. G. Ward has been encountered off Brighton in a boat by three whales — For half an hour he was in extremis. By the bye, I am sorry to say we have a most anxious account of his health.

We are getting on well here

Ever Yrs affly J H Newman of the Oratory

P.S.   I have *no wish at all* to give up the Smethwick School. The simple question is whether Miss F's £200 is to be used upon it — and

[1] i.e. Mrs Bowden's nephew, Henry Bowden's son Harry who had been at Eton until he became a Catholic in 1852.
[2] i.e. an estate at Rathtarman, County Sligo.

again whether *we* are to make it a *centre of operations*. To these two questions, I answer in the negative.

Stanislas is just come. He returns on Saturday. Give my love to Frank [Kerr], and say I don't want him *till after Christmas*. I will take him back with me. I will write today to his Father.

TO LORD HENRY KERR

6 Harcourt Street Dublin November 15/54.

My dear Lord Henry,

I am much pleased at the thoughts [sic] of having Frank here — I once saw his face across a table, when I had the pleasure of dining in your company, and am sure I shall like him.

I did not make it clear that he was to come *after Christmas* — Unless he goes up to you for his holy days, he shall go back with me, when I return from Edgbaston to Dublin — I suppose the first day of term will be the octave of the Epiphany —

He will want no Tutor — we have a private Tutor in each house as a part of the system —

I shall not give him a fireplace in his *own* room, but will take good care, tell Lady Henry, that he is never in the cold — I shall view him as an extern of the University lodging and boarding with me — and propose to charge him £60 for the 38 weeks, including all extras, such as coals, lights, and washing —

Very sincerely Yours in Xt   John H Newman of the Oratory.

Lord Henry Kerr.

P.S.   I wish you and Lady Henry would bear Mr Ward in mind (of Cowes and Old Hall Green) if you have not yet heard about him. All his friends are in serious anxiety about his health. We fear paralysis, or the like —

TO HENRY WILBERFORCE

6 Harcourt Street Nov 15/54

My dearest H W

The day for the Classical Examinations is fixed for the 29th instant. It seems a shame to call you all the way from London — tho' of course your expenses will be paid. Yet of course also, I shall be disappointed, if you do not come. I can take you in.

However, if you really have good reasons for not coming, I must get you to write to Myles O'Reilly, and to ask him to take your place, (subject to my approval.) I cannot ask him myself (for it would be a bad compliment to ask him second) while his being asked would still be a compliment.

I hope you still get on well — let me know about you[1]

Ever Yours affly J H N

TO T. W. ALLIES

6 Harcourt Street Dublin Nov. 16./54.

My dear Allies,

Thank you for consenting. Come if you can a day or two before the 21st December, for I set off for Birmingham for my short holyday on the morning of the 22nd, and you indeed will be glad to get back for your Christmas.

Tell me too by *December 1.* whether you can give a course of Lectures next Term. I do not press it, because I know your existing engagements, but of course I wish it, and I must know, whether or not, by the date I have fixed.

I mean to bring out a good Programme, consisting of 10 or 12 courses of Lectures, lasting from January 13 to April 1, though not *all* of them through the *whole* time. If you were to give 9 (e.g.) during three weeks, you might run from February 25 to March 18.

As to theology, the discussion would come into your Inaugural Lecture, and you might state my view and refute it, if you will.[2] For myself, I cannot help thinking that laws are a sort of facts *in* the subject matter which is in question. In chemistry latent heat involves certain laws. These the religious mind rightly considers to have been determined by the Creator for a good end; but the end is not part of the law, as in the corresponding case of morals, 'finis praecepti non cadit sub praeceptum.' Bacon seems to me to state correctly, that the doctrine of final causes (when actively introduced) spoils physics. First let us ascertain the fact — then theologize upon it. Depend upon it, when once the laws of human affairs are drawn out, and the philosophy into

[1] See the letters of 23 Nov. to Wilberforce.
[2] Allies, replying to Newman's letter of 11 Nov., wrote on 13 Nov., 'There is a question about the exclusion of theology on which I feel inquisitive, and rather sore—but of that hereafter.'

which they combine, it will be a movement worthy of the Lawgiver, but if we begin speaking of Him first of all, we shall never get at His laws. I can quite understand a Professor drawing religious conclusions from historical laws or ordinances, as from physical, but he must find his laws. Excuse this and believe me

Ever yrs affly John H Newman

TO HENRY HENNESSY

6 Harcourt Street, Dublin. November 16th. 1854.

My dear Mr. Hennessy,

I have to thank you for two very interesting and important letters.[1] No one can regret more than I do the delay which has occurred in setting up the medical and engineering schools — but in truth we began too late in the year, and in consequence could not make our arrangements in time for November. I was not put into my situation till June, and the engagements for the year are made in August. We had to find a school building, and thought ourselves fortunate in finding one as soon as August. And so as regards the engineering department, men in good business must have a sufficient time before they can separate themselves from their existing engagements. I wanted to have come over the first day in the year — I actually did come over in the beginning of February, but the time was all but wasted till June. I could get nothing done. At the same time, in a great undertaking, which is to last (we trust) long, a year sooner or later will not be much to look back upon hereafter.

I propose, when I can get persons together (before long, I trust) to put the whole matters connected with the useful science schools into the hands of two or three experienced men, who will consult together and advise me on matters on which I am of course ignorant myself. Meanwhile, what you propose seems to me to promise well.

Do you think then you could give a course of Lectures on some general subject, which would be at once useful to the Students generally, not to say the public, and in particular to the students in engineering? There are several such students already. If you wish a room *set apart* for the purpose, I should recommend a room in the (empty) medical school — but this we can talk of afterwards. The course of

---

[1] Newman had offered the Professorship of Natural Philosophy to Hennessy, who wrote on 11 and 14 Nov. about its subject matter. This he held to include Mechanics, Astronomy and General Physics. Hennessy regretted that the Schools of Medicine and Engineering had not been opened simultaneously with that of Arts.

Lectures, say on Mechanics, would extend from (say) January 29 to March 24 that is, *8* weeks, and with two Lectures a week — Or, if you prefer, a popular course on Astronomy.

As to the remuneration, of course I should wish to do what is fair on the side both of yourself and the University. When you are formally established here as Professor, the salary attached to the Chair would be £300 a year — but from what you say, I suppose some little time would pass first — and during this interval, I suppose the simplest way is to remunerate according to the sets of Lectures delivered.

You have touched upon a subject, on which I feel a great interest. For the last six months, I have been trying in vain to get an Observer. From what I hear, he must have special qualifications for his Office — I mean, it is not every scientific man who will do. He need not be a first rate mathematician, but he must have considerable patience and endurance, he must not mind drudging, he must have clever fingers, able to make nice adjustments with his instruments, he must not mind being up at nights, and must have the strength of constitution which that implies. He should be *apprenticed* to his work, as a youth.

I have been trying to find a young man with these qualifications, zeal for the occupation being of course presupposed. I should propose, when I found him, to send him to the Astronomer at Bonn — and, when he returned taught, I should propose to the Trustees to lay out £500 in instruments etc, and should at once set him observing, and on publishing his observations annually. If you could recommend me any one for the purpose, or suggest anything on the general subject, I should be much obliged. It must be a really good person for the work, or it is of no use thinking of it at all.[1]

I am, My dear Mr. Hennessy, Very truly yours in Xt.

John H. Newman of the Oratory.

H. Hennessy Esq.

TO THOMAS SCRATTON

Thursday [16 November 1854]

My dear Scratton

Archdeacon Wilberforce's present of books to the University lies at 16 Harcourt Street, and must be *at once* placed in a dry place. Can it be lodged in Cecilia Street?[2]

I want for *tonight* a man to keep the reserved seats at the University

[1] Hennessy replied on 22 Nov., 'Your views as to an astronomical observer are perfectly correct and show that you must have already given the subject a great deal of attention.'   [2] See letter of 1 Sept. to R. Wilberforce.

House. Would your porter do? Anyhow, send me up a trusty man *here*
(6 Harcourt Street) at 7 P M, and I will go with him to the Room

Ever Yrs J H N

TO EDWARD CASWALL

6 Harcourt Street Dublin Nov 17/54

My dear Edward

Stanislas begs an extension till Monday, his land business being
still unfinished.

I inclose Mr [F. R.] Ward's letter and legal statement. Send the
letter to him by the first post — (Sunday night) having added to it in
pencil any remarks in addition to mine, after a meeting of the Fathers.[1]

As to the £200, I told you in my last letter to let Fr Bernard accept
it of the Miss Farrants with many thanks, at once.

My opinion on the whole is this:—

1. Any how, the preaching at Smethwick must be discontinued — I
wish this, because it does not answer its purpose, viz to bring people to
our chapel. In this *fact*, Bernard, Stanislas and yourself agree together.

2. I do not object to, though I do not prefer, the £200 going to a school
room at Smethwick — so that it is a bonâ fide school room, with a clear
statement on our register, in which Miss Farrants' donation is entered,
that we are giving the money out of our hands to Smethwick, which
happens at present to be part of our mission, in the same way that we
gave the £160 to Alcester Street. It is money which we might spend
upon our own place, which we give to a place which any moment we
might lose.

Ever Yours affly J H N

P.S.   Perhaps some of you may be able to give poor Monsell a Mass
on the 21st as the inclosed letter asks.[2]

TO C. J. LA PRIMAUDAYE

6 Harcourt Street Dublin. November 17. 1854

My dear Mr La Primaudaye

It would give me great pleasure, and would be a great service to the
University, to be able to connect Mr Pollen with it.[3] If I do not at once

[1] This refers to Lady Olivia Acheson's legacy.
[2] See letter to Monsell of this day.
[3] La Primaudaye, who had known Newman before the latter became a Catholic
in 1845, wrote on 18 Oct. to ask that his name and that of his future son-in-law, John

ask you formally to propose it to him, it is because the Archbishops are away at Rome, and I have besides to consult for difficulties which surround us in every step I take. We expect too that the Statutes of the University will come back from Rome soon, and till they are settled, I do not quite know what may be my powers.

I wonder whether he has any idea what a Fine Arts Professor ought to be and to teach. It would be most important to get a person like Mr Pollen to give the subject a Christian character and separate it from the sensuality which is often considered part of it, without running into the extravagancies of the Ultra-Puginians. It is a subject which I am sure, would be most popular here. He might include in it the principles of taste which apply to any subject matter — vulgarity, affectation, over elaborateness, technicality, refinement, would form chapters of a treatise which would lay down canons for prose and poetical composition as well as for the Fine Arts. The History of the Fine Arts is another and obvious branch of this subject. And so the connexion of the Fine Arts with national character and political institutions.

Supposing in a month or two we were able to make any arrangement, I should, when we got as far as that, next recommend his name being mentioned at once, but his lectures not commencing for six months, to give him time for preparation.

I mention all this to suggest thought to Mr Pollen with a view of interesting him in the work which I shall venture to propose to him.[1]

Very sincerely Yours in Xt   John H. Newman of the Oratory.

C. J. La Primaudaye Esq

Hungerford Pollen, might be put on the books of the University, in token of their support. Newman replied by asking whether Pollen would be prepared to help in the department of the fine arts. La Primaudaye answered on 2 Nov., 'I have sounded John Pollen on the subject you hint at in reference to him. And it has evidently stirred the spirit within him. . . . His qualifications are of a high order *practically*. Theoretically, that is in acquaintance with the rules and history of Art, such as would be required in one called upon to teach in such a Place as your University, he is as yet quite deficient. But with an object in view, has that love for Art, and such readiness that I think he could profitably apply himself with success to the acquirement of what is needed.'

[1] For an account of the delight of Pollen (who had heard Newman in the pulpit of St Mary's, Oxford, but had never met him), at the prospect opened up by this letter, see Anne Pollen, *John Hungerford Pollen*, London 1912, pp. 252–8.

TO WILLIAM MONSELL

6 Harcourt Street November 17 1854

My dear Monsell,

I am indeed concerned at your news[1] — and most gladly will say the Mass you ask for on the 21st.

Stanislas, who happens to be here, will do the same. And I will try to get you some others

Ever Yours affly in Xt   John H Newman of the Oratory

W Monsell Esqr M P

TO AMBROSE ST JOHN

⌜6 Harcourt Street Novr 17/54

My dearest Ambrose,

I suppose you have not much to say in your favor yet.⌝ [[as regards asthma?]]

Don't send me the Univers — they charged /4d on each of two which came this morning.

As to poor Frederic [Thomas Godwin], I think he meant no impudence. It was 'tandem liber equus —' so I think. He is luxuriating in his freedom. I have taken him for six months — and afterwards, he is to give me a notice of three months before he leaves.

We are going on very well. Stanislas goes tomorrow — to get to Edgbaston on Monday.

⌜My leg has somewhat retrograded the last week. It requires patience. Mr Babington gives precisely the same direction as Dr O' Ferrall.

I am building a chapel out over the pantry.⌝ (*Private*) Frank Duke has thoughts of coming into my house — all I can offer him is to chum with his brother. Don't mention this, because Dr D. [Duke] should hear it first through Frank.[2]

⌜I have great anxiety lest I should not make both ends meet. My expences are near £1050 a year.⌝

Ever Yrs affly J H N

---

[1] Monsell's wife was dying.
[2] St John was staying with Dr Duke at St Leonards.

TO J. D. DALGAIRNS

6 Harcourt Street Dublin Novr 19/54

My dear Fr Bernard

I go to Bm [Birmingham] if all is well December 22. I return January 11. If between these dates, I can do any thing for the [Birmingham] Catholic Association, I will gladly. So should you and Father Edward.

Dont say *one syllable of any kind* to Mr Fullerton. I have my reasons.[1]

You *may* thank him for the Trust Money; i.e express satisfaction that Mr Ward informs us that we have a sum of which the *interest* is to be given us for the *poor*.

But pray don't hint one single word about the very *existence* of any thing else.

All is going on well as to the matter, as I learn from the post which brings your letter.

And tell all our Fathers to identify in talking, the *trust* money with 'Lady O A's [Olivia Acheson] legacy.' Don't *talk* as if any more money were coming to us

Ever Yrs J H N

TO H. E. MANNING

6 Harcourt Street Dublin. Novr 22/54

My dear Manning

I write to you on a matter which Monsell has opened — but, considering his present anxieties, I don't like to trouble him with.

He asked whether I could take into my house Mrs Blunt's son. At the moment I had but one room, which I had reserved for Harry Bowden. His father declined it yesterday — and I prefer to offer it next to Mr Blunt.[2]

---

[1] This and what follows refer to the bequest of nearly £6000 which Lady Olivia Acheson wished to go to the Oratory, in addition to the interest on £1900 in trust for the poor. On the reasons for secrecy see letter of 15 Oct. to St John. Fullerton, the executor, had been advised to deal with the Oratorians through an intermediary. Hence Newman's instructions to Dalgairns.

[2] Newman hoped that Francis Scawen Blunt (1839–72), and also his brother Wilfrid Scawen Blunt (1840–1922), later famous as poet and politician, would enter the University. Their widowed mother became a Catholic in 1850 and her two sons followed her in 1852. They were sent first to Stonyhurst, and then in April 1853 to Oscott. Their mother died in the following June, leaving Bishop Grant as their guardian, and commending them to Newman, *Campaign*, p. xlvi. However, the Court of Chancery

As I have other negociations and plans about it on hand, I should like an answer soon

We are getting on very well — far better than I had dared to hope — but I am not forgetful that a storm may come any day

Do not forget us & believe me Ever Yrs affly J H N

TO AMBROSE ST JOHN

⌐6 Harcourt Street Nov 22/54

My dearest A

I was in bed this day year, and just now getting up to preach. Every year brings its changes and mercies —[1] we hope to have Lady O A's [Olivia Acheson] money soon — do help us with a few Masses. As to this place, we are succeeding far better than I could have expected. Dr Leahy's Inaugural Lecture, as mine before it, has done us great good among Queen's College Catholics and Protestants. Ornsby follows tomorrow.[2] Then again the University Hall is getting on well.[3] I am building a little Chapel in Number 6 — which I suppose will be out of my pocket (£75) — simply so — not out of my *salary* — for, *giving* £300 a year to the House,[4] Stanislas and I make out, I shall have a great chance of being minus at the end of the year. Harry Bowden does not come. M. de Vaulchier is a nice boy. Sir Reginald Barnwall is coming daily.

My leg has been somewhat stationary for the last three weeks — and last week retrograded, and I had to go again to the Doctor. I can't tell why. He said quite a new and distinct evil was come — viz a swelling of the veins under the knee —⌐ which, I suppose, may arise partly from want of exercise, partly from the elastic stocking ending there — It is only tiresome — and I want exercise.

appointed two Protestant relatives as guardians, who allowed the boys to remain at Oscott, since their mother had placed them there. Bishop Grant feared to suggest moving them from Oscott to Dublin, lest the guardians should decide to send them to a Protestant school instead.

[1] [[This day two years I was up on the Achilli matter, and Fr Joseph took to his bed.]] In 1853 Newman preached at the opening of the church at Edgbaston.

[2] Leahy's lecture 'The Church and the Bible,' was delivered on 16 Nov., and Ornsby's 'The Utility of Classical Studies,' on 23 Nov. A corrected report of Leahy's lecture was published in the *Catholic University Gazette*, (18 Jan. 1855), pp. 284-94. For Newman's lecture see letter of 11 Nov. to Allies.

[3] This was St Patrick's, the University House, at 86 Stephen's Green, of which Michael Flannery was the Dean. Cf. *McGrath*, p. 341 and *Campaign*, pp. 43-4.

[4] [[for, though giving £300 a year out of my salary to my housekeeping,]]

⌐I am glad to hear a good account of you from Dr Duke —⌐ whom
thank very much for his kind letter

Affly Yrs J H N

TO THE EARL OF DUNRAVEN

6 Harcourt Street November 23. 1854

Sent in substance.

My dear Lord Dunraven,

People here are asking me, Why do you not get Lord Dunraven's
name for the books of the University? I say, Why, we put on them no
names but Catholic names. Then they answer that he has distinctly
professed himself, by very definite acts here, to be a Catholic.

So you see I am forced, lest I should be wanting in respect to you,
and in due consideration of the interests of the University, to ask you
for your name. And I really do trust you will not refuse me.[1]

We are going on very well here — and ought to be most thankful
for the success which has hitherto attended on us.

It gave me very great concern to hear of Lady Anna Maria's
indisposition.[2] I have had no news of her for some days now

Ever Yours affectly in Xt   My dear Lord Dunraven,

John H Newman of the Oratory

The Earl of Dunraven

TO HENRY WILBERFORCE (I)

Wednesday Nov 23/54 6 Harcourt Street

My dear H W

I suspect the inclosed is not worth much.

When I said I should be 'disappointed,' if you did not come, I
meant that I had hoped you would have had furniture or other matters

[1] Lord Dunraven replied on 30 Nov. as to giving his name, 'it appears to me
simply to amount to a public declaration of Catholicism: and as I most solemnly, in
the sight of God believe that my doing so would cause my wife's death: I cannot, and
will not do it—' Dunraven hoped his wife would come round to accepting his conversion, 'I know she has been making efforts to look the thing in the face, and prays
to have strength to do God's will: I also feel that latterly I have felt more earnestly my
own desire to place myself unreservedly under His guidance in the matter; and more
at present I cannot do—Oh pray forgive me if I have written any thing amiss.' Lord
Dunraven, whose wife remained firm in her Protestantism, became a Catholic in 1855
and gave his name to the University.

[2] Lady Anna Maria, William Monsell's wife, was the only sister of Lord Dunraven.

which would have required *last words* here, and made a journey necessary. You had better not write to O'Reilly, if you have not, for I shall get some one else.

⌐Dr Leahy's lecture went off capitally — and so I expect Ornsby's will to-night.

Will you order the Catholic Standard for me at your office,⌐ to come to me at 6 Harcourt Street? ⌐Don't be discouraged at your initial work; it will be far lighter when you get into it. I can fancy what a mess you must be in — I shall say some Masses for you soon.

As to Arthur [Wilberforce], his desk shall be taken care of. My only anxiety is, that I shall not have room at *any moment* for him.⌐

Ever Yrs J H N

TO HENRY WILBERFORCE (II)

6 Harcourt Street Nov 23/54

My dearest H W

Your letter has just come, and I write a hasty line.[1]

I *could not* be so unreasonable as to suppose you must come at all hazards — indeed I distinctly showed I thought you could not. What I *did* want was an immediate answer, whereas I have had a week in suspense. Also, I asked you about Myles O Reilly — and you do not say a word in answer. I *suppose* you have not written to him, but, if you have, I shall be appointing *two* persons! for I cannot leave longer time without appointing some one.

I was glad to be able to put down your name — but, from the first, I never disguised from myself the probability that you would not be able to come. And I said so to you.

Thank you for what you say about T.M. and my brother —[2] I

---

[1] Wilberforce wrote on 21 Nov. from London, excusing himself for not answering Newman's letter of 15 Nov. in which he was asked to come as an examiner to Dublin or get Myles O'Reilly in his place. Wilberforce had that week taken over the editorship of the *Catholic Standard*, he had no sub-editor, and all depended on him.

[2] Wilberforce wrote about Newman's brother-in-law Tom Mozley, on the staff of *The Times*, who gave news of Francis Newman: 'Mozley is kind beyond anything that I can express. He seems also in a much more religious state of mind than I had expected to find him. His work is desperate—so much so, that high as his pay evidently is I do not think I should be for a moment tempted to undertake it. It is not the exact amount of hours but the time. He leaves home at 8.30 each evening and lets himself in with a latch key getting to bed I believe about 4, in the morning, breakfasts at 10 and is ready to gossip etc all morning with anyone. He has a most beautiful house in one of the best situations in London and elaborately furnished. Keeps a Brougham and

heard of my poor Frank's absurd beard — but I cannot believe his absurd vow — to whom is it made? — to what god or devil? Does he pray to Mazzini by rapping? or will he end by being a Jew?

As to Mozley, tell him by all means to keep the plate, which I am sure must be worth nothing. ⌜I have no plate here but a few electro plated spoons and forks — and feel the full value of 'Cantabit vacuus etc'[1] It is odd, I should *begin* to keep house at 53. For the first time I heard the cook (Martin Jones) call me 'master.' It shocked me so much that I forbid the word — and am to be called 'the Rector,' 'the Father —'⌝ any thing or all things but it

Ever Yrs affly J H N

TO JOHN STANISLAS FLANAGAN

Friday Nov 24 [1854]

My dear St

Your letter has just come with the £100 note for which I thank you.

It flashes on me that I drew £100 on myself at Bm [Birmingham] Bank on a paper from your cheque book. What on earth became of it? I am utterly in the dark. Please write a line about it by return of post.

Tell Edward by all means to go to his mother.

riding horse for himself and Grace. [His only child, Newman's niece.] The latter however is at school at Brighton. Of religion we have talked—he says that if he had to sign the articles again he should reconsider some of them with which he feels difficulty and these difficulties he implies are on the *Roman* not the Latitudinarian side (as I feared). . . . He regards himself as a clergyman still. . . . On the whole there are many things which seem much more hopeful than I had expected. I must get prayers for him. With regard to you he has not spoken much. All he ever says is in the utmost tone of kindness. He wants to know whether as you are now keeping house, it will not be convenient to you to have part or all of the plate you gave Harriett but does not like to ask you lest he should seem to be "returning the gift" . . . I hope you will seek occasions of intercourse. He owns to me that he is *afraid* of them, i.e. of the effect they would be likely to produce on his mind . . .

Of your brother Frank he gives a strange account—he says he is singularly little changed in appearance and not aged, but that of late he has taken to nourish a long beard and hair—he has (as you know) by nature so very little beard that M says each hair stands separate and distinct giving M. the idea as if it took a line of its own as independent of all the others as Frank's own, and his hair is brushed back from his forehead behind his back hanging down far below his collar. Mozley suspects (for he does not profess to know) that he has made some resolve not to cut them till he hears of the fall of the House of Hapsburgh against which he has a fanatical animosity.

I must conclude

Your most loving and grateful H W W.'

[1] Cantabit vacuus coram latrone viator. Juvenal, *Satires*, x, 22.

I think it would be well for the Oratory to subscribe £5 towards the 'Patriotic Fund'[1] *I* subscribe *here*.[2]

mind writing to Hardman, if the Congregation wished — i.e. if I am in possession of the facts of the case.

I have scratched out the word 'Priests' in the inclosed — for there is no need to bring evidence against ourselves[3]

Ever Yrs J H N

TO T. W. ALLIES

6 Harcourt Street Nov. 27. 1854.

My dear Allies,

By all means you must come here and be my guest, if you will, and will excuse the bustle the house may be in, à propos of my settling things before I go.

Will you give me the exact *thesis* of your Inaugural Lecture, that I may publish it?[4]

Ever yours J. H Newman

TO JOHN STANISLAS FLANAGAN

6 Harcourt Street Nov 27/54

My dear Stanislas

I have some difficulty, and some compunction, in persuading the University Finance Committee to let me build with their Funds a *temporary* Church. I see I shall not be able to effect it with comfort to myself.[5]

What do you think of the first blush of the following project:—

A Church to hold (if only) 200 persons with a good sermon and good music, may charge, i.e. will get, 1/ a sitting once a week. That is, £10 a Sunday or £380 for 38 weeks, i.e. the academical year.

[1] The Patriotic Fund was in aid of the widows and orphans of the soldiers who lost their lives in the Crimean War.
[2] The first line of a new paragraph began after this, but has been torn out.
[3] This was a description of the Oratory for insertion in a guide to Birmingham.
[4] Allies replied on 1 Dec., 'I propose simply to draw out the idea of the Philosophy of History . . .'
[5] For the great importance Newman attached to a University church see the Memorandum of 29 April 1854, in Appendix 1, p. 560. 'It symbolized the great principle of the University, the indissoluble union of philosophy with religion.' *Campaign*, p. 290; see also pp. 305–09.

The space next to my House is 110 feet by 24; and would make a (gothic) chapel to hold 200 persons. Since our own temporary chapel (just the same length) cost under £2000 *furnished*, and about £1000 unfurnished, and, as in this case, the two side walls are in great measure built, and the space of the roof narrower, I conceive that a church or chapel might be built in the space I speak of, (including shell, flooring or tiling, plastering, painting, plain wainscotting and plain seating, and gas fittings, and architect's charge (warm air pipes?)) for £2000. Adding to which £1000 for decoration, makes the whole expence £3000.

I shall ask to borrow of the University Funds £3000 on good security while I give, at 3 per cent interest (as a *favor*) to be repaid by the end of 20 years.

My good security is the Achilli money. My payments are arranged as follows:

	£	s.	d.
Rent of the *ground* from Mr Egan, say £30 to —	40		
Expences of gas and firing and cleaning —	60.		
Interest on £3000 at 3 per cent —	90.		
Instalment on principal to be repaid in 20 years $\frac{3000}{20}$ —	150		
	340		
yearly profits	380		
margin	£40		

1. The Church *will* hold *more* than 200.
2. Will *as many* as 200 come?
3 Am I likely to be hindered asking a shilling a head?
4. The Church will be my property at the end of 20 years.
5. You will observe I throw the expence of sermons and of choir on the University Funds. But, such is the inconsistency of man, I think I should have as little difficulty in charging £200 for preaching, and £300 for choir, as £300 or £200 for a *Professor*; whereas, if I asked for £100 a year for a temporary church (which in the event the Oratory or some other body might *buy* of the University) I should be refused or permitted grudgingly

Ever Yrs affly John H Newman

P.S.   I am treating with Mr *Bianconi* about it.[1]

[1] Flanagan replied on 30 Nov., 'Your project appears to be an excellent one, and would, I cannot doubt, work out the results you show on paper.'

TO PETER BRETHERTON

6, Harcourt Street, Dublin December 1st. 1854.

My dear Mr. Bretherton,

Your letter, dated the 23rd. of November, came here, I think, yesterday; or I would have sent an earlier answer.

As you kindly give me my choice of days, I will fix the 1st. Tuesday *in February* — which, I think, will be the 6th.[1]

Hoping Mrs. Bretherton and the children are well, and Miss Smith.

I am, My dear Mr. Bretherton, Very truly yours in Christ,

John H. Newman, of the Oratory.

Peter Bretherton Esq.,

P.S. You will be glad to hear that we are getting on very well in the University.

TO AMBROSE ST JOHN

6 Harcourt Street Decr 1. 1854

My dear Ambrose,

If I had time I would write a long letter.

Wm's [William Neville] room had better be got ready, he is in bed just now with tooth ache and bile. I must apologize to the Congregatio Deputata (read this to them) for not getting him to renew his leave of absence — but, to tell the truth, ⌐my leg has quite baffled my expectations, and in this especially, that I thought it was always getting well,⌐ and that he would be going back constantly, and then again, that, if he *was* to stay, *how many* days were to be named of longer leave, considering the progress of my leg was so unfathomable, and its prospects so mysterious? This must be my excuse.

⌐As to the deeds of our House, they had better, I think, go to Mr Ward at once, if the Congr. Dep. so decide.[2]

Thank Mr Fullerton etc for the courtesy and kindness of having them lodged with Mr Ward. Of course Mr W. will give us a formal receipt. *Where* will he keep them? I know lawyers keep deeds, as⌐ Maule

[1] This was for Newman's lecture to the Birmingham Catholic Association.

[2] As a security for Lady Olivia Acheson's £6000, which Fullerton was handing over to the Birmingham Oratorians, he was to hold the deeds of their property in Edgbaston for ten years. He proposed that these should be kept by Newman's friend, the lawyer F. R. Ward. Cf. letters of 15 Oct. to St John and 19 Nov. to Dalgairns.

did ⌜in Paper Buildings — but I always have a feeling of insecurity, from the idea that they may be dying, and what becomes of their Papers?⌝[1]

As to the *reversionary* legatees of the Trust money, I see no objection to what you propose.[2] Would it be possible to leave it to the Bishop's Seminary Burse fund? But I suppose it is only a name — for we *cannot* forfeit it, while we leave 200 sittings for the poor.⌝ Is it not so? ⌜I have no other observations, and give my assent to all you say.⌝

I leave the whole matter to the Congregation — ⌜I suppose the £2500 is [[in government]] *stock* — else, the interest will be *more* than £100, which it is not. Is the £5200 stock? If both are *money*, and stock is at 90 (which it is not) then £7700 ought to fetch £7700 + 770 in stock = £8470⌝ — the interest of which at $4\frac{1}{2}\%$ = £380 and more. And I hear talk of past interest.

Ever Yrs affly J H N

P.S. ⌜I like old Fr Wilfrid softening you again. It is his delight to fill you with an admiration of Wilfridiance.⌝[3]

TO JOHN STANISLAS FLANAGAN

6 Harcourt Street Advent Sunday [3 December 1854]

My dear Stanislas,

You are to send me a £100 as *a loan* (e.g. from the Achilli money) and I shall not be able to get away without it. Poor Lady Barnewall is still stickling, partly or principally on the money question. But I have seen Mr B. your friend, and hope it is all right. As it stands, he ⟨Sir R.⟩ [Reginald Barnewall] is to come tomorrow. I suppose I shall have Mr O Meagher's son from Paris. *How* am I to stow Arthur Wilberforce and the two Blunts?

F. [Frederic] is certainly tripping, like Charlie.[4] The servants

---

[1] [[but I feel an insecurity that they may die, and can no longer be guardians of such deposits.]]

[2] This refers to the money left in trust by Lady Olivia Acheson, on which see letters of 18 and 20 Aug. to F. R. Ward. Reversionary legatees had to be appointed, to whom this money would go, if the conditions of the trust were not fulfilled. St John suggested for this purpose the Birmingham Catholic Mission.

[3] St John wrote from the London Oratory, pleased with his welcome there and with the beauty of its newly built house.

[4] i.e. Frederic (Thomas Godwin), Newman's servant in Dublin. Charlie was the pony at Rednal.

(Jones and Margaret) have been kept waiting half an hour to be let in
in the morning. In consequence *Jones* is not punctual. Twice I have let
Margaret in. Twice I have found the hall door not locked and bolted,
through the night. Once I had to sit up for F. till near 12. Dont mention
all this. 'Tis the cares of housekeeping. As to Renouf, I gave him up as
a helper, from the moment he could not take off that chicken's wing
without turning the poor beast upside down. I suspect he will be able to
do *nothing*, in my absence.

Well, but all this does not cause me to write — but the £100
additional. And don't send it in *a note*. I have to present it — and I
have not dared yet to present your former note — from dread of the
long ceremony which will ensue.

As to the chapel costing £3000, I allow for extras — and I think
with reason. *Now* my plan is *to take in Mrs* Segrave's stables etc, the
coach house would make a choir gallery above, reached by a staircase
from the lane at the back, and opening into nothing. Under it would be
the sacristy. Behind would be two dwelling rooms — where I could put
two of our party — e.g. Victor [Duke] and Harry [Ryder] — of course
they would be good rooms. This might lead to the necessity of a
covered way from the house, but this I should not include in the £3000.

I would rather say thus:—

Rent	40. 0. 0
Expences of Chapel	60. 0. 0
Interest 3 per cent on £3000 =	90. 0. 0
Instalment of principal	150. 0. 0
	340. 0. 0
(over entrance)	
40 Gallery seats at £2	80. 0. 0
300 at /6 for 38 weeks	285. 0. 0
	365. 0. 0

The vestibule will be 10 feet deep — I put over it a gallery — I let
the gallery project 10 feet into the church — so that it is 20 feet deep —
and takes 4 rows of benches (not to say 5) with 10 (not to say 12) in a
row = 40. I let them at £2 the Session = £80. The rest at /6.

It must be determined *what* we give them for their money. High
mass, as well as Vespers and Benediction? There is this difficulty in it,
that it will be *only* for 38 weeks — so that they cannot make it their
habitual Church, as the Gesù.[1]

If it were better, I could merely take 1/ for the gallery seats every

[1] The Jesuit church in Rome.

time — or allow people to have them for the session or not, as they pleased.

Ever Yrs affly J H N

P.S.   Wm [William Neville] proposes to leave on Friday morning. This is a proof I am better.

By all means paper Rednall at once, but [see] *the walls are fit for it.*

Keep in mind, or *begin preparations* for the bodies being deposited in the cemetery. February 13 next. This must be *fixed.*

TO J. B. O'MEAGHER

6 Harcourt Street Dublin Decr 3. 1854

sent the same
in substance — but
not so uncivil or abrupt.
Dear Sir

I thank you very much for your kind and confidential letter about your Son — and I thank him too for the trust he is so well inclined to place in me.[1]

The delay in answering you has arisen from perplexity in finding room for him. I really wish to do so, wishing to make our new Institution serviceable to as many as I can. I have arranged that two brothers shall have one room — and in this way am able to offer to receive him. As I shall go to England for the Holy days, and only return by the 12th January, I propose his remaining with you till that date.

I have said that it is my zeal for the University which has made me desire to have a youth, of whom you speak so satisfactorily, after all natural deductions on the score of your affection for him. It is that zeal which has brought me here, and led me to open my house at all to young men. You think the terms high. I can only say that, while each of my inmates pays only £100 for being with me, I pay £300 for taking them in. So far from any profit accruing to me, a friend calculates for me, that, *after* I have put in £300 in behalf of the house expences, I have a chance

---

[1] O'Meagher lived in Paris and was introduced to Newman by Robert Belaney, Vicar of Arlington in Sussex, who had become a Catholic in 1852. O'Meagher's Spanish wife had just died, and he had thoughts of sending his son Ernest to Oxford, now open to Catholics. Ernest went to the Catholic University in Jan. 1855 and became a Scholar there in July 1856.

of having a deficit still — and something to pay besides. I do not know what advantage I have in the arrangement, except the feeling that I am promoting a great Catholic work.

I do not say this as if any thing you actually said required it — but only, since you are surprised at the terms, to state how things really are. One cannot tie down young men in expences — they are extravagant in coal, in candles, in washing, all which are included in the £100. They give a great deal of trouble merely from thoughtlessness. Were I a Protestant clergyman in a living in England, I should ask £300 from each pupil. Were your son to go to Oxford or Cambridge, he would cost you £300 a year, or near upon it.

You will not, I hope, think it out of the way, if I add that my rule is to receive the half year's payment (£50) at the *beginning* of each half year — in order to keep the house going.

I look with great pleasure on making your son's acquaintance. We have already a French youth in the house (the Vicomte de Vaulchier) who speaks English remarkably well. The others are English youths except Sir Reginald Barnewall.

Pray thank Mr Belaney for his kind letter, and for introducing me to you.

Very faithfully Yours John H Newman

J B O'Meagher Esqr

P.S.   On reading over my letter, I fear you may think I have laid too great stress on what you say about terms — But might I ask you to be so good as to consider that I have spoken in case *others* should speak of our University *in general*. The world is unreasonable on the subject and has brought down the charges at the University House to 40 guineas! which of course throws a large deficit upon the funds.

TO JOHN STANISLAS FLANAGAN

6 Harcourt Street Dec 5/54

My dear Stanislas

I am very sorry still to plague you — but my matter is a dissolving view, and requires fresh treatment.

Mr Egan has just sent in his *facts* — his *proposal* is to come.

He offers his property, which is his for 229 years from this date subject to a yearly rent to Mr Singe of £46. 3. 1.

I find he lets *above* ground for £70 a year — and the cellars for £18 a year Taxes (which *he* does not pay) are £5 or £6. If Mr Singe still pays them, he has more to do with the matter than I like.

Well, since he pays £46. 3. 1. to Mr Singe his gain is the difference between this and £70 + £18.

Suppose him to *keep* the cellars, or to let me rent them of him (I leasing them in turn for the same as now, i.e. guaranteeing him the rent of them, which however, I suppose is awkward for 229 years) then his profit which I have to make good to him is £70 − £46. 3. 1 or £23. 16. 11, which represents the worth of his *buildings* and his *situation* — As I suppose the situation is taken into account in his ground rent to Mr Singe, it represents his *buildings*, and, as buildings should bring £10 per cent, it represents £240.

It would seem then, as if the *utmost* I need give him is £240 for his interest in the place — Since, I suspect, it would be a convenience to him to get rid of it, the buildings being out of repair, he might take considerably less.

I do not know how to calculate the present waste of the cellars.

Of course I must put the matter into a lawyer's hands — but I should like your opinion first.

—

Another part of it.

I have given up having *any thing* to do with the University Funds in borrowing money. Fr McNamara recommends me to do it all myself.

Therefore (is it not fair? please, consider) I mean to charge the University (1) *rent*. (2) expences of gas etc i.e. for rent of sittings £50 a year, for gas etc £60 more or less, as by previous statement.

The great advantage of this will be that I shall be able to pay back the principal quicker — and so be saved *the chance of their building their* OWN *Church* for themselves *sooner* than the end of 20 years, and so cutting me out, and ruining me. (There is not a chance of their laying out £20.000 on a Church *and its being finished* under 12 years)

On the other hand I should have to pay *more* for my interest.

— Payments.

Interest of £3000 loan at 4½ per cent (to include purchase money to Mr Egan)	135.	0.	0
Rent to Mr Synge	46.	3.	1
Yearly gas, coal etc	60.	0.	0
Instalment of Principal	200.	0.	0
Sundries	29.	16.	11
	471.	0.	0

Receipts.

Gallery — 40 seats at 1/-	76.	0.	0
Body of Church — 300 at /6	285.	0.	0
University Rent	50.	0.	0
University payment of expences	60.	0.	0
	471.	0.	0

In this way I should wipe off £1000 in 5 years (to say nothing of the diminution of interest.)

In the beginning of the 6th year the debt would be only £2000 — (to say nothing of diminution *during* the following years) or there will be a saving of interest of £45 which added to the current instalment will clear off the second £1000 in 4 years.

So that, at the end of 9 years, only £1000 debt will remain.

This last £1000 will be cleared off in little more than 3 years — so that in 12 years the whole £3000 will be cleared off.

But the £46. 3. 1. will *remain* — what is to be done with this?

Where am I to borrow the money? I think of claiming the first £2000 of Lady O A's [Olivia Acheson] money, which is due to me for the temporary Church. (How to get the 3rd thousand is another matter which I won't talk of now. Perhaps the Congregation will *invest* the 3rd thousand on the security of the Achilli money)

I don't wish to deprive the Congregation of the interest, which I will pay at 4½ per cent, as above.

In this way (1) I gain a *successor to me* in the transaction if I die — viz the Oratory. (2) I give the Oratory a place in Dublin, and a small Church to begin with.

Ever Yrs J H N

P.S. The sea has frightened Wm [William]. He goes tomorrow. (*Dont answer this, till you hear again.*)

TO AMBROSE ST JOHN

6 Harcourt Street Decr 5/54

Charissime

I am afraid you are not so well as you should be.

What you say is most distressing — but, alas, very natural.[1] Your

[1] St John wrote that his mother was not being treated well and he did not know how to remedy it. 'With 5 or £600 a year she is treated like an old servant.'

316

brother is of course the proper person to talk with. Have you spoken to him? — It is quite clear he will join with you.

Ever Yrs J H N

P.S.   The sea frightens William. I have nothing to say on Mr [F.R.] Ward's letter. I assent.[1]

TO JOHN STANISLAS FLANAGAN

Dec 6/54 6 Harcourt Street

My dear St

I suppose I have made some great floor in my figures — let me try again.

Supposing stocks at 90 then

£90 in cash buys £100 stock and

£100 in cash buys £100 + £11· 11 (decimal·) stock i.e. £111· 11 stock

Then, £2500 + £5300, or

£7800 cash buys £78 × 111· 11 stock = £8666·58 stock.

Now suppose the stock be railway at 4½ per cent. The interest of

£7800 cash or £8666·58 stock is $\dfrac{4\frac{1}{2}}{100} \times 8666\cdot58 = \dfrac{9}{200} \times 8666\cdot58 =$

£389·9961 near £390.

Dec 13.

Your and Ambrose's letters are just come. I thank you both.

First I ought to have answered Ambrose before this, that the tax for the poney carriage sticks in my throat.[2] I have no objection myself at all to ride in a tilt,[3] if the *springs* defend one from joulting. I think the poney carriage will have an evil beyond itself. It will make people think us very rich.

I have just seen that detestable article in the Times about the Immaculate Conception. The force of it is *this* — that hitherto they have ever said that they did not attack the religion of Catholics, — doctrine was nothing to them, — but the politics — that we were a political body — that the Convents confined British subjects — but now it takes quite a new line, and shows the devil that is at the bottom. What is it to

[1] About the arrangement for Lady Olivia Acheson's legacy.

[2] St John wrote on 5 Dec., 'I find the duty on any four wheeled carriage is £6. o. o.'

[3] i.e. a two-wheeled cart, which was not taxed. St John corrected himself on 18 Dec. The tax had in fact been more than halved and it applied to all vehicles.

it, though we worshipped the lamp-post? this is what it used to say. However . . .[1]

Thank you much for the pains you have taken about my calculations — Egan hangs fire — so I am not sanguine or eager.

Meanwhile, St Audoen's revives in my mind, and I and Wm [William] have just been to see it.[2] It is very tempting. What made me go was this — I reflected that Ch Ch [Christ Church] and St Patrick, which had the two fashionable choirs, were close by it — and that, if people came to them, they would come to us.

It is a fine, large, bare Italian Church, and would hold any number. If I got it for nothing, I could spend on the decoration what I should spend on the site and building on the ground next me. I should get over Denouelle to give me decorations, and would tell him to go as far as £1000 — this would be £2000, which I could afford. It would pay much better than any other place. Dr Cullen said he would give it the *Oratory*, if we would have it — so I suppose I could get it for the University. It is of easy access *except* from Stephen's Green — and I am not over much attached, as you know, to this quarter.

As to the domestic arrangement, I find the plan I mentioned to you[3] has so grown on my mind that I shall, I think, act upon it — tho' you but partially assent, and Ambrose dissents.

1. I *must* have two women. We shall be 11 in family.

2. And I really do not see how one person *can* wait at dinner on 11 people statedly, and perhaps 15.

3. It seems absurd to pay Jones £26 and his board for blacking shoes and opening the door.

4. Frederic, unless he is sanguine, says he knows an Elton youth, who is a penitent of Father Henry's who has been in service — whom he can fully trust. Do you know him? He would sleep at the University House.

5. As to F. himself, he is contrite, and has been a good deal better, or rather unexceptionable ever since — if he does not relapse.

Paint the cottage what colour you please — and paper it, if it be dry enough. You are putting the cemetery wall in hand I suppose.

Thanks for your notice of your Butler. Also for your x, y, z calculation, which is as inexpugnable as Sebastopol.[4]

[1] The third leading article in *The Times*, 9 Dec. 1854, was a violent, even scurrilous, attack on the doctrine of the Immaculate Conception itself. Of the definition it said, 'If this claim of the Pope be admitted, he may as well cancel the whole Bible, and leave the doctrines of Christianity to be taught anew at his pleasure.'

[2] Newman thought of using St Audoen's church, High Street, as the University church. See letter of 9 April 1855 to Patrick Mooney, and *Campaign*, pp. 293 and 305.

[3] i.e. in the letter of 8 Dec. to St John, written before the latter part of this one.

[4] Flanagan had proposed a former butler of his family for Newman's house, and had sent an elaborate calculation of the cost of a university church.

Ambrose's letter has just run away, in one of those remarkable ways in which letters always make off from my table, but I don't think I have to do more than to thank him.

Reginald [Barnewall] and Louis [de Vaulchier] *promise* very well — Reginald is sharp and a good scholar.

I can get nothing but either sloppy or muddy ink

Ever Yrs J H N

P.S.   Could we ask the Bishop for an ad interim leave for the Deeds, without opening to him?

Perhaps it would best for you as Treasurer, or Ambrose, to send a formal letter from me or us to the Cardinal, asking him to get leave. He could give it perhaps *himself* — His powers are very great.[1]

TO MANUEL JOHNSON

6 Harcourt Street Dublin Decr 7/54

My dear Observer

I am still hunting for your double. I am not going to inflict on you more than an answer 'yes or no' to the question 'Is the inclosed promising at first sight? is it worth pursuing?' Please return it.[2]

I see in the Paper an announcement about Mrs Johnson, upon which I must offer you and her my congratulations.[3] I hope all is going on well

Ever Yrs affly John H Newman

M. Johnson Esqr

P.S.   We are making a very promising beginning here.

Thank you for your kindness to Penny.

TO ARCHBISHOP CULLEN

6 Harcourt Street   In fest. Concept Imm. B M V [8 December] 1854

My dear Lord,

While you are in St Peter's taking part in the greatest event of the day,[4] from which I hope some good will come to the University as well

---

[1] See letter of 12 Jan. 1855 to Wiseman.

[2] This was an application for the post of Director of Newman's proposed Observatory, from Hugh Breen; see letter of 20 Dec. to Johnson.

[3] On the birth of their fourth child, Richard.

[4] i.e. the definition of the doctrine of the Immaculate Conception of our Lady.

as to the Church at large, I take up my pen to write to you, because you must wish for a letter.

Thank God, we have hitherto gone on very well. We have had five Inaugural Lectures — every one has been successful. Signor Marani comes next week and Mr Allies finishes the Term.[1] The Lectures have done us a great deal of good. We have now above 60 names down for matriculation — and, whereas the Lecture List a month ago had but 17 names, we have advanced [to 27?][2] In my own house I am stowing as many as 9 young men.

We are going to increase (double) the size of the Gazette with the new year. I shall no longer be Editor, but shall keep my eye on it.

I trust we shall be able to provide some courses of lectures on Natural Philosophy, which will be one way of using the Medical School. I shall present Mr Hennessy, (who is a person of considerable name in scientific circles) for the appointment of the Archbishops on their return.

I have placed the Secretary's office at present, in the Medical School — and must have hired a lodging, if we had not got the School. I have made Mr Scratton Secretary — he has nothing whatever to do with the Funds — but there is great deal of work for him — He is at his office 4 hours a day.

I propose to build a Church or Chapel out of my own money (*not* the Achilli money) — if I get your Grace's and Mr Flanagan P.P.'s leave. I shall let it to the University at so much a year — (beginning with a small sum, and increasing when the numbers increase) — I think it will pay me — and, when the University chooses to build a Church itself, then it may leave mine. I will not use a penny of University money in the building — I foresee I should have difficulties, if I did. Unforeseen difficulties may come in the way — but at present, except that I want your leave, the prospect is pretty clear.

I have nearly built my little chapel in the House — in order to receive the Blessed Sacrament, if I am fortunate enough by your Grace's good offices, to obtain the privilege of reserving it.

Will you please do something towards our getting at least the loan of the Irish MSS at St Isidore's?[3]

[1] For Newman's Inaugural Lecture on 9 Nov. see letter of 11 Nov. to Allies; for those of Leahy and Ornsby which followed, see letter of 22 Nov. to St John. On 30 Nov. Renouf gave his Inaugural Lecture, 'The Literary History of France,' on 7 Dec. MacCarthy, 'The Nature and Meaning of Poetry.' Marani's subject was 'The Origin and Rise of the Italian Language and Literature,' and that of Allies 'The Object and Idea of the Philosophy of History.'

[2] The top corner of the page, folded over when the autograph in Dublin was microfilmed, is illegible. Unfortunately the autograph has since been mislaid, and the omission cannot be repaired.

[3] See letters of 5 June to Talbot, and 8 Oct. to Cullen.

Begging your Grace's blessing, and with kind remembrances to Dr Kirby I am My dear Lord Very affly & obly Yours in Xt

John H Newman of the Oratory

The Most Revd the Archbp of Dublin

P.S.   May I ask your permission to build my church (if I can manage it) on condition of my getting Mr [Matthew] Flanagan? The ground will be in *Harcourt* Street.[1]

TO THE COUNTESS GRANVILLE

6 Harcourt Street Dublin. Decr 8/54

Madam,

I thank you very much for your kindness in thinking of Dr Logan as a person who could serve us in the New University.[2] Whatever circumstances may have set him at liberty to offer himself, it is quite clear to all who have the pleasure of his acquaintance, that the University would gain by receiving him.

Knowing well his talents and learning in the departments of mathematics and metaphysics, I have long had the thought of connecting him with us, before me — but I do not think there is any chance at all of my being able to effect it, even if he consented.

It is not wonderful, considering that Ireland has contributed, and will contribute, the greater part of the Funds, that Irishmen should be unwilling to see appointments made of Englishmen and Scotchmen — and metaphysics and mathematics are two of the special departments of science for which they have a genius. I know a Scotchman, a convert, with a large family and very slender provision for them, who has a reputation for metaphysics; but he too has no prospect of being appointed to the chair of that science.[3] The only department in which the

---

[1] Cullen replied on 20 Dec., 'I will give you permission to build the new church— but I think it would be well to select a site where it would be of the greatest public utility. . . . I expect to get permission for you to keep the Blessed Sacrament.' Flanagan was the Parish Priest of St Nicholas Without, the parish concerned.

[2] Countess Granville, the mother of Sir John Acton, wrote on 4 Dec. asking if a place in the University could be found for Dr. Logan. He had been chaplain to the Duchess of Leeds at Hornby Castle, but they had quarrelled, and he had been forced to leave.

[3] This must be William MacLaurin, Dean of Moray and Ross, who became a Catholic in 1850, and in 1851 asked Newman for a professorship in 'Mental Philosophy and Ethics.' He was at the time almost penniless.

Irish are not equal, or are inferior to English, is that of classical literature — and in it alone I have been able to appoint Englishmen.

I am very sorry to return such an answer to your letter, and to have had to add so long an explanation,

and am, Madam, Your Ladyship's faithful Servt in Xt

John H Newman of the Oratory

The Countess Granville

TO MRS JOHN MOZLEY

6 Harcourt Street Dublin Decr 8/54

My dear Jemima

Thank you for your affectionate letter. Hardly had I last written to you, and the very first walk I took in the beautiful place where we had pitched ourselves, when I broke a fibre of my calf in going up hill, and have been laid up ever since. Luckily it has not affected my health — but I am now very slowly getting to walk, and it took place three months ago. This is the whole matter.

As to the war, I was always opposed to it, and am now. Were it a mere matter of practical expedience, I should feel that others know better than I can, but my *principles* in the matter are bolder than most people can bear. It seems to me insufferable to go to war for the sake of the Turks; and, though I most fully acknowledge that, so far as we have made promises and treaties in their favor, we must abide by them, yet to do more than this is intolerable — and to say we mean to set them up when we don't mean it, is worse — for it is hypocritical.

That we have a right to be afraid of Russia, I grant — but I hate taking a *negative* side. Russia is developing — it is most ungracious, and I think impolitic, because it promises ill, merely to resist a growing and (I will add) an improving nation. The proper way is for us to develop too. In short, the true policy, to my mind, is not one of jealousy, but of compensation. I have no mercy on Turkey, and (except so far as I have made promises to the contrary) I should imitate the man in the story, who, when another cried out 'Stop thief, he has got my hat, and I am too drunk to run after him,' said, 'Well, if you are quite sure you can't, I will make bold to take your wig.'

The Czar pointed to *that* — he wished us to share the spoil between us — We were too virtuous to listen to the proposal. We did not say, it is not for our interest, but 'it is so very wicked.' Now the Yankees went out against the Mormons, and would have put them down if they

322

could — and did not, because they *could* not. And, in like manner, the Turks are a simple nuisance, and ever have been, and have no business in Europe, and have never settled down or been domesticated there, have never had a place in European congresses and treaties, and are like the Mormons, only a great deal worse, and act the dog in the manger in the most beautiful countries of the world — and the only reason they were not put down long ago has been, because Europeans could not — but now, not only they can, but the Turkish power is really in its last stage of existence — and *must* go — and something *must* take its place.

This is what I mean by the timid, narrow, jealous system which we are pursuing. The Turks *must* go — Russia proposes a bold *constructive* policy — let us propose another — but we don't — we propose nothing — we have nothing to say but ' *You* shan't have the country;' and then, when driven from our ostensible reason, we add 'We will defend the *integrity* of Turkey —' what a piece of fudge!

In the long run that power will gain which has a clear bold distinct policy, and dares avow it — but the English policy trims.

People say 'Russia is a persecutor of the church —' well, she avows it — England persecutes, and dare not avow it. Moreover, I dread the liberalism and infidelity, which would follow the sway of England in Turkey, more than the bigotry of Russia.

I had no notion, when I began, of thus running on.

I am sorry Herbert's accident has lasted so long. I thought it was reckoned one of the slightest of severe ones

Ever Yrs affly J H Newman

TO AMBROSE ST JOHN

6 Harcourt Street Dublin Dec 8/54

My dearest A

Buona festa. I said Mass for both Oratories today — for you yesterday, for Nicholas the day before — for Lady O A's [Olivia Acheson] legacy the day before that, and for the Birmingham Benefactors tomorrow — so Bm has a long spell.

I am bothering Stanislas, so much that I am going to bother you. Show this to him, and to no one else and write to me your and his opinion.

It is quite impossible that I can do without a second waiter at dinner. I expect 9 youths — with Renouf and me it makes 11 — even without a single guest. I fear this *demands* an alteration in my domestic economy, and there is abundant reason for it, independent of this — though I should bear it for a while, but for this. I am afraid of going further, and faring worse; and I recollect Cowper's advice to 'Beware of dangerous steps.'[1]

Well. — My *thoughts* go in this direction.

1. to depose unhappy Jones — thereby letting loose £55 (25 wages + 30 board) He cooks very so - so, so much so that Margaret is now installed as a sort of private tutor, with the understanding of a douceur (£5) from him out of his pay. I will never trust the exquisite Scratton again.

2. To bring in (as a day labourer, as Margaret is, her sister) giving her (say) altogether £20, if that will content her — engaging her month by month — she is so engaged now at the University House. Margaret becomes cook.

3. To get a boy — cost, his living £30 and wages £5. Here you have the £55.

This involves three extra and occasional expences.

1. pensioning off old Jones till April — viz: from January 13, about 10 weeks — his wages 10/ a week — his board 10/ altogether £10.

2. contriving part of the furniture room — in the basement, for the two women to put their bonnets in, and putting a stove into it

3. knocking up *some where* (!) a closet for the boy.

These things, though laughable, annoy me — they kept me awake part of last night.

Ever Yrs affly J H N

If you can think of any thing better, let me know.

TO AN UNKNOWN IRISH PRIEST

Decr 9. 1854

Dear Revd Sir[2]

I have received your letter containing your request, and I will gladly offer the most Holy Sacrifice for your intention on the Octave of the Immaculate Conception Friday next.

---

[1] 'Beware of desp'rate steps. The darkest day (Live till tomorrow) will have pass'd away.' *The Needless Alarm*, 132–3.

[2] This priest, who was dying, sent Newman £190 for the University, under strict anonymity, and announced he was leaving to it his books. Newman cut out the address and signature on the priest's letter, and made a note that he thought of spending the money 'in altar furniture for the University Church.' See also letter of 25 Jan. 1855 to V. B. Dillon.

I hope I direct to you rightly, but I can find neither your name nor your direction in the Catholic Register Believe me, with every sincere wish and good prayer for you &c

J H N

TO J. D. DALGAIRNS

6 Harcourt Street Dec 12/54

My dear Bernard

Poor Mrs Ward should not have asked — but grief makes us selfish. And I dare say she is at her wits' end.

I am much vexed — but what strikes me is, that, were anything to happen to Ward, we should be very sorry you had not gone.[1]

You must go, and be back as soon as you can; the latest day, Saturday the 23rd

Ever Yrs affly J H N

TO LORD HENRY KERR

6 Harcourt Street Dublin. Dec. 12/54

My dear Lord Henry,

I can only excuse my troubling you further on the plea that we are in so unsettled a state that plans alter. I am in great want of room in my house, and my question is whether Frank can be asked to share his room with a boy of 15 — I would put up a skreen between the beds, so as to make it as near two rooms as possible.

It is a son of the Countess de la Pasture, a cousin of Mr Lisle Phillips. She is a convert with her children, and has lost, I believe, the reversion of considerable property by that step. She has earnestly desired that the boy should be an ecclesiastic and be with me, these five years — and now she has written to me on the subject. I am told he has a good chance of having a vocation, though it is not yet certain.

Should you have any unwillingness, I *fully rely* on your expressing it without any reserve —

How is Mrs Hope Scott. Will you tell James [Hope-Scott], I said Mass as he wished me —

Very sincerely Yours in Xt   John H Newman of the Oratory

Lord Henry Kerr.

[1] W. G. Ward was ill at Brighton.

TO AMBROSE ST JOHN

⌐6 Harcourt Street Decr 17/54⌐

My dear Ambrose

⌐I propose to make my appearance (with Wm) [[William]] on Friday, starting by the 8½ AM boat.⌐ Will you let my fire be lighted *several* days — for you know I am sensible of damp — and all my bed furniture put before it.

⌐As to your letter to the Cardinal, I do not see *why* we must wait for the answer. At least, I suppose there is no doubt at all of our getting it. I shall be disappointed if we do not *at once* get the money.⌐[1]

Tell Stanislas with my love that he seems oblivious of the message of Monsell, twice delivered to him, that ⌐the Trustees wished to put the money out to 4½ per cent interest, and that they would be obliged to him (Stanislas) to recommend some Irish security.

As to the cemetery wall, I am aghast, but will talk when we meet.[2]

Tell Victor, Harry, and Ralph to look at the *Scholar's Examination* in Gazette of last Thursday for of course they must undergo it. Let them choose their books⌐[3]

Ever Yrs affly J H N

TO THOMAS SCRATTON

Dec 18/54

My dear Scratton

Some of the letters I now send are *important* — as being my vouchers for putting down foreign names

Ever Yrs J H N

TO THOMAS SCRATTON

Tuesday Decr 19/54

My dear Scratton

Will you dine here today or tomorrow?

And will you tell me *how much* remained in my name and Dr

[1] This and the following paragraph refer to Lady Olivia Acheson's legacies.

[2] This wall at Rednal seemed likely to be expensive.

[3] Victor Duke, Henry Ryder and Ralph Kerr, as candidates for the Scholar's Degree at the University, must choose their Latin and Greek set books for examination. See the *Catholic University Gazette*, (14 Dec. 1854), p. 226.

Cullen's, *before* the £700 paid in — and draw me a cheque of £10 in favor of Allies

Ever Yrs J H N

TO MANUEL JOHNSON

6 Harcourt Street Dublin Decr 20/54

My dear Observer

I should be very much obliged by your asking Airy about Mr Breen.[1] His being an Irishman, and so long at it, is much in his favor — but I certainly do want a good article.

Do you know any thing of the Catholic men of science at Bonn, or elsewhere? I want a Professor of Pharmacy, and a Professor of Pathology.

Ever Yrs John H Newman of the Oratory

M. Johnson Esqr

P.S.   It seems to me that Henry [Bowden] lets Harry have his own way too much.

TO LORD HENRY KERR

6 Harcourt Street Dublin Decr 20/54.

My dear Lord Henry

Thank you for your permission[2] and your hint about Francis.

As to the terms I would take the full sum and thank you if I could at present do so with a safe conscience. When F gets older, he shall have a room to himself and with a fireplace in it; and then, when he is on a par with the others, he shall pay as they — but his is not the only room which I have been forced to divide — and when that was the case, I have acted in one and the same way. Should I find I have made a wrong calculation at the end of the year, I would not mind telling you and others, and profiting by your liberality, but if I can make the house go on as I am intending, I shall have done all I wish to do.

[1] Hugh Breen, an Irish Catholic, had been working at the Royal Observatory, Greenwich, for sixteen years, under G. B. Airy, the Astronomer Royal. Airy's opinion was that Breen lacked the initiative and force of character that Newman would look for in his first astronomer. His son James Breen was a calculator at Cambridge Observatory 1846–58.   [2] See letter of 12 Dec. to Lord Henry Kerr.

The best and kindest wishes of the season to yourself and Lady Henry. Alas to how many does the war sober it.

Yours very sincerely in Xt   John H Newman of the Oratory.

The Lord Henry Kerr.

TO HENRY WILBERFORCE

6 Harcourt Street ⌐Decr 20/54⌐

My dear Henry

You may get any number of the Gazettes at Burns and Lambert's, 17 Portman Street, Portman Square, London.

I asked you to order for me the Catholic Standard — if you would kindly do so. I have not seen any one number of it. It was better to send to 'Oratory, Hagley Road, Birmingham.' I go there in a day or two.

I am going to deliver a Lecture on something or other at Birmingham — and you shall have it if that will do.[1]

⌐We are doing well here. Our Inaugural Lectures are telling. We began with 17 youths in lecture — we have risen in the course of the Term to 27. We commence next Term with 33 certain. I have 8 in my house. It would be impossible for me now to take Arthur [Wilberforce] for some time, and that is why I wrote to you about him, before I was so full. He may well wait at Ushaw some time. I am to have in my house 2 English, 2 Scotch, 2 Irish, and 2 French.⌐[2]

Ever Yrs affly J H N

TO JOHN ENNIS

6 Harcourt Street Dublin Decr 21. 1854

My dear Dr Ennis,[3]

I had just put on my coat this morning to call on you at Booterstown, when Mr Rock called on me and explained the cause of your calling

[1] Newman was to have lectured on the British Constitution but changed his subject at the last moment. See letter of 5 Feb. 1855 to Faber, and diary for 6 Feb. 1855. The lecture on the British Constitution was developed into the letters 'Who's to Blame?' which appeared in the *Catholic Standard* in the Spring of 1855. *D.A.* pp. 306–62.

[2] i.e. Henry Ryder and Victor Duke; Lord Ralph Kerr and Francis Kerr; Sir Reginald Barnewall and Ernest O'Meagher; Charles de la Pasture and Louis de Vaulchier.

[3] John Ennis, D.D., was the parish priest of Booterstown. It was he who was sent by Archbishop Murray of Dublin to represent him in Rome in 1839, when the contro-

at the University House. This seemed to me to remove the necessity of troubling you with a visit — so I laid aside my intention. I will take care that every attention is paid to his proposal.

I came down stairs the day before yesterday, on receiving information of your call, and found you just gone. As I was in the midst of examining one of our youths, I could not leave him at the moment. I was very sorry I was not in time.[1]

Very truly Yours John H Newman

The Revd Dr Ennis

TO GEORGE RYDER

6 Harcourt Street Dublin Dec 21/54

My dear Ryder,

I start for Birmingham tomorrow. You do not say where Harry is. If you are of opinion that he ought to act as if he had a vocation, i.e. that he should *try* his vocation, you should have him tonsured before he came to me.

I should like him to be at Dublin before the 12th of January. If I saw him, I could explain to him all about it. His best way will be to come to Birmingham about the 10th, and I would send him on, two days before myself, with full instructions etc.

Ever Yrs John H Newman of the Oratory

George D Ryder Esqr

TO F. R. WARD

Edgbaston Dec 23/54

(Copy)

My dear Mr Ward

I have just returned in time to receive your letter to Fr St John, inclosing the cheque for £5724. 11. 4 and the Agreement which I am to sign.[2]

I thank you very warmly for the zeal you have shown all through this business.

versy as to whether the national schools, involving mixed education, should be accepted. Murray was in favour of them.

[1] Ennis replied on 22 Dec. to Flannery, having heard that Newman had left Dublin: 'I never called at the University House, nor do I know of any Mr Rock.

If any mistake be the cause, of course it is only a mistake etc—but there might be *some trap.*'   [2] This was Lady Olivia Acheson's legacy, received at last.

On talking over the matter with Fr St John, I learn that you said to him in conversation that Mr Fullerton would leave us at liberty at any time to substitute any other security for that which we are now giving in the Articles of Agreement, provided that the proposed substitution were satisfactory to Mr Fullerton, and on the condition on our part, supposing we could not satisfy him, of returning to him the £5724. 11. 4. Will you allow me then to trouble you thus much further, as to ask you whether Fr St John has rightly reported your words.

I do not think this need delay the completion of this matter more than the return of the post — and am etc

J H N

F Ward Esqr Clifton

TO HENRY WILBERFORCE

Edgbaston. Birmingham ⌐Dec 23/54
Charissime,

I have just returned, and am pained to see that you have inserted in one of your first Numbers two attacks on Lucas.[1] For one of them I am told you have apologized, but the other seems to me worse. The writer speaks of 'rebellion against episcopal authority,' as his offence, of his being a neophyte etc.[2]

[1] The quarrel between the two parties in the Irish Tenant League was at its height. On one side were those led by Frederick Lucas and Charles Gavan Duffy who were pledged to fight for tenant right and for justice for Catholics, and to accept no office until they attained their objects. On the other side were those, (some of them in spite of pledges to the contrary), who were ready to accept favours from the Whig Government and work with it. Archbishop MacHale and many priests supported Lucas, while many others and most of the bishops, notably Archbishop Cullen, were for co-operating with the Government. Matters came to a head in the autumn of 1854 when the Bishop of Ossory forbad the Parish Priest of Callan, one of the founders of the League, to take any further part in public affairs. This was a blow at the only class of leaders available to the Irish in their struggle for their rights, and so threatening that the Tenant League decided to appeal to Rome against the Bishop. Lucas set out for this purpose and was supported in Rome by MacHale. One consequence was that the latter became more than ever opposed to Cullen and all that came under his control. Thus the Catholic University found itself drawn into the vortex of Irish party and ecclesiastical politics. See also the letters of 30 Dec. 1854 to Ornsby and 24 Jan. 1855 to Cullen.

[2] Wilberforce had just taken over the *Catholic Standard* and in the number for 9 Dec. inserted two letters against Lucas. The first claimed that few English Catholics supported him, and on 16 Dec. the editor apologised for anything disrespectful in this letter. The second letter, signed 'Clericus,' spoke of how a priest was 'admonished by his bishop . . . to abstain from politics . . . Mr. Lucas, a layman, a neophyte, and having no connection with either the parish or the diocese in question, immediately takes offence, and comes forward at a public meeting to vindicate what he calls the liberty of the priest, and to denounce at the same time the act of the bishop . . . If this be

Now I think this most *unfortunate*. It is a very bad throw off. But what makes me notice it, is the embarrassing position you have put *me* in. I must be friends of *all* parties. You have at once dubbed yourself in all Irish minds as the opponent of Lucas. How can I possibly write in the Standard with my name, without identifying myself with Lucas's opponents?

I have been foremost in protesting against Lucas's attacks on Monsell — I cannot be party to an attack on Lucas. Really I do not see how any one, who would ignore the party politics of Ireland, can connect himself with an English paper which goes out of its way to introduce them. The very reason men give up the Tablet is 'because of its Irish politics —' are we to be pursued by them in an English paper?[1]

Ever Yrs affly J H N

P.S.   All kind thoughts of the season to you and yours.

TO JOHN STANISLAS FLANAGAN

The Oratory Dec 24/54

My dear Stanislas,

Thank you for your letter, which was very welcome, though the news was such as it was.[1] I cannot call it sad news, considering all you say. Assure Philip we do not forget him, and shall not tomorrow.

Ever Yours affectly in Mary and Philip

John H Newman of the Oratory

P.S.   The cheque for the money is come, £5724 that is, deducting Ward's bill £5690. Of this we might buy with £5500, stock in an Irish Rail way which pays 4½ per cent. As soon as you have time, I shall ask you to see to it.

TO JOHN HUNGERFORD POLLEN

The Oratory. Hagley Road Birmingham. Dec 24/54

My dear Mr Pollen,

I am very much obliged to you for your letter, and assure you that I was not expecting to hear from you. It would have been most

Catholic respect for episcopal authority, it is something I have yet to learn.' Clericus went on to condemn in violent language the throwing off of allegiance to bishops.

[1] Flanagan had gone to see his cousin Philip Molloy, now a Redemptorist novice at Bishop Eton. He was dangerously ill, but 'in the most perfect dispositions—calm and resigned.'

unreasonable in me to expect it, when you had not heard from me —
and it is very kind in you to waive ceremony, and to write to me first.[1]

I want very much to be able to induce you to come to Dublin — in
the capacity of Professor or Lecturer in the Fine Arts in our University.
I consider such an occupation would be of great benefit to the Catholic
community. As you know, I have not the disposal of the office in my
hands absolutely, and have nothing to do with the Funds, and am
obliged to move with great circumspection and deliberation; but I am
sanguine that I should succeed with the Irish Episcopate and laity if I
succeeded with you.[2]

As to the decoration of an University Church, of which you kindly
speak, we *must* have a Church, temporary or permanent, and it must be
decorated — and I should be very much obliged by your assistance in
the decoration.

With the best wishes of the season to you, and to your hosts,[3] I am,
My dear Mr Pollen, Very truly yours in Xt

John H. Newman of the Oratory

John H. Pollen Esq

TO F. W. FABER

Edgbaston Dec 26/54

My dear Fr Wilfrid,

I write to wish you and the London Fathers all the blessings of the
Season, and to assure them I do not cease to think of them.

Also, I have heard with great concern of your accident — and
earnestly and anxiously expect a good account of you.[4]

I have nothing to tell you, except what you know — that at Dublin

---

[1] C. J. La Primaudaye had never answered Newman's letter of 17 Nov. which
proposed that Pollen should become Professor of Fine Arts at the University. See the
notes there. Pollen, who now had received a second message through Allies, wrote on
20 Dec. that he gladly accepted Newman's proposal and also a further one that he
should decorate the University church.

Pollen added that he had already begun his work of preparation, and that Newman's
letter of 17 Nov. to La Primaudaye was of great value, 'as it has opened the way not
a little to arrangement of thoughts on the subject.'

[2] Pollen replied on 26 Dec., 'I suppose the delicta of our ancestors have over and
above brought down on the heads of Englishmen the very natural penalty of national
jealousy from which even Catholics cannot expect to be entirely freed.

I myself owe a great debt to Ireland. The practical life of the Irish removed from
me difficulties, which arguments ought to have superseded, but failed to affect as they
ought to have done.'

[3] Pollen was staying with the Henry Bowdens at Chiselhurst.

[4] It had become necessary to operate on Faber for a rupture.

we are going on remarkably well, and that whatever trials we may expect, they have not come yet. I indulge myself in visions of leaving at the end of a moderate time — and then when I have fairly committed myself to them, some rude reverse will come, and I shall find my work beginning.

Philip Molloy seems to be dying. Stanislas has gone down to him. I am here for three weeks. I have got in my Dublin House 2 Englishmen, two Scotchmen, 2 Irishmen, and 2 Frenchmen.

Ever Yrs affly John H Newman

TO MRS WILLIAM FROUDE

The Oratory. Hagley Road Bm. Dec 26/54

My dear Mrs Froude

A happy Christmas to you and Wm. Will you thank him for his letter? which was very welcome, though I don't know why he should seem to think I had a claim on one. It so happened I had mistaken some one's hand for his a day or two before, so it was doubly welcome. Tell him, I quite understand his suspicion about poor Lumley for it has long crossed my own mind, uncharitably or not.[1] I am only annoyed he has so much trouble. Perhaps Duffy may be making some proposals for the Church of the Fathers — but, if so, I will take care that he has no trouble then.

How dreadful this war is! From the first I have stored up with quite a feeling of resentment Lord John's declaration, that a war with Russia was not much of a war, last February![2] It was so detestably cruel

---

[1] William Froude wrote on 18 Dec. of delays over the new edition of *The Arians of the Fourth Century* which Lumley was to publish. Froude said that if Lumley were not such a good man, there might occasionally be 'the shadow of a misgiving that he is a little "fast and loose"—' Froude held the copyright of *Ari.* for Newman.

[2] Newman is referring, as his letter of 22 Feb. 1855 to Mrs John Mozley shows, to Lord John Russell's speech when introducing a Reform Bill on 13 Feb. 1854: 'If there were an apprehension of an immediate invasion . . . our thoughts would be directed to nothing but the means necessary for the defence of our country. But, much as I abhor war, much as I deprecate the evils of war, I confess I do not view war with that apprehension with which some hon. gentlemen seem to regard it. I conceive that we should be able to provide all the means necessary to carry on war with vigour . . . and, at the same time have full time for deliberation on those of our domestic concerns which appear most to require consideration. This apprehension of our being unable to attend to these topics from the time war should be declared—this idea that there is such danger in Russian armaments and forces, appears to me, I confess, one of those thoughts that may be described as having in it only one part of wisdom and three parts of cowardice, and I must say it does not affect me.' *The Times*, (14 Feb. 1854).

333

in a Minister thus to get John Bull into a scrape, who is ever ready enough to run his head against a wall, at that critical moment. And then Lord Palmerston and Sir James Graham with their Reform Club dinner![1] It is a great question whether with our newspaper system, our national tenderness of individual rights and interests, and our developed and refined sensitiveness, a war is possible, for any long time. A North American savage bears the severest bodily tortures without quivering — the delicately or morbidly organised Englishwoman would die under the least of them. The whole nation is *morally* in the latter case. It is enabled vividly to realize every movement which goes on in the Crimea, and it witnesses and sympathises in every wound of every soldier. Moreover, it is not *bound* down, for this moral operation, it has its arms free, as well as its voice; and it has no governing principle with in it to enable it to endure with fortitude the unavoidable anguish, and to create an internal momentum of resistance antagonist to the infliction. If the pain does not intermit, if disaster follows on disaster, where are we? War implies the movements of masses, in which the individual units, which compose them, are forgotten. The soldier, like the monk, at least in his idea, has no attachments of this world, he is cut off from human affection, at least for the time being, and goes out with his life in his hand devoted to a cause. Many letters, I presume, do the Russian soldiers send home to their friends! much definite information does the Russian public receive of the fortunes of the particular soldiers which swell the Czar's army! But we are like a set of Children on a rainy day who spend hours, yet not unconcernedly like children, in tracing the wayward course of each particular drop of rain, as it strikes against the window pane, and runs down to the frame at the bottom in its own way. I suppose the new instruments of destruction have certainly for the moment made a battle more hideous — Still on the whole this war is like other wars and the late battles like others — Had we been present or had a photograph representation of Agincourt or Blenheim or Vittoria, I suppose we should have been as much horrified as with the recent accounts of the newspaper correspondents; but up to this date parents and friends have seen their warriors off, and welcomed them back with scars and mutilations, but have known little or nothing of the process. I think, in the Agamemnon of Aeschylus, (Wm will declare I am making a mistake, and thinking I am writing to him — but it is all one,) the fore runner of the King of men proses to the natives of the miseries of the past war, or at least of the shipboard. His satisfaction at his return is swallowed up in the keen memory of past suffering.[2] What is past is over and can't be undone; now the home public feels the operation as it

---

[1] For this, see letter of 12 March 1854 to St John. [2] *Agamemnon*, 560–77.

goes on, and is sorely tempted to stay the operator's hand. Well we want one more advance in investigation — and Lord John as much as any one, viz to anticipate beforehand as vividly, as we feel during the operation. Had this been our wisdom, we should perhaps, before beginning, have looked twice in order to be sure that our cause was just and war unavoidable. Is this the reason for the foreign mercenaries?[1]

Thank Wm too for his account of Mrs B——, of whom I had heard nothing at all, before, except, what I was most gladly [sic] to hear, that she was a good manager.[2]

As to your own question, you know there is no *authorized* interpretation of Scripture in the Church, for the simple reason that none was ever given to her. When it is said that she interprets by the Fathers, (which is most true) it means that their doctrinal teaching is the *rule* of interpretation. This being premised, I should say, that it is generally considered that the woman in the Apocalypse is the Roman power, i.e. the temporal. That this will never revive, and become Antichrist, is more than I can say. Rome ever shows a recollection of its pagan greatness — in 1848 it drove out the Church, and established triumvirs. The Roman population seems to me like the ruins of the old city and the malaria which lives among them, and I never should be surprised at an outburst of Paganism. The church has ever been seated upon those ruins, and thus upon the cinders of a volcano. There have been Anti-Popes enough before now — and I can fancy one of them arising with a pagan ceremonial, proclaiming himself the true Pontifex Maximus instead of the Pope, pronouncing the Papacy a poor imitation of Imperial Sacerdotalism, and inaugurating the worship of Jupiter Optimus, Maximus [sic] in St Peter's. I have no reason to depart at present from the substance of the Tracts on Antichrist in the Tracts for the Times.[3]

I am very well, thank you, and I rejoice, and am most thankful, to say that the Catholic University is progressing as well as ever I could expect — most satisfactorily[4]

---

[1] The Foreigners' Enlistment Act passed through all its stages in ten days, and received the Royal Assent on 23 Dec., the day on which *The Times* began its exposure of the calamitous state of the army in the Crimea.

[2] The reference is evidently to Edmund Bastard's wife Florence Mary, eldest daughter of Simon Scrope of Danby, Yorkshire. They were married on 22 Nov. 1853.

[3] *Tract 83*, 'Advent Sermons on Antichrist,' 1838, now *D.A.* pp. 44–108, 'The Patristical Idea of Antichrist.'

[4] The last two or three lines had already been cut off when this letter was copied.

TO MISS M. R. GIBERNE

Oratory Hagley Road Birmingham Dec 27/54

My dear Miss Giberne

Your letter came last night, and was a sort of welcome to my Festa. Don't suppose I am not well and strong, for I am; and I shall live, please God, many years yet, for I am not fit to die, tho' not so many as poor old Routh who died a few days ago, having seen 100 years, and fulfilled 99 of them.[1] We have been prospered very much in Dublin, in which your prayers have had a share; I have a house-full myself, 2 English, 2 Scotch, 2 Irish, and 2 French. I am come here for my holidays, and go back soon after the Epiphany. The first thing I did on coming back was to put out your pictures for framing, and I hope they will be done and put up in the Refectory before I go. Lady O A's [Olivia Acheson] money has just come to us, and we ought to be very thankful — for, now it is over, I may say that we have been in considerable pecuniary difficulties for want of annual income, and I really don't know what we should have done unless the money had come in. We must make some offering to our Lady and St Ph. [Philip]. Is it not pleasant that it just comes to us with the definition of the Immaculate Conception, like a bounty of the Great Queen upon her festal day — I am going to see our new cottage at Rednall, and we hope to bring down Fr Joseph and Aloysius there by February 13 his anniversary. I shall return here for the day.[2]

Thank you for the intended vestments. I have been very anxious to hear about where you were. I should like to put you under obedience to make yourself comfortable. Have you taken care that your London lawyer ever sends you any money? You *must* feed well. I forget prices, but I think your dinner should cost you at least 6 pauls[3] and no more cats meat, if you please, such as you used to eat. It does not answer letting the spirits sink — and living by yourself must try you — so, please, do indulge a bit in the pleasures of the table. Recollect the caricature of old Lord Eldon, who, when he was turned out of power, was presented by some admirers in Lancashire with a large cheshire cheese — and whom the H.B. represents sitting before it and saying 'My cheshire cheese is now my only consolation.'[4] Also, do, please keep

[1] Martin Joseph Routh, President of Magdalen College, Oxford, died on 23 Dec.
[2] Joseph Gordon died on 13 Feb. 1853, Aloysius Boland, the laybrother, on 19 March 1852, and they were to be reburied at Rednal.
[3] A paul was worth about 5d.
[4] The H B caricatures were those of John Doyle (1797–1868), painter and political caricaturist. The signature 'H B' was formed by placing two J D's one above the other.

yourself warm, and furnish your room; those brick floors are frightful. I am quite in earnest in all these injunctions. I suspect your man of business sends you nothing.

Philip Molloy is (apparently) dying, and Stanislas has gone to see the last.

F. Ambrose has just come in, and is impatient for some recognition of a letter which he wrote to you putting aside his penitents and office, on the spot, in answer to yours. He says he has sent you four letters —

Ever Yrs affly John H Newman

TO THOMAS SCRATTON

The Oratory. Hagley Road Bm December 29/54
My dear Scratton,

I cannot make out the signature of the inclosed — nor do I know in what part of Ireland St Michael's and St John's is — and I have no Directory here. Will you make out for me and answer the letter?

Will it shock you, if I say that I mean if I can *to beg* the money? since I have none to go on with. Therefore I should be obliged to you, if you could get 'Mr R.' whose name I cannot read, PP of St Michael's and John's, to pay it into the 'Cullen and Newman account' at the Hibernian.[1]

There is some one or other who ought to have £5. I cannot think who it is and it annoys me.

Do you think you could find out what *habitual* pew renters there are to the Protestant Patrick and Ch Ch [Christ Church]? It bears on the point of taking St Audoen's as our University Church. It is very central, and near the Quays.

Between 1829 and 1851 Doyle produced nearly a thousand of these caricatures.

Eldon, after being Lord Chancellor for a quarter of a century, resigned in 1827, and was bitterly disappointed at not receiving the office again a year later when the Duke of Wellington became Prime Minister. He then threw his energies into opposing Catholic Emancipation, and for this was presented with a cheese by 'the Protestants of Cheshire.'

Doyle's caricature, Number 25, 7 Oct. 1829, 'Consolation, or, Otium cum Dignitate,' shows Lord Eldon sitting in a chair with a huge glass of beer and an enormous cheese before him, and saying 'My Cheshire Cheese and my Glass form now my only consolation.'

[1] Newman was sending to Scratton a letter which announced the amount of the collection for the University at the church of SS Michael and John, on the Quay, at Dublin. When Scratton approached Nicholas Roche the parish priest he learned that the money had already been paid into the Catholic University account, and so could not be touched. At the end of the year Dr Leahy succeeded in liberating for the current expenses £1000 from this account.

Your brother seems very well — he is soon going to Mr Nugent's. We feel he has done the boys good here.[1]

Ever Yrs affectly in Xt   John H Newman of the Oratory

Thos Scratton Esqr

P.S.   Please write a line of *acknowledgement* of the letter I inclose, saying that I am away.

2 P.S.   Your letter just come (I had fancied I had not even £10 at the Bank.) — and another for me from Dr Keane. Will you kindly acknowledge it and say that I am away

TO T. W. ALLIES

The Oratory Hagley Road Birmingham Dec. 30/54.

My dear Allies,

A suggestion comes from Rome this morning of our holding an Academia in Dublin in honour of the Immaculate Conception.[2] We *must* have a copy of Greek verses from you. You need not be present, nor your name known as the author. Would not the   [3] suggest something to you? I am asking various others for English etc, etc.

Ever Yrs J H Newman

TO F. W. FABER

Bm Decr 30/54

My dear Fr Wilfrid

I am just in possession of a suggestion from Rome that we should hold in Dublin an Academia in honor of the Immaculate Conception.

---

[1] James Scratton had been living at the Oratory during the autumn, and was about to go to the Catholic Institute at Liverpool.

[2] Cullen wrote on 20 Dec., describing the scene at the definition of the doctrine of the Immaculate Conception and added, 'I think it would be most desirable for us to have in Dublin something like the Roman academies—to commemorate this great event. If you would employ some good English Poets ⟨F. *Faber*, McCarthy etc⟩ to write compositions on the subject, and get some lines in Greek and Latin, and the modern languages, a display might be made worthy of the new university and the church of Dublin. . . .'

[3] The copyist has left a blank here.

I want from you a copy of Verses, English or Latin, for the occasion — and, asking it in the name of Mary I shall get it. Breathe them out as you wake some morning.

Ever Yrs J H N

P.S.   Your name need not be given, if you object.[1]

TO ROBERT ORNSBY

The Oratory Hagley Road Decr 30/54

My dear Ornsby

We must get up an Academia in celebration of the Immaculate Conception. I wish you would think *who* will write for it. It will consist of ornate composititons in prose and verse in *all* Languages with select pieces of music — and will be held in the Cathedral, which is dedicated to the Immaculate Conception. These names occur to me McCarthy — De Vere — Faber — Oakeley — Paley (?) — Allies —

Will you, please, tell Duffy to send from January 4th the Gazette to Dr Cullen, Collegio Irlandese, Roma. And to Mr Scott Murray, Poste Restante, Roma. And to send it STAMPED *to me here*, for January 4 and 11. And to send me the two quarterly parts *at once, done up in their covers.*[2]

As the Gazette is just going to Rome, *we must be very careful what we insert.* Depend upon it, we must expect a *very great deal* of criticism. Our success will create it by itself — but, consider, since I see clearly Dr McHale (entre nous) will not get his way, we must expect his opposition. This began before he left the country. I am *told* that he and another Bishop would not dine with the other Bishops at a formal dinner at the Irish college. All this to yourself[3]

Ever Yrs affly J H N

P.S.   Could you ransack any Catholic Latin Poets for verses on the subject of Mary?

[1] On 16 March 1855 Faber wrote to Newman at Wiseman's suggestion, urging him to write on the Immaculate Conception, because both converts and old Catholics were said to be disturbed at the manner in which it had been defined. Newman did write a Memorandum on the subject for Robert Wilberforce, which has been printed in *M.D.* pp. 115–28.

[2] Ornsby was now taking over the editing of the *Catholic University Gazette* from Newman.

[3] Cullen wrote from Rome to Newman on 20 Dec., 'The Pope has approved all the regulations [for the University] we made last may—and to prevent attempts to change them, he has ordered that they have a fair trial of five or six years so that during that time at least the presentation of professors etc will depend on you.

Dr McHale has made every effort here to prevent the confirmation of those regulations or to get it withdrawn—He says now that he will have nothing to do with the

TO THOMAS SCRATTON

The Oratory Hagley Road Bm Jan 1/55

My dear Scratton

A happy new year to you. I have received £401. 10. 8 from Dr Kilduff, which I mean to bag for the Cullen and Newman Account.

I send you these items — will you put them into the Tablet as far as items are put in (i.e. in the usual way) saying 'The Very Revd Dr N. begs to acknowledge etc'

Ever Yrs J H Newman

Thos Scratton Esqr

TO J. WALKER OF SCARBOROUGH

The Oratory Hagley Road Bm — Jany 1. 1855

My dear Mr Walker

Your kind and encouraging letter arrived here about an hour ago, just in time for me in my answer to wish you a happy new year — though, as far as public affairs go, it promises at best to be a very anxious one. ⌈I have hated the war heartily from the first, thought it unnecessary, and considered Whig pride to be the moving principle of it. I have thought it a simple piece of Johnbullism — and now we seem to have put our foot into it indeed — but I suppose we shall have our successes as well as our reverses. Any how, I hate the war ten times as much as I did this time year.

The University is succeeding far above my expectations, and every one is in very good spirits about it. Of course we must expect rubs and crosses, but it has begun well, and must advance. We have above 60 youths' names entered on our books; in my own house I have 2 English, 2 Scotch, 2 Irish, and 2 French.⌉ At present things are going on so much better than I had anticipated, that really I have hopes of getting back here at the end of my three years.

Mr Curry, our Professor of Irish History, is the first Archeologist in Ireland. We shall begin with the beginning, if we open out new sources of information.

university—so much the better—but I fear that he will excite a storm against it—Of course Haec omnia inter nos sint—It is as well not to let Dr Leahy know this matter, lest Dr Slattery should be displeased.'

See also first note to letter of 23 Dec. 1854 to Wilberforce and letter of 24 Jan. 1855 to Cullen.

Fr St John unites with me in congratulations to you on the new year, and I am, My dear Mr Walker, Sincerely Yrs in Xt

John H Newman

The Ver Revd John Walker

TO MRS WILLIAM FROUDE

The Oratory. Hagley Road Bm. Jan 2/55

My dear Mrs Froude,

The best wishes of the new year to all of you. I am so full on [sic] the subject of the war, that I cannot tell *what* I said to you — but I know well, not a tenth of what I feel. War is not *necessary*, till we have attempted to keep peace — and that we did not. The very opponents of government only complain that we did not *threaten* the Russians soon enough. The Russians threw out plans of accommodation and compromise — we would not even entertain them. And, whereas Turkey lies below water mark, and that water is the great ravening empire of Russia, we have attempted, not like Mrs Partington with a broom,[1] but by mounds and dykes, to keep the ocean out. Turkey must go; yet we have attempted to set Humpty Dumpty on the wall again — and have enveloped ourselves in illusions and shams, as John Bull always does, instead of looking at things as they are, and having the manliness to confess the truth. And then, having resolved that the Turk shall be alive, when he is dead, we next resolve that Russia shall be a contemptible enemy, when she is a most formidable one — and we cheer Lord John when he has the grave inconsiderateness to declare that we are undertaking only a little war. Three years before we had undertaken the Pope, whose arms are spiritual — we go on to the Czar, whose arms are fleshly — Perhaps the second blunder is the punishment of the first.

Well — but as to your question. I answer thus:—

There is a marked contrast in Catholicity between the views presented to us by doctrine and devotion respectively. Doctrines never change, devotions vary with each individual. Catholics allow each other, accordingly, the greatest licence, and are, if I may so speak, utter *liberals*, as regards devotions, whereas they are most sensitive about doctrine. That Mary is the Mother of God is a point of faith — that Mary is to be honored and exalted in this or that way is a point of

[1] Sydney Smith, in his speech at Taunton in Oct. 1831, compared the rejection by the House of Lords of the Reform Bill to the efforts of Mrs Partington, who lived in a house on the beach at Sidmouth and tried to keep out the Atlantic during a great storm in 1824.

devotion. The latter is the consequence indeed of the former, but a consequence which follows with various intensity, in various degrees and in various modes, in various minds. We know from the first that St Joseph was our Lord's foster father and the guardian of Mary — we know nothing more now than was known by St Irenaeus and St Cyprian — yet till two or three centuries ago the devotion to St Joseph was almost unknown in the Church; now it is one of the dearest devotions, and closely connected with the affections and enshrined in the hearts, of myriads. It is not to the purpose here to inquire the philosophy of this — but so it is, we live in devotions to which our next door neighbours are dead; we do not find fault with them, nor they with us. Fr Spencer comes to me, and preaches at me for not taking up his particular devotions of Prayers for England — I say, 'Well, *mine* at present is that of Prayers for the souls of the dying and the dead in this terrible war.' I feel my own most keenly — I am not denying his—the duty of prayers for England, and for the dying and the dead, we both admit, — and practice; but when it takes the shape of a devotion, one takes one, another another.

As far as I can make out from history and from documents St Chrysostom had not the devotion to Mary, which St Buonaventura had or St Alfonso — but they agreed together most simply and absolutely that she was the Mother of God. And in like manner, while you and I admit this doctrine, and while we both admit and maintain that God is to be worship [sic] with an honor of His own, infinitely distinct from any honor we give His creatures, even Mary, the first of them, *I* shall not quarrel with any form of words *you* use about her, or to her, so that it *does not state some untruth*, and shall expect *you* not to quarrel with *me*, who refuse to use your forms and devotions.

'We praise thee, O Mary; we acknowledge thee, to be our Lady.' Is it the doctrine, or the taste of this, to which you object? I expect, the taste. You mean, 'the words in themselves are not strong — but it is exceedingly indecorous, it is a mere parody, a profane parody, thus to parallel the Te Deum.'

Well. I turn to the Anglican service for the 30th of January — and read 'The people stood up, and the rulers took counsel together, against the Lord and against His anointed.' That is, against Charles the first — here is not even a parody — but *the very words* are used, which belong to our Lord.

The non-conformist is furious with you — and he calls the service blasphemy. And so on, 'The *breath of our nostrils*, the *anointed* of *the Lord*, was taken in their pits: of whom we said, UNDER HIS SHADOW(!) we shall be safe.'

Now what do you say in answer? You say this — 'My good friend, you are quite ignorant of the whole structure of Scripture. It is founded on the principle of mystical interpretation. Every sentence has a score of meanings — one under another — one rising above and through another. I suppose, originally and primarily, the 'anointed of the Lord' meant David. David was a type or shadow of Christ — and so was King Charles. You may dispute this *doctrine*, that Kings are Christ's Vicegerents — but they who hold it, are committing no blasphemy in using words of King Charles, which have a higher meaning, unless the inspired writer committed blasphemy, in uniting in one sense Christ and David. Moreover, what applies to Kings, applies to all Christians — we are all Christs — we are all 'gods —' there is no attribute of the Supreme God, which He has not in His love communicated, in the way of grace, to us.'

Now all this is *our* explanation also. If even Anglicans use the mystical interpretation, we do still more freely. He who called judges 'gods,' is our warrant for applying all that is included in the idea of God, and all that is said of God, to the regenerate, and especially to its higher specimens, though in what is called an 'improper' sense. The Breviary is full of such adaptations. E.g. on a Bishop's festival. 'Thou art a priest for ever, after the order of Melchisedech.' In Compline office 'He shall give His angels charge concerning thee, to keep thee in all thy ways.' etc etc.

I really do think then, no objection can be made to 'We praise thee O Mary — etc' except that it is 'very bad taste.' And if this is all, let us recollect that, using our own judgment, we should call the Oriental-isms of Scripture 'very bad taste.' Every nation and age has its own taste — and though there are invariable principles, we must allow a great latitude for such accidents. Think of the condescension of Almighty God comparing Himself to an eagle, with His Saints between His shoulders etc etc. — There is no end of this, if you go on. Use your own taste, and let me use mine.

To answer then your question precisely, I say, that the Church has not expressly *authorized* the formularies of devotions you speak of, but, as far as I know, she has not interfered with them

Ever Yrs affly JHN

TO SIR JOHN ACTON

The Oratory Birmingham Jany 7. 1855

My dear Sir John Acton,

I am so busy to day that I much fear I shall not get this off by the post this evening — but I have set about it without delay.

It is very difficult to answer your question without some considerable knowledge of the circumstances of your place.[1] My first impression is, that it would be best to avoid the subject of religion altogether — or at least to speak of it as little as possible — and in the most general terms. Kind mutual feeling makes way for the introduction of religion — but this is the work of time. It would seem most natural to introduce yourself in that character only or mainly, which gives occasion to the festivities. The other is sure to follow in proportion as you are known.

As to the Queen, every one must respect her private conduct. There is but one opinion as to the excellent way in which she brings up her family — and she is the keystone of the social fabric — so that all our political happiness is bound up in her welfare. Moreover, as being a lady, it is right to have certain chivalrous feelings about her. Yet I doubt whether I could be enthusiastic in her favor, knowing how opposed she is to the Catholic religion. I agree with you that it would have a bad effect for the priest and the Protestant clergyman to divide the grace between them.

Excuse this hasty letter. I have not given myself time to wish you and your place joy on the event, which I do most sincerely.

I hope it will not be taking a liberty to say Mass for you on Tuesday morning

I am, My dear Sir John, Very truly Yours in Xt

John H Newman of the Oratory

Sir J. D. Acton, Bart

TO THOMAS SCRATTON

Jan 7/55

My dear Scratton

Thank you for your paper. We will talk about it when we meet.

I don't send you the order for the £400 — as £1000 has been paid in to me, I have not signed it and made it money — nor shall I take it. Will you keep it till I come?

Ever Yrs J H N

P.S. I am sorry to say, I have not the power of blessing.

The Mr Murphy is the poor man in bad health at Kingstown Mullcote Avenue.

[1] Sir John Acton wrote for advice as to the line to take during his coming of age celebrations at Aldenham, Shropshire. He was born on 10 Jan. 1834.

TO J. WALKER OF SCARBOROUGH

The Oratory Bm Jany 8/55

My dear Mr Walker

Our students are not in one large House, but separated College fashion into various — according to the plan in many places insisted upon in the University Gazette — vid pp 80, 91, 109, 210, 221 etc Accordingly, we have already three houses — my own is mentioned with the University House at p 241. It is also referred to p 180.

My house is more than full even at present — and I have so many besides wish to come that it looks as if I must turn the stables into rooms. At present I have two English, two French, two Irish, and two Scotch — and among these, Lady Lothian's son, Lord H Kerr's son, the Countess de la Pasture's son, the Vicomte de Vaulchier, and Sir Regd Barnewall.

In the University House nearly all are Irish. As to my own, if they did not go on to my entire satisfaction, I should get rid of them without scruple. At present, I ought to be very thankful, for many of them are as devout and innocent as novices, and all of them are gentlemen. As far as I can make out, they have a number of good youths in the University House too.

As to your other point, *from the first* I proposed to go only for a few years. My three years are already out! but I must give another three of *work*. The Pope has only given me leave of absence from Birmingham for three years, not more.[1]

Reciprocating your good wishes for the new year (I wish Fr St John were well, but he has got into an uncomfortable state of health) I am, My dear Mr Walker,

Most sincerely Yours in Xt   John H Newman

TO WILLIAM MONSELL

The Oratory Bm Jany 9/55

My dear Monsell

I write to express my deep sympathy with you in your affliction.[2] I had just been saying two Masses for your intention. Of course this

[1] See note to letter of 5 June 1854 to Wiseman.
[2] Lady Anna Maria Charlotte Wyndham Quinn, whom Monsell had married in 1836, died on 7 Jan. She was the only sister of the Earl of Dunraven.

requires no answer. Poor Lord Dunraven, how much he is tried too! I ought to say perhaps, yet, though I think it is a consolation, feel it needs an explanation to say it, that nothing I have ever seen or heard, made me think her near the Church. I mean it looks like invincible ignorance and good faith

Ever Yours affly in Xt with every sincere wish & prayer for your support,

W Monsell Esqr M P.   John H Newman of the Oratory

TO MRS JOHN MOZLEY

Bm Jan 9/55

My dear Jemima

I have made a sad mistake. I thought it was my old cousin Henry. I did not know the other's name — of course I shall be glad to return *his* call, and so shall be thankful for his address any how.[1]

But you must set me right, if you please, about the *absurd letter*, which he will read as addressed to him, and stare.

Ever Yrs J H N

TO ROBERT ORNSBY

Bm ⌈Jan 9/55⌉

Private
My dear Ornsby

⌈I am very much annoyed just to have heard that Dr Leahy has altered one of my notices in the Gazette.[2] Those Notices are mine, and no one ever must alter them without my consent. Let this be understood, if you please, by the Printer, as a rule for the future.

By accident, I suppose, the Sedes Sapientiae etc was omitted in the Number of last week,[3] *which marked the transition between what was of authority and what was not.* It should have come *before* the notice of

---

[1] Newman's old cousin was Henry Fourdrinier, the son of his Uncle Charles. It would appear that another Fourdrinier cousin, probably James Fourdrinier, the son of Charles's brother Sealey, wished to call.

[2] Leahy appears to have postponed his own lectures by ten days.

[3] i.e. in the *Catholic University Gazette* of 4 Jan. Newman's articles, which became 'The Rise and Progress of Universities' in *H.S.* III, were headed 'Sedes Sapientiae, ora pro nobis.'

Allies' Lecture. ⌐It was from fear of such accident I had wished to have seen the number before it was printed off.

I am quite in ignorance *what* Dr Leahy has put in instead of my announcement. When announcements are once made, I have an almost insuperable repugnance to altering them — and when they are on practical matters, as the days of [[public]] Lectures, I should have been very hard to persuade. I should rather have given the Lectures myself.¬

Ever Yours John H Newman of the Oratory

P.S. ⌐I suspect the Whig opposition to my appointments will turn out to be nothing beyond the *dis*appointment of certain Trinity College [[(private)]] Tutors and candidate Barristers.¬¹

WEDNESDAY 10 JANUARY 1855 Harry (*Ryder*) went with John (the boy) to Dublin
THURSDAY 11 JANUARY Charles de la Pasture came to Edgbaston

TO MRS J. W. BOWDEN

The Oratory Edgbaston January 11. 1855
My dear Mrs Bowden,

I am sorry to hear from Fr Faber this morning that Emily has not got rid of her bronchitis. There is a bad influenza going about here, and in Dublin — and perhaps in London, which she must be careful of. I dare say it has something to do with the late visit of the Cholera.

I am starting for Dublin — and my real and anxious work is beginning — for I have a housefull of 8 youths, and have no one, I may say, to divide my responsibility — for, though Mr Renouf, who is in the House, has a hundred recommendations, he is not a Priest, and cannot take my place, either when I am there or away. I ought to be very thankful at the style of youths I have got — The French Vicomte, the Irish Baronet, and our own Lord R Kerr, are three of the most amiable innocent youths you can fancy, and if I can keep them so, will be great gain to us — but you may fancy it is a great anxiety.

Have I told you that we have had a great care taken away from us lately, in having received Lady O Acheson's legacy? I trust it will put us straight for the future, but the interval has been trying.

I congratulate you on your servant's conversion, which must be a great personal comfort to say nothing else. Was not tomorrow Sister

¹ Ornsby wrote on 2 Jan. the gossip that there was 'a strong feeling of jealousy against the English appointments [at the University], on the part of the ministerial party—the Whigs.'

Mary Dominica's profession-day? I shall not be in time to say Mass at Dublin tomorrow — but I will say Mass for all of you including your servant on Saturday instead. Love to Emily.

Ever Yrs affly in Xt   John H Newman of the Oratory

TO FRANCIS KENRICK, ARCHBISHOP OF BALTIMORE

The Oratory Birmingham January 11. 1855

My dear Lord,

What a sad disappointment to me that I have missed you! Had I known the time of your coming, I certainly would have made some arrangement which would have hindered such a piece of bad fortune. I have heard nothing of Dr Hughes or any other American Prelate; so I hope they have not passed Dublin also, since my absence.[1]

The truth is, I had been four months away from this place, and my presence here was imperative. The Holy Father has given me leave of absence hence for Dublin, but only for three years, and I must not be away from the Oratory longer time than Dublin actually requires — so that in the vacations I am bound to be here.

We are getting on very well, I am glad to say. We have above 60 on the books for entrance — between 30 and 40 in Lecture. In my own house I have eight — 2 English, 2 Irish, 2 Scotch, and 2 French. I hope I shall one day add, 2 American.

We have watched with the greatest interest, as you may suppose, the late proceedings at Rome — they have issued in a most wonderful event, which employs the minds of Protestants almost as much as ours, tho' in a different way.

We were much pained to see by the papers, that the good priest who was tarred and feathered, has died in consequence of the ill usage. Is he your first martyr? I think not —[2] Begging your Grace's blessing, I am, My dear Lord, Yr faithful servt in Xt

John H Newman of the Oratory

The Most Revd the Archbishop of Baltimore.

[1] Archbishop Kenrick passed through Dublin on his way back from attending the definition of the Immaculate Conception in Rome. Dr Hughes, Archbishop of New York, had also been in Rome.

[2] 'The reference is most likely to Father John Bapst, s.j., who was tarred and feathered, by a nativist mob at Ellsworth, Maine, on October 14, 1854. However, the press report of his death was false, as he lived to serve a term as president of Boston College after this incident.' (Note by John Tracy Ellis in *American Essays for the Newman Centennial*, edited by J. K. Ryan and E. D. Benard, Washington 1947, p. 33.)

P.S.   I am sorry you should have occasion to notice errors in the American list of names.[1]

FRIDAY 12 JANUARY 1855   Lisle *Ryder* and Charles *de la Pasture* went to Dublin went at night ⟨mid day?⟩ to Dublin   got to Dublin at night?

TO LADY GEORGIANA FULLERTON

The Oratory Bm. Jan 12. 1855.

My dear Lady Georgiana

For many reasons it is difficult to write to you on a subject, as to which the Birmingham Congregation of the Oratory owes you and Mr Fullerton, and feels a great deal of gratitude.[2]

It is pleasant to acknowledge a benefit at all times but there are no persons whom it is more pleasant to us to consider as benefactors and to have in our thoughts than yourselves.

We are thinking what small memorial of the whole matter we can prevail on you to accept from the Oratory, trifling indeed in itself, but which may convey thanks and to be a pledge of prayers, better than ours, — I think we may say, St Philip's own; meanwhile we hope you will not be displeased if our nine Priests here say 3 masses apiece at once for your and Mr Fullerton's intentions

I am &c. J H N

TO FORTUNAT DE MONTÉZON, S.J.

L'Oratoire, Birmingham 12 Janv. 1855

Mon Révérend et Cher Père,

J'ai attendu pour répondre à votre excellente lettre jusqu'à mon retour ici, où je pensais recevoir l'ouvrage du célèbre Père de Ravignan, que vous m'avez été assez bon pour m'envoyer.[3] Mais hélas! ce que c'est que d'avoir un grand nom, et d'avoir écrit un livre qui intéresse les Catholiques! Un ami l'a retenu et le lit avec attention; et maintenant que je retourne à Dublin, je ne l'ai pas encore vu. J'en commencerai la

---

[1] Probably the list of contributors to the University.

[2] This was due for the arrangements Alexander Fullerton had made about Lady Olivia Acheson's legacies to the Oratory.

[3] It is not clear what work of de Ravignan was sent. Perhaps his *Clément XIII et Clément XIV*, Paris 1854.

lecture avec un grand plaisir, étant bien sûr d'y trouver à méditer et à m'instruire. Je serais bien heureux de vous revoir, et je regrette beaucoup de ne pouvoir pas parler français.

Je vous en prie, présentez mes profonds respects au Père de Ravignan, et croyez moi avec les sentiments les plus vifs de bienveillance De votre Révérence le fidèle serviteur en J.C.

John H. Newman de l'Oratoire

Le Rd Père de Montézon S.J.

TO ROBERT ORNSBY

Bm Jany 12. 1855

My dear Ornsby

I hope to start tonight (Friday) I have been detained by the mishaps of my cargo. Two have got the influenza, and one sticks in London having lost his baggage — and one is taking care of them.

You will have no one to examine except the two Ryders and Mr Charles de la Pasture (pronounced Delāpăture) — of whom two of them are extempore candidates viz Lisle Ryder of the University House, and Charles Delāpăture of my house. They are mazed as to what books to name.

Lisle R. will give Medea and some Satires of Juvenal.

Charles D. will give part of the Anabasis and any Latin you will.

Charles D's history seems fair, but I have not examined him in the classics.

Lisle R. ought to do well, but will be unequal   Harry Ryder, the elder of the two, takes up some Herodotus and Juvenal.

Ever Yrs au revoir John H Newman of the Oratory

P.S.   ⌜I have got your second Gazette and think it a *very good* number. I am amused at your getting into a scrape about the Tablet — I thought you would. But it will soon be all right.⌝[1]

[1] Ornsby inserted in the *Catholic University Gazette*, (4 Jan. 1855), an article from the *Tablet*, (23 Dec. 1854), on 'Education in Ireland,' and found himself obliged to explain in the next number of the *Gazette* on 11 Jan., p. 269: 'An article having appeared in a contemporary, commenting in severe terms on the publication of extracts from some other papers in the *Catholic University Gazette*, we beg to state that this journal has nothing to do with politics, and that in quoting paragraphs of news, or expressions of opinion on educational matters (to which its province is strictly limited), it does so simply as a matter of convenience, for the information of its readers . . .'

TO CARDINAL WISEMAN

Jany 12. 1854 [1855]

My dear Lord

I think it possible that your Eminence has powers which may enable our Birmingham Congregation to obtain from you a permission which we believe to be a mere matter of form.

We have lately had some property left us. It comes to us through a friend, who wishes a security lest the law should claim it back of him before a certain number of years run out by means of some technicality, which of course he does not foresee or think more than barely possible. He has asked us to call the money a sum raised as a mortgage on our Birmingham dwelling house — and to give him a *promise* that we will execute a mortgage, if he calls on us to do so; he on the other hand engaging to destroy our promise at the end of a certain number of years. We have given him this promise, fearing to lose the money from some unforeseen accident, and knowing we could recall it and restore the money, if authorities at Rome objected to the proceeding. We should have applied to your Eminence first, had you been in the country. Now we write to you instead, that our letter may meet you immediately on your return.

Our Treasurer, Father Flanagan, will wait on you in London at any time you please to appoint to explain the matter more fully. And at the same time he will take the opportunity of asking you several other questions.[1]

We have also read with great interest the proceedings at Rome, as you may suppose — and congratulating you on your return to [England] and kissing the sacred purple

I am &c J H N

SATURDAY 13 JANUARY 1855   *I went to Dublin?*

TO AMBROSE ST JOHN

6 Harcourt Street Jan 13/55

Charissime

Have just arrived and said Mass after a prosperous journey, and found every one here who should be.

[1] Wiseman replied on 8 March that no permission was required since no real alienation of property was intended.

The time went very quick and we got in by ¼ to 6. The time went quick because I had only one thought on my mind almost the whole time, unless I was asleep You little think that within me the same clearness which makes me see other's failings makes me see[1] my own, or at least, and rather, makes me see what people think about me or may think; and in consequence, not from any supernatural feeling, but naturally, I am most keenly troubled, when I feel I might have on any occasion done better. Sometimes I have for hours quite writhed with pain. My one thought through my journey has been 'Forgive the sin and remove the scandal.'[2]

Stick up the inclosed in the Congregation Room, and with love to all I am Ever Yrs affte

J H N[3]

MONDAY 15 JANUARY 1855   long frost, I believe, began   Lectures began

TO EDWARD CASWALL

Jan 16. 1855 6 Harcourt Street
My dear Edward

I am in a whirl of business, and do not do half I have to do. The three came safe last night — Ralph should not come till he is *strong* enough to bear the journey, and it is a question whether he should not sleep at Holyhead. The boxes are come — and cheaply. I have not yet time to unpack mine

I wish all the matters, which have to be decided on February 2 in General Congregation to be brought before it *in shape* by the Congregatio Deputata. The report of the three Fathers about Miss F's [Farrant] £200 — Fr William's report about Rednall — and any thing that Fr Stanislas, or any other Father has to work out for the Congregation should be discussed and resolved on at latest in the Congr. Deput. of the last Monday in January. Though not entered in the Register. I think it would be very good, if the Congr Deputata brought down to the General Congregation definite propositions *in writing*, for discussion.

[1] The bottom third of the page has been torn out after 'unless I' and supplied in St John's hand. The reference must be to Dalgairns's faults. See letter of 22 Jan. to him.
[2] On the verso, the bottom third of the page is missing at this point, and has not been supplied by St John.
[3] St John replied on 15 Jan., 'How shall I ever repay, dearest Father, all your care and anxiety for me and for us all.—I fear you had a poor night of it. In spite of self will I do say now and then to myself, the Father is always right in the long run.'

If we had done so before the last General meeting, instead of contenting ourselves with verbal resolutions it would have been better.

I think the *reading* in the morning should be very short, so that the doubting[1] might not keep us waiting, as it commonly does — I conceive breakfast need not last beyond a quarter of an hour or 20 minutes — so that after reading Scripture etc. there would hardly be time for 5 minutes *general* reading. It would be a great pity to lose time merely by the doubting. What would you say to the morning recreation (which will be closed when the clock strikes 10) being only of Fathers — the evening of Fathers and strangers — and the tea at a ¼ to eight of Fathers and brothers.

As to your book, as it has passed the Congr Deput. and has been revised by F. Bernard I can have no objection to the prefixing of your name. I will send it on; thank you for letting me look into it[2]

Ever Yrs affly J H N

TO THOMAS SCRATTON

6 Harcourt Street Jan 17/55

My dear Scratton,

Certainly if Ladies attend the Poetry Lectures, it ceases to be an academical meeting.[3] The mixed Lectures of last term were the sort of exception or anomaly, by way of advertisement, which is not uncommon. I do not object to Ladies being admitted to Mr Mc Carthy's lectures; but, if so, it is quite impossible that I can send young men with pencil and paper to take down notes. However, let it be so — the circumstance that the Lectures are paid for will be the excuse for making a distinction

Ever Yours John H Newman

T Scratton Esqr

[1] The questions proposed for discussion at the meal.
[2] *Hours at the Altar*, from the French of M. L'Abbé de la Bouillerie, edited by Edward Caswall, Dublin 1855.
[3] Scratton wrote on 16 Jan., 'Will ladies be admitted to McCarthy's lecture? He seems to think they ought to be and I am in some perplexity as I shall have shoals applying here.'

TO THOMAS SCRATTON

January 19/55

My dear Scratton

As to Jones, I must speak with you. I ought to see the *proof* of our Lecture List. I would not enter into any conversation with Mr Mooney.[1] Please stamp and post the letter to Mr Buckeridge which I send. Will you write to Mr Burke officially from me, a *very civil* letter, thanking him *from me* for his book, and saying that, as he wishes, I will place it in the University Library.

Will you be so good as to draw a cheque in favor of Mr Connelly for £12. 10 and send it to me here. It is in point of his Exhibition.[2] I send a receipt which belongs to you.

Ever Yrs J H Newman

TO EDWARD CASWALL

Sat. Jany 20 [1855]

(Private)

My dear Edward

I send you the inclosed before I answer it, as not knowing *when* Mr L's[3] time is up, and *how long time* he has had. I am very unwilling to give longer leave than a month — but, if you think it well, I don't mind proposing a fortnight more to the Congregation, lest we seem unkind. Let me have the letter back.

I have very much fear lest I should not be able to get to you by February 2. The difficulty is, the confessions I hear here on Saturday evening — You can easily understand how ticklish a thing it is to put young persons out of their regular habit of coming. Moreover, some may be coming for the first time to me, for of course there are those who are only now getting into the habit

Ever Yrs affly J H N

---

[1] This was a person Newman had never met and not the parish priest of St Audoen's.

[2] Patrick Connolly had been awarded a mathematical exhibition (minor scholarship) in Nov. 1854.

[3] Henry Lynch, who was a guest at the Birmingham Oratory.

TO WILLIAM NEVILLE

Sunday Jan 21/55

My dear Wm

Your letter is just come, and I hasten to answer it.[1]

We must first decide the *application* of our money.

There are five applications, perhaps more 1. — house and grounds — 2 furniture — 3 cemetery, 4 annual taxes etc. 5 maintenance.

We must make our money go as far as it can.

One application may imply another, as the cemetery (3) implies a fence round the grounds (1).

Some applications are *necessary*, as to taxes (4).

Some money has been given for one purpose, some for another — Mrs Hope does *not* give for the cemetery — I do not give for furniture.

1. As to the first application, I do not know it is at all necessary, except perhaps chimney pots, and so much fire as suffices to air the house. As to Hansom's wages, he gets a lodging for nothing — say £5 to £8 a year — *what* on the other hand does he do for us? Well, whatever it is, could we not allow him to farm the garden for it, i.e. give him the rent of the garden? At least this should go towards his wages. A house, a large garden and £31. 4 seem to me very great wages indeed.

The garden wall accidentally becomes necessary if we decide in favor of No 3 below.

2. Furniture — very little seems necessary at present — but if money has been given to us which we cannot otherwise apply, well and good — chimney pots will come under furniture.

3. The cemetery. I certainly do hold that it is absolutely necessary to remove the bodies and to have in consequence a cemetery by the summer i.e. by July 1. This, besides, was *the sole reason* why we have Rednall at all. I think we should not have accepted it except *with the object* for which it was offered. Furniture and carriage, chimney pots and meat and drink, vanish before this purpose.

4. annual taxes etc. These are necessary.

5 maintenance. It seems to me the Congregation should let out the rooms, and charge each Father for every 24 hours so much. The poney, I suppose, comes into the maintenance. £25 seems a great sum for him. As much as for a Christian

If it be said, that Mrs Hope gives maintenance, well and good, if she *does* give it. But she only gives a certain sum *towards* it — and it may be used to *bring down* the sum which the Fathers' maintenance cost —

---

[1] It concerned the expenses of Rednal.

but cannot liquidate it. Maintenance includes 1. taxes. 2. board. 3 servants. 4 coals. 5 lights. 6. poney. 7 chapel expences. that is, according to Fr Ambrose

(For our Fathers)

—	Taxes —	20. 0. 0
	Board say —	25. 0. 0
	servants (moiety)	15. 0. 0
	coals —	5. 0. 0
	lights —	– – –
	poney	25. 0. 0
	chapel expences	10. 0. 0
		100. 0. 0
Deduct Mrs Hope's		35. 0. 0
		65. 0. 0

cost for one Father through the year — 65. 0. 0

Therefore, (dividing by 52) per week 1. 5. 0

per 24 hours 3. 6 6/7

This is reckoning that a Father is always there. Accordingly, if a Father was there only every other day the congregation would lose 12/6 a week, (not taking into account its saving of his board.)

Since the board is put at £25 a year or 9/7 a week, half of which is 4/9, the real loss to the Congregation would be 12/6 − 4/9 = 7/9 a week or (say) £20 a year.

Ever Yrs affly J H N

I suggest this as a basis for the Congregation to decide upon:—

House Expences

Received			Pd	
Mrs Hope	35. 0. 0		For one Father every day in the year — (as above)	100. 0. 0
Payments of Fathers for lodging at Rednal (if so) — every other day	32. 10. 0			
half £65 saving of the Father's board every other day	12. 10. 0			
chance gifts through the year	20. 0. 0			
	100. 0. 0			

General Fund

Received			Paid		
From Congregation	63. 0. 0		Completing fence round our ground where wanted, open paling, dead thorns or any other way	40. 0. 0	
From Fathers	10. 0. 0				
	73. 0. 0		Trenching and planting laurels round cemetery	10. 0. 0	
			Moiety of servants —	16. 4. 0	
to be made up by chance gifts	5. 4. 0		cart and harness	12. 0. 0	
	78. 4. 0			78. 4. 0	

I confess I should like to know the uses of the cart, before buying it. If for carrying produce from the land, we ought to be sure, it pays to grow our own meat and drink.

Furniture

Received			Paid		
	£	S D			
From Mrs Hope for furniture	50. 0. 0		Carriage	12. 0. 0	
			Harness	8. 0. 0	
			Chimney Pots etc		

The only article of yours I have not included is 'Stable in town £5,' which some how I think the Edgbaston House should pay. All then you require, according to your letter, may be done with chance gifts of £20 + £5. 4. 0. This might be much better — I put it down as a basis

J H N

TO J. D. DALGAIRNS

6 Harcourt Street Jan 22. 1855

My dear Fr Bernard,

I think you had better finish St Ignatius etc than go to St Philip. If Mother Margaret only wants four days a year, I don't see why you should not give them to her.[1]

I spoke severely to you in the Congregation, because I thought you

---

[1] Dalgairns was acting as occasional confessor to Mother Margaret Hallahan's nuns. He was also engaged on a life of St Ignatius of Antioch.

gave evidence of that deep self conceit (for I know you wish me to speak plainly) which you sometimes show. It would have been better, if you had come *directly after* the meeting to me, and I would have explained it to you, instead of waiting till now.[1]

Thank you for what you say about Victor [Duke]. I will attend to it.

I have just received from Dr Cullen leave for reserving the Blessed Sacrament. He incloses the Bull of the Immaculate Conception. *The* point you were speaking to me about in connexion with Scotus is left open apparently. The words are 'Declaramus etc. doctrinam quae tenet, Beatissimam V.M. in primo instanti suae Conceptionis fuisse singulari omnipotentis Dei gratiâ et privilegio, *intuitu meritorum Christi Jesu Salvatoris humani generis*, ab omni originalis culpae labe praeservatam immunem, esse a Deo revelatam, atque idcirco ab omnibus fidelibus firmiter constanterque credendam.' Perhaps, however, the word *Salvatoris* decides it — is Salvator as strong as Redemptor? — It is remarkable that the Bull does not define the doctrine, but defines that it is *revealed*, and *therefore* of faith.

Yrs affly J H N

TO ARCHBISHOP CULLEN

6 Harcourt Street Jan 24/55

My dear Lord,

I was rejoiced to receive your letter with the leave to keep the Holy Sacrament in my private chapel. Thank you very much for your kindness and the trouble you have taken. I feel also very much the Holy Father's condescension and indulgence.

As soon as I received the letter before this last, at once I sent about a number of letters to collect materials for the Academia — I think I had better do nothing more till your Grace's return.[2]

As to my projected Church, I have not advanced further — and, various persons thinking that it would be better to take St Audoen's, I went to Mr Mooney P P [Parish Priest] and had a talk with him about the possibly of hiring the *use* of it at certain hours. He was willing — but I shall call on some other persons and get more information.

---

[1] Dalgairns's restless zeal was leading him to act as a censor and reformer. He replied, '. . . I am often conscious of the fault you mention. In the midst of so much to dishearten one, it is not encouraging to know that at the age of six and thirty, such a fault is still so little subdued as to be visible. However it is better that it should be out than in; and I beg of you to let me know whenever you perceive it.'

[2] See the letters Newman wrote on 30 Dec. 1854.

I had your copy of the important Bull put in type at once, and it is to be in the Gazette tomorrow.[1]

Soon I hope to be able to put your wish in execution of having lectures in the Medical Hall; indeed to take steps towards filling up some of the Chairs. I trust most earnestly that *politics* will not come into the University. If they do, it will be utterly against my wish. There are persons such as Mr John O'Hagan who (I have been *told*) once were called Young Irelanders — all I know is, that they are admirable persons now, and, I am sure, would show nothing of the spirit of which your Grace complains so justly. I may meet with others as far from any political spirit *now*, who *once* had the name — and if so, should they be eligible men, I do not see the harm of employing them — but I feel deeply that we shall be ruined, if we let *politics* in.[2]

This being my intense feeling, you may think how absurd the reports are of my having said any thing in favor of Mr Lucas against your Grace. Why, the notion of *my* coming to Ireland, and pretending to take the *part* of the Irish Church, and saying it was *betrayed*, would be coxcombical enough — but the truth is, whenever Mr Lucas's *facts* (if they are his, I mean *such* as his) have been named to me, I have never scrupled to say that, if he stated them, he was under a simple *delusion*. I know him and respect him highly — but I think he is simply mazed and wild, when he speaks of your Grace having done this or that, *if* (as people say) he says it. And, I suppose, he does say it, though the *Tablet* has been *silent*. Some things which have been reported, I have on my own knowledge, simply denied. I have said 'I know nothing of politics

---

[1] Cullen sent a copy of the Bull of Definition of the Immaculate Conception, and suggested that it should be inserted in the *Catholic University Gazette*.

[2] Cullen wrote on 12 Jan., 'I regret very much to be obliged to be absent so long from Dublin—but I believe it is necessary at the present moment to be here. You are aware of the active agitation got up against me by Mr Lucas, Duffy, and some priests. They were quite determined to make the world believe that I wish to sell the Irish Church, and the price is to be a charter for the University. They think I must be very easy in making a bargain. Well—we must suffer reproach with patience as our divine master has taught us by word and example. You will be surprised perhaps to learn that your authority is quoted to prove that I am really become a slave of the government, tho' in the deluge of lies that has been let loose in the country, nothing can surprise us. Of course I did not attach the least importance to vague rumours.

I trust you will make every exertion to keep the university free from Young Irelandism—of which the spirit is so evident in the Nation.' [i.e. the organ of the Young Irelanders.]

Cullen had already in his letter of 20 Dec. 1854 complained of the support Lucas was receiving from Dr Whitty and others in England, and remarked then, 'I know many of Lucas' adherents in Ireland are anxious to assail yourself—but I am confident that you will be supported by everyone that has the interests of religion at heart. For my part I heartily despise all this paltry political and provincial spirit.' See also letter of 30 Dec. to Ornsby.

— I know nothing of Ireland — but this I know, that so and so is an absolute mares nest and piece of fudge, and nothing else. And I have informally protested, that *you* have had nothing to do with politics either. It seems, the Pope had told Mr Lucas distinctly, that it was right to prefer a government which was *better* inclined to the Church to one that was less so — and this is all which I suppose is laid against your Grace, when the charge is coolly examined.[1]

We have not much news to tell the Holy Father about the University, except that things are getting more into shape weekly. Perhaps the less we have to say, the better — so that we are at work. The Inaugural Lectures last term had great success — the *courses* of Lectures now

---

[1] Newman's friendliness with Irish nationalists was a major cause of Cullen's alienation, as Newman explained in 'Memorandum about my connection with the Catholic University,'

'But a cause of offence to Dr. Cullen, far greater than my desire of a lay Finance Committee, was my countenance of those whom he considered young Irelanders, and generally nationalists—and to these he added a very different party, the friends of Lucas, up to the Archbishop of Tuam. I never of course would give up Lucas as a friend. I differed from him, but I thought him an honest good man—Dr. Cullen's treatment of him at Rome is too painful for me to talk of. As soon as the Archbishop thought I was on what may be called speaking terms with him, he grew cold towards me, then warned me against him, and I of course would not be warned.

But again there was a knot of men who in 1848 had been quasi rebels—they were clever men and had cooled down most of them. I did not care much for their political opinions—Dr. Moriarty introduced them to me, and I made them Professors. They are the ablest men who had belonged to the University—such as Professor O'Curry —and Professor Sullivan. I can never be sorry for asking their assistance—not to take them would have been preposterous—There you had good men, Irishmen, did Dr. Cullen wish Irish? had he not warned me against English and Scotch? If I did not take men made ready to my hand, desirable on their own accounts, desirable because their fellows were not to be found, I must put up, if not with English and Scotch, with incapable priests—is this what Dr. Cullen wanted?

He, however, seems to have been in a great alarm, what was coming next. I saw a great deal of Mr. Pigot, now dead, the Chief Baron's son—he talked like a republican —but he was full of views and a clever man. I had a thought of giving [him] a law Professorship—or I did. Dr. Cullen brought down with him to me, an excellent man the Archbishop of Halifax, Dr. Walsh?, to dissuade me by telling me things against Mr. Pigot. I have forgotten every word he said. It made no impression on me—I dared say he had said and done a number of wild things—he was a fanatic even then—but I did not see that therefore I should separate myself from him. But Dr. Cullen always compared young Ireland to young Italy—and with the most intense expression of words and countenance assured me they never came right—never—he knew them from his experience of Rome.

I cannot pursue these things at this distance of time—but the consequence was that Dr. Cullen became alienated from me, and from an early date either did not write to me, or, if ever he did, wrote by a secretary.' *A.W.* pp. 328–9.

The double tragedy of Lucas's death later in the year, and of Gavan Duffy's self-imposed exile in Australia, which brought the Tenant League to an end, dashed many Irish hopes, and had repercussions that were crippling for the Irish University. See also *McGrath*, pp. 230–1.

commenced have very few attendants besides University youths — and it is a question whether we shall go on with them after this term. I am speaking of the evening *display* lectures — the morning lectures are the Lectures of *business* — and they go on as well as I could wish. I have some very nice youths in my own house — 8 — One, alas, is away — Lord Ralph Kerr from indisposition — but I say, 'alas,' because his dear brother John at Ushaw seems dying — poor Lady Lothian, if this [is] to be the case.[1] He is given over — If he is taken, it will be because he is too good for the world. Poor Ralph (*my* pupil) is kept abed at Edgbaston, and cannot go to him. His uncle, Lord Henry, is with him. We shall be, I think, 37 in lecture this term — and we have above 60 names of youths on the books, come or coming. I am quite satisfied as far as we have gone. Dr Leahy is ill of the bronchitis at Sandy Cove. Fresh youths are continually applying — 3, I think in the last six days —

I am so low about poor Lady Lothian — If I can *say* any thing by way of contradicting the rumour you allude to, pray let me know.[2]

Begging your Grace's blessing, and the Holy Father's and kissing his feet I am, My dear Lord, Ever Yrs affly & faithfully in Xt

John H Newman

The Most Revd Dr Cullen.

TO JOHN LEAHY, COADJUTOR BISHOP OF DROMORE

6 Harcourt Street Dublin Jan. 24. 1855.

My dear Lord,

Mr Brennan called here today about an order for money sent from your Lordship to me, in behalf of the Catholic University and not acknowledged by me.[3]

I told him I knew nothing of it — and he went away. However, I have to make a deep apology both to him, and your Lordship especially.

For, since he has been here, I have found it. It came *in my absence*, and was safely lodged. It lay in a private place with other valuable papers. It was my own fault that you have had no acknowledgement of it. All I can say is, that, as the money matters are generally transacted by the Vice Rector, as the *Secretary* of the original Committee, I have not directed my thoughts that way.

[1] See letter of 27 Jan. to Lady Lothian, who, like Cullen, was in Rome at this time.
[2] i.e. the rumour that Newman had said Cullen was 'a slave of the government.' Cullen returned to Dublin in the middle of July but did not write to Newman in the interval. Cf. letter of 16 April to Manning.
[3] John Brennan was the Parish Priest at Warrenspoint in the diocese of Dromore.

Hoping you will kindly accept this explanation, and now acknowledging formally your order for £80. 15. 4, and availing myself with
great satisfaction of the opportunity of asking your Lordship's blessing,
I am, My dear Lord, Your faithful friend and Servt in Xt

                                        John H Newman of the Oratory

The Rt Revd Dr Leahy

P.S.   I have to thank your Lordship for your letter by Mr Hennessy.
It was a great gain to receive it from a person like yourself.

THURSDAY 25 JANUARY 1855   Wm Pusey called and dined

TO V. B. DILLON

                                                        Jan 25/55
Dear Sir
     I thank you for your letter just received and I will write to Mr
McDonough, telling him, it is your wish, that I should ask information
from him on the very acceptable news which you communicate to me[1]

                                        I am etc J H N

TO THOMAS SCRATTON

                              6 Harcourt Street Jany 25/55
My dear Scratton
     Will you help me to form a list of payments to University Officers?
     They seem to me the following:
Quarter from November 1 1854 to February 1. 1855

1 Rector .... $\frac{400}{4}$ ... 100

2 Vice Rector and Professors   ... $\frac{350}{4}$ ... 87 . 10

3 Professor Classics   ... $\frac{300}{4}$ ... 75

---

[1] Michael Dillon, curate at Tibohan, Frenchpark, Roscommon, to his uncle Michael
McDonogh, had just died and left his books to the Catholic University. A relative wrote
to inform Newman of this. Michael Dillon is perhaps the unknown priest to whom
Newman wrote on 9 Dec. 1854.

4 Lecturer Ancient History ... $\frac{200}{4}$ ... 50

5 *Acting* Professor Mathematics (Mr Penny) ... $\frac{300}{4}$ ... 75

6. Lecturer in Poetry ... $\frac{200}{4}$ ... 50

7 Lecturer in French ... $\frac{150}{4}$ ... 37 . 10

8 Lecturer in Italian⎫
9. Secretary   ⎬ ... $\frac{150}{4}$ ... 37 . 10

Penny was the de facto Professor last term and should be paid as such. He has nothing the next, for the *Hall* itself should pay him.

Mc Carthy I have considered to run from November, because the lectures he is now delivering must have taken him a good deal of time *before* delivery.

Signor Marani's emoluments must be considered. He said he got (I think) £2 a quarter from pupils — and besides he is giving lectures, which must have taken him time. He has had £20.

As to yourself, I should like the opinion of two or three persons. James O'Ferrall as one person is most satisfactory. What has Mr Bedford at All-hallows?[1]

Ever Yrs J H N.

TO AUBREY DE VERE

6 Harcourt Street Jan 25/55

My dear Mr de Vere,

I am very glad to get your letter, and to find that you do not extinguish my hope of getting your [sic] for the Lectureship on English Literature.[2]

[1] Scratton replied on 27 Jan., 'The Directors of all Hallows, of whom Bedford is one, are not allowed by their Rule to receive money for work done. They all have their board etc. and every expense paid . . .' Henry Bedford (1816–1905), a convert clergyman, spent nearly fifty years on the staff of All Hallows College.

[2] Newman wrote in his University Journal on 25 Jan., 'Thompson (without speaking to me) with Monsell's advice lately offered to Aubrey de Vere the Lectureship in English Literature, which he (T.) is obliged by bad health to relinquish—writing to me that he had done so. I wrote to De Vere in consequence—He writes this morning saying he could deliver some lectures in October ⟨Autumn⟩ Term, and then, or before then, could determine whether he could continue to hold the Lectureship and to discharge its duties, without abandoning other and long formed plans etc. I am writing to say that this will hardly be enough; that I wanted lectures after Easter—and that the Lectureship is an important one; and that a lecturer must throw himself into his work with zeal.'

It will be my object to get Lectures delivered next Term, i.e. after Easter — and Thompson's sad indisposition has been, as you may think, already an inconvenience to me. The importance of the chair has grown with the late Report of the Commissioners on the India Civil Service. They make the province of which it treats equal in weight, in their prospective examinations, to Latin and Greek together, and half as much again as mathematics.[1] And it was named to me as one of those departments to which I must attend in the first instance.

Of course I may fail every where in getting a lecturer on so short a notice — but I certainly must attempt to get one for next term.

I will not allow myself to anticipate that this necessity will interfere with the attainment of the object, which I have so long and sincerely aimed at, your connexion with us — It is plain from what I have said that the Lecturer in English Literature must throw himself into his work, and labour in it with zeal.

I am much vexed that you have not received the expression of my sincere and grateful acknowledgements for your volume and its dedication.[2] A letter of my own to you I fancy must have miscarried — if not, I sent you a formal message in a letter to Monsell or Thompson.

Forgive my apparent negligence — and believe me to be, My dear Mr de Vere   Sincerely Yours in Xt

John H Newman

Aubrey de Vere Esqr

TO J. D. DALGAIRNS

Jany 26/55

My dear Bernard

I have written an explanation this morning to Henry, which he can show you.

I have quoted to F. Ambrose Vincent of Lerins, who is stronger than the Pope — tho' a Pope is a Pope.[3]

[1] By the India Act of 1853 the Indian civil service was thrown open to competition. Commissioners were appointed, with Macaulay as Chairman, to make the new arrangements. In their *Report* they fixed the relative value of subjects in the qualifying examination by allotting 750 marks each to Latin and Greek, 1500 to English, and 1000 to Mathematics. The *Report* of the Commissioners was described in the *Catholic University Gazette*, (25 Jan. 1855), pp. 306–08, 'The Throwing open of Haileybury.'

[2] Aubrey de Vere's *Poems*, London 1855, was dedicated 'To the very Reverend John Henry Newman, D.D. Rector of the Catholic University of Ireland, etc. etc. . . . with the utmost respect and gratitude.'

[3] See letter of this day to St John.

The news has just come to me from Durham of dear Johnnie Kerr's death. Poor Lady Lothian and her daughters — poor Ralph.

I may tell the Fathers, *but no one else*, that the Pope WANTS to make me a Bishop. Develop the word 'wants.'[1]

I am aware about the Lisbon Oratory.[2] I found it out at Rome — but I doubt the possibility just now of gaining the privilege. It would require two sides, I mean the Bishop must be heard. And it is a great question. Endowments will in time destroy the difficulty.

Ever Yrs affly John H Newman

TO THE MARCHIONESS OF LOTHIAN

[26? January 1855].

I have heard that dear John has been thought too good for this world by Him who so lovingly brought him near Himself a year ago.[3] Ever since I heard of his illness I have been thinking of him. I saw him last year at Ushaw, and was so struck by him that I talked of him to others for some time after. He came into my room of his own accord, and made friends with me in an instant.[4] For him, how can I but rejoice that he should be taken out of this dark world in the freshness and bloom of his innocence and piety. But it comes over me most keenly that if once seeing him made me love him so much, what must it have been to you? And oh! how sad in a human light that you and his sisters should have been so far away — and poor Ralph in bed and unable to go to him![5]

[1] Newman learned this from Archbishop Dixon of Armagh. See letter of 27 Jan. to Ullathorne.

[2] Dalgairns wrote that the Lisbon Oratory had the right of having its members ordained 'titulo missionis et mensae communis,' i.e. without a patrimony having to be provided for them. Dalgairns wanted the Birmingham Oratory to obtain this privilege, 'Could we not represent as a reason the absence of our Superior, which certainly increases our difficulty of getting novices? Who would come to Birmingham except for you? I have heard it given as a reason for our never getting novices. Do we not deserve something from the Holy See, for having given you up at its bidding?' Nearly a hundred years later the privilege Dalgairns wanted was granted to all Oratorians.

[3] Lady Lothian's youngest son John, not yet fourteen, died at Ushaw College of pneumonia on 25 Jan. 1855, while his mother was in Rome. He had become a Catholic a year earlier.

[4] See letter of 3 June 1854 to St John.

[5] John's elder brother, Lord Ralph Kerr, was ill with pleurisy at the Birmingham Oratory.

TO AMBROSE ST JOHN

6 Harcourt Street Jany 26/55

My dear Ambrose,

I was sending a letter to you yesterday and who should come in but Wm Pusey. He stayed here about four hours, dined with us, and I think was a *little* scandalized at our 'luxury.' He had nothing to tell.[1]

I have been saying Mass two, not to say three, mornings for the 2 Kerrs; and am rejoiced and thankful to find that Lord John is somewhat better. I was expecting a telegraphic message all through one day with great dread, but happily none came.

The inclosed came today. When you are at home, you can open my letters and put them into an envelope, leaving them to Wm [William] to stamp and direct.

An Irish nun asks the prayers of the Confraternity for her brother in England who has apostatized.

Thank you for your kind zeal in sending me the Pope's words. I had the Bull from Dr Cullen, who wished me to put it in the Gazette. It is in, and I thought of anticipating the English papers, but forgot the Univers.[2]

You recollect the words of Vincentius Lirinensis, the author of the Quod semper etc? I don't mean to put the words of an individual of the 5th century against a Pope of the 19th, but they bear quoting.

Vincent Lirinens.   Commonitor. 29, 30

Imitetur animarum religio rationem corporum, quae, licet annorum processu numeros suos EVOLVANT et explicent, eadem tamen, quae erant permanent. Multum interest inter pueritiae *florem* et senectutis *maturitatem.* etc . . . ut, quamvis unius ejusdemque hominis status habitusque *mutetur,* una tamen nihilominus eademque natura, una eademque persona sit. Parva lactentium membra, *magna* juvenum; eadem ipsa sunt tamen;[3] et si qua illa sunt, quae aevi maturioris aetate *pariuntur,* jam in *seminis ratione* proserta [sunt], ut nihil novum postea proferantur [sic] in senibus, quod non in pueris jam antea LATITAVERIT. Unde non dubium est, hanc esse *legitimam* et rectam *proficiendi* regulam,

---

[1] William, the younger brother of E. B. Pusey, went up to Oriel in 1827 and was Vicar of Langley, Kent, from 1842 until his death forty-six years later.

[2] The Oratorians at Birmingham had seen in *L'Univers* the Bull defining the Immaculate Conception, which Newman had thought would appear first in England in the *Catholic University Gazette* of 25 Jan. St John and Dalgairns pointed out how the Bull supported Newman's theory on the development of doctrine, and St John remarked of Flanagan who did not follow Newman, 'Stanislas is fairly stumped by it.'

[3] Newman omits here the words 'quot parvulorum artus tot virorum.'

hunc ratum atque pulcherrimum CRESCENDI ordinem, si eas semper in *grandioribus* partes et formas numerus detegat aetatis, quas in parvulis creatoris sapientia praeformaverat. . . . Christianae religionis dogma sequatur has decet *profectuum* leges, ut annis scilicet consolidetur, DILATETUR tempore, sublimetur, aetate. . . . De incrementis triticeae institutionis, triticei quoque dogmatis frugem demetamus, et, cum aliquid ex illis *seminum primordiis* accessu temporis *evolvatur*, et nunc latetur et excolatur, nihil de germinis proprietate mutetur; addatur licet FORMA, species distinctio, eadem tamen cujusque generis natura permaneat. etc

Ever Yrs affly J H N

TO BISHOP ULLATHORNE

6 Harcourt Street, Dublin. Jany 27. 1855.

My dear Lord

It is more than a year ago that I had some conversation with your Lordship on the subject of music at Mass and Benediction — I mean at *Low* Mass. And you said you did not see any difficulty in *English* words being used at such a *Low* Mass.

I am not certain whether you gave your deliberate judgment, or spoke, as one may, in the course of conversation.

My reason for asking your view of the matter now, is this — I do not, if you please, wish it mentioned, but it is just possible, that, from mere want of funds, we may be obliged at the Oratory to give up High Mass. Year by year a debt comes on our books from the Music, which we have no means of meeting. Accordingly, I am looking about, without speaking to others, to see what we are to do, if we cannot continue our Choir. At the last moment indeed some assistance may turn up — still this is our present prospect. I want to know then, whether you would feel any difficulty in our accompanying a Low Mass with congregational singing, if we give up the High Mass. It may be possible, that you do not wish to give an opinion one way or the other. If so I should act according to the best of my own judgment, if I could be satisfied I was going counter to no wish of yours.[1]

---

[1] Ullathorne wrote on 2 Feb., 'In reply to your question, I think I ought to mention my impression that the Holy See has looked with dislike on the singing in the vulgar tongue at Mass in Germany. If I do not mistake, it is considered to have been one of the causes which led to that widely spread desire manifested during the last Pontificate in Germany to have the Mass in *lingua vulgari*. It was a handle to the Hermesians.' Then, after quoting three seventeenth-century Roman decrees on the

You will be kindly glad to hear, that the Archbishop of Armagh, who is just returned from Rome, has brought to me the kindest of messages, directly or indirectly, from the Pope — and I am convinced, (though I do not say the Archbishop said so,) that he would be showing me marks of his favor, did he not feel some anxiety as to the effect of it in Ireland.[1]

Begging your Lordship's blessing I am, My dear Lord, Yr faithful & affte Servt in Xt

John H Newman

The Rt Revd the Bp of Birmingham

TO CARDINAL WISEMAN

6 Harcourt Street Dublin Jan 28. 1855

My dear Lord Cardinal,

I have just been reading Fabiola, and, as your Eminence is just now returning, I cannot help sending you a line, which may be taken, if you are so kind, as a sort of greeting, to thank you for the instruction and interest which have attended my perusal of it.[2]

It is impossible, I think, for any one to read it, without finding himself more or less in the times of which it treats, and drawn in devotion to the great actors who have ennobled them.

I trust we shall have the Church of the Basilicas from the same pen — for I do not know any other which can do it. And from certain papers of yours in the Dublin, it is plain you have the matter so prepared that at any moment it may be carried to your fingers' ends and be poured out upon paper.

This requires no answer. I have nothing new to say of our work

use of vernacular hymns, Ullathorne added, 'I do not myself think that the Sacred Congregation or the Holy See would look with satisfaction upon the use of vernacular singing at the principle mass of a congregation. Though I may be wrong. In France, in country places, cantiques are certainly sung, at some of the Masses. But the Holy See has been always anxious to see France a little more attentive to its Congregational Decrees. . . .' Ullathorne thought that at Rome they would not like 'the Oratory to set the example of singing at the Principle [sic] Mass in the vernacular, even though it were a low Mass,' and suggested an unpaid choir. 'Could not a few persons be induced to sing for the love of God?'

[1] Ullathorne replied to this reference to Newman's intended bishopric, 'I cannot make out why certain prelates should have opposed the Pope's intentions already conveyed to yourself, or how it can help the University, or how it accords with so many precedents practised at Rome especially. I of course subscribe to the Pope's judgment, though I do not see through it. I suppose it is but a present delay.' Cf. *A.W.* p. 319.

[2] Wiseman's '*Fabiola; a Tale of the Catacombs*,' was published at the beginning of 1855.

here — We are going on very well — and I am quite satisfied — of course to do the work well, we must aim at inward improvement rather than any great external manifestations — To commence and fix traditions is our first object — and I am content to be employed on that

Kissing the purple, I am, My dear Lord Your Eminence's affte friend & Servt in Xt

John H Newman of the Oratory

The Cardinal Wiseman

TO GEORGE RYDER

6 Harcourt Street Dublin Jany 29/55

My dear Ryder

I hope you have good accounts of your boys from themselves — I inclose a receipt for Lisle's half pension.

As to their pocket money, Harry has already earned for himself £20 this year — which I think should do for journeys, clothes and books — his only expences during the academical year — so that you need not think of him.

As to Lisle, I cannot tell what will be enough, more than *you* can — but his extras are just those three, clothes, books, journeys. There is nothing at the moment which he can stand for, to bring him in any thing — but I trust there may be.

The twenty guineas, to which the inclosed relates, will carry him very near 20 weeks — that is, to about the 8th of June.

W Pusey called here the other day, sat and gossipped, and dined

Ever Yrs J H N

TUESDAY 30 JANUARY 1855   I stopped all the evening lectures about this time, on account of the frost.

TO JOHN HAMILTON, ARCHDEACON OF DUBLIN

6 Harcourt Street Jan 30. 1855

Copy

My dear Archdn Hamilton

A friend of mine has called on me to-day, and wishes to consult the Freeman between the years 1830 and this date. He says there is a copy among the late Archbishop's books.

I am sorry that the Bookcases, (for which I gave orders directly after your call before Christmas) are not finished nor the books in them. Would it be asking too much of you to let Mr Scratton the University Secretary carry away the box containing the Freeman to the Medical School in Cecilia Street, where our other books are in course of collection, and where my friend who called on me may have an opportunity of inspecting it.

Mr Scratton is the bearer of this.

I am &c J H N

TO LORD HENRY KERR

6 Harcourt Street Jany 30. 1855.

My dear Lord Henry

Your presence must have been a great comfort to dear Ralph [Kerr] and I hope you left him as consoled as we can expect.

Do you know I am seriously disappointed at Dr Evans' decision? And perhaps a little rebellious against it — on a ground, however, on which, though I have as good a right to an opinion as Dr Evans, I cannot of course venture to oppose your own should it be clear —

Everyone knows how miserable it is for an invalid to be sent away for his health where he will be solitary — several of our own party will speak to the distress, with which they have passed and exhausted their weary time at Hastings or St Leonards. If Ralph knows people well there, the case is altered — but come there, a small house, close when shut up, draughty and otherwise inconvenient, the chapel at a distance and nothing to do, remain as substantive miseries. And this when dear Ralph is depressed in mind.

I did not indeed suppose he would come to us at once — but I am anxious about his going into such banishment — at the same time, if I must speak, I should think he would be as well here as anywhere —

The snow is on the ground — but I never have been cold indoors. The climate is much milder than England — We have his friends here, who would keep him cheerful. He should read just as much as he wished and no more — He has Mass, he has the Blessed Sacrament in *the house*. Nothing need take him out of doors, unless he wished it. The Father[1] hears from home that it is bitterly cold at St Leonards.

However you will decide what is best — As I am going to Birming-

[1] The copyist has misread here. Newman must be referring to what Victor Duke heard from home.

ham in a few days for a purpose, I am glad to think I shall see him before his departure —

Very sincerely Yours in Xt   John H Newman of the Oratory.

The Lord Henry Kerr.

TO THOMAS SCRATTON

Jan 30 [1855]

My dear Scratton

I am not aware I have any need of gum or paste just now — and am curious to think who has told you I have.

Also I never gave any orders to the Porter about Jones, nor did it come into my head to do so. Your orders about his not leaving the University House seem very good.

I can't quite say at the moment what is to be done about Mr Bourke's £5. I want you to be so good as to go as soon as you can in a cab to Archdeacon Hamilton's, 111 Dorset Street, and ask leave to carry away with you, if it can be done, the package of Dr Murray's Library containing the Freeman.

Read and keep the copy of my letter to the Archdeacon which I send — and present the letter itself

Ever Yrs J H N

I send the Catalogue, which Mr Shaw has just brought.

TO ROBERT ORNSBY

⌜February 1855

Duffy write me word that 'there has been a great falling off in the circulation of the Gazette.' He incloses me the letter of one person of name, who says he 'has observed with much pain a departure from the system at first adopted etc' I find it costs £10 a number

J H N⌝

TO AMBROSE ST JOHN

Febr 1/55

My dear Ambrose

Please, let my room be ready *at once* — I don't know when I shall come — perhaps Friday night, perhaps Saturday — perhaps Sunday night — perhaps Saturday late

Ever Yrs affly J H N

FRIDAY 2 FEBRUARY 1855. said mass in *my* new chapel *in Harcourt Street* and got into it by this day

TO THOMAS SCRATTON (1)

6 Harcourt Street Febr 2/55

My dear Scratton,

1. You will see I have put an advertisement in the Paper to the effect that Lectures (*Evening*) will be discontinued till further notice *on account of the severity of the weather*. Will you therefore write to Mr Curry, Signor Marani and Ornsby to say so. I have written to Dr Leahy and Mr Mc Carthy, and spoken to Renouf.

2. I find you will have to pay *me* £33. 6. 8 *more* — my three months terminated on January 1. Therefore to bring me up to the others you must pay me January i.e. $\frac{£400}{12}$

3. Has Hodges and Smith's bill been paid — If not, I wish it paid at once; i.e. taking out (Maitland's two works and Wilberforce's) such as are *mine* personally.

4. As to Duffy's cheque, which you sent me yesterday, I do not wish it entered except as you have already entered it — because it is a loan in favor of the Gazette, which he assures me will be paid back — and thus will not appear in the accounts.

Ever Yrs J H N

TO THOMAS SCRATTON (II)

Febr 2 [1855]

My dear Scratton

There is no harm your having entered Duffy's draft in the book. All I wanted was that you should not put it under my head of account.

As it stands, I am bound to go to England at once for a day or two — but I am looking, perhaps with a vain hope, for being let off on account of the weather

Ever Yrs J H N

SATURDAY 3 FEBRUARY 1855   wind and snow hindering me going to England

TO PETER BRETHERTON

6, Harcourt St. Dublin. Feb. 3rd. 1855.

My dear Mr. Bretherton,

I have got my travelling Bag ready, and made all my preparations for leaving, and was going by the 1 o'clock Boat to-day; but, tho' it is not only a disappointment to me to change my mind, but a considerable inconvenience to undo my various arrangements here, with the prospect of having to make them over again at some future time, yet the weather appalls me, and I must beg you to gain me the Association's indulgent acquiescence in my postponing my Lecture.[1]

It is a little more than a year since I was confined to my room or bed for 3 weeks with a severe cold by having to go to Liverpool to deliver a Lecture, the journey being extended to Dublin and back without sufficient rest.

I have now had a cold on me for this fortnight, and since I wrote to you it threatened me with rheumatism.

It is now snowing thick, and the strong wind which has been blowing all through the night, is necessarily filling the cuttings of the railway with snow drifts. Did I set out, I might be detained at Holyhead, Chester or[2] might not be in a condition to lecture on Tuesday evening

All this being considered, sorely against my will, my judgment

[1] See diary for 6 Feb. Bretherton was the Vice-Chairman of the Birmingham Catholic Association.
[2] The page has been cut here for the sake of the signature on the verso.

determines me to stay here, and to ask the forgiveness of the Association for doing so.

Here we have stopped all the evening Lectures of the University, tho' they had been advertised, in consequence of the severity of the weather. It was the only thing that could be done,

Believe me, My dear Mr. Bretherton,

TO EDWARD CASWALL (I)

6 Harcourt Street Dublin Feby 3. 1855

My dear Fr Edward[1]

It is now snowing thickly and has through the night, and a strong wind is drifting it.

I have packed up and made all my preparations, and was going by the 1 o'clock boat today — but at length I think I must get you to represent to the Association[2] my hope that they will allow me to postpone my lecture, which was fixed for Tuesday.

We have postponed by Advertisement all our evening Lectures at the University — it was the only thing, which could be done.

Did I set off, the chance is I should be stopped at Holyhead, Chester, or some other intermediate point by snow-drifts — and thus lose my time, and be absent from this place for nothing. Or the train might be stopped between station and station. And when I got to Birmingham what with my cold, and its increase in consequence of fatigue and the weather, I might not be able to lecture after all. Last year I was three weeks in my room and in bed at Birmingham[3] in consequence of fatigue and cold in a forced journey I made to Dublin, lecturing at Liverpool in my way. So I fear I have a precedent to recur to. And I could not afford to lose three weeks now

On the whole then I must ask

My dear Fr Edward

As perhaps my letter to Mr B will be shown about or read, I think I must write a more formal one. So send you this for yourself and the Congregation by way of notifying my stopping him

Ever Yrs affly J H N

[1] Newman began this as a letter to Bretherton, first beginning it 'My dear Mr Bretherton.' See the last paragraph.

[2] Newman added later in pencil ⟨Catholic of Bm?⟩

[3] Newman later underlined 'Birmingham' in pencil, and wrote above it '(when I got there).'

P.S. I will write you a second letter, if I possibly can before eleven A M today. If you do not get it with this, you will get it on Monday *evening* — So postpone (in that case) the end of the Congregatio Generalis till *Tuesday*.

TO EDWARD CASWALL (II)

6 Harcourt Street Febry 3. 1855

My dear Edward

Though this does not go till 5 today, I think you will get it on Monday *morning* — and I shall be considerably disappointed, if you did not get the letter I sent just now by Sunday morning, and Mr Bretherton his — for I would not have committed myself now to not coming, unless I thought I had delayed to the last moment, which will not be the case, if it makes no difference whether I send this morning or tomorrow

I am altogether put out by being kept from going — because, to say nothing else, the prospect of a journey keeps me unsettled — I wished to have got it over, and had put off various things till over the time of my return — but, for the reasons I gave you in my letter just now, there is no help for it.

I could have wished Mr Bretherton had anticipated me, by telling me that the Association had put off its meeting, as we have put off *our* evening public lectures in the University House.

I wish to recommend to the Congregation your re-appointment as Rector up to the period of my return, which will be, I suppose, before Easter, since I do not come now. The entry in the Register (keeping the forms we used before) might be, 'the Father having been hindered by the weather from being present at this Congregation, wishes to continue Fr E.C. till his return etc' I am not certain however, if your *particular appointment* was inserted in the *Register*.

As to the Music, which now must be settled without me, I wish to propose something of this kind to the Congregation. I am not certain that a decree will be necessary, except so far as the *money* comes into question.

It is quite plain, we are not in circumstances just now to have high mass and Vespers as public Services — for no one will come to hear voices without instruments — unless they are superlatively good. Whatever then is done as regards Mass and Vespers, will be an Oratory matter, not a people's matter.

The question is what public service will take the place of High Mass.

I propose, a Low Mass with congregational singing. Perhaps we might be even allowed to sing vernacular, as in Germany — but, whether or not there are various Latin Hymns etc which we could manage — Ave Maris Stella, Salve Regina, and other Antiphons etc. to our Lady — Tota pulchra es etc. the Litany of Loretto — other Litanies — the Lauda Sion — Tantum ergo — Ave verum etc etc. These would require only the same sort of practice which our English Hymns require, which is next to none. One or two Psalms, Quàm dilecta etc. might also be learned.

As to expence, if a singer can get more elsewhere, of course he will do so. Else, it would hardly be more than his being at the service, at which he *otherwise* would be. One would require one or two persons, *simply* to take the place of Frederic — Francis perhaps might go off to some other choir — but if he did not, he ought not to ask much, if *he does it at all*. I think we ought to get a Frederic £10 a year — Tom Ford and Br Wm [William] would assist him, perhaps others. The expence would then be Organist, Organ, and one leader — to which I should add Emma Webb — to whom we might give a £1 a quarter, without telling any one. This would stand

Organ	10?
Organist	25?
Singer	10?
Emma Webb	4?
	49

In this calculation, I consider, that, Jewsbury doing work *in the house*, the Congregation takes a portion of his pay on itself.

Now the Offertory could spare at least £30 towards it.

Sacristy	120?
Missioners	50 at most
Music	30
	200

All this is on the supposition of no Father finding he can take up the music, and make himself responsible for it.

I am not strong about the plan I have proposed, if any one will think of any other. All I feel is that the *Congregation* should not commit itself to more than it can reasonably expect to discharge.

I think that Fr Frederic's maintenance of the choir for a month or 6 weeks since Christmas should be put down and read among the benefactions of the year (on next Purification)

Then as to the *Oratory* services, if we chose to have mass and vespers as private services, by way of keeping the rule, we should have as voices Frs Frederic, Stanislas, Nicholas, Robert, and your own, any of whom might be cantors — and besides Fr Ambrose and myself to sing High Mass.

Ever Yrs affly J H N

If it *can* snow cats and dogs, it is doing so now. It was simply impossible to come to you — Ornsby tells me that the sea was frightful at Kingstown. And I am just now susceptible of rheumatism and hoarseness in an unusual degree. But I am very much vexed at it.

SUNDAY 4 FEBRUARY 1855   at night went to England

TO LORD HENRY KERR

6 Harcourt Street Dublin. Feby 4. 1855.

My dear Lord Henry,

I am very glad Ralph is to be in London or at Rome.

As to St Leonard's it so happens we have had a good deal of sending people of our own there. There is an excellent physician, Dr Duke, of whom only just now poor Mr Monsell was speaking in the highest terms — but we have had three Fathers and one lay brother there at different times, (to say nothing of Fr St John who happens to have private friends there) and we know how dismal they found the place, in spite of Dr Duke's kindness. I have myself too been three weeks alone in a convalescence in a sea place — and know what support it requires —

Yours very sincerely in Xt   John H Newman of the Oratory

The Lord Henry Kerr.

P.S.   I am anxious to hear you speak so seriously of Ralph's health —

MONDAY 5 FEBRUARY 1855   got to Bm [Birmingham]

TO F. W. FABER

The Oratory Birmingham 5 Febr 1855[1]

My dear Fr Wilfrid

I am exceedingly concerned at your news — They say *here* that Antony's throat is affected — but I am glad to find you give the true

---

[1] The date, added later in pencil, is confirmed by the postmark.

account of it. Even his absence is a severe loss, but it is pleasant to be able to trust that he will be soon restored to you. Give him my love, and say I will not forget him.[1]

I reciprocate your congratulations on the Purification. St Philip has done great things for us in seven years. I was going to give a lecture tomorrow in the Bishop's House on 'The English Constitution' — but hearing they have invited Mr Scholefield M.P. I have been obliged at the last minute to change my subject for a less ambitious one

Ever Yrs affly J H N

TUESDAY 6 FEBRUARY 1855 gave Lecture on the Three Patriarchs[2] at the Bishop's House St Chad's

THURSDAY 8 FEBRUARY snow and wind hindering my return

SATURDAY 10 FEBRUARY set off at night for Ireland

SUNDAY 11 FEBRUARY got to Dublin early

TO F. W. FABER

6 Harcourt Street Dublin Febr 11. 1855

My dear Fr Wilfrid

Perhaps Antony has set off. If not, I am thinking whether he could [do] any thing, if he goes to Rome, about the Office for the Heart of St Philip.[3] Perhaps he could get Naples, or Florence, or Turin to join with us in a petition.

The reason I mention it just now, is this: since my Bishoprick is blocked against the Holy Father's wish, it may be a moment when he may be disposed to do me some favor. He has already in the most condescending manner written me leave of absence from Bm [Birmingham] for three years — and I should not be sorry if St Philip gained an (accidental) glory, instead of me, if I can compare the two.

Fr Neville may be going to Town for a few hours, and I will instruct him to bring up several copies of the Service, *provided* Antony is not gone yet.

Ever Yrs affly John H Newman of the Oratory

[1] Hutchison was going to Italy for his health.
[2] Newman lectured to the Birmingham Catholic Association on 'The Three Patriarchs of Christian History, St Benedict, St Dominic, and St Ignatius.' Some of Newman's notes on this subject have been preserved. See also *H.S.* II, pp. 365–70.
[3] See letter of 19 March 1851 to Stanton, and those of 30 March 1851 and 28 March 1853 to Faber.

P.S.   John [Bowden], I believe, is away, at the Isle of Wight. I suppose
the things are locked up; else, I should very much wish Father Neville
to bring down to Bm with him the following articles.

1. Mrs Bowden's chain to the Cross.
2. Hope's ring.
3. Mrs Bowden's Rochet.
4. The Three Mitres to which I wish added
5. the razor case of mine which John has

Will you tell some one to write a line to Fr Neville to say whether the
things are to be got at, *and whether Antony is gone abroad.*

TO JOHN STANISLAS FLANAGAN

6 Harcourt Street. Febr 11/55

My dear Stanislas,

Do you think you could take Ralph [Kerr] to Town when he goes,
since you said you wanted a day there?

On the other hand, I wanted *William* to go with him, if the said Wm
could do for me a service, which may not be in his power. John Bowden
has various properties of mine, which I wish brought to Bm [Birming-
ham] and I thought Wm might bring them back with him; viz

1. Mrs Bowden's chain
2. Hope Scott's ring.
3 Mrs Bowdens rochet
4 three mitres

and 5 a razor case which was to have gone out to Naples.

John Bowden is in the Isle of Wight — and perhaps the things
cannot be got at. I have written to Fr Faber to let William know. If he
cannot bring them down, I don't wish him to go. If he goes, I will pay
for his journey; but if you go, the House must pay it, both because the
Cardinal is House business,[1] and because Ralph falls to the House.

I had a famous journey — the passage only 4 hours — the cabin
crowded with the passengers of three days; the boats did not go on Friday,
I am told. No news here, except that I have got into a scrape by the
Editor's omitting Mr Mc Carthy's name in the last Gazette, as among
those who gave inaugural Lectures last term. He writes to me seriously

---

[1] Flanagan was to consult Wiseman about the arrangements in connection with
Lady Olivia Acheson's legacy. Cf. letter of 12 Jan. 1855 to Wiseman.

to complain. Lisle is as bad or worse than ever. I can't think what is to be done[1]

Ever Yrs affly J H N

P.S.   In the pigeon-hole *immediately under* (I think) the Deeds in my closet, is a paper bundle containing some copies in slips of our office for the heart of St Philip. If Fr Faber writes to say that *Antony can take them with him*, will you send up by William or yourself take, or send by post, *three* copies — not else.

TO PATRICK KENNEDY

6 Harcourt Street Febr 12. 1855

Sir,

I feel much obliged by your courtesy in sending me the copy of Mr Whitney's work, and beg to thank both you and him for the very kind expressions towards myself with which you accompany the present.

Both your publication and your letter are acceptable to me, and I am sure to read the former with as much pleasure as I have read the latter[2]

Very faithfully Yours John H Newman of the Oratory

Mr Kennedy

TO J. B. MORRIS

6 Harcourt Street Dublin Febr 13/55

My dear Morris

Thank you for your inclosure, which I return. I am truly glad of any news you tell me showing a return to better sentiments on the part of one who has gone so fearfully astray.[3]

As to dear William Froude, I think we must pray for him. Is Bastard gone abroad this winter? and are you snowed up, as we have been here?

[1] Lisle Ryder's habit of staying in bed in the morning was causing anxiety to his father and friends. See letter of 24 Feb. to Ryder.

[2] Patrick Kennedy, a Dublin bookseller, published a collection of folk-tales, *Legends of Mount Leinster*, 1855, under the pseudonym of Harry Whitney.

In 1856 Newman selected a fairy tale from this work as the subject for the English verse prize in the University.

Kennedy, evidently pleased at this academic recognition from the patron of O'Curry, sent Newman copies of his later works, *Evenings in the Duffrey*, 1869, and *Fireside Stories of Ireland*, 1870.

[3] The next name mentioned suggests that the reference is to James Anthony Froude.

Allies is at Number 10, John Street, Adelphi; so that you are as able to send him my compliments, as I yours. Renouf is out of the way just now — but will be glad to hear tidings of you.

Sir John Acton was one of the first to put his name on the books. I thank you for yours.

Report is, that you are to lose your Bishop — also that Dr Clifford is going to Rome to take some one's place — I hope his health is fair[1]

Ever Yours affectly in Xt   John H Newman of the Oratory

The Very Revd J. B. Canon Morris

TO EDWARD CASWALL

6 Harcourt Street Febr 16/55

My dear Edward,

Will you represent next Monday to the Congregatio Deputata that, under the Decree of General Congregation of February 13, which you send me,[2] I wish to recommend to the Congregation yourself, Fr Edward Caswall, to represent me in my absence up to St Philip's Day next.

I wish, though I cannot wonder it should be impracticable, that the quasi members of the Orat. Parvum, having failed in Green's Village, should think of Smethwick.[3]

Tell Stanislas (and the Congregation) that as his paper stands, there seems some confusion between the Holy See's 'failing to confirm' or 'confirming' and 'beneplacet.' Till the words 'notwithstanding' it is assumed that the H.S's confirmation or interference is *not* necessary

The order seems to be[4]

I can't do it — and am writing against time — so I must keep S's [Stanislas] paper.

As to the new school room and Nowel's estimate, I would have you keep quite close to the Decree about it of February 2nd, 7 and 8.

---

[1] George Errington, Bishop of Plymouth, was about to become Wiseman's Co-adjutor with the right of succession at Westminster. William Clifford lived with Errington at Plymouth, while Morris was the priest at Yealmpton.

[2] This empowered Newman until 2 Feb. 1856 to appoint a representative in his absence.

[3] Caswall was seeking a sphere for the charitable work of the men who belonged to the Oratorian confraternity. The priest at the neighbouring St Peter's did not want their help in Green's Village, a court near New Street Station, Birmingham.

[4] Newman tried to set out the question about the purely nominal mortgage in connection with Lady O. Acheson's legacy, for explanation to Wiseman, and then cancelled his attempt.

It is curious the Pope should have interfered about Oxford. I almost think I have seen it before.[1]

I am glad Ralph [Kerr] has at length gone — the change will do him good — and he will see his brother the sailor.[2]

I was surprised that Monsell resigned, seeing he was in *possession* — though when he was out and possession the other way, 2 years ago, I was sorry he went in. But the Morning Post says he has *not* resigned[3]

Ever Yrs affly J H N

TO J. D. DALGAIRNS

6 Harcourt Street Febry 17. 1855

My dear Fr Bernard

Fr Austin is kind enough to undertake to do something towards forwarding the Catalogue of the Library — and, to begin properly, I should wish him to know what has really been done by the *novices*, which you alone can tell. So I wish you would be so good as to tell him.

Edward had some notion of his beginning a catalogue according to the *position* of the books, but that is not what I wanted of him, but an *alphabetical* catalogue, which will do for *use*.

Please tell him I do not want him to put himself out of the way — but only to give to it such hours as he has vacant.

Victor is getting on in mathematics

Yrs affectly J H N

P.S. Since writing this, your letter has come. I shall say 'No' distinctly to the Cathedral request about you, if it comes. Thank Mrs Hope for her book just come.[4]

[1] Caswall had quoted to Newman on 13 Feb. from the Bull *Immensa aeterni Dei* establishing the Roman Congregations, issued by Sixtus V in 1588. The Pope claimed to protect Oxford as well as other Universities: '. . . nec ipsam Oxoniensem, quantum in nobis est, deserentes, sed ex intimo animi affectu ad matris gremium et ad viam salutis revocantes; omnesque intimo cordis affectu prosequentes, ac sub nostra et B Petri Apostolorum Principis protectione iterum suscipientes . . .'

[2] This was Lord Walter Kerr. He was said to be convinced he ought to become a Catholic, and his brother Ralph persuaded Darnell to accompany him to London in order to meet him. Lord Walter was received into the Church after a visit to his mother at Ryde in the Isle of Wight in May.

[3] Monsell, who had become Clerk of the Ordnance in 1852, wrote to tell Flanagan that he had resigned, because he did not think it 'decent or proper to hold office under the Premiership of such a man as Lord P— [Palmerston].' The *Morning Post* was right; and Monsell remained in office until 1857. Cf. Newman's Memorandum at the end of Dec. 1852.

[4] *The Acts of the Early Martyrs*, London 1855. Anne Hope (1809–87), widow of James Hope physician to St George's Hospital, became a Catholic in 1845. This was

TO AMBROSE ST JOHN

6 Harcourt Street Febry 17/55

My dearest Ambrose,

It is not likely you will soon go on your expedition to St Leonard's and Paris, but when you do, you had better hint privately to Dr Duke the state of *Frank*. You must not speak *from* me, or F. will be hurt, but you must say that you have *gathered* from me. Mind this. He fancies, and IS SURE, his head is growing continually smaller, and will not bear reasoning. I asked him if any one else had observed it, because *others* see more of his head, than he does himself, but it is almost a point of faith with him. He spoke to me about a month ago — and then wished to see a Doctor. He came again two days ago, insisting on the same uncomfortable symptom, his head — at length I advised him to go to Dr Corrigan. He returned from him disappointed. In fact I suppose he expected Dr C. to have cut off, or open, his head — whereas he only gave him pills of hyocyamios.[1] This medicine is significant. I think he wished to have a surgeon, who perhaps could scalp him.

You *must not* tell his father about HIS HEAD — but generally, that I think him nervous and imaginative.

Poor Lisle is going on very ill. For two days I am trying to see Penny about him. Scratton has heard, and is interfering, and, being of the Channel-Fleet school,[2] is going instanter to cure him — and only asks two days for him at Kingstown with him. The only fault we have to find, but it is a sufficient, is, that he will not get up in the morning.

I fear this weather tries your chest a good deal — but I am afraid to say so, since you will not believe I think about you. Why did you go away so abruptly at last, merely because I had to say something to Stanislas relating to a Confession?

Ever Yrs affly J H N

P.S.   Are the Corporals and Palls blest, which Mrs Wootten has so kindly given us, ask William.

2 P.S.   Since writing the above, your letter has come. I think the list[3] very good, and return it.

the first of a number of works on Church history that she published. She was a friend of the Oratorians, especially of Dalgairns.

[1] i.e. Henbane, which was used as a sedative.

[2] The British Baltic fleet after cruising about ineffectually for months, had returned home and the sailors were paid off. The Channel Fleet school was represented by the sailor who exclaimed in a letter to *The Times*, (15 Feb. 1855), 'Only give us heads to command, and someone who will lead us into the thick of it, leaving us to fight our own way out . . .'   [3] Of Lenten Services.

J.H.N.—2 C   383

TO THOMAS SCRATTON

Saturday [17 February 1855]

My dear Scratton

I suppose I did not understand you when you spoke to me about the receipt form; certainly I very much object to it, now I have seen it — and wish it not to be struck off. It is as great an inconvenience to me, as it can be to any one, that people will send me money which ought to go to others; but it would make matters worse, were I to sanction it as regular by printing or engraving a form.[1]

Should Dr Leahy give you written leave to receive sums I should have of course nothing to say — but in that case you must sign yourself 'assistant to Dr Leahy for the Committee appointed by the Synod of Thurles' or the like, not 'For the Catholic University, T.S. Secretary.'

I shall be very seriously distressed at any act which directly or indirectly implies that the Secretary to the University has any thing whatever to do with the subscriptions or the Fund

Ever Yrs John H Newman

T Scratton Esq

SUNDAY 18 FEBRUARY 1855 began reserving the Blessed Sacrament in the Tabernacle in the New Chapel

TO JAMES HOPE-SCOTT

⌐6 Harcourt Street. February 18. 1855.

. . . Here comes a question, on which I wish to ask your opinion legally, academically, and in any way you can give it. (e.g. how the thing will look) Can the said Oxford, Cambridge, Dublin (Examiners) were [sic] their M A gowns?[2]

While I am about it, I must ask you a second question. Where shall I place the Bishops? in a sort of Ambassadors' box or bench? or in line behind and above the Rector? In a procession, I suppose the Bishops

---

[1] Scratton had already had a plate engraved for printing receipt forms. See letters of 19 and 28 Feb. to him.

[2] Hope-Scott replied on 24 Feb. that there was nothing to prevent M.A.'s of the English Universities from wearing their gowns, even though they had become Catholics, unless they had been degraded.

would go in the higher place, but at Oxford they were in the lower place. What is done abroad? Of course I can write to Louvain.[1]

This is the more important, now that there seems to be, in *consequence* of certain Irish Bishops, a hitch in my consecration.

Lady Henry [Kerr] gave me yesterday a very pleasant account of you, Mrs Hope Scott, and M M.[2]

TO THOMAS SCRATTON

Febr 19/55

My dear Scratton

I don't mind your using the plate altered *as I now send it back*

As to Mr Errington's request, I will send it at once to Dr Leahy, or you can take it to him — but I should not like to do so merely of my own authority.

If he is going to Kingstown, *he* could tell Dr Leahy that at first sight I have no objection

Ever Yrs J H N

How is the library getting on?

WEDNESDAY 21 FEBRUARY 1855   Ash Wednesday.   Ashed the youths etc.[3]

TO WILLIAM NEVILLE

6 Harcourt Street Febry 21/55

My dear William,

I am sorry to hear of your cold, but what wonderful weather it is. Our Chapel is very cold, but I began reserving the Blessed Sacrament

[1] 'Your second question is more difficult and English precedents will not meet it. In Oxford and Cambridge the Chancellor and, as his representative, the V.C. [Vice-Chancellor] is *Ordinary*—i.e has Episcopal jurisdiction over members of the University, and *within the University* is entitled to the place of Bishop thereof. I think you had better write to Louvain. I have always dreaded the desire of show likely to occur —but so long as you adhere to strictly ecclesiastical forms I think you may do well.'

[2] Mary Monica, Hope-Scott's daughter.

[3] Newman's essay on 'University Preaching,' *Idea*, pp. 405–27 was first published in the *Catholic University Gazette*, (8 March 1855), pp. 394–400, see also 5 April 1855, pp. 416–19, as a letter addressed to David Moriarty, Coadjutor Bishop of Kerry, and dated 21 Feb. When Newman included it in *Lectures and Essays on University Subjects*, London 1859, pp. 187–220, he made some alterations. This revised version is that reproduced in *Idea*.

with Quinquagesima. The Chapel is now quite finished, and looks so nice, that I shall not hesitate to apply part of your money to the inside decorations, and tell every one that they are your present.

The inclosed direction of a friend of mine[1] will explain why the letter it conveyed came to me four days after date. Which was the cleverer, you or the post-person in London.

I have no news.

Ever Yours affly J H N

Will you send my Catholic Standard of last Saturday?

TO HENRY WILBERFORCE

Harcourt Street Dublin. Febry 21/55

My dearest Henry

I have just heard from dear Ralph Kerr, whom the doctors pronounce not well enough to come to me yet. The consequence is, ⌐I have a room disengaged, and I offer it at once to Arthur.

As you know, I have been seriously anxious how I should find room for him; so, I write to you at once.[2]

You must not think me sharp in my practice, if I look out for some one else, if he cannot come.⌐ The truth is, since I am calculating on laying out £300 a year of my own on my establishment, I cannot afford to lose *more* — and it has already been a trouble to me that Ralph has been neither coming nor not coming. This post has decided it.

⌐I have liked your Paper,[3] as far as I have seen it —⌐ but, please, *give directions for its being sent to me at No 6 Harcourt Street, Dublin —* else, I am not sure of it. ⌐Serjeant O'Brien wished you to know that he had succeeded in getting various copies taken in⌐

Ever Yrs affly J H N.

TO MRS JOHN MOZLEY

6 Harcourt Street Dublin Feb 22. 1855

My dear Jemima,

Your kind letter came here today, and I thank you for it.

Certainly the weather is portentous — snowing thick this morning!

---

[1] i.e. Neville himself. See letter of 13 March to him.
[2] Arthur Wilberforce remained at Ushaw. See first letter of 27 Feb. to Wilberforce.
[3] i.e. the *Catholic Standard*.

I am thankful to say that on the whole I have escaped cold. In the worst part of this weather, the fierce wind drifting the snow into the cuttings of the rails, and simply stopping the packet boats, I had to go to Birmingham and back, and got both ways with a calm sea, a quick passage, and no suffering from cold. What a great thing the Magnetic Telegraph is! it makes its way, though trains and boats cannot — and enabled me to communicate from hence to Bm [Birmingham] and from Bm back again, when I had to delay going till a fine day came. Yet I was there and back, and kept my appointment there, which was a fixed day, within the week.

I got my letter back again safely, thank you.

In the neighbourhood of Sligo the sea is frozen. The lakes in the Shannon, 7 miles across, are frozen over — and they say that it is still worse, if that can be, at Cork. If the cold takes this South West direction, perhaps the Crimea will escape, and our poor people there.

From the first I have looked at this war with horror — and have been saying several times a day a prayer for those who are dying or who are dead in it. A war with Russia is the most terrible of wars — and I have felt, since the time he spoke it, on introducing his precious new Reform Bill this time year, as if I could never forgive Lord John Russell for calling it a *little* war.[1] We should have had no war, if the Duke and Sir Robert [Peel] had lived.

Maria Giberne is in Lodgings in Rome somewhere — but a letter directed to 'Palazzo Borghese' would find her

Ever Yours affectly John H Newman

TO AMBROSE ST JOHN

⌐Febr. 22 (1855⟨?⟩)

Charissime,

I shall say a Mass every week for you, till you are in a better humour — it shall be Fridays — so, it is your interest to remain as you are, as long as you can

Thank you for your congratulations.

Ever Yours most affectly⌐

---

[1] On 13 Feb. 1854. See second note to letter of 26 Dec. 1854 to Mrs William Froude.

TO RICHARD STANTON

6 Harcourt Street Dublin Febr 22. 1855

My dearest Richard

I have sent back the lists with notes made as correctly as I can without having the books by me.[1]

Thank you very much for your congratulations. I am now getting into what they call the vale of years, and can't believe it.

I am not over worked now and have so many blessings. I don't know how to enumerate them. You know I have a Chapel with the Blessed Sacrament here.

I am quite sure of the truth of what you say, that favors, such as the Bishoprick, require to be pressed — and I have long thought it.[2] But, as I never thought of such a thing as it, I am not likely to go out of my way to lift a little finger in order to get it — and this, not I trust from any want of respect to it or the honor of it, but because I feel myself much happier or more independent without it. That it would do me good *here*, I feel clearly — indeed, else, why should it have been objected to? But I do trust I am not to remain in this banishment for ever — and of course a Bishoprick would have put a difficulty in the way of my departure.

I have no news. I am very anxious about your Father.[3]

Ever Yrs affly J H N

FRIDAY 23 FEBRUARY 1855   long frost of six weeks went

TO ARCHBISHOP CULLEN

6 Harcourt Str Dublin Febr 23. 1855

My dear Lord,

As they say there is no chance of your coming home before Easter, I write again. I am seriously concerned that you should be at last, if

[1] Stanton wrote on 21 Feb. that, not having much space for books in his room, he wanted 'to get rid of all Puseyite works except yours.' He sent a list of *Tracts for the Times* and other pamphlets for Newman to mark those of which he was the author.

[2] Stanton wrote, 'I was somewhat disappointed about the bishopric, particularly fearing lest it might be injurious to your influence in Ireland. . . . It is however, I am sure, always expected that favours of this kind should be solicited or pressed when half promised by influential friends.'

[3] i.e. Faber who had been ill, and was at the seaside, at Littlehampton.

what I hear is correct, inconvenienced by the deputation, which seemed to have gone off — but perhaps it may still come to nothing.[1] All I can do is to show my concern in the *way* I can — which will be to remember your Grace before the Blessed Sacrament which to my great joy and thankfulness is now in the little chapel I have built. I propose saying a Mass once a week for your Grace till you return.

I have not much to tell you, first because your absence suspends my operations — next because the weather has frozen up all business that was not indispensable — and because, more than all, being busily engaged in the internal routine working, which is the real thing after all, we have nothing to *show* of a novel kind. Every thing is going on well, and we are very fortunate in our set of youths.

A number of them mean to take advantage of the bonus of 2 years to those who have been at approved schools, and are in May presenting themselves for their first examination. It must be somewhat a formal thing and public. Do you see any difficulty in *our* wearing our Oxford and Cambridge etc *Master of Arts* gowns, till we get gowns of our own? They are badges of our fitness for teaching *Arts*, and have nothing to do with theology.

I think soon of coming to some agreement with Mr Mooney about St Audoen's. Time is getting on, and it certainly will do us harm if we don't make more of a *show*. The sort of impatience you feel at Rome to hear that something is *doing*, is only a specimen of what is felt here. Now there is nothing which will *tell* so much in this way as a University Church. The post went yesterday — I have already talked to Dr Yore and Fr Mc Namara on the subject, and I shall go over to Dr O'Connell in a day or two. I have also consulted Dr Leahy, Mr Bianconi, (on the business part) and tried to find Dr Maher, the V.G. [Vicar General].[2]

I want to appoint the following Professors — Mr Henessy [sic], Natural Philosophy — Mr Sullivan to lecture in chemistry — Dr Lyon (of Dublin) to lecture on Physiology (These would occupy the Medical School.) And Mr Pollen (the late Proctor etc at Oxford) the Fine Arts — he himself painted and decorated Merton Chapel, Oxford, which is one of the finest buildings there.

It is very inconvenient for us that Dr Dunne sleeps at St Laurence's, while he is Tutor in the University House — but he does not like to shift his quarters without your Grace's knowledge.

The Secretary writes to me 'I have a notice from the Catholic Secretary of the Bequests' Board to the effect that the executors of the late Mr Desmond have lodged in the Kilkenny Bank £150 for our

[1] Lucas's deputation on behalf of the Tenant League was still in Rome.
[2] i.e. William Meagher, Vicar General and Parish Priest of Rathmines.

University. It is placed to the credit of Dr Cullen, so that only he, or some one authorized by him, can receive it.'

Begging your Grace's blessing, I am, My dear Lord, Yr affte friend & Servt

J H Newman

P.S. I have already troubled your Grace with a message to the Holy Father — but I should very much like him to know how much it *rejoices me* to have the Most Holy Sacrament in my House.[1]

TO J. WALKER OF SCARBOROUGH

⌐February 23. 1855

... For years and years it has been a pain to me to write. I have overworked my hand, and this makes me write so obscurely. If you have as good an excuse, I will commiserate you on your difficult hand also. All I can say is, that, *when* I can get at your words, I profit by them very much.

I am very much obliged to you for your zeal in our behalf, and I should covet having any youth from you. At the same time I assure you I should be very jealous of any youth I took into my house — and should be afraid of any beautiful snake getting among us, though I don't expect such from the shades of Everingham. I am amused at any one being afraid of our hurting *him*.⌐[2]

TO EDWARD CASWALL

6 Harcourt Street Febry 24/55

My dear Edward,

As you seem afraid of the School House scheme which was conditionally passed by the Congregatio Generalis when I was in Birmingham, would it not be well to see, by way of getting time to determine, if it is possible to rent a house or houses at the interest of the 200£?

If this will not do, and all plans fail, we must not be dogs in the manger, but give the money up, and let it go to Smethwick. A school

---

[1] Cullen did not reply to this letter of Newman's. See that of 5 July to Cullen.

[2] Walker had presumably suggested that Marmaduke, eldest son of William Constable-Maxwell of Everingham, Yorkshire, might enter Newman's house. Marmaduke born in 1837 was the eldest of a large family. His father established his claim to the barony of Herries in 1858.

room might be built there according to the original plan, that is, a bonâ fide school room, for that purpose and nothing else. The one thing I clearly object to, is putting a preacher or mass at Smethwick for the sake of Smethwick.

I have heard nothing of the two points which we want leave from Rome about.[1]

Ever Yrs affly J H N

TO GEORGE RYDER

Feb 24/55

I dont know whether I can advise you to speak severely to him.[2] I know him so little, it might make him sullen and obstinate, — at least I see that he retires into himself whenever he is treated with severity, whatever be the cause, though I am sure no one has treated him severely here, as he knows well.

Yours affectly J.H.N.

P.S.   I have *told* Lisle that I have written to you about him

TO HENRY BITTLESTON

6 Harcourt Street, Dublin Febry 27. 1855

My dear Henry,

I am very sorry to hear from Edward just now that you were ill in London. This makes me write, not as hoping to hear a good account of you, but knowing where you are to be addressed.

Strange to say, though don't mention it —, you are in a House I have known for near 20 [50?] years. To my surprise years ago I found that Isaac William's [sic] Father lived on the opposite side the street, but No 17 was my own residence in London more or less from 1803 to 1821. Two of my sisters were born there — and one of my first memories even before the first of these events in 1803 is my admiring the borders of the paper in the drawing rooms. I have not seen the house since the month of October 1821; but of course every part of it is as clearly before my mind, as if I had lived in it ever since.[3]

---

[1] These were permission for Oratorians to be ordained titulo mensae communis, i.e. without a patrimony, and permission to reserve the Blessed Sacrament in the house.

[2] i.e. to Lisle Ryder, about his laziness.

[3] Bittleston wrote to Newman from 17 Southampton Street, on 16 Feb., 'I am come to see an old friend and connexion of my family who is in a dying state. She has

I have heard nothing of the friend whom you have gone to see there.

I say, Don't mention about the house, for this among other reasons — when one gets old, it is most painful to talk when there *can* be no sympathy, for all who have known me young are gone, or almost so — so that to go to see places I knew in former years is a great pain to me.

Ever Yrs affly J H N

TO EDWARD CASWALL

6 Harcourt Street Febry 27. 1855

My dear Edward

I think it would be a very good plan to have some Father to undertake the schools — I will not undertake to appoint one, for I don't know your respective engagements and wishes enough to do so, but I will name any one whom the Congregatio Deputata thinks best.

Whatever you do in the way of Mr Sherlock's mission will be good — I can only wish, what I suppose is impossible, that it was in *our* Mission.[1]

I congratulate you on your success with Mr Duffy[2] — How is it that you hit it off with him, and Formby does not? Will you tell the latter, when you see him, that I thank him for his letter, but am too busy to undertake the (more excellent) work he wishes.[3]

Thank you for apprising me what the subject of Fr Ambrose's communication is to be.[4]

Tell William I am sorry to give him the trouble — but should be much obliged if he would send on my Tablet — It is directed to Fr Ambrose.

been ill a long time . . .' This friend lived in Stepney, and Bittleston stayed at his brother's house in Southampton Street until the end of Feb. The Newman family moved to 17 Southampton Street, now Southampton Place, Bloomsbury, in 1802. In 1816, when the Newman bank came to an end, the house was let for about three years.

[1] This refers to the men in the confraternity at the Oratory helping in the district of John Sherlock, whose church was in Park Street.

[2] Caswall's *Hours at the Altar* was selling well.

[3] Formby had given up his efforts to spread the Plain Chant, and was now trying to 'bring about a better knowledge of the Scriptures and the Catholic faith by publishing works profusely illustrated with instructive pictures.' (*Gillow*, II, p. 310.)

[4] i.e. the permissions in note to letter of 24 Feb. to Caswall. The second page of this letter is missing, and what follows is a postscript written at the head of it.

TO AUSTIN MILLS

6 Harcourt Street Febr 27/55

My dear Austin

Thank you for the trouble you are at in the Library, which seems to promise very well. I certainly should wish my subscription to the Church Education Fund continued.

Today is oppressively mild, after the frost.

The inside of the Tabernacle smells of white paint. Had we not that trouble once in Birmingham? How long did it last? can it be got rid of? Is there any chance of its infecting the consecrated particles?

Ever Yrs affly J H N

TO HENRY WILBERFORCE (I)

6 Harcourt Street 27 Febry 1855.

My dear Wilberforce

⌐Thank you for your speedy answer.⌐ I think I should have decided for Arthur as you have. ⌐Whenever a vacancy occurs again, you shall know. It is my fear of losing him which made me write. You must keep in mind that the Holy See has given me leave of absence from Birmingham for *three years* only, and that I shall have an earnest desire to get back there at the end of the time.⌐

As to my dear Frank[1], he is most absurdly unreasonable. The French ambassador! and I am never quite without a suspicion that he is treating Catholics like children, and trying to use them. I have inclosed a letter which you may read and send him, if you will

Ever Yrs J H N

TO HENRY WILBERFORCE (II)

6 Harcourt Street Febry 27. 1855

My dear Henry

As to my brother Frank's wish as to M. Janko as far as Ireland is concerned, there are, you know, very few convents for men here — the

---

[1] Francis Newman. See next letter.

393

members of religious orders not being yet in a condition always to live in community.[1]

But besides this greatest of difficulties, there is another which might not strike a person who is not a Catholic, and that is, that each religious order has a character of its own, and it does not prove that Mr Janko would be a Dominican, Jesuit, or Capuchin, because he has a high moral character, great devotional absorption, and such zeal for converting others as to be disagreeable in a Protestant family. Perhaps he would find no religious body in the whole Catholic world suit him — and would find it best to remain in a secular state.

This is supposing that I could be sure that he was all that my brother believes him to be; whereas he only speaks from others whom he can trust.

It seems to me that any recommendation of him to Catholics should come from people *who know him*, nay from *Catholics* who know him. Fr Brownbill's introduction would have great weight.

Excuse haste Ever Yrs affly J H Newman

H W Wilberforce Esqr

TO THOMAS SCRATTON

Febry 28. 1855

My dear Scratton

As you feel the direction I gave somewhat subtle and mysterious, I think it better to write this, which you can keep by you.

1. *As Secretary*, you take *no* money for the University. Therefore any receipt or notice signed by you 'Secretary,' much more if it is to be engraven on copper, is to be avoided.

2. As 'Mr Scratton' you may take as much money as ever you please.

3. When you *have* taken it, you are not to take it to the Bank or advertise it in the Paper — but simply to deliver it to Mr Star as Dr Leahy's acting man, making him give you a private acknowledgment for it.

Indeed, in all things I wish you to do in this matter, as I do myself. *I* do not give receipts signed 'Rector,' nor do I publish in the paper — but I take to Mr Star — and, when you next come here, I will show you the sort of receipts he gives me. They are all on one piece of paper with a Queen's head stamp on it.

[1] Francis Newman was a zealous upholder of the Hungarian Nationalist exiles in their struggle against the Hapsburgs. Among them was the devout Mr Janko. See letter of 6 March to Wilberforce.

It is a great inconvenience, I know, that Priests should bring you money, *when you have nothing to do with it* — it is a great inconvenience that they bring it to *me*. We neither of us can help it — we must not complain — we must not give copper plate receipts — we must not give our names to the public — but we must get rid of the money, as easily as we can.

For me, I see nothing recondite in this mode of acting under a difficulty — and if I have a difficulty, it is why you cannot do just the same as I do.

Yrs most sincerely John H Newman

TO EDWARD CASWALL

6 Harcourt Street March 1. 1855

My dear Edward,

I have thought over the scheme of going into Mr Sherlock's mission, and I really do not relish it. It does not please me that the Orat. Parv. should actually make work for itself in another parish. Rather call them a set of young men assisting Mr S. and let him be the head of them. For that is the fact; and if the Missioner was any one but he, whom we get on so well with, we should have collisions. If I understand you, you are already disappointed in Green's Village, by means of that sort of thing — and you don't know how long Mr S remains in his post.[1]

Our great object seems to me to be in all things to aim at making Catholics *about* us. We have uphill work. We have to make a mission. We made one in Alcester Street but under more promising circumstances. It will be several years before we get a Catholic population in the growing streets about us. And then the boys have to grow up, which may take ten or fifteen years. In Liverpool, they have already a Catholic youth. I don't expect much of the Bm Orat. Parv. for some years — but I almost could say, I had rather there should be none, than that we should not tend to strengthen St Philip. I don't think employing youths to labour in Park Street strengthens St Philip. Even to help Mr Nugent would be strengthening him more.

Ever Yrs affly J H N[2]

[1] Cf. letter of 16 Feb. to Caswall.

[2] Newman pasted two newspaper cuttings at the bottom of his letter: 'This day is published, price 1s. 6d., THE JUDGMENTS OF GOD *upon the* NATIONS—Pius Ninth the last of the Popes. London, Wertheim and Macintosh, 24, Paternoster-row. Just published, price 2d., or by post, 3d.' The second cutting was: 'PUSEYISM, *the Curse of England*: a Letter to the Labouring Men of this Country, suggested by a consideration of our disastrous Campaign in the Crimea. By a *Berkshire Tenant Farmer*. Reading, R. Welch; and of all booksellers.'

TO THOMAS SCRATTON

Thursday March 1/55

My dear Scratton,

Thank you for your hint about Mr Pigot — I have written to him. Your note was the first thing I had heard of his calling.[1]

There is no reason you should not mention to me about the ground behind the Medical School. I wish very much it could be bought. *I always give my opinion*, when I have one. E.g. I have asked Mr James O'F [O'Ferrall] to try to get us the lease or some kind of possession of a portion of the ground behind the University House — it is much wanted by us as playground, but I cannot get him. Mr Bianconi said that he could do it, and no one else.

As to their employing you to make the purchase etc of the Medical School ground, it is nothing to me.[2] It is a great deal to you that you are sure they *can* do so — Else, if the Committee does not ratify, the ground will be thrown upon you. Whether they have power, I cannot tell — but you know. Every one ought to feel your generosity.

It seems to me that some medical man, as Mr Ellis, through whom we have the place, would best give a judgment whether the ground was wanted.

The truth is, I never bargained for the money matters. I have always said I would have nothing to do with them. The University House itself is thrown upon us, sorely against my will.

Ever Yrs J H Newman

TO T. W. ALLIES

6 Harcourt Street, Dublin March 2. 1855.

My dear Allies,

What would you say to the proposal of taking modern history into your Professorship? Then I could offer you £300 a year. We want a Lecturer in Modern History, particularly ENGLISH, and I do not wish to make a new appointment. This would not remove from you the subject of the 'Philosophy' — but would only add another to it.

Ever yours John H. Newman

[1] John Edward Pigot had been asked to deliver lectures and on calling twice or thrice had been told Newman was engaged.

[2] Errington and O'Ferrall of the University Sub-Committee wanted Scratton to arrange this purchase.

6 Harcourt Street Dublin March 2. 1855.

My dear Lord Henry

Thank you for the account you give me of dear Ralph. Give him my love and tell him that if it is decided that he should go to Rome, there is no need he should come here for his clothes. If he will send his orders, they shall be attended to. My servant Frederic, tell him, unpacked his boxes out of civility, to save him the trouble, when we thought him coming in a day or two. We will put by safely whatever he does not send for.

Fr Darnell gives me an account of him which makes me very anxious — however, all things are right —

As to your other subject, to tell the truth, I think, Master Francis has the gift of spending. I gave him a sovereign not many weeks ago — and I find that he has, besides this, borrowed 30/ of my servant. If you please, you must not say a word of this to him. Now some of the things doubtless were necessary which he got — e.g. a few shelves to put his books on, 6/6 etc Then again, the skaiting is a temptation, which will not come again, and cost him a shilling a time. However, as the season advances he *must* have some outdoor expences. He has been to two concerts (3/6 a piece) under the charge of ladies he knew. I thought they might have franked him, till I found the contrary this morning.

I think it will be best, not to repress him in detail, but, as you say, to give him an allowance which will make him careful, and pinch him, if extravagant. He is the youngest son, and I suspect, spends most.

Even for those who are of full age, I consider a comparitively [sic] small sum will be necessary for all expences. I consider that, beyond the University Pensions, there should only be three ordinary bills — *clothes, travelling, books* — to these one must add what is meant by *pocket money.*

de Vaulchier, who will be a person of large property and of station in his neighbourhood, had only £7 given him by his father on parting, and his Tutor declares to me it will last him through the year for pocket money. I dont know what is given to a boy at an English public school. A youth is less than 9 months in the year here. Ten shillings a month ought to be very handsome for *mere* pocket money. I do not know whether you will think this narrow, if so, you must recollect that my office is to diminish expence. I have been ambitious to bring the expences of some youths four or five years older than Francis, within £20 a year for clothes, travelling, books and pocket money. I should add

397

that Francis has bought at least one *book* (perhaps more) out of money he has had but (as I am told) in a foolish extravagant way. As to the 30/- *I* must speak to him about that, and you need know nothing about it. My servant says that, 15/- of it was actually *borrowed*. He ought not of course to have lent it to him, and it will not occur again — but as he had so lately come to me for money, he ought not to have gone to my servant — but I repeat, I will speak to him, and you must not know it.

Very sincerely Yours in Xt   John H. Newman of the Oratory.

The Lord Henry Kerr.

P.S.   You might tell him that he should get his books, as his clothes, *through me*.

TO THOMAS SCRATTON

March 2 [1855]

My dear Scratton

I don't think there can be any thing better than your plan about St Columba's for the youth. It is a lamentable case.

Mr Bianconi had some difficulty in any one acting but Mr James O'Ferrall.[1] I suppose Mr. J. O'F. has let the favorable time slip by. It would be well if you wrote to Mr Bianconi, saying that I wanted to rent two or three acres, and that I wanted his advice what to do.

Ever Yrs, J H N.

TO JOHN STANISLAS FLANAGAN

6 Harcourt Street March 3/55

My dear Stanislas

Household cares. After seven weeks trial, Margaret cannot cook. It is no good talking. Well — Myles O'Reilly gives me the name of the Stephen's Green Club Steward, to consult for a successor. I have called twice and can't get to see him. I sent in my name to him, and he sent out word that he was engaged.

Now can you recommend me any one who will get me a cook? Would Mr Foley? If so, what is his direction, that I may see him.[2]

---

[1] This refers to obtaining the ground behind the University House. O'Ferrall was a friend of the former agent of the property.

[2] Michael Foley, University Hotel, 31 Wicklow Street.

As to my expences, I ought to be thankful — With *all* debts of the current *establishment*, washing lights, fire, chapel, wages[,] sundries, jobs etc etc. January makes up £71, and February makes up £71 — though in different items. And what is more to the purpose the Butcher and several other great bills, are not much increased in February — though we were not here in strength till January 13th. Moreover, these are heavy months in coal.

$$
\begin{array}{lr}
\text{Now } \pounds72 \times 9 \text{ months} = & \pounds648 \\
\text{to which must be added — Rent —} & 110 \\
\text{Board Wages} & 13 \\
\hline
& \pounds771
\end{array}
$$

These are, I think, my WHOLE expences of every kind.

On the receipt side —

$$
\begin{array}{lr}
5 \text{ at } \pounds100 — & 500.\ 0.\ 0 \\
1 \text{ at } \pounds80 & 80.\ 0.\ 0 \\
2 \text{ at } \pounds60 & 120.\ 0.\ 0 \\
\text{my own —} & 300.\ 0.\ 0 \\
\hline
& 1000.\ 0.\ 0 \\
\text{Surplus} & 229.\ 0.\ 0
\end{array}
$$

(Lord Ralph's £100 is wanting to me; to which his expences would not approach)

On the other hand it must be recollected that getting into the House (*besides* the Chapel) will come to a good £150

Tell me, if you see any flaw[1]

Ever Yrs J H N

TO WILLIAM NEVILLE

6 Harcourt Street March 3. 18[55][2]

My dear William

I am very sorry you should be troubled about the fence.

First, are the laurels moved from St Wilfrid's? next, is the (cemetery) ground marked out which they are to bound? I say this, because the Season for planting may pass by. The time for evergreens is different from that for other plants — but I forget it.

This might be done at once?

[Is][2] your difficulty about the fence knowing *whose* trade it is to

---

[1] Flanagan could find none.

[2] The corner of the page has been torn. This letter concerns Rednal.

undertake such jobs? If so, could not Nowell get you some person whose trade it was, or put you on finding one?

Is Nowell willing to undertake it, or Hansom, only you can't agree on terms?

Do you think you could not get some hedger and ditcher, who, if the materials were found for him would work at it by the piece?

Would not such a person tell you *what* materials would do for the purpose, and what they *cost*?

Who planted the shrubs in the garden at Edgbaston? perhaps he would be of use to you?

The one object of these questions is, not to get you to make an *engagement*, but to enable you to make out *what it will cost*, that you may submit your plan to the Congregation

Ever Yours affectionately J H N

TO HENRY WILBERFORCE

Saturday March 3/55

My dear Henry

⌐How inconsistent one is or rather how one sided! here am I desirous of peace and thinking war will upset the constitution — which I *do* think — but then, when the very chance of peace comes, rises the chance of an English Know-nothing-ism. I suppose, especially since the Peelites have been shivered, nothing stands between us and persecution, if there is peace.[1] Do you not think I ought to hesitate, before I go on with my letters? [['Who's to blame?']]⌐ — Since I have not had time to change my signature, ⌐I suppose you have not yet published the first — but n' importe, if you have. I will trust even if there be peace, that the British Constitution will bring us through the attacks [[on us]] of British Protestantism⌐[2]

Ever Yrs affly J H N

[1] The Peelites, including Gladstone, Sir James Graham and Sidney Herbert, resigned on 23 Feb. from Palmerston's newly-formed ministry, and Lord John Russell joined it. The Nativist 'Know-Nothings' in America attacked especially Catholics and Jews. Palmerston and Russell represented the Protestant and Liberal forces most opposed to Catholics.

[2] The first of Newman's letters 'Who's to blame?' signed 'Catholicus,' was published in the *Catholic Standard*, (3 March), p. 9; *D.A.* pp. 306–10. There Newman wrote, p. 307, 'I have a decided view that Catholicism is safer and more free under a constitutional *regime* such as our own, than under any other.'

SUNDAY 4 MARCH 1855   swelled gum — unwell

TO THOMAS SCRATTON

March 4. 1855

My dear Scratton

I will pay Beardwood's bill for the Medical School, and thank you for the pains you have been at about it.

I know how much we are indebted to your zeal and diligence generally — and am very sorry if I have on any point expressed myself obscurely to you.[1] I have no obscurity in my own mind on the matter we talked about last night, and if you do not mind the trouble of reading, I will set down the one *principle* which will clear the whole matter up.[2]

1. The Synod of Thurles appointed a *Committee*, as for other University matters, so for University *finance*.

2. I think this committee is *still in existence* — If so, Dr Leahy is the secretary.

3. But let us suppose that it is *not*. Then, since a Synod's act is a grave and formal matter, any other committee, secretary etc for a like purpose, must have a *parallel appointment*.

4. *I* have had no such appointment.

5. Consequently, I cannot give what I have never received.

6. Therefore, you, as University Secretary, have nothing whatever to do with the finance matters.

Now comes my *principle*

You have quite a right to aim at the finance Secretariship, if it be vacant, and I have no right to hinder it,

but

you must not use the University Secretariship as a stepping stone to obtain the Finance Secretariship

I lay down this Principle,

1. because it cannot be done without implying that at present you have something to do with finance

2 because in my private opinion, to which of course *I* have a right, I see great difficulties in the Finance Secretary being a layman.

Now all I want you to avoid is *what compromises this principle*.

---

[1] Scratton wrote to Newman on 2 March that for the previous fortnight he had had very little to do and felt that the sphere of his duties ought to be enlarged.

[2] Newman copied the draft of this letter in the Appendix to 'Memorandum about my connection with the Catholic University.' The draft is less explicit than the letter sent.

I think it *unfair* if you *use* the office you hold of the Rector for an object, of which he wishes to stand clear.

E.g. Money is paid you by the P.P. [Parish Priest] of Kilbeggan. It is an unfortunate misconception that he should fancy you have to do with finance. You should *dis*courage the idea. You wish to encourage it. You wish to advertise it in connexion with your name. Would it have been paid you, *had you not been* University Secretary? Is it given to you as 'Mr Scratton'? Not a farthing would you have had to acknowledge in the Paper, except you were Secretary. That is, you use the University Secretariship as a lift towards the Finance Secretariship.

2. Again, You have a copper plate receipt-form with 'Secretary' at the end. You meant to use it for cases like the P.P. of Kilbeggan. What was this but encouraging the notion that the *one* Secretary was the *other*? I proposed you to have 'Rector' instead of 'Secretary' — (the wrong word could have been got out from the Plate) No — you did not like this — because it would simply have overturned the object for which (among other objects) I conceive you had it done. The *only* act of yours which you have not drawn out for me in *detail* first, before it was done, was *this*. You showed me proofs or written copies of the *Register* — you consulted me about the *binding*, about the *tickets for* the lectures — about details of every kind. One thing you do not show me, viz the *wording* of the receipt form. And it was the most important of all.

I give these instances as illustrations of the *one principle* I wish to lay down, — which I do feel to be *personally binding on me* to enforce

Ever Yrs John H Newman

P.S. Now that Dr Leahy has come into residence, I have thought of making over all such money matters as I have to him.[1]

TO LORD HENRY KERR

6 Harcourt Street Dublin March 5. 1855.

My dear Lord Henry

I am sorry to say that Francis has spent more than I thought, though some of the things are necessaries. He first had a £1 from me — then

[1] In the draft 'I have thought of making over the "Cullen and Newman account" to him. [[(vid April 24. 1855)]]' Newman preserved a note of what he wrote to Leahy on 18 Oct. 1854 'that he could not have any thing to do with the money—and that he was sending any sums that came to him to Mr Star.'

Scratton thanked Newman for his 'very kind and explicit letter,' but said he 'should be glad to have more work and *more pay*.'

saying he had no money 5/-. I find his bill with my servant is as much as £1. 14. 9. Altogether as near as possible £3 —

Of this, bookshelves 7/- a parcel 2/3 Horace 2/- devotional book 2/- necktie 3/6 knife and scissors 5/- etc came to £1. 1 and more, crape for his hat 1/-

He seems to have gone skaiting for near a fortnight, which with cars, has made nearly another £1.

The third pound is made up of needless expenses. It seems he went and subscribed to a circulating library for half a year at 12/6 then finding he had no time for reading the books, he bought books to that amount — religious books I think — but I suspect old fashioned and bad copies.

Then he seems to have bought two pipes at 5/- each one of which he gave away.

I have asked him, if he has got any bills anywhere, and am sorry he has got one. He bought a pair of skaits which he has not paid for. The cost is 12/-

I have asked him to put everything on paper and let me send it to you. But I suppose, his accounts are not very correctly kept, as I foresee the post will go before it comes.

This east wind is bad, I fear, for Ralph.

Very truly Yours John H Newman

The Lord Henry Kerr

TO JOHN EDWARD PIGOT

March 5/55

. . . It pleased me . . . to find that you were not indisposed to give us your valuable assistance.[1]

I was for a moment made anxious by seeing that you added something about *politics*. As I hope you saw in the conversations I have had the pleasure of holding with you, I myself have no political opinions adverse to those which you expressed. In England itself I am not a politician — much less should I presume to have any quarrel, with an Irishman in Ireland holding opinions which his patriotism dictated. But what makes me anxious is that I suppose there are zealous supporters of the University who would be much distressed if politics were introduced into it; and indeed I will confess myself that I think it one of the

[1] Pigot wrote on 3 March that he would be glad to become professor of practical law and treat of the Law of Real Property, unless his political opinions would be compromised by connection with the University. Pigot was a Young Irelander.

faults of Oxford as a University that it has been made the seat of special political opinions. Again, I ought to add that, conceiving as I do that politics do not enter into an academical body, I could not make it an objection to a person of different political opinions from your own, supposing such a person, being well qualified, did not introduce them into his teaching.

But I shall be able to talk of these and other questions with you when I have the pleasure of seeing you.[1]

TO HENRY WILBERFORCE

6 Harcourt Str March 5 [1855]

My dear Henry

It is very hard that your people will not send the Standard from your office to me *here*. Here is Monday afternoon, and I have not seen it. In consequence ⌐I do not know whether I am in print or not.[2] I have the 3rd and 4th done — but I don't like going on without the certainty they will be wanted.⌐

Ever Yrs J H N

TO HENRY WILBERFORCE

6 Harcourt Street Dublin March 6/55

My dear H W

Your letter has just come — I have not yet seen Saturday's Paper. As you have begun with Catholicus, *go on with it*. I will send Numbers 3 and 4 directly to you.

⌐Register seems a good name — and your way of dropping Catholic Standard is the best.[3] The Leader apes the Guardian in arrangement.

---

[1] Pigot replied on 7 March thoroughly agreeing that politics did not belong to a university, but adding that he had feared some of the law professorships might 'be made the vehicles of the inculcation of opinions which I hold to be not only false but so peculiarly criminal in Ireland' and that he would thus be compromised in conscience. Pigot alluded to 'that class of exaggerated opinions touching the British "Constitution" on the one hand, and the *necessary* "allegiance" of *my* country to the laws and government of that particular *English* nation on the other, with which most English law books teem. . . .'

[2] i.e. the first of the letters 'Who's to blame?' in the *Catholic Standard* of 3 March.

[3] Wilberforce wrote of his plan of combining two papers. The first combined number appeared on 19 May as the *Weekly Register and Catholic Standard*, and a leading article explained that for a newspaper to assume 'a title implying that it is the standard-bearer of the Catholic Church' was thought presumptuous.

I am not quite satisfied you should do so too. The first page of the Guardian, being necessarily concise, becomes sententious, antithetical, priggish, and flippant. What I do detest is the wood cuts.[1]

I can't read your last sentence. I hope your wife is getting better — there has been a vast deal of influenza every where. You see Lord Stanhope has died of it, as well as the Emperor Nicholas.[2] ⌜We stopped our [[public]] lectures here, owing to the weather — Now we resume them.⌝

As to my brother, all that I say (and you, I suppose) is that his devout Hungarian should come to you, *not from* him, but from persons you know. He must *bring his introduction* — not set you to *seek* his strong points — I am *very sorry* you 'desire a personal interview with Mr Janko,' if you are to go to Lord Clarendon about him.[3] And, as to Mr Pulzky, I have not one grain of faith in him.[4]

Ever Yrs J H N

NB. I *must ask your kindness*, if you observe any mistakes in *facts* (even the Feudal system), to give me an opportunity of correcting them. What is the exact meaning of 'seaboard' — ? in Number 4 or 5 I use it for a sea margin round a *boundary* of a country.

About the plan of a *cheap* Catholic Standard I can give no opinion. It is a business question.

TO DENIS FLORENCE MACCARTHY

6 Harcourt Street March 8. 1855

My dear Mr McCarthy,

Mr Curry proposes to give four Lectures before Easter, now that the bad weather is gone. Perhaps Dr Leahy may do the same. Are you

[1] The woodcuts in the *Catholic Standard* were dropped on 19 May, but the arrangement of the leading article was unchanged.

[2] The fourth Earl Stanhope (1781–1855), and Nicholas I (1796–1855), Czar from 1825, both died on 2 March.

[3] The Earl of Clarendon was Foreign Secretary.

[4] Francis Newman was a friend of Louis Kossuth's chief lieutenant and fellow exile Francis Aurelius Pulzky (1814–97), the Hungarian politician and archaeologist. Pulzky joined the Nationalist movement in 1849 and between 1851 and 1860 was a constant visitor to England. He had plans for organizing a Hungarian legion during the Crimean War. When he and Kossuth left for good in 1860, Francis Newman was told by the former that they were glad to leave behind in him one Englishman who knew all their secrets and could be trusted to expound them. Francis Newman, *Reminiscences of Two Wars and Two Exiles*, London 1888, p. 1. Pulzky became Minister of Finance under the constitutional monarchy, and in 1866 Director of the National Museum.

disposed to do so, or will you wait till after Easter? Whichever you do, will be equally pleasant to me.

I am told that from four to six lectures, coming close together, are most likely to obtain and keep an audience through the course. And time has got on so, that, supposing you gave any this term, I suppose you would be obliged to take more than one a week, to get through them. But whatever you determine to do or not do, will please me. My only wish is that Lectures such as yours should not be thrown away on partially empty rooms

Very truly Yours John H Newman

D F McCarthy Esqr

P.S.   As far as I can make out at present, Dr Leahy and Mr Curry will lecture thus

> March 13. Tuesday — Mr Curry
> 15 Thursday — Mr Curry
> 20 Tuesday — Mr Curry
> 21 Wednesday — Dr Leahy
> 22 Thursday   Mr Curry
> 28 Wednesday   Dr Leahy

Your lectures stood for

> March 16 23 30

TO EUGENE O'CURRY

6 Harcourt Street March 9/55

My dear Mr Curry

Would these evenings suit you, the 13th, 15th, 20th, 22nd? If so, I will advertise them.

If Monday at ½ past 3 will suit you, I will avail myself of your kind invitation to call on you at the Royal Academy at that time.

Very truly Yrs John H Newman

E. Curry Esqr

TO THOMAS SCRATTON

Sunday [11 March 1855]

My dear Scratton

I dare say Mr Curry has written to you, as he told me he should, but I write to make assurance double sure, to say that he had much rather no money should be paid for his tickets.

406

So you had better merely advertise 'Tickets will be given, or may be procured etc.'

Ever Yrs J H N

Will you advertise Dr Leahy's continued indisposition; as by note inclosed.

TO T. W. ALLIES

6, Harcourt St, Dublin March 12. 1855.

My dear Allies,

I hope Mrs Allies has found, as in other matters that suspense and uncertainty are the great trials, and now that Almighty God has decided one way, her distress is at an end. What can parents wish for better than that their children should go to heaven?[1]

Thank you for your news about Wm Palmer, which was most welcome.[2]

I fear I have not clearly stated to you my proposal about Modern History or you would not have returned me so ready and acceptable an answer. Of course it would require *residence* here. Do you think you could do *this*, if you really do think of it? viz; come here for six weeks about June. You should not give public lectures unless you wished, but you should give a private course on e.g. the history of the 16th century. In this way you would both see what materials you had here to tutorize, and get into the state of the place, and also you would try the stimulus of lecturing by getting up subjects which would do either for Philosophy of History or Modern History. Of course, nothing would be more agreeable to me than that you should close with my offer at once, but, if you could not do that, here is a middle course.

Ever Yrs John H Newman of the Oratory

TO BISHOP ULLATHORNE

6 Harcourt Street Dublin March 12/55

My dear Lord,

I thank you very cordially for the present of your new publication.[3] I shall read it with great interest — the primâ facie appearance of its

[1] Allies's fifth son Bernard died on 7 March a month after birth. See Mary H. Allies, *Thomas William Allies*, London 1907, pp. 79-81.

[2] William Palmer of Magdalen was received into the Church at Rome on 27 Feb.

[3] *The Immaculate Conception of the Mother of God: an Exposition*, London 1855.

contents shows me what instruction I shall get from it. Does it not seem as if the effect of the Definition was already showing itself? I cannot be very sanguine about peace at the moment — but, as things stand, both England and Russia have each in their way had a severe blow, and France and Austria, the two Catholic powers, are on the ascendant. But we must not be premature in our conclusions. If peace were made now, England would have the mortification of having lost her prestige of military glory, without opportunity of recovering it. If the war goes on, what are our 10.000 in the Crimea to the French 90.000?

I wish I could have heard your lecture last Tuesday. The Aborigines of Australia must be a curious study to the philosopher and theologian.

Dr Cullen is still detained at Rome. The state of things is very serious, I fear. They talk of a Rescript to be addressed to the Irish Church.[1]

Begging your Lordship's blessing, I am, my dear Lord, Yr faithful and affte Servt in Xt

John H Newman of the Oratory

The Rt Revd The Bp of Birmingham

TO HENRY WILBERFORCE

6 Harcourt Street Dublin March 12/55
My dear Henry

⌐I am sorry to say I cannot bring my subject to an end, as speedily as for both our sakes I wished. I send by this post Letter 5. Letter 6 is written, but I shall keep it a while. I hope to finish in Letter 7 — and to devote an 8th, as you will or not, to the consideration of the effect of peace upon the position of Catholics.⌐[2]

You must not think me precise, if I am anxious my letters should be *printed correctly*. When one writes with as much condensation as is possible, the mistake in one word may be serious. There is an error, of no consequence at all luckily, in Number 2 — but if there is one, there might be another. Did you send them *me*, I would not *alter* from the MS I sent to you, but would look after such mistakes. As you do not,

---

[1] The dissensions between Archbishops Cullen and MacHale continued, and the latter had left Rome against the wishes of the Pope. In April Pius IX sent a circular to the Irish bishops blaming MacHale.

[2] The eighth of the 'Who's to blame?' letters was on English jealousy of Church and Army, and appeared in the *Catholic Standard*, (21 April 1855), p. 9.

I must be indebted to you to keep a careful eye on your printer. The mistake in Letter 2 is 'and, this being kept in view, *as showing my statement*,' I *suppose* it ought to be 'as shown by my statement.'[1]

I hope you will think twice before you attack the French Government for their Gallican mode of admitting the Pope's brief. Ultramontane as I am, I do not see how they could avoid doing so, unless they wished the question to go by default. The Pope every year protests, I believe, against the King of Naples not sending him a mule, or an ambassador to ride into St Peter's on a mule, or some silver pence, or something or other; he could not do otherwise, till the matter is finally arranged, yet he may be good friends with Naples for all that.[2]

Ever Yrs affly J H N

P.S. I hope your wife is getting well by this time.

TUESDAY 13 MARCH 1855 The Music Lessons began for the youths here. Resumed in [the?] public evening Lectures in the University Rooms — viz Dr Leahy's, Mr Curry's Mr McCarthy's

TO CATHERINE ANNE BATHURST

6 Harcourt Street. Dublin March 13/55

My dear Child,

I said Mass for you the other day, and have been going to write to you for some days. Your letter has just come — I shall burn it after writing this.

I think Pride is what you are looking for. In all your resolutions, consequent on reading Fr Faber's book, take advice.[3] I mean, a remark may be very good in itself, but for various reasons bad for the individual.

As to the discipline, I do not object to it, so that you are *taught* to apply it. I have known persons most imprudent, from not knowing

---

[1] This passage has been re-written in *D.A.* p. 315.

[2] In virtue of the Organic Articles the Conseil d'État insisted on giving its *Placet* before the Bull on the Immaculate Conception was published in France, and only did so after considerable opposition.

The Popes claimed that Naples was held as a fief of the Holy See, and the feudal due was the annual gift of a white mule.

The *Catholic Standard* said nothing about the French attitude to the Bull, but reported its acceptance by the French at Algiers, where public officials attended the solemn services in honour of the Definition.

[3] It is clear from the letter of 4 April to Catherine Bathurst that *Growth in Holiness* is Faber's book in question.

better. Striking the *neck* behind, sometimes I believe affects the eyes. Of course you will take advice of Reverend Mother.

Such little mortifications as you mention, you need not ask about, but you should be on your guard lest they should be so many as to be considerable *altogether*. I think it would be *better* abstractedly if you mentioned them to Revd Mother, but I do not press it.

When I shall come to town, I do not know — but I rejoice to be assured, even without seeing you, that God is very gracious to you.

I will not forget you. Pray for me and us here; we are going on well, I trust — but it is a *long* work, and I do not wish to be many years at it.

We have the Blessed Sacrament in our Private Chapel here, which was a great allowance from Rome[1]

TO JOHN STANISLAS FLANAGAN

6 Harcourt Street March 13. 1855

My dear Stanislas,

Pray wish Mr Lynch every good wish from me and offer him my best congratulations.[2] A Limerick Priest told me the other day that it is believed in Limerick and the Ordnance that Monsell is to enter the Ecclesiastical State, and that 'those Oratorians at Bm [Birmingham] have done it.' I said I had lately been to Bm and had heard nothing of it.

I went to the Railway Secretary the morning after your letter came — signed the papers and left them there *with the certificate.* Perhaps Fr Frederic has heard from the people there.[3]

Thank you for your kindness about my domestic wants. *Ever since* I gave her warning, poor Margaret has changed her cooking so marvellously, that it seems a fright does good. Before we had raw beef, raw mutton, raw *veal — daily —* in spite of warnings. From the very day she had warning, she and her sister were in great excitement. They came up to me separately, and, I believe, abused me — for I could not understand one word they said — as Frederic prophesied. Then they set to abusing him and John. Margaret ended in reforming — and *not one* day since has the dinner been badly cooked. As to her sister she has become a pattern of clean dusting — so as to make me laugh. Perhaps then I shall give them a month more, and keep them, if I can.

---

[1] Conclusion and signature have been cut out.
[2] Lynch had apparently decided to become a priest.
[3] Shares were being transferred to Frederic Bowles.

I inclose the Cardinal's letter.[1] I should like the opinion of the Congregatio Deputata upon it.

I don't think I had any thing else to write to you about

Ever Yrs affly J H N

P.S.   You see the Times thinks that Dr McHale is getting his way in regard to the University. If he does, it means, that he can reverse my appointments, and put in people of his own. This I won't stand, and will resign rather than allow it — But it won't come to that.[2]

P.S.   By the bye, did I ever tell you to pay the £5 for the Catholic Association — do it, if you haven't, I'll not give another — but don't say so

I signed the transfer for Fr Frederic on faith in you — for I don't know what money it was.

TO WILLIAM NEVILLE

6 Harcourt Street. Dublin March 13. 1855

My dear William

Had I not been busy, you should have heard from me before.

I am very sorry you have had the trouble about the Newspapers. I have told them in London to send on the Catholic Standard direct here, since you have one already in Bm [Birmingham]. The Post Office never accused you of sending me the News of the World, but of sending the cover so loose upon the Cath. St. that it came off, and they could only guess at which paper was mine, and guessed wrongly.

I did not like at all the way the ground was laid out at Rednall, when I was there with you. As to the fences round our piece, the very first question is, what will putting it right cost? next who will formally *engage* to do it for what? You think the fence on the side behind the house will about £10. 10. The next question is, Is a fence wanted on the

[1] Dated 8 March. See letter of 12 Jan. to Wiseman.

[2] *The Times*, (12 March 1855), p. 7, quoted a private letter from Rome as saying 'Archbishop Cullen was decidedly of opinion that the exclusive management [of the Catholic University] should be vested in the hands of the Metropolitans; and before the arrival of Archbishop MacHale his opinion was shared by the Propaganda. I have reason to believe, however, that the management will be left to the whole Irish episcopacy.'

MacHale left Rome in the middle of March, although Pius IX expected him to remain for the investigation of his differences with Cullen. In fact the Decrees on the University left its management in the hands of the four Archbishops. See letter of 25 April 1855 to Hope-Scott.

other sides — and what will it cost. I put the whole (I think) at £40 in the sketch of calculation I gave you before February 2. When you say £5 for the other sides, do you mean £5 for each side? that would make £15. Any how the whole would be £25, much short of £40, but there is the cost of labour to come. Should it not be done *by the piece*? If you are satisfied on this point you might enter into an engagement with some one. But consult Stanislas first. I congratulate you on your success so far.

I wish you could get the laurels in ⟨⟨on three sides, if the fence is the fourth or two sides, if two sides are fence.⟩⟩ — but in order to this, of course you must mark out the ground. This *I* cannot do. I made a calculation when I was at Edgbaston, and showed it to some of the Fathers, but somehow it fell to the ground. The Congregatio Deputata must settle it. As to the number of square feet in the cemetery, the first question is, for how many bodies is it to be prepared? next are they to be buried in brick graves, one above another, or not? 3. what are the dimensions in length and breadth of a coffin?

I hope Miss Giberne has been written to and her presents suitably acknowledged. As to her presents to me, I should *be very glad to have them sent here.*[1]

The only view I have about the roads in our ground is, that they should not be drawn so, as to *hinder* our having, if we choose it here-after, a terrace covering the lowest floor of the house, as at a a a — so that the lowest floor and

windows would *not be seen* in front.

Does Fr Nicholas contemplate a *vault*? If so, I am surprised, for I thought the very reason of having Rednall, was to allow of a *ground*.

Ever Yrs affly J H Newman

TO EDWARD CASWALL

6 Harcourt Street March 14. 1855

My dear Edward

Thank you for the Paper of Holy Week Services. I wish I could promise myself being at Edgbaston to take part in them. But I don't see that more than 2 or 3 of my party will be going away — and I don't like to leave the rest here by themselves. It is possible too Renouf may be away. But I won't give up the idea.

[1] Miss Giberne sent Newman a set of Low Mass vestments.

Pray say every thing kind from me to Lady Shrewsbury, when you write.

I am very glad to hear of the new roads, which are important,[1] and of your taking the School Finance.

We have begun our public lectures again for 10 days — three Irishmen, Dr Leahy, Mr Curry, Mr McCarthy. Mr Curry maintained tonight that Ireland was in the flower of its literature in the time of Henry ii and thrown back by the invasion and conquest. This startled me for he is a very learned man.[2]

Ever Yrs affly J H N

TO RICHARD STANTON

6 Harcourt Street Dublin March 14/55

My dear Richard

As soon as your letter came, I wrote to Chirol, as you advised, asking for his *advertisement*. I suspect he is hurt, for he has not answered me.[3]

[1] New roads, Beaufort and Duchess Roads, were being cut near the Oratory, which would thus be able to develop as a mission or parish.

[2] Newman attended all O'Curry's lectures and arranged for him to deliver further ones. When these lectures of 1855–6 were published as *Lectures on the Manuscript Materials of Ancient Irish History*, Dublin 1861, O'Curry wrote in his Preface, pp. vii–viii,

'Little indeed did it occur to me on the occasion of my first timid appearance in that chair, that the efforts of my feeble pen would pass beyond the walls within which these Lectures were delivered. There was, however, among my varying audience one constant attendant, whose presence was both embarrassing and encouraging to me, —whose polite expressions at the conclusion of each Lecture I scarcely dared to receive as those of approbation,—but whose kindly sympathy practically exhibited itself, not in mere words alone, but in the active encouragement he never ceased to afford me as I went along; often, for example, reminding me that I was not to be uneasy at the apparent shortness of a course of Lectures, the preparation of which required so much of labour in a new field; and assuring me that in his eyes, and in the eyes of those who had committed the University to his charge, quantity was of far less importance than accuracy in careful examination of the wide range of subjects which it was my object to digest and arrange. At the conclusion of the course, however, this great scholar and pious priest (for to whom can I allude but to our late illustrious Rector, the Rev. Dr. Newman),—whose warmly felt and oft expressed sympathy with Erinn, her wrongs and her hopes, as well as her history, I am rejoiced to have an opportunity thus publicly to acknowledge,—astonished me by announcing to me on the part of the University, that my poor Lectures were deemed worthy to be published at its expense. Nor can I ever forget the warmth with which Dr. Newman congratulated me on this termination of my first course. . . .'

Cf. *McGrath*, p. 394.

[3] Stanton wrote on 26 Feb. that Alexander Chirol, a clergyman who became a Catholic in 1847 and had an invalid wife, was in distressed circumstances. Chirol had

Meanwhile, Ornsby asked me to let my name stand among names who would *take subscriptions*. To this I decidedly objected. It would fill me with scruples, and I should end in having to pay lots of money as possible restitution money. Mrs C (I forget her name) *without my leave* used my name in this way, and I was pestered with small sums as 10/- which I did not know how to get to her, or how to remember. And so in this case, I should have post office orders, anonymous shillings, inquiries involving correspondence etc. I told Ornsby, I would gladly give my *name simply*, but not to receive money and there it has ended.

I tell you all this, because his first putting my name (without my leave) and then withdrawing it, will force him to give some account unfavorable to me. I think he is not treating me well. Let me know what people are giving, and I will send something to Fr Faber for him — but I almost fear the money will be thrown away — it is sure to be, unless 1. a sufficient sum is collected 2 he uses it for a definite object. He has told us nothing *how much* he wants, or *for what*.

I hope your Father is pretty well — your account cheered me — When you write to him, congratulate him from me on his second book being out. I hear people praising it.[1]

Ever Yrs affly J H N

TO F. S. BOWLES

6 Harcourt Street Dublin. March 15. 1855

My dear Fr Frederic,

I am very sorry to hear from Henry that you are invalided. Get well as soon as you can, or the Easter Music will suffer. I wish I could promise myself the hearing of it.

I have engaged a singing master to come here — and twice a week the youths are to practise. What will come of it I don't know — but we aim at Mass and Vespers. Frederic plays and sings in public, but not in the solo line. I must get him to take to the bass, for the doublebass is now at his finger's ends.

I have not a dream where the Cività is just now either in fact or

a scheme for raising money, and was using Newman's name without asking permission. Stanton suggested that Newman should ask him for particulars of his scheme.

[1] *Growth in Holiness* had appeared towards the end of 1854. It was now followed by *The Blessed Sacrament*, dedicated 'To my most dear Father, John Henry Newman, to whom in the mercy of God I owe the Faith of the Church, the Grace of the Sacraments, and the Habit of Saint Philip, with much more that love knows and feeds upon, though it cannot tell in words, but which the Last Day will show,' dated 2 Feb., 'Seventh Anniversary of the English Oratory.'

opinion but, as Jack Morris has just been informing me of Wm Palmer's reception, I think it safest to inform you, that the Czar is dead. Are you with Alexander ii? or is this a graceful moment to rat?[1]

Will Bloxam follow Wm Palmer? and had the President's death any thing to do with Palmer's move?[2]

Tell Henry that I said Mass for all of you on St Gregory's day — and he must not fancy that he was forgotten. Congratulate him, and thank him for his letter.[3]

Ever Yrs affly J H N

TO W. J. O'NEILL DAUNT

6 Harcourt Street Dublin March 16. 1855

My dear Sir

I fear I cannot from memory answer your question — and I have not books here to consult. The books, comparatively deficient in evidence, which are received by Protestants, are the Epistle to the Hebrews, the Catholic Epistles of St James and 2nd St Peter, the 2nd and 3rd of St John, and the Apocalypse. I am not quite sure of St James being one of them. It was rejected by Luther, but, I fancy, on its internal evidence, as being contrary to his doctrine of justification by faith alone. Of the Hebrews and Apocalypse, the former was not received generally in the West, nor the latter in the East.

As to the Old Testament, the books Protestants take, depend on the authority of the Jews, so that that of the Fathers is superseded by them. However, the book of Daniel (which Protestants acknowledge) was but doubtfully received, I think, by the Jews — and is not found in the Septuagint Version. Or rather I think it was translated so badly, that the Christians substituted Theodotion's — and the version of the Septuagint was discovered in the course of last century. Any how, the Jews are said to have looked doubtfully on the book of Daniel.

Would not Dr Dixon's work on the Canon give you all the information you require?[4]

[1] Morris and Bowles must have been readers of the conservative Jesuit monthly in Rome, *Civiltà Cattolica*. Palmer was received on 27 Feb. and Nicholas I, who died on 2 March was succeeded by Alexander II.

[2] Bloxam and Palmer were Fellows of Magdalen and close friends of Martin Joseph Routh, the President, whose death on 22 Dec. 1854, may have made it easier for Palmer to become a Catholic.

[3] St Gregory's day, 12 March, was the fifth anniversary of Bittleston's admission into the Oratory.

[4] Joseph Dixon (Archbishop of Armagh), *A General Introduction to the Sacred Scriptures*, Dublin 1852.

I do not know what the Second Council of Carthage says about clerical continence.[1] I hardly know what is meant by being a *rule*. It was not a precept — or de fide. It is a point of discipline. There seems to have been a difference in East and West. St Jerome speaks, I think, as if the Apostles allowed married men to be in sacred orders, propter duritiam cordis.

As to Protestant Handbills, what would become of the country, if Catholics posted bills up as well? I often marvel at the meekness of Catholics here. If they began a furious retaliation, government would be sure to interfere and stop both sides.

I am, My dear Sir, Very faithfully Yours

John H Newman

W. J. O'N. Daunt Esqr

TO A. LISLE PHILLIPPS

6 Harcourt Street Dublin March 16. 1855.

My dear Mr Phillipps,

I have been reading your new book with great interest. I believe you have been kind enough to send it me — if so, accept my best thanks. Anyhow, I have to thank you for the pleasure and the instruction which I have gained from its perusal — and for the honorable mention you have made in the course of it, of my little book on the Turks.[2]

It is important, over and above the sound views you put forth, that Catholics should handle the Apocalypse. Protestants are too apt to think that we *give it up* into their hands, as confessedly their weapon, not our property; — as Dr Pusey's low Church friend, who, when P quoted some text of St Paul in expounding the Catholic view of baptism, said 'Stop, stop, you have got hold of one of *our* texts;' just as if he had taken off a friend's hat or umbrella on purpose or by accident.

My only difficulty in following you absolutely and altogether is, that Catholic tradition seems to teach that Antichrist will come shortly or immediately before the coming of Christ. That Mahomet is one most special type of him, I do not at all doubt. Hoping you will excuse this

---

[1] The Council of Carthage in A.D. 390 forbad priests and deacons to live as married men.

[2] *Mahometanism in its Relation to Prophecy; or, an Inquiry into the Prophecies concerning Antichrist, with some reference to their bearing on the Events of the Present Day,* London 1855. Phillipps argued that Mahomet was Antichrist and the break up of the Turkish Empire the end of his reign. Newman's *Lectures on the History of the Turks in its Relation to Christianity* are praised on p. 149.

superfluous criticism, and with kindest regards to Mrs Phillipps, I am,
My dear Mr Phillipps Most sincerely Yours in Xt

                                        John H Newman of the Oratory
Ambrose Lisle Phillipps Esqr

P.S.   Harry Ryder is in this house, fagging hard. Lisle over the way.[1]

TO JOHN HUNGERFORD POLLEN

                                  6. Harcourt Street. Dublin March 16. 1855
Private
My dear Mr Pollen,

Some weeks back, when I found that Dr Cullen's delay was pro-
tracted, I wrote to him to mention your name for the office which you
were kind enough to allow me to impose upon you. He has not yet
answered me.

Also, within this week, I had determined, since he did not return,
to begin my University Church without him. I have hardly moved,
when a person who has a right to be heard, has scruples about my plan
— and begs a fortnights delay. I am obliged to grant it, or I should have
been consulting you in this letter.[2]

You shall hear from me again as soon as I can write. Meanwhile I
hope you will believe that it is not my fault, however I may regret it,
that I have kept you in this suspence.

Very faithfully Yours in Xt

                                        John H. Newman of the Oratory
J H Pollen Esq.

TO THOMAS SCRATTON

                                        6 Harcourt Street March 17/55
My dear Scratton

If you will draw Byrne's bill, I will pay it — I take *for granted* that it
is all right. It is a great sum.[3]

I meant to have sent you back the green cloth and candlestick and

---

[1] i.e. in the University House, 86 Stephen's Green.
[2] This person was perhaps Dr Leahy, the Vice-Rector.
[3] £109 for fifty-one benches and a desk.

scissors yesterday. He has sent nothing else included in the bill I sent you.

As to the Library rules, it will be a long time before they are wanted — sorting, cataloguing, and placing will be laborious works. When the place is ready you will have to send to James R. Hope Scott Esqr, Paper Buildings, Temple, for *his* books.

Ever Yrs J H N

TO T. W. ALLIES

Dublin Mar 20. 1855

My dear Allies,

I do not know how to answer your reasons and [or] to wonder at your decision, but I grieve about it very much, because it has brought out clearly that we can never have you here. The highest sum which has been assigned for a Professor is £300 a year.

Modern and English History will be a most important subject of teaching, and, I suppose, will occupy the more advanced youths, and the Professor, as much as classics ordinarily does. I do not see how the instruction could be carried on by a non-resident Professor, coming at intervals.

We are getting on very well, and though fierce winds blow through the Irish sky and howl at our windows, we are very warm and comfortable indoors.

Ever yrs affly in Xt   John H Newman of the Oratory

P.S.   I shall be glad to have your lectures in the summer, but I do not press for them till the autumn. Before you write I must talk to you about the number, etc.

TO EDWARD BADELEY

6 Harcourt Street Dublin March 20. 1855

My dear Badeley,

A friend of mine is writing a life of Cardinal Mezzofanti; and is collecting anecdotes of all sorts. I happened to say that the Cardinal had spoken to you about Hudibras — and he wishes very much to know the particulars. Could you detail them to me?[1]

[1] Dr Russell of Maynooth was preparing his *The Life of Cardinal Mezzofanti*, London 1858. Badeley had seen the Cardinal a year before his death in 1848, and the

I have nothing to tell you except that it would be very pleasant to have a long chat with you — and that, if I come to Town ever, I shall try to make you postpone 'tua seria ludo,'[1] and gossip with me. We are going on very well here, but I am blocked in my attempt to do more, by some sinister influences, which I hope will not last.

Ever Yours affectly John H. Newman

P.S.   How is the Trust Bill (Catholic) going on?[2]

TO EDWARD CASWALL

6 Harcourt Street March 20/55

My dear Edward,

Thank William for his letter, and tell him, (and yourself) that I propose, if all is well, to come to you on Spy Wednesday; so to be in readiness to celebrate on the Three Days. I shall depart on the following (Easter) Wednesday.

I hope Fr Frederic is well again. I hope I gave my acquiescence in your undertaking the school. I was very glad of it.

I wish you would be cautious in going to the leads.[3] Fr Ambrose whisked round the Library sky light in a way which might easily have sent him off.

As to your thoughtful and very liberal offer about the £1000, you must look back at our register. We have got the money interest on certain conditions, and it must remain ours, I suppose, by Church rules. Your plan does not interfere with this, but you must look at it carefully.

anecdote is given, pp. 406–07. Mezzofanti was astonished to learn that *Hudibras* had been translated into French, 'But how is it possible to translate such a book? The rhymes, the wit, the jokes, are the material points of the work—and it is impossible to translate these—you cannot give *them* in French!' During the rest of the interview he kept exclaiming 'Hudibras in French! Hudibras in French! Most extraordinary—I never heard of such a thing!' Russell inserted the story as an example of Mezzofanti's minute knowledge of English language and literature.

[1] *Eclogue*, VII, 17.

[2] When the Charitable Trusts Act was passed in 1853, the Government promised to deal later with Catholic objections but nothing came of this. Cf. letter of 6 Oct. 1853 to Hope-Scott.

[3] Caswall wrote on 19 March that after a view from the lead roof of the Oratory house, he had been struck with the importance of buying some unoccupied land near, which would otherwise be built on and turned in to a 'grove.' He suggested an arrangement by which he could provide £1000 purchase money.

Your plan seems a very good one, tho' I don't know what a 'grove' is.[1] Take care you don't give *too much.*

Ever Yrs affly J H N

P.S.   I forget whether I ever thanked Henry for his letter. I hope he is quite strong again.

TO THOMAS GRANT, BISHOP OF SOUTHWARK

6 Harcourt Street Dublin March 20. 1855

My dear Lord,

Your letter was as pleasant and encouraging as it was kind.

I should be truly indebted to you, if you would keep in mind our poor youths here, and commend them to our dear Lady. They are a very good set, and, judging from their way of going on, (I am speaking of them all, 30 or 40 of them altogether) I do trust they are in a state of grace, and going on hopefully. Of my own in particular I speak with great confidence — and consider that of the many blessings with which we have been favored here, the greatest is the set of youths who make up my own house. Alas, youths are so changeable, that I must not boast, yet it can't be wrong in saying it in thanksgiving, that I could not ask a more religious innocent set of fellows than I have. And it is most important, for, as you know, the Irish love rank and that sort of thing, and the example of youths, such as those of whom I have charge, being attentive to their duties, gentle and modest, has great influence on the whole body. Their minds are well occupied with reading, and they are making progress in their studies. Harry Bowden is not one of them. His Father has preferred he should be an extern, and he is reading with Mr Ornsby. Francis Kerr is my youngest here — and is a boy — but a very pleasant one, as you know, and we get on very well. Thank you for all you promise me, when need occurs, of your aid, which I shall value very much.[2]

But this is 'private and confidential.'

Thank you for all your kindness, My dear Lord, and believe me Yr Lordship's affecte friend & Servt in Xt

John H Newman of the Oratory

The Rt Revd the Bp of Southwark

[1] Caswall defined this on 24 March as 'an alley of trees with small houses of an inferior description on each side.'

[2] A new paragraph begins here, of which the first line has been cut out at the bottom of one page, and the second and third erased at the top of another. It seems to refer to the controversy between Archbishops Cullen and MacHale, and the objection to English professors.

TO THOMAS SCRATTON

March 21 [1855]

My dear Scratton,

Mr Curry is going to give two more Lectures next week, on Tuesday (27) and Thursday (29) — So they will be advertised.

Send a civil answer to the inclosed, telling him that since we break up in July, it will be hardly worth while the Youths' coming for a week or two. And send him November 1 (I think) of the Gazette, which gives the information about entrance.

Ever Yrs J H N

P.S. You might suggest their coming after Easter.

TO MRS WILLIAM FROUDE

6 Harcourt Street Dublin March 22/55

My dear Mrs Froude

I am amazed at your extract. There was a controversy about it when it came out, unless I mistake. I don't know — but I fancy the passage turned out to be a squib of [parody][1] of the Jesuits, which Wordsworth had taken in earnest — but I will send it to some Jesuit friend, and you shall hear his account of it.[2]

[1] There was a word here which the copyist could not decipher.

[2] The Jesuits seem not to have replied to Newman. See letter of 8 June to Mrs Froude. The page torn from a book by Wordsworth is now lost. The indications are that it came from one of the early anti-Catholic books of Christopher Wordsworth, who has many references to the Jesuits. The following 'Profession' which Wordsworth quotes from *Libri Symbolici Ecclesiae Catholicae*, editi a Streitwolf, Göttingen 1838, II, p. 343, in his *Letters to M. Gondon on the Destructive Character of the Church of Rome*, 2nd ed., London 1847, pp. 69–71, would seem to fit very closely to Newman's description:

'Confessio Romano-Catholica in Hungariâ Evangelicis publicè praescripta et proposita.'

'I We confess that we have been brought from heresy to the Roman Catholic faith by the diligence and aid of the Fathers of the Society of Jesus.

II We confess that the Pope of Rome is Head of the Church, and *cannot err*.

III We confess and are certain that the Pope of Rome is Vicar of Christ and has plenary power of remitting and retaining sins according to his will, and of thrusting men down into hell (in infernum detrudendi).

IV We confess that whatever *new* thing the Pope of Rome *may have instituted* (quicquid Papa instituerit novi), whether it be in Scripture or out of Scripture (sive

You see, the passage comes to me with the same characters of absurdity, and excites my sense of the ludicrous just as if I were told that the lines in the Rejected Addresses 'Heaven bless the guards — Heaven bless their coats of scarlet — etc. Heaven bless their pigtails, tho' they are now cut off —[1] was the prayer of a Tory, and definitely, of the 'Squires and Parsons of Devonshire.'

Excuse my bad writing. Love to William.

Ever Yrs affly J. H. N.

P.S. Alas! before I saw your P.S. I damaged the precious portion of Wordsworth by tearing off part for my Jesuit friend — but I have begged him to send it back to me, and you shall have all. However, you set me the example of mutilation.

TO THOMAS SCRATTON

Friday March 23/55

My dear Scratton

I suppose I had better pay the Insurance of the University House As to the Clerical Library, I know it is doubtful.[2]

Ever Yrs J H N

infrà sive extrà Scripturam), is *true, divine and salvific*; and therefore ought to be regarded as of *higher* value by lay people than the *precepts of the living God* (*ideoque a laicis majoris aestimari debere Dei Vivi praeceptis*).

v We confess that the Most Holy Pontiff ought to be honoured by all with *divine honour* (honorari divino honore), with more prostration than what is due to Christ Himself.

vi We confess and affirm that the Pope is to be obeyed (*audiendum*) by all men in all things, without exception, and that whoever contravenes his decrees is not only *to be burnt without mercy*, but to be delivered, *body and soul, to hell*.

vii We confess that the reading of Scripture is the source of heresy, and the fountain of blasphemy. . . .'

[1] Newman quotes the last lines of the first of the *Rejected Addresses*, 'Loyal Effusion':

> 'God bless the Army, bless their coats of scarlet,
> God bless the Navy, bless the Princess Charlotte;
> God bless the Guards, though worsted Gallia scoff,
> God bless their pig-tails, though they're now cut off . . .'

[2] Scratton wrote on 21 March that 'the Clerical Library had been voted unanimously to the Catholic University, as the Clergy find it merely a source of expense to them—We are obliged to them but it seems they will expect corresponding privileges in the use of our Library.'

TO MISS M. R. GIBERNE

6 Harcourt Street Dublin March 24. 1855

My dear Miss Giberne,

Your letter came a day or two ago — and, tho' I have nothing to say, still, since I have no very great work on my hands just now, and may have soon, I think it best to write to thank you, not only for it, but for some vestments which I am told have come for me, and left Bm [Birmingham] for this place last Monday, I hear. I am sure I shall like them very much, and am particularly obliged to you. Dr Cullen has got me leave to have the Blessed Sacrament in the house — so I have built a chapel — and we have reserved it since Quinquagesima. I am amused at your trying to get intimate with Dr C. [Cullen]. He is full of business, and I could have prophesied he would not have returned your call. He has not written to me since January, and I want a letter. I fear we shall have a good deal of trouble in this country, and only hope the University will not suffer. It was said the Pope determined the Irish Prelates should not go, till all was clear — but Popes are not omnipotent, and there are substances, which, when ignited, become gas, and you cannot kept [sic] them in your possession, if you would.

The University Gazette seems dying from inanition. There is no one to edit it. I put it into the hands of an Editor, and it fell off in the way you have seen. Now I have changed it to once a month, intending to finish it in May, and to take the very next two months April and May myself — but it is a great nuisance giving it up.[1]

I am very much pleased to hear your account of Mr Lyons — and I will not forget him. I think I saw him once — I dined with Lord Arundel the day his son and heir was born — and two Mr Lyons were there — one is in command of a vessel. This one, I think, is a Ch Ch [Christ Church] man.[2]

Henry Wilberforce edits the Catholic Standard, and there have been so [sic] good leading articles in it. It is provoking that it is so difficult to get you newspapers to Rome. His wife has been ill with influenza, worse than she has ever been since 1838. We have had snow again in England, and even here a sprinkling.

Palmer's conversion is a great point. I wish Mr Lyons would follow

[1] The last number of the *Catholic University Gazette* was that of 7 Aug. 1856.

[2] For Richard Lyons cf. letter of 6 Nov. 1854 to Miss Giberne. He went up to Christ Church in 1835. His younger brother Edmund Mowbray Lyons commanded the *Miranda* in the Black Sea, and died in the Crimea. Newman met the two brothers on 28 Dec. 1847. See diary for that day. Lord Arundel's heir, later fifteenth Duke of Norfolk, was born on 27 Dec.

his example instead of criticizing him — I see in today's paper that Mr Deane of All Souls has just been received too.[1] With your letter came one from R. Wilberforce from Paris. I am glad to say, he is going to pay me a visit here in May.[2]

Jemima was asking how to direct to you. I told her that the 'Palazzo Borghese' would find you. You are wrong in supposing I do not make a great deal of such remarkable little events, as you describe about the Madonna's picture. I will tell you one which occurred to myself the other day — Don't laugh, for I am quite serious. I went out of doors, and when I got two paces, I said 'Something is the matter with my person. I think I am not brushed.' So without a word and not being able to say why, ⟨⟨Don't you tell any one⟩⟩ I at once turned, knocked at the door, went in, and said to my servant 'Brush me.' I was quite well brushed enough, but, to my surprise, I had no (long) gaiters on — and there should I have pranced about Dublin showing my worsted stockings! I can't account for such things at all — I think it is my Guardian Angel. I am perfectly *sure* I had no sensation of cold about my calfs. The contrary — my accident of the autumn not being well, I had just been obliged to put on my elastic stocking again — and *that* is how I came to think I *had* gaiters on — for I felt a thickness of covering. I really cannot fancy my distress, if in the midst of the fashion of Dublin in Sackville Street, I had found my situation. A more remarkable thing of the same kind occurred to me years ago.

I wish you would buy yourself a writing desk — and get two candles to see by. You laugh at me when I say all this.

Mr Grenside is a convert — a pious good man — who has done a good deal in his parish with little means — he is an awful proser and bore.[3]

[1] Edward Dean was the son of Richard Betenson Brietzeke, a barrister, who was at Christ Church, changed his name to Dean, became Chairman of the Board of Customs, and died in 1850. His son Edward Dean, matriculated at Christ Church 10 Nov. 1831 at the age of 17, was a Fellow of All Souls 1836–55, B.C.L. 1838, D.C.L. 1843, and also Vicar of Lewknor, near Oxford.

[2] Robert Wilberforce wrote from Paris on 20 March, '*I long to see you* after our ten years separation.

I have stopped here instead of going to Rome, because I found I could not talk French, and I didn't like to see the Holy Father in dumb show. Next winter, if I live, I hope to see him and ask his blessing. Meanwhile I have been learning French, and studying Geology and mineralogy, which may perhaps be useful, if I ever settle in Ireland, as I think likely. Have you anyone to lecture on such subjects in your University?

But towards the middle of May I think of returning for a time to England, and my first object would be to renew my old intimacy with the man I most value in the British Islands.'

[3] John Grenside built the church, school and priest's house at Rugeley, and lived there in great poverty. He died on 29 Dec. 1867.

If you want to do me a kindness, think sometimes when you are painting your Madonna, of the 8 poor youths here with me, and beg her to take them into her keeping

Ever Yrs affly John H Newman

6 Harcourt Street Dublin March 25. 55

My dear Lord Henry

I could wish with you that Francis showed some great penitence, but I think he is only thoughtless and a boy — and as he did not reflect then on what he was doing, so he does not reflect now enough on what he has done. He may feel it a good deal more than he seems to do — And the proof of it will be his being more careful in future. I shall look anxiously for that —

On his saying you wished him to have some clothes I sent him to my own tailor, who is also the Oratorian Tailor in London, a well known man as a good Catholic. From what I hear since from the other youths, I suspect the Dublin tailors are generally cheaper than he is, and I have had some compunction in consequence. I have no doubt his cloth and work is much better than theirs, but this may not be necessary for a boy, who is not likely to suffer his clothes to last so long as to enjoy the benefit of this superiority. Will you be so good to give him instructions on this point?

Were it not that his brother's return from the Black Sea is an unanswerable reason, I am sorry he is going away at Easter.[1] There are no vacations here except the Long — i e in such sense that the youths are *sent down*; though they may go if their friends please. I hope his going away will not unsettle him. I propose to leave for Birmingham on Tuesday week, the 3rd. He can remain here (with my friend Mr Renouf, who is in the house) as the others do, or go with me to Bm [Birmingham] and there wait till his brother returns — as you please — Our term recommences on the 22nd of April. I should be sorry for him to be away then but a brother's return under such circumstances would be taken at Oxford as an excuse for absence and will be here — Since he *is* to go, it does not matter whether he goes on the 3rd or on the 10th as far as unsettlement is concerned — so if you prefer him to go to Bm [Birmingham] I will take him with me and we shall be all very glad of his company

---

[1] Henry Schomberg Kerr was serving on H.M.S. *Vengeance*.

there. Indeed I think that will be the best arrangement; and then you can send to us for him, when you will —

Thank you for your good news about Ralph He should not be over-worked if he came here.

Very sincerely Yrs in Xt   John H Newman

TO AUBREY DE VERE

6 Harcourt Street Dublin March 26/55

My dear Mr de Vere,

I did certainly despair of having the advantage of your aid in the English Literature — and that, because I doubted how far I could persuade you to take a *large* subject upon you.[1]

The feeling of the day, and the opinions and views expressed in the India Civil Service Report, lead us to lay a great stress on English Literature. There will be many, perhaps the majority, who will give up the classics, as soon as they can — that is, at the end of the first two years. Such there will be very soon, since at present the two years at a school count as if residence here.

Now English Literature is next best to Latin and Greek — and, though it is difficult to do it, we must attempt to lecture the young men in it — I think they must know Shakespeare, Bacon, Addison, Clarendon etc in some shape or other. The *history* of English Literature, of English *Philosophy*, etc etc. will be a great field for taking a Catholic view, of what is in itself an engine against us.

I had certainly thought that the *real constant work* which carrying out a scheme of this kind involves had been more than you felt you could give us — and with great reluctance and sorrow I had come to the conclusion that you declined the post which carried with it a responsibility. Your letter gives me hopes it is not so.

In consequence of my impression I had offered the Professorship of English to another person; the letter went on Saturday last. This is Monday. But I can *most easily* reverse it, if you only will rejoice me by saying that you will make yourself *one with* us.[2]

---

[1] See letter of 25 Jan. to de Vere, for this and the next paragraph.

[2] The rest of this letter is missing. De Vere became eventually Professor of Political and Social Science. There seems to be no record of the name of the friend to whom Newman had offered the Professorship of English Literature; possibly it was Robert Wilberforce. In the end MacCarthy combined it with that of Poetry.

TO HENRY WILBERFORCE

Monday [26 March 1855]

My dear Henry

If you can avoid it, I wish you would *not* put the part of the May-nooth Report, which is about the *Professors' want of intimacy with the Students*, in your paper of *Saturday next the 31st*. I am putting it in the Gazette of *April 5*, and we have great difficulty to make the Gazette interesting.[1]

Ever Yrs J H N

TO AMBROSE ST JOHN

6 Harcourt Street March 27. 1855

My dear Ambrose

I continue saying Masses for you, and shall till you notice properly my last letter but one.[2]

As to the sounds, I told him to send them here, and much regretted he made the mistake of sending it to Bm.[3]

Ever Yrs affly J H N

WEDNESDAY 28 MARCH 1855   Terminal Examinations began

TO AMBROSE ST JOHN

⌜March 28 1855?⌝[4]

As to the line I wrote about the Sermons, I like the subjects each Father has chosen. Tell Stanislas there is *not a* chance of my subject

---

[1] See letter of 28 March to Wilberforce.

[2] Newman's last extant letter but one is that of 17 Feb. It would seem probable that an intervening letter has been lost, and that Newman is referring to his letter of 22 Feb. to St John, with its promise to 'say Mass every week for you, till you are in a better humour.' St John complained on 26 March that his letters were being left un-answered. See Newman's letters of 12 and 18 May.

[3] A gift of cod sounds ('the sound or air-bladder of the cod,' *OED*) had been received at Birmingham. St John wrote on 26 March, 'we have found out the way to dress them, and they are very good indeed . . . the first time I had them no one liked them . . . Frying was the great mistake. The receipt for stewing has happily retrieved them . . .'   [4] Newman added the year and question mark in pencil.

clashing with his, (if I come) — Don't let him fancy it. He will preach on lapses and relapses — I on loss of final perseverance.⌐

TO HENRY WILBERFORCE

6 Harcourt Street Dublin March 28. 1855

My dear Henry

I propose to go to Birmingham on Tuesday next.

After all I shall not perhaps use the Maynooth Report till the Gazette of May — so, I must not hinder you.[1] At the same time *education* is so much *my* line, not yours, that I really should be obliged to you, if, though you insert the Report in your paper, you did *not* call attention to Dr Moriarty's evidence and the others on the Patriarchal and constitutional systems which is so much to *my* purpose.[2]

Your letter has just come — and I was very much concerned at you and your wife's continued indisposition. Both together makes it very trying.

⌐As to my Letters, [[[(signed Catholicus, 'Who's to blame?')]]] I think altogether your wish is *not to be entertained*

  1. If they are known as mine, you *separate them off* from the Standard. What you should aim at is that people should say 'Really there was a very good letter in the Standard on such and such a subject.' You had better let the idea rise, as it gradually will,[3] that 'N. writes in it,' than point out specifically *what* I write. If you get Badeley to read, *because* it is *mine*, he does not read the paper because it is *yours*.

  2. Next, You will see a letter on 'Public evening Lectures' in the

---

[1] This was the *Report of Her Majesty's Commissioners appointed to Inquire into the Management and Government of the College of Maynooth*, Dublin 1855. The Royal Commission was appointed in 1853 to inquire into 'The Management and Government of the College of Maynooth; the discipline and Course of Studies pursued therein; also into the effects produced by the increased Grants conferred by Parliament in the year 1845.'

[2] Dr Moriarty, at the time President of All Hallows College, was examined at great length about the absence of close relations between professors and students. He thought it a great mistake and contrasted it unfavourably with the opposite practice of his own College. The Commission recommended that the junior professors should be represented on the Council of the President. Newman extracted the evidence of Moriarty and others, from the *Report*, and published it in the *Catholic University Gazette*, (3 May 1855), pp. 425–30. The *Catholic Standard*, which summarised the *Report* on 24 March, had nothing further except a general leading article on 31 March.

[3] [[You had better let the idea be started, as it will]]

Gazette of April which is to the point here.[1] People may not read the 1st 2nd or 3rd — but some one or other will read the 4th — he won't read 5th or 6th — but he will take up the 7th. Then it will come on him, 'well, really there is a good deal in these letters — whose can they be?' My Catholicus in the Times [[February 1841]] was ascribed to Phill-potts.[2] The *mystery* will make people begin to read. But even supposing they are but half read by any one, by the end of them the idea is created and grown up. 'There are clever writers in the C. [[Catholic]] Standard.' People won't recollect *what* was cleverly done — but there will be a general feeling — 'I recollect reading one or two very good letters' etc etc.

Don't be impatient — be content to work, work on. I shall do you more good by being half read, and *not* known, than entirely read and known.

3. I am not sure whether you will follow me to *the end*, and will not think me severe and unjust.

4. I have an enormous dislike to puffing. S. Wood used to find fault with my writing [[publishing]] 'Parochial Sermons —' he said that, if I gave another name [[e.g. 'Essays']], people [[intellectual people]] will read. And then he quarrelled with the *titles* of particular sermons, [[as unfair to myself because they]] which had more in them than the titles promised. From a child a description of Ulysses's eloquence in the Iliad seized my imagination and touched my heart. When he began, he looked like a fool. This is the only way in which I have done anything. φαίης κεν ζάκοτόν τινα ἔμμεναι etc.[3]

5. I have the greatest diffidence in what I have written — feeling I am no lawyer, and think that most people will think me sour and soured.

Well, on the whole — when you have read to the end of the 8th, if you *still* think it desirable, you may in confidence tell Manning, and ask him if it is desirable [[to disclose my name]]. If you both agree that it is, you may tell it privately, in the way you propose⌐

Ever Yrs affly J H N

P.S.   I think Mirror does very well.

[1] The *Catholic University Gazette*, (5 April 1855), pp. 420–22. This letter empha-sised that the purpose of public lectures was to attract attention, 'They do not invite an audience, but an attendance.' See *Appendix* 3, p. 568, and *Idea*, pp. 490–4.
[2] *The Letters* by Catholicus, i.e. 'The Tamworth Reading Room,' *D.A.* pp. 254–305, were said to be by Henry Phillpotts, Bishop of Exeter.
[3] *Iliad*, III, 220.

THURSDAY 29 MARCH 1855   Public Evening Lectures ended

TO THOMAS SCRATTON

Thursday 29 March [1855]

My dear Scratton

The Quarter days are 1st of Novr, Febr, May and August.

As I said the other day, so I repeat, if you will but draw the cheques, I will sign them. I have expected Byrne's bill from you for the benches some time.

I send Beardwood's bills, which I will pay, if you testify to the University Rooms bill. Mr Flannery has looked over the other

Ever Yrs J H N

TO HENRY WILBERFORCE

6 Harcourt Street 9 am Thursday [29 March 1855]

My dear Henry

At the very last moment 9 am your people send the proof. It cannot get back till midday Friday. And so stands a chance of appearing not corrected at all.

I send it back at once. Why cannot they send me all those 6, 7, 8 at once?

Ever Yrs J H N

P.S.   And your people gave *no direction*. So I make a shot!

FRIDAY 30 MARCH 1855   Terminal Examinations ended

TO EDWARD CASWALL

6 Harcourt Street March 30/55

My dear Edward

If we borrow money of you at 4 per cent, it adds £16 to our debt.[1] Some how I am annoyed at this. Whence is the money to come? As it is,

[1] The land referred to in the letter of 20 March to Caswall was offered for sale at £1400.

Fr Stanislas has always thought we shall be minus. Then there is Rednall to provide for.

Is not the *first* question, the ways and means? can I be expected to have an opinion till that question is answered?

In your plan I recollect you named another piece of ground, nearer us — what has become of *it*?

If it were contiguous to Fr Ambrose's ground, more might be said for it. At first sight it is not more convenient to us than if it were at the same distance in any other direction.

£1400 is a very large sum. Consider what might not be done with it. Might you not buy several of the small houses with the ground they stand on, which continue the line of our back wall?

However, I trust I shall see you soon, and will talk over it.

Please tell Fr Wm [William] that I am pleased at his getting the fencing so advanced, and that I approve of the plan he details amounting to £57

We have just finished collections. Poor Louis [de Vaulchier] has fallen ill of excitement. Ralph [Kerr] is ready to come any day, unless his mother strongly urges his going abroad.

Thank Fr Ambrose for his letter

Ever Yrs affly John H Newman

P.S.   You may tell Stanislas to tell Mr Bretherton that on no account will I allow myself to receive a single penny for coming to lecture — or allow it to be given eo nomine, to any Oratory purpose.[1]

SATURDAY 31 MARCH 1855   Vacation began

TO THOMAS SCRATTON

Saturday 31 March [1855]

My dear Scratton

Will you kindly direct and send to the Post the inclosed to Mr. B from H Ryder?

I inclose a letter from Mr McDonogh, which I have told him you will answer. It would be a good thing, if he sent a catalogue, before the books are moved. The moving and packing will cost something, and we ought to be sure the books are worth it, if we can.[2]

---

[1] i.e. for the lecture delivered on 6 Feb.
[2] Cf. letter of 25 Jan. 1855 to V. B. Dillon.

You know far more about accounts than I do; but I do not see why the account of expenditure cannot be drawn out without any knowledge of receipts. But I think you imply some disappointment, which I do not see how to remedy. I assure you I have done nothing to hinder you knowing what the balance is — *and I have no means of letting you know*. I have not the Banker's book and never had. They told me at the Bank that Dr Cullen had it. I fancied you told me that *you* had it. Certainly *I* have not set my eyes on it. I *believed* money was paid into my name, because (not at your second, third, or fourth) but at your first naming the matter I applied to Dr Leahy, and he told me he would certainly attend to it. And I never could make out why after naming it to me, you went on assuming I had none [?]. I think I told you I should mention it to Dr Leahy.

I should be *very much obliged* to you to tell me, as you have done before, when the money is failing — but I declare I don't know how to let you know. For if *you* have not the Banker's book, Dr Cullen has.

Will you ask Ornsby to check Duffy's £30 bill for books

Ever Yrs J H Newman

TO AUBREY DE VERE

March 31. 1855 6 Harcourt Street

My dear Mr de Vere,

Thank you for your long letter. I answer it at once. It has just come.

A year or a year and a half ago I offered many persons a year for preparation, which, you will easily understand, I could not now, when we have actually begun. This will account in part for my doing last Autumn, what I could not so well do now. ⟨The theological school does not begin till Autumn 1855. Also the medical — and engineering.⟩

Another thing is this — that some Professorships are far more of a catechetical nature than others. It would have been too good news to have been able to take for certain that you would consent to help us in so intimate a way — and therefore, not being able to rely upon it, I offered you what either was in its nature merely professorial, or for a time would be such; e.g. the professorships of poetry, of criticism, of political science, of philosophy of religion, and of medieval history. Of these all but the last are in their nature professorial — and the last would have been for a time.

As to English Literature, for the first term or two it might have been professorial only — but not after that. It comes into the course of studies of the second two years, and these we expected would have commenced with some of our young men at this Easter. They have been obliged to put off their examination; and, when that is over, whether in May, June, or July, at once the English Literature becomes a subject, not for mere Professorial Lectures, but for catechetical instruction.

You will see the reason then why I laid such a stress upon lectures in next term (i.e. before the Long Vacation) and also why I did not venture myself to offer you the Professorship of English Literature. It involved as much drudgery as the Professorship of Classics, and seemed to be more than I could persuade you to undertake. It did not require much preparation — it did not require, tho' it admitted, of brilliant composition — but it imperatively demanded drudgery. When, however, Thompson and Monsell wrote to me that they had proposed it to you, you cannot wonder that I should be delighted at the chance of connecting you so intimately with the University — and you cannot fancy I should have been so unjust and unkind to it as to throw obstacles in your way. And Thompson said that he thought if you once began any how, you would go on. In consequence I willingly co-operated in what I should not have myself initiated.

I cannot recollect all that passed but I fancied that two months ago, or whenever it was that we last corresponded, you absolutely declined it — that is, you said you could not be ready till after the long Vacation. Then it came upon me, that we had asked too much of you — and I first (as I told Lord Dunraven or Monsell) proposed to give lectures next term myself, (indeed I have sketched them) and next I got another Professor to undertake a course for me — and lastly having an opportunity, I offered the Professorship to a friend.[1]

If I have been wanting in bringing any point of this out to you, which was necessary for your forming your judgment, pray pardon me — though I am not aware that I have not. We never got so far, as made it necessary for me to say more than I did.

You now so distinctly say that you could not ultimately reside or act as a Tutor, (i.e. a *catechist*) that I fear I must conclude that the Professorship of English Literature will not be one you can accept.

You will see now more clearly why I did not think it unreasonable to insist on lectures without much preparation — viz because I did not want Professorial Lectures so much as familiar general expositions such as beginners especially require, and an educated person can throw off. If you stood up on a sudden and said any thing which came uppermost, you would be sure to do them good.

I cannot help thinking that, if I had the pleasure of some conversation with you, I should express myself much better, and less run the risk

---

[1] See letter of 26 March to de Vere.

of leaving on your mind impressions which I did not mean to convey, than by writing.

I trust Robert Wilberforce will be here in May

Ever Yrs very sincerely in Xt

John H Newman of the Oratory

Aubrey de Vere Esqr

P.S. The young men having put off their examinations, I could do without the catechetical lectures till after the Long Vacation—and do not *especially* want the Professorial before. But I can talk much better than I write.

TO HENRY WILBERFORCE

Saturday March 31 [1855]

My dear Henry

I go to Birmingham on Tuesday — therefore, if the proof comes to me, it must be directed *there*.

But your man must either send it earlier, or not at all. I had no time to correct it this week. It came when I was in the midst of business, and, unless I sent it *directly*, it would have been no good to send it at all.

You correct so well, that I am quite satisfied. This week there are faults, *because* I had hardly time to read it over

Ever Yrs J H N

P.S. ⌜I really am anxious about being known, for it *is not my line* — and a person who knows more history or law may say 'ne sutor etc' with justice.⌝[1]

TO EDWARD CASWALL

Palm Sunday April 1/55 6 Harcourt Street

My dear Edward,

I have just heard from Stanislas that Philip Molloy is gone, and that he is going down to day.[2]

As last year, I will take the Christus — on Friday, if you cannot do better.[3]

---

[1] [[Ne sutor ultra crepidam.]]
[2] Philip Molloy, Flanagan's cousin, had just died.
[3] i.e. the Christus part, in the singing of the Gospel on Good Friday.

How strange it is, Stanislas is always called away at a great function —more times than I can count.

Ever Yrs affly J H N

TUESDAY 3 APRIL 1855   Went with Victor [Duke] to Bm [Birmingham] at night

TO A. LISLE PHILLIPPS

6, Harcourt Street Dublin. April 3/55

My dear Mr Phillipps,

I have no cause for writing to you, except that of thanking you for your letter — but it was so very kind to me personally, as well as valuable in itself, that I do not like to put it by without a word of acknowledgment to you.[1]

I trust every year, as it passes, will tend to knit together in one the Catholics of England more and more — and certainly the events, of various kinds, which have been happening for some time, have through God's mercy had that effect.

And not only the Catholics of England, but of Ireland too. Alas! what a great Catholic country this would be, if it could but agree together.

Renouf has been very urgent with me to remember him to you. He is busy here, and very useful.

Lisle Ryder is not directly under my care, and I cannot say so much about him — but Harry is in my house, and is as diligent and good as any one could wish. They would both desire me to name them to you, were they in the way. Lisle is a sharp boy, and is getting on very well.[2]

Ever Yrs most sincerely in Xt,

John H Newman, of the Oratory.

A. L. Phillipps Esqr.

[1] Phillipps wrote on 18 March a long defence of his views on prophecy, in reply to Newman's letter of 16 March. He ended by congratulating Newman on the definition of the Immaculate Conception, 'because I think it must have been personally most precious and interesting to *you*, in as much as It involves an indirect sanction of the highest kind of your own Theory of Development. . . . I acknowledge I *was* one of those, who very much, and as it turns out, very wrongly, objected to that Theory—I need not *now* say, there is an end of all that in my mind.'

[2] Phillipps had sent his love to the Ryders, who were his cousins.

TO HENRY WILBERFORCE

April 3/55

My dear Henry

Your letter is just come. Put what heading you choose. I never meant to limit you, and am sorry I did not express it more distinctly.

⌐I think you are making too much of what is a mere trifle as a composition. The Oxford Tracts were a work and had a principle.⌐

Ever Yrs affly J H N

⌐P.S. I am nervously afraid of your making too much of a trifle.⌐ Your title 'Why have we failed before Sebastopol' will do very well. ⌐I could write you some more letters on the subject, if you are not tired and if I have time.⌐[1]

WEDNESDAY 4 APRIL 1855 arrived there [Birmingham] early in the morning

TO CATHERINE ANNE BATHURST

Oratory Hagley Road April 4/55

My dear Child

I am just arrived, and find your letter.

It strikes me, I told you to go by the advice of your Revd Mother. It will never do for you to act except *under the tradition* of a religious house. To say nothing of moral evils, there will be physical ones. You must go by the tradition of your community. I don't think it will do to ask Stuart[2] any more than me — and I don't like your making me so independent in a matter of this kind of your community. I don't know how I can *act* as your Confessor absolutely, tho' I am very glad to give hints or suggestions.

I can say nothing till I know you proceed under your Revd Mother. *We* are not a regular body, yet even we should not act in such matters except under our Superior.

As to Fr Faber's book, I suppose it is a perfect magazine of valuable

[1] Newman's seventh letter, published in the *Catholic Standard*, (14 April), pp. 9–10, was headed 'Who is to Blame?' In *D.A.* p. 345 it became 'English Jealousy of Law.' The eighth letter, 21 April, p. 9 was headed 'A Free State or a Standing Army;' and in *D.A.* p. 353 'English Jealousy of Church and Army.'
[2] Her brother, Stuart Eyre Bathurst.

thoughts — but it must not make you scrupulous. What suits one person, does not another. To say that *every one* is joyful at first, is as untrue as the Evangelical notion, that every one must pass through certain stages of conviction etc etc.[1]

I shall not forget you in Mass tomorrow

Ever Yrs affly J H N

MAUNDY THURSDAY 5 APRIL 1855   was celebrant these three days

TO D. B. DUNNE

April 5/55

My dear Dr Dunne

I am truly glad of your good report of Mr B.[2] Since he is so fair in his Latin, he only wants, what is much less difficult, some rubbing up in Chronology, Geography, Geometry etc.

You will see what you think about it, and what Mr Flannery wishes, but it seems to me that you could not do better than take him into your House at once, and then grind him for a few weeks, after which he could be examined.

Since he is so certain, after some preparation of passing, it seems to me no breach of rule to take him in at once — as a sort of catechumen in an Academical view

Very sincerely Yrs John H Newman of the Oratory

D Dunne Esqr

TO CATHERINE ANNE BATHURST

Good Friday [6 April 1855] Bm.

My dear Child

I did not think or say that you were proceeding without authority, but without tradition. The discipline may be dangerous if used without *teaching*. Nor can Stuart teach you. Women alone can teach you — Some persons object to the shoulders altogether. You are likely to do yourself as much harm as Puseyites in fasting, unless you are *taught*.

This is all I meant

Ever Yrs affly J H N

[1] By Faber's book, *Growth in Holiness* is meant. See chapter one there.
[2] Perhaps Alfred Byrne, who became a scholar of the University.

437

The Oratory Hagley Road Birmingham April 7/55

My dear Mr de Vere

Your notion of my paying you a visit is too pleasant to be easily possible. Whenever I get away from Dublin, I have duties here — but I will not quite despair of it.

Why will you not accept the province of the Belles Lettres? You have some Lectures written, which would come under that head — and when you have finished them, you might go to the literature of any other nation you choose. Do see if this will not do.

I do not quite make out from your letter whether you understand, that Thompson from his great and kind zeal for the University, wrote to you on the subject of the Chair of English Literature before he wrote to me that he had done so.

Very sincerely Yours in Xt   John H Newman of the Oratory

Aubrey de Vere Esqr

P.S.   The best wishes of this sacred season to you.

TO PATRICK MOONEY

Edgbaston April 9/55

My dear Sir

It seems so very difficult to pronounce when the Archbishop will return, that I do not think it right to wait longer without making you a definite proposal on the subject about which I had the pleasure of conversing with you before Christmas. And I have the less scruple in doing so, because I feel sure that, if we can come to an agreement upon it, Dr Cullen is not likely to make any objection.

I propose then to take for a term of the Parish Priest and the parishioners of St Audeon's the whole of the two transepts of the Church, including the High Altar, ⟨communion could be given at the rail which cuts off the transept from the nave.⟩ and the present sacristy for ten years; during which time I (and my executors, being Catholic Priests) should have exclusive occupation and use of these portions of the building with full leave to erect galleries, alter sittings, and in any other way determine the internal arrangements; and permission to appoint services at any hours on Sundays or weekdays, except between 6 and 11 A M; and with exclusive right to make collections at the door during such services as I or my representatives may appoint.

I should draw a barrier across the top of the nave continuing to the walls of the two opposite transepts and that should be the rail for communion.

In return for this accommodation, I propose to build a Parish Sacristy for the convenience of the Priest and otherwise to improve and embellish the building to an expence of £1500, and, as soon as the gross yearly receipts arising from my services pass £300 to pay 20 per cent upon them to the Parish Priest and Parishioners[1]

J H N

TO HENRY WILBERFORCE

Oratory Hagley Road Bm April 9/55

My dear Henry

I wonder if you could give me dinner on Wednesday (the day after tomorrow) at 6. I think I will try, and, if I find you engaged, I can get dinner at the Oratory where I shall sleep. As my teeth are in a very bad condition, I must ask Mrs Wilberforce literally for some pap or something equally soft.

Don't *speak* about my coming. I shall be at the Dentist's at 3 — then I shall run down to Mr Babington, and then I shall come straight to you.[2]

Ever Yrs affly J H N

EASTER TUESDAY 10 APRIL 1855   Victor [Duke] went back to Dublin

WEDNESDAY 11 APRIL   went to London — to Dentist — to Greenwich to Miss Bathurst — to Badeley — Wilberforce in Fleet Street   dining with Wilberforce in Onslow Square   sleeping at Oratory *Brompton*   saw Mr Monteith

THURSDAY 12 APRIL   breakfasted with Badeley — called on Cardinal — Lord H Kerr etc.   went back to Bm [Birmingham]

MONDAY 16 APRIL   set off midday for Dublin, where arrived at night.

[1] Newman made a careful calculation of the cost of his proposal. For the reply see letter of 22 April to Mooney.

[2] Newman, receiving no answer to his application for an appointment, did not see Dr Babington. The latter, who was ill, wrote on 3 May, 'Your very kind letter would have found me, a month since, quite unable to reply to it, and looking forward with no doubtful expectation to the close of my earthly career.' On this letter Newman wrote, 'The last that I had from him. He died while I was abroad (I believe) in January 1856.' Babington had been Newman's medical adviser since 1827.

TO H. E. MANNING

The Oratory Bm April 16/55

My dear Manning,

I am on the wing for Ireland, having been kept here longer than I had expected. It was very provoking that, how I do not know, I had fancied you were out of town, when I was there last week — and H W [Wilberforce] and Badeley either created, or did not remove, this impression, so I did not call on you.

When I came back, I got your letter, on the subject of which I should have liked to talk with you.[1] It pleased me to read your suggestion about my going to Rome, which I had already projected, if things were bad. Indeed, it is now above a year since I was going, had not Dr Cullen stopped me.[2]

Hitherto Dr C. has concurred entirely with me — but, perhaps from over anxiety, I am foreseeing difficulties even in that quarter. I can't help fearing he thinks I do not simply enough throw myself into his cause, and he is getting stronger against young Ireland, as such, than I think it is good for the University that we should be. Two or three

---

[1] Manning wrote:

'78-South Audley Street April 12. 1855.

My dear Newman,

I showed your letter to Hope and to Bellasis: and I think their mind was as follows.
1. That if the present arrangement by which you have real power in the selection of men be destroyed by the influence of the opposite section, it would place you in a position in which you could not continue: but
2. That this is not the state of the facts; nor as we thought from all we hear of Rome, likely to be so: and that as yet there seems no danger of such an alternative: again:
3. That if such a state of facts should arise it would be advisable before you give the slightest expression to your thoughts as to the future, to go in person to Rome, and to lay before the Holy Father the whole case from your point of view: with its consequences as bearing on yourself.
4. Lastly I add what has been always in my mind.

If you should find the national element in Ireland insuperable, would it not be well to re-consider the site of the University.

All your arguments of centrality would apply to the West Coast of England as much as to the East Coast of Ireland. From the first I have rather acquiesced than assented to the present site: except as a balance to the Queen's Colleges. In the sense of your paper on Attica in the 2d or 3d University Gazette, England is even more central to the Anglo Saxon Race than Ireland. [*H.S.* III, pp. 18–32]

The difficulties of contributors would be overcome by the motives which would satisfy the Holy See.

This alternative would I hope be considered before that of your resignation.

I hope you are well. All Easter joys.

Ever yours affecly Henry E. Manning.'

[2] See note to letter of 20 Jan. 1854 to J. I. Taylor.

months ago he wrote (entre nous) to say he heard that I spoke against him; he did not believe it, and I wrote to say it was simply absurd —[1] but still he has not written again (his letter was in January) though I have written to him several times. If, as is not at all unlikely, he objects to young Ireland appointments, while *others* object to our not cursing the Protestant Government, my choice of professors will be still more limited than now.

The worst of my going to Rome would be, that, if I succeeded there, I should be tied by the leg to the University longer than I bargained for.

Hitherto we have been marvellously prospered — so much so, that I do not see that it can last. We have a very good set of youths, and the authorities and professors pull very well together. We have about 40 youths in *lecture*, which, I think, good — and we have need of opening a new house.

Ever Yours affly in Xt   John H Newman of the Oratory

The Revd Dr Manning.

TO F. S. BOWLES

6 Harcourt Street Dublin April 17/55

My dear Frederic

T. Ford came to me between 8 and 9 yesterday morning, and said that he was going at 10 o'clock, at F. Stanislas's direction. I said 'Have you told Fr Frederic?' he said, 'No' — I said 'I will' — and tried to catch you as you left recreation at 10 o'clock; but did not succeed. F. Stanislas perhaps will tell you more.[2]

I had a very calm and good passage, and found all here well. I travelled to Chester with an officer who would have asked me to dine, had I stopped there — and I should have liked it. He was a Cambridge man, perhaps 25 years ago; and began speaking of Mr 'Frowde', as he called him. He could not help making out I was a convert priest, unless he thought me a very far advanced Puseyite. I was very much taken with him.

Tell Stanislas that Beardwood will build me and make *fit for going in to*, four rooms with staircase etc., rooms about 14.6 square, and 10 feet

---

[1] Letter to Cullen of 24 Jan. 1855.

[2] Thomas Ford, a singer in the choir, went to Mount St Bernard to discover whether he could become a Cistercian. He returned to Birmingham on 28 April.

high for £150 — what does he think of this? Perhaps Fr Ambrose too may give an opinion on this weighty point.

Victor has not yet got over his sea sickness

Ever Yours affly J H N

P.S. I have heard from Lady Lothian, who consents to Ralph [Kerr] coming. He *must* be idle, Francis [Kerr] *is* idle, Frederic Thynne, *wishes to be* idle, and Reginald [Barnewall], if not idle, loves amusement, and these four somewhat frighten me.

TO AUBREY DE VERE

6 Harcourt Street Dublin April 18/55

My dear Mr de Vere,

I hope you will not think it rude, if I ask you whether you think you can comply with the suggestion I threw out to you in my last. I do not like to lose your name, your assistance, or your Lectures already completed — is it impossible that there is not some way or other of my having them? I am ashamed of thus teasing you, and, when, I recollect it is not the first or second time I have done so, I feel that nothing but my sincere and strong desire can excuse me — And I think it better to write than to stand the chance of subjecting you, against my will, to some inconvenience by my silence, as perhaps before now.

I wrote my last letter very hastily, and, being absent from my memorandum books, I did not make an abstract of it — but I believe I am right in saying that I asked whether the subject of Polite Literature generally, taking in *all* Languages, would not embrace your present lectures, those you thought of on Dante etc. Would 'Criticism' be more exact?

Very sincerely Yrs in Xt   John H Newman of the Oratory

A. de Vere Esqr

THURSDAY 19 APRIL 1855   Requiem Mass at Jesuits' for Fr Meagher[1]

[1] Thomas Meagher S.J., Rector of Belvedere College.

TO THE EARL OF SHREWSBURY

6 Harcourt Street Dublin April 20. 1855

My dear Lord Shrewsbury,

When I got here from England, I saw your Lordship's letter on my table, and thank you very much for it, pained as I was at what you felt it necessary to write.

There is no great chance of an Englishman obtaining a Professorship here, because the Irish are competent on most subjects, and, caeteris paribus, ought to be taken. Classics are the only province in which Englishmen have a right to be located, and they do not furnish many chairs.

As far as appointments go, matters are at a stand still in consequence of the absence of Dr Cullen, and the most contrary accounts are spread of the time of his return. However, we are going on steadily with the schools which have been opened; and last term had about 40 youths in lecture, which we consider very good. We hope to have a public examination before the Long Vacation.

I beg my best respects to Lady Shrewsbury and Miss Talbot, and beg their good prayers for our success. You have escaped great severity of weather here this winter; Hyères, I suppose, is always mild, in spite of the cold in various parts of France.

I am, My dear Lord Shrewsbury, Your Lordship's faithful Servt in Xt

John H Newman of the Oratory

The Rt Honble The Earl of Shrewsbury

SATURDAY 21 APRIL   Term began

SUNDAY 22 APRIL   Louis [de Vaulchier] came back in time for mass   dined with Harry [Ryder] at Allhallows   opened the term with an address as before. tea [?] at Sergeant O'Brien's

TO T. W. ALLIES

6. Harcourt Street Dublin April 22. 1855

My dear Allies,

Mr Bianconi has placed a monument over O' Connell's heart in St Agatha's at Rome, in which he is represented rejecting in the House of

Commons the antipapistical oath. He wants an *inscription* and has been wandering about, receiving the merest coppers which have been flung at him as such. One thing he said, that the inscriptions offered him might be shorter, or in other words, that he should be better off if he could change their worth into silver and gold. And here common sense stood for him in the stead of witticism.

He has sent me once or twice a number of specimens, which I have done nothing but reject, by degrees they have improved, but still he complains of their length. Yesterday he came with a lot of them for me to look over. I am too wise to attempt one myself, but I have taken phrases etc, out of various of them and made them stand in the shape which you will find enclosed.

Now will you be so good, as to read it over, and tell me, if there is any fault in the Latinity which I have over looked. The *matter* is fixed, for the heart must be mentioned and O'Connell's *attitude* and *words* are made a point of by Mr Bianconi.

I don't ask you for more than five minutes literally.[1]

Yours affectly John H. Newman

P.S.   I hope Mrs Allies is well now.

TO PATRICK MOONEY

Copy

April 22/55

My dear Revd Sir

I have just received your letter, and thank you sincerely for the promptness with which you have taken my request into consideration.[2]

Of course we are each of us bound to consult for the interests of the side we represent in the negociation which I have been opening.

All I want is to secure the interest, and to get back my principal of my outlay

I would ask you to modify or alter my proposal, were your objections to it less strong than they are; but as you cannot receive either 'principle

[1] This inscription, the matter fixed as Newman describes, was written after all in English. 'Bianconi, as was his habit, sought the views of a great many people; then, as was also his habit, he finally did what he himself wanted to do.' M. O'C. Bianconi and S. J. Watson, *Bianconi, King of the Irish Roads*, Dublin 1962, p. 156, where the inscription is printed. The monument is now at the Irish College in Rome.

[2] Mooney replied on 19 April to Newman's letter of 9 April, '. . . your late proposal is of such a nature both in principle and detail that it cannot even be submitted to my Parishioners.'

444

or detail' I do not think it worth while to take up your time with any further remark, and wish hereby to withdraw from what I see would only cause trouble and disappointment.

I am &c.

TO THOMAS SCRATTON

[22 April? 1855]

My dear Scratton

Stewart has taken Mr Robertson's Lectures last term and must have his quarter's salary that is $\dfrac{£150}{4} = £37.\ 10$

As to yourself, I asked you to take the Library, because you said you had not enough to do as *Secretary*. If you really think you *have*, then the Library shall be a separate matter.

Another person has spoken to me on an increase of salary, and, as I fancy, on the ground that you have £150. I say this, merely to show the difficulty I am in.

Ever Yrs J H N

MONDAY 23 APRIL 1855   Reginald [Barnewall] came back

TO LORD HENRY KERR

6 Harcourt Street Dublin. April 23/55.

My dear Lord Henry,

It has struck me whether Mr Coffin[1] could not be made useful for Ralph. A servant would be some expence, I dont know what — At the moment, I have nothing to offer Mr Coffin in the University, worth his acceptance in itself, and I have not room for him in the house — but I could offer him what with the sum you consider a servant would cost, might induce him to remain here for a while, at the end of which time I might have something to offer him. I thought before your letter of this morning, that Mr C was certainly to accompany Lord Ralph here —

We have begun lectures again today and I am glad the idle time is over. *Supposing* his brother comes again in the autumn as I understood you to say, it might be well to leave Francis here at present —

---

[1] Edmund Coffin, the brother of R. A. Coffin.

445

I was quite ashamed so to intrude on you and Lady Henry in London.

Very sincerely Yours in Xt   John H Newman of the Oratory

The Lord Henry Kerr.

TO THOMAS SCRATTON

Monday 23 April [1855]

My dear Scratton

I asked Signor Marani to say what he thought fair *on the basis* of what he got at St Columba etc — and am disappointed he has not named a sum.

As to Renouf's income, it is £150 — and he has about 30 youths in class, and has had a lecture a day, and is now to have 3 in 2 days. I do not think Signor Marani has as much as this — nor is Italian so important a language as French — If he will make a return to me of the number he has in class, and how many classes, I will determine for him on that basis. As to public lectures, I suppose Renouf has ready and has delivered far more than Signor Marani. As to yourself, if you had 4 hours a day work, I think £150 certainly would not be too much. If the Secretaryship requires this, the Librarianship should be extra — also, it might make up the Secretary's time. I don't think that the circumstance of being *obliged to be at the office* can be made to tell; for this very ground has been put before me in favor of *uniting* offices. E.g. Dr Leahy has only £50 as Vice-Rector, *because* he is Professor — and I suppose Mr Flannery would do the Secretariship for less than £150, because he is always obliged to be in Dublin, and has not to come in from Kingstown.

It rather pains me to find how people are making money the first thing in the University. For myself I am conscious, I have lost hitherto by my situation, and I suppose am likely to do so. I spent near £100 because [before] I had got a penny from it.

Ever Yrs affly J H N

P.S.   The place I first offered you, and with which you were content, was £100 and board and lodging — about £150 in all — and this, being a tutor's, would have involved *far more* work than 4 hours a day, including, i.e. the responsibility and occasional cramming.

TO THOMAS SCRATTON

April 24. 1855

My dear Scratton

Did I not exercise your 'penetration,' perhaps you would say I was, not obscure, but rude. Ask your categorical question, and I will answer it.[1]

Certainly I have ever wished to make the Secretariship a better thing — but it must have more *work* first — I never meant to make University offices pieces of patronage.

I wished and wish the Librarianship to be additional — but, since I said so, you have shown me that work is wanting to the Secretary. Do which you will; keep the Library distinct, and diminish the Secretary's pay, or make out the Secretary's work with the Library. I shall be best pleased, when it turns out that the Secretary has full work, and does not need the Library.

You have alluded to the Secretary of the Propagation of the Faith. *Would you be content* to have your salary fixed by the standard of his work and confinement? I should like to know this, for it would end disputes.

You should not say 'I know very well' what I rather know contrariwise. For I *suppose* Mr F. [Flannery] has no more pay for his confinement at the office of the Prop. than you.

I do not see you should be paid because you have to come from Kingstown — persons could be found, as I said before, who are already in Dublin. And as to Cecilia Street, I might retort your 'you know very well' that the Secretary is not fixed to Cecilia Street, but might be in any part of Dublin he chose.

I too am obliged to say Mass here every morning. I do not call it 'confinement,' because I am on the spot. When I go away, I have sometimes been forced to pay a Priest, because I was *obliged* to take him from a distance. Of course if we were obliged to take a Secretary from

[1] Scratton wrote on 23 April, 'I am always very much afraid of misunderstanding you and I confess I do not now quite penetrate your meaning. Though the Secretary is not fully employed from ten till two, people expect to find him at the Office and so I may say the Secretaryship *does* require the time to be occupied. You speak as if you thought I was not content. The Secretaryship is paid quite enough, but I thought you wished £50 to be added for the Library, which it is well worth. You may remember that last quarter you expressed concern that even the Secretaryship could not be made a better thing and that you were really pained at it.

Flannery could not be at an Office from ten till two, being Secretary of the Propaganda, and I do not know of any Ecclesiastic of this country who would consent to be so tied; as you very well know.'

Kingstown, he might plead 'confinement' and demand payment. But what will the Bishops say when the accounts are brought up, if I let you make a merit of living at Kingstown?[1]

You seem to forget my accounts will be audited. *Will* you let me *shelter myself* by the example of the Propagation? I don't know what Mr F. gets or what he does — but it is your own reference — and I will gladly use it.

Take care of your strain. I cautioned you against ladders

Ever Yrs J H N

TO JAMES HOPE-SCOTT

⌐6 Harcourt Street. April 25. 1855

I was in Birmingham at Easter, and saw for the first time your beautiful presents — which pleased me very much, and have been going to write to you ever since to thank you for both morse and ring; but something has come in my way — so I do it now.[2]

I heard yesterday that the Holy See has sent a circular to the Irish Bishops, in the course of which it expresses its dissatisfaction at Dr McHale's conduct at Rome.[3] I suppose he has not the slightest influence there; but what I fear is his intriguing at home.

The Statutes, or rather Decrees, came to me yesterday.[4] They are pretty much what I expected. They are to hold for six years. The Bishops are not to meet every year, but the four Archbishops to take their place. I have not a *safe* majority in either body. Between their meetings I can only make provisional appointments.[5]

Lord Ralph has just heard from Lady Lothian that he is to remain at St Leonard's till her return. I fear this is ill judged. I have never spoken against his going to Rome; but always against his being at St Leonard's, — from its loneliness, and now again from the continual *fretting* produced by his disappointments, which must hurt his health,

[1] Newman copied out his draft of this letter in the appendix to 'Memorandum about my Connection with the Catholic University,' adding, 'vid. March 4. 1855.'

[2] These were for Newman to use as a bishop. A morse is the decorated clasp on a cope. That given by Hope-Scott was ornamented with the jewels of his wife.

[3] See last note to letter of 13 March to Flanagan, and letter of 27 April to Monsell. Cf. *McGrath*, pp. 352-4.

[4] The Decrees of the Synod of 1854 were confirmed in Rome and the management of the University placed in the hands of the four Archbishops, who were to meet annually. See *Campaign*, p. 92.

[5] The Rector was given the right of presenting professors, who could hold their appointments until the Archbishops met to confirm or reject them.

and I fear is making him *believe* that he is very ill, which is not desirable. He writes me word 'There is no one here, and it is horribly slow — and today I felt a slight return of my old pains in the side.' Apparently he has nothing else to think of but himself.⌐

TO HENRY WILBERFORCE

6 Harcourt Street Dublin April 25/55

My dear H W

Is this your birth day or your Father's? yours — his was St Barth's.[1]

When I talked of more papers, it was when I had only sent you a few — you have as many as eight,

I am so busy now, I can write nothing more.

You must not bring in *my* name, but so it is that ⌐a circular has gone out from Rome to the Bishops or Archbishops of Ireland expressing dissatisfaction at Dr McHale's behaviour at Rome. But I fear him, not at Rome, but here.⌐

If this is your birthday (I am ashamed of my doubt) many happy returns. How old are you? 48? Were you not 20 in 1827?

Ever Yrs affly J H N

P.S.   You and your wife were ill, because you went into a *new* house.

TO LORD HENRY KERR

6 Harcourt Street April 26/55.

My dear Lord Henry,

The inclosed note has just been sent me from Birmingham and in confidence I send it to you.[2]

I [like?] you I cannot help being very much distressed at Ralph being so thrown on himself. You know how very much I have disliked his being at St Leonards — Would it not be better his going to *Edgbaston* till Lady Lothian returns than his remaining at St Leonards? No woman, not even a mother, can know a youth's heart. This letter frightens me.

I have thoughts of getting one of our Fathers to go down to him.

---

[1] Newman was writing on St Mark's day. Henry Wilberforce was born on the day after St Matthew's day 22 Sept. 1807 and his father, the philanthropist, on St Bartholomew's day, 24 Aug. 1759.

[2] See the end of the letter of 25 April to Hope-Scott.

He is continually in my thoughts, dear fellow — and I do earnestly hope that the Blessed Virgin and his good Angel will help him. I am glad that Dr Grant is going there.

Do send him to Birmingham at least if he does not come here.

Ever Yrs most sincerely John H. Newman.

P.S. I have come to the conclusion of filling up Ralph's room here, at once, but I intreat you to send him to Birmingham, unless you have grounds I have not —

TO WILLIAM KIRBY SULLIVAN

6 Harcourt Street April 26/55

(*Private*)

My dear Mr Sullivan

The day before yesterday I received the Statutes (provisional) of the University, and now know where I stand, and proceed to do what I can in the department of Medical Science.

I am led to believe that the following is the staff I should aim at

1 Physiology, one Professor, two assistants.
2 Chemistry one Professor, one assistant.
3 Pathology, one Professor
4 Theory and Practice of Medicine one Professor.
5 Surgery one Professor
6. Midwifery one Professor
7 Materia Medica and Therapeutics one Professor
8 Medical Jurisprudence — one Professor.
9 Botany

I do not know whether Pharmacy could be united to Botany. Have you any remarks to make upon my division of subjects?

Can you in confidence name to me any persons who would be competent and willing to take any of these chairs?

May I not reckon upon your own assistance in Chemistry?

I will call on you at any hour you will appoint[1]

Very sincerely Yrs John H Newman

Professor Sullivan &c &c.

[1] Newman wrote in his University Journal for 27 April, 'I have called on Mr Sullivan, and had a talk with him on the Professors in the Faculty of Medicine. I offered him that of Chemistry, with the reserve of what the Bishops would say considering his connection with the Government Institution [The Industrial Museum]. In consequence of my talk with him I have written 1. to Dr Lyons at Scutari, asking him to be Professor of Physiology, not mentioning what the salary — 2 to Dr Griffin

6 Harcourt Street Dublin April 27. 1855

My dear Mrs Bowden,

It was a great disappointment to me just to have missed you when I was in London. I reckoned on seeing you — not that I had anything particular to say, but it now is a year since we met.

We are getting on here as well as possible — by which I mean that a beginning must be a beginning, and that if we got on better, I should be anxious, lest our progress had something unsound in it. We have now about 40 youths in lecture, and hardly a week or fortnight passes without an addition to the number. They are a good set of youths, and hitherto give us very little trouble; and, though it must always be uncertain how youths turn out, and a change might take place any minute, they have given us no trouble to speak of hitherto. They range from 14 and 15 to 21 — In this house I have one 21, one 18, four 17, one 16, one 15, one 14. Have I told you all this before? I talk of building on my spare ground, and must not lose the season, yet do not like to commit myself to bricks and mortar.

The University statutes have just come from Rome, and I now for the first time know what my powers are; and in consequence am setting to work more vigorously than I could before.

Dr Cullen is likely to be kept much longer at Rome, but is getting on well

Ever Yours affly in Xt   John H Newman of the Oratory

P.S.   Love to Emily and Charles.

TO ROBERT D. LYONS[1]

Dublin. April 27th 1855.

'I wish to know whether you will allow me to name you to them' (The Bishops) 'for the chair of Physiology (as distinct from Anatomy).

asking if he can help us, and for advice. 3 to Mr Hughes of Carlow, asking after Mr O'Meara, whom I travelled with, of whom Mr Sullivan (and Mr Butler) spoke highly, and 4 to Dr Denvir, asking if he could name any persons from the neighbourhood of Belfast.'

[1] Lyons was at the Military Hospital at Scutari near Constantinople, and was expected home by the end of the Summer, although he did not in fact return until May 1856. He had not accepted a post under the Government, a fact which John Edward

I cannot say what the salary will be at the moment, but it will be my wish to make it equal to the importance of the Professorship.' . . . 'I have made great use of the paper which you sent me nearly two years ago, it has been the basis of various questions I have addressed to friends in the subject. . . .'[1]

John H. Newman.[2]

TO WILLIAM MONSELL

6 Harcourt Street Dublin April 27. 1855

My dear Monsell,

What did you say to me when last I saw you about advancing money for purchasing a house? Will you tell me what you meant, and whether you are able still to be of the same mind?

The reason I ask is, because I have the opportunity of buying the house I am in, and finding [sic] that possibly I could so combine it with a purchase of the ground next to me, which I have some chance of effecting, as to make it an object.

I have just received the University Statutes, and now for the first time know my powers. In consequence I am beginning to work more freely.

It must not come from *me*, but I don't know whether you have heard that Dr Cullen sent in to the Pope a full statement of what he had to say, and the Pope called on Dr McHale to answer it, paragraph by paragraph. That, instead of doing so, Dr McHale sent in some general answer, and departed from Rome without taking leave. In consequence a circular has gone round to all the Bishops, in which it is [sic] introduced an expression of the Pope's dissatisfaction — which has been also signified in a letter addressed to Dr McHale himself. However, it is not his influence at Rome which is to be feared, but in Ireland. It seems as if Dr Cullen would not return for some time yet.

Ever Yours affectly in Xt   John H Newman of the Oratory

Pigot, who was to become his brother-in-law in 1856, pointed out to Newman. His temporary engagement as Pathologist in Chief was for purely scientific work. The variety of diseases at Scutari presented a great opportunity for scientific research and experiment, and Lyons was to investigate, and also lecture and demonstrate to the medical officers there.

[1] This paper, of 22 May 1854, entitled 'A View of the State of Medical Science in Ireland, with suggestions relative to the Proposed Medical Faculty of the Catholic University of Ireland' is preserved at the Birmingham Oratory.

[2] This letter reached Lyons at Scutari on 13 May, and he wrote the same day to accept the Chair of Physiology.

P.S. Let me congratulate you on your new honors, of which the direction of this letter will speak, before you open it.[1]

6 Harcourt Street Dublin April 27. 1855

My dear Father O'Reilly,

I hope I shall not be intruding upon your occupations, if I write you a few lines about our Theological School.

We shall set it up in November; indeed as soon as we receive power to grant degrees, though the *work* will not begin till November; and I am sanguine we shall fill our classes. I cannot help hoping that your Fathers in Gardiner Street will send you some hearers — the younger secular clergy will furnish others — and I trust Allhallows will do something for us. I have been talking to Dr Woodlock on the subject, and he kindly said he would write to you, and take your advice.[2]

My notion is, which I wish to submit to your better judgment, to set up the school with three Professors or Lecturers — dogmatics, Scripture, and Ecclesiastical History — and to use them as my advisers in 'designating' (to use the word of the Statutes just returned from Rome) the other Professors — Canon Law, and Moral Theology, and any others.

I have failed in several attempts to obtain a Professor in Ecclesiastical History, and my present idea is not to fill it up till I can quite satisfy myself, and in the meanwhile to lecture myself in that department. Dr Leahy, as you know is Professor of Scripture.

It seems to me that the Lectures should all of them be beyond the routine of a Seminary course. E.g. I could conceive the Loci gone through, or the notes of the Church, with a special reference to present controversy, and a special application to the present state of the world.

My present opinion is that the Theological School should be in the neighbourhood of the Archbishop, the Jesuits' Church, Allhallows, and the Dominicans — and not at our end of the city.

Might I ask from your kindness any views you have on the points I have introduced into this letter, or on any others?[3]

[1] Monsell was named a Privy Councillor.

[2] Bartholomew Woodlock had been Professor of Dogmatic Theology at All Hallows College, Drumcondra, from its opening in 1842, and succeeded David Moriarty as President in 1854.

[3] Replying on 30 April O'Reilly considered that more than one Professor of Dogma would be necessary, and that, besides the lectures of a high standard, a regular course

Begging your good prayers, and those of your holy community,[1] I am, My dear Fr O'Reilly Most sincerely Yrs in Xt

John H Newman of the Oratory

The Revd Fr O'Reilly

TO THOMAS SCRATTON

Friday April 27/55

My dear Scratton

I inclose the receipt of a sum I lodged in the names of Cullen and Newman yesterday at the Bank

Ever Yrs J H N

SATURDAY 28 APRIL 1855   Frederic Thynne came for first time

TO MESSRS HOPE

Dublin April 28/55

Copy

Sir

Mr Lewin writes me word by this post that you want to hear from me. By this time I had expected he would have been applying for the injunction.

If you have any *proposal* to make me, pray state it *at once*. I fear I cannot wait very long. My delay hitherto has been from Mr Lewin fancying I was in correspondence with you.[2]

Yr obt Servt J H N

Mr Hope

would be needed for those who were preparing for the priesthood. Newman seems to have explained that he did not mean for the present to provide the usual full education for the priesthood. On 4 May O'Reilly wrote, 'either provision should be made precisely for those who are supposed to have gone through an ordinary seminary course, or precisely for those who are desirous to go thro' their first and perhaps only course . . .'

[1] O'Reilly was at St Beuno's, the Jesuit College in North Wales.

[2] James Joseph Frew, an Anglican clergyman, had brought out *Tracts for the Times No. 90. Reprinted with an introduction and notes*, London 1855, the publishers being Messrs Hope. Newman's solicitor in the Achilli trial, S. R. Lewin, had been dealing with the piracy. Messrs Hope agreed no longer to sell their edition of the *Tract*.

TO THOMAS SCRATTON

Saturday [28 April 1855?][1]

My dear Scratton

I was waiting for Bowden's return to ask you to preside at a Committee of 'men' (you will then be ἄναξ ἀνδρῶν)[2] to choose a cricketing ground. I wish very much to have a word with you on the subject.

Why won't you dine here today or tomorrow

Ever Yrs J H N

Thos Scratton Esqr

SUNDAY 29 APRIL 1855 breakfasted at Serjeant O Brien's

TO DAVID MORIARTY, COADJUTOR BISHOP OF KERRY (I)

6 Harcourt Street Dublin April 29, 1855

Private

My dear Lord,

I have received the Statutes of the University from Rome, and at once have begun to move in the matter of Professors. Till now, I did not know what I could do, and what not. I find I can appoint provisionally till the next meeting of Bishops or of Archbishops — And at all events, that I have the absolute power of *presentation*.

Accordingly I am looking about for Professors in the Faculty of Medicine. I wish to ask you in confidence how the appointment of Dr Corrigan (*if* we [he?] would accept it) would strike you, connected, as he is, with the Queen's Colleges. The appointment gives him no *power*. On the other hand, his name is great, he lectures well — he knows well the state of the medical Profession in Dublin, and could give me a good deal of good advice — and, they say, he can do much, either for us or against us.[3]

I have offered Dr Lyons the Professorship of Physiology — and

[1] This note can be dated by Scratton's apology on 9 May for his slowness in finding a cricket ground.

[2] 'Lord among men,' Homer's title for Agamemnon. Harry Bowden had been in the Eton Cricket XI in 1852.

[3] Moriarty replied on 1 May, 'There is no doubt that Corrigan's name and Corrigan's talents would be of immense service to the University. His being one of the Senate of the Queen's University seems a difficulty, but I do not think it likely that the two institutions will come practically into collision. It is most desirable to secure Corrigan.'

455

Mr Sullivan that of Chemistry (subject to the question whether his connection with the Industrial Museum will be an impediment — I consider you to think, not;) — Mr Ellis will have Surgery. I should offer Dr Corrigan the practice of Medicine.[1]

There is a Mr O'Meara (I think) — a scientific man at Carlow. Do you know any thing of him?[2]

I have had from time to time a good deal of talk with Mr J. Pigot — and he promised me to entertain the proposal of lecturing on Real Property. Lately (I mention it in great confidence) Dr Cullen has said to me, 'I hope you will have no young Irelanders in the University.' I answered, that I considered his Grace did not mean, now who *once* had the *name*, for that would include Mr John O'Hagan and Mr McCarthy, but those who really would introduce hot politics into the place. Now Mr Pigott assures me he thinks it would be the worst taste possible to bring in politics at all — and moreover, 'Real Property' is not a subject which admits it — but there is no denying he has very definite political views — and I should not wonder, (but perhaps you know better than I,) that he does not like Dr C's political course, as far as he has had any — Have you any advice to give me on this point?[3]

I was sorry to hear your Lordship still had the rheumatism but, if you will sit a whole day in the Confessional in damp places, what can we expect?

Begging your blessing, I am, My dear Lord, Affectionately Yours in Xt

John H Newman of the Oratory

The Rt Revd Dr Moriarty

[1] Moriarty continued, 'The other appointments you propose are very wise, and Sullivan's connection with the industrial Museum [a Government Institution] need be no bar. . . .

You are very safe in Lyons and Sullivan, and if you could have the advice of Ellis and Corrigan, for the remaining appointments I trust good ones could be secured.'

Newman noted in his University Journal at this time, 'I consulted Fr MacNamara, who was afraid of an outcry against the Archbishop [Cullen], as if we were becoming Government men — but he [McNamara] said he would see if Dr McHale, who was a patient of Dr Corrigan's, could be got to move — for, if so, all would be well. Mr Sullivan was decidedly for Dr Corrigan, and advised me to take his *advice*.' See also letter of 22 June to Moriarty.

[2] Moriarty replied that he had known O'Meara when he was a medical student in Paris. He was clever, but Moriarty had 'some impression that his manner was rather vulgar.'

[3] Moriarty answered, 'I do not at all share in Dr Cullen's distrust of those he calls Young Irelanders. I hope his Grace will live to know them better; but whatever estimate is to be made of them Pigott cannot be ranked amongst those Dr Cullen would distrust. He is a truly estimable young man, working quietly at his profession.—In obedience to his father he withdrew from his political party in 47, and never that I remember took part in politics since.'

TO DAVID MORIARTY, COADJUTOR BISHOP OF KERRY (II)

April 29/55

My dear Lord

I forgot to ask one question — Did you not once speak to me of Dr Hayden? What did you say of him? are there not two Dr Haydens?[1]

Yours afftely in Xt   John H Newman

MONDAY 30 APRIL 1855   Mr Robertson, who has just come, to breakfast.

TUESDAY 1 MAY   Mr Knight dined with us, the last day before his return to England

TO WILLIAM MONSELL

6 Harcourt Street Dublin May 1. 1855

My dear Monsell,

What a nuisance about the Oath — however, it will turn out well any way, and I doubt not you will in some way or other be the cause of its removal. Only I wish it soon settled.[2]

Mrs Segrave, and Sergeant O'Brien, said at first £1200. I should have been willing to close with this. She gave £2600 for it 30 years ago. It has a head rent on it of from £25 to £30. However, it seemed fair to submit the matter to valuation — and it may turn up to be more.[3]

When you are in a position, and have time to write about it, you must tell me what interest you propose, and when the loan is to be repaid.

[1] Moriarty replied, 'I am sure I never spoke to you of Dr Hayden ⟨⟨there are *two* Dr Haydens⟩⟩. We should have nothing to do with the man of that name who lives in your street and advertises continually in the papers.' This was George Thomas Hayden, author of *Physiology for the Public* . . . London 1842; *An Essay on the Wear and Tear of Human Life and the Remedy*, Dublin 1846; *A Dialogue on Religious Equality or the Road to the Revival of Christianity*, Dublin 1852; and *Remedies for Ireland. The Voluntary System; or every Sect self supporting*, Dublin 1853. He died at 82 Harcourt Street in 1857. Cf. letter of 1 Aug. 1855 to Cullen. Thomas Hayden, who became a lecturer on Anatomy, was a very different person, as his nickname 'Gentle Thomas' suggests.

[2] Monsell had already objected to the promise of allegiance only to the heirs of the Electress Sophia, in the Catholic Emancipation Act Oath, as a slur on Catholic loyalty. When sworn as a Privy Councillor on 13 Aug. 1855, Monsell was evidently allowed to amend his oath, omitting the reference to the Royal Supremacy. Cf. *Ignaz von Döllinger Briefwechsel mit Lord Acton, 1850-1869*, Munich 1963, p. 65. In 1865 he introduced a private bill for altering the Catholic oaths, which passed the Commons but was thrown out by the Lords. It led, however, to the Parliamentary Oath Acts of 1866, which introduced a universal oath, and removed the special Catholic ones. Cf. also letter of 28 June 1854 to Monsell.

[3] See letters of 27 April and 4 May to Monsell. Mrs Segrave was the owner of 6 Harcourt Street.

457

Mrs Segrave says she has no idea of pressing me for the money. So I might pay it at different times — or you might lend me part of it

Ever Yrs affectly in Xt   John H Newman of the Oratory

WEDNESDAY 2 MAY 1855   Mr Robertson to dinner

TO CATHERINE ANNE BATHURST

6 Harcourt Street, Dublin May 3/55

My dear Child

I will, if all is well, say Mass for you every Friday through this month, beginning with tomorrow.

I so little know my own movements, that I cannot say when I shall be in London. Certainly not this month.

Depend upon it, you are going on well as regards your vow, and need not be frightened.

I continue what I said about your not confessing except in the extreme case you mention — and I wish you to say the Miserere every Saturday, as you propose.

The intentions you name could not be better —

Thank Revd Mother about the Benediction. It is almost as difficult to me to go to London, as to go to the Crimea — i.e. it requires a great effort.

Mind, I am not up to teach you your duty as a nun, or to confess you as a nun, or answer any really important questions. I can only go by common sense. Otherwise its not my line.

It's no sin not to attend to the dry old French Sermons, and, so that you do not give scandal, you may use devotions or spiritual reading. It is a great cause of thankfulness you don't go to sleep, which I should do for certain

Ever Yours, my dear child, in the heart of Jesus & Mary

J H N

TO WILLIAM MONSELL

6 Harcourt Street Dublin May 4. 1855

My dear Monsell

I write you a hasty letter, lest you should be putting yourself to trouble, that this morning my negociation about the House I am in is absolutely off.

Mrs S. [Segrave] said £1200. When we went to valuers, they have said, one £500 the other £585. And the consequence is that Mrs S. *won't sell*.

I say all this to you privately — What makes it a great difficulty to me personally is that I have *bought* the next ground on the notion that I was sure of buying this in some way or other (for she said she would not press me for the money) and what I am to do with my purchase I can't think

Ever Yrs affly J H N

Wm Monsell Esqr M P

TO AUBREY DE VERE

6 Harcourt Street Dublin May 5. 1855

My dear Mr de Vere,

What do you say to the Lectureship in 'Political and Social Science'? Under this the kind of lectures you propose will come. You may go on with them as long as you please, viz on the action of Literature on Society, and of Society upon Literature. By the time this subject is exhausted and you ought to go to Politics, you may have given us as much of you as you propose to do — or you may by that time see your way to proceed further, which would be more acceptable to us.

This Lectureship would not require residence or catechetical teaching. It would require from 4 to 6 lectures a term delivered close together; and the remuneration would be £5 a lecture.

We should be ready to hear them this term, if it suited you.

Very sincerely Yours in Xt   John H Newman of the Oratory

Aubrey de Vere Esqr

TO EDWARD CASWALL

6 Harcourt Street May 7. 1855

My dear Edward

I wished to hear something about your brother, and am much pained at what you tell me. But recollect our Lord said 'they know not what they do — ' and this applies to words still more than to deeds. And His

Eternal Father doubtless heard the 'Forgive them,' though they would have at the moment scorned the forgiveness.[1]

Thank you for the sight of Richard's letter. It operates no sudden conversion in me.[2]

I don't forget I owe you a letter about your Masque — but I am very busy.[3]

As to the Orphanage, of course I follow whatever you all think best[4]

Ever Yrs affly J H N

P.S. We don't expect Dr Cullen home till July.

TO J. D. DALGAIRNS

6 Harcourt Street May 7. 1855

My dear Fr Bernard

I wrote in haste to say that my last accounts (a day or two ago) from O. [Ornsby] were favorable about your sister.[5] O. thinks certainly that every thing is going on well. They are in their new house. The only difficulty at the moment is, lest there should any thing come of the nearness to her of the school where her little girl is. O. has quite given in about her friends. I don't think he is at all annoyed at you. She seems to be behaving most exceedingly well. And I should go and call, except I fear she connects me with his advisers.

Ambrose Phillipps has asked you to preach, and I have said no.

Ever Yrs affly J H N

P.S. I did not forget yesterday, and wished to say Mass for you, but am under an engagement with Mrs Seagrave, that I will say Mass for her every Sunday when I am in this house. I shall say Mass for you tomorrow on the Feast of the Archangel. Thank you for your Mass.

[1] Caswall's brother Alfred was dying, and strongly opposed to the Catholic religion. He asked his Oratorian brother to pray for him 'as a brother though not as a priest,' and said, although not to Caswall himself, 'No Mass for me, living or dead.'

[2] Stanton said St Philip's Feast could be kept on Whitsun Eve. See letter of this day to Mills.

[3] Caswall's *The Masque of Mary and other Poems* was published in London in 1857.

[4] It was proposed to have a church collection for the orphanage at Maryvale.

[5] Dalgairns asked about his sister, Ornsby's wife.

TO AUSTIN MILLS

Monday May 7/55

My dear Austin

I was taking up my pen to know the state of the case, when your letter came.[1]

I don't know what a solemn votive mass means. Is it only a *high* mass? are all other masses low masses of the Virgil? — how will, in that case, June 5 be kept? And then as to Office, vespers e.g. what will they be, and what colour?

At first sight, unless the solemn votive mass transforms all the masses into St Philip, and Vespers, and the whole Church, I don't know what is gained. It seems a non-descript concern.

They have no such solemn votive mass at the Chiesa Nuova — and I suppose they could have got it, if they had thought it best.

I must know more about it, before I see my way to like it.

Is it not, because the London House has got it, that you think it must be some wonderful privilege?

Ever Yrs affly J H N

P.S. Since writing this, I have opened Edward's letter. It answers some of my questions, but I still fear we should make a mess of neither one thing nor the other. At all events, since *permissions from the Holy See when gained, are obligatory*, I think we should not act upon our idea hastily.

TO A. LISLE PHILLIPPS

6 Harcourt Street May 7/55

My dear Mr Phillipps

I do not like to say nay to any proposition of yours, but I fear I must do so in the case of the present one. There are, I know, few persons whose wishes have the claim upon zealous Catholics which yours have, and I know how interesting a ceremony yours is at Grace Dieu.[2] But we have so many requests for aid, that we should get into difficulties elsewhere, if we complied with yours; it would be a delicate and ungracious

---

[1] As to the feast of St Philip, 26 May. It fell on Whitsun Eve in 1855, and so was transferred to 5 June. The London Oratorians had obtained leave for a votive mass on 26 May.

[2] Phillipps wanted a preacher at a Sunday Procession to his out-door Calvary.

thing to draw the line, and really we have so much work at home, that it would not be fair on Fr Dalgairns or the rest, if I did what would be pleasant to myself indeed, and no trouble at all, but a good deal of trouble to them. I hope you will allow these reasons to plead my excuse for what you must not think, and I am sure will not think, unfriendly.

The remarks of the Presbyterian Review only confirm my persuasion that it is unfair to ourselves, and unkind to Protestants not to put out our own view of the drift of the Apocalypse.[1] Their argument consists not so much in the evident correctness of their own interpretation, as in there being no other producible. 'If it does not mean this,' they seem to say, 'what else does it mean?'

We are getting on very well here, and have quite a galaxy of high people in this house. You know your relative Charles de la Pasture is here — a very dear boy, and sharp withal.

My best remembrances to Mrs Lisle Phillipps and believe me Most truly Yours in Xt

John H Newman of the Oratory

Ambrose Lisle Phillipps Esqr

TO THOMAS SCRATTON

May 8/55

My dear Scratton

Will you draw a cheque in favor of Mr Butler for £25; and enter it in your accounts 'Mr Butler, for the period ⟨month⟩ between his giving up his Inspectorship and the commencement of the Quarter,' or some other form similar.

As to Signor Marani, we have no time here as yet for Italian — nor at Dr Quinn's. (The *first two years* of the course will never give much time) If he will do what I proposed, or rather *he*, say what his terms were (e.g.) at St Colomba — put down his hours a week in Michaelmas and Lent Terms, and number of students attending him, I will calculate his sum.

Ever Yrs J H N

---

[1] Phillipps wrote on 4 May, that he had been sent the *Edinburgh Guardian*, with a review of his book on Antichrist, 'in which the Presbyterian (?) writer calls upon his coreligionists who believe the Pope and the Papacy to be the Antichrist of Prophecy to read my treatise, which he evidently admits to be a satisfactory set off on the other side, if not a complete refutation of their Theory.' Cf. letter of 6 March to Phillipps.

WEDNESDAY 9 MAY 1855   Mr [F. R.] Ward of Bristol called

TO EDWARD CASWALL

May 9/55

My dear Edward

I write a hasty line as I forgot the preacher. I suppose Dr Moore, if he will condescend to St Philip. When you write to him, excuse the short notice, and say that it was my fault. I suppose June 5. I have just got your inclosure of F Richard's letter but have not time to read it.

How does the negociation with Fr Ambrose for the bit of ground for a school go on

Ever Yrs J H N

TO HENRY HENNESSY

May 10/55

My dear Mr Hennessy

My last letter was occasioned by your saying that, if you gave up a situation for the Professorship I have offered you, the Episcopal meeting would be sure to confirm you in it.[1] I wrote to bring home to you just how things stood. I have the designatio and praesentatio of the Professors, the Bishops have the nominatio. Of course I have the greatest confidence in the Bishops, else I should not hold my present post. But I know well by experience how bodies of men move as if independently of the intentions of the individuals composing them. Their action is like the result of combined forces in mechanics, something distinct from the act of any one of them. You know how anxious I have been all along

---

[1] On 26 April Newman wrote to Hennessy to offer him the Professorship of Natural Philosophy at £300 a year, from the date of the Bishops' meeting whether June or Oct. Hennessy replied that he was sure any appointment of Newman's 'would be certain of confirmation by the Bishops,' and that they would take into account the sacrifice he would have made of his present post of Librarian to the Queen's College at Cork. Newman then offered him the Natural Philosophy Professorship, to begin immediately, and Hennessy accepted. However, as Newman noted in his University Journal, 'I got nervous as to the chance of the Bishops interfering, since he *could* not well lecture till *after* their meeting,' (owing to the preparations required) 'and I only had the absolute appointment *till* their meeting, and they might say "Why didn't you wait?"' Newman therefore decided to write to Hennessy that his Professorship should be revocable on a year's notice. Hennessy answered on 9 May, 'I think nothing could be fairer but I trust it does not imply any doubt as to the duration of the Professorship itself.'

not to outstep my powers. And when you spoke of relying on the view which the meeting would take of your surrender already of your present position, I again fell something [sic] into my former vague anxiety. Should you and Mr Sullivan after perfectly taking in, what I say, still determine that you should connect yourself with us at once, I am quite willing on my part. Suppose, e.g., the Bishops ⟨meeting⟩ were to pass a rule that no Professorship should be held above 3 years? suppose they were to make some grave change at the end of six, which is the time for which the Statutes are at present to stand — or suppose they were at the end of a certain period to lower the salary. I have no reason to believe such changes likely. I should not be a party to such acts, nor do I think them likely, but I wish you to see every thing before you decide.

Should you decide on accepting it at once, I should advise your coming up to Dublin and delivering 2 or 3 lectures as soon as possible — that you actually may be in harness at once[1]

I am &c J H N

TO MRS JOHN MOZLEY

6 Harcourt Street. Dublin May 10, 1855

My dear Jemima

I have just received your letter, and its inclosure.

Frank wrote to me lately — but I have no opinion. What I said was, 'how can I prescribe in a case, where 18 years have elapsed since I saw the patient, and 30 years since I could be said in any sense to know him?'[2]

I also said, what I should like best would be to pay his Butcher's and Baker's bills — or his clothes bill — viz to lay out a certain sum which would be necessary, and of which he would not have the control. His lodging bill, for instance.

I also said that, though I promised at present £18 a year, yet I really did not know whence it was to come. Indeed hitherto I have rather lost· than gained by my situation here, and I don't know how long it will last

---

[1] Hennessy accepted the Professorship at once, relying on the fairness of the Bishops and their interest in the University. Newman thought it wise to tell him that when he began to lecture he should explain that he held his post ad interim. Hennessy's brother-in-law W. K. Sullivan in a letter of 13 May to Newman pointed out the necessity for an immediate appointment, since it would take at least four months to collect diagrams and apparatus.

[2] This letter refers to Newman's brother Charles, who about this time, or at least by 1858, settled for good at Tenby.

I said that, taking away my journeys, I supposed I did not spend £70 a year on myself — and it did not seem therefore that he should have more.

I still say, if I were left to myself, I should bargain with the lodging house keeper to give him board and lodging at a certain rate — and never let the money come into his hands.

To attempt to treat him as a patient, to argue etc etc. is a thing quite beyond me.

And I think I never will have one word with him. I will speak to his tradespeople.

At the same time, If F. is kind enough to take trouble, I will so far co-operate with him, as to pay him any money which I can give and he will receive

Ever Yrs affly J H N

TO AMBROSE ST JOHN

May 12/55

My dear A

⌐I have just got your letter — and shan't say one mass for you!!¬[1]

I opened *by accident* the Analecta¬ which Wm [Neville] sent me — (having intended to bring it back as he sent it —) ⌐and out dropt the inclosed. I send it that you may tax the local Post about it. It seems to be a letter, sent to them, which they have allowed to slip into my parcel.¬ If so, it is a serious matter. Of course they must send it according to its destination.

I have written something to that effect on it — but I have only stated the fact, I have not accused the Post Office.

⌐My leg was so uncomfortable 10 days ago, that I went to Cusack — he examined it — said all was right — but that these were tedious matters — and I must have patience — he would not pledge himself *when* I should be quite well. He gave me something to rub in.[2] Edward tells me your breath is worse. I suppose it is the East wind.¬ And you confirm it.

[1] See letters of 22 Feb. and 27 March to St John, who wrote on 11 May, '. . . I was in a grumpy state I suppose, but somehow *I really did* quite think you were out of sorts with me. I dont exactly know why, except that it seemed a very long time since you had written me anything about yourself, or you will say I mean "myself." Well perhaps I do a little but not altogether[.] I really do desiderate more about yourself. There. That is all.'

[2] James William Cusack (1788–1861) of 7 Merrion Square North, was thrice President of the Royal College of Surgeons in Ireland, and was made Surgeon to the Queen in Ireland in 1858.

You see we are both invalids, and our letters for the future must be such as the child's 'Dear Papa — I am well — I hope you are well, etc etc.'

⌐Your house negociations promise well, and I trust you will be quite right in time. 7 years lease is a great temptation. I wish Mr B's [Bretherton] especially¹ was better⌐

Ever Yrs affly J H N²

SUNDAY 13 MAY 1855   Pollen with Mr Laprimaudaye to dinner³

TO AUBREY DE VERE

6 Harcourt Street Dublin May 13. 1855

My dear Mr de Vere,

I was much pleased to have your letter.⁴ Now I write to you on the subject of your lecture.

It would please me most to have three lectures from you, but this depends, not only on your consent, but on another circumstance which I proceed to mention. As you must know, we have not yet sufficient students, to be able to rely for an audience on our own people. We must depend on the public.

Now, we have found the Inaugural Lectures very well attended, but not the *courses*. And this agrees quite with what friends who know the state of things in Dublin witness upon their own experience.

Accordingly I should suggest to you, that you had better let me announce that you will give one Lecture — Then we shall see what our

¹ Newman wrote 'esp' and in copying read it [[age]].

² St John replied, 'Your dear good letter has been a great comfort to me. I am out of the dumps . . .'

³ Pollen wrote to Maria La Primaudaye, his fiancée, the same evening, describing his first meeting with Newman and this dinner, 'I found him most kind, ever so nice, and full of fun. We had a long conversation, and I told him I was very dubious of my own sufficiency for his purposes. However, I am going to write a lecture and deliver it as soon as I can . . .

. . . The Rector begged us to be punctual for dinner at five. . . . We were in very good time, and the redoubtable Newman appeared in the "short dress," and we had a plain but very good dinner. After *pranzo*, the *giovanotti* retired to their drawing-room, and I, Newman, and Renouf sat and cosed over some port wine and biscuits for an hour. He was quite charming, so very simple and so fond of his old Oxford recollections.' Anne Pollen, *John Hungerford Pollen*, London 1912, p. 253.

⁴ De Vere accepted Newman's offer of 5 May that he should be Lecturer in Political and Social Science.

466

audience is — and at the end of the Lecture you can announce you mean
to give another. And at the end of[1]

TO THOMAS SCRATTON

May 16/55

My dear Scratton

When Signor Marani has a regular class of 15, I have no objection
to offer him the same terms as Trin. Coll. [Trinity College]. 15 is a
respectable number. At present his office with £130 a year would be
considered a sinecure.[2] I never held out any expectations to him, and
insisted to him at Dalkey that we were beginning in a very small way.

If he still thinks such terms necessary, we cannot hit off any arrangement, and he does in fact decline the Professorship.

De la Pasture may go with you. It is enough that *he* should put
himself into a car at Westland Row on his return.[3]

Ever Yrs J H N

TO ANDREW ELLIS

May 17/55

My dear Dr Ellis

I have seen Dr Corrigan and had a long talk with him. He was very
kind and suggestive. I fear we have not made progress[4]

Very truly Yours John H Newman

FRIDAY 18 MAY 1855   Stanislas made his appearance (from Boyle)[5]

TO HENRY BITTLESTON

6 Harcourt Street May 18/55

My dear Henry

I am very much concerned to hear your account of Mr Betteris's
eyes; and wish you had known, to tell me, *what was the matter* with

[1] The rest of the letter is missing.
[2] In the first term Marani had fourteen in his class, and in the end it varied between
seven and three.
[3] Scratton wished to take de la Pasture out to dinner.
[4] See letter of 2 June to Corrigan.
[5] Whither he had gone to see an aunt who was dangerously ill.

them. Is it organic or functional mischief? Tell him that I do not forget him at mass.[1]

Stanislas has not yet made his appearance. Will you tell Robert I should be much obliged by his copying out and sending to me a few lines of MS which introduce a Novena of the Passion and Resurrection pasted into the end of the Scripture Extracts which we read in Refectory.[2]

F Wilfrid, if his account is prosaically true, says that Fr Antony's physician has given him up, as 'incurable.' This is deplorable, if it is prose.[3]

I have great fears lest I should not be able to stay when I come to Bm. [Birmingham]. I am so busy here just now.

Dr Cullen at last is coming. I cannot help thinking there is some sort of shade between us. I have not heard from him since January. I *somewhat* defended Lucas to him—and he, as every one, likes people to go the whole hog.[4]

Ever Yrs affly J H N

Fr Stanislas just come. Tell Fr Edward, that, as Stanislas does not preach on Sunday, I shall keep him here a day or two on my own business.

TO T. F. KNOX

May 18/55

My dear Francis

Thank you for your extracts. I keep all of them. One you once showed me on Development, and I have never been able to get from me. It is a few words of some Avignon Pope, I think[5]

Ever Yrs affly J H N

[1] Betteris had been one of Newman's parishioners at St Mary's, Oxford.

[2] What appears to be a printed copy of these lines of MS is all that can be found. It runs: 'A NOVENA OF THE PASSION, CRUCIFIXION, AND RESURRECTION.

The narrative of the Passion and Resurrection of our Lord and Saviour has not been included in the above course:—

1. From the difficulty of finding a suitable place for its introduction.
2. Because it is sure to be so much better known than other parts of Scripture.
3. Because it is perhaps less suitable than other parts of Scripture for reading in Refectory.

It is thrown in the following pages into a course of nine days' reading, which might begin on the Monday in Holy Week, and end on the Tuesday in Easter.'

[3] Hutchison recovered from this first breakdown in health and did not die until 1863.

[4] See letter of 24 Jan. to Cullen, and cf. Cullen's letter of 28 July 1855 to Barnabò, quoted in the last note to Newman's letter of 26 July to Cullen.

[5] Newman preserved two extracts in Knox's writing bearing on *Development*, one from Gerson's *Sermo de Conceptione B.V.M.* and one from Sanchez, *de Matrimonio*.

TO AMBROSE ST JOHN

⌐6 Harcourt Street May 18/55⌐

My dear Ambrose,

You seem somewhat oblivious that my only letters are business letters. This makes it so difficult to write to you and to Henry. And you both attack me.

Accordingly, ⌐I am seeing whether I have power, to change the Rector [[of the Oratory]] — and I shall, if so, make you Rector, out of compassion for you, and comfort to myself.

I am struggling against a load of difficulties to my movements in every direction — and though I trust I am making progress, yet it is slowly.⌐

I want, pace tuâ, to consult Stanislas upon some Dublin and Irish points and he is kept at Boyle, when every day is valuable to me.

⌐I doubt whether I shall stay many days at Edgbaston⌐

Ever Yrs affly J H N

TO EDWARD CASWALL

May 20/1855[1]

My dear Edward

I appointed you Rector till St Philip's day (June 5) — Can you tell me whether the Congregation has given me the power to *change* the Rector during the year? If so, I am inclined to do so, by way of filling out the idea with which I originally began[2]

Ever Yrs affly J H N

MONDAY 21 MAY 1855   Stanislas went for Bm [Birmingham]
THURSDAY 24 MAY   Fred Thynne left for Pollen's

TO STANISLAS FLANAGAN

6 Harcourt Street May 24/55

My dear Stanislas

No letter has come to you from Boyle. I inclose Nicholas's letter, which should have gone before.

[1] Newman later added the year, in pencil.
[2] Newman, who had appointed Caswall as Rector until the Feast of St Philip, had the power of changing the Rector. His original idea had been to make the appointment for six months at a time.

Ask him or Austin what I must do, having (as I always am in dread of) in taking off the lid of the Pyx, touched one of the particles with the fringe (I suppose) of the silk veil (of the pyx.)

I grieve to say that Thynne is going off instanter to Pollen. He has already begun corrupting my youths, if they could be corrupted[1]

Ever Yrs affly J H N

P.S. Perhaps I shall make my appearance on Thursday morning, the 31st.

Thank you for the Post Office order.

TO LORD HENRY KERR

6 Harcourt Street. May 24th/55

My dear Lord Henry,

I write in a great hurry. Francis will set out tomorrow (Friday) at 1, and will get to you at the same hour on Saturday. He goes by Belfast, as you proposed.

I have a good account to give of him. The Professor of Mathematics speaks well of him, and he seems to me generally attentive, and to have a good conscience.

Give us your prayers, for we need them much.

Most sincerely Yours in Xt   John H. Newman.

P.S. I have been rejoicing over your good news about your son. Pray convey my congratulations to Lady Henry — [2]

TO JOHN HUNGERFORD POLLEN

Thursday. [24 May 1855]

My dear Pollen,

I take it for granted Thynne is with you. He need not move his things. Tell him I shall merely tell our people that, since he knew La

[1] Frederic Thynne came to the University in April aged not quite seventeen, and besides being idle, had evidently disgraced himself. See letter of 27 May to St John. He stayed for a few days with Pollen, who was a friend of his family, until Lord Charles Thynne, his father, came to fetch him. He was taken in at the Oratory in Birmingham for a few weeks. From there on 13 June Darnell reported of him that he was not very regular at his work, but 'wrote to his Mama on Sunday Evening—and was at Communion in the morning. . . . is quite like an Eton boy and exhibits nothing bad—no inclination to the Town or spending money.' He obtained a commission in the Army later in the year.

[2] Henry Schomberg Kerr became a Catholic on 22 May, while on leave from the Navy.

Primaudaye and . . . he required more time than I could give, I had let him, as was natural, take up his abode with you. This is what every one here will say about him.[1]

Most truly Yours John H. Newman

FRIDAY 25 MAY 1855   Francis Kerr went home for a week

TO DAVID MORIARTY, COADJUTOR BISHOP OF KERRY

6 Harcourt Street May 25/55

My dear Lord

I am getting on very well with the Medical appointments — but I have one hitch, which affects them nearly all:—   viz:—

Can I promise the persons with whom I am in treaty that they are sure to remain in their places and salaries, except in case of bad conduct?

As some of them are giving up a *certainty* for the University, and some others are very tender of their reputation, which to a Professional man is every thing, I seem hardly able to get on, till this question is answered.

We have no reversal of the news about Dr Cullen's return, I am glad to say.

We are making a move as you know in the theological department; and shall be much indebted to All hallows

Ever Yrs affly in Xt   John H Newman of the Oratory

The Rt Revd Dr Moriarty

TO J. D. DALGAIRNS

May 27 [1855]

My dear Fr Bernard

I wrote to Mother Margaret, that, if she wanted you *this year*, I would mention it to you, and ascertain what you thought of it, if she would name the time.[2]

You had better write to her, if you assent. If not, wait till I come home

Ever Yrs J H N

[1] Pollen wrote on 2 June, 'Accept my most sincere sympathy . . . for such a grief as this must have been to you, who are so sympathetic for other people.'

[2] i.e. for giving a retreat to Mother Margaret Hallahan's nuns at Stone.

TO AMBROSE ST JOHN

6 Harcourt Street May 27. 1855

My dear Ambrose

⌈By all means close with Mr Lee and Mr Talbot[1] — and let the [[poor]] school ground take its course.⌉ I can talk of it when I come to Bm [Birmingham]. ⌈If, as you report, Misses Farrant think the money should be used, we must give it over to Smethwick, though we ultimately lose it.

I am pleased at your description of Rednall — and hope you will all get good from it — For myself, I will not sleep there, till Fr Joseph does. Si ascendero in lectum strati mei etc.[2]

I expect to arrive at Bm Thursday morning, or evening, or midnight. Perhaps Robert Wilberforce will soon be paying us a visit, and go back with me to this place. Perhaps I can manage to stay a week — ⌉ but, in addition to other cares, Thynne has left me — and I grieve for his parents more than I can say. I fear they are now overwhelmed in grief — as I do not hear from them. The circumstances attending this as you may conceive, do not make it easier for me to stay away. It must not *be said* that he has left me — but that he found Pollen's house more to his purpose, under all circumstances. He is still an extern of this house — but how many days he will remain in Dublin is a problem.

⌈It pained me rather to find you express such ready joy at the prospect of being Rector. We are not praised in Scripture for desiring the upper seats, and to be called Rabbi. I shall ever call you, while you are Rector, my Rabbi. You have fairly teased me into it.

Ever Yours affly, My dear Rabbi, J H N⌉[3]

Thank Fr Austin for his letter.

MONDAY 28 MAY 1855   Lord C Thynne came to Dublin about now, and took away his son.

[1] The tenants of St John's two houses next to the Oratory wished to renew their leases for three years. For the Misses Farrant's money see letters of 7 Nov. 1854 to St John and later.

[2] Ps. 131: 3. Joseph Gordon's body had not yet been buried at Rednal.

[3] Newman misinterpreted an exclamation in St John's letter. He wrote on 28 May to explain that he felt his office of Rector to be a painful charge and concluded, 'Now add hypocrite to Rabbi, scribe Pharisee or what you please. I'll be any thing you like for peace with you

Yr loving Child Ambrose—'

May 28 [1855]

My dear Scratton

The following is a corrected list of the Lecturers, as far as they are settled.[1] Advertise once a week in the weekly Dublin Catholic Papers — and on the day of the Lecture in the Freeman, giving the subject as well as Lecturer, if possible.

You had better write to each Lecturer, telling him of his days, to prevent the chance of a mistake

Ever Yours   John H Newman

TO EDWARD WALFORD

6 Harcourt Street, Dublin May 30. 1855

My dear Walford,

I don't know whether it would suit you, supposing our arrangements were so far advanced, but I can't help asking you whether you will examine here a few youths for our *Littlego*[2] in July.

There will not be many of them, and you may suppose easily they will not make any great display, but it will put them on the qui vive to find that you are coming from London for the purpose of examining them.

Your colleague would be Mr Myles O'Reilly of Knock Abbey. We are not quite certain the examination will come off, but things promise for it, and I must not delay looking about for examiners

Very truly Yours in Xt   John H Newman of the Oratory

E Walford Esqr

THURSDAY 31 MAY 1855   went at 1 o'clock to Bm [Birmingham], wretched passage

FRIDAY 1 JUNE   R Wilberforce came to Bm *as a Catholic*, first time I had seen him since I was a Catholic

[1] i.e. those for the first three weeks of June. They included Inaugural Lectures by J. B. Robertson, Lecturer on Geography, by Henry Hennessy, Professor of Natural Philosophy, by Aubrey de Vere, Lecturer on Political and Social Science, by John O'Hagan, Lecturer on Political Economy, and by J. H. Pollen, Lecturer on the Fine Arts.

[2] The popular name of the first examination for the first degree of B.A. at Cambridge.

TO JOHN MOORE

[1 June 1855]

My dear Dr Moore

I am very much distressed to find, on coming here, that we have put you to an inconvenience in asking you to preach on Tuesday. It must be owned that St Philip has not chosen a suitable day this year.

Will you promise us faithfully, if all is well, to preach for us *next* year? The day will be the Monday in the Octave of Corpus Xti. If this will suit you better, we will consent to give up the pleasure and advantage of your presence this year

        Very sincerely Yrs in Xt   John H Newman of the Oratory

The Very Revd Dr Moore

SATURDAY 2 JUNE 1855   Lord C Thynne came about now to Bm [Birmingham] or last night   went with R W [Wilberforce] to Oscott

TO D. J. CORRIGAN

Bm June 2/55

Dear Sir

In the last conversation I had the pleasure of having with you, I showed you a written engagement I had drawn up on the subject of the Professorship I had offered to your acceptance in the Catholic University — [1] You objected that the offer I made you contained no mention of the permanence of the Professorship. This deficiency I am now able to supply — and accordingly inclose a paper which I flatter myself you will consider satisfactory[2]

        I am, Dear Sir &c J H N

D Corrigan Esqr

[1] This formula, dated 12 May, began: 'Acting under the existing Statutes of the Catholic University, by which the Rector is empowered to designate and present to the Bishops for definitive nomination its Professors,

I hereby offer to D. Corrigan Esq M.D etc etc the Professorship of the Practice of Medicine from November next. . . .'

[2] On 1 June Dr Ellis wrote to Newman that he had interviewed Corrigan, whom it was so desirable to obtain for the University (cf. first letter of 29 April to Moriarty), and found his manner 'cold cautious and reserved.' Corrigan, however, promised that if he received a proposal in writing he would reply.

The amended formula which Newman now sent, and which he used for other medical appointments, was as follows:

'Acting under the Decree of the Conventus Episcoporum Hiberniae of May 1854,

TO PETER LE PAGE RENOUF

The Oratory. Hagley Road Bm. June 3/55

My dear Renouf,

I never had so terrible a passage — but however, it is over.

Robert Wilberforce will be passing from this place through Dublin on *Tuesday* or *Wednesday*. Please tell Frederic to get ready for him the room which *Thynne* was in.

Thank Frederick for his letter which has just come, and which is very satisfactory. Tell him the slab may be got for the hearth, which he speaks of.

My love to the Boys — so Francis [Kerr] has got a cold by going home

Ever Yours most sincerely in Xt

John H Newman of the Oratory

P Renouf Esqr

P.S. Wilberforce has settled to leave this at 8 PM on Tuesday: so he will arrive in Harcourt Street early Wednesday morning — Tell Harry [Ryder] he must act as his page. He wants to find out Pollen.

MONDAY 4 JUNE 1855 went with R W [Wilberforce], Ambrose and Wm [Neville] to Rednall

TO LADY GEORGIANA FULLERTON

Birmingham. June 4, 1855.

My dear Lady Georgiana,

If I seem intrusive you must excuse it on the ground of the interest which has always accompanied the thought of you in my mind, since

since confirmed by the Holy See, by which a Catholic University is erected in perpetuity, consisting of the five faculties of Theology, Law, *Medicine*, Philosophy and Letters, and Mathematical and Physical Sciences, and its Rector is entrusted with the designation and presentation of Professors whether ordinary or extraordinary,

I hereby offer to Dr Corrigan Esqr M D etc etc the office of Professor of the Practice of Medicine in the said University in permanence from November next, at a salary of £150 per annum, in addition to the fees of students attending his Lectures, the fees being £2.2 for each course, and 5 per cent being paid out of them to the University

In making this offer I reserve the right of the Bishops to remove any Professor of the University, if, (in the words of the decree) he is ever "sui muneris ac promissionis immemor, quod Deus avertat."" See letter of 7 June to Corrigan.

475

the day you let me call on you years ago, as you passed through Oxford. I have already been saying Mass for your intention, though a black Mass has been impossible. And so have others here.[1]

It would be presumptuous in me to speak to you and Mr. Fullerton of submission. However, let me bear witness, not only as a matter of faith, which we all receive, but as a point, which the experience of life has ever been impressing on me, more and more deeply, from my early youth down to this day, that unusual inflictions, coming on religious persons, are proofs that they are objects, more than others, of the love of God. Those whom He singularly and specially loves, He pursues with His blows, sometimes on one and the same wound, till perhaps they are tempted to cry out for mercy.

He loves you in proportion to the trials He sends you. I am telling you no news: but a testimony, external to oneself, strengthens one's own: and perhaps my testimony may be given with greater energy and fervency of conviction than another's.

We are in His hands — and cannot be in better.

With every respectful and earnest feeling of sympathy with Mr. Fullerton, I am, my dear Lady Georgiana, &c., &c.

TO JOHN HUNGERFORD POLLEN

Monday June 4/55

My dear Pollen

Thanks for your plan just arrived, which I like very much.[2] I am glad also to hear about the Racket court.

R. Wilberforce is to be at 6 Harcourt St on Wednesday morning and is rejoiced to hear that you are in Dublin. I wish you would make him a Professor. Try to persuade him.

I am so knocked up that I could almost think I should not be able to come back by the day. The passage was hideous, but that is the least of it, if one did not feel it afterwards. It takes so much out of one.

Lord Charles says that Fred *changed* directly he got upon English ground — and [he] cannot help being hopeful.

Yours most sincerely John H Newman of the Oratory

[1] The death on 29 May 1855 of Lady Georgiana's only child, Granville Fullerton, at the age of 21, was the great tragedy of her life.

[2] The scheme for using St Audeon's as the University Church having broken down (see letter of 22 April to Mooney), Newman bought ground beside the University House in Stephen's Green, and asked Pollen to draw up plans for a church there. In his reminiscences in 1890 Pollen wrote of the church that 'It covered the garden in rear

TUESDAY 5 JUNE 1855   St Philip's day kept   Sang high Mass.   preached (short)
in Evening R W [Wilberforce] went in evening to Ireland

TO HENRY (SEBASTIAN) BOWDEN

The Oratory June 6/55

My dear Harry,

Thanks for your exertions. He took off £30 for me for the substitution of Yorks for granite — but nothing else would do. So you have
gained £30 there. Also, I could not move him about the height of the
wall. I congratulate you upon your success.

I don't quite understand about the FRONT wall. Would it not be a
better job, to pull down the front coach house wall, (if it is that) to take
advantage of the stone flags already laid down, and to pave 20 feet short
at the end of the court, than to leave the coach house standing behind
the high wall? But I don't think he proposes this really.

The sea so knocked me down that I have not yet righted. We had a
very successful Festa. Robert Wilberforce was here.

Ever Yours affectionately John H Newman of the Oratory

H Bowden Esqr

TO THOMAS SCRATTON

The Oratory, Hagley Road Bm. June 6/55

My dear Scratton

I find I cannot get the ground next me, Mr Egan's! So all is off. It
strikes me I should be obliged to you to look at Judge Burton's House,
which Mr Butler mentioned to me, as being in the Encumbered Estates
Court. It is in Stephen's Green, not far, I think, from the University
House.[1] Perhaps I might *move* there, if there was room to build a Church
— But — a preliminary question is, in what *Parish* it is.

of the University House; a plain brick hall with an apsidal end, timber ceiling etc.
somewhat in the manner of the earlier Roman basilicas. He [Newman] felt a strong
attachment to those ancient churches with rude exteriors but solemn and impressive
within, recalling the early history of the Church, as it gradually felt its way in the
converted Empire, and took possession.' The *Month*, (Sept. 1906), p. 319.

Although Pollen and Newman had only met on 13 May, the contract was already
being negotiated with the builder, as the next letter illustrates. But Newman was still
looking out for a better site and did not sign the contract for the ground beside the
University House until 23 June.

[1] The University House was 86 and Judge Burton's 80 Stephen's Green.

I should be glad if any thing enabled you to make out what day of the week would be best for a Professorial tea at the University House, which I hope to institute on my return. You could ventilate the subject. The library, I suppose, would be the best room for the purpose

                                        Ever Yrs John H Newman

TO D. J. CORRIGAN

                                        Bm June 7. 1855
Dear Sir,

I have to acknowledge your obliging letter, and, from the kind tone of it, have no scruple in writing to you again.

I do not think there has been any misconception between us as to the upshot of our late conversation. Your wish to speak to me on one subject is no reason why I should not wish to speak to you on another.[1]

However, I thank you heartily for repeating your willingness to give me your valuable counsel on the undertaking generally on which I am engaged, and will at once avail myself of it.

I would ask then your experience to advise me, in what words I ought to embody, and with what engagements, stipulations, and conditions I should accompany, my offer of the Chair of the Practice of Medicine in order to make that offer respectful and acceptable to any gentleman of wide practice and high repute in his profession; — without reference to any particular individual.

Instruction upon this point will be an essential service to me, and one for which I shall feel grateful

                                        J H N

Dr Corrigan Esqr

TO CATHERINE ANNE BATHURST

                                        The Oratory Bm June 8. 1855
My dear Child

It is a difficult thing for me to say you should go to Communion every day, considering I am not near you. Yet I think with your present

---

[1] To Newman's letter of 2 June Corrigan replied on the 6th 'that in all our conversations, any opinions I expressed or information I was able to give you, in reply to your inquiries had reference solely to general views or arrangements and were distinctly to be understood as having no application whatever directly or personally, to myself.' See letters of 22 June to Moriarty and 1 July to Corrigan.

occupation you might — or might for a week or two; and then reconsider it. I forget how many times you have lately been going.

I know how great a trial your occupation must be. Poor Miss Ryder, in addition to it all, has good part of the management of the House, and is sorely straitened for money to live by.[1] So you have fellow workers, and God will support you all.

You have every thing to encourage you — You have more and more of grace given you — and you are doing a great work — I will not forget you

Ever Yours affly in Xt   John H Newman of the Oratory

P.S.   I expect to go back to Dublin tomorrow, having come here for St Philip's day, which we kept this week.

TO MRS WILLIAM FROUDE

The Oratory, Hagley Road, Birmingham. June 8/55

My dear Mrs Froude,

I was much touched by dear Hurrell's[2] remembrance of me— may God lead him — I can ask nothing better for him.

It is a wonder to me that I have not heard about your leaf of Wordsworth — and I shall write to Father Collyns about it.[3] The English Jesuits are queer people, intensely cautious and scared just now, as if they were on the eve of being turned out of the country, and it may be they are afraid to write to me. I dont mean Father Collyns himself. They have not even let me pay them the compliment of putting the names of some of them on our University books, for fear of 'il Governo.'

I am here a day or two for St Philip's feast — and expect to go back to Dublin tomorrow. My passage here was miserable, and knocked me up for the week I have been at home.

Thank you for letting me see Mr Stevens's letter.[4]

[1] Sophie Ryder, Sister Mary of the Sacred Heart, was assistant to the Prioress of the Good Shepherd Convent at Bristol.

[2] Mrs Froude's eldest son, Richard Hurrell Froude, born in 1842.

[3] See letter of 22 March 1855. Charles Henry Collyns, after being at Christ Church, was curate at St Mary Magdalen's, Oxford, in 1844, leaving the following year to become a Catholic and then a Jesuit. By 1855 he appears to have been already quarrelling with the Jesuits, which was probably the reason for his not replying to Newman. In 1858 Collyns abandoned both the Jesuits and the Church.

[4] Evidently a letter from Thomas Stevens, founder of Bradfield College, where Richard Hurrell Froude was at school. Stevens was Warden of the College 1847–81.

As to dear F. Rogers, it is a mournful thing to think how life changes us, and often for the worse. I have not seen him these 12 years — and, I suppose, we, who were so intimate, should have only a few thoughts in common, were we to meet.[1] Is it not better to cherish and enjoy the image of the past, than to dissipate it by the present? Robert Wilberforce has just been here. I had not seen him for the same length of time. Wonderful it is to see him now, a Catholic. He has aged a good deal — and when I see people after such an interval, I make them my looking glasses, and think how I must look to them. He has suffered a great deal in various ways; his spirits used to be as lively as Hurrell's; you may think he was brought to our minds by seeing each other[2]

Ever Yours affecty John H Newman of the Oratory

P.S. You know another of Lady Lothian's sons, as well as of Lord Henry's, has been received.[3]

TO MISS HOLMES

Oratory Hagley Road Birmingham June 8/55

My dear Miss Holmes

I take the chance of the vague direction you have given me finding you, though you seem yourself not without doubt whether it will. I am glad you have at last come to light, for I did not know whether you were in Italy, France, or Ireland. A week or two ago (shortly before your last letter,) a letter came to me from you, directed to Rome (!) and brought by a friend who said it was found in the Porteria of the Chiesa Nuova. I was pleased to find that you seemed more satisfied with the family you are now with, than with those before them for some time past; nay perhaps since Mr Leigh's, which is going back a long way.[4] It pleased me too to hear about your niece. I heartily wish she may be found to

---

[1] Frederick Rogers renewed his friendship with Newman on 30 Aug. 1863. Cf. *Trevor* II, pp. 311–13.

[2] Richard Hurrell Froude, Robert Wilberforce and Newman had been Fellows and Tutors of Oriel together more than a quarter of a century earlier.

[3] Besides Henry Schomberg Kerr, Lord Walter Kerr had just become a Catholic. Both were in the Navy. Mrs Froude knew the family of Lord Henry Kerr, who had been Rector of Dittisham in Devon, not far from Dartington.

[4] Miss Holmes, to whom Newman addressed his letter 'Poste Restante Boulogne sur Mer,' was still with the family of Thomas Preston. At the time of her conversion in 1844 she entered the family of William Leigh, who moved to Woodchester Park the following year.

have a vocation in Belgium but vocations are rare things. Of course I will say Mass for her, when she will let me know.

We are getting on very well in Dublin, though very slowly — It is truly slow and sure — and I feel convinced [?] that the only way in which we could move surely is to move slowly. In my own house I have two English, two Scotch, two French, and two Irish — and all of them very excellent youths.

I came here to keep St Philip's Feast — and met my dear and most intimate friend, Mr R. Wilberforce, who has lately been received, and whom I had not seen for ten years and more. He had a succession of trials in that time, the last, before his conversion, being the loss of his wife. His two sons are Protestants. Time goes on silently but powerfully, and is making all sorts of changes. Every one seems getting old and dying. And this dreadful war may be making revolutions. May all this instability teach us to love more what is unseen

Yours, my dear Miss Holmes, affectly in Xt
John H Newman of the Oratory

SATURDAY 9 JUNE 1855   went to Ireland at night to Dublin   Sergt O Brien etc etc. in boat
SUNDAY 10 JUNE   where arrived early in morning

TO AMBROSE ST JOHN

⌜June 10 [1855]

I think I never have had a bad passage *hither*, only *thither* — from which I infer that the sea is calmer by night than by day.⌝

TO EDWARD WALFORD

6 Harcourt Street Dublin June 10. 1855
My dear Walford,

I had hoped to have offered you hospitality in my own house — but we have been seized with scarletina. So I have thought it better to get you a bed two doors off. You shall judge for yourself, when you come, how far there is cause of fear.

You need not bring your cap — We are quite beginners here, and have to learn our A B C. Ornsby is too flourishing in his account.

The boats are altered lately — but I suppose you will get here by 10 on Saturday morning. You have [sic] better tell the car man to drive here, and then you shall be shown your lodging

Very sincerely Yours in Xt   John H Newman of the Oratory

Edwd Walford Esqr

TO JOHN STANISLAS FLANAGAN

6 Harcourt Street June 11. 1855

My dear Stanislas,

Judge Burton's house, it is thought, I could buy by private contract for £2500 — not that I should offer more than £2000. (It has no head rent) His daughter, the inmate, will not let any one see it, which is a difficulty. It is sold in Court August 1. So that before that date there is no chance of beginning to build the Church.

The simple question is, whether it would be a safe investment of the Achilli money. Of course I don't know what repairs it wants or what the repairs of a Church and House would be.

Properly speaking, it would not be the Achilli money, for that would go to the Church. M. [Monsell] must lend me the money — if he can't so large a sum, (and I don't suppose he can) the whole matter is at an end.

I wish you would see your way through the subject. I am almost tempted to give up the whole as a bad job.

In my calculation of a Church next door, I allowed £46.3.1 for yearly rent, and £200 as yearly instalment of the principal. £46 (rent of present house) £80 = 126. It is what I should [have] been paying here yearly for Numbers 5 and 6 Harcourt Street. £2500 at 5 per cent (is *that* enough for house property?) is £125. *If* then £5 per cent is enough (do they say £10 per cent for houses or furniture?) I should not lose by giving £2500 (it would be a finer Oratorian House and site ultimately)

But supposing M. cannot lend the money, what am I to do?[1]

Return the lawyer's paper inclosed

Ever Yrs affly J H N

P.S.   The offices must be pulled down to build the Church on.

[1] Flanagan replied on 12 June, 'If you have the money, I think the house would be a bargain at £2,500. It is hard to conceive how property of this kind should have so fallen in value since 1819, when Judge Burton gave for it £4500.' Flanagan did not think Newman could safely raise the money required.

TO THOMAS SCRATTON

June 11. [1855]

My dear Scratton

Have Mr Hennessy and Mr de Vere, who lecture this week, responded to your official summons? One is nervous about people not coming to the scratch

Ever Yrs, J H N

TO THOMAS SCRATTON

June 12 [1855]

My dear Scratton

Thank you for your notice. It has been the basis of the one I have drawn up, and which I could not have written without it. Let me see it, please, in proof. Tell me if I have left any thing out, or made other mistake.[1]

Dr Leahy goes on indefinitely — you had better ask him — he was not sure, when last he spoke to me

Ever Yrs J H N

TO F. W. FABER

6 Harcourt Street In fest. S. Antonii [13 June] 1855

My dear F Wilfrid,

I have left at Bm [Birmingham] Lady G. F's [Fullerton] direction — will you complete the inclosed?

I have been saying mass this morning for Antony, as I do every June 13.

Your book[2] has come, superbly bound, I have begun to read it with great interest and instruction

Ever Yrs affly J H N

[1] The notice was an invitation: 'Catholic University Stephen's Green. The Rector will have pleasure in meeting the Authorities, Professors and other officials of the University in the Library at 8 o'clock, on Monday evenings between this date and July 21 when the Sessions ends.
The pleasure of Mr   's company is requested on Monday June 18 and following weeks. June 12 1855'

[2] *The Blessed Sacrament; or, The Works and Ways of God*, London 1855.

TO LADY GEORGIANA FULLERTON

6, Harcourt Street, Dublin. June 13, 1855.

My dear Lady Georgiana,

I was very grateful to you for your letter, which I did not expect. This requires no answer.

I hope to say Mass for you and Mr. Fullerton every Thursday between this and Michaelmas Day.

Would that I could use words of real comfort. Words are weak — but the Mass is strong. Most sincerely yours in Xt., &c.

TO THOMAS LONGMAN

6 Harcourt Street Dublin June 13. 1855

My dear Mr Longman[1]

Lady Jervis called on me yesterday. She is a pleasing lady-like person, and I was quite sorry I had nothing to say which would promote her wishes. Here we have no need at present of Oriental Professors; and two or three, of great pretensions, have already been named to me. It seemed very cold comfort to say that converts have a time of trial after they have joined the Church — but it is true, and Mr J. must prepare himself for it. If I had any way of showing my sympathy, I would gladly avail myself of it. I fear they thought me unfriendly, but really I had nothing to say[2]

Very truly yours in Xt   John H Newman of the Oratory

The Revd Thos Longman

TO WILLIAM MONSELL

6 Harcourt Street Dublin June 13. 1855

My dear Monsell,

Since I wrote to you, I have had all manner of ons and offs about houses. At present I have neither ground for house nor church.

[1] Thomas Longman was the priest at Hampton-on-Hill, Warwick.
[2] Lady Jervis was the wife of James Walter Jervis, a convert clergyman, who had been an Anglican chaplain in Bombay.

I am thinking of buying Judge Burton's or Judge Ball's house in the Green. Don't mention it, please. I find that the interest, at 5 per cent, of the outlay will be less than what I pay for this house with the ground (could I have got it) next to me — and a much larger house into the bargain — whereas here I must build. I suppose I should want from £2000 to £2500. I don't know whether you have found you could lend me any sum. You see, I could give you £4 or £4½ per cent in interest, leaving £1 or £½ per cent for repairs. Perhaps, however, that would not be enough?

Can you tell me *where* a box of books is, which Allies told me to tell Duffy to send to Scutari[1]

Ever Yrs John H Newman of the Oratory

W Monsell Esqr M P

P.S.   A de Vere is nailed — and gives his inaugural Lecture on Friday. He comes to this house tomorrow for a week, I hope.

TO W. G. WARD

6 Harcourt Street June 13. 1855

My dear Ward,

Your letter, dated the 10th, has just come. I had not the slightest suspicion that [J. M.] Capes thought disadvantageously of Fr Faber's books. I had not observed they were not reviewed in the Rambler, and am very sorry he should have any such feeling as you suppose. I will think about writing to him, but my fear is, it might make things worse, if they are as you think. He will bring out to himself more strongly than he knows at present, and might defend to me, his differences from Fr F. whereas, if not insisted on, they may die away. However, I will think about it. I am just beginning with extreme interest F's last book. As to the two others, strange to say, I have hardly heard a word against the first, but I know persons who threw up the second, religious persons too, yet I have not a dream why.[2]

The truth is, where you have a number of intellectual persons, where you have a number of schools, a number of orders, you *must* have a number of differences. In English Catholicism these are crowded

---

[1] These were books that Monsell had asked should be sent out for the sick soldiers See letter of 3 Nov. 1855 to Allies.

[2] By Faber's first book is meant *All for Jesus*, 1853, and his second *Growth in Holiness*, 1854.

together on a narrow field — in France, they are scattered and diluted over a large surface. Our only hope is to bear and forbear.

I sent you a message by Dr Weathers the other day. After all, Mr Molloy has come here, and seems very happy and content.[1]

It gave me great pleasure to hear so good an account of you — but don't presume on your improvement. Mrs Ward must keep you from that. My kindest remembrances to her, and believe me, My dear Ward, Affectly Yours in Xt

                                    John H Newman of the Oratory

W G Ward Esqr

P.S. I don't think I have written a word to Capes or he to me these two years. If so, it must have been something very accidental or trivial. I recollect, he wrote to me about St Alfonso.[2]

THURSDAY 14 JUNE 1855   de Vere came for his lecture and put up with me

TO LORD HENRY KERR

                              6 Harcourt Street Dublin June 14. 1855.
My dear Lord Henry

We must dun you for money, for our exchequer is low and I have the less compunction because our rule is, as at the English Universities, that payment should be made in advance. It will do, if you pay by the end of the first week in July. The money should be paid into 'Dr Newman's private account at the Hibernian Bank, Castle Street Dublin — ' I will put the items on the opposite page.[3] Francis (and the rest)

[1] This was James Lynam Molloy the song writer. He was at school at St Edmund's College, Ware, and thus known to W. G. Ward. Molloy, who won a classical scholarship at the University, went to St Patrick's House, and was nearly expelled in Dec. 1857. See the correspondence then.

[2] Newman wrote seven letters to Capes on the subject of St Alfonso during 1854, but otherwise after 1852 sent him only three short and unimportant letters.

[3] Mr Francis Kerr,

		£	s	d.
Due to the Rectors House up to July 22. 1855.		44.	0.	0.
Feb.	given him.	1.	5.	0.
April.	Butlers account.	2.	13.	0.
May.	Journey home	3.	0.	0.
		50.	18.	0.
Journey in July home?		–	–	–

have taken to boating and he distinguishes himself — I was glad of it for as far as I can make out, it is a cheap as well as a healthy recreation — He has been going on very well, and did I tell you the Professor of Mathematics praised him to me? Should there be nothing to prevent it when the time comes and should he like it, I hope you will let him go home by Edgbaston —

Very sincerely Yours in Xt   John H Newman of the Oratory.

The Lord Henry Kerr.

MONDAY 18 JUNE 1855   began evening Soirées at the University House in Library

TO EDWARD WALFORD

6 Harcourt Street. June 18/55 Dublin

My dear Walford,

The day for the Examination, if it suits you, will be July 16, Monday. If you can, you had better come several days before it. Bid the carman drive here to me, and if I can't give you a bed, at least I will get one for you, and shall be truly glad to show you all hospitality but a bedroom, at all events. You will be able to get back on Tuesday or Wednesday the 18th. Tuesday would be a *better* day for the examination, unless you are pressed to get back.

It is not more than a littlego in fact — and we have nothing out of the way to produce, but it will give some eclat your coming. Your colleague is Mr Myles O'Reilly, who took his degree at the London University. I don't know whether we shall be able to wear them, but if you have your ⟨(Oxford)⟩ gown and hood, you have better bring them.

The books will be such as these:—the three first books of Herodotus — four first books of Homer — Alcestis, Hippolytus, Philoctetes, Cicero's Offices — Virgil — Greek History —

They will not succeed in Latin Composition, tho' they must be examined in it.

Very sincerely Yours in Xt   John H Newman of the Oratory

E Walford Esqr

TUESDAY 19 JUNE 1855   Stanislas came   H Ryder unwell   de Vere unwell

TO AMBROSE ST JOHN

6 Harcourt Street June 19. 1855

My dear Ambrose,

If the Hebdomadarius is weekly, as the word means, its duties would clash with the doubting once in so many weeks.[1] Any how *you* are not the only person affected — Fr Bernard would in his turn be affected as well. If all feel it, all cause it in their turn also. If all feel it, let all alter it. I left word, what I suppose has not reached the particular Fathers, that Fr Henry and Edward should take any doubting and waiting — i.e. it would not come to any other Father, if you were not at Table, to doubt in your place.

In like manner no one should go out to Rednall on his doubting or waiting day.

⌐There may be any redistribution of doubting waiting or Hebdomadariasm, which is desirable.

Fr B's magisterialism is only what he exercised against *me* at Christmas⌐

Ever Yrs affly J H N

⌐I inclose an answer to Mr Wyse (lucus à non lucendo)⌐[2]

[1] One whose week it was to be the confessor on duty might be prevented from taking his turn as waiter in the refectory or as proposer of questions for discussion there. This happened frequently to St John, and Dalgairns had, as the former put it, exercised his 'magisterialism' by complaining 'at recreation very angrily and rudely,' about the matter.

[2] The priest at Alcester Street complained unjustifiably that collections were still made in that district for the Oratory. St John wrote on 17 June, '*Whatever* shall I say. I suppose anything will offend the donkey.' The answer Newman sent for St John's use was as follows:

'My dear Mr Wyse

I sent your letter to Fr Newman, our Superior, for whom I conceive it was intended. He writes me word to express his concern that any thing should have happened as regards the collections for our new church and schools which you have reason to think interferes with the rights due to your position as Missioner in Alcester Street. He feels how zealously you are engaged in that Mission, and would be very sorry in any way to offend you. He also begs me to say that he really hopes that you will find that in the present instance no offence has been committed, and that in consequence you will have no need to take the public notice of it which you contemplate. I shall be glad to transmit to him any thing else you have to say on the subject, and am etc

A. St John'

Two years later Wyse apologised for his letter. See letter to him of 14 May 1857.

WEDNESDAY 20 JUNE 1855   H Ryder *had* scarletina   got all the youths out of the house but F. Kerr, who at first seemed unwell too.   Reginald [Barnewall], Victor [Duke], Charles [de la Pasture], and Ernest [O'Meagher] to Scratton's at Kingstown.   Renouf and Louis [de Vaulchier] to Pollen's.   attended marriage and breakfast of Captain Latham and Miss Molloy, Stanislas officiating.[1]

TO LADY HENRY KERR

6 Harcourt Street June 20. 1855.

My dear Lady Henry

Scarletina is in the air here owing to this most sad weather and Henry Ryder has just caught it. I shall send Francis for the week to Kingstown or more likely to Birmingham with Fr Flanagan who goes back to night.

In this way he will not lose his time, and will pass a quarantine before he comes home at the end of next month

Most sincerely Yours in Xt   John H Newman of the Oratory

The Lady Henry Kerr.

P.S.   On second thoughts I am sending Francis with one or two others to Kingstown to Mr Scratton our Secretary in whose house he will be

THURSDAY 21 JUNE 1855   F. Kerr went to Ornsby's
FRIDAY 22 JUNE   de Vere Scarletina too[2]

TO DAVID MORIARTY, COADJUTOR BISHOP OF KERRY

6 Harcourt Street Dublin June 22/55

My dear Lord

I have just returned from Allhallows, and was grieved to find you were gone. It was said you were to remain till the end of the month. I tried to find you on the evening when you were at the Lecture, but was too late. And I unluckily missed you when you called. Since then, I have been in some trouble. The Scarletina has seized one of our Youths,

---

[1] Joanna Molloy was Flanagan's cousin.

[2] 'When I had been but a few days in Newman's house I fell ill of scarlatina, and the first of my lectures had to be read aloud by another person. . . . and every day, in spite of countless other engagements, Newman found time to sit by my bedside occasionally, and delight me by his conversation. When advancing towards convalescence I went to Bray for sea air, and he drove out to see me.' *Recollections of Aubrey de Vere*, London 1897, p. 268.

Mr Ryder, and Mr de Vere, who came up to give a Lecture, is seized too, as the Doctor pronounced this morning. Another youth alarmed me, but has got well. Dr Leahy and Mr Flannery were both attacked in the throat, like Mr de Vere. And I am suffering under something of a sore throat myself.

I wanted some confidential talk with you on subjects, either too delicate or too much in detail to write about. As to your answer to this, you may not like to express an opinion, or you may not like to say much — And I will burn it, whatever is in it, more or less.

1. We must now *at once* come to a conclusion about Dr Corrigan. I think he *wishes* the appointment, but he has some notion, though he has not said so to me, that the Bishops have not well treated him at Maynooth — and he does not like taking a Professorship without some security that the Bishops 'will go on with the Medical Faculty.'[1] He professes to think that in a year or two they may, for want of funds for example, give it up. I don't suppose he has any difficulty in the Bishops having the ultimate power of removing a Professor, for heterodoxy, immorality, or neglect of his duty, but saving and allowing this, he wishes some *guarantee* of the continuity of the office. The Decree of the Synodal Meeting, confirmed by the Holy See, he does not understand.

As I consider that your Lordship's judgment will be the most favorable for him I can have, I shall give up, exceedingly against my will, the thought of having him, if I find that you think it not safe to proceed. He will be a great loss to me, but there are sacrifices which we must be content to make.

I thought of *this*:— viz, letting him *buy* his Professorship with a sum, — nominal, if so be, — which he would receive back on *selling* it to the University again, on his retiring. This would give him the right of being Professor with a certain Salary, except in case of the exertion of the Bishops' supreme power as above.

Again I thought of giving him a mortgage to a certain amount on the Medical School, which we bought.

A third plan would be promise him (except in case of dismission as above) *two* (say) years' salary, in advance, if he were removed.

And this is all I have to say on this subject.[2]

[1] Corrigan was the physician to Maynooth. The *Report* of the Royal Commission on Maynooth, published earlier in the year, included a number of serious complaints from the students about the medical department.

[2] Moriarty, who had recommended Corrigan so strongly in his first letter of 29 April, replied on 25 June, 'If Dr Corrigan ceases to hold connexion with the Queen's University you may safely make his appointment in the most absolute manner. Not a Bishop in Ireland but will be delighted to have him associated with the University. . . .

If he continue to hold his place in the Senate of the Queen's University we may

2. My second chief subject is that of the Financial matters of the University, on which I could say a great deal in very various aspects.

The most obvious grievance at present is the want of a Secretary and Treasurer. The parochial collections come in *any* how, and to *any* one. And the confusion is great in consequence. Dr Leahy, I, Mr Flannery, Mr Scratton, Mr Star, the Vicars General, the Bank, all receive sums at random.

Next, I have no one to go to or treat with, when I want money. Once or twice I have been run dry.

Several laymen of influence have the strongest feeling on the subject, and declare that nothing can go right till a small committee of Finance is appointed. They prophesy that the subscriptions will gradually cease, unless there is a good organization.

There is *no one to do* it. Dr Cullen hitherto has refused to move. I would gladly move, if the Bishops had given, or would give me power — Did they tell me to put the matter in shape, I should try to get three or four good men of business as a Committee, with a clerical Secretary. (perhaps a lay Secretary too)

We shall in a little time be wrecked unless this is done.[1]

Begging your Lordship's blessing, I am, My dear Lord Affectly Yours in Xt

John H Newman of the Oratory

P.S.   The University, thank God, is decidedly making progress.

TO THOMAS SCRATTON

June 22. [1855]

My dear Scratton,

Will you be so good as to provide monthly tickets for Barnewall, O Meagher, and de la Pasture for the Kingstown Rail, and charge them to me overleaf? And for V. Duke for a fortnight, if they issue such.

And will you take care that none of them goes out *by himself* after dinner?

expect a protest from a certain quarter, and we should therefore make sure of support. In this supposition it were better to ascertain Dr Dixon's opinion and if we can Dr Cullen's. If they coincide with us we need fear no opposition.'

See also letter of 1 July to Corrigan.

[1] Moriarty agreed that a financial committee should be appointed, but felt that nothing could be done until Cullen returned to Ireland. Cf. letter of 26 July to Cullen.

And will you look at the accounts overleaf?[1] and, if they are correct, I will draw the drafts at once

Ever Yrs With thanks for your kind arrangements

J H N

TO F. S. BOWLES

Saturday June 23/55

My dear F Frederic

Will you tell me what sort of an *Organ* you would recommend me to get, as to stops etc etc. for £250? I have signed the agreement for the ground this day — and shall begin building my Church at once. I have already been with an organ builder, Telford, who is a good man.[2]

Harry [Ryder] is getting wellish. The eruption has come out thick on De Vere. Both are having it lightly All besides well

Ever Yrs affly J H N

TO JOHN HUNGERFORD POLLEN

Saturday [23 June 1855]

My dear Pollen,

Thank you for your kind letter. R. Wilberforce comes to-day, and lodges at the Hairdresser's. I am engaged to dine out to-morrow, and,

---

[1] Scratton.

Barnewall, O'Meagher and de la Pasture for a month at £11. 0. 0.	33. 0. 0.
Duke for a fortnight ———————	5. 10. 0
(3 monthly tickets for the Rail)	
(1 ticket for a fortnight)	
	£38. 10.
Ornsby	
Kerr for a month ———————	11. 0. 0
Duke for a fortnight ———————	5. 10. 0
Kerr's car hire———————	12. 0
	17. 2. 0
Pollen	
Renouf and de Vaulchier at £1. 10.——	12. 0. 0

[2] William Telford, 100 Stephen's Green.

c. . . .[1] if I don't, he mayn't think it right to come here. Can you give him dinner? If so, I would come to *wine* or tea — but perhaps you are engaged.

Ever Yours John H. Newman of the Oratory

P.S.   Could you give him tea *to-night*.
I don't know when he comes.

MONDAY 25 JUNE 1855   R Wilberforce came from the West, sleeping at next door but one.   Dr Ellis left his patients.

TUESDAY 26 JUNE   R Wilberforce went.   my buildings in Harcourt Street began — or this day week?

TO JOHN STANISLAS FLANAGAN (I)

6 Harcourt Street June 26/55

My dear Stanislas

Thank Nicholas for his letter which has just come. Fred. [Thynne] should pass into your hands before this, since N's fortnight is over. Do not let us entangle ourselves with him. I don't mind his merely being in the *house* — but, since we decided there were to be no lessons, let there be none. I don't know who has time to give them.

I write to you, because I am very much down in the mouth, as about other things, so about my Church. I don't know how I can shut my eyes to the fact that it will cost £4000 from first to last. Then again, what if the Bishops turn round and say, 'since we give sermons and music, we must have a portion at least of the incomings'? May not they say, 'You are getting a wonderful interest for your money (500 seats at /6 for 40 weeks) £500 for an outlay of £4000 — viz 12½ per cent.'

How am I to answer this? how am I to raise the £4000?

Ever Yours affly J H N

P.S.   Harry [Ryder] and de Vere dine with me at 5 today. Harry is at his violin.

One of my troubles, *not to be repeated*, (for he may change) is that George Ryder is going to take away his two sons at the vacation![2]

---

[1] Word illegible to copyist.
[2] See letter of 14 Aug. 1855 to Harry Ryder.

June 26. 1855

My dear Stanislas

I can't help thinking my last hit in the accompanying paper is a good one. When you have toiled through it, let me have it again.

I take the Choir on myself, and charge on the University

Rent of ground	—	10. 0. 0
Gas and coal	—	60. 0. 0
Use of organ (10 per cent)		25. 0. 0
Use of choir	—	75. 0. 0
100 sittings at /6 for 40 weeks	—	100. 0. 0
Sundries	—	30. 0. 0
		300. 0. 0

which just pays the choir

Ever Yrs J H N

TO THOMAS SCRATTON

June 26/55

My dear Scratton

Mr Robertson goes this week — I suppose you should pay him £50, besides his bill at Mrs Porter's.

Will you try to calculate how much money I shall want for the Professors etc who ought to be paid by the 20th of July, in anticipation of August 1. — The two Examiners, Mr Myles O'Reilly and Walford must be remembered — and O'Reilly's bill set against us as Pro-Procurator last summer, which I think he has promised, and never given in.

De Vere, Pollen, O'Hagan, ought (I suppose) to have £5 a piece for their Inaugural Lectures. (Was there any precedent to guide us in November? Allies came from a distance and returned.) I inclose the cheque which I drew some days ago

Ever Yrs J H N

WEDNESDAY 27 JUNE 1855   de Vere and H Ryder went out for the first time.

TO F. S. BOWLES

6 Harcourt Street June 27. 1855

My dear Frederic

What do you think of the inclosed, which, please, return?

And give the inclosed to Stanislas; (no. I inclose to Edward.)

Harry has been taking a ride with me to-day — and de Vere is to do so after lunch. The Doctor is gone from both of them.

Your letter is this moment come. Thank you for it, but you have left out the first sheet, I suppose — for it begins 'I believe the waldflute etc.'[1]

Ever Yrs affly J H N

TO EDWARD CASWALL

June 27/55

My dear Edward

I don't suppose the proposed building is to be on the Oratory (Church) Ground — but I can't make out any thing which shows that it is not. I should like to have this clear. The only plan I heard of was, as Henry said, a *room over the stable* — £400 is a large sum, which will become £500, and whence is the money for a *temporary* building?[2]

Ever Yrs affly J H N

THURSDAY 28 JUNE 1855 de Vere left for Bray went out with Harry

TO THOMAS SCRATTON

June 28/55

My dear Scratton,

Will you send me a £5 cheque for de Vere, who goes to-day. Mr Robertson too goes, I believe, this week.

The rule, I have observed is, that residents are paid by the Quarter — non-residents by the work or piece

Ever Yrs J H N

[1] Bowles's letter of 25 June about organs in the end reached Newman complete. The second sheet begins 'I believe the Waldflute is very beautiful for a Solo stop . . .' Newman's first-mentioned enclosure must also have concerned organs.

[2] This and the letter of 1 July refer to a school building.

FRIDAY 29 JUNE 1855   went to Clongowes with Victor [Duke][1]

TO JOHN HUNGERFORD POLLEN

Friday [29 June 1855?]

My dear Pollen

I should like very much to answer these questions, which have just come, by the 12 o'clock post, if possible

Ever Yrs J H N

1. I consider the pipes are merely to air and dry, not to warm, the church.
2. The gratings will add so considerably to the expense, that I shall wish much to avoid them.

FRIDAY 30 JUNE 1855   went with Harry to call on de Vere at Bray

TO JOHN STANISLAS FLANAGAN

[End of June 1855?][2]

My dear Stanislas

From your knowledge of Dublin give me some advice.

My youths are taking to the Billiard Tables in Dawson's Lane.

The tables are kept by a good Catholic who professes to keep a strict eye over them.

Mr Barnewall recommends them — and Priests play there in private.

I have wished to get a billiard table for the University — the want of a room, and the expense has delayed it.

It won't quite answer the purpose, for *the youths wish to see play*.

Here we come to the cardo of the difficulty.

I had thought of formally taking references of Mr Burnell the Keeper, and then of formally licensing him, and forbidding them to go elsewhere.

But, it is the great billiard place in Dublin.

[1] Clongowes Wood was the Jesuit College twenty miles west of Dublin.
[2] This letter is undated, but during the summer vacation Newman had stables at the back of University House converted into a billiard room at a cost of £160, which was borrowed from the University. The work was finished by the end of Sept. See also postscript to letter of 10 Oct. 1855 to Scratton.

Query. Will they form undesirable acquaintance, hear undesirable betting news, etc etc. there?

As you know Dublin perhaps you can answer.

Ever Yrs affly J H N

P.S.   The inclosed goes, I think, to Fr Edward — or is it Fr Ambrose?

TO EDWARD CASWALL

July 1/55

My dear Edward

It does not seem to me a great difficulty the incroachment on the Church ground.

But the £400 will be £500 which is a prodigious sum. And, without giving an opinion against its adoption, I do not wish to be answerable for it — and the more so, because I never have liked Nowell — and think that his first act should be making good the boards of the floor at Rednall. I am not so certain what we shall think of his work ten years hence.

Ever Yrs affly J H N

TO D. J. CORRIGAN

July 1. 1855

(Copy)

Dear Sir

I have given my best attention to the points, which you offered to my consideration as conditions of your giving us your important assistance in the University Medical School; and I am sorry to say that, as regards two of them, I fear I shall not be able so to arrange matters as to satisfy your wishes.[1]

I do not contemplate a difficulty in the question of the *salary* to be attached to the Professorship of the Practice of Medicine or that of the *Gentlemen* who are to be associated with you in the School; but I await

[1] Corrigan's letter is not to be found but its tenor can be sufficiently gathered from Newman's reply. Cf. letter of 22 June to Moriarty.

497

with some anxiety the ultimate view you will take upon other points which you set before me.

You felt it necessary, if I understood you, for me to give you some assurance of the *continuance* of the Institution, and of your place in it, supposing you took part in it, *greater* than the solemn determination of the Holy See and the National Synod, carried out in the act of the Bishops upon my presenting to them your name. I would gladly give you something beyond this, if I could; but the more I think of it, the less do I see how it can be done. It is the very guarantee on which I thought it worth while to leave my own home in England to take part in what I felt to be a great work; and, while I considered, and still consider it sufficient myself, I am obliged to say I cannot devise any thing which you may think more satisfactory.

And in like manner, as to the other point, *the School in Cecilia Street*, I bought it on such available advice as I had, and with which I am still perfectly satisfied, the advice of able and experienced practitioners, and I cannot ask the University authorities to reverse an act, which has involved great expense, and which I recommended to them.

It grieves me to relinquish the hopes which I have so long entertained of your assistance — nor indeed will I yet do so. But I am obliged to send you the letter which I promised you in answer to the distinct considerations to which you directed my attention.[1]

I am &c J H N

D. Corrigan Esqr M D &c.

TO JOHN STANISLAS FLANAGAN

6 Harcourt Street July 1. 1855

My dear Stanislas,

I am in that state of mind that I forget every thing, and cannot master yours and Mr [F. R.] Ward's letter as I should. Do just what you think right.[2]

Thank you for your account of Fred. Thynne — and thank Nicholas for the mundatories. De Vere is gone some days, Harry [Ryder] moves slowly through his convalescence. I have great exertions to make for the close of the Session, and dread them.

I am very sorry indeed about your annoyance as to John Smallman

[1] Corrigan did not become one of the Medical Professors at the Catholic University.
[2] This refers to the plan to borrow from Monsell money for the University church, and give as part security land in Roscommon.

— I ought to have asked you — somehow I took it for granted that a Treasurer was ever a treasure house[1]

Ever Yrs affly J H N

6 Harcourt Street Dublin July 1. 1855.

My dear Lady Henry,

I did not understand till your last that Lord Henry had gone to Aix precisely for his health. I am very sorry for it, it must be a great trouble both to him and you. He was kind enough to write me a line the other day — There is not more than a fortnight more of it now, before his return.

Francis is very well, and was with Mrs Wyse at a sort of fête of the Lord Lieutenant's yesterday, in the Lodge Gardens — I am thankful to say, all the youths are well and Mr Ryder more than convalescent. He has had the complaint very slightly, nor can I make out that there has been any peeling of his skin at all.

Thank you for your explanation about the Post Office orders, which was very simple. I think I am right in saying that you told me to pay Francis for *July* — Francis as perhaps you know from him is lodged at Mr Ornsby's with Mr [H.] Bowden for a companion (as after[?] it will be with Mr Dunn[?]) I got the whole house out of doors immediately on the medical man's [advice] except him. I kept him here a night in some anxiety, for he had a little sore throat, and looked heavy — But Fr Flanagan of Birmingham, who was here, gave him something hot, and put his feet in hot water, and put him to bed in the afternoon: he at once slept like a top, and was quite well in the morning as he has continued ever since — He and Mr Ryder had both been bathing too much or imprudently, I think, this very inclement unseasonable weather. What a midsummer it is! Mr Aubrey de Vere, who was sleeping in the room between Mr Ryder and Francis has had the complaint too — Both are up today and indulging in chicken and sherry. So we ought to be very thankful —

I put Francis with Mr Ornsby because I feared he would be idle, if he had been at Kingstown with batchelor Mr Scratton or those others.

Excuse this long explanation and believe me Most sincerely Yours in Xt

John H Newman of the Oratory.

The Lady Henry Kerr —

[1] Flanagan had had to borrow journey money for a servant.

MONDAY 2 JULY 1855   soirée at University House in evening

TO THE EARL OF DUNRAVEN

6 Harcourt Street July 2. 1855

My dear Lord Dunraven

Your most welcome letter has come on this Feast, as a special favor of our dear Lady to me — I congratulate you most sincerely on what you tell me — not the least, from the feeling all your friends must have had that your health was suffering severely from the great anxieties under which you laboured so long.[1]

I rejoice in having your name, and am very thankful for your promise of aid for my Church. It is very munificent, and, I assure you, you could not have done me a more seasonable, welcome kindness.[2]

The same post, which brought your letter this morning, brought one from the other end of the earth, showing the working of God's grace in a way so wonderful, that it is distressing to have it all to oneself, and not be at liberty to mention it. As I happen to be writing to you, I say as much as this — but shall not even say so much to any one else.[3]

If we *were* to have the scarletina in the house, we could not have had it more lightly. Poor Aubrey de Vere, it seemed hard on him though. I hear since, it has been all about the Street. He is at Bray, and I am going this morning to see him. He speaks as not being quite well.

Ever Yours, My dear Lord Dunraven, Affectionately in Xt

John H Newman of the Oratory

The Earl of Dunraven

P.S.   I propose to say a Mass of thanksgiving for you tomorrow morning

[1] After hesitating for years, and in spite of the strong opposition of his wife, Lord Dunraven had become a Catholic.

[2] Lord Dunraven promised £200 towards the University church.

[3] This was a letter from the second son of Arnold of Rugby, Thomas Arnold, Inspector of Schools in Tasmania, who became a Catholic in Jan. 1856. See letter of 25 Oct. 1856 to him. Arnold's daughter later wrote of him that, 'he who had only once crossed the High Street to hear Newman preach, and felt no interest in the sermon, now, on the other side of the world, surrendered to Newman's influence.' Mrs Humphry Ward, *A Writer's Recollections*, London 1918, p. 19.

TO AMBROSE ST JOHN

[4 July 1855]¹
My dear Ambrose

I earnestly trust you will not let a day pass without getting water in some other way.²

It is a question whether we shall not be compelled, till we can afford the alteration of the Pipes, to use city water, which I suppose I am right in saying we can get for a few shillings or Pounds.

Any how, I doubt how we can clear ourselves of the guilt of murder and suicide, if we do not give over the lead water at once

Ever Yrs J H N

Letter from Bloxam this morning

'Wm Palmer has been breakfasting with me this morning, and giving me an account of his reception at Rome.

You will be sorry to hear that poor Mariott has had a paralytic attack, and is dangerously ill at Oriel.'

Lead brings on paralysis. The way of proceeding would, I think, be this — 1. to leave off the lead water *at once*. 2 to get Dr Evans to confirm or reject Southall's judgment. 3 not to return to the water unless Southall was utterly confuted.³

I tease William out of his existence — Show him the inclosed direction etc of the Tablet which came this morning.

THURSDAY 5 JULY 1855   very hot weather these weeks.

TO ARCHBISHOP CULLEN

6 Harcourt Street Dublin July 5. 1855
My dear Lord,

I have just heard from Mr Lyons that your Grace is likely to be by this time in London — ⁴ and I write at once to express my great pleasure that at last you are so near Dublin.

¹ Dated from St John's letters.
² It was discovered that the well water used at the Oratory was contaminated by the lead of the pipes through which it flowed.
³ The doctor fully confirmed the analysis of the chemist.
⁴ Richard Lyons had presumably told Newman this when writing from Rome about the death in the Crimea on 23 June of his younger brother Edmund Lyons, R.N.

I have not written to you, because things have remained much or entirely, in the same state as they did in Lent.[1] We have been busy with the young men whom we have collected; but I have been able to do little on the points about which I consulted your Grace. Of course Dr Dunne remains in Harcourt Street still — since you did not give me leave to move him. As to Dr Lyons, about whom I wrote to you, I did not speak to him for some months, but, when I found he was going off to Scutari, I wrote to secure him, though I should have liked a word from you first.[2]

In like manner I have found it necessary to appoint provisionally several gentlemen, as Mr de Vere and Mr Pollen, who have been giving Inaugural Lectures within this last week or two with great effect.

I have been, as every one else, constantly thinking your Grace was coming home — Else, though I had nothing to say, I should have written to you.

The last two or three weeks have been important ones for us. At last, after many fruitless efforts, I have been enabled to get ground for my Church. We have got a lease of Mr Carmichael's House,[3] next the University House, and I have taken the garden part for my purpose. Also, I have secured several gentlemen for the Medical Chairs — and I have been obliged to promise to begin the Theological School in October, thinking you particularly wished it, though I would rather take your opinion on it, directly I see you.

Mr Lyons has just told me you have been at Louvain. I should have been very glad to have known it, as there are questions I should have liked you to allow me to suggest to you to ask.

Our examinations for the Scholar's Degree begin on *Monday the* 16th — and we all break up in the course of that week. I am sorry to say, I must be in England by the end of it — and shall not return till November.

But I rely on seeing your Grace here *next* week — when a few hours conversation will settle all I have to ask you[4]

I am, My dear Lord begging your Grace's blessing, Yours affte friend & Servant in Xt

John H Newman

His Grace the Archbp of Dublin.

---

[1] Cullen had never answered the pressing questions in Newman's letter of 23 Feb. at the beginning of Lent, nor indeed replied to his letter of 24 Jan.
[2] See letter of 27 April to Dr Lyons.
[3] 87 Stephen's Green.
[4] See diary for 13 July and letter of 26 July to Cullen.

TO J. R. BLOXAM

6 Harcourt Street Dublin July 7. 1855

My dear Bloxam,

Your two books have arrived, and I thank you very much for the acceptable present — but I shall be afraid of writing to you, if such consequences follow.

What you say of Marriott fills me with the greatest concern.[1] I see it mentioned in a London Paper that the seizure is severe. The Oxford Paper seems to say nothing of it, as far as I can see.

You do not say whether Palmer is making a stay at Oxford. Should he be still there, tell him, with my kindest remembrances, that I shall be in Birmingham in the course of a fortnight, should he be coming that way. What a shame you are not following his good example.[2]

Ever Yours affectly John H Newman of the Oratory

P.S. If you have any thing to tell of Marriott, I should be most grateful for a line.

MONDAY 9 JULY 1855   soirée at University House in evening

TO ISY FROUDE

6 Harcourt Street Dublin July 9. 1855.

My dearest Isy

I am very glad to have your present. A pen wiper is always useful. It lies on the table, and one can't help looking at it. I have one in use, made for me by a dear Aunt, now dead, whom I knew from a little child, as I was once. When I take it up, I always think of her, and I assure you I shall think of you, when I use yours. I have another at Birmingham, given me by Mrs Phillipps of Torquay, in the shape of a bell.

This day is the anniversary of one of the few times I have seen a dear brother of mine for 22 years. He returned from Persia, I from

---

[1] See letter of 4 July to St John. Charles Marriott had a stroke on 30 June, and was removed in Aug. to Bradfield, Berkshire, where his brother was curate, and where he lingered on until his death in Sept. 1858.

[2] i.e. in becoming a Catholic.

Sicily, where I nearly died, the same day.[1] I saw him once 15 years ago, and now I have not seen him for 9 years.

My dear Isy when I think of your brother, I will think of you. I heard a report he was to go and fight the Russians.[2] I have another godson, called Edward Bouverie Pusey, who is a sailor already, fighting the Russians either in the Baltic or at Sebastopol[3]

Ever Yours affectionately John H Newman of the Oratory.

P.S. You will have a hard matter to read this letter

TO JOHN STANISLAS FLANAGAN

July 10/55

My dear S

I am disgusted at Terence coming, just when we are breaking up, when Mr Hennesy and Mr Sullivan have left — when I shall be busy with the Archbishop, with Examinations. and with the various jobs involved in leaving for the Vacation. I have said he had better come here by Saturday next.[4]

I hope [F. R.] Ward won't be long with his hitch, as I must sign the contract before I leave.[5]

1. Do I pay the servants their ordinary money *besides* board wages, during the Vacation? e.g. do I give Frederic for August $\pounds\frac{.25}{12}$ + 10s a week? If I do *not*, I must give Margaret something for keeping the house. If so, how much?[6] Your letter is dated the 8th, but has just come.

Ever Yrs J H N

TO J. B. PAGANI

Dublino, 10 luglio 1855.

Scrivo due righe all R. V. per condolermi con voi e coi vostri Padri per la perdita del vostro rinomato e santo Fondatore . . . Un uomo come

[1] Newman returned from his Mediterranean tour, and his brother Francis from his missionary journey, to their mother's house at Iffley on 9 July 1833.

[2] Isy Froude was fifteen and her brother Richard Hurrell, Newman's godson, thirteen.

[3] Edward Bouverie Pusey (1838–1921), Captain R.N., was the second son of William Pusey, Rector of Langley, Kent, the younger brother of E. B. Pusey.

[4] Terence Flanagan, the Professor of Civil Engineering, had just returned from Portugal, where he had been constructing the railway from Lisbon to Cintra.

[5] There was a difficulty about raising money on the Roscommon estate.

[6] Flanagan replied that the 'ordinary money' should be paid.

lui sino a tanto che rimaneva sulla terra era una proprietà di tutta la Chiesa. Io temo che le tribolazioni da lui sofferte quaggiù debbano avere abbreviata la sua vita.[1]

TO WILLIAM KIRBY SULLIVAN

6 Harcourt Street Dublin July 10. 1855

My dear Mr Sullivan

I am sorry for your answer, but I can't be surprised — and I thank you for the trouble you have taken in considering my proposal.[2]

Also I thank you for your valuable hints about the Medical Chairs.

You say that Mr Gayes might fill the two chairs of Chemistry and Pharmacy as far as *Medicine* is concerned — but could he fill chemistry for engineering purposes? I am expecting Mr Flanagan, the Professor of Engineering, in Dublin in a few days — and I should be much obliged, if you could answer me this question.

Also if you could get me in confidence some opinion about Mr Murney's qualifications, I should be much obliged. Dr Denvir spoke strongly in his favour. You, when I mentioned his name, said that you had heard well of him, though you did not know him. His Chair would be Materia Medica — Since, others have spoken less warmly about him.[3]

Very sincerely Yours John H Newman of the Oratory

Wm K Sullivan Esqr &c &c.

TO AMBROSE ST JOHN

6 Harcourt Street July 11 1855

My dear Ambrose,

I did not forget you on the 29. I was necessarily engaged for Mass — but I will say Mass for you instead on the Octave. Poor Captain Lyons's death has quite depressed me. And now Lord Raglan's.[4]

[1] Antonio Rosmini-Serbati died on 1 July at Stresa.

[2] Sullivan declined the Professorship of Chemistry, being already Professor of Chemistry in the School of Science at the Museum of Irish Industry in Dublin. He only became Newman's Professor of Chemistry in 1856.

[3] Henry Murney was a young Irish doctor recommended by Dr Denvir, Bishop of Down and Connor. He did not come to the University.

[4] St John's birthday was on 29 June. Edmund Mowbray Lyons, Captain R.N., commanding the *Miranda* in the Black Sea, was mortally wounded in the attack on the sea defences at Sebastopol on 18 June, and died in hospital on 23 June. Lord Raglan, the Commander in Chief in the Crimea, died of fever there on 28 June.

Tell William with my love that, if he has money for an Indian matting for Rednall, costing £3.15, I have nothing to say against getting it. Also tell him, that I can excogitate nothing better than the mark O.R. for the Rednall Oratory linen.

Harry gets strong slowly.

Ever Yours affly J H N

FRIDAY 13 JULY 1855 Walford came — he lodged at Hairdresser dined etc with me Archbishop (Dr Cullen) returned from Rome. Called on him at night
SATURDAY 14 JULY Myles O Reilly came, or tomorrow?

TO AMBROSE ST JOHN

⌐July 14/55⌐

My dear Ambrose,

⌐As to the way the graves should run, there is, I think an ecclesiastical rule — and there I am obliged to leave it.⌐ If there is none, he ⟨W. [William]⟩ may please his fancy.

⌐If there is one Cross or (Crucifix) in the middle, the boys will pelt it. I doubt whether a crucifix should be on each grave. I should prefer a simple cross. Any how, leave the crucifix to the future.

I have great doubt whether either of the bodies should be brought under a roof.⌐ I doubt whether especially ⌐in this weather,⌐ we should not have a fever in consequence.[1]

⌐Both ought, surely, to be taken straight to the ground.⌐ A temporary place might be made and covered over, till the mass begins. If we could have the mass in a tent, so much the better — but perhaps this would not be possible.

⌐A few persons may come with tickets.

I will write to Mr Poncia, but my hand aches, so, and it is so painful to me to write, and I write so badly in that state, and am so full of business just now, that you must give me time.

I am sorry you can't do without a hearse — but of course you can't.⌐ The same hearse after depositing Aloysius, might proceed to the rail station. *It must be in time* at the station; say, an hour before hand.

[1] The bodies of Aloysius Boland and Joseph Gordon were to be buried in the cemetery at Rednal, the first from the crypt of St Chad's Cathedral, the second from Bath. See also letter of 24 July to John Poncia.

⌐I can't write just now to Lady Arundel.⌐ I have long ago sent a message to her thro' Fr Faber — [1] ⌐My wrist is so uncomfortable.⌐

Ever Yrs affly J H N

So, that portentous man, Lord John, is out. What fools we are making of ourselves abroad. Lord John went a Saul and returned a prophet.[2] You see the Times says that he has never prospered since 1850[3]

TO WILLIAM KIRBY SULLIVAN

6 Harcourt Street Dublin July 14. 1855

My dear Mr Sullivan

I thank you very much for your letters, and your information on the special point on which I asked you in my last.[4]

We shall be very much obliged by your getting us the chemical apparatus. I am providing money, when it is wanted for the purpose, and meanwhile shall be very thankful to have the estimate you promise.

I think I have decided on postponing the Chemical, Botanical and other similar appointments.

My reasons are, because since Dr Corrigan will not be persuaded to take the Practice of Medicine, we cannot start in November with a perfect school. So that nothing would be gained by filling up these appointments.

[1] Lady Arundel was not fully recovered after the birth on 1 June of a son, Edmund, who was to become the first Viscount Fitzalan, when she heard of the death on 23 June, of her brother Captain Lyons in the Crimea. Also her second son Philip, aged two, was ill, and died on 24 July.

[2] Lord John Russell, who represented Great Britain in the peace negotiations at Vienna, agreed there to a compromise with Russia, until he received instructions to the contrary. On his return he spoke in favour of continuing the war, and when the Austrian minister revealed that he had assented to the compromise he was forced to resign on 13 July. Cf. 1 Kings (Samuel), 19: 22–4.

[3] *The Times* castigated Lord John Russell for advocating the continuance of slaughter that he really considered unnecessary. Newman must have added his post-script on 16 July when the first leader in *The Times* contained the passage to which he refers:

'It is not to be supposed, however, that the fall of Lord John Russell . . . has been the result of any sudden pique or extraordinary incident. . . . the decline of his influence and of his reputation has long been perceptible. . . . on looking back to that period of six years [when Lord John Russell was Prime Minister] we must say that so inoperative and unsuccessful an Administration has never existed for so long a period in this country.'

[4] Probably the question about Murney, whom Sullivan thought fully competent.

Moreover, I hear murmurs about the appointments of foreigners, and these are likely to decrease or cease, after a time; and after the visible gap in the school, testifying to the want of Irishmen just now for certain chairs, and to my reluctance to introduce strangers — and lastly by the idea of strangers becoming familiar to the public mind, by remaining before it. But if suddenly foreign appointments were made, people would be sure to say, that persons might have been found for them at home, with a little looking about.

I am told that, as more courses of Surgery and Anatomy are necessary, than of Practice of Medicine etc the students may for the first year confine themselves to the Lectures which we are able to give.

Of course I shall keep your list of names and thank you for them
> Very sincerely Yours John H Newman of the Oratory

W. K. Sullivan Esqr

SUNDAY 15 JULY 1855   Mr T. Flanagan came.   ill with teeth

TO ARCHBISHOP CULLEN

> 6 Harcourt Street July 15. 1855

My dear Lord,

Mr Walford, one of our Examiners, is afraid he should not see you, and has called with this note, to pay his respects to your Grace, before you go to Maynooth.

Is it impossible you should come up to us for a quarter of an hour tomorrow (Monday) morning? I had every one in waiting for you yesterday.

And can you tell me whether you have the two Exhibitions, of £35 each, to give away the ensuing Autumn, as at the last?[1]

> Yours affte Servant in Xt John H Newman of the Oratory

P.S.   I shall write down on paper a number of things I am doing, for your Grace's inspection, as soon as I get quiet at Birmingham.

MONDAY 16 JULY 1855   The Examinations for Scholar's degree   Walford, Myles O Reilly and Mr Flanagan Examiners   Soirée in evening

[1] There appears to be no record of a reply to this letter, nor of a visit by Cullen to the University. On 14 July, however, he attended the prizegiving at Dr Quinn's St Laurence O'Toole Seminary.

TO JOHN STANISLAS FLANAGAN

July 16 [1855]

My dear Stanislas

I lost the post yesterday. I have written a duplicate of this to Mr Lynch. Renouf etc are crossing for London on the 19th or 20th. Why did you not tell me the boy's address here, that I might have communicated straight

Ever Yrs J H N

TUESDAY 17 JULY 1855   Examinations concluded   de Vere made his appearance and slept

TO THOMAS SCRATTON

July 17/55

My dear Scratton,

I fear the passages you refer to prove that there is *no such* resolution as we hoped.[1]

As to the subcommittee, of which you speak, they *have* acted since I was in Ireland — and I have always consulted the members of it — so that, practically, it always has gone on as far as *I* am concerned. I bought the Medical School, with the advice *of those persons*, intentionally.

I see no difficulty at all in that subcommittee going on, and perhaps it would be the best thing of all, *if the members would act*. This is the *only difficulty*. I repeat I have, in furnishing the University House, in the Medical School, and every thing financial, consulted intentionally, because they were a subcommittee, those very persons. Mr Errington has been in my room at St Laurence's before now — and I dined with Mr J O'Ferrall, as he kindly allowed me, last Lent year, once a week — *with this very purpose*.

Ever Yrs J H N.

P.S.   I must make some engagement with you about the next term[?].

[1] The resolution hoped for was one concerning the separate financial management of the University. Scratton on 17 July quoted to Newman passages, none of which provided for this. The sub-committee was that set up on 21 Oct. 1853, by the University Committee to represent it, especially on financial matters, with the Rector. Its members were Archbishop Cullen, Dr Leahy, James O'Ferrall, Michael Errington, and Myles O'Reilly. See letters of Aug. and Oct. 1853 to Dr Taylor, and the second letter of 4 Sept. 1855 to Monsell.

P.S. I have thought this subcommittee *superseded*, and as *far as I was concerned*, the whole Committee — which has led to Mr Errington's misconception about us, perhaps.

WEDNESDAY 18 JULY 1855 Terminal examinations began de Vere went

TO D. B. DUNNE

July 18/55

My dear Dr Dunne

From Jan 13 to May 1 is about 15 weeks. This, (at the rate of £100 for 38 weeks,) is £39 — and board and lodging for 15 weeks about, is £16. Which two sums I set down to your account some months ago.

In like manner from May 1 to July 20, is about 11 weeks — which gives at the same rate, £29 for salary

11 for eleven weeks board

——

£40 the sum due to you

Yrs most sincerely John H Newman

Dr Dunne etc etc

THURSDAY 19 JULY 1855 Terminal examinations concluded I came off late at night with 2 Ryders

FRIDAY 20 JULY arriving at Bm [Birmingham] for Mass

TO JAMES HOPE-SCOTT

The Oratory, Hagley Road, Birmingham, July 20, 1855

My dear Hope Scott

I am building a University Church in Dublin on my own hook — and wish to borrow money on good security, which I can offer.

It is just possible that you may have some floating money, and, if so, I want to know whether you will not turn your thoughts to lending me some. I can give you £4 per cent, if you will think that enough.

I do not use *University* money for several reasons: — 1. I wish to have my own way as to site, building, decoration etc etc — whereas a

Committee would bother me. 2. I do not wish to commit the University to a *permanent* Church at this early date. It ⟨(The U.)⟩ may leave it on my hands, when it will. 3. In that case, and in any case ultimately, I have an Oratorian Church. We calculate that I shall be paid back by sittings etc my £4000, which will be the whole cost, in 14 years, with its yearly interest. And I could undertake to repay the money I borrow by yearly instalments.

I should be glad to borrow of you, or any friend £1000 or £2000, or more.

I still hope to be able to borrow of Lady O. Acheson's trustees the £2500 which she has left us. I offer a first mortgage on our Irish property, which cost us £5000 and now would sell for £7000.[1] There is a *technical* hitch here, which [F. R.] Ward may or may not be able to get over. But though it may be a hitch in the case of a trust, I dont think it would be such to *another* lender.

I can offer also to mortgage a head rent which I bought for £2100 (of the Achilli money) on a large property in Roscommon. Or I could *sell* this head rent. It pays £48 odd a half year gross and certain — the present deductions for Income tax etc being £7. or £8 a half year — leaving nearly a clear £40 or £4 per cent.

Very affly Yours John H Newman of the Oratory

P.S. They say the Church is certain of great success. It will be in Stephen's Green.[2]

SATURDAY 21 JULY 1855   went into retreat for 3 days   Mr T. Flanagan came
SUNDAY 22 JULY   F Nicholas went down to Bath to bring up F Joseph's body Mr Flanagan went

[1] This was property of the Flanagan family at Rathtarman, County Sligo, which the Oratorians had bought.

[2] Hope-Scott replied on 22 July, 'I am arranging all my money matters just now with a view to a special object; and have no floating money available for your purpose— But, even if I had, I should be tempted to offer my advice to this effect, that, as far as you have good security to offer, you should transact with *strangers*, and as a mere matter of business. And then, to the extent to which your wants exceed your commercial means, you should fairly ask from friends for donations—In this way all parties learn exactly where they stand, and business is partitioned off from Friendship and Almsgiving—but in the case of *friendly* loans, (except where some great emergency requires them,) there is doubt upon both sides—the Borrower relying upon having a friendly Creditor—the Creditor on the other hand perhaps having need of the money but not liking to ask it etc etc.'

Hope-Scott concluded by saying that when Newman had raised all the money he could in the ordinary way, 'tell me and your other friends, and I, for one, will look, not into my Ledger, but into another account, and see what I can do.' See also letter of 1 Aug. to Hope-Scott.

MONDAY 23 JULY   Frederic (Thos Godwin) came from Dublin
TUESDAY 24 JULY   burials of Fr Joseph and Br Aloysius in our ground at Rednall

TO JOHN PONCIA

24 July 1855

My dear Mr Poncia

I cannot allow this day to pass in which you give up to us a precious deposit of ours, without thanking you in the name of our whole community for the charity which has led you and Mrs Poncia now for three years to take charge of it. You have greater thanks than ours, because you know it is one of the seven corporal works of mercy to bury the dead, and if more must be said, then, considering how we were at the time of Aloysius's death perplexed how to find a temporary resting place for him, and how unusual as well as acceptable a favor you did us then, you may be said to [have] brought yourselves within the blessing expressly pronounced by our Lord Himself on those who when he was a stranger and homeless have at any time hospitably received him.[1]

With thanks [?] & good wishes & prayers for both of you,

I am etc.

TO LORD HENRY KERR

Hagley Road Bm July 25/55.

My dear Lord Henry

I was very glad to hear so good an account of you and hope you have gained more than all you expected, by your journey —

Francis acquitted himself well at the Terminal Examination and has not been idle; he might have done *more* but this was partly my fault —

I have set him to prepare himself for standing for two prizes, which he will tell you of. There is always a great chance in these things — but really he is not unlikely to succeed in one or other. I ought to have asked him how much Virgil he has done. He has read the greater part of Horace so I think he had better get on with the Aeneid — I wish he would get some Virgil by heart. Have you any wish he should do any Greek in the vacation? I almost think I have given him enough without—

I hope you will find he has spent nothing unnecessarily.

[1] The body of Aloysius Boland was buried at first in the Poncia vault at St Chad's Cathedral, Birmingham.

I subjoin our account as it stands — unless I have made some mistake — If so, you must set me right —[1]

Very sincerely Yrs in Xt   John H Newman

TO JOHN HUNGERFORD POLLEN

The Oratory, Hagley Road Bm July 25/55

My dear Pollen,

Thank you for your great care about the Church, in spite of your own troubles and occupations. I have been in retreat several days, or I should have answered you at once. Yesterday we buried Fr Gordon and our other brother. Every thing went off very well, and it is a good work done and over, which is pleasant.

Your arrangement about the payment is very fair — I will be ready; at least, I mean to be so. I am glad they are on the ground, and sorry I have to lug out, but I suppose the bitter and the sweet must go together. I have not yet got any money.

You were quite right in not touching the boundary wall. And I suppose with you, that Beardwood's care for his own reputation will be our best surveyor of works. I have no taste for Mr Butler.[2]

I don't want the specifications, for I should not understand them. I am sorry you don't go to Dublin this way. There are many things I might have said to you. What ails you to take 24 hours at sea?

Very sincerely Yours John H. Newman of the Oratory

J. H. Pollen Esq.

[1]	Received			As by account			
	by Lord H. Kerr			already sent.	50.	18.	0.
	July 2.	55.	0. 0.	coat. (mourning)	3.	5.	0
	by Lady H. Kerr	10.	10. 0.	Tailor	6.	3.	6
				Linen	3.	16.	0.
		65.	10. 0.	Books	1.	14.	0
	to balance	4.	8. 6.	Hat		17.	6.
				July pay		10.	0.
				Buttery		4.	6
		69.	18. 6.	Journey July	2.	10.	0.
					69.	18.	6.

[2] i.e. the architect.

513

THURSDAY 26 JULY 1855   sang high black mass for the soul of Lady Annabella
Acheson

TO ARCHBISHOP CULLEN

The Oratory Hagley Road, Birmingham July 26. 1855
My dear Lord[1]

I wish to bring before your Grace more distinctly than I was able
to do in the conversation I had with you on the day of your arrival, how
we stand as regards the commencement of the Theological School. I did
not like to negative the idea of starting it in November, knowing how
much you wished it; accordingly, when Fr Curtis asked me whether
we should want Father O'Reilly at that time, I told him of your wish
and that I could not in your absence say we did *not* want him. In consequence of my saying this, they have not included him in their arrangements for the ensuing year, but have reserved him for the University.

I have done what I could to get him a class from Allhallows — but
the authorities there do not really want him, and, though they have
signified, I believe, that they will send some of their students to us, they
do so as a favor to us, and not from any view they entertain of advantages
they will gain from such an arrangement themselves.

[1] Newman copied out his draft of this letter, at the end of 'Memorandum about my
connection with the Catholic University' as follows:

'I wish to put before you more clearly than I did in the conversation I had with your
Grace on the day of your return, how things stand as regards the theological school.

About April last Fr Curtis wrote to me to ask whether we wanted Fr O'Reilly
in November, as it was important for him to know before arrangements were made
for the coming year. Had I acted on my own view of the matter, I should have answered
him in the negative; but I told him, that, knowing how desirous your Grace was of
setting up the school, I could not possibly say that it would not be set up—and therefore he has reserved Fr O'Reilly for us.

On the other hand, I do not clearly see how he will get a class. It is true that the
authorities of Allhallows College have offered to send some of their youths, but they
do not wish to do so, and they do so as a favour to us. Now then that your Grace is
returned, it is desirable that Fr Curtis should have a distinct expression of your wish
on the subject.

Should you decide on setting up the school, I shall have to ask your Grace for the
letter concerning the Louvain Professors, which I sent you to Cork in October last.

After I spoke to you on the subject of the appointment of a small Committee and
a Secretary, to manage the accounts, I was shown a Resolution of the Thurles Committee to the effect that the laymen of their body should form a subcommittee for that
purpose. This has stopped me; for I should be putting myself into antagonism with a
Committee, not only appointed, but lately recognized by the Holy See, if I interfered.

I ought to tell your Grace, unless you are already aware of it, that I have reason
to believe, that a strong opinion and much soreness exist on the subject among the
laity of the educated class, and that we shall not gain the names of the Catholic gentry,
till the money matters of the University are in their hands.'

It seems then that we are bringing Professor and Students together, against the will of both parties, neither of them wanting the other.

This being the case, it would be very desirable, and I should be much obliged to your Grace, now that you are returned, if you would state your own wishes to Fr Curtis on the subject.

In case you decide on establishing the School in November, I shall have to trouble you for the foreign letter I sent you down to Cork, shortly before you went to Rome in October last, on the subject of the Louvain Professor of Canon Law.[1]

How do we stand as to the power of conferring degrees? Is any thing wanting on the part of the Holy See to enable us to do so?

After I spoke to you on the appointment of a small committee and a Secretary to manage our accounts, I was shown a resolution of the Thurles Committee, which entrusted this office to the laymen of their body.[2] This has stopped me; for I found I could not move in the matter, without putting myself into antagonism with a body, not only appointed by the Irish Church, but lately recognised by the Holy See. And it certainly seems to me that the laymen in question ought to act. I suppose they would do so at once, if they had any encouragement from your Grace.

I ought to add, what I dare say you are aware of already, that some soreness exists on the part of the educated and upper class through Ireland on the ground that they are allowed so little share in the management of the money matters of the University. I think they would have joined us before now, if they had been more definitely recognised.[3]

[1] See letter to Mgr Vecchiotti placed at the end of June 1854.

[2] See letter of 17 July to Scratton, and second letter of 4 Sept. to Monsell.

[3] Cf. letter of Richard More O'Ferrall quoted in note to that of 12 May 1854 to James More O'Ferrall. Newman copied out parts of two letters he received from James More O'Ferrall, the first dated 17 Dec. 1854: 'If a money secretary is wanted, I conceive he should have been appointed preparatory to the collection in October . . . I know nothing of the Revd Mr Mullen—but from my experience I do not consider clergymen much suited for such an office, nor that office suitable for them.

I know it is not necessary as regards your opinion to add, that I fear, and hear that such fears generally exist, that the tendency is to make the University a close borough of clergymen and a clerical College, which was neither the intention or wish of those who have encountered much obloquy in trying to establish it.'

From the second letter from O'Ferrall, which Newman dated 'after Dec. 1854?,' he copied as follows: 'I regretted the appointment of Dr Leahy as Vice-President, because, the Rector being a clergyman, if a Vice Rector was really necessary, I think a layman would be more acceptable to the laity. Knowing the good motives which occasioned that appointment, I do not blame it. It is the effect upon others which I regret.

Dr Leahy being Vice Rector and a clergyman, the appointment of a clergyman to the Revd Mr Flannery's post [Dean of St Patrick's, the University House] was at all events unnecessary. But what called forth my letter particularly was the appointment

Begging your Grace's blessing, I am, My dear Lord, Your affte friend & Servt in Xt

John H Newman of the Oratory[1]

His Grace the Archbp of Dublin.

TO HENRY MURNEY

The Oratory Hagley Road Birmingham. July 27. 1855

Dear Sir,

I hoped to have fulfilled my promise of writing to you before now, on the subject of our conversation, but have not been in a position to do so.

My first wish was to have filled up at once all the chairs in the Medical School — and I had hoped to have effected this. Unexpected difficulties, however, have hindered me.

This being the case, I have come to the resolution of leaving things just as they are, that is, with only those subjects provided for, (as a beginning) which belong to one particular department of the Faculty, viz anatomy, physiology, pathology and surgery.

Materia Medica the practice of medicine, chemistry, botany, pharmacy etc. must, I am sorry to say, stand over.

I am, Dear Sir, Very truly Yours John H Newman

— Murney Esqr

of Revd Mr Mullens for a post the most unsuited for a clergyman and which one would not expect a clergyman to look for.' See also *A.W.* pp. 325–8, and *McGrath*, p. 502.

[1] Cullen did not reply to Newman until 8 Sept. See his letter, placed before Newman's of 13 Sept. On 28 July, however, Cullen wrote as follows in the course of a letter to Barnabò at Propaganda:

'Your Excellency will be pleased to hear that the Catholic University has begun with the happiest prospects, and that there is every hope that it will succeed. The only point on which I have heard some complaint is that Father Newman shows a certain ignorance of practical affairs, and has therefore permitted the introduction of things which could be very inconvenient as the years go by. For this reason I should be very glad if he were not yet made a bishop, and I hope that no step will be taken until the affairs of the university are well launched. Although this most worthy Father is deserving of every honour, it is better that he should continue as he is for some time, since if he were a bishop he would not, and could not, attend to the details and minutiae that must be dealt with while the university is being established.' Archives of Propaganda, *S.R.C. Irlanda*, 1854–6, f. 510, translated and quoted by J. H. Whyte in *D R* (Spring 1960), pp. 34–5.

TO ARCHBISHOP CULLEN

The Oratory, Birmingham July 28th 1855

My dear Lord,

I write to your Grace and to the other Archbishops to say, that I have designated and propose to present to the Coetus Episcoporum the following professional Gentlemen of Dublin, to fill chairs in the Medical Faculty of the University: —

Dr Ellis to be Professor of the Practice of Surgery.

Dr Hayden and Dr Cryan to be Professors of Anatomy.

Dr Lyons to be Professor of Pathology.

I have not found it practicable just now to fill up the remaining chairs; but I am assured that more is not requisite for the commencement of the School.

I inform your Grace of these arrangements at this moment, because the custom of the Medical Schools of Dublin obliges me to publish the names by anticipation, though subject to the Bishops' definitive nomination, in order that the School may open in November.[1]

Begging your Grace's blessing, I am, My dear Lord, Your faithful Servt in Xt

John H Newman Rector

His Grace The Archbishop of Dublin

TO THE COUNTESS OF ARUNDEL

The Oratory Hagley Road Bm July 29. 1855

My dear Lady Arundel

I would not write to you, did I think you would suppose I expected an answer. Nay, I almost fear to intrude upon you at all, yet the many kindnesses I have received from you and Lord Arundel make me earnestly desire to express to you how much I feel the succession of trials which a good Providence has brought upon you.[2]

However, such a visitation (as you know so well,) is the greatest mark of His love: — or rather, who would have any encouragement to hope that his name was written in heaven, if he passed through this life

---

[1] The identical letter to Archbishop MacHale is printed in B. O'Reilly, *John MacHale Archbishop of Tuam*, II, pp. 509–10. For MacHale's reply see letter of 6 Aug. to him.   [2] See second note to letter of 14 July to St John.

without affliction! Be sure, you are dearer to God and His Angels than ever you were, now that you are suffering so much, and, unwelcome as suffering is, so willingly.

You know, we are saying Mass for you and your intention. Pray say everything kind and respectful from me to Lord Arundel, and believe me, My dear Lady Arundel, Most sincerely Yours in Xt

John H Newman of the Oratory

The Countess of Arundel

TO HENRY TAYLOR

The Oratory Hagley Road Birmingham July 30. 1855

Dear Sir

It is with very great pleasure that I have just now received the present of your Poems gained for me by the kind offices of Mr Aubrey de Vere.[1] It is a confession which I make with shame, that, since it so happens they have not actually come in my way, I have not made a point of obtaining works which the whole world admires and which I have ever desired to study. It is no poetical justice, that, in requital of this negligence, I should at length have them given to me by the poet himself.

The pleasure which I shall derive from the perusal of them will be enhanced by the interest and respect due to a friend of Mr de Vere's; and this feeling will carry me through one of them, which, if common report speaks truly, will, I fear, somewhat run counter to principles and persons I account sacred.[2] I am sure you will allow me this honesty of speech, which is a guarantee of the sincerity of the thanks which I have been expressing for the favor you have done me.

I am, My dear Sir, Very faithfully Yours John H Newman

Henry Taylor Esqr

[1] This was a copy (still in Newman's room at the Oratory) of *The Eve of the Conquest and Other Poems*, London 1847. Henry Taylor (1800–86), poet best known for the drama *Philip Van Artevelde*, 1834, worked in the Colonial Office 1824–72. In 1839 he married Theodosia Spring Rice, a cousin of Aubrey de Vere, who became his close friend. De Vere wrote to Newman on 10 July 1855 that he had asked Taylor to send his poems and added, 'He has got your early sermons. Poor fellow; there is something touching in his expression, when challenged in theological matters. "It is only by mortifying the speculative intellect that I believe as much as I do—"'

[2] This refers to 'Alwine and Adelais,' an attack on the dedicated celibacy of the conventual and monastic life. In 1868 Newman sent Taylor a copy of *Verses on Various Occasions*. Cf. *Recollections of Aubrey de Vere*, London 1897, p. 270, who says that Newman and Taylor had 'a singular sympathy for each other, though they had never met, and though there was so much antagonistic in their opinions. . . .'

WEDNESDAY 1 AUGUST 1855   Lady Lothian, Ralph [Kerr], and Wm Palmer came (or tomorrow?)

TO ARCHBISHOP CULLEN

Bm August 1/55

My dear Lord

I think you will find Dr Hayden is a Catholic. The advertising Dr Hayden is a Protestant. Dr Ellis would give your Grace any information on this head.[1]

Yr affte Servt in Xt   John H Newman of the Oratory

His Grace the Archbishop of Dublin

TO JAMES HOPE-SCOTT

⌐The Oratory. August 1. 1855

Thank you for your most kind letter of this morning.[2] I am quite as mindful, I think, of the principle you so justly laid down as you can be — but I did not think I infringed it in my question to you. You spoke as if I wanted to mortgage the rents of my *prospective* Church; whereas I meant to offer existing rents arising from lands, which could not revert to me before the money was paid back without an *act* on the lender's part, which (however generous in him, if ever made ⟨⟨done?⟩⟩) I, from my own sense of honour, should never for an instant have countenanced. Nay, I offered to sell one of them out and out. And really, kind as it is in you to hold out the idea of it, I am not conscious that I want any money given me; and, were it given, I should spend it in embellishments, not a substantial work. In this way I hope to give £250 myself (for in Ireland, though not here, I am a rich man) and Lord Dunraven has out of his own head promised £200 — and a Priest, just before he died, sent me under secrecy, near £200 for any University

[1] Cullen wrote on 31 July, 'Perhaps you may not be aware that Dr Hayden is a protestant—at least the only Dr Hayden I know of is such. Before I answer your letter, I wished to mention this to you. . . .' Newman endorsed Cullen's letter, 'N.B. This supposed fact was a simple mistake. J H N' See second letter of 29 April 1855 to Moriarty.

[2] Hope-Scott, who had written on 22 July (see second note to Newman's letter of 20 July), wrote again on 31 July, '. . . My last did not require an answer—still I should have liked one—even a scolding—for I wrote hastily, and I fear too freely, and it vexes me to think I may have hurt you.'

purpose I liked,[1] and I shall spend it in an Altar or something of the kind, I am glad to receive such money, but I should be quite unfair if I said I needed it. To be sure, the Church may not fill, and that would be a great smash; but if any thing is improbable, that is; and I must let the difficulty come, if it is to come, and meet it when I see it. At present it has neither length nor breadth, weight or measure.

I am in correspondence with Dublin lawyers about the money, which I hope to raise, but they are slow. That was the difficulty.

Your books will be the cream of our library, and we shall be very grateful for them.⌐[2]

TO S. M. MACSWINEY

The Oratory, Hagley Road, Birmingham. August 2/55
My dear Sir,

I hasten to inform you, in answer to your letter just received, that the only chairs, which are filled up in the Medical Faculty of the Catholic University, are those of the Practice of Surgery, of Anatomy, and of Pathology. I have no intention of going further at present.

You are quite right in supposing, that, as I said to you, I should not forget your application; nor have I done so.[3] By which I did not mean to say, that I should certainly have an opportunity of availing myself of your talents, but that it was impossible for me not to take into account in the appointments, and to weigh with great respect and consideration claims like yours

I am, My dear Sir, Very truly Yours John H Newman

S. M. MacSwiney Esqr

TO RICHARD STANTON

The Ory Hagley Road August 2. 1855

My dear Richard

I hope to be here without let or hindrance till November. And rejoice at the prospect of seeing you. Give my love to you all, and believe me

Ever Yours affectly J H N

[1] See letter of 9 Dec. 1854.
[2] Hope-Scott was sending, for the University Library, 198 volumes, chiefly folio, nearly all on Canon and Civil Law. The holograph ends here.
[3] See letter of 15 Sept. 1854.

TO CATHERINE ANNE BATHURST

The Oratory Bm August 5/55

My dear Child,

I was on the point of writing to you that I meant to come to you to-morrow week, the 13th. I shall go up, if all is well, by the early train, which getting to London by ½ past 10, will bring me to you about ½ past 11. I must leave you at 1; as I have an engagement at 3, and must get back here in the evening.

I shall rejoice to see you — but, mind, you are to ask me no difficult questions about the Profession, Vows, Duties etc etc — of a nun, for I am not up to them.

Your kind gift of '£10 each year to the Oratory' will be most acceptable — as we are in considerable distress for want of money — We have had a debt every year.

Ever Yrs affly J H N

TO JOHN MACHALE, ARCHBISHOP OF TUAM

Bm ⌐Aug 6/55¬

My dear Lord

⌐I am much obliged by your Grace's letter, just received, and lose no time in replying to the question it contains.[1]

[1] Newman's letter of 28 July to the four Archbishops, announcing that he had designated and proposed to present at the Bishops' meeting four professors in the Medical Faculty, produced from Cullen the inquiry whether Dr Hayden was a Protestant. Michael Slattery, the aged Archbishop of Cashel, replied on 31 July that he was about to go on Visitation, and added, 'Having no opinion to offer one way or the other on the persons to which it has reference I have the honor to remain in extreme haste Dear Sir your faithful Servt + M Slattery.'

Joseph Dixon, Archbishop of Armagh, wrote on 1 Aug., 'Of course, whatever may be the value of my poor approval, you have it by anticipation for every arrangement which you may make. It is a cause of great regret to me that being so much occupied ... I have not called more frequently to the University, nor exerted myself sufficiently to promote its interests; but I hope by good conduct in future to make amends for past neglect.'

On 3 Aug. John MacHale sent his reply from Tuam:

' My dear Dr Newman

I am in receipt of your letter of the 28th ultimo and beg to know whether in forwarding to the Archbishops the list which it contains, you consider it only as a communication of courtesy or whether it is meant to submit it to their approval.

I remain My dear Dr Newman Your faithful Servt + John MacHale'

521

In answer then to your inquiry whether 'in forwarding to the Archbishops the list' of names 'I consider it only as a communication of courtesy, or whether it is meant to submit it to their approval,' I beg to reply that I send it to them in the spirit of the Regulae Fundamentales de designatione et nominatione Professorum approved by the Synodal Meeting held in Dublin in May 1854, in which it is said 'Decernimus in praesentiarum, et donec aliter coetui Episcopali visum fuerit, Professorum tam ordinariorum quam extraordinariorum, quorum designatio ac praesentatio ad rectorem spectabit, definitivam nominationem à nobis duntaxat ratam et firmam habendam esse, etc'[1]

As the Coetus Episcopalis, had not yet met, it seemed respectful to inform the four Archbishops of my designatio in the cases specified.

Begging your Grace's blessing I am &c⌝

J H N

TO JOHN HUNGERFORD POLLEN

The Oratory, Hagley Road Bm August 8/55

My Dear Pollen

I can't help fearing there has been some stupid mismanagement on my part, and that I might have saved you taking a house for a quarter of a year by offering you mine. I have been trying to make out when I first heard of your intention of taking one. I knew you had been looking out for a long while — but, as far as I can recollect, I think your *immediate* intention of *occupation* took me by surprise (for I thought you were looking out in prospect) and, I suppose, I was wanting in presence of mind, being full of my own difficulty from the   [2]. However, it is no good bewailing my conduct now.

I am glad to hear of your report on the progress of the Church. I cannot understand the matter of the boundary wall, and leave it to your conscience to do as you will.

Thank you for Mr Trevor's announcement. I *suppose* it is from Lady CastleStewart.[3] *The money must not go to Scratton.* I must do everything to prevent the notion of its being a University matter, not my own. I

---

[1] See *Campaign*, pp. 89–90, and letter of 20 May 1854 to Dalgairns.

[2] Word omitted as illegible by the copyist.

[3] The Countess of Castle-Stewart appears to have sent Newman £5 for his Church. Cf. letter of 9 Aug. to Scratton. She was a granddaughter of Henry Bathurst, Bishop of Norwich, and in 1830 married the third Earl of Castle-Stewart who became a Catholic in 1854, and died three years later. In 1867 at Rome she married Alessandro, only son of General Pistocchi.

shall soon open an account at the Bank of Ireland (I will give you notice) and it must be paid — there 'to my account.'

You have acted very wrong in not coming here. I would have paid your fare, and thanked you — but you have been punished by your [1] — that's one satisfaction.

Please have a look at *my own buildings* at number 6.

Ever Yours most sincerely J. H. Newman

P.S.   I send the inclosed to Scratton by *you* — because it is private, and I don't want it mislaid, if he is away.

TO HENRY HENNESSY

[9? Aug 1855]

My dear Mr Hennessy,

Thank you for your paper etc.

I think great caution is necessary in bringing the University as such before scientific bodies just now.[2]

I see they put you down 'M.R.I.A.' — and do not seem to recognise the University but this need not hinder the Science Faculty, as (e.g.) the Medical School (the University allowing, but not introduced) acting for itself, if you think you can speak of Mr Butler and the other Professors without consulting them

J H N

TO THOMAS SCRATTON

Thursday [9 August 1855?]

My dear S

The inclosed from poor Lady Castle-Stewart is just come.

I think it best for you to take it to the Bank — (1.) to ask if she has an account there (2.) if she has power to draw — and if so — then I think you must ask to see a *really confidential person* and show him Lady S's letter, saying that we cannot appropriate it without her friends knowing

Ever Yrs J H N

---

[1] Word omitted as illegible by the copyist.

[2] Hennessy was attending the meeting of the British Association at Cheltenham, and wanted the Catholic University to join Trinity College and other bodies in inviting the Association to hold its next meeting in Dublin.

For Newman's view of the British Association see last note to letter of 15 Sept. 1847 to Mrs Bowden.

FRIDAY 10 AUGUST 1855   Mr Bethell called
SUNDAY 12 AUGUST   Fr Robert Tillotson ordained Subdeacon by the Bishop in our Church.
MONDAY 13 AUGUST   went to London   to see Miss Bathurst at Greenwich (who is to be professed tomorrow)   called on Badeley   — went to the Dentist (Lintott) called on Burns, and back by 1 a.m.

TO HENRY WILBERFORCE

Monday [13 August 1855][1]

My dear H W

I am in London for two hours to see my perpetual Dentist, so I have come on for the chance of seeing you.

Ever Yrs affly J H N

P.S.   There is not a chance, it seems, of your coming here today — but, to let you know, my engagement at 23 Wimpole Street is at half past one

TUESDAY 14 AUGUST 1855   Harry Ryder called one of these days   taking his brothers to Oscott.

TO HENRY (IGNATIUS) DUDLEY RYDER

Bm August 14/55

My dear Harry

I will say mass for your intention next Saturday — the mass de S. Philippo.

As to your Father, I will say no more than that he is losing an old friend, who has served him many times, and has, as I trust the great day will show — never had any thought towards him inconsistent with truth and love. Meanwhile, God will make up to me, I know, whatever His Almighty Will puts on me.[2]

[1] The date is added in another hand, and 'H W Wilberforce Esqr' on the middle fold of the last page shows it was not sent through the post. It was probably left for Wilberforce at the office of the *Weekly Register*.
[2] Harry Ryder wrote that he was not to return to Dublin, and that his father proposed to send him to the English College in Rome. 'I am extremely sorry not to go back to you but what can I do I have said all I can without being disrespectful.' George Ryder had begun to quarrel with Newman in the summer of 1855. The latter, on 19 Nov. 1862 wrote to console Henry Wilberforce, Ryder's brother-in-law, who was

One thing I will say about the English College — (and this applies, as far as I could make out from Dr English last year, to the *new Collegio Pio*, which the Pope has lately set up;) viz that those who go there are partly paid (by Burses) from the Bishops, and therefore are the Bishops' priests through life.[1]

Further, that even when they have paid for themselves, they have sometimes from moral reasons found it exceedingly difficult to avoid taking the oath which binds them to the Bishop. I have known several such cases — As far as I can recollect, Fr Spencer, Montgomery and Bernard Smith are instances at home — when I was at Rome (I think) Mr McMullen found himself taken by surprise (by nobody's fault) though he had paid for himself, and took the oath. I think I am right in my memory.

When the time comes, should you *deliberately* make up your mind to take it, then you will have a clear course. But should you feel surprise or reluctance; recollect there are friends in England, who, as far as money matters are concerned, will readily get you out of the difficulty.

I will get your things from Dublin, when you tell me. I should like to say a word about your *health*, if you go to Rome.

Recollect the words in Scripture which the Holy Father has quoted to encourage *me*.

> Quia acceptus eras Deo, necesse fuit
> ut tentatio probaret te.[2]

Whenever I say mass for my Dublin youths, which I do at Dublin every Saturday, I shall include you. I said Mass for you, as well as other Harries, on St Henry's day — and for you and Lisle the day following.

Give him my love Ever Yrs affly J H N

then in the same predicament: 'It was just the same to *me*; I was nursing his son who had the scarlet fever, and had written and not sent a letter to him about it, when I received to my utter astonishment a letter from him [about 24 June 1855] charging me in express terms of duplicity, underhandedness, and making categorical statements contradictory to plain, patent facts. . . . He said he acted towards me under a priest's direction, adjured me by the coming of the day of judgment, and addressed me "Revd Sir."' On 14 Oct. 1856, Ryder quoted what Newman (in the postscript to the letter giving an account of Harry Ryder's scarlet fever) had replied to this attack: 'I certainly shall not answer one word to your letter just received. It grieves me to think how you are letting your mind brood upon itself and upon phantoms. You are not wise if you quarrel with good friends.' See also Newman's letter of 15 Oct. 1856 to Ryder. Ryder appears to have thought that Newman was in some way coming between him and his sons.

[1] Harry Ryder had already decided to become a priest, and was studying at Dublin with that end in view. See Newman's letter of 17 Aug. 1854 to Ryder. The Collegio Pio was founded in Rome for late vocations. See also letter of 21 Aug. 1853 to Hope-Scott.

[2] *Tobias*, 12:13.

TO RICHARD STANTON

The Oy Hagley Road Bm Augst 15. 1855

My dear Richard

I send your Father and all of you our gratulations on the Festa. Thanks for your kind letter.[1] Of course it gave me great comfort to hear what you said about my Development argument. That I should have written it very differently, had I been a Catholic, I know well, and have always said — and the reason, when at Rome, I declined to enter into controversy with old B. [Brownson] was, as I expressed it, that I had come there to learn my religion, not to hold a theological polemic.[2] I always said that my book was a philosophical, not a theological one; and it was on that very distinction that the Cardinal passed it without correction.[3] Nothing has happened from that time to this to make me think the *principle* of the book false — but I had rather, by waiting, let better hands than mine set right the details, than attempt a censureship myself which might need censuring.

I have been always puzzled myself at people taking to Passaglia, as they do. He is a simple minded, amiable man, as well as an able, learned,

[1] Stanton wrote from London on 7 Aug.,

'I do not know whether you saw Mgr Talbot, when he was over, or not.

If not, you may not have heard a piece of gossip, which I think you are entitled to know—

Mgr T. did not tell us—He told Mr [W. G.] Ward, who told F. Faber, who told me—As it thus passed through so many hands, you must not rely too much on the details, but it must be substantially correct—

P. Passaglia, as one of the theologians employed, made a draft for the Bull of the definition of the Immaculate Conception totally different from the one adopted, in which he declared that it was the explicit tradition of the Church all along—The Cardinals and Bishops to whom it was shewn, all cried out that he was wrong, and that it was only *implicitly* the Catholic doctrine, and the Bull was framed accordingly.

I do not know in what esteem you hold Mgr's [Talbot] theological opinions, but perhaps they indicate the impression of the Court.

He says, that though there are things in your Essay which you would not have said as a Catholic, he has no doubt the theory is substantially true.

What is more important, he says that though it ought not to be publicly talked of, he knows it to be the private opinion of the Holy Father himself—

I cannot say what pleasure it gives me to think, what service you may have done to our Blessed Lady, having perhaps been the means of hastening what might otherwise have been delayed for years.

By the way, the Cardinal once told us, that some French Bishops said to him, that it was evidently the adoption of your theory—

I am surprised to find what influence P. Passaglia has on the English converts. They quote him for every thing and swear by him. He is very eloquent, and I suppose really clever, and has very strong opinions—I have not however heard what the said converts say of Development.'   [2] See letter of 10 May 1847 to Knox.

[3] See letters of 2 Nov. 1845 to Hope [Hope-Scott] and 7 Nov. 1845 to Wiseman.

and eloquent one; but he is too rhetorical, too wrapt up in his own notions, and too little ministrative to other minds, (if I may so express it) to elicit my own admiration. The more an intellect aims at imitating our Lord, so should it more and more take an apron and napkin, and go round washing the disciples' feet. Passaglia seems to me ever in the teacher's chair.[1]

I have discovered when too late, I am writing to you on a shameful 'outsider.' A most disgraceful sheet, indeed.[2]

As to Dr Cullen, Talbot seems to me so to have hit the mark, that I could have said beforehand it was so.[3] Dr C. has an extreme dread of Dr McHale. Dr McH. has just made a fresh protest against my appointments — but don't talk of this

Ever Yrs affly J H N

THURSDAY 16 AUGUST 1855 Henry Bethel came and slept? The Blunts came over from Oscott and dined? FF Frederic and Austin went to Belgium, and Victor Duke went home.

TO ANDREW ELLIS

The Oratory, Hagley Road Birmingham August 16. 1855

My dear Dr Ellis

I thank you for the pains you are taking about the opening of the School.

I have decided to begin only with

     1. Surgery.   2. Anatomy.   3. Pathology.

and to put off the other appointments.

I will keep Dr Byrne's letters.

There is one word I propose to alter in the advertisement. I must

[1] On Passaglia's part in drafting the Bull on the Immaculate Conception see D T C, VII, 1199–1204. Passaglia was one of those who held that the Pope should voluntarily give up his temporal power. On account of this opinion he resigned his professorship at the Gregorian University in 1857 and two years later he left the Jesuits. In 1861 Pius IX sent him on a diplomatic mission to Turin, where he became the leader of the 'liberal' clergy in Italy, and was suspended from his priestly functions. He was reconciled shortly before his death in 1887.

[2] The slightly soiled outside sheet of a packet.

[3] Stanton concluded his letter, 'Another thing that Mgr T. said, was that the Archbishop of Tuam said nothing against your bishopric, but that Dr Cullen said what *he supposed* Dr McH. *would* say—this, he says, caused the hitch.' See also last note to Newman's letter of 26 July to Cullen.

keep the technical word 'designated' instead of 'selected.' I may get into difficulties else.

Very sincerely Yours John H Newman of the Oratory

A Ellis Esqr M D

TO THOMAS SCRATTON

Oratory Bm Augst 16/55

My dear Scratton

Thanks for your letters I hope it won't put you to inconvenience to beg you to alter *one word* in the Advertisements.

I think I must say, not 'these gentlemen have been *selected*,' but '*designated*.' I have had a second unpleasant letter from Dr McHale, *entre nous*.[1]

Thank you for your proposal about coming here. It was merely our wish to see you, since you were in England — I had nothing particular to say to you

Ever Yrs J H N

P.S.   Will you thank Pollen for me for his letter, and tell him that I have now an account (for the new Church, and that only) at *the Bank of Ireland*.

I think I asked you to be so good as to see Star about the painting at Number 6. Or was it Pollen?

FRIDAY 17 AUGUST 1855   Henry Bethel went away?

TO THOMAS SCRATTON

The Oratory Bm August 17. 1855

My dear Scratton

The Professorship of the Practice of Medicine is far too important to give away off hand.

For a year and more I have been in correspondence with Medical

---

[1] See letter of 6 Aug. to MacHale. The first unpleasant letter was presumably that placed before Newman's of 8 Oct. 1854 to MacHale.

Men, on the subject of the Medical Chairs — not the least, that of Medicine, and not one has once mentioned our friend.[1]

I could not act now as you propose merely because there is no one else.

Ever Yrs J H N

MONDAY 20 August 1855   Fr Bernard went over to Stone

TO WILLIAM PHILIP GORDON

The Oratory Bm August 20. 1855

My dear Philip

I don't suppose you require any answer, but I send a line to say how glad we shall be to see you.

Say every thing kind and respectful from me to your hosts

and believe me Ever Yrs affly J H N

TO THOMAS SCRATTON

The Oratory Hagley Road Bm Augst 20/55

My dear Scratton

Thank you for your anxiety about the 'Designation' — I think you have managed very well.

As to my name coming in, at first sight I did not like it — but I suppose that Dr Ellis urged it. With 'designated' it is better in, than out — with 'selected' better out than in.

Will you be so good as to lodge £300 from the Cullen and Newman Account at the Hibernian (i.e. a draft which I have signed and left with you) to my account AT THE BANK OF IRELAND. It is a temporary loan for the Church till my Church money is paid in.

When the £300 is lodged, there, please, give Beardwood the inclosed on his receipt.

I fear I must give Number 87 to Mr Moylan's Gas Company (the

---

[1] Scratton wrote on 15 Aug. that the doctors of the Medical School wanted more of the Chairs filled and they recommended that Joseph O'Ferrall, the surgeon who attended Newman for his knee, should be appointed to that of the Practice of Medicine. 'There were some trifling objections to him,' but 'positively no other Catholic physician in Dublin' who was suitable, Scratton reported.

other)[1] The pipes are ready laid down in the Street. But it's not clear it will be wanted

Ever Yrs affly J H N

TUESDAY 21 AUGUST 1855 Stanislas went into full retreat

TO WILLIAM MONSELL

The Oratory Hagley Road Bm. August 21/55

My dear Monsell,

I wish you would learn for me whether I am to keep two rooms for the Blunts next Easter. It is a shame to trouble a man in office about such sublunary matters; but it was you who wrote to me about them, and I don't know whom else to apply to. They have nothing to say themselves, and Manning whom I asked could throw out no suggestion where I could learn.[2]

Fr Stanislas is just going into an eight days retreat — else I would say, why cannot you run down here? I have a good deal to say about the University. I trust we are getting on, but there's no one to support me — and some of course against me.

Ever Yrs affly J H Newman of the Oratory

The Rt Honble Wm Monsell

TO JOHN HUNGERFORD POLLEN

The Oratory. Hagley Road Birmingham. Aug. 21/55

My dear Pollen,

Thank you for all your anxiety and your success — and your report. I have sent Beardwood £200 through Scratton — but as yet have not got the money, though I hope it will not be long delayed.

As to the   [3], I am glad you are coming here. It can be made flat. You shall see it.

[1] This Company had a prior claim for supplying gas at 87 Stephen's Green to that of the Alliance Gas Company, on whose behalf Scratton had been approached.
[2] See letter of 22 Nov. 1854 to Manning. Francis and Wilfrid Scawen Blunt were at Oscott, and never went to Newman's University.
[3] Word illegible to the copyist.

The tiles will come from *Mintons* in our neighbourhood — and the agent in Birmingham is one of our penitents[?]. Perhaps you had better talk with him when you come.

I will say Mass for your Aunt. I am very sorry for the News. I am told the London Oratory is *very bad* for music. Really I am not sorry at all about the open roof.

My account is now open at the BANK OF IRELAND. Any money may be paid in *there*, which comes for the church.

It is very kind of you with so important a personal matter on your hands, to give so much time to me.[1]

Ever Yours most sincerely in Xt.

John H. Newman of the Oratory

J. H Pollen Esq.

WEDNESDAY 22 AUGUST 1855   F Henry went

TO HENRY IGNATIUS DUDLEY RYDER

The Oratory Birmingham August 24. 1855

My dear Harry,

I don't know Louis's direction, and the worst is, he has two or three houses. He is near Besançon properly — if you went there you could learn. We could give you an introduction to the Cardinal Archbishop.[2]

The project of your going abroad has proceeded so rapidly, that I shall seem to you abrupt perhaps in what I am going to say, in consequence of my not having been prompt enough in saying it. I fancied you would go in October; you tell me you are going in a fortnight.

I did not write to you by return of post because I wished to say Mass on the subject before I wrote.

My dear Harry, you have told me distinctly you have a Vocation to the Oratory and you have asked me to speak out to you.[3]

It is my deliberate judgment then, which I am not likely to change, that you must consider yourself under us from this time. As matters

[1] Pollen's marriage to Maria La Primaudaye was fixed for 18 Sept.

[2] Harry Ryder was to leave for France early in Sept., en route for the English College at Rome, and wished to visit Louis de Vaulchier, his fellow student in Dublin. Newman met Cardinal Mathieu, Archbishop of Besançon, in Sept. 1846.

[3] Harry Ryder in his letter said, 'Do write to me as often as you can and say what you feel about me. . . . Do not be dissatisfied with anything I do or say without letting me know.'

have gone so far, before I had the means of making up my mind, I acquiesce in your going to Rome for a *year*, but no longer. Any how, you must come to us by Advent 1856, if you are to be ours.[1]

Ever Yours affectly in St Philip

John H Newman of the Oratory

H D Ryder Esqr

SATURDAY 25 AUGUST 1855   Mr Howard called and dined[2]   Fr Philip Gordon came   Monsell came   Mr Green came
SUNDAY 26 AUGUST   Mr Green passed the day here[3]

TO ANDREW ELLIS

The Oratory, Hagley Road, Birmingham August 26. 1855

My dear Dr Ellis

Thank you for your letter and its information. You must be kind enough not to think me rude, if I send you at any time a letter inclosed without any note of *mine* — as I often have so many letters to write.

I had not observed your letter to me was not stamped

Never mind people's smiling at our deficiencies. The great thing is to *make a beginning*, and those who are first in the field will have more honor

Very sincerely Yrs John H Newman

A Ellis Esqr M D

P.S.   I must have, please, Mr Nolan's letter back to acknowledge.[4]

[1] Newman wrote at the end of his draft of this letter, 'N B from memory I have settled his not coming at once, 1. because he had made his arrangements and was almost starting with a friend whom he might inconvenience. 2 since he had already put aside the notion of being admitted to the Oratory before he went, I thought it might be too great a trial for him. 3 he will have a year of probation. 4. meanwhile, we may say masses and pray to get money ⟨a patrimony⟩ for him, which we cannot give him at once. 5 He ought any how to be a year at Rome, and this will give him it.' See letter of 25 Sept. to Ryder.

[2] Presumably Philip Henry Howard (1801–83) of Corby Castle, with whom Newman had corresponded at the end of 1850.

[3] John Philip Green (1830–83), was at London University, B.A. 1849, LL.B. 1853. After his visit he wrote that the lives of St Philip and passages in Newman's writings had made a great impression on him, as also the life led at the Oratory. He became a barrister, went out to Bombay in 1862, and was a Judge of the High Court there 1873–1881. In 1874 he became a Catholic.

[4] Dr Nolan, who wanted to be Demonstrator in Anatomy, was to be refused.

P.S. I re-open this letter to ask you *in strict confidence* what you would say to an eminent Irishman and physician being brought from elsewhere to Dublin for our Professorship of Medicine, and a good *Lecturer*.[1]

TO MISS HOLMES

The Oratory Hagley Road Birmingham. August 26. 1855

My dear Miss Holmes,

I congratulate you on getting home. I expect to be here till November. However, very glad as I shall be if you come this way, don't suppose I can be of use to you in the Confessional now. I have no Confessional, nor have had for some years. Direction is a science, and I am not up to it. Any use I can be to you short of this religious use, I will most gladly.

I send this to Woodchester, since you do not give me your present address, yet I don't know how to spell Mr Ley's name, nor what his Christian name is[2]

Yours affectly in Xt   John H Newman of the Oratory
Miss Holmes

MONDAY 27 AUGUST 1855   Monsell went   Mr Charles Weld called?
TUESDAY 28 AUGUST   Fr Philip Gordon went   Mr Herbert called[3]   Northcote called
WEDNESDAY 29 AUGUST   Fr Bernard went to Bath   Fr Frederic returned from Belgium
THURSDAY 30 AUGUST   Fr Stanislas out of retreat   Augustus Bethel came

TO CATHERINE ANNE BATHURST

The Oratory Hagley Road Bm August 30/55
My dear Child
The books came quite safe — but they were very badly done up, so it's a wonder they did — I mention it in case you have another parcel to go any where

[1] Ellis replied that '*no* one could lecture on the Practice of Medicine in Cecilia Street during the ensuing medical session who is not an established and *recognised* Lecturer, and a physician to an hospital in Dublin.'

[2] i.e William Leigh of Woodchester Park, Gloucestershire. See letter of 8 June to Miss Holmes.   [3] Probably John Herbert of Llanarth.

I will write to Miss Ryder (not Rider) you know you will have to pay — they are as poor as rats.[1]

It concerned me very much to hear of your pain — it must be anxiety. I won't forget you.

Thank you for the St Francis, though I can't find it — I dare say I shall.

Mortifications of intellect

1. Not to ask for reasons why
2. Not to say, 'I hope it will turn out well' (with the Vicar of Wakefield)[2]
3. Not to say 'I told you so.'
4. Not to desire to hear the news
5. to be willing to be ignorant of many branches of knowledge etc
6. not to be eager about history
7. not to be eager for the explanation of Scripture difficulties, or difficulties and mysteries of faith
8. in a conflict of opinions and judgments, instinctively to feel you are less likely to be right than another

Ever Yrs affly in Xt   J H N[3]

Miss Ryder's direction is Arnos Court Brislington Bristol.

FRIDAY 31 AUGUST 1855   Fr Robert *Tillotson* went to America

TO MRS J. W. BOWDEN

The Oratory Hagley Road Bm. August 31/55

My dear Mrs Bowden,

I have just felt like you — wishing to write, and having nothing to say. We must remember each other at holy times and seasons the more.

[1] Cf. letter of 8 June to Catherine Bathurst.

[2] The reference is presumably to Dr Primrose's words at the end of Chapter XXI, when his disgraced daughter returns, 'Have patience my child . . . and I hope things will yet be better,' or else more generally to his attitude of optimism.

[3] Newman enclosed the following note in his own handwriting:
'*From Viva.*
It is certain, that the Incarnation was not simply necessary, even sin being supposed; for God might have willed either not to pardon sin, or to pardon it whether by (inward) grace, or *by a condonation external to the sinner*, *without* any previous manifestation of a condign satisfaction.
*   *   *
The satisfaction of Christ cannot be refused by God, against whom the offence has been committed. It is true indeed universally that parties who have been offended

What I heard from Henry [Bowden], that you were troubled with rheumatism, annoyed me, because I really feel you do not take care of yourself, as you should.

We are getting on with the University as well as we possibly can. It is swimming against the stream, to move at all — still we are in motion. The great point is *to set up* things — That we are doing. The medical schools will begin in October — the Church is building — and an Institution for Physical Science in course of formation. It will be years before the system takes root, but my work will be ended when I have made a beginning. Four years are now gone since I have been engaged upon it — the Holy Father has given me leave for two years more — and, as you may think, I shall be heartily glad when they are at an end. A Rector ought to be a more showy, bustling man than I am, in order to impress the world that we are great people. This is one of our great wants. I feel it vividly — but it is difficult to find the man who is this with other qualifications too. Do you recollect how we used to laugh at poor Goldsmith's 'My Lord Archbishop' uttered from one extremity of a long room, crowded and in hubbub, to the other? — that voice is the symbol of what we want in Dublin.[1] I ought to dine out every day, and of course I don't dine out at all. I ought to mix in literary society and talk about new gasses and the price of labour — whereas I can't recollect what I once knew, much less get up a whole lot of new subjects — I ought to behave condescendingly to others, whereas they are condescending to me — And I ought above all to be 20 years younger, and take it up as the work of my life. But since my qualifications are not those, all I can do is to attempt to get together a number of clever men, and set them to do what is not in my own line. I think of St Gregory of Nazianzus at Constantinople, and see, that at least I resemble him in his deficiencies[2]

My best love to dear Emily Ever Yours affectly in Xt

John H Newman of the Oratory

Mrs Bowden

are at liberty to refuse such satisfaction as is offered for the offender by a third person, (as, for instance, a creditor is at liberty to refuse the full *value*, should it be offered, of a stolen horse, in a case when the very individual horse might be restored) but still, when *a contract* has actually been made between Christ on the one side, and on the other Almighty God *consenting* to that satisfaction which is to be set forth by Christ as our bail ⟨surety⟩, in such a case, God could not refuse that satisfaction.'

[1] This reference has not been traced.

[2] Cf. *H.S.* II, 'The Church of the Fathers,' Chapter IV and *Apo.* p. 59.

31 AUGUST 1855

TO W. J. O'NEILL DAUNT

The Oratory Birmingham August 31. 1855
My dear Sir,

I do not see how a doctrine can be called 'an article of Christian faith' till it has been proposed by the Church. Since then certain books of the Canon were not so proposed in the earliest times, I do not see how they were articles of Christian faith in those times.

Next, till they were so proposed, they might, I conceive, be 'doubted or denied without heresy' — certainly without formal heresy.

The argument you maintain from the parallelism of the circumstances of the doctrine of the Canon and that of the Immaculate Conception seems to me correct.

I am sorry my answer has been delayed, and am, My dear Sir, Very truly Yours in Xt

John H Newman of the Oratory

W J O'N. Daunt Esqr

TO ROBERT ORNSBY

The Oratory Bm ⌜August 31. 1855⌝
My dear Ornsby

⌜Unless you find it disagreeable, I wish you would call on the Archbishop from me, to ask categorically whether we have the power of granting degrees *in Arts* — as we are pledged to give the Scholars' Degree in November.

I wrote to him on the subject as soon as I got here, that is, as soon after his return as I could — 6 weeks ago — and on that, as on other subjects, I cannot draw from him one single line of answer.[1] If we have *not* the power, I suppose we can get it on asking. The words of the Irish synodal meeting are 'Rectori potestatem decernimus, ut, servatis servandis, et habitâ auctoritate a sede Apostolicâ, quoscumque gradus academicos conferre valeat.'

The Decree of the Holy See upon this adds '*supplicandum* vero SSmo D. N. quoad expetitam facultatem pro ejusdem Universitatis Rectore ad gradus Academicos conferendos.'

The question is, *Has* that supplication been made? — if not, *who* is to make it?⌝

Ever Yrs affly J H N[2]

[1] See Newman's letter of 26 July to Cullen.
[2] For Ornsby's reply on the morning of 3 Sept. see letter of 4 Sept. to Monsell. Ornsby also wrote a second letter in the evening, giving a report from Dunne, who

536

SATURDAY 1 SEPTEMBER 1855   Augustus Bethel went
SUNDAY 2 SEPTEMBER   Mr Lynch here and Rankin
MONDAY 3 SEPTEMBER   Mr Lynch and Mr Rankin went.   F Edward went for his holiday?

TO ALFRED WILLIAM WORTHINGTON

The Oratory Hagley Road Birmingham Sept 3. 1855

Dear Sir

I am here the whole of this week — and shall be glad to see you whenever you call

Very faithfully Yours John H Newman

Alfred Wm Worthington Esqr

TUESDAY 4 SEPTEMBER 1855   Frs Antony and Alban came

TO WILLIAM MONSELL (1)

Bm Sept 4/55

My dear Monsell

I send you the inclosed as a specimen of Dr Cullen's way.

I wrote to him six weeks ago to know whether we had got from the Pope *the power of granting degrees*, which they exercise independently of the State in Belgium, which the Irish Bishops put into my hands, and which the Holy See has said should be given to the Bishops, *provided they asked for it.*

had just been in the south of Ireland. There 'he found people well satisfied with the University, i.e. with the officials, but much disappointed at the lack of support on the part of those who ought to be its principal strength. It was in vain to conceal that the Bishops did nothing for it. The cause of this was their jealousy of Dr Cullen. At the Irish Synodal meeting last May twelvemonth, *after* the resolutions were passed constituting the four Archbishops the supreme power of the University, Dr Cullen produced a Brief constituting himself Apostolical Visitor of the University, in fact supreme over it and thereby setting aside the authority of the four Archbishops which their resolution had just established; upon this, as Dr Dunne knew from good authority, two bishops left the room. It was a question whether the resolutions passed at that meeting were approved in Rome—they had not been published at all events, though some of them had already been put into force which referred to Maynooth. We were at present in the anomalous position of not knowing who our head or supreme power really is. There was talk in Rome of an idea of making Dr Cullen Chancellor of the University.'

It was one of MacHale's complaints that Cullen, who had been appointed Apostolic Delegate in Ireland in 1850, had used his power to control the University. See *McGrath*, pp. 352–3.

The question was, *had* the Supplica been presented, and accorded.

Dr Cullen has to this day sent me no answer. About a week ago, I asked Ornsby to *call* on him to get me a categorical answer; he went *from me* and for me

You will see his answer opposite.[1] Independently of the want of businesslike carefulness as regards the University (for we are pledged to give the Scholar's Degree in November, and ought to have the Supplica presented and granted before then) is there not something of rudeness as regards myself? Might he not at least have said, 'I will write to Dr Newman?'[2]

Ever Yrs affly J H N

The Rt Hon Wm Monsell M P

Let me have this back please, Ornsby had called on him once before and could not find him.

[1] Newman wrote this letter to Monsell on the unused second sheet of Ornsby's morning letter of 3 Sept., in which the latter said, 'I called this morning on the Archbishop, and asked him, from you, the question whether we had the power of granting Degrees in arts? He replied he could not say at present,—he would look into the papers and see whether we had or not. I then referred to the question of the supplication to the Holy See, but his Grace only repeated his previous answer. He was just going out, and the interview lasted scarcely a minute.'

[2] Monsell answered on 7 Sept., 'I cannot account for Dr Cullen's conduct except in one way—In Ireland one often meets with people of his class, kind and considerate after their fashion, but moving in a sphere completely different from ours and therefore acting in a manner in which if we acted we should shew a want of consideration and respect for others. . . . Want of thoughtfulness and want of respect are very different things—I cannot conceive that there can be intentionally any want of the latter towards you—One or two plans for getting an answer have occurred to me—I hope to try tomorrow to bring one of them to bear.' Cf. letter of 30 Sept. to Monsell.

Newman later commented, when copying this letter for the appendix of 'Memorandum about my connection with the Catholic University':

'Decr 2. 1872.

I account for Dr Cullen's silence in another way. He had lived too long at Rome not to have known the received rules of courtesy as well as Monsell—but he had begun to treat me as one of his subjects, to whom no such observance of rules was due. I can't help thinking he learned another rule from Rome, viz not to commit himself in writing —Thus one would think that at least the Archbishops could have corresponded *with each other* on certain questions which I wanted answered—but no, he must always wait "till the Archbishops met." Even then he would not have them answer my questions— but simply passed them over in silence. I was *not* to act, and for their purpose it was enough for them to be *silent*. Another thing he had learned from Rome, was the virtue of delay; he simply left questions to settle themselves.'

TO WILLIAM MONSELL (II)

Tuesday Evening [4 September 1855]

My dear Monsell

I have just heard from Ornsby that the Financial Committee is called for next Monday — this is a good move — perhaps from you[1]

Ever Yrs J H N

TO THOMAS SCRATTON

The Oratory Hagley Road Bm Sept 4. 1855

My dear Scratton

I must throw myself on your kindness to do me a favor. Harry Ryder wants his books, clothes etc, If you go to my house, Margaret will show you his room, and perhaps you will kindly put them together. Whether he has a box there or portmanteau I know not. If not, I suppose some very common deal packing will do.

The box must be directed to Mrs Roberts, 78 South Audley Street London.

Ever Yrs John H Newman

P.S.   While you are there, will you kindly inspect the new buildings — and send in the painters (Star) to do what is necessary at as little expense as possible.

WEDNESDAY 5 SEPTEMBER 1855   Frs Antony and Alban went   F Austin returned Mr Worthington called

TO J. D. DALGAIRNS

Oy Bm Sept 5/55

My dear Fr Bernard

There seems a feeling among some of us, as if it required considering, in what way the Rule of the Oratory allows of any member of it ever

[1] Ornsby wrote that the financial sub-committee for the University was to meet on 10 Sept., in order to wind up its affairs. Cf. letter of 26 July to Cullen. On 4 Sept. Scratton wrote the further information, 'James O'Ferrall says he will not attend, but will write a letter to say that he did not know that the Committee existed.'

Monsell replied to Newman 7 Sept., 'I do not know whether the committee meeting is caused by my letter to Serjeant O Brien as I have as yet received no answer from him —From whatever cause it meets I trust that it will settle the financial question and once for all put it in a safe and satisfactory state.'

The sub-committee met, adjourned to 4 Oct., and was heard of no more.

giving a Retreat, or being extra-ordinary Confessor to a Convent. I say this, because I think we shall have to consider it on your return.

My way of answering the difficulty has been that the Sisters of Mercy and Third Order of St Dominic are not nuns but I don't know whether this will stand[1]

Ever Yrs affly J H N

TO JOHN HUNGERFORD POLLEN

The Oratory. Hagley Road. Bm Sept 5. 1855

My dear Pollen,

I think it best to propose to trouble you with the inclosed, as you can talk with Mr Telford about the depth ofthe Gallery, its height above the ground, the depth of the nitch ⟨recess⟩, if there is to be any etc. etc.

Will you tell him 'I accept his proposal of June 25 for an organ,' £250, and wish him to send me the specifications.

Also, that I should like it better, if he could construct the framework so that it may at some future time be fitted up with stops to the amount of £600 altogether.

And that I should like to dispense with the Grecian grained oak case.

On second thoughts I do not inclose his paper as I have no copy.

Ever Yours John H Newman

P.S.   Ain't you coming here on your way to London?

J. H. Pollen Esq.

FRIDAY 7 SEPTEMBER 1855   Fr Richard came

---

[1] i.e., not solemnly professed, 'moniales.' The Sisters of Mercy had convents in or near Birmingham at Handsworth and Maryvale. The Third Order of St Dominic were Mother Margaret Hallahan's nuns at Clifton and Stone. Later in Sept. it was decided that Dalgairns should no longer act as confessor to nuns. See letter of 5 Nov. 1855 to him. Newman did not realise until the middle of Oct. that the London Oratorians had, on 14 Aug., without telling him, written to Propaganda on this very subject of hearing nuns' confessions, which was forbidden by the Rule, as taking Oratorians away from their proper work. Dalgairns, an interested party, either now, or perhaps after Stanton's visit 7–10 Sept., was aware of the London application. See letter of 18 Oct. 1855 to Cardinal Fransoni, and first letter of 23 Oct. 1855 to Flanagan.

TO EDWARD CASWALL

The Oratory Hagley Road Bm Sept 9. 1855

My dearest Edward

Do you think your Oration would be ready by the 29th? We could not have a better day.[1]

No news here. Fr Stanton is with us. Antony and Alban have passed through. Victor [Duke] is hovering near, we don't know where.

Ever Yrs affly J H N

MONDAY 10 SEPTEMBER 1855   Fr Richard Stanton went   Miss Bathurst in Birmingham   Dr Errington called   Pollen came   Victor [Duke] returned
TUESDAY 11 SEPTEMBER   confined to my room with a cold   Burns called   Harry and Lisle Ryder came and slept
WEDNESDAY 12 SEPTEMBER   H and L. Ryder went   H. to the Continent   L. (soon) to America

TO ANDREW ELLIS

The Oratory. Hagley Road Birmingham Sept 12. 1855

My dear Dr Ellis,

I quite concur in your recommendation of Mr O Reilly for the office of Demonstrator of Anatomy; and beg you to offer it to him.

As to Mr Hennessy, he is in Paris. His *Faculty* is a distinct one from the Medical Faculty, by the Episcopal Statute.[2] However, if the Advertisement were headed 'University Medical School, Cecilia Street,' since in matter of fact he *will* have his things there at first, if there is room for them, his name might appear as belonging to the House. If Mr Sullivan is in Dublin, he would decide whether you could go further than this.

[1] Newman was beginning a custom which lasted several years, of presenting, on the feast of St Michael, to the Oratorian Community and the congregation around them, an annual review of events. In 1855 Caswall gave a history of the Oratory in England from its inception, together with biographical accounts of Aloysius Boland and Joseph Gordon, who had died in 1852 and 1853. Cf. letter of 19 Sept. to Stanton.

[2] Ellis was anxious to fill out the Medical Faculty, and besides obtaining O'Reilly as a Demonstrator, wished to associate Hennessy, the Dean of the Faculty of Natural Philosophy, with it. Hennessy was to lecture in the building of the Medical School, and Ellis remarked that his subject 'bears strongly on medical education and is often associated with it.'

As to the Practice of Medicine, as I understand from you that the Lectures are not imperative the first year, I think I would rather take a little more time, and actually talk with you, before I did any thing. And so of the Chemistry

Very sincerely Yours John H Newman of the Oratory

A Ellis Esqre M D &c &c

TO LORD HENRY KERR

The Oratory Birmingham Sept. 12. 1855.

My dear Lord Henry,

Mr Stewart, I should think, would take Francis and would suit him — His brother[1] was with Mr S who always speaks of him with great affection — I suppose he is at home — His address Francis must know — I think it is 'Milburne House Drumcondra Dublin.'

Will you thank Lady Henry for her letter and tell her that, I think, if anyone can, under God, convert Mrs Froude it will be she —

We are taking holyday here and wandering about. Those who are on the spot join me in all kind remembrances, to Francis as well as yourself.

Very sincerely Yours in Xt   John H Newman of the Oratory

The Lord Henry Kerr —

THURSDAY 13 SEPTEMBER 1855   Fr Ambrose went away for a fortnight to the Kent and Sussex coast   F Bernard returned   Wenham and Edward's brother called   Palmer came

TO EDWARD CASWALL

Oy Bm Sept 13/55

My dear Edward

Do you think you can get ready your Oration by the 29th? Answer me at once, please.

I wrote to you at 6 Harcourt Street, but you have not got the letter.

Ever Yrs affly J H N

[1] His eldest brother, William Hobart Kerr.

542

FROM ARCHBISHOP CULLEN

Dublin 8th Sept. 55

My Dear Dr Newman

I must beg ten thousand pardons for so long a delay in answering your letter.[1] My only excuse is that I was endeavouring to get more information about the state of the university before I should write, and not being successful all at once I delayed from day to day in the hope of being able to write with more knowledge of the question. I must now say that I still remain in great ignorance of the real state of things. All I can do then at present is to beg of you to spend some days here before the end of vacation, and to prepare a most minute account of every thing for the meeting of our bishops. I think they will meet in October I dare say about the middle of it. At all events the Archbishops will meet on the 18th. I hear many complaints about the expenditure of money, and some disciplinary matters — but I suppose by a little explanation every thing will be made clear. Any how, it will be well to be ready for the bishops, and also to have the principal rules prepared for their approval.

I beg now to add that I have received for the *University Church* fifty pounds, which I will hold until you direct me to dispose of it.

Excuse this hurried line. I have deferred writing so long that I thought it better to send a hurried line than to delay an answer any longer

Believe me to be with sincerest esteem Your devt Sert

+Paul Cullen[2]

V. Revd Dr Newman

[1] i.e. that of 26 July. Cf. letter of 5 July to Cullen.

[2] Newman commented: 'Decr 2. 1872 1. This is a Tu quoque. 2. If he wanted information how could he hope to gain it in the depth of the Long Vacation except from me, yet of me he had asked no question. 3 How could he expect me to be at Dublin in the Vacation, when I had duties at Birmingham? (as it happened, at that very moment, most serious duties; which led me at Christmas to go to Rome, but this he could not know.) 4 "Expenditure!" then why did he not give me a finance committee, which I earnestly pressed from first to last, but in vain, instead of saying to Butler as he did "All is in Dr Newman's hands"?—5 "Discipline!" then why did he not give me a Vice Rector? 6 "Prepare a most minute account!" Why, by the Episcopal Decrees it was my *duty* once a year, in the Autumn, to present a Report of the year's proceedings to the Bishops; I needed no instruction from him for that purpose; he *knew* that Report was coming—and it did appear at the proper time to the length of 52 octavo pages, dated Oct. 13. 1855.

I consider then the above letter a mere pretence—but I did not take notice of it to him.'

Newman preserved another 'Very important paper, tracing the quarrel between Dr C and myself,' and written at the time: 'N B. Dr Cullen tells Mr Butler that "every thing is in my hands" then why not at once confirm my appointments? Why say I am spending a good deal of money etc.'

TO ARCHBISHOP CULLEN

The Oratory Hagley Road Birmingham. ⌐Sept 13. 1855¬

My dear Lord,

⌐I thank your Grace for the letter you have sent me. I am sorry to find that the Bishops think of meeting in October — as I shall find it difficult to alter my arrangements of remaining here till the end of that month.¬[1]

Thank you also for your notice of the £50 given to the University Church. Its best destination, I think, will be the 'Cullen and Newman Account' in the Hibernian Bank — whence I will draw it as a Separate Sum, when I want it.

⌐I wrote to your Grace from this place in July, begging you to be so good as to instruct me what I was to do as regards Father O'Reilly,[2] whose coming I did not like to stop, without your Grace's sanction, though I did not see myself how to employ him just now. Since I wrote, he has come to Dublin for our purposes, and I have had to commence his salary as Professor, without any clearer idea than before, what we are to make of him.[3] This will give us some trouble.¬

Begging your Grace's blessing I am, My dear Lord, Your affectionate Servt in Xt

John H Newman of the Oratory

The Most Revd Dr Cullen.

FROM ARCHBISHOP CULLEN

Dublin. 16th Sept 1855

My Dear Dr Newman

From your last letter I perceive that you are doubting about the success of a class of theology connected with the university. I have made some enquiries on the matter and I think I can assure you that such a class will probably be very well attended. There are several young priests, and some friars anxious to assist at lectures in theology. It should not however be an elementary class of theology,

---

[1] Newman noted, [[The *term* began November 3. I went to Dublin in fact October 18.]]

[2] i.e. on 26 July. Newman noted, [[This important point asked in July Dr Cullen did not write about till Sept 16, 1855.]]

[3] Newman noted [[I think I am right in saying, that, in the event, Fr O'Reilly refused to take any salary, as he was not employed.]]

but lectures on the most important points. The lectures also should not be too frequent — twice a week would suffice.[1]

It would not be necessary to engage a house for this purpose, as for the present lectures could be given at one of the parochial houses ex. g. at Marlboro' Street or at SS. Michael and Johns where there are rooms sufficient to accomodate [sic] fifty persons.

I write this line to remove any difficulties that may have presented themselves. But if you were here it would [be] easy to come to a better understanding about every thing. During your absence in the beginning and before things are settled, it is impossible to know what should be done. I suppose Dr O Reilly would require some instructions, so that he may know what he is to do.

It will be altogether necessary that you should be present at the meeting of the bishops or have some thing prepared for them. However the time for their meeting is not fixed and perhaps it may be deferred. The Archbishops meet for Maynooth affairs on the 18th October. Believe me to be with great esteem Your dev sert

+Paul Cullen

V. Revd Dr Newman

FRIDAY 14 SEPTEMBER 1855   Pollen went

TO F. W. FABER

The Oratory Bm Sept 14. 1855

My dear Fr Wilfrid

I am truly glad to have your own assurance of what I hoped would be the case, and considered was the case, from the information Fs Edward and Joseph sent me.[2]

---

[1] On 26 Sept. 1855 Edmund O'Reilly, the Professor of Theology, wrote to Newman about the form his lectures should take, and added, 'With regard t o hearers, I know of none except secular priests (how many I have no definite idea, and I fear they may be somewhat of a *floating population*) some few regulars—I have heard Carmelites chiefly spoken of—and perhaps some *few* from All-Hallows.'

Three years later, on 24 Oct. 1858 O'Reilly wrote to Newman, asking whether his lectures were to be continued, 'My only hearers last Session, or nearly so, were the young men [Carmelites] of Aungier Street Convent. They were most punctual and attentive; nothing could be better. But the number was small—about eight. Now it appears to me that this number is not respectable for a Theological Class in a University. I think it has the look of a sham. The awkward appearance is increased by the circumstance of *all* coming from one community, that community not being created by the University, as would be a Seminary established for Divinity Students. Nor can this small school be looked on as *a commencement* which, with time, will grow into something considerably greater. . . .'

[2] Faber who had been ill in Dublin, was now at Sydenham. Edward Bagshawe and Antony Joseph Ball had written long accounts of his state. Faber was thought to be suffering from gravel in the kidneys and wrote further details on 13 Sept. 'The whole

The great thing is to know what a complaint is — to what it tends — and how it is to be met. Though I trust you will not have the very severe pain again with which you are threatened, yet, it is so great a thing to know one's trial (for at least medically we may say, ἐν φάει καὶ ὀλέσσον)[1] that I think it is better than the vague illnesses which seemed to haunt you.

We do not forget you, be sure Ever Yrs affly

JHN

TO THOMAS SCRATTON

[14 September 1855?]

My dear Scratton

Thank you for the cheque for £200. I will send it direct to the Bank of Ireland — and I inclose a cheque for Fr Flanagan to the same amount, *dated September 16.* which please pay in to the Cullen and Newman account of that date

Thank you also for your calculation of the cost of the Medical School of which I am not unmindful.

As to the Erringtons, of course it is a pity if they don't come, but it does not do to hurry people. Thank you for your suggestion.

Is there any chance of your coming this way? I will give your salutation to Nicholas

Ever Yrs John H Newman

P.S.   I will write to Dr Ellis about the expences.

TO EDMUND O REILLY, S.J.

The Oratory Hagley Road Birmingham. ⌈Sept 16/55⌉

⌈(Sent in substance)⌉
My dear Father O'Reilly

⌈I have thought a good deal of you and of your department lately, and in consequence have written another letter to Dr Cullen, hitherto

matter then resolves itself into a *temporary* idleness, and the subsequent endurance of some sharp pain. . . . I have the best advice and Lord Arundel insists on paying all the expenses incurred. . . . and friends will send me as much game as I am allowed to eat, and more [butcher's meat being forbidden]. . . .

Light reading bores me, and I must read, and thinking fatigues me; and not saying mass for I can't *stand* at all, tho I can hobble about, is a great penance. . . .'

[1] *Iliad*, XVII, 647. 'Once there is light, let it be that though slayest us,'—the prayer of the Greeks fleeing in the mist.

without success — however, he may still speak to you or write to me.[1]

He was so earnest before he went to Rome, about the commencement of the Theological School even before this Autumn, that I felt I could not go against his wishes in his absence, when F Curtis wrote to me about April last on the subject — and while I did not do any thing more than decide on having you in his absence, yet I did all I could, by addressing myself to Dr Woodlock etc. to prepare matters for his consideration.

Up to this time, however, I cannot extort one single word from him — and therefore have great difficulty in answering your questions, which are most natural and kind, being without any materials for doing so.[2]

I said to Dr Cullen⌐ as to the question of the School altogether — ⌐You are bringing together Professors (as F O'Reilly) and hearers, who are, both parties, well employed already, and neither of them wish to come — Is this to be done?

Now, however, that the step has been taken, the question is, what is to be done?

For myself, I do not see my way to opening the School in November next. The All hallows people are very unwilling to move in the matter, for the best of reasons, because they do not want us and we can at present but disarrange them; and I really am much perplexed what to do.⌐

(I wanted to have provided for the chair of Canon Law, if the School was to begin, but Dr Cullen has not only not answered my letters, but has mislaid a letter on the subject of some Louvain theologian, about whom I meant to inquire. At least he neither returns the letter, nor notices it, when I have asked him. All this I need not say, I mention to you in confidence.)[3]

Then go on to speak of Dr Errington's two suggestions. 1. of a Canon Law professorship or 2 of a course of lectures for laymen etc.[4]

MONDAY 17 SEPTEMBER 1855 Palmer went

TUESDAY 18 SEPTEMBER Mr John Flanagan came about now

WEDNESDAY 19 SEPTEMBER Miss Holmes came

[1] Cullen wrote this same day the letter printed after Newman's of 13 Sept.

[2] O'Reilly wrote on 13 Sept., asking what subjects he was to lecture on, and how often, in the autumn term.

[3] See letter of 26 July to Cullen. Newman put this paragraph in the draft of his letter to O'Reilly in brackets, and wrote at the top of it '(I have just mentioned it)' i.e. the subject of the paragraph, in the letter as sent.

[4] Archbishop Errington, now Wiseman's Coadjutor with the right of succession, had visited Newman on 10 Sept.

TO RICHARD STANTON

Hagley Road Sept 19/55

My dear Richard

Will you put on paper a few words from [for] me by Michaelmas Day, which I may work up for our people, as an account of your progress etc. at Brompton? We are going to have a domestic party on that day, and I should like to say something to them on the subject.[1] And can Edward [Bagshawe] tell me what year the State first recognised the London University Degrees? Not before the *Queen's* London University was set up, I suppose — If so what year was that?[2]

Ever Yrs affly J H N

THURSDAY 20 SEPTEMBER 1855 Miss Holmes went
SATURDAY 22 SEPTEMBER Fr Edward returned Allies came
MONDAY 24 SEPTEMBER Allies went confined to my room with face ache[3]

TO HENRY (IGNATIUS) DUDLEY RYDER

Bm Sept 25. 1855

My dear Harry

But a very few words from you were necessary to set every thing right with me, and you have altogether done so by your letter which has just come.[4]

[1] Stanton replied on 23 Sept., that the move to Brompton had consolidated the London Oratory and given it influence in its neighbourhood, which was not possible in the centre of London. The attendance at the church was more satisfactory, although fewer converts were received. The Oratorians had the care of one convent of nuns and heard confessions in at least two others, but had 'applied for instructions' as to whether to continue this work. As to this last matter, see letter of 18 Oct. 1855 to Cardinal Fransoni.

[2] No letter from Bagshawe is to be found. The Anglican King's College received its charter in 1829. That for the non-sectarian University College, founded in 1827, was bitterly opposed. It received its charter in 1836, and at the same time the University of London was set up by the Government, with the power to grant degrees to students from both colleges.

[3] Altered in *Chronological Notes* to 'tooth ache.'

[4] Harry Ryder had avoided replying to Newman's letter of 24 Aug., merely writing on 2 Sept, 'Thank you for your last letter.' Newman noted on 13 Sept., '. . . He came to take leave September 11 and went next day September 12—but—said nothing.
Therefore, if next Autumn, he proposes to come to us, which I do not much expect, he must bring a pension—that will be the condition on which we receive him. J H N'
Ryder had told Newman he was sure he had a vocation to the Oratory and Newman

You may be sure, my dear boy, I do not forget your great trial. It is sent you to do you great good. I will not fail to remember you at holy times, and to pray that you may be carried well through it.

You cannot wonder at my backwardness, under the circumstances, to speak to you, after I had already written, without your commencing the subject. Quite in the dark as I am, what is at the bottom of the strange events, by which we both are sufferers, I naturally feel it safer to do nothing towards you, which I am not actually called on to do.

However, your present letter shows me most strikingly, what you have already told me of yourself, that you have a vocation to the Oratory. You must recollect that personal attachment to the members of the congregation, (unlike the case of a religious vocation,) is one of the marks of an Oratorian vocation.

And, feeling you have a true vocation to us, I should be wanting in my duty, if I did not repeat the summons of my last letter, viz that I expect you here by Advent 1856

Ever Yrs most affly J H N

Love to de Vaulchier — and my best respects to his Father, the Comte[1]

TO THOMAS SCRATTON

Bm Sept 25/55

My dear Scratton

Dr Ellis may in conversation have said wax work would be a good thing, but I recollect nothing of his having asked for a definite £100 and it took me by surprise.[2] It would be safer, if you had my warrant for every cheque you draw. I am little disposed to give a second £100 — as I have a hint that people think I am going ahead.

Ever Yours affly J H N

Thos Scratton Esqr

had written on 24 Aug. that he must consider himself as belonging to it, i.e. that he would be taken in irrespective of whether his father or family agreed to provide for him. Ryder now appeared anxious to avoid accepting this offer. He was therefore putting himself in the position of an applicant who had no claim to particular consideration.

Ryder's letter which put things right is not to be found. His great trial was evidently his father's attitude towards him,—taking him away from Dublin and insisting that he should go to the English College at Rome.

[1] On his way to Rome Ryder was staying with Louis de Vaulchier.
[2] This money was wanted for the School of Medicine.

TO ROBERT WHITTY

The Oratory, Birmingham. Sept. 25, 1855.
My dear Dr. Whitty,

I return with many thanks the letter which you have so kindly sent
me. It has concerned and distressed me most deeply. I have the warmest
attachment and, I may say, affection for Lucas. And it is so wonderful a
dispensation, ecclesiastically considered.[1]

Will you say every thing kind from me to him, and tell him I shall
say Mass for him once a week, till I hear that God's good Will has been
declared as regards him one way or the other.

We all share in my feelings.

Yours ever affectly in Xt., John H. Newman of the Oratory

The Very Revd. Dr. Whitty.

FRIDAY 28 SEPTEMBER 1855   F Ambrose and F Henry returned

FROM ARCHBISHOP CULLEN

Dublin, 27th Sept 1855
My Dear Dr Newman

I have just heard and I believe it to be true that Dr Leahy has been appointed
parish priest of Cashel and Dean of that diocese. This will, I suppose, leave his
place vacant.

I beg to add that there are great complaints here that no one is doing any
thing for the university, and no one is charged to give information about what is
to be done next year. When those concerned are asked, they say they have no
instructions. I fear that if things be left in this state, we cannot expect any
success. I beg and implore of you to take some steps to set things right

Believe me to be with great esteem Your dev Sert

+ Paul Cullen
V. Revd Dr Newman

[1] Frederick Lucas returned from Rome to London on 23 May, in very bad health, his
appeal to the Pope against Cullen still undecided. He was suffering from heart disease,
and on 23 Sept. dropsy set in. He bore his pains joyfully and died on 22 Oct., aged
forty-four. Whitty, whose sister was married to Lucas's brother, visited him frequently.

TO ARCHBISHOP CULLEN

Birmingham ⌐Sept 28/55⌐

My dear Lord

⌐I have just received your Grace's letter.⌐¹ I very much regret Dr Leahy's retirement. I hope he will keep his Professorship, though he is obliged to resign his Vice Rectorship²

⌐The Secretary of the University attends at his Office in the new portion of the University House every day from 10 to 2 — and either by application then or by letter will answer all questions.³

This has been advertised [[(in the Papers)]] again and again, but I will take care it is put afresh into the Newspapers⌐

Yr affte Servt In Xt   John H Newman of the Oratory⁴

The Most Revd The Archbp of Dublin

¹ Newman noted: [[Still a Tu quoque]]

² Leahy remained nominally Vice-Rector of the University until 1857. In the appendix to 'Memorandum about my connection with the Catholic University' Newman made a note, which he marked '*Very Private*':

'Decr 1872. From 1854 to 1857 Dr Leahy was Vice-Rector. I always got on well with him—from first to last—we never had even a momentary misunderstanding—no sharp or cold word ever passed between us—but, as to his presence in the University, he was hardly there at all. First he was at Thurles; then he was PP of Cashel and Vicar General; then he had a bad accident which kept him away, then he put off his resignation till the next meeting of the Bishops. When he had resigned, which he did not till he became Archbishop, I was left without a Vice Rector up to the time I resigned. The Vice Rector by the Statutes had the care of the discipline of the place—this was all thrown on me. Dr Cullen was from the first, dissatisfied with my not residing in Dublin more than I did—I have no reason to think that he ever expressed dissatisfaction with Dr Leahy.' Cf. *A.W.* pp. 294-5.

³ Scratton wrote to Newman on 29 Sept., 'Really I think it rather too bad of the Archbishop as I have only been absent from the Office for three weeks during the whole Long Vacation and have rarely left Dublin till late in the afternoon, having been fairly detained by business nearly every day.'

Newman copied a sentence out of a letter to him from Dr Ellis of 23 Aug., 'Mr Scratton is constantly at his post, and as vigilant as possible.'

⁴ Towards the end of Oct. Cullen wrote to Tobias Kirby, the Rector of the Irish College in Rome, a letter which he passed on to Propaganda, where it was endorsed as having reached there on 4 Nov. The final paragraph ran:

'With regard to the university, we have done nothing. For more than three months Father Newman has been in England, and has left a convert Englishman called Scratton here to take his place. To the Vice-Rector he gave no instructions. I have not therefore been able to find out how things stand, but they don't seem to me to be going in a way that can be defended. The continued absence of the Rector cannot be approved. Then the expenses have been very large, and furthermore the discipline introduced is unsuitable, certainly to this country. The young men are allowed to go out at all hours, to smoke etc., and there has not been any fixed time for study. All this makes it clear that Father Newman does not give enough attention to details. I hope that when he returns from England, it will be possible to induce him to introduce a better system.

TO PATRICK LEAHY

The Oratory Bm Sept 28/55

My dear Dr Leahy

I have just heard that there is a fear of our losing you. I hope not. But any how I write to express my great regret, and to thank you for all your kindness since you and I have had any thing to do with the University, which is four years at least, as I have cause to know.

Be sure I entertain the most pleasant recollection of our acquaintance, and will be still more pleased if you tell me the report is illfounded.

I write in great haste to get the post, having only just heard the report

Ever Yrs very sincerely in Xt

John H Newman of the Oratory[1]

The Very Revd Dr Leahy &c &c

TO ROBERT D. LYONS

Bm Sept 28/55

My dear Sir

I have read your letter of September 14 just received with extreme surprise and concern, and I really think I should not be right in complying with your (to me) most unwelcome wish, that your name should be withdrawn from our medical list, till you renew it after receiving my explanation.[2]

Surely it is never right to act to the injury of others (and such an act would be to our injury) without hearing what they have to say for them-

It is true we shall always have the difficulty that "Nemo potest duobus dominis servire", and Father Newman cannot be excepted. He cannot spend a great part of the year in England and govern a university here. I hope they won't make him a bishop in Rome until he has properly arranged all the affairs of the university.' Archives of Propaganda, *S.R.C. Irlanda*, 1854–6, f. 567, quoted by J. H. Whyte in *D R*, (Spring 1960), p. 35.

Cf. letter of 25 Oct. 1855 to Cullen.

[1] Leahy replied on 5 Oct. that he was ready to remain for a short while connected with the University. He thanked Newman for his letter, and said, 'be assured I account it the greatest honour of my life to have been associated with a man of whom every Catholic in the realm, and beyond it, is justly proud.'

[2] Lyons wrote from the General Hospital in the Camp before Sebastopol to resign the Professorship of Physiology, which Newman had offered him in his letter of 27 April. He wished his name withdrawn from the advertisement at once. His ground was that Thomas Hayden and Robert Cryan had been advertised as professors of 'Anatomy and Physiology,' in July, while he was described as Professor of 'Pathological Anatomy,' which he felt to be a mere nominal title.

selves. If it be true, as you say, and most true it is, that in my position the state of 'medical affairs in Dublin cannot well come fairly under my notice,' it is true also that what is passing in the Catholic University cannot fairly come under your notice at Scutari.

For every thing that has been done I am the only person responsible — but still I took the advice of two of your friends, as I believe they are, Mr Sullivan and Mr John Pigott, both persons for whom I have a great respect, with the very object of not interfering with your views of a Medical school, and I should be surprised if I find that I have done any thing which they considered disrespectful or inconsiderate to you.

I cannot here refer to your last Letter, but really my belief is that it was yourself who suggested Pathology for your chair, instead of Physiology.[1]

However, I have never had any idea whatever of separating Scientific Physiology from it; I wished and wish the chair called the chair of Physiology and Pathology.

When the Anatomical Professors spoke of their being also professors of Physiology, I objected because I said you were to have it; and it is expressly understood that Physiology is added to Anatomy in the designation of this Professorship, merely to satisfy the students, who require it, especially in your absence.

I assure you I have never had any doubt of the wisdom of your views (as far as I have a right to have an opinion) and have never had any idea I had done any thing to interfere with them. I fully intend on your return, should I be fortunate enough to retain your services, to carry them out.

Might I ask you to have the kindness to refer the matter to any persons, as the two gentlemen I have mentioned?[2]

I am &c J H N

TO MISS M. R. GIBERNE

Bm Sept 30 1855

My dear Miss Giberne

I have been going to write to you some time, but did not know how to direct.

[1] In his letter of 13 May Lyons had spoken of being Professor of Clinical Medicine and of giving lectures in Pathology.

[2] Lyons was completely pacified by this letter, and his name was presented to the Bishops in Oct. for the Chair of 'Physiology and Pathology,' the Chair of Hayden and Cryan being described as of 'Anatomy' only. *Campaign*, p. 50. However, in the University Calendar, 1855–6 and subsequently, Hayden and Cryan were described as Professors of 'Anatomy and Physiology,' while Lyons appears as Professor of the 'Practice of Medicine and Pathology.'

Even now I do not know. I direct this to the Palazzo Borghese. Please acknowledge it at once — that we may know you have got it.

You will be doing a very great service if you are able to manage this matter.[1]

We hope to get the Church open at Easter, if the pictures are ready.

Since coming here, I have seen the vestments you have sent, they are most beautiful — and a *very great addition* to the sacristy

I did not forget you on St Rose's day but said Mass for you

Ever Yrs affly J H N

TO WILLIAM MONSELL

The Oratory Bm Sept 30. 1855

My dear Monsell,

Thank you sincerely for the trouble you have taken — and for the letter you have elicited.[2]

The secretary of the University is installed in an office, and is to be found every day between 10 and 2 at the University House.

This has been advertised many times.

He is in constant correspondence with me, and my rule is to answer his letters by return of post.

I was in Ireland 46 weeks running; except 6 Sundays.

If any one wrote to me in Harcourt Street, the letter would be forwarded here

Ever Yrs affly J H N

P.S.   I congratulate you on having taking Sebastopol, or at least the South Side.[3]

[1] Newman was writing on the last page of a letter from Pollen to Miss Giberne, in which he asked for her working drawings of certain pictures, in order to have enlarged copies made in Dublin for the decoration of the University church.

[2] Monsell wrote on 28 Sept. 'At length we have elicited from Dr Cullen a reply. Will you put his letter in the fire when you have read it—

It appears odd that none of the anxious enquirers whose enforced ignorance he bemoans should ever have thought of committing their questions to a penny stamp and directed them to you at Birmingham—

It is well at all events to know what is passing in his mind and I think it probable that the letter to which the enclosed is a reply will make him more easy to deal with and more attentive than he has been. [Cf. Monsell's letter of 7 Sept. quoted in note to Newman's of 4 Sept. to him.]

I have heard no more as to how the financial confusion has been dealt with.'

[3] The south side of Sebastopol was captured on 8 Sept.

Appendixes

Appendix 1

Memorandum on the Objects of the University and the
Means for attaining them[1]

April 29. 1854

1.

I BEG to submit to the Most Revd and Rt Revd Prelates, the Archbishops
and Bishops of Ireland, the following Remarks, on the subject of their
present design of founding a University for the Catholics of Ireland and
of other countries which speak the English tongue.

Their object, I conceive, is that of providing for Catholic Education,
(in a large sense of the word 'education') in various respects, in which at
present we have to depend upon Protestant institutions and Protestant
writings. For instance, they propose

1. To provide means of finishing the education of young men of rank,
fortune, or expectations, with a view of putting them on a level with
Protestants of the same description.

2. To provide a Professional education for students of law and medicine; and a liberal education for the mercantile class.

3. To develop the talents of promising youths in the lower classes.

4 To form a school of Theology and Canon Law, suited to the needs
of a class of students, who may be required to carry on those sciences
beyond the point of attainment sufficient for parochial duty.

5 To provide a series of sound and philosophical Defences of Catholicity and Revelation, in answer to the infidel tenets and arguments, which
threaten us at this time.

6. To create a national Catholic Literature.

---

[1] On the back of this Memorandum Newman wrote 'This Paper was for Dr Cullen
to show to the Synodal Meeting which took place at the end of April   J H N   Jany 28.
1879.'

The original MS, which is here printed, had been returned to him, from among the
papers of J. I. Taylor who had died in 1875.

The Paper received a few alterations before being read at the Synod in May. The
corrected version is printed in *Campaign*, pp. 93–100. Cullen sent his approval of the
first version through Dr Taylor, but suggested two additional points, 'that it would be
well to lay it down in express terms that the University is the property of the Archbishops and Bishops of Ireland,' and 'that the faculty of Theology should be particularly mentioned as an integral part of the University.' Newman felt that he had already
provided for the second point, but altered his final paragraph to emphasise the Bishops'
responsibility for the cost of the University.

7. To provide school books, and, generally, books of instruction, for the use of Catholics of the United Kingdom, the British Empire and the United States.

8. To raise the standard, and to systematise the teaching, and to encourage the efforts, of the Schools, already so ably and zealously conducted throughout Ireland.

9. To give a Catholic tone to Society in the great Towns.

10 To respond to the growing importance to [of] Ireland, arising from its geographical position, as the medium of intercourse between East and West, and the centres of the Catholicism of the English tongue, with Great Britain, Malta, perhaps Egypt, and India on one side of it, and North America and Australia on the other.

2.

The means, by which these great objects must be attempted by those to whom the most Revd and Rt Revd Prelates commit the work, is the appointment of Professorial Chairs for the cultivation of the most important and seasonable branches of knowledge, and of men of high name to fill them.

Considering we have the whole weight of government, not only against us, but in favor of a rival system, it is imperative that the Professors appointed should be men of celebrity. Such celebrity is the only (human) inducement for students joining us in preference to the Government Colleges. Even able men, if they have not yet made a name, will be insufficient. It were better to leave some of the Chairs empty for a time, than to fill them with men whose names are not in themselves an attraction. It is desirable to substitute, at first Lecturers for Professors, if by so doing we secure the temporary services of men of name who can assist us on no other terms.

3.

An additional conclusion follows. If students are to be gained to us by the celebrity of our Professors, our Professors (or Lecturers) must be appointed prior to and independent of the presence of our students. This has been the case in the history of all Universities. Learned men came and opened schools, and drew followers. Even when schools were set up by sovereigns the process was the same. The schools rose into importance, not simply by royal favor, by civil privileges, by degrees, or by emoluments, but by the enthusiasm kindled by distinguished teachers, and by the popularity and recognised importance of the subjects on which they lectured.

This brings us to another practical conclusion. We must commence by bringing into position and shape various large departments of knowledge; by founding institutions, which will have their value intrinsically, whether students are present or no. This, if we can effect it, will have double advantage; such institutions will attract students, and will have a sufficient object before students come.

I will give some illustrations of the sort of institutions I mean, though they are not all possible at once, and it is not easy to determine at a moment which of them are more likely than the rest to be brought into effect.

1. A school of useful arts, developing and applying the material resources of Ireland; that is, comprising the professorships of engineering, mining, agriculture etc.

2. An observatory with the Professorships it involves.

3. An archaeological department, employing itself on the language, remains, MSS etc of ancient Ireland, with a special reference to its Catholicity.

4. A Hospital, with the Professorships it would involve in medicine.

Such institutions, I repeat, would give an immediate dignity and importance to the University, before, during, and until the actual formation of classes of students, for whose sake they are really set up, and whom they would attract. Astronomers might be taking observations, physicians attending patients, archaeologists deciphering and printing MSS, and chemists and geologist variously serving the public, though their lecture rooms were at first but partially filled.

4

Such institutions, could not be contained under one roof — nor need they. A definite local position in a city or town is rather the attribute of a College than of a University. A University fills the city in which it is placed. The University of Paris occupied the whole extent of hills and gardens on the south bank of the Seine; it included in its circuit the great monasteries of St Victor and St Germanus, and it had a legal connexion with St Genevieve; — besides the hold it had upon the island, and, as many think, on portions of the north up to Montmartre. The University of Oxford to this day reaches from one end of the city to the other; the Anatomy School, the Observatory, the Botanical Lecture-rooms and gardens, are each half a mile distant from the other.

5.

The Unity of the University, thus locally distributed, will consist in the Unity of the Catholic dogma and spirit. I think their Lordships will see the desirableness of providing a University Church, for all those high occasional ceremonies, in which the University is visibly represented. But, besides this, it will be the place for ordinary preaching on Sundays and holydays, when the pulpit will be filled by some distinguished theologian or sacred orator, called for the purpose from the scene of his labours in Ireland or England. No one can over estimate the influence of an instrument of this kind in inculcating a loyal and generous devotion to the Church in the breasts of the young.

6.

But of course the more obvious means of securing Catholic Unity in this great institution is that of throwing the students into small communities, in the neighbourhood of the Lecture-rooms which they have to attend. These communities will be formed, as students come, and should consist of about 20 students each. They should be presided over by a Dean, who should be a young Priest, who would enforce discipline and serve the community chapel.

The Dean of these small communities should have with him two or three young men who have already passed the course and public examinations, and are therefore of several years standing. These should be the private Tutors or 'Preparers' of the 20 students who constitute the community, in subordination to the Professors.

As such Tutors, from the nature of the case, cannot be provided at once I should propose meanwhile to be allowed to commit the whole Tutorial work to a board of three or four good scholars, whose duty it would also be to systematize a plan of studies and to form a list of standard editions of works, critical helps, and course of reading.

7

As to the charges to which a student will be subject, it is impossible as yet to estimate them exactly; but I consider they need not exceed those of the better class of schools, say 40 guineas a year. Moreover, I should recommend to their Lordships a certain number of burses or money prizes, to be obtained by concursus, which may serve both to stimulate exertion, and diminish the expences of those who obtain them.

8

I conceive the normal age of coming to the University should be 16. For the first two years, the student will be engaged in classics, the elements of mathematics and logic, ancient history etc. At the age of 18, he will pass an examination, which will gain an initial degree. We must contemplate losing the majority of our students at this age; which is compatible with having imparted a certain amount of liberal knowledge to those who are then entering on the duties of their particular calling.

Those who remain will give themselves for the space of a second two years to a course of modern history, political economy, law, metaphysics etc which will terminate, at the age of 20, after an examination, in the degree of B.A.

After this none would remain, except such as desired, at the end of three additional years, by a degree of M.A. or the Doctorate, to qualify themselves for a Profession or Professorship.

Modifications and exceptions to these rules will occur in particular cases, which are too minute or complicated to notice here.

9.

I submit to their Lordships that a trial of seven years must be given to this institution, which, if successful, will have so important bearings on Catholic interests, whatever be the degree or promise of success in the course of them. And that, during these years of experiment, an annual outlay be contemplated of £5000

John H Newman

Appendix 2

The Autumn Term, 1854[1]

Postremo pereunt imbres, ubi eos pater aether,
In gremium matris terrai praecipitavit:
At nitidae surgunt fruges, ramique virescunt
Arboribus; crescunt ipsae foetuque gravantur.

Lucret., i. 251.

PERHAPS it may interest the readers of the *Catholic University Gazette*, to lay before them a brief account of the doings and progress of the University up to the close of the year 1854.

At the end of the preceding year, 1853, a great many persons whom we casually met in society and elsewhere, could be scarcely brought to believe that our University was a reality at all; that it was projected no one could deny, but many believed, in consequence of the long delay which had so often disappointed them of their expectations, that it was doomed never to take its place among the things of this world as a living and moving body. We are thankful to say that our best hopes are now realized, and we have to congratulate the Catholic Church in these kingdoms upon what we dare to call a great fact; we have really a Catholic University. We wish to sketch the history of the actual events connected with it during its first Term.

The Classical and Mathematical schools of the University were opened on the Feast of St. Malachi, November 3, 1854. There was no pomp and circumstance to set off the event; no crowds assembled to behold a spectacle; all this was rendered impossible, by the absence in Rome of our archbishops, and so, quietly and peacefully, without noise or ceremony, our Institution commenced its career.

The examinations for entrance were conducted by the Vice-Rector (Very Rev. Dr. Leahy); the Professor of Classical Literature (Mr. Ornsby); and the Lecturer on Logic (Dr. Dunne). The examinations consisted of Latin composition and of questions submitted to the candidates on paper; after which a further trial was given to each student separately, by questions asked and answered viva voce. Above twenty passed successfully and immediately afterwards commenced the University course. Among the students who were thus enrolled on the books,

[1] This article, which appeared in the *Catholic University Gazette*, (1 Feb. 1855), pp. 320–3, was written by the editor, Robert Ornsby. See also *Campaign*, pp. 313–24.

there was one who requires special mention at our hands. This was Mr. Daniel O'Connell, grandson of the illustrious leader, in consideration of whose name the authorities presented his descendant with an Exhibition, enabling him to reside at the University House, and in consequence to attend the University Course, for four years free of expense.

On Saturday, Nov. 4, the classes were formed, and the lecture-list was arranged.

On Sunday, Nov. 5, the Rector (Very Rev. Dr. Newman) gave a *soirée* at the University House, by way of introducing the students to their academical career. The Dean of Residence (Very Rev. Mr. Flannery), the Professor of Classical Literature, the Lecturers in Logic and French Literature, and fifteen of the newly admitted students were present. They assembled in the Refectory, after which the list of names was read over by Dr. Dunne, and the students were successively introduced to Dr. Newman and to the Dean. This ceremony being concluded, Dr. Newman addressed the students to the following effect. He began by saying that the first question before them was: 'What are they here *for*?' and the most obvious answer was, to prepare for their respective professions, — law, medicine, the ecclesiastical state, engineering, or mercantile pursuits. But that was not all that a university education was intended for. He would explain his meaning by a story which he had heard many years ago, in early life. There was a widow lady who had suffered some reverses of fortune, and was left with a large family. One of them was obliged to accept a situation, which appeared beneath his rank, and expressed naturally some regret at this. The mother, who was a wise person, said: 'My dear Charles, remember *the man makes the place, not the place the man*.' They were here to receive, no matter what their intended profession was, an education which would alike fit them for all. Of course, the University was also intended to provide an education of special use in the professions but it was more than that; it was something to fit them for every place and situation they might meet with in life. For instance, a man, as life goes on, suffers adversity; great changes befall him. If he has a really cultivated mind, he will act under these changed circumstances with grace and propriety. Or again, if sudden alterations the other way befall him, he will act in them too with calmness and as he ought to do. You often see people who cannot do this; who, if they come into a great fortune, don't know how to spend it properly, and throw their opportunities away. A well-trained mind will act under such circumstances with propriety. It will not be thrown off its balance by any of the changes of life, but will turn all to proper account, and conduct itself exactly as it should do throughout them all.

He went on to explain what a University was, and the nature of that University education from which hitherto, from the circumstances of the country, Catholics had been debarred. The Holy See had thought it was time this state of things should come to an end, and that the Catholics of this country, and all speaking the English language, should have the means afforded them of that higher education which hitherto the Protestants had monopolized. The idea of a University was, that it was a place of education to which people resorted from all quarters. They would here meet with men of various conditions, and from various places, and would add to each other's knowledge by that means. Again, a University ought to be in the capital of a country, and that was the reason why the Catholic University was established in Dublin. Other places had their recommendations, but to the capital talent and distinction resorted. Hence it was that the Queen's Colleges, of the members of which he spoke with all kindness, never could be a University. He proceeded to speak of the discipline of a University, and reminded them that they were no longer boys, but verging on manhood. Children must be governed to a great extent by fear. That was no longer the case with them. They were, to a certain extent, their own masters, the guardians of themselves. The authorities believed them to be intelligent youths, and would repose confidence in them, and believe their word, and they hoped to be met by a similar spirit of confidence. He alluded to the Romans putting on their *toga virilis*, and quoted the beautiful passage of St. Paul about putting aside childish things. In one sense, we were always children — children of our Heavenly Father, and we should be fools if we forgot that; but in a certain sense they should now feel that manhood had arrived, and they must endeavour to show a manliness of mind. They must begin well, and there would reign over the whole place a *genius loci*, a good general character and spirit.

The Rector then made some remarks on the time that had been selected for the opening, which was St. Malachi's day, Nov. 3. This was partly from devotion to the saint whose name has always been held in much reverence in Ireland — he divided Ireland into the four archbishoprics which still remain — partly as the time when colleges in general open, and allowing for their long vacation, which would be from August to October inclusive.

He went on to allude to the qualifications of those in whose charge they would be placed, the Vice-Rector, the Dean of Residence, and the Professors, and mentioned the hours of the academical day. There would be Mass at eight o'clock, breakfast at nine, lectures from ten till one or two, including French, which he thought necessary for all, and after that hour they would be their own masters till dinner at five, after which the

hours would be settled by the Dean of Residence. He ended by speaking
of their numbers, with which he was well pleased, though some of them
might have expected more. They would look back with great pleasure
if they lived to be old, to St. Malachi's day, 1854, on which they had
taken part in the founding of the University, which would then be so
great; and the fewness of the numbers with which they began would
happily contrast with the magnitude to which in the course of years it
will have arrived. It reminded him of the scene of Shakespeare, in which
Henry the Fifth, before the battle of Agincourt, when some of his
attendants are discouraged by the fewness of his soldiers, bravely tells
them that he would even have the numbers fewer rather than more.
Westmoreland wishes but one ten thousand of those men who were that
day idle in England, were there to help them. The king replies:

> What's he that wishes so?
> My cousin Westmorland? No, my fair cousin;
> The fewer men, the greater share of honour.
> God's will! I pray thee, wish not one man more.
> . . . O do not wish one more.
> Rather proclaim it, Westmorland, through our host,
> That he which hath no stomach to this fight,
> Let him depart; his passport shall be made,
> And crowns for coming put into his purse.
> This day is called the feast of Crispian:
> He that outlives this day and comes safe home,
> Will stand on tiptoe when this day is nam'd.
> He that shall live this day, and see old age,
> Will yearly on the vigil feast his neighbours,
> And say: To-morrow is Saint Crispian
> . . . Then shall our names,
> Familiar in his mouth as household words, —
> Harry the King, Bedford and Exeter,
> Warwick and Talbot, Salisbury and Glo'ster, —
> Be in their flowing cups freshly remembr'd:
> This story shall the good man teach his son;
> And Crispin Crispian shall ne'er go by,
> From this day to the ending of the world,
> But we in it shall be remembered;
> We few, we happy few, we band of brothers.
> *Henry V.*, act IV. sc. iii.

After this beautiful and animating discourse (of which we have only
been able to give a most inadequate outline), the youthful academics
separated, highly delighted with their first evening in college.

On Monday morning, November 6, the lectures commenced, and were proceeded with throughout the term. These lectures were given by the Professor of Classical Literature (Mr. Ornsby), the Lecturer on Ancient History (Mr. Stewart), the Lecturer on French Literature (M. Renouf), the Lecturer on the Italian and Spanish Literature (Signor Marani), and by the Rev. W. Penny, as the substitute for the Professor of Mathematics, who was not able at the moment to commence the duties of his office. They were attended by the students with great regularity, and considerable progress was made in various branches of science during even this short term.

On Thursday, the 9th of November, an Inaugural Lecture was delivered at the University House, by the Very Reverend the Rector. . . . The following Thursday evening an Inaugural Lecture . . . was delivered by the Professor of Sacred Scripture (Very Rev. Dr. Leahy) . . . On the succeeding Thursday evenings throughout Term, Inaugural Lectures were delivered by the Professors and Lecturers in the several departments of classical, French, and Italian literature, and the Philosophy of History.

Our space only enables us to add, that these lectures were heard with the deepest interest by an assembly so crowded, that it became a matter of regret, that the University was unable to place at their disposal a larger room for their accommodation.

On Wednesday, the 29th of November, an examination was held for the election of four Exhibitions, two classical and two mathematical, to be chosen out of candidates of Irish birth, for the Session 1854–1855. The Examination was conducted for the Classical Exhibition, by the Very Reverend Dr. Leahy, Vice-Rector, the Professor of Classical Literature (Mr Ornsby), and the Lecturer on Logic (Dr. Dunne); and for the Mathematical Exhibition, the Professor of Mathematics (Mr. Butler), Rev. W. Penny, and Rev. M. O'Ferrall, S.J.

On Thursday, 30th of November, the Rector, on the report of the Examiners, announced the election as follows. For the Classical Exhibition (£35), John Henry Bracken. For the Mathematical Exhibition (£35), Patrick Conolly. For the Classical Exhibition (£25), Andrew Washington Kirwan; and for the Mathematical Exhibition (£25), Bernard John Mazon.

A Classical Prize was awarded to Francis Leo Tobin. . . .

On Wednesday and Thursday, the 20th and 21st days of December, the Rector, assisted by the University officers, held the first Terminal Examination at the University House. With these Examinations, in some places called Collations, the Term concluded, and the Students were dismissed for the Christmas Recess.

On the same evening, at eight o'clock, an Inaugural Lecture was delivered by the Lecturer on the Philosophy of History (Mr. Allies). As might be expected from the fame and talents of the distinguished lecturer, a more satisfactory conclusion to the business of the first term of the Catholic University of Ireland could scarcely have been desired, than was afforded by Mr. Allies on this occasion.

Appendix 3

Public Lectures of the University
A Letter to the Editor of the University Gazette[1]

Sir,

I dare say it will look like presumption in me, but an anonymous person cannot be reached, and a mask cannot blush; so I will venture to give you my thoughts on the *object* of the evening public lectures, lately delivered in the University House, which, I think, has been misunderstood, and which I have a notion is better understood by myself.

I attended them, and I can bear witness, not only to their remarkable merit as lectures, but also to the fact that they were very satisfactorily attended. Many, however, attach a vague or unreasonable idea to the word 'satisfactory,' and maintain that no lectures can be called satisfactory, which do not make a great deal of noise in the place, and who are disappointed otherwise. This is what I mean by misconceiving their object; for such an expectation and consequent regret arise from confusing the ordinary with the extraordinary object of a lecture, — — upon which point we ought to have clear and definite ideas.

The *ordinary* object of lectures is *to teach*; but there is an object, sometimes demanding attention, and not incongruous, which, nevertheless, cannot be said properly to belong to them, or to be more than occasional. As there are kinds of eloquence, which do not aim at anything beyond their own exhibition, and are content with being eloquent, and with the sensation which eloquence creates; so in schools and universities there are seasons, festive or solemn, any how extraordinary, when academical acts are not directed towards their proper ends, so much as are intended, like fireworks, to amuse, to astonish, and to attract, and thus to have an effect upon public opinion. Such are the exhibition days of Colleges; such the annual commemoration of Benefactors at one of the English Universities, when the Doctors put on their gayest gowns, and the Public Orator makes a Latin Oration. Such at the Protestant University of Durham are, or were, the terminal Lectures, at which divines of the greatest reputation for intellect and learning have before now poured forth sentences of burning eloquence into the ears of the congregated ladies and gentlemen of the Palatinate. The object of

[1] The *Catholic University Gazette*, (5 April 1855), pp. 420–2. This letter, mentioned in that of 28 March 1855 to H. Wilberforce, is included, with some omissions, in the address on 'Discipline of Mind,' *Idea*, pp. 490–4.

568

all such Lectures and Orations is to excite or to keep up an interest and reverence in the public mind for the Institutions from which the exhibition proceeds.

Such we have suitably had in the new University. Of this nature, before it was instituted, were the Rector's Discourses in the Rotunda this time three years. Such, Mr. Editor, I conceive, has been in a great measure your own publication itself. Such were the Inaugural Lectures delivered before Christmas. Displays of strength and skill of this kind, in order to succeed, should attract attention, and, if they do not attract attention, they have failed. They do not invite an audience, but an attendance; and perhaps it is hardly too much to say that they are intended for seeing rather than for hearing. And this was the result in some measure of the Inaugural Lectures I have mentioned; they were, as you recollect, honoured and rewarded by so large a crowd of literary and distinguished persons, not to mention the ladies who attended, that the only fault to be found with the demonstration was, that it was too large for the rooms which were the scene of it.

Such celebrations, however, from the nature of the case, must be rare. It is the novelty which brings, it is the excitement which recompenses, the assemblage. It is too much, it would be disrespectful, to ask the circles of so large a city, where each has his own business, to find time and to feel a taste to become students again, and to re-enter the University schools. The academical body, which attempts to make extraordinary acts the normal condition of its proceedings, is putting itself and its Professors in a false position.

It is then a simple misconception to suppose that those to whom the government of our University is confided by their Lordships, the Bishops of Ireland, have aimed at an object, which could not be contemplated without a confusion or inadvertence, with which no considerate person will charge them. Public lectures, delivered with such an object, could not be successful; and, in the present instance, have, I cannot doubt (for it could not be otherwise), have necessarily, ended unsatisfactorily in the judgment of any zealous person, who has assumed for them an office, with which their projectors never invested them.

What their object really was, the very meaning of academical institutions suggests to us. It is, as I said when I began, *to teach*. Lectures are, properly speaking, not exhibitions or exercises of art, but matters of business; they profess to impart something definite to those who attend them, and those who attend them profess on their parts to receive what the lecturer has to offer. It is a case of contract: — 'I will speak, if you will listen:' — 'I will come here to learn, if you have anything worth teaching me.' In an oratorical display, all the effort is on one side; in a lecture it is shared between two parties, who co-operate towards a common end.

This being the case, I am almost sorry, as it has turned out, if I may excuse the impertinence of saying it, that the evening lectures of the term just completed were so sedulously advertised. Of course it is desirable that the Dublin public should know when men like Dr. Leahy, Mr. Curry, and Mr. M'Carthy give lectures; it might think itself aggrieved, if it did not. It is natural too, and necessary, that at the beginning of *term* a table should be issued of the lectures which are to be given in the course of it; but our Professors are too well known to need to be cried in the market-place. The men and the subjects will bring such an audience as is suitable, an audience really wishing to learn what is set before them. They should deliver their lessons to us, not with open, but with closed, though not close, doors. There should be something, on the face of the arrangements, to act as a memento, that those who come, come to gain something, not for mere curiosity. And in matter of fact, such were the persons who did attend, in the course of last term, and such as those, and no others, will attend. Those came who wished to gain information, on a subject new to them, from informants whom they held in consideration, and regarded as authorities. It was impossible to survey the audience, which occupied the lecture room, without seeing that they came on what may be called business. And this is why I said, when I began, that the attendance is satisfactory, — not which is numerous, but — which is steady and persevering. In the instances, of which I am speaking, it consisted, either of ecclesiastics or other strangers, or of the University students themselves. But it is plain, that to a mere by-stander, who came merely from a general interest or good will to see how things were going on, and who did not catch the object of advertising the Lectures, it would not occur to look into the faces of the audience, he would think it enough to be counting their heads; he would do little more than observe whether the staircase and landing were full of loungers, and whether there was such a noise and bustle, that it was impossible to hear a word; and if he could get in and out of the room without an effort, if he could sit at his ease, and actually hear the lecturer, he would think he had sufficient grounds for considering the attendance unsatisfactory.

There is a rule in Horace which may be applied with much appositeness to the matter before us. 'Non fumum ex fulgore, sed ex fumo dare lucem.'[1] The stimulating system may easily be overdone, and does not answer on the long run. A blaze among the stubble, and then all is dark. I have seen in my time various instances of the way in which Lecturers really gain upon the public; and I must express my opinion, that, even

[1] *De Arte Poetica*, 143.

were it the sole object of our great undertaking to make a general impression upon public opinion, instead of that of doing definite good to definite persons, I should reject that method, which the University indeed itself has *not* taken but which young and ardent minds may have thought the more promising. Did I wish merely to get the intellect of all Dublin into our rooms, I should not dream of doing it all at once, but at length. I should not rely on sudden startling effects, but on the slow, silent, penetrating, overpowering effects of patience, steadiness, routine and perseverance. I have known individuals set themselves down in a neighbourhood, where they had no advantages, and in a place which had no pretensions, and upon a work which had little or nothing of authoritative sanction; and they have gone on steadily lecturing week after week, with little encouragement, but much resolution. For months they were ill-attended, and overlooked in the bustle of the world around them. But there was a secret, gradual movement going on, and a specific force of attraction, and a drifting and accumulation of hearers, which at length made itself felt, and could not be mistaken. In this stage of things, a person said in conversation to me, when at the moment I knew nothing of the parties, having learned what I have hitherto said afterwards: 'By the bye, if you are interested in such and such a subject, go by all means, and hear such a one. So and so does, and says there is no one like him. I looked in myself the other night, and was very much struck. Do go, you can't mistake; he lectures every Tuesday night,' or Wednesday, or Thursday, as it might be. An influence thus gradually acquired, endures; sudden popularity dies away as suddenly.

I cannot help thinking that the University authorities view the matter in the same light with myself, and it is that feeling which removes the reluctance I should otherwise feel in obtruding my remarks upon you.

I am, etc., C.

List of Letters by Correspondents

List of Letters by Correspondents

Abbreviations used in addition to those listed at the beginning of the volume:

A.	Original Autograph.
Bayswater	Oblates of St Charles, Bayswater, London.
C.	Copy, other than those made by Newman.
D.	Draft by Newman.
Georgetown	The University of Georgetown, Washington, D.C.
H.	Holograph copy by Newman.
Harrow	Dominican Convent, Harrow, Middlesex.
Lond.	London Oratory.
Magd.	Magdalen College, Oxford.
Oriel	Oriel College, Oxford.
Pr.	Printed.
Pusey	Pusey House, Oxford.
Rankeillour	The Lord Rankeillour.
S.J. Dublin	The Jesuit Fathers, 35 Lower Leeson Street, Dublin.
S.J. Lond.	The Jesuit Fathers, 114 Mount Street, London.
Stoke	The Dominican Convent, Stoke-on-Trent.
Todhunter	Mrs Todhunter, Gillingham Hall, Norfolk.

The abbreviation which describes the source is always the first one after the date of each letter. This is followed immediately by the indication of its present location or owner. When there is no such indication, it means that the source letter is preserved at the Birmingham Oratory. It has not been thought necessary to reproduce the catalogue indications of the Archives at the Oratory, because each of Newman's letters there is separately indexed, and can be traced at once.

After the source and its location have been indicated, any additional holograph copies (with their dates) or drafts are listed, and then, enclosed within brackets, any references to previous publication in standard works.

Lastly, when it is available, comes the address to which the letter was sent.

Correspondent	Year	Date	Source	Location, Owner, Address
Acton, Sir John	1854	5 June	A	*Ad.* Sir John Acton/at Dr Döllinger's Munich/Bavaria. Postmark: Munich, 9 June
	1855	7 Jan	A	Mr Douglas Woodruff
Alemany, Joseph	1854	22 Jan	D	
Allies, T. W.	1854	18 May	C	(*McGrath*, p. 296)
		3 Sept	C	
		22 Oct	C	
		8 Nov	C	
		11 Nov	C	
		16 Nov	C	
		27 Nov	C	
		30 Dec	C	
	1855	2 Mar	C	
		12 Mar	C	
		20 Mar	C	
		22 April	C	
Arundel, Countess of	1855	29 July	A	The Duke of Norfolk
Badeley, Edward	1854	11 May	A	
		17 May	A	
		28 June	A	
	1855	20 Mar	A	
Bathurst, Catherine Anne	1854	12 Feb	A	Harrow
		10 Mar	A	Harrow
		21 Oct	A	Harrow
		14 Nov	A	Harrow
	1855	13 Mar	A	Harrow
		4 April	A	Harrow
		6 April	A	Harrow
		3 May	A	Harrow
		8 June	A	Harrow
		5 Aug	A	Harrow
		30 Aug	A	Harrow

Correspondent	Year	Date	Source	Location, Owner, Address
Bittleston, Henry	1854	8 June	A	
		23 June	A	(*McGrath*, p. 320)
		27 June	A	
	1855	27 Feb	A	
		18 May	A	
Bloxam, J. R.	1855	7 July	A	Magd. MS. 307
Bowden, Emily	1854	16 July	A	Lond. Vol. 14
Bowden, Henry Sebastian	1855	6 June	A	Lond. Vol. 15
Bowden, John Edward	1854	5 Jan	A	Lond. Vol. 15
		23 Jan	A	Lond. Vol. 15
		15 Aug	A	Lond. Vol. 15
Bowden, Mrs J. W.	1854	18 Jan	A	Lond. Vol. 14
		30 Mar	A	Lond. Vol. 14
		15 April	A	Lond. Vol. 14
		20 April	A	Lond. Vol. 14
		5 July	A	Lond. Vol. 14
		9 July	A	Lond. Vol. 14
		16 July	A	Lond. Vol. 14
		23 July	A	Lond. Vol. 14
		16 Aug	A	Lond. Vol. 14
		14 Nov	A	Lond. Vol. 14
	1855	11 Jan	A	Lond. Vol. 14 (*McGrath*, p. 347)
		27 April	A	Lond. Vol. 14
		31 Aug	A	Lond. Vol. 14 (*Trevor* II, p. 68; *McGrath*, pp. 363–4)
Bowles, F. S.	1854	11 Feb	A	
		28 Feb	A	(*Trevor* II, p. 39)
		18 Mar	A	(*McGrath*, p. 269)
		15 June	A	
	1855	15 Mar	A	
		17 April	A	
		23 June	A	

577

Correspondent	Year	Date	Source	Location, Owner, Address
Bowles, F. S.	1855	27 June	A	
Bretherton, Peter	1854	1 Dec	C	
	1855	3 Feb	C	
Brown, Thomas Joseph	1854	17 June	C	
Brownson, Orestes	1854	6 June	A	University of Notre Dame (H. F. Brownson, *Orestes A. Brownson's Middle Life: from 1845 to 1855*, Detroit 1899, pp. 479–80; Theodore Maynard, *Orestes Brownson*, New York 1943, p. 206) *Ad.* Dr Brownson/*Boston*/United States/Postmarks: Dublin 6 June; Boston 22 June
		23 Aug	A	University of Notre Dame (*Orestes A. Brownson's Middle Life*, pp. 481–2; *Orestes Brownson*, p. 207)
			D	
		27 Sept	A	University of Notre Dame (*Orestes A. Brownson's Middle Life*, p. 484)
Burke, James	1854	14 Feb	D	
Butler, Edward	1854	10 July	A	(Postscript only)
			D	
Capes, J. M.	1854	4 Jan	A	
		5 Jan	A	
		15 Jan	A	
		21 Jan	A	
		15 June	A	
		20 July	A	
		15 Sept	A	
		11 Oct	A	
Caswall, Edward	1854	25 Feb	A	(*Trevor* II, p. 40)
		22 Mar	A	
		8 Sept	A	
		11 Sept	A	
		14 Sept	A	
		17 Sept	A	

Correspondent	Year	Date	Source	Location, Owner, Address
Caswall, Edward	1854	22 Sept	A	(*Trevor* II, p. 53)
		4 Oct	A	(*Trevor* II, pp. 63–4)
		8 Oct	A	
		12 Oct	A	
		15 Nov	A	
		17 Nov	A	
	1855	16 Jan	A	
		20 Jan	A	
		3 Feb (I)	A	
		3 Feb (II)	A	
		16 Feb	A	
		24 Feb	A	
		27 Feb	A	
		1 Mar	A	
		14 Mar	A	
		20 Mar	A	
		30 Mar	A	
		1 April	A	
		7 May	A	
		9 May	A	
		20 May	A	
		27 June	A	
		1 July	A	
		9 Sept	A	
		13 Sept	A	
Clifford, William	1854	18 Aug	A	Diocesan Archives, Clifton
Coffin, R. A.	1854	28 Feb	D	
Corrigan, D. J.	1855	2 June	D	
		7 June	D	
		1 July	D	
Cullen, Archbishop	1854	12 April	A	Diocesan Archives, Dublin
		15 April	A	

Correspondent	Year	Date	Source	Location, Owner, Address
Cullen, Archbishop	1854	1 May	A	Diocesan Archives, Dublin
		11 May	D	(*McGrath*, pp. 293–4)
			H	1870–3
		17 May	A	Diocesan Archives, Dublin
		27 May	A	Diocesan Archives, Dublin
		12 June	A	Diocesan Archives, Dublin
		18 June	A	Diocesan Archives, Dublin (*McGrath*, pp. 319–20)
			D	
			H	1870–3
		23 June (i)	A	Diocesan Archives, Dublin
		23 June (ii)	A	Diocesan Archives, Dublin
		1 July	A	Diocesan Archives, Dublin
		12 July	A	Diocesan Archives, Dublin
		5 Aug	A	Diocesan Archives, Dublin
		17 Aug	A	Diocesan Archives, Dublin
		27 Aug	A	Diocesan Archives, Dublin
		9 Sept	A	Diocesan Archives, Dublin
		27 Sept	A	Diocesan Archives, Dublin
		30 Sept	A	Diocesan Archives, Dublin
		1 Oct	A	Diocesan Archives, Dublin
			D	
			H	1870–3
		3 Oct	A	Diocesan Archives, Dublin
		4 Oct	A	Diocesan Archives, Dublin
		6 Oct	A	Diocesan Archives, Dublin
		8 Oct	A	Diocesan Archives, Dublin *Ad.* Al Reverendmo e Colmo Il Monsignore Cullen &c &c/Collegio Irlandese/Roma
		8 Dec	A	Diocesan Archives, Dublin
	1855	24 Jan	A	Diocesan Archives, Dublin (*McGrath*, pp. 349–50) *Ad.* The Most Revd/Dr Cullen/Collegio Irlandese/Roma/*Italy*

Correspondent	Year	Date	Source	Location, Owner, Address
Cullen, Archbishop	1855	23 Feb	A	Diocesan Archives, Dublin
		5 July	A	Diocesan Archives, Dublin
		15 July	A	Diocesan Archives, Dublin
		26 July	A	Diocesan Archives, Dublin
			H	(Two) 1870–3
		28 July	A	Diocesan Archives, Dublin
			D	
		1 Aug	A	Diocesan Archives, Dublin
		13 Sept	A	Diocesan Archives, Dublin
			D	
			H	1870–3
		28 Sept	A	Diocesan Archives, Dublin
			H	1870–3
Dalgairns, J. D.	1854	28 Feb	A	Lond. Vol. 12
		4 Mar	A	Lond. Vol. 12
		10 Mar	A	Lond. Vol. 12
		16 Mar	A	Lond. Vol. 12
		28 April	A	Lond. Vol. 12
		15 May	A	Lond. Vol. 12
		20 May	A	Lond. Vol. 12 (*McGrath*, p. 296) *Ad.* The Revd Fr. Dalgairns/The Oratory/Hagley Road/Birmingham/England/Postmarks: Dublin 20 May; Birmingham 22 May
		7 June	A	Lond. Vol. 12 (*Trevor* II, p. 57)
		19 June	A	Lond. Vol. 12 (*McGrath*, p. 320)
		22 June	A	Lond. Vol. 12
		7 Sept	A	Lond. Vol. 12
		18 Sept	A	Lond. Vol. 12 *Ad.* The Revd Fr. Dalgairns/The Convent/Stone/Staffordshire/England
		4 Nov	A	Lond. Vol. 12
		7 Nov	A	Lond. Vol. 12
		19 Nov	A	Lond. Vol. 12

Correspondent	Year	Date	Source	Location, Owner, Address
Dalgairns, J. D.	1854	12 Dec	A	Lond. Vol. 12
	1855	22 Jan	A	Lond. Vol. 12 (*Trevor* II, p. 58)
		26 Jan	A	Lond. Vol. 12
		17 Feb	A	Lond. Vol. 12
		7 May	A	Lond. Vol. 12
		27 May	A	Lond. Vol. 12
		5 Sept	A	Lond. Vol. 12
Daunt, W. J. O'Neill	1854	11 Oct	A	The National Library of Ireland
	1855	16 Mar	A	
		31 Aug	A	St John's Seminary, Camarillo, California
Dillon, V. B.	1855	25 Jan	D	
Dixon, Joseph	1854	3 June	A	Dr Günter Biemer, Tubingen
		9 July	A	St Patrick's College, Maynooth
		30 Sept	A	Diocesan Archives, Dublin
Dodsworth, William	1854	18 Aug	C	(*McGrath*, p. 343)
Döllinger, J. J. Ignaz von	1854	18 Aug	A	Döllingeriana II, Bayerische Staats-Bibliothek, Munich
Dunne, D. B.	1854	25 July	A	Miss Doreen Powell, County Cork
		28 July	A	Miss Doreen Powell
	1855	5 April	A	Miss Doreen Powell
		18 July	D	
Dunraven, Earl of	1854	17 Feb	A	
		23 Nov	A	
	1855	2 July	A	
Ellis, Andrew	1854	21 July	A	
	1855	17 May	A	*Ad.* A. Ellis Esqr/&c &c 110 Stephen's Green
		16 Aug	A	*Ad.* Andrew Ellis Esqr MD/&c &c/ 110 Stephen's Green/Dublin/
		26 Aug	A	*Ad.* the same
		12 Sept	A	*Ad.* the same
Ennis, John	1854	21 Dec	A	

Correspondent	Year	Date	Source	Location, Owner, Address
Estcourt, E. E.	1854	24 Feb	A	Diocesan Archives, Birmingham
Faber, F. W.	1854	13 Jan	A	Lond. Vol. 9
		10 Feb	A	Lond. Vol. 9 (*Trevor* II, p. 33; *McGrath*, p. 243)
		4 Mar	A	Lond. Vol. 9
		14 Mar	A	Lond. Vol. 9 (*Trevor* II, p. 42)
		18 Mar	A	Lond. Vol. 9
		26 April	A	Lond. Vol. 9 (*Trevor* II, p. 43)
		27 April	A	Lond. Vol. 9
		28 April	A	Lond. Vol. 9
		7 May	A	Lond. Vol. 9
		11 May	A	Lond. Vol. 9
		24 May	A	Lond. Vol. 9
		28 June	A	Lond. Vol. 9
		13 Aug	A	Lond. Vol. 9
		27 Aug	A	Lond. Vol. 9
		8 Sept	A	Lond. Vol. 9
		26 Dec	A	Lond. Vol. 9
		30 Dec	A	Lond. Vol. 9
	1855	5 Feb	A	Lond. Vol. 9 *Ad.* The Very Revd Fr Faber/The Oratory/*Brompton Road*/London
		11 Feb	A	Lond. Vol. 9
		13 June	A	Lond. Vol. 9
		14 Sept	A	Lond. Vol. 9
Feilding, Viscount	1854	6 Jan	A	
		9 Aug	C	
Flanagan, John Stanislas	1854	9 Feb	A	(*McGrath*, p. 252)
		28 Feb	A	(*Trevor* II, pp. 38–9; *McGrath*, p. 259)
		4 Mar	A	
		6 Mar	A	
		10 Mar	A	(*McGrath*, p. 267)

Correspondent	Year	Date	Source	Location, Owner, Address
Flanagan, John Stanislas	1854	14 Mar	A	
		16 Mar	A	
		13 May	A	
		8 June	A	
		28 June	A	
		2 July	A	
		6 Oct	A	
		12 Oct	A	
		24 Nov	A	
		27 Nov	A	
		3 Dec	A	(*McGrath*, pp. 245–6)
		5 Dec	A	
		6 Dec	A	
		24 Dec	A	
	1855	11 Feb	A	
		3 Mar	A	
		13 Mar	A	
		24 May	A	
		11 June	A	
		26 June (I)	A	
		26 June (II)	A	
		End of June	A	(*McGrath*, p. 346)
		1 July	A	
		10 July	A	
		16 July	A	
Froude, Isy	1855	9 July	C	(*Ward* II, p. 317)
Froude, William	1854	10 April	C	
Froude, Mrs William	1854	2 Mar	C	(*Ward* I, p. 336; *Harper*, p. 95)
		17 Mar	C	
	1854–5	placed at 10 April 1854	C	(*Ward* I, pp. 622–4; *Harper*, pp. 84–9)

Correspondent	Year	Date	Source	Location, Owner, Address
Froude, Mrs William	1854	5 May	C	(*Harper*, pp. 100–1)
		26 Dec	C	
	1855	2 Jan	A	*Ad.* Mrs Wm Froude/Dartington Rectory/Totnes/Devon
		22 Mar	C	
		8 June	A	*Ad.* Mrs Wm. Froude,/Dartington Parsonage/Totnes/Devon
Fullerton, Lady Georgiana	1855	12 Jan	D	
		4 June	Pr	The *Month*, cxxix (April 1917), p. 335
		13 June	Pr	The *Month*, cxxix (April 1917), p. 336
Giberne, Miss M. R.	1854	22 Jan	A	*Ad.* Miss Giberne,/Palazzo Borghese/*Roma*/Italy
		9 Mar	A	*Ad.* the same
		15 May	A	*Ad.* the same Postmarks: Birmingham 15 May; Rome 24 May
		18 Aug	A	*Ad.* (in St John's hand) Miss Giberne/Palazzo Borghese/*Roma*/*Italia*
		6 Nov	A	
		27 Dec	A	*Ad.* Miss Giberne, Inglese,/ 5 Via S. Ignazio/ultimo Piano/Roma/*Italy*
	1855	24 Mar	A	(*Trevor* II, p. 63)
		30 Sept	A	
Godwin, Thomas	1854	11 June	A	
Gordon, William Philip	1854	In note to letter of 18 Aug. to M. R. Giberne	A	Lond. Vol. 11
	1855	20 Aug	A	Lond. Vol. 11
Grant, Thomas	1854	19 June	A	Georgetown
	1855	20 Mar	A	Georgetown
Granville, Countess	1854	8 Dec	A	
Hamilton, John	1855	30 Jan	A	The Jesuit House, Gardiner Street Dublin
Hanmer, A. J.	1854	27 Aug	A	S. J. Lond.

Correspondent	Year	Date	Source	Location, Owner, Address
Hanmer, A. J.	1854	1 Nov	A	S. J. Lond.
Hendren, Bishop	1854	5 Feb	D	
Hennessy, Henry	1854	16 Nov	C	
	1855	10 May	D	
		9 Aug	D	
Holmes, Miss	1854	12 April	A	*Ad.* Miss Holmes/Casa Macquay/ Via Sta Anna del Maglio/Firenze/ Italy Postmarks: Birmingham 12 April; Florence 19 April
		18 Aug	A	*Ad.* Miss Holmes (Inglese)/Casa Stefani/Bagni di Lucca/Toscana/ Tuscany
	1855	8 June	A	*Ad.* Miss *Holmes,*/chez Madame *Preston*, Poste Restante/Boulogne sur Mer/*France*
		26 Aug	A	
Hope, Messrs	1855	28 April	D	
Hope-Scott, James	1854	1 Jan	A	Rankeillour
			H	1870–3
		6 Jan	A	Rankeillour
			H	1870–3
		15 Jan	A	Rankeillour
		23 Jan	A	Rankeillour
			H	1873
		24 Feb	A	Rankeillour
			H	1873
		4 April	A	Rankeillour
			H	1873
		7 April	A	Rankeillour
			H	1873
		27 Aug	A	Rankeillour
			H	1873
		30 Aug	A	Rankeillour
		8 Nov	A	Rankeillour
		11 Nov	A	Rankeillour

Correspondent	Year	Date	Source	Location, Owner, Address
Hope-Scott, James	1855	18 Feb	H	1873
		25 April	H	1873 (*McGrath*, p. 352)
		20 July	A	Rankeillour
		1 Aug	H	1873
Hughes, John	1854	12 July	Pr	The *Tablet*, xv (2 Sept. 1854), p. 549
			D	
Johnson, Manuel	1854	5 May	A	(*McGrath*, p. 330) *Ad.* M. Johnson Esqr/Observatory/ Oxford/England
		11 June	A	(*McGrath*, pp. 330-1) *Ad.* Manuel Johnson Esqr/The Observatory/Oxford/*England*
		15 June	A	*Ad.* the same
		1 Aug	A	*Ad.* Manuel Johnson Esqr/Observatory/Oxford
		7 Dec	A	*Ad.* the same
		20 Dec	A	*Ad.* M. Johnson Esqr/Observatory/ Oxford/England
Kennedy, Patrick	1855	12 Feb	A	Irish Folklore Commission Library
Kenrick, Francis	1854	Nov?	D	Diocesan, Archives, Dublin
	1855	11 Jan	A	Baltimore Cathedral Archives (*American Essays for the Newman Centennial*, edited by J. K. Ryan and E. D. Benard, pp. 32-3)
Kerr, Lord Henry	1854	27 Aug	C	Todhunter
		8 Nov	C	Todhunter
		15 Nov	C	Todhunter
		12 Dec	C	Todhunter
		20 Dec	C	Todhunter
	1855	30 Jan	C	Todhunter
		4 Feb	C	Todhunter
		2 Mar	C	Todhunter
		5 Mar	C	Todhunter
		25 Mar	C	Todhunter
		23 April	C	Todhunter

Correspondent	Year	Date	Source	Location, Owner, Address
Kerr, Lord Henry	1855	26 April	C	Todhunter
		24 May	C	Todhunter
		14 June	C	Todhunter
		25 July	C	Todhunter
		12 Sept	C	Todhunter
Kerr, Lady Henry	1855	20 June	C	Todhunter
		1 July	C	Todhunter
Knox, T. F.	1854	27 Sept	A	Lond. Vol. 9
	1855	18 May	A	Lond. Vol. 9
La Primaudaye, C. J.	1854	17 Nov	C	(*McGrath*, pp. 357–8; Anne Pollen, *John Hungerford Pollen*, pp. 252 and 258)
Leahy, John	1854	28 June	Pr	The *Irish Monthly*, XVIII (Dec. 1890), p. 648
	1855	24 Jan	A	S. J. Dublin
Leahy, Patrick	1855	28 Sept	A	Cashel Diocesan Archives
Longman, Thomas	1855	13 June	A	Diocesan Archives, Birmingham
Lothian, Marchioness of	1855	26 Jan	Pr	*Cecil Marchioness of Lothian*, edited by Cecil Kerr, London n.d. [about 1920], p. 146
Lyons, Robert D.	1855	27 April	C	
		28 Sept	D	
MacCarthy, Denis Florence	1854	14 Mar	A	Bodleian Library, MS. Eng. Letters, e 48 *Ad.* D. F. McCarthy Esqr/29 Blessington Street,/Dublin
	1855	8 Mar	A	Bodleian Library, MS. Eng. Letters, e 48
MacHale, John	1854	13 June	Pr	Bernard O'Reilly, *John MacHale, Archbishop of Tuam*, New York 1890, II, pp. 502–3
		17 Aug	Pr	*Op. cit.* II, p. 504
		3 Oct	Pr	*Op. cit.* II, pp. 504–6
		8 Oct	Pr	*Op. cit.* II, pp. 507–9 (*Ward* I, p. 360; *McGrath*, p. 326)
			D	(Two)
			H	1870–3

Correspondent	Year	Date	Source	Location, Owner, Address
MacHale, John	1855	28 July	Pr	Bernard O'Reilly, *John MacHale, Archbishop of Tuam*, II, pp. 509–10 (*McGrath*, pp. 360–1)
		6 Aug	D	
			H	1870–3
Maclachlan, John	1854	17 Aug	A	St Mary's College, Blairs
Maclean, H.	1854	6 Sept	C	
MacSwiney, S. M.	1854	15 Sept	A	The Newman Preparatory School, Boston
	1855	2 Aug	A	The Catholic University of America
			D	
Manning, H. E.	1854	13 June	A	Georgetown
		17 Aug	A	Bayswater
		22 Nov	A	
	1855	16 April	A	Bayswater
Mills, Austin	1854	22 Feb	A	(*Ward* I, pp. 339–41; *Trevor* II, pp. 36–8; *McGrath*, p. 256)
		29 June	A	
	1855	27 Feb	A	
		7 May	A	
Monsell, William	1854	8 Mar	A	
		16 Mar	A	
		28 June	A	
		29 June	A	
		1 Aug	A	
		21 Aug	A	
		8 Sept	A	
		17 Nov	A	
	1855	9 Jan	A	
		27 April	A	
		1 May	A	
		4 May	A	
		13 June	A	
		21 Aug	A	

Correspondent	*Year*	*Date*	*Source*	*Location, Owner, Address*
Monsell, William	1855	4 Sept (I)	A	
		4 Sept (II)	A	
		30 Sept	A	
Montalembert, Comte de	1854	29 June	A	Comte de Montalembert, La Roche-en-Brenil, dossier 478 *Ad.* A. Monsieur/M. le Conte de Montalembert/40 Rue de Bac/ Paris France. [Re-directed: A courtrexville.]
Montézon, Fortunat de	1854	12 April	A	Archives of the Jesuit Province of France, Chantilly. [The text is taken from a copy authenticated by the archivist.] *Ad.* A. Monsieur/M. le Rev. Pere Montézon S.J./18 rue des Postes/ Paris/*France*
	1855	12 Jan	C	Archives of the Jesuit Province of France, Chantilly. [The text is taken from a copy authenticated by the archivist.]
Mooney, Patrick	1855	9 April	D	
		22 April	D	
Moore, John	1855	1 June	A	The Sacred Heart Convent, Hammersmith
Moriarty, David	1855	21 Feb	Pr	(See note to diary for 21 Feb.)
		29 April (I)	A	
		29 April (II)	A	
		25 May	A	
		22 June	A	
Morris, J. B.	1854	17 Aug	A	St Edmund's College, Ware
	1855	13 Feb	A	St Edmund's College, Ware
Mozley, Mrs John	1854	2 Mar	A	J. H. Mozley, Haslemere, Surrey
		9 Mar	A	J. H. Mozley
		16 Mar	A	J. H. Mozley
		27 July	A	J. H. Mozley
		11 Sept	A	J. H. Mozley
		8 Dec	A	J. H. Mozley
	1855	9 Jan	A	J. H. Mozley
		22 Feb	A	J. H. Mozley

Correspondent	Year	Date	Source	Location, Owner, Address
Mozley, Mrs John	1855	10 May	A	J. H. Mozley
Mozley, Thomas	1854	28 Mar	A	
Murney, Henry	1855	27 July	D	
Neville, William	1855	21 Jan	A	
		21 Feb	A	
		3 Mar	A	
		13 Mar	A	
Northcote, J. Spencer	1854	9 April	A	Stoke
Nugent, James	1854	25 July	C	
O'Curry, Eugene	1855	9 Mar	A	St Patrick's College, Maynooth
O'Ferrall, James More	1854	12 May	A	
O'Meagher, J. B.	1854	3 Dec	D	
Oratorians at Birmingham	1854	23 Feb	A	(*Trevor* II, p. 38; *McGrath*, pp. 258–9)
O'Reilly, Edmund	1855	27 April	A	
		16 Sept	D	
			H of D	1870–3
O'Reilly, Myles	1854	23 Sept	C	
Ornsby, Robert	1854	7 July	A	
		10 July	A	
		15 July	H	1870–3
		19 July	A	
			H	1870–3
		20 July	A	
		21 July	A	
		30 Dec	A	
	1855	9 Jan	A	
			H	1870–3
		12 Jan	A	
			H	1870–3
		Feb	H	1870–3
		31 Aug	A	

Correspondent	Year	Date	Source	Location, Owner, Address
Ornsby, Robert	1855	31 Aug	H	1870–3
Pagani, J. B.	1855	10 July	Pr	Francesco Paoli, *Vita di Antonio Rosmini-Serbati*, Turin 1880, p. 555
Paley, F. A.	1854	20 May	D	
Patterson, James Laird	1854	9 Mar	A	(*McGrath*, p. 267) *Ad.* The Revd J. L. Patterson/ Palazzo Vaticano/Roma/*Italy*
Phillipps, A. Lisle	1854	13 June	C	
	1855	16 Mar	C	(*de Lisle* II, pp. 102–3)
		3 April	C	
		7 May	C	
Pigot, John Edward	1855	5 Mar	D	
Pollen, John Hunger-ford	1854	24 Dec	C	
	1855	16 Mar	C	
		24 May	C	
		4 June	C	
		23 June	C	
		29 June	C	
		25 July	C	
		8 Aug	C	
		21 Aug	C	
		5 Sept	C	
Poncia, John	1855	24 July	D	
Poole, Sister Mary Imelda	1854	4 April	C	
Pusey, E. B.	1854	11 Mar	A	Pusey (Liddon's *Pusey* III, p. 394)
		16 Mar	A	Pusey
		21 April	A	Pusey
Renouf, Peter le Page	1854	20 Feb	A	Pembroke College, Oxford (*The Life Work of Sir Peter le Page Renouf*, Vol. IV, p. xlvii) *Ad.* A Monsieur/Monsieur Renouf/ chez M. le Conte de Mauclerc /Ougney/par Baume les Dames/Doubs/France/[Re-directed; a Consolation]

Correspondent	Year	Date	Source	Location, Owner, Address
Renouf, Peter le Page	1855	3 June	A	Pembroke College, Oxford
Rivington, Francis	1854	20 Jan	D	
		28 Jan	D	(Two)
Robertson, J. B.	1854	21 April	D	
Ryder, George	1854	3 Jan	A	
		8 Jan	A	*Ad.* G. D. Ryder Esqr/Mrs Roberts's/Petersham/near London
		17 Aug	A	*Ad.* George D. Ryder Esqr/The Warren/Grace Dieu/Whitwick/Ashby de la Zouch
		21 Dec	A	*Ad.* G. D. Ryder Esqr/25 Wilton Place/Hyde Park South/London
	1855	29 Jan	A	
		24 Feb	C	
Ryder, Henry (Ignatius) Dudley	1855	14 Aug	A	
		24 Aug	A	
		25 Sept	A	*Ad.* A Monsieur Monsieur Henri D Ryder/chez M le Vicomte de Vaulchier/Chateau des Dechaupes/Jura/France/to be forwarded/[re-directed to Lucerne]
St John, Ambrose	1854	8 Feb (I)	A	(Trevor II, p. 34; *McGrath*, p. 252)
			H	1875
		8 Feb (II)	H	1875
		11 Feb	A	(*Trevor* II, p. 34; *McGrath*, p. 253)
		17 Feb	A	(*Ward* I, p. 337; *Trevor* II, p. 35; *McGrath*, p. 254)
		21 Feb	A	(*Trevor* II, p. 36; *McGrath*, p. 255)
			H	1875
		26 Feb	A	
			H	1875
		2 Mar	A	(*Ward* I, p. 336; *McGrath*, p. 266)
			H	1875
		4 Mar	A	(*McGrath*, p. 267)
			H	1875

Correspondent	Year	Date	Source	Location, Owner, Address
St John, Ambrose	1854	10 Mar	A	
		12 Mar	A	
			H	1875
		26 April	A	
		27 April	A	
			H	1875
		11 May	A	
			H	1875
		16 May	A	
			H	1875
		3 June	A	(*Trevor* II, p. 52)
			H	1875
		4 June	A	(*McGrath*, p. 315)
			H	1875
		8 June	A	
		15 June	A	(*Trevor* II, p. 59)
			H	1875
		1 Sept	A	
			H	1875
		2 Sept	A	
		4 Oct	A	
			H	1875
		8 Oct	A	
		12 Oct	A	
		15 Oct	A	
			H	1875
		27 Oct	A	(Trevor II, p. 64)
			H	1875
		6 Nov	A	
			H	1875
		7 Nov	A	
			H	1875

Correspondent	Year	Date	Source	Location, Owner, Address
St John, Ambrose	1854	17 Nov	A	
			H	1875
		22 Nov	A	
			H	1875 (*Ward* I, p. 360; *McGrath*, p. 345)
		1 Dec	A	
			H	1875
		5 Dec	A	
		8 Dec	A	
		17 Dec	A	
			H	1875
	1855	13 Jan	A	(*Trevor* II, pp. 58–9; *McGrath*, p. 350)
		26 Jan	A	
		1 Feb	A	
		17 Feb	A	
		22 Feb	H	1875
		27 Mar	A	
		28 Mar	H	1875
		12 May	A	
			H	1875
		18 May	A	
			H	1875
		27 May	A	(*Trevor* II, p. 59)
			H	1875
		10 June	H	1875
		19 June	**A**	
			H	1875
		4 July	A	
		11 July	A	
		14 July	A	
			H	1875

Correspondent	Year	Date	Source	Location, Owner, Address
Scott, W. H.	1854	31 July	A	
Scratton, Thomas	1854	27 June	A	S. J. Dublin
		9 July	A	S. J. Dublin
		15 Aug	A	S. J. Dublin
		17 Aug	A	S. J. Dublin
		21 Aug	A	S. J. Dublin
		24 Aug	A	S. J. Dublin
		5 Oct	A	S. J. Dublin
		11 Nov	A (and two notes)	S. J. Dublin
		16 Nov	A	S. J. Dublin
		18 Dec	A	S. J. Dublin
		19 Dec	A	S. J. Dublin
		29 Dec	A	S. J. Dublin
	1855	1 Jan	A	S. J. Dublin
		7 Jan	A	S. J. Dublin
		17 Jan	A	S. J. Dublin (*McGrath*, p. 351)
		19 Jan	A	S. J. Dublin
		25 Jan	A	S. J. Dublin
		30 Jan	A	S. J. Dublin
		2 Feb (I)	A	S. J. Dublin
		2 Feb (II)	A	S. J. Dublin
		17 Feb	A	S. J. Dublin
		19 Feb	A	S. J. Dublin
		28 Feb	A	S. J. Dublin
		1 Mar	A	S. J. Dublin
		2 Mar	A	S. J. Dublin
		4 Mar	A	S. J. Dublin
			D	
			H	
		11 Mar	A	S. J. Dublin

Correspondent	Year	Date	Source	Location, Owner, Address
Scratton, Thomas	1855	17 Mar	A	S. J. Dublin
		21 Mar	A	S. J. Dublin
		23 Mar	A	S. J. Dublin
		29 Mar	A	S. J. Dublin
		31 Mar	A	S. J. Dublin
		22 April	A	S. J. Dublin
		23 April	A	S. J. Dublin
		24 April	A	S. J. Dublin
			D	(Two)
		27 April	A	S. J. Dublin
		28 April	A	S. J. Dublin
		8 May	A	S. J. Dublin
		16 May	A	S. J. Dublin
			D	
		28 May	A	S. J. Dublin
		6 June	A	S. J. Dublin
		11 June	A	S. J. Dublin
		12 June	A	S. J. Dublin
		22 June	D	
		26 June	A	S. J. Dublin
		28 June	A	S. J. Dublin
		17 July	A	S. J. Dublin
		9 Aug	A	S. J. Dublin
		16 Aug	A	S. J. Dublin
		17 Aug	A	S. J. Dublin
		20 Aug	A	S. J. Dublin
		4 Sept	A	S. J. Dublin
		14 Sept	A	S. J. Dublin
		25 Sept	A	S. J. Dublin
Shrewsbury, Earl of	1854	8 Mar	A	*Ad.* The Right Honble/The Earl of Shrewsbury/Toulon/*France*. [Redirected: Voir a Hyères]

Correspondent	Year	Date	Source	Location, Owner, Address
Shrewsbury, Earl of	1854	29 June	A	
		3 Aug	A	
	1855	20 April	A	
Simeon, Sir John	1854	19 June	A	Sir John Simeon, Bart. *Ad.* Sir John Simeon, Bart/Swainston/Isle of Wight/England/
		1 Aug	A	Sir John Simeon, Bart.
Slattery, Michael	1854	17 Aug	A	Cashel Diocesan Archives
		3 Oct	A	Cashel Diocesan Archives
Stanton, Richard	1854	23 Jan	A	
		5 Feb	A	
		14 Feb	A	(*Trevor* II, p. 33: *McGrath*, p. 243)
		28 Feb	A	
		12 Mar	A	(*McGrath*, p. 268)
		3 Aug	A	
		3 Oct	A	(*McGrath*, p. 324)
	1855	22 Feb	A	
		14 Mar	A	
		2 Aug	A	
		15 Aug	A	
		19 Sept	A	
Stewart, James	1854	24 May	C	
		21 June	C	
		26 June	C	
		5 July	C	
Sullivan, William Kirby	1855	26 April	A	
		10 July	A	
		14 July	A	
Talbot, George	1854	5 June	A	English College, Rome *Ad.* Al Sign Revmo e Colmo/Il Signor Monsignore Talbot,/Palazzo Vaticano/Roma/*Italy*
		29 June	A	English College, Rome *Ad.* Al Signor/Monsignore Talbot/ Palazzo Vaticano/Roma/*Italy*

Correspondent	Year	Date	Source	Location, Owner, Address
Taylor, Henry	1855	30 July	A	Bodleian Library, MS. Eng. Letters, C.I.
Taylor, J. I.	1854	15 Jan	A	(*McGrath*, pp. 239–40)
		20 Jan	A	
		23 Jan	A	
		24 Feb	A	
		7 April	A	
Ullathorne, Bishop	1854	28 Jan	A	Diocesan Archives, Birmingham
		5 Feb	A	Diocesan Archives, Birmingham
		5 June	A	Diocesan Archives, Birmingham
		19 Oct	A	Diocesan Archives, Birmingham
	1855	27 Jan	A	Diocesan Archives, Birmingham
		12 Mar	A	Diocesan Archives, Birmingham
Unknown Irish Priest	1854	9 Dec	D	
Vaughan, Frances Angela	1854	19 Jan	A	The Visitation Convent, Waldron, Sussex
Vecchiotti, Septimius	1854	End of June	D	
Vere, Aubrey de	1854	21 Aug	A	National Library of Ireland
	1855	25 Jan	A	National Library of Ireland
		26 Mar	A	National Library of Ireland
		31 Mar	A	National Library of Ireland
		7 April	A	National Library of Ireland
		18 April	A	National Library of Ireland
		5 May	A	National Library of Ireland
		13 May	A	National Library of Ireland
Walford, Edward	1854	27 Aug	A	*Ad.* Edward Walford Esqr/30 Chepstow Place/Bayswater/London
	1855	30 May	A	St John's Seminary, Camarillo, California
		10 June	A	
		18 June	A	
Walker, J., of Scarborough	1854	27 Aug	A	
		3 Sept	A	

Correspondent	Year	Date	Source	Location, Owner, Address
Walker, J., of Scarborough	1855	1 Jan	A	
			H	1873
		8 Jan	A	
		23 Feb	H	1873
Ward, F. R.	1854	18 Aug	C	
		20 Aug	C	
		23 Dec	D	
Ward, W. G.	1855	13 June	A	Lond. Vol. 9
Weld, Frances de Sales	1854	6 Feb	A	The Visitation Convent, Waldron, Sussex
Whitty, Robert	1855	25 Sept	C	
Wilberforce, Henry	1854	19 Jan	A	Georgetown
			H	1876
		23 Jan	A	Georgetown
			H	1876
		26 Jan	A	Georgetown
		14 Feb	A	Georgetown
			H	1876
		13 June	A	Georgetown
			H	1876
		17 June	A	Georgetown
			H	1876
		5 July	A	Georgetown
			H	1876
		12 July	A	Georgetown
			H	1876
		19 July	A	Georgetown
			H	1876
		3 Nov	A	Georgetown
		15 Nov	A	Georgetown
		23 Nov (1)	A	Georgetown
			H	1876

LIST OF LETTERS BY CORRESPONDENTS

Correspondent	Year	Date	Source	Location, Owner, Address
Wilberforce, Henry	1854	23 Nov (II)	A	Georgetown (*McGrath*, p. 345)
			H	1876
		20 Dec	A	Georgetown
			H	1876
		23 Dec	A	Georgetown
			H	1876
	1855	21 Feb	A	Georgetown
			H	1876
		27 Feb (I)	A	Georgetown
			H	1876
		27 Feb (II)	A	Georgetown
		3 Mar	A	Georgetown
			H	1876
		5 Mar	A	Georgetown
			H	1876
		6 Mar	A	Georgetown
			H	1876
		12 Mar	A	Georgetown
			H	1876
		26 Mar	A	Georgetown
		28 Mar	A	Georgetown
			H	1876
		29 Mar	A	Georgetown
		31 Mar	A	Georgetown
			H	1876
		3 April	A	Georgetown
			H	1876
		9 April	A	Georgetown
		25 April	A	Georgetown
			H	1876
		13 Aug	A	Georgetown

Correspondent	Year	Date	Source	Location, Owner, Address
Wilberforce, Robert Isaac	1854	13 Jan	A	Miss Irene Wilberforce
		15 Aug	A	Miss Irene Wilberforce
		21 Aug	A	Miss Irene Wilberforce
		1 Sept	A	Miss Irene Wilberforce
		21 Sept	A	Miss Irene Wilberforce
Williams, Isaac	1854	28 Jan	A	Revd. R. H. Isaac Williams
			D	
Wiseman, Cardinal	1854	2 Jan	A	(Trevor II, p. 32) *Ad.* All' Emo e Remo Principe/Il Signr Cardinale/*Wiseman*/Collegio Inglese/Roma/*Italy*
		23 Jan	A	(*McGrath*, pp. 240–1) *Ad.* the same
		1 Feb	A	*Ad.* All' Emo Principe e Pdre Colmo/Il Signr Cardinale Wiseman/Collegio Inglese/Roma/*Italia.* (*Ward* I, p. 331; *McGrath*, p. 242; W. Ward, *The Life and Times of Cardinal Wiseman*, 2nd edition, London 1897, II, pp. 74–5)
		5 June	A	(*McGrath*, p. 315)
		25 June	A	(*McGrath*, p. 322)
		20 July	A	
		1 Aug	A	
		13 Aug	A	Bayswater
		Nov?	D	Diocesan Archives, Dublin
	1855	12 Jan	D	
		28 Jan	A	(W. Ward, *The Life and Times of Cardinal Wiseman*, II, pp. 99–100)
Woodward, J. H.	1854	19 June	C	
Worthington, Alfred William	1855	3 Sept	A	St John's Seminary, Camarillo, California

*   *   *   *

MEMORANDA, Etc.

On the Objects of the University and the Means for attaining them	1854	29 April	A	(in Appendix 1, p. 557)
Expenses of a Student in the University House	1854	23 Sept	A	

Correspondent	Year	Date	Source	Location, Owner, Address
Newman's Dispensation from Residence at Birmingham	1854	20 Dec		(in note to letter of 5 June 1854 to Wiseman)
The Autumn Term of 1854 (by Robert Ornsby)	1855	1 Feb		(in Appendix 2, p. 562)
Public Lectures of the University	1855	5 April		(in Appendix 3, p. 568)

(For the letter 'On Latin Composition,' the *Catholic University Gazette*, (18 Jan. 1855), pp. 294–6, see *Idea*, pp. 366–71, and for the second letter intended to follow this up, see *A.W.* pp. 50–3)

*   *   *   *

LETTERS TO NEWMAN

		from	Inserted before Newman's of
1854	20 Jan	Cardinal Wiseman	1 Feb
	3 April	William Froude	10 April
	6 Oct	John MacHale	8 Oct
1855	8 Sept	Archbishop Cullen	13 Sept
	16 Sept	Archbishop Cullen	after Newman's of 13 Sept
	27 Sept	Archbishop Cullen	before Newman's of 28 Sept

Index of Persons and Places

Index of Persons and Places

The index to Volume XI contains notices of almost all the persons who occur in that volume, and the indexes to subsequent volumes notices of those who occur in them for the first time. These are not repeated, and so, for persons and places already mentioned in those volumes, reference back is here made by an (xi) or (xii) etc. inserted after such names.

References are given, in the case of persons mentioned for the first time in this volume, to *The Dictionary of National Biography* or *The Dictionary of American Biography*, and failing them, to Frederick Boase, *Modern English Biography*, or Joseph Gillow, *Bibliographical Dictionary of the English Catholics*; also occasionally to other printed works. Much of the information is derived from the correspondence and other material in the archives of the Birmingham Oratory, and from various private sources.

Bernard, see Dalgairns, John Dobrée.

Bernard (XIII), laybrother, Bernard Hennin, 3, 149.

Bethell, Henry (1836–1908) and Augustus (1838–1912), sons of John Bethell, 527–8, 533, 537.

Bethell (XIV), John (1804–67), 524.

Betteris, Mr, 467–8.

Bianconi, Charles (1786–1875), born near Como, came to Ireland at sixteen as an itinerant print seller. He made a fortune by establishing a public car system in the country parts of Ireland. In 1831 he was naturalized, and, in 1846, purchased the estate of Longfield in Tipperary. He was a friend and supporter of O'Connell, whose monument he erected in the church of the Irish College at Rome. During the Famine he took care of his own tenants and gave employment on his estate to others. (*DNB*, II, 462; M. O'C. Bianconi and S. J. Watson, *Bianconi King of the Irish Roads*, Dublin 1962), 203, 222, 309, 389, 396, 398, 443–4.

Bittleston (XIII), Henry (1818–86), 35, 54, 70, 80, 93, 151, 164, 172, 175–6, 249–51, 268, 270–1, 277, 282, 288–9, 318, 364, 391–2, 414–15, 419–20, 467–9, 488, 531, 550.

Bloxam (XI), John Rouse (1807–91), 118, 415, 501, 503.

Blunt, Francis Scawen (1839–72), son of Francis Scawen Blunt of Crabbet Park, Sussex, was received into the Church in 1852 two years after his mother, who was by then a widow. He held a commission in the 60th Regiment, and also became a Franciscan tertiary. He died in 1872 of tuberculosis and was buried in the Franciscan Church at Crawley, 303–4, 311, 527, 530.

Blunt, Wilfrid Scawen (1840–1922), brother of the above, and like him educated at Stonyhurst and Oscott after becoming a Catholic. Neither brother went to the Catholic University, nor came into contact with Newman at that period, but Wilfrid spent three days at Edgbaston in May 1876, and was impressed by the kindness of Newman, whose touch, he claimed, had cured him of toothache. Wilfrid was in the diplomatic service until his marriage in 1869 to Lady Anne Isabella Noel, only daughter of the first Earl of Lovelace by his first wife, Lord Byron's only child. Wilfrid Blunt was an eccentric—a poet, a breeder of Arab horses and a champion of oppressed nations. He became an Irish home ruler, and in 1887 was arrested after a meeting in Galway, and spent two months in gaol. He had for many years been hesitant in his religious faith, and he was buried, at his own wish, without religious rites. (*DNB*, 1922–1930, 84), 303–4, 311, 527, 530.

Bonavia (XIV), Dr Vincent, 8, 24, 215.

Borghese, Princess Agnes, 133, 226, 287.

Boston, Bishop of, see Fitzpatrick, John Bernard.

Bowden (XI), Elizabeth Swinburne (1805–1896), widow of J. W. Bowden, 15–17, 96–7, 105, 112–14, 118, 140, 187, 190, 197–8, 205, 217, 294, 347–8, 379, 451, 534–5.

Bowden (XI), Emily (1832–1909), 15–18, 96, 112, 187, 190, 197–8, 205, 217, 295, 347–8, 451.

Bowden (XI), Henry (1804–69), 105, 191, 224, 295, 303, 327, 332, 420, 535.

Bowden, Henry George (Sebastian) (1836–1920), son of Henry Bowden by his first wife, was at Eton from 1848 until 1852. In the latter year he was in the football XI and played for the Eton cricket XI against Harrow and Winchester. At the end of the same year he was received into the Church at Gibraltar, while travelling with his cousin John Edward Bowden. From Oct. 1853 to July 1855 was a private pupil of Ornsby in Dublin. In Sept. 1855 he joined the Rifle Brigade, transferring in 1856 to the Fusilier Guards, in which he remained until 1867. He then left the army to join the London Oratory, and was ordained priest in 1870. From 1889 to 1892, and from 1903 to 1907 he was Superior there, 198, 295, 303–04, 327, 420, 455, 477, 499.

Bowden (XI), John Edward (1829–74), 8, 24, 84, 215, 379.

Bowden (XI), John William (1798–1844), 65, 122–3.

Bowden (XI), Mary Anne (1831–67), 8, 12, 15–17, 24, 243, 348.

Bowles (XI), Frederick Sellwood (1818–1900), 35, 41, 47, 59–61, 63, 69, 71, 79, 85, 92–3, 120, 151, 160–1, 164, 217, 230, 254, 256, 277, 288, 376–7, 410–11, 414–15, 441–2, 492, 495, 527, 533.

Bowyer (XIV), George (1811–83), 105, 158.

Breen, Hugh, 318, 327.

Brennan, John, 361.

Bretherton, Bartholomew, seemingly a brother of the following, 133.

Bretherton, Peter, engaged in business in Birmingham where he had a horse and carriage repository, was connected with the Oratorians both at Alcester Street and Edgbaston. Newman baptised his daughter Elizabeth in 1850. Another daughter, Eleanor, born a year earlier, used to go to confession to Newman, and he was always anxious for her welfare, and for that of her family after she married. Bretherton was Vice-

Hamilton, John, Archdeacon of Dublin, Parish Priest of St Michan's, 369–71.

Hamilton, Sir William Rowan. (*DNB*, VIII, 1119), 123–4.

Hanmer (XI), Anthony John (1817–1907), 237, 285.

Hansom (XII), Joseph Aloysius (1803–82), 142.

Hansom, Mr, Caretaker at Rednal, 280, 355, 400.

Hardman (XII), John (1812–67), 97, 127, 142, 238, 240, 252, 308.

Harington, Richard. (*Boase*, I, 1338), 76.

Harold, John, 191.

Hayden, George Thomas. (*Boase*, I, 1395), 457, 519.

Hayden, Thomas (1823–81), of a Tipperary family connected by marriage with the Duke of Wellington, became a Licentiate of the Royal College of Surgeons in Ireland in 1850. He was Professor of Anatomy and Physiology at the Catholic University from 1855 until his death, and Physician of the Mater Misericordiae Hospital from its foundation. He contributed articles to medical journals and also to the *Atlantis*. From 1875 to 1877 he was Vice-President of the College of Physicians in Ireland. 'Hayden was so remarkably courteous, and his demeanour was always so calm, that he received the soubriquet of the " Gentle Thomas." ' Sir Charles A. Cameron, *History of the Royal College of Surgeons in Ireland*, Dublin 1886, p. 603. (*Boase*, V, 615), 457, 517, 519, 552–3.

Hely, Francis Haly (1785–1855), educated at Maynooth and consecrated Bishop of Kildare and Leighlin in 1837. (*Boase*, I, 1297), 48.

Hendren (XII), Joseph William (1791–1866), 34, 71, 80.

Hennessy, Henry (1826–1901), of Cork, brother of Sir John Pope Hennessy and brother-in-law of William Kirby Sullivan, was a self-taught mathematical physicist. His earliest paper was published in 1845 when he was only nineteen, and an article on ' Researches in Terrestrial Physics,' appeared in the *Transactions of the Royal Society*, 1851. In 1849 he was made Librarian of Queen's College, Cork, and in 1855 Newman appointed him Professor of Natural Philosophy at the Catholic University. He was elected a Fellow of the Royal Society in 1858, and from 1874 to 1890 was Professor of Applied Mathematics at the Royal College of Science, Dublin. (*DNB*, 1901–11, 247), 298–9, 320, 362, 389, 463–4, 473, 483, 504, 523, 541.

Henry, see Bittleston, Henry.

Herbert, John (1815–95), 533.

Hodges and Smith, 189, 372.

Holmes (XII), Mary (1815?–78), 110–11, 227–8, 480–1, 533, 547–8.

Hope (XIV), Alexander James Beresford (1820–87), 46.

Hope, Anne. (*Gillow*, III, 373), 355–7, 382–3.

Hope-Scott (XI), James Robert (1812–73), 3–4, 11, 14, 24–5, 33, 51, 55–6, 71, 95, 97–9, 105, 108, 121, 125, 134, 140, 144, 158, 161, 182, 186, 208, 210, 225, 238, 240–1, 261–2, 291, 293, 325, 379, 384–5, 411, 418–19, 440, 448–9, 510–11, 519–20.

Hope-Scott (XV), Mary Monica (1852–1920), 3, 385.

Howard (XIV), Philip Henry, 532.

Howley, Sir John. (*Boase*, I, 1561), 124.

Hughes, James. (*Boase*, I, 1572), 48, 50, 451.

Hughes (XI), John (1797–1864), Archbishop of New York, 194–6, 348.

Hutchison (XII), William Antony (1822–1863), 13, 152, 278, 377–80, 468, 483, 537, 539, 541.

Irons, William Josiah (1812–83), at Queen's College, Oxford, Vicar of Brompton 1840–70. He was a theological writer who defended Anglicanism and wrote against the doctrine of development. Newman noted Irons's death in his book of anniversaries. (*DNB*, X, 482), 119, 124.

Ivers, Bernard, 41.

Ives, Levi Silliman (1797–1867), became Episcopalian Bishop of North Carolina in 1831, and was attracted by the Oxford Movement. He formed in 1848 the religious Brotherhood of the Holy Cross, which, owing to its Tractarian ideas, soon had to be dissolved. At Christmas 1852 he resigned his see and submitted to Pius IX at Rome. His wife, a daughter of Bishop Hobart, became a Catholic at the same time. He wrote *Trials of a Mind in its Progress to Catholicism*, Boston 1853, and returned to the United States in 1854. There he found work as a Professor at St Joseph's Seminary, New York, and at St John's College, Fordham. (*DAB*, IX, 521), 105, 207, 212.

Janko, Mr, 393–4, 405.

Jeffries, George, Canon of Birmingham and Vicar General, 139, 152.

Jenkyns, Richard. (*DNB*, X, 755), 76–7.

Jervis, Lady, 484.

Jewsbury, Mr, Sacristan and organist at the Oratory, 82, 85, 117, 241–2, 246, 376.

Johnson (XI), Manuel (1805–59), 118, 123–4, 155–6, 161–3, 209, 319, 327.

Joseph, see Gordon, John Joseph.

in Classics, M.A. 1823. He then taught in England, and wrote in the *British Critic* for J. H. Rose, whose friend he was. At an early period in his life he became an Episcopalian and by 1840 was the clergyman at Elgin. From there he wrote to Newman at Oriel to say he felt increasingly drawn to the Roman Church, and hoped for clear guidance from Oxford. Newman urged him to wait and see how the Tractarian experiment proceeded. He became Dean of Moray and Ross, but in 1850 was received into the Church with his wife and family. In 1851 he hoped to become a professor at the Catholic University, and told Newman that he was about to spend his last five pound note. In 1854 he wrote from Yarmouth giving his name to the University, and still hoping for a professorship, 321.

Maclean, H., 245.

Macmullen (XI), Richard Gell (1814–95), 525.

MacNamara, Thomas (1808–91), ordained as a priest of the diocese of Meath in 1833, was one of the founders of St Vincent's College, Castleknock, in 1835. In 1841 the priests there were affiliated to the Congregation of the Mission, the Vincentians, and MacNamara may be said to have been one of the founders of that Congregation in Ireland. Besides giving missions, he was in charge of the Vincentian house at Phibsboro, Dublin, until 1864, when he succeeded Philip Dowley as President of Castleknock and Provincial. From 1868 to 1889 he was Rector of the Irish College in Paris. (*Boase*, II, 667), 270, 272, 315, 389, 456.

MacSwiney, Stephen Myles (1821–90), who was born in Killarney, pursued his medical studies locally, then in the School of the Apothecaries' Hall, Cecilia Street, and at St Vincent's Hospital, Dublin. He became a Member of the Royal College of Surgeons in England, 1844, Doctor of Medicine at St Andrew's, 1847, and a Licentiate of the Royal College of Physicians, 1854. Newman appointed him Professor of Medical Jurisprudence at the Catholic University in 1855, 253, 520.

Maher (XIII), Michael (1798–1862), 60, 142, 164.

Mai (XI), Angelo, 272–3.

Manning (XI), Henry Edward (1808–92), 7, 15, 32–3, 75, 105, 116, 140–1, 158–9, 161, 169, 198, 219–20, 239, 242, 303–04, 361, 429, 440–1.

Manning, William Henry, 141.

Marani, Augustus Caesar, of Modena, a supporter of United Italy, was at the Jesuit College and University there about 1830, and came to Ireland a few

years later. He was first deputy Professor and then Professor of Italian at Trinity College, Dublin, and also acted as a tutor in private families. In Oct. 1854 Newman appointed him Professor of Italian and Spanish at the Catholic University, 265, 268, 320, 363, 372, 446, 462, 467, 566.

Marriott (XI), Charles (1811–58), 501, 503.

Marshall (XI), Henry Johnson (1818–75), was working as a priest in Dublin 1854–55, 40, 167–9, 186.

Martindale, Robert, Mallow, Cork, according to Newman's diary, received an alms of £3 from him in 1854, 191.

Maskell (XIII), William (1814–90), 105.

Mathieu (XI), Jacques Marie (1796–1875), Cardinal Archbishop of Besançon, 531.

Maxwell, Patrick (1817–97), solicitor, 37 North Great George Street, with Pierse Kelly. (*Boase*, VI, 188), 185, 200, 203, 216.

Meagher, Thomas. (*Boase*, II, 826), 210, 442.

Meagher, William, ordained priest at Maynooth, was a Dublin priest much trusted by Archbishops Murray and Cullen. He wrote the life of the former, and was an executor of the latter's will. In 1848 he became Parish Priest of Rathmines and later Vicar General. He had been made a member of the Dublin Chapter in 1834, became its Dean in 1876, and died in 1881, 389.

Meath, Bishop of, see Cantwell, John.

Meyler (XV), Walter (1784–1864), 39.

Meyrick (XII), Frederick (1827–1906). (*DNB*, 1901–11, II, 617), 9.

Mezzofanti (XII), Giuseppe (1774–1849), 418.

Mills (XI), Henry Austin (1823–1903), 35, 51–4, 60, 163–4, 180, 247, 249, 251, 256, 259, 277–8, 382, 393, 460–1, 470, 472, 527, 539.

Molesworth, Sir William (1816–55). (*DNB*, XIII, 570), 82.

Molloy, James Lynam (1837–1909), born in Ireland, was educated at St Edmund's College, Ware, and the Catholic University of Ireland, where he won a classical scholarship in 1855. He was nearly expelled at the end of 1857 for going out at night from St Patrick's House. See the correspondence Dec. 1857—Jan. 1858. However, he also read his poetry to the literary Society, of which he was Vice-President, and showed musical ability, his singing during the Holy Week services attracting attention. Molloy was called to the English Bar from the Middle Temple in 1863, but from 1865 distinguished himself, chiefly as a song writer. By the end of the century he had written nearly a hundred songs, including

brother and a sister. He became the friend of Mother Mary Aikenhead, and was appointed by her Chief Surgeon at St Vincent's Hospital, from its opening in 1834. He practised at 15 Merrion Square, North, and wrote numerous articles on medical subjects, 254, 259, 302, 529.

Ogle, Miss, 124.

O'Hagan, Arthur, solicitor in partnership with Charles Cavanagh, 9 Harcourt Street, Dublin, 200.

O'Hagan, John (1822–90), the son of a merchant at Newry, went to Trinity College, Dublin, and, in 1842, was called to the Irish Bar. He was an active member of the Young Ireland Party, and one of the counsel for Charles Gavan Duffy in 1848. He was also a poet and wrote patriotic songs. He was a good scholar, a contributor to the *Atlantis* and later published literary essays. As a lawyer he was respected for his integrity and described as ' a nineteenth century edition of Blessed Thomas More.' In 1854 Newman appointed him Lecturer in Political Economy at the Catholic University, and the two became close friends. After Newman's return to Birmingham, O'Hagan frequently visited him there. He was made a Commissioner of the Board of National Education in 1861, and Gladstone appointed him Chief Judicial Commissioner for the Irish Land Commission in 1881, with the rank of a judge. In 1865 he married Frances, daughter of Thomas, later Lord, O'Hagan. (*DNB*, XIV, 947; the *Irish Monthly* (Feb. 1903), pp . 61-85), 117, 135, 173, 199, 232, 263, 265, 359, 456, 473, 494.

O'Hagan, Thomas, first Baron O'Hagan (1812–25), was called to the Irish Bar in 1836, and became a Queen's Counsel in 1849. He was a friend of Daniel O'Connell but opposed to the repeal of the Union. He acquired a reputation as a lawyer and in Dec. 1855 successfully defended the Redemptorist Fr Petcherine, who had publicly burned a copy of the Authorised Version of the Bible at Kingstown. In 1861 O'Hagan became Solicitor General for Ireland and in the following year Attorney General. In 1868 he was appointed Lord Chancellor of Ireland, the first Catholic since the reign of James II, and in 1870 was made a peer. He was interested in Irish education and in Feb. 1854 Newman offered him unsuccessfully any professorship he would take. He was elected Vice-Chancellor of the Royal University of Ireland on its foundation in

1880. (*DNB*, XIV, 947), 48, 71, 121, 247–8.

O'Meagher, Ernest, son of J. B. O'Meagher, an Irishman with Spanish connections, who lived in Paris. Ernest entered the Catholic University of Dublin in Jan. 1855, and won a scholarship there in July 1856, 311, 313–14, 328, 489, 491–2.

O'Meara, Thomas, a doctor at Carlow, Member of the Royal College of Surgeons of England, 1839, M.B. London University, 1840, 451, 456.

Oratorians, life and vocation, 3, 25, 30, 33, 35, 40–1, 47–8, 57–63, 68–70, 74, 120, 131–2, 146, 149–50, 152, 168, 175–6, 206–07, 238–9, 259, 266–7, 278, 290, 349, 365, 395, 495, 539–40, 548–9.

O'Reilly, Edmund Joseph (1811–78), born in London, was six years old when his parents returned to Ireland. His father died when he was young, and his mother was, with her four sisters, co-heiress of Edmund O'Callaghan of Kilgorey, County Clare, who though mortally wounded in a duel, lived for five days and repented. Of Mrs O'Reilly's sisters, one became a Visitation nun at Westbury, one married J. J. Bagot of Castle Bagot, another Gerald Dease of Turbotstown, and the last became the Countess of Kenmare.

Edmund O'Reilly was at school at Clongowes, then at Maynooth for four years until 1830, when he went to the Irish College at Rome under Cullen. He gained his doctorate in divinity at the Collegio Romano in a ' public act ' and was ordained in 1838. In the same year he won, by competitive 'concursus,' the Chair of Theology at Maynooth. There he remained until June 1851, when he resigned in order to become a Jesuit. He entered the novitiate at Naples and in 1853 was appointed to teach theology at St Beuno's, the Jesuit College in North Wales.

Newman chose him as Professor of Theology at the Catholic University and wished to have him as Pro-Vice-Rector in 1857. In 1859 O'Reilly became the first Rector of the House of Retreats at Milltown Park, Dublin, and was the Jesuit Provincial in Ireland 1863–70.

In *A letter to the Duke of Norfolk* Newman quoted from O'Reilly's writings, calling him ' one of the first theologians of the day,' and a ' great authority,' *Diff*. II, p. 338. After he died Newman wrote on 17 Nov. 1878 to Dr Russell of Maynooth of ' his largeness of soul, and his sweetness and gentleness in his intercourse with

returned the following year as Chaplain to the exiled Sisters of Compassion. In 1854 he joined the London Oratory, where he was known as an artist, a poet and an author, 177.

Pigot, John Edward (1822–71), son of Chief Baron Pigot was called to the Irish Bar in 1845. He was a Young Irelander and one of the poets of the movement, author of 'Up for the Green.' Newman wanted him as Professor of Practical Law, and he was ready to work for the University as long as it was not made a vehicle of English domination. It was not, however, found possible to establish the Faculty of Law. Pigot was a friend of Eugene O'Curry and collaborated with him. In 1865 Pigot went to India, made a fortune as a barrister, and returned to Ireland to die. (The *Irish Monthly*, May 1896, pp. 225–37), 138, 145, 360, 369, 403–04, 451–2, 456, 553.

Pius IX (1792–1878), xiii, 31–3, 36, 60, 73–4, 101, 110, 112, 121, 144–7, 152, 170, 174, 180, 183, 209, 213–14, 236, 273, 339, 341, 345, 348, 358, 360, 365–8, 382, 390, 395, 408–11, 423–4, 440, 452, 525–6.

Plater (xv), Edward Angelo (1834–97), (*Gillow*, v, 320), 34–5, 37, 40.

Polding (xii), John Bede (1794–1877), 275.

Pollen, John Hungerford (1820–1902), great-great-nephew of Pepys and nephew of Sir John Walter Pollen, second Baronet, of Redenham, Hampshire, was at Eton and Christ Church. He was a Fellow of Merton 1842–52, and came under the influence of the Tractarians. In 1844 he was curate at St Peter-le-Bailey, Oxford, and from 1847 to 1851 worked on the staff of St Saviour's, Leeds. In 1850 he refused the living of Kibworth in Leicestershire, nearly £1000 a year, because he was unsure of his religious position. He returned to Oxford for a year, and was Senior Proctor. In 1852 he became a Catholic, following the example of many of his friends. He decided to devote himself professionally to art and architecture. In 1855 he came to Dublin as Newman's Professor of Fine Arts, and built the University Church. Two years later he settled in London and was always busy with artistic work. He was at the South Kensington Museum from 1863 to 1867, when he became private secretary to the Marquis of Ripon. He married Maria La Primaudaye in 1855 and had a large family. Two of his sons became Jesuits and one joined Newman at the Oratory. Pollen himself was one of Newman's most devoted and faithful

friends. (*DNB*, 1901–11, 122), 300–01, 331–2, 389, 417, 466, 469–76, 493–4, 496, 502, 513, 522–3, 528, 530–1, 540–1, 545, 554.

Poncia (xv), Eliza (1820–73), wife of John Poncia, 227, 246, 512.

Poncia (xiii), John (1814–74), 506, 512.

Poole (xi), Maria Spencer Ruscombe, Sister Mary Imelda (1815–81), 98, 132.

Preston, Thomas (1817–1903), 110–11, 170, 480.

Pugin (xii), Augustus Welby (1812–52), 142, 301.

Pulzky, Francis Aurelius. (I. Giberne Sieveking, *Memoirs and Letters of Francis W. Newman*, London 1909, pp. 247–62), 405.

Pusey (xi), Edward Bouverie (1800–82), 5, 19–20, 28–9, 77, 80–1, 88, 105–06, 108, 114, 366, 416.

Pusey, Edward Bouverie (1838–1921), 504.

Pusey (xi), William Bouverie (1810–88), 362, 366, 369, 504.

Quinn (xv), James (1819–81), 38, 173, 206, 462, 508.

Raglan, first Baron (1788–1855). (*DNB*, xviii, 645), 505.

Ram (xv), Pierre François Xavier de (1804–65), 5.

Ranken (xv), George Elliot (1828–89), 537.

Ravignan, Gustave Xavier de, 16, 286, 349–50.

Rednal, Birmingham, cottage and cemetery of the Oratorians, xv, 207, 227, 236, 240–1, 247, 268, 271, 277, 280, 283, 311, 313, 318, 326, 336, 352, 355–7, 399–400, 411–12, 431, 472, 475, 488, 497, 506.

Reisach, Karl August, Count von (1800–69), Rector of the College of Propaganda, where, with Perrone he examined the teaching of Hermes, which was condemned in 1835. In 1836 he became Bishop of Eichstätt, and later Archbishop of Munich, but his defence of Church rights after 1848 displeased Maximilian II. In 1855 Pius IX transferred him to Rome and made him a Cardinal in Curia. He became Prefect of the Congregation of Studies. In 1866 he came to England to enquire into the Oxford question, but did not visit Newman, 166, 194.

Renouf (xi), Peter le Page (1822–97), 48–9, 260, 265, 288, 295, 312, 320, 323, 347, 372, 381, 397, 412, 425, 435, 446, 466, 475, 489, 492, 509, 566.

Rhodes (xv), Matthew John (1817–91), 7.

Richard, see Stanton, Richard.

Richards, Joseph Loscombe. (*Boase*, iii, 139), 75–6.